International Economics:
Theory and Context

Wilson B. Brown
University of Winnipeg

Jan S. Hogendorn
Colby College

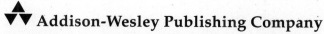
Addison-Wesley Publishing Company
Reading, Massachusetts ▪ Menlo Park, California ▪ New York
Don Mills, Ontario ▪ Wokingham, England ▪ Amsterdam ▪ Bonn
Sydney ▪ Singapore ▪ Tokyo ▪ Madrid ▪ San Juan ▪ Milan ▪ Paris

Sponsoring Editor:	Marjorie Williams
Managing Editor:	Kazia Navas
Production Supervisor:	Kathy Diamond
Production Services:	Beth Stephens
Composition:	Sigrid and Michael Wile
Copyeditor:	Karen Stone
Cover Designer:	Eileen Hoff
Pre-press Consultant:	John Webber
Technical Art Coordinator:	Susan London-Payne
Technical Illustrations:	TechGraphics
Senior Manufacturing Coordinator:	Judy Sullivan
Marketing Manager:	David Theisen
Indexer:	Jo-Anne Naples

Library of Congress Cataloging-in-Publication Data

Brown, Wilson B., 1938–
    International economics : theory and context / Wilson Brown, Jan
S. Hogendorn.
      p.   cm.
    Includes bibliographical references and index.
    ISBN 0-201-55445-3
    1. International economic relations.   2. International trade.
3. Commercial policy.   I. Hogendorn, Jan S.   II. Title.
HF1359.B76   1993
337--dc20   93-25797
                                          CIP

ISBN 0-201-55445-3

1 2 3 4 5 6 7 8 9 10-MA-96959493

Preface

International Economics: Theory and Context explores the field of international economics in its institutional, historical, and political contexts, addressing the key international economic issues of the 1990s. To allow breadth of coverage, the book avoids extensive theoretical elaboration and mathematical presentation; as a tradeoff, it gains the opportunity to apply theory to real situations, to synthesize ideas, and to evaluate theory and policies. The resulting text is challenging and sophisticated, yet accessible. It gives students a broader canvas than other more theoretical texts and a chance to develop more complex intellectual skills as they learn to use theory, synthesize material, and make evaluations.

International economics courses, unlike those in economic development, industrial organization, or money and banking, have not had a good field text. The books that present only the basic theory also fail to develop the context or show the usefulness of the models they do develop. The main thrust of the more advanced books, despite their claims to the contrary, is not in application of models but in further model building. *International Economics: Theory and Context* strikes a very different balance: It deals not only with theory, but also with the institutions and politics, creating a richly textured introduction to the field.

THEORY AND CONTEXT

The table of contents gives some idea of the range of subjects covered: (1) historical background to most key subjects, such as increased integration, trade policy, and international monetary arrangements; (2) new policy developments, such as tariffication, strategic trade policies, and savings and investment approaches to trade imbalances; (3) treatment of key institutions and arrangements, such as GATT, fair trade laws, the European Community, the gold standard, Bretton Woods, the IMF, Eurocurrencies, the Maastricht Treaty, and the Basle Accord.

This book keeps a keen eye on political contexts, whether they are the growth of the state in an increasingly integrated world (Chapter 1), the sources of protectionism and its continued vitality (Chapter 6), the unjustness of fair trade laws (Chapter 7), or the underlying economic structures that make international adjustment difficult (Chapters 17 and 18).

At the same time, the book maintains a sharp theoretical focus. Its use of a limited number of models aids this task. Demand and supply and production possibilities curves are amazingly flexible and powerful tools as are, in the macroeconomic arena, the income absorption approach, aggregate supply and demand, and the T-account. Although the text introduces many new models, its focus is on explaining the real world, and if it can use a model students do not have to be taught anew, it does so.

B&H takes an international view. While American examples and problems certainly are of critical concern, Canadian, European, and Third World data and examples are also plentiful.

TEACHING FEATURES

We have designed the book with the students' learning very much in mind. The writing is lucid and richly textured, with plentiful examples, carefully examined. Many charts illustrate the points the text makes. Flow diagrams, which represent an economic shock and the path of the reaction, clarify complex relationships. Descriptive captions accompany each diagram or graph, summarizing its meaning or mechanics. Boxed text and charts supplement the main ideas of the chapters. On-page footnotes explain points that may puzzle some readers, or they add interesting sidelights. Several appendixes explore specific topics more closely. Clear statements of objectives precede each chapter, and key concepts and vocabulary followed by thought-provoking questions end the chapters. Each chapter has extensive end notes providing a considerable bibliographical source.

INTENDED AUDIENCE

International Economics: Theory and Context has four related audiences:

1. Undergraduate international economics courses where the object is to explore the field rather than to develop specific modeling and mathematical skills. Its emphasis on breadth and the skills of application, synthesis, and evaluation challenge and engage students. It is also eminently suitable for courses where no intermediate economics is required and in which numerous nonmajors are enrolled.

2. One-term courses dealing with both trade and finance, where the students are expected to learn much on their own and class time is necessarily limited.

3. Graduate courses in business, public administration, or international relations, where students usually do not have extensive academic economics background, yet want a book that is sophisticated and addresses a range of topics.

4. Advanced students, using a text emphasizing theory, yet wishing to broaden their perspective with supplementary material.

ADAPTING THE BOOK TO DIFFERENT CLASSES

With a group of undergraduates with limited training and horizons, instructors can restrict the material examined to basic knowledge and comprehension, omitting the appendixes to several of the chapters and steering the students away from many of the more challenging questions at the end of the chapters. They may also wish to skip the more difficult parts of Chapter 8 and Chapter 15. For students with more economic background or greater sophistication, the instructor should use the various appendixes and may wish to try some of the projects suggested at the ends of chapters or in the instructor's manual. The endnotes give many additional references to form the basis of student essays. Those interested in management and public policy will want to emphasize more heavily the policy chapters: 4–9, 15, 17–19.

ACKNOWLEDGEMENTS

This book has been in process for a number of years and has benefited from the advice of many readers and students. We would like to thank Stephen Smith at Gordon College for his many helpful comments, Don Daly at York University for his long-term championing of the manuscript, and the many readers: Leonardo Aurenheimer of Texas A & M; Akorlie Nyatepe-Coo at the University of Wisconsin—LaCrosse; John Devereux, University of Miami; James A. Dunlevy, Miami University; R.W. Gillespie at the University of Illinois, Urbana/Champaign; Jonathan Harris of Boston University; Jack Hou at California State University–Long Beach; Gerald Lage of Oklahoma State University; Elden Liechty at Gordon College; Richard McIntyre at the University of Rhode Island; Craig MacPhee of the University of Nebraska–Lincoln; Steven Matusz at Michigan State University; and Ike Van de Wetering at Iowa State University. Katherine Rogers, chief assistant at Colby College, provided valuable aid. The students who have studied the book from manuscript pages, caught errors, confessed their confusions, and shown their appreciation deserve a hand. We would like to thank those students in Wilson Brown's honors seminar at the University of Winnipeg, who helped develop much of the national income data—William Lai (Korea), Karla Petri (Ireland), Raymond Chan (Thailand), Roger Martini (New Zealand), Rick Schroeder (Australia), and Ken Kroeker (Sweden). Lastly, we would like to acknowledge the many people who helped at Addison-Wesley; Karen Stone, our enthusiastic copy editor; and the editorial work of Beth Stephens, who helped us do the final difficult trimming of the manuscript.

Wilson B. Brown
Winnipeg, Manitoba

Jan S. Hogendorn
East Vassalboro, Maine

Contents

Chapter 1

The Nature of International Economics

OBJECTIVES

Overall Objective: To show and suggest the problems of the increasing integration of the world economy against a background of increasing state participation in the economy.

- To show how the world economy has become more and more integrated, often in subtle ways that people do not notice.
- To demonstrate that higher degrees of integration have been associated with improvements in communication and transportation and with increasing prosperity.
- To argue that, as governments have grown larger and more pervasive within their own economies, they have created many economic differences that would not otherwise exist.
- To surmise that the increasing integration and increasing influence of the state create considerable tension.

INTERNATIONAL ECONOMICS IN DAILY LIFE

The Sony clock radio (Japanese made, with a number of parts from Korea and Thailand) awoke Mr. and Mrs. Peoria one morning in their home in America's Midwest, the announcer babbling about the latest crisis in the Middle East. Mr. P. wondered vaguely whether the events would increase the cost of gasoline and whether he should buy that (German-made) Mercedes he always wanted on the excuse it had a diesel engine, or stick to his stylish and peppier but far less classy Honda (Japanese made). Mrs. P. was already up, deciding which blouse to wear (both carried the names of European designers, although one was made under license in the United States, the other in Bangkok), when Mr. P. meandered to the bathroom and debated whether he should shave with his Philips (Holland) electric razor or his Gillette 2-track (designed in Britain).

The stock market had done well that morning (principally due to foreigners' heavy buying in the market). Mr. P. had ordered his broker to sell some shares that day, so he was in a good mood. Admittedly, with the price of corn down (due to Europe's failing to import much American grain or meat), business in town was not as good as before, but it seemed that something was taking up the slack locally (indeed, a number of smaller manufacturers had seen their exports increase). Mrs. P. suggested that instead of a new car they should add a room to the house, but they were concerned because the price of lumber had just risen. (They had not noticed or understood how the U.S. government had just forced Canada to raise the price of its lumber exports to the United States.) Maybe, they thought, that long-awaited return trip to Britain would be a better thing, but they worried about the cost of the pound, since they had been rather shocked by the prices the last time they had traveled there.

The Peorias downed their (Brazilian) orange juice as the doorbell rang. It was Maria come to clean the house (and send some of her earnings to her family in Mexico). The French coffeemaker, fueled at that moment by energy released as a Canadian river gushed through a dam on its way to the Arctic Ocean, sent the aroma of freshly ground (in a German-made grinder) coffee, a blend of Indonesian, Brazilian, and Colombian beans, into the air. "Oh well," Mr. Peoria said, finishing his muesli (Swiss made) and toast with strawberry jam (Bulgarian) and butter (for which they had paid an unnecessary premium due to import restrictions), "perhaps we should just keep our money here; it's certainly good to have a 100% American day."

Like Mr. and Mrs. Peoria, we all are affected by international economics all the time, but rarely and then only dimly realize how and in what ways it affects us. In 1991 Americans spent about 11% of their income (GNP) on foreign goods and services, three quarters of that on goods and the rest on services, including foreign travel. They earned slightly less, about 10.4% of their income coming from exports of goods and services. In addition, they earned about as much from foreign investments as they did from rendering foreign services. Since they spent somewhat more than they earned, they borrowed a sum from abroad—less than 0.33% of their income, down sharply from their borrowings in the 1980s, which were closer to 2%.[1] Even Mr. Peoria helped the borrowing, because when he sold his stocks, they were purchased by a Japanese; and so another claim on American assets was transferred abroad, the Japanese giving up the use of his money so that an American could use it.[*]

Mr. and Mrs. Brandon, average Canadians, had a similar day, awaking in the western plains and watching "Good Morning, America" (U.S. produced) on cable TV, but their connection to the world's economy was even stronger. In 1991 Canadians earned just over 28% of their incomes (GNP) from abroad, over 80% of that from exports of goods.[**]

They spent about the same amount abroad, about 70% of that on goods and the rest on services. The Brandons, being typical Canadians for 1991, borrowed

---

[*] Whether it was a net loss or not depends on whether Mr. Peoria spent the money on the house (in which case it would be investment) or on a vacation (in which case it would be consumption).

[**] We use GNP rather than GDP in this chapter because many of our calculations include factor income and payments. For most countries, the two figures are within 3% of each other. See Chapter 11 for a more detailed discussion.

about 4% (net of what they lent) from abroad; part of their mortgage was from funds the bank borrowed in the United States, but the Brandons' bank invested some money in American treasury bills when Mrs. Brandon deposited money received unexpectedly.

We could continue with typical families on a country-by-country basis, but Fig. 1.1 shows more efficiently, though with less flair, some of the key factors of interdependence in a selection of different nations.

Figure 1.1 shows trade as a percentage of GNP, indicating also how much of that is a good and how much is a service.

Figures such as those in Fig. 1.1 often surprise people who are unfamiliar with them. Generally speaking, smaller nations have higher percentages of international trade than do larger ones. That is a physical fact having to do with the number of possible interactions, as true of mice and elephants as of nations. If California were a separate nation, all its trade with the other U.S. states would be international trade; if Belgium were merely part of a United Europe, all its trade with other European countries would be subtracted. The United States is the world's largest trader—13% of all the world's traded goods originated in the United States and 17% of trade ended up in the United States—despite the fact that trade as a percentage of GNP is one of the smallest among those countries listed. (Among major countries only India and the former Soviet Union have had

Figure 1.1 **Export of goods and services as a percentage of GNP in selected countries, 1991.** Trade is shown here as a percentage of GNP, indicating also how much of that is a good and how much is a service.

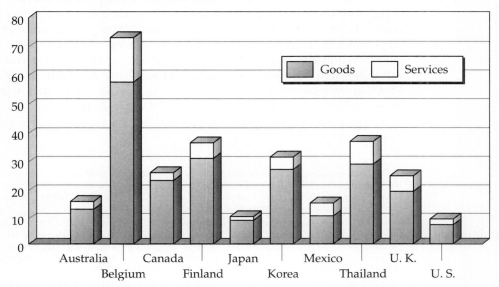

The figures are derived from the country pages of International Financial Statistics, *1991* Yearbook, *and the* IFS *monthly publication, February 1992.*

smaller figures.) Like the United States, Japan also has a vigorous and large internal economy; it is the third most important trader, yet trade makes up only around 13% of its GNP, the second-lowest ratio among the industrial countries.[*] The highest percentage of GNP accounted for by foreign trade in countries of any economic importance is Belgium, with well over 60%.[**]

Figure 1.1 also shows the large and growing trade in services. The services counted here do not include what is paid or received for interest or profits (taken up below), but only those expenditures on such things as shipping, tourism and travel, royalties, insurance, consulting, and data processing. Service payments and receipts vary considerably from nation to nation. Britain, with its well-developed financial, insurance, and shipping base, has always had a large percentage of its income in the form of services. Among the Third Woooorld countries, high receipts of services are usually associated with tourism. In Thailand, for instance, tourism has just replaced rice, that country's leading export for over a century, as the number-one foreign exchange earner.

Modern trade is not simply a matter of a German toaster, a Japanese car, or a Chinese-made shirt. Rather, many of the products themselves contain parts or ingredients made in other countries. The Ford Escort, for example, made in Europe, has parts from 15 different nations and is assembled in both Britain and Germany. Even at the level of parts, however, we miss other elements—the rubber to make the tires, the nickel for the stainless steel, the payment for the technology used, the rewards for marketing skills and strategies developed, the interest paid lenders in many countries, and ultimately the dividends that reward the shareholders for their capital and risk-taking.

The Peorias and the Brandons may not have noticed another international aspect of their lives: Some of the income from their holdings of stocks and bonds had its origins in profits and interest payments from foreign sources. Technically, payments received for lending money—interest and profits (dividends)—are service payments, but it is often instructive to separate these *factor services* from other services, and most international accounts normally do so. The United States in 1991 received about $132 billion in interest and profits in *factor income*— over $500 a person, about 2.3% of GNP.[†] Countries that have invested substantially abroad over the years such that they have a great stock of wealth in foreign

---

[*] The leading trading nations as measured by their combined exports and imports in 1991 were: (1) the United States, $931 billion; (2) Germany, $803 bn; (3) Japan, $552 bn; (4) France, $448 bn; (5) United Kingdom, $394 bn; (6) Italy, $352 bn; and (7) Canada $252 bn. Source: *International Financial Statistics 1992 Yearbook,* International Monetary Fund.

[**] In some circumstances trade as a percentage of GNP can exceed 100%. This can happen if imported inputs into production are very large and are worked on by domestic labor, and then the resulting finished products are exported. The imported inputs are (rightly) not included in GNP, so that trade as a percent of GNP can be very high. Hong Kong provides a good example. Its exports of goods and services in 1988 were 136% of GDP.

[†] *Net,* the figures are much lower, as the United States spent $110.5 billion on profits, interest, and related payments to foreign residents, leaving a surplus of about $25 billion—still half of one percent of GNP.

countries have high returns on their *net factor incomes;* those that have been net borrowers over the years have net outflows. Canadians, for instance, make over $1000 per person in factor payments abroad, receiving only $250 per person from abroad. While in recent years the United States has been borrowing, the stock of wealth is such that the United States is still able to come out ahead in its net payments. Figure 1.2 shows a typical sampling; the countries in deep debt must make high payments, but the reader should be careful not to assume a high ratio of debt necessarily means trouble—at least not one where the outflows are in the range of 4 or 5%.

Trade in goods, services, and factor payments is just part of the interconnectedness of the world economy. Also vitally important is the movement of capital from one nation to another. The bank loans and the international sale of corporate and government securities are enormous. Statistics are not so easy to gather on capital movements, but those available show substantial amounts. The International Monetary Fund (IMF) has calculated the amount of assets and liabilities that commercial banks* have outside their own countries. Such banks

---

* The IMF calls these "deposit banks" to distinguish them from central banks. They are equivalent to "member banks" in the U.S. or "chartered banks" in much of the British Commonwealth.

Figure 1.2 **Net factor payments and receipts.** Net factor payments act as a fair proxy for payments on debt. The chart shows a number of nations' payments or receipts, ranging from Ireland's payments of nearly 15% of GNP to Switzerland's receipts of 5%.

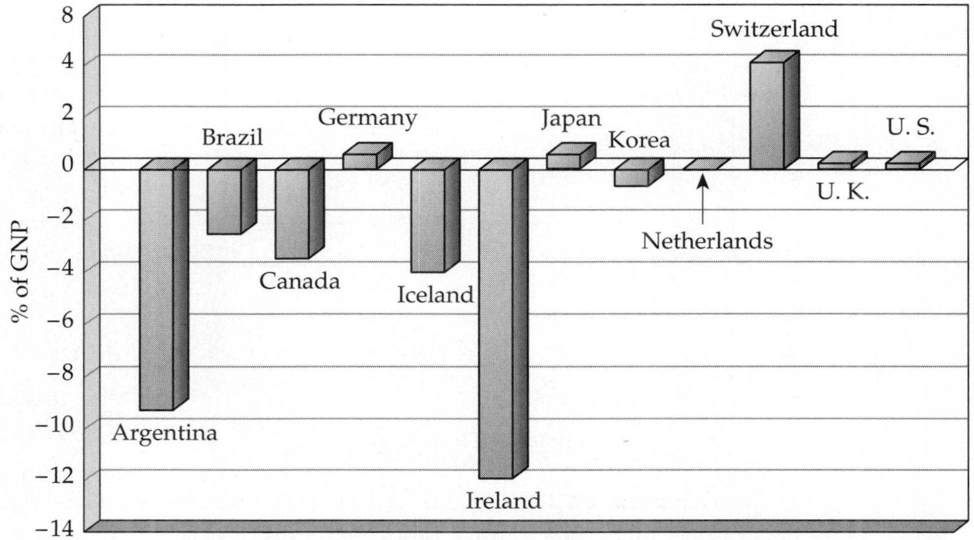

Source: National income accounts from International Financial Statistics. *Most figures are from 1991; Argentina's is 1989, Brazil's and Ireland's from 1990. The different years are not critical for the present demonstration because such figures do not change rapidly from year to year.*

had at the end of 1991 some $6.8 trillion of assets (loans and other foreign credits). (Approximately four fifths of these loans were made to other banks, which in turn lent the money to their customers.) Figure 1.3 shows the size and growth of such activity in 1985 dollars.

Bank lending and deposit taking is only part of the picture. In the last decade, increasing proportions of total lending have been made through security markets. New corporate bond issues sold abroad totaled close to $300 billion in 1991, having doubled in seven years. Purchases of corporate shares have also been high: 1991 saw *net* (the change at the end of the year) purchases of shares (for portfolio, not control purposes) of over $50 billion, out of a *gross* flow of nearly $1.5 trillion.[2]

The foreign exchange markets, where currencies are traded, have expanded greatly to handle the increase in trade and investment. Figures in those markets tend toward the astronomical: Daily turnover in 1990 in the world's markets is $650 billion.[3] That comes to more than $22 trillion a year. Earlier figures are

Figure 1.3 **Commercial banks' foreign assets: World, United Kingdom, and United States, 1970–1991 (1985 dollars)** Commercial banks' foreign assets have skyrocketed, rising in real terms some thirteenfold in the two decades following 1970. The largest lender (and borrower) is the United Kingdom, the center of the large Eurodollar market (discussed in Chapter 15), and the second in size is the United States, but the bulk of the increase in assets has been spread among banks in many countries. In 1991, there was a slight downturn in bank lending (measured in 1985 U.S. dollars).

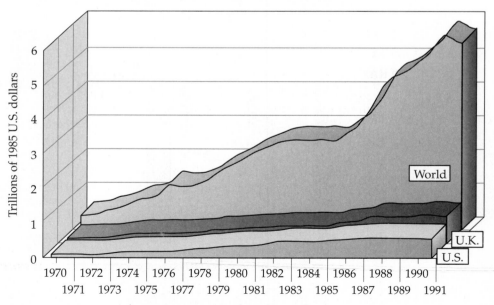

Source: International Financial Statistics Yearbook, *1992.*

guesswork, but all specialists agree that the volume in the markets has been doubling every few years.

Not only capital, but also labor is mobile. Despite restrictions on entry, there were an estimated 20 million migrant workers in the world in the late 1970s, 12 million of those from less developed countries—6 million in North America, 5 million in Western Europe, and 3 million in the Middle East, the rest scattered about. Workers' remittances to their home countries grew from $3 billion a year in 1970 to $24 billion in 1980, and are a major source of foreign exchange earnings for some Third World countries. A more recent indicator the IMF has developed is a measure of the earnings of residents of one country working in others. This figure doubled (in nominal terms) between 1984 and 1990, and stands at $22 billion.[4]

The extent of the integration of the world economy has profound significance not only for individuals, but also for policy makers and economic institutions. Today's interpenetration is the culmination of a long historical process, unlikely to be reversed. Simultaneously, national governments, which control currencies, manage the microeconomic environment, and determine macroeconomic policies, have grown strong and have played an increasing role in shaping their national economies. Yet, almost paradoxically, extensive economic integration has meant that the national governments are less and less able to control economic activity within their own borders. In the following section of the chapter we look at how all this happened. In the rest of the book, we examine the way the world economy affects the individual nation, and how the nation reacts.

THE GROWTH OF ECONOMIC INTERDEPENDENCE

TRADE AND CURRENCIES BEFORE THE MODERN ERA

The study of international economics can make a claim to be the oldest branch of the discipline. The first acceptable figures for gross national product date from the 1930s—anything before is guesswork, however sophisticated—but foreign trade data can be traced back to medieval times. English trade statistics, for instance, date back to 1355, in the reign of Edward III. Agents of the crown or city-state could tax and measure foreign trade funneled through relatively few ports or highways. Domestic trade, however, was far too various and complicated to control or count. For the same reasons, economists today find that in many less developed countries trade statistics are reasonable while many other economic figures are not.

Trade among kingdoms and empires is of great antiquity. A recent underwater archaeological find highlights the early origins. It is of a Bronze Age merchant ship, which, some three thousand years before the Christian era, heading for some port of Asia Minor and laden with, not surprisingly, bronze, sank off the coast of Turkey. Some two millennia later, but still a thousand years before the Christian era, we have evidence of agreements between kingdoms. A case in point is the story of Solomon's temple. In the King James Bible's version:

> *And Hiram sent to Solomon saying, I have considered the things which thou sentest to me for: and I will do all thy desire concerning timber of cedar, and concerning timber of fir. My servants shall bring them down from Lebanon unto the sea: and I will convey them by sea in floats unto the place that thou shalt appoint me.*
>
> *. . . So Hiram gave Solomon cedar trees and fir trees, according to all his desire. And Solomon gave Hiram twenty thousand measures of wheat for food to his household and twenty measures of pure oil; thus gave Solomon to Hiram year by year.* [*]

This was not the last time that oil and wheat have figured in trade agreements.

Ancient times saw not only extensive trade but also problems of currency exchange. Currency changers were common throughout the ancient world; indeed, it was foreign exchange traders whom Jesus drove out of the temple (for profaning the temple, not for changing coin). Kingdoms used a variety of metals for coinage—gold and silver, electrum (a gold-silver alloy), copper, bronze, and even iron, though gold and silver came to predominate. The prices of these metals varied against one another as the demand and supply of the metals changed over the centuries, making the job of trading the coins even more difficult. In addition, rulers frequently debased their coins, manufacturing them from less precious metal than their markings indicated. Cleopatra and her father unleashed a serious inflation in Egypt, as did Nero (who rebuilt Rome with the profits from debasement) and many of the late Roman emperors. In Egypt, the value of a pound of gold increased from 1125 denarii in AD 179 to 3000 denarii by AD 191, and over 3 billion denarii at the end of the third century. The currency problems of recent years are hardly new—nor are the means of handling them. Even such seemingly modern and sophisticated devices as forward exchange rates (discussed in Chapter 13) and the use of units of account to denominate debt date back at least to medieval times.[5]

The ancient trade of the West diminished in the early Middle Ages. A decline in public safety, with a rise of marauders and pirates, the collapse of the Roman roads, the decline in literacy, and the disappearance of good coinage all discouraged growth and trade. Signs of revival occurred in the twelfth century, and the invention of vessels that could sail against the wind helped to lower the cost of trade. Still, it was the fifteenth century before the development of premodern institutions—banks, well-developed markets, credits for trade, double-entry accounting, or insurance.

While international trade grew in these centuries, it never penetrated people's lives the way it does today. Only a small part of national production could be exported or imported. A sailing ship had a small capacity to carry

---

[*] Norman Crump, *The ABC of the Foreign Exchanges*, London, Ayer, 1965, quotes this from I Kings 5:8–11.

goods, and internal roads were usually too miserable to sustain extensive or heavy shipments. Normally, each city or rural estate was supplied almost entirely from the countryside around it, and only the items that had a high value per cubic foot could be transported great distances.[6] There was a silk trade, a carpet trade, a fur trade, and a spice trade, but no wheat trade, coal trade, or meat trade—indeed, very little wine trade until means of preservation were improved. Travel was very difficult—the word itself is a twin to *travail* and derives from a medieval torture instrument in which people were confined so they could not move. It was not undertaken lightly or for fun until well into modern times. Tourism did not begin until the eighteenth century.

The nineteenth and early twentieth centuries brought enormous changes of dimension not seen earlier. In 1800, it took a hard full day to get from New York to Philadelphia, and a week to get to the Alleghenies. In 1830, the persistent traveler could get somewhat further west into Pennsylvania in a day, but not much further in a week. Yet by 1857, the traveler could be well into Ohio at the end of the first day and across the Mississippi at the end of the week. The steamboat, the railway, the telegraph, and the telephone all allowed trade on a vastly greater scale. The amount of goods that could be carried in railway cars and steamboats was vastly greater than wagons, barges, and sailing ships could carry. (Steamships were not at first faster than sailing ships, just more reliable and far more capacious.) Wheat from lands in Argentina, Saskatchewan, and North Dakota, beef grazed in the plains and slaughtered in the prairie cities of North and South America, or bananas grown in the Caribbean could be shipped thousands of miles to hungry buyers. Transportation costs, which frequently accounted for 100% or more of the original cost of the goods, fell to small fractions (10 or 20%) of the costs, often with the remarkable result that prices rose for the exporter while falling for the importer. Thus the price received in the Argentine pampas by the producers of grain or meat rose at the same time that the price the Londoner paid to consume these commodities fell.

Communications improved the flow of trade. What was needed in the importing country and what was available in the exporting country could be matched, and the shipowner no longer had to wait until his ship came into port to find out what was on board. Payment could be made by telegraph (the line across the Atlantic was established in 1868). By the early years of this century, trade and international finance were no longer affecting only small groups within nations or just a few key products—in many countries 20 and 30% of all wealth was being generated by goods and services that were traded, and that figure was destined to rise even more in the last half of the century.

Historical figures are difficult to evaluate, but Fig. 1.4 helps visualize how the changes in the nineteenth century stimulated trade. The period 1720–1820 saw slow growth of both national economies and commerce; the period after 1820 until the First World War, which was the period described above, showed a growth of trade far in excess of the growth of income.

Figure 1.4 **Growth in real GDP and exports of selected countries.** High levels of economic growth are associated closely with high levels of growth in trade.

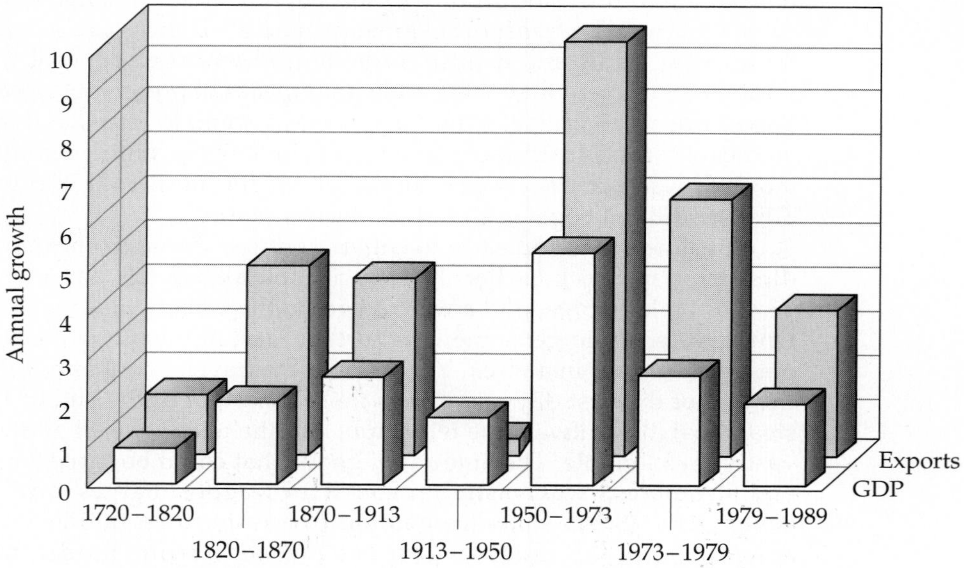

Britain and France for 1720–1820, these plus Germany and the United States for 1820–1870, and these four plus Italy and Japan for the later dates.

TRADE IN THE TWENTIETH CENTURY

The basic technological changes allowing the expansion of trade had been set in place before the First World War. While the cost of transportation had continued to decline to an important degree, it cannot have had the same impact as nineteenth-century changes. If the cost of moving $100 worth of goods fell from $100 to $20, another fall of even 50% in costs would represent only 10% of the price of the good. Only air traffic (and that after the middle of the century), with its ability to move vast numbers of tourists, has made a difference as dramatic as the nineteenth-century changes did.

Trade in the present century, as Fig. 1.4 shows, is divided into two distinct periods. In the period from just before World War I to just after World War II, both income growth and trade growth were low, and it is the only period in the table when trade grew at a slower rate than income. The two wars disrupted trade itself, but national policies erecting high tariffs on imports, and later quantitative barriers, also made trade difficult. Finally, the Great Depression of the 1930s reduced incomes and, combined with the protectionism of the period, depressed imports.

The third quarter of the twentieth century saw dramatic declines in tariff barriers, reductions of capital controls, and attempts at international standardization of safety, health, and labeling requirements. It saw enormous capital movements on a scale never before witnessed—whether or not desired by governments. Transportation costs declined sharply and speed of delivery rose with the introduction of large, highly automated ships capable of unloading their cargoes in a single day. (Indeed, the problem today is to store and move the cargo that has been unloaded. Thus the New York City piers are rotting, while the New Jersey ports of Newark and Elizabeth, with their enormous meadows of marsh that can be used for storage, have virtually all the business.) With rising fuel costs, too, ocean transport became relatively cheaper than land transport. Once a ship is loaded, the marginal cost of sailing another one hundred miles is very low. Astonishingly, it is cheaper today to move cars from Japan to California than it is to get them there from Detroit. Sea-rail links have made coastal cities in Japan little more than a week away from Chicago. Winnipeg, not far from the geographical center of North America, regularly has fresh fruits from Argentina, Chile, and, in season, rambutans and lychee from Southeast Asia. A map of the world drawn according to freight rates, not geographical distances, would show the oceans shrunken to the size of the Mediterranean Sea.

National tastes, too, have been converging. As large parts of the developing world come to enjoy high per-capita incomes, high levels of education, and high levels of urbanization, they evolve many tastes similar to those of the developed world. The spread of motion pictures, magazines, television programs, books, and extensive interpersonal contact all press toward a certain uniformity in taste. The once uniquely Western business suit, for instance, is well-nigh ubiquitous among business leaders and government people. Blue jeans and Coca-Cola seem as popular in Japan and France as in the United States. Mechanization has brought with it its own physical demands, lending a certain sameness to cities and factories everywhere. Except for some surface styling, an elevator is an elevator even when it is called a lift; a petrochemical factory is just that; even automobiles vary little from country to country.

The third quarter of the century also saw the rise of a tremendous amount of nongovernmental cross-border activity—what has come to be called transnational activity, as opposed to international activities involving relations between governments. The ready communications of satellites and fast jets put people into contact with an ease never before imagined. IBM, for instance, has all of its European operations tied together on telephone lines, and one computer can send to any other detailed plans and specifications on any project. It is not unusual for an executive to fly across the Atlantic to meet with other executives in some airport hotel for a few hours and then fly back. As a result of this easy communication, growth has mushroomed with all kinds of transnational contacts—charities like Foster Parents; service organizations like the Rotary; myriads of professional societies of engineers, architects, and economists; interest groups like the Audubon Society; and, not least, those profit-making enterprises known as multinational corporations. Solomon's Temple today might have been built by international contractors from Rome, designed by an international architectural firm in New York, and constructed of wood supplied by an international conglomerate.

Statistics support these observations, even though the public is little aware of the extent to which the growth of trade has surpassed the growth of output and income over the past 40 years or so. Figure 1.5 reveals this tremendous expansion. World trade grew nearly ten times in real terms between 1950 and 1990, much higher than growth in real GNP in those years, which quadrupled. This enormous increase in trade made new kinds of goods broadly available, contributed to real output growth because of scale economies and specialization that could not be realized in small national markets, increased competition in national markets, and was a major contributor to the high growth rates of GNP that characterized the global economy after World War II.

As an inevitable result of trade growing faster than domestic economies, the vast bulk of nations have seen trade rise as a percentage of national income. In the early 1950s, barely more than 3% of U.S. GNP came from exports; by 1965 it was 5%, and had climbed to nearly 11% by 1991. Canada's exports rose from 19% of GNP in 1965 to 28% in 1991, and the pattern is similar in other countries, as Fig. 1.6's sampling reveals.

A significant decline in the growth of world trade set in during the recession of the 1980s, however. It started in 1981 and was not reversed until 1984; contributing to the fall was the reduction in oil shipments as countries substituted other energy for petroleum. By volume, world trade had risen 5.2% per year on average between 1972 and 1981, but it fell between 1981 and 1983. Rapid growth

---

Figure 1.5 **Value of world trade in 1980 U.S. dollars.** Total world trade expanded nearly ninefold in real terms between 1950 and 1990, using a U.S.-based deflator. Other, more sophisticated methods (but with older data) show growth to be somewhat higher. See the *World Development Report* for 1988. Note also that, logically, world exports should equal world imports, but that they do not: imports always appear to be higher. Chapter 11 discusses such statistical problems in greater detail.

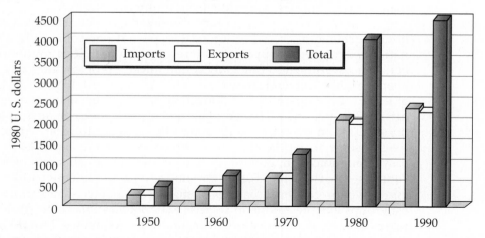

Source: World Development Report, *1990, pp. 194–195,* International Financial Statistics Yearbook, *1992.*

Figure 1.6 **Exports of goods and services as a percentage of GNP in selected countries, 1965 and 1990.** In the vast majority of countries, exports have grown as a percentage of GNP since 1965, usually substantially.

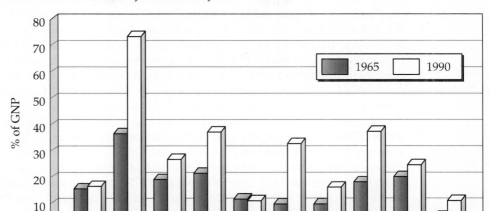

resumed in 1984 and continued through 1990, when it, along with world output, slowed considerably. Trade as a percentage of world income is now at an all-time high of over 20%.[7]

The historical thrust has been for greater interdependence in the world economy. The forces behind that thrust have been powerful; if we may make a preliminary observation to be supported in later chapters, those nations that have chosen—or have been compelled—to buck the forces of integration have not on the whole done well. With the exception of big oil exporters, virtually all the nations with trade declining as a percentage of national income, or those with low percentages of trade, have very low incomes per capita. When the world as a whole has tried to resist the forces of interdependence, as between 1914 and 1950, incomes have fallen or risen only sluggishly.

We turn now to the actor in this drama who must choose whether (and how) to ride or to fight those forces: the nation-state.

TRADE AND THE NATION-STATE

INTERNATIONAL AND INTERREGIONAL TRADE

Ask the lay person why international trade exists and the answer is likely to have something to do with national characteristics. Malaysia is in the tropics and exports rubber. Industrious Germans produce high-quality cars. Creative French designers produce the latest clothing styles. That type of explanation, clothed in its proper theoretical vestments, is only partially correct. Natural differences of soil, climate, even national temperament often do coincide with nations. Oceans, seas, jungles, deserts, and mountain ranges not only form militarily defensible lines, but also more or less incidentally serve to hold a nation within climatological boundaries. Often, too, national borders delineate cultural differences, as cultural groups have struggled to preserve themselves or have eliminated competing cultural groups within their borders. Religions change with the border, as from Israel to Jordan, Pakistan to India, or Thailand to Malaysia. Languages change, as from Mexico to the United States or Uruguay to Brazil, and with that comes much other cultural baggage. Surely an exposition of cultural and climatic differences should explain trade between such nations. But such explanations also serve to explain why Florida sends oranges to Massachusetts and Massachusetts sends computers to Florida—that is, they are basically explanations of *interregional,* not international trade. To the extent that nations have different regional characteristics, the explanations are useful, but in themselves insufficient.

To make the point more conclusively, let us look at something that is international but not interregional. Consider the satellite photograph in Fig. 1.7 of part of the border between the United States and Canada. The border stands out as clearly as the edge of a carpet: There is farming on the U.S. side and ranching on the Canadian side. Yet the land is the same. The winter wind blows just as cold, the summer's grasshoppers munch just as greedily, and there is in short no geographical reason why the land use patterns should vary so sharply. There is no cultural reason either: Both Canadians and Americans eat wheat and beef, and each country has both farmers and ranchers. Both groups of farmers are English-speaking of European ancestry. Indeed, the forty-ninth parallel is just a line drawn by far-away negotiators. Yet that artifact has determined, somehow, a pattern of land use.

Suppose we follow Mr. and Mrs. Peoria, who decide to take a two-week holiday in Canada, starting in the western plains and ending driving east to Toronto. They drive north across that border between North Dakota and Manitoba—a day's drive east of where the satellite picture was taken. Consider what differences they would see that are not due to regional variations.

1. They have to pick their route carefully to find a place to cross the border. The transportation system, built largely by government money or subsidies, is not as dense near the border, and access is controlled. It certainly is not a serious problem for their car, but it is for a truck because the roads leading to many crossings are not all that suitable for heavy transport. What is more, there are only two railway crossings between the Winnipeg area (where there are several) and the Rockies.

2. Immigration is controlled. The Peorias spot this immediately when a uniformed customs officer walks over to their car to inquire about their citizenship. Since they are not Canadians, the officer inquires further as to the

Figure 1.7

Source: Landsat image courtesy of the Canada Centre for Remote Sensing, Energy, Mines and Resources; Ottawa, Canada.

purpose of their visit and when they intend to leave. As usual, he is satisfied, but young people, especially those traveling in a van, might raise suspicions, and might be subjected to a long session of questions, for fear they might wish to stay on and find work in Canada. People from a rather long list of countries must have passports to enter, and some even are required to obtain visas before arriving in the country. Without these, they will be turned back at the border or will not be allowed to land, and the process can at times be rather arbitrary.

3. Imports are controlled. The officer will inquire what the Peorias are bringing in that they will not be taking back, and whether they have any firearms or liquor (one bottle per person is allowed). If they had any gifts for Canadians, they might find themselves paying a tariff, plus the far more costly sales taxes levied by the government and provinces, which could amount to nearly 15% of the value of their purchases.

4. They go for a bite to eat, and find they need a different currency. (Yes, the restaurants will take their U.S. dollars in the border areas, but not always at the best rates, because they cannot use the U.S. dollars to pay their bills and have to take them to the bank, which has to send them back across the border.)

5. The Peorias' youngest daughter, Gloria, is twenty years old, and they all want a beer. In North Dakota, she could not be served; indeed, she was not even supposed to be in a place serving beer. In Manitoba, she is of legal drinking age.

6. They ask the part-time, obviously pregnant waitress something about her medical coverage, and she tells them that the restaurant does not provide any insurance, but that she gets a great deal of coverage through the province. To most people in industrial economies, that would be familiar, but to the Peorias, whose health insurance is privately provided and who are aware that part timers often are not covered by their employers' policy, the Canadian system is surprising.

7. The Peorias wonder, however, about what might be the resultant higher taxes, but find that in the brief discussion they cannot really discover whether Canadian taxes are higher or lower than those paid by Americans because deductions, exemptions, tax rates, and the like are all so different.[*]

8. Half the label on the ketchup bottle is in French. They learn that a company cannot sell ketchup in Canada without a label in French and English, even if its target market is a thousand miles away from any concentration of French speakers, and further from any monolingual Francophones.

THE SOURCES OF NATIONAL DIFFERENCES

None of the differences noted above is regional; all deal with the existence of separate governments. Each nation has different codes or rules that make its economy different from those of its neighbors. Taxes may be principally on income in one nation and on value added in another. One nation may subsidize farming, another industry. Pollution, safety, labeling, and branding requirements differ enormously—and often for no better reason than that they have evolved separately. Habits that are basically customary become sanctioned by law—as in which side of the road to drive on, and therefore which side the steering wheel is on.

National laws also tend to isolate each nation from its neighbors, making a considerable difference in the way trade is conducted within a country and between countries. Within the United States, for example, labor, management, and capital move freely. Great movements these can be, as with the pioneers to the frontier, blacks to northern cities, or businesses to the so-called Sunbelt. In Europe one finds the Welsh moving to London, the provincial French to Paris, or Germans to Bavaria. Capital moves too. New textile plants are built in the American South, leaving old ones idle in New England; electronics firms have moved to the circumferential highway around Boston, robotics plants to the road between Detroit and Ann Arbor; and capital raised through the sale of stocks and bonds sold in any area of the United States can serve to finance operations in any other area.

---

[*] To answer the question: Canadian taxes are about 40% of GDP, compared with about 30% in the United States. The difference is made up of higher interest on Canadian debt, higher transfers (including Medicare), and higher expenditures on goods and services, each accounting for about a third of the difference. (*The Globe and Mail*, Toronto, Sept. 18, 1992, reporting on an OECD paper.)

Between countries the situation is different. In the United States, Ellis Island, the point of entry for millions of immigrants for over a century, is now a museum, and legal immigration slowed to a trickle (but has recently risen substantially). Canada and Australia, which until recently had virtually open doors for (white at least) immigrants, now have them open just a crack, and the bulk of new immigrants are refugees. While the number of people working across borders is still substantial, the flow is not what it used to be.

Modern governments also try to restrict the movement of capital, although they are often unsuccessful. Many nations require a business or individual to have government permission before sending money abroad—what is called exchange control. Several nations have tried to restrict the inflow of capital; the Swiss, for instance, actually charge foreigners a fee instead of paying interest on Swiss accounts. Many nations limit any capital movement associated with a controlling ownership, particularly of natural resources. A firm may be able to move fifteen hundred miles from New York to Alabama, but if it went just a few miles to Quebec, it would have to fill out a long document explaining why it was investing and why it should be allowed to make its investment. (Until a few years ago, the Canadian government rejected many applications.) In Japan, Mexico, and most of the Andean countries, foreign firms cannot invest unless they share ownership with domestic citizens. Communist countries, of course, prohibited extensive private ownership on principle, but that era appears to have ended.

The nation-state shapes its own economy in many subtle, often unintended, and frequently ill-understood ways. Every tax, every subsidy, every regulation causes economic reactions, which we understand only partially. Economics can tell us something about the incidence of taxes (who ultimately pays a tax[*]) or the incidence of a subsidy (who ultimately benefits). But answers to such questions are difficult both theoretically and statistically. The costs and benefits from regulation are even more difficult. Find two side-by-side nations and the differences, as with the forty-ninth parallel, may be clear, but the causes of those differences may not be at all apparent. Is the difference between U.S. and Canadian land-use patterns caused by a U.S. subsidy to grain farmers? (The picture was taken before the high subsidies of recent years.) Canadian subsidies on meat? Transportation policy? Tax structures? The value of the Canadian dollar? You could make an argument on each point.

THE NATURE OF THE MODERN STATE

Many of the differences just described derive from the nature of the modern nation-state, both in its jurisdiction and in the extent of its activities. A law made in Paris applies in equal force anywhere in France, and stops at the border.

---

[*] A tax may be levied on a merchant, but the merchant may be able to raise prices and pass the tax on to customers, in which case the incidence of the tax is on the customer.

Table 1.1 **Early U.S. government expenditure as percent of GNP or national income**

Year	Federal expenditure as % GNP or NI
1799	1.4[*]
1859	1.7[*]
1889	2.9[*]
1909	2.6[**]
1929	2.3[**]

[*] of national income   [**] of GNP

Source: Dennis C. Mueller, "The growth of government,"
IMF Staff Papers, *Vol. 34, No. 1, March 1987, p. 116.*

It was not always so—a medieval king could hardly hope to have his laws applied equally in all parts of the country, because many of the nobles who were presumably loyal to him were not willing to enforce them, and there was nothing the king could do about it. It is even true today in many countries that the power of the central government diminishes in distant areas. Burmese control over its northeastern area or Bolivian control over the coca-growing regions resembles more the struggles of some medieval king dealing with half-rebellious barons than the patterns of a modern state. In this sense, we must have modern, consolidated nation-states to speak of international economics.

The second element in modern nation-states is the extent of their intervention in the economy, which in turn determines the degree to which the governments shape those economies. Certainly, the kings of Europe had intervened in the economy, created monopolies, even tried to set prices, but their power and scope were limited. Large centrally controlled standing armies and even police forces are basically nineteenth-century developments. The percentage of national income the government could extract in taxes was necessarily small because there was little surplus income above subsistence. Heavy taxation is basically a phenomenon of the last hundred years. Gathering the historical data is necessarily difficult, but the following sampling should help make the point. Table 1.1 gives some early U.S. figures for the federal government alone, while Fig. 1.8 brings figures up to date. Such figures are for total expenditures and taxes and include income transfers. (Transfers, such as pensions and Social Security, were not large percentages of the budgets until the 1940s.)

Other nations have shown similar increases. Most Western European governments have rather higher total taxes and expenditures, due principally to higher transfers.

The rise in taxation and expenditure has increased the government's effect on the national economy. Tax rates of 5 or 10% are unlikely to alter substantially firms' or households' actions, particularly if those taxes are collected from many

Figure 1.8 **Government expenditures as percent of GNP federal and other (U.S.).** Governmental expenditure has risen steadily as a percentage of American GNP. Note that the additional growth in recent decades has come principally from the state and local levels.

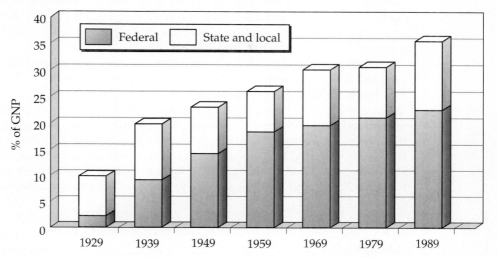

Source: Mueller, as in Table 1.1, and Government Financial Statistics Yearbook, *1991, for more recent figures.*

different tax bases (some excise, some imports, some real estate). When, however, taxes and expenditures are at current levels, they have major effects in changing (or distorting, to use a more loaded word) the allocation of resources. Since the taxation and subsidies are different in each nation, the shape of their economies differs also.

POLITICAL-ECONOMIC CONSIDERATIONS

Political considerations loom large in the way the state confers benefits and extracts penalties. The national state is the focus for compromise and tradeoffs, carrying a *legitimacy* that far exceeds its ultimate physical powers to enforce its laws. We each pay, albeit grudgingly, taxes to support many things we do not like, and we each get the benefit of subsidies and expenditures paid for by others. We all recognize that the state is an arena in which various interest groups contend for their piece of the pie, but most of us also feel that much of what the state does is good for virtually everyone. The vast bulk of the population accepts the compromises and tradeoffs made at a national level. Many citizens may begrudge the import controls that cause them to pay extra money for their shoes or chickens, all in support of some far-off town, but they expect that there will be some other compensating benefit, if not now, then at the next round.[8]

Internationally, there is less sense of legitimacy and of tradeoff, and tradeoff is much harder to accomplish between nations. We accept the domestic shaping of the economy, even if it involves major distortions from a hypothetical free-market result and even if those distortions hurt us individually. We do not accept similar distortions when they have foreign origins. With the focus of our political activity on the national level, the international arena is secondary, even when it is not secondary in importance.

Subsequent chapters will demonstrate what occurs when small groups are able to harness the considerable powers of the modern state to their own ends, frequently fighting integrative pressures that will increase economic efficiency at their expense. To prevent the state from bridling as the harness is placed on, they use smooth and soothing phrases, explaining the benefits of some greater good, disguising or ignoring its actual costs, to provide their actions with the moral legitimacy required for acceptance. As economists, our concern is with a demonstration of costs and benefits. As students of policy, however, we take our roots to Adam Smith and J.S. Mill seriously; we are still moral philosophers.

LOOKING FORWARD

The chapters that follow explore the way international and national economies are related, and the patterns of policy that emerge domestically. Part I of the book explores the microeconomic side of the economy: the benefits of trade, the problems of trying to restrict trade, and the development of free trade between groups of countries.

Part II examines most of the key macroeconomic issues—growth, full employment, inflation, and debt. No change in the money supply and no change in the level of taxation is without its international repercussions, and any nation, even the very biggest, that tries to act alone does so at its peril. At the same time, the highly integrated world economy imposes constraints on domestic policies that make impossible policies that once benefited certain groups. Moderate inflation, for instance, increases real taxes, allowing legislators to spend without having to declare an increase in taxes. It also causes real wages to fall, without anyone having to renegotiate a contract. If international factors force deflation or limit inflation, some groups will be hurt, and others will benefit. The final chapter addresses foreign direct investment, a topic closely related to investment and finance, although the analysis required is in fact basically microeconomic.

VOCABULARY AND CONCEPTS ————————————————

Capital movements   **Interregional trade**
Commercial banks   **Nation-state**
Economic interdependence   **National differences**

Economic intervention
Exchange control
Factor income
Factor services
Foreign exchange markets
Gross national product (GNP)
Income
International trade

Net factor income
Protectionism
Services
Tariff
Taxes
Transfers
Transnational activity

QUESTIONS

1. Do small or large countries typically find that trade is a large percentage of their GNP? Why?

2. For most purposes, is it important to distinguish trade in goods from trade in services?

3. What indications exist to show that the world is more interdependent (or more integrated) today than 30 years ago?

4. Why have the changes noted in question 3 occurred?

5. Why did trade and economic integration expand so much in the nineteenth century?

6. What is the evidence that expanding trade is linked to economic prosperity?

7. "International economics is basically a study of the economic phenomena wrought by the nation-state." Explain, distinguishing international economics from interregional economics.

8. "We cannot have international economics without nations, for if the world were one nation, no trade could be international." What in the nature of the modern state has made differences across borders greater than they were 75 years ago?

9. Explain the difference between interregional and international economics. Use the photograph of the U.S.–Canadian border as a point of departure for your discussion.

10. A tension has arisen between the growing influence of national governments and the increasing integration of the world economy. Explain.

11. As will become ever-more apparent as the book progresses, our laws and enforcement are applied far more arbitrarily and probably unjustly against foreign businesses than domestic ones. How might the sense of legitimacy and the pattern of tradeoffs lead to such a situation?

NOTES

[1] For those who need to know the latest data, the numbers are from the International Monetary Fund's International Financial Statistics, available in most university libraries.

[2] Morris Goldstein, David Folkerts-Landau, Mohamed El-Erian, Steven Fries, and Liliana Rojas-Suarez, *International Capital Markets, Development, Prospects, and Policy Issues,* International Monetary Fund, 1992, pp. 33–36. Total outstanding bonds is harder to figure. The Bank of International Settlements estimated the amount at around $1 trillion in 1988, and the total was probably about $1.3 trillion by 1991. See Research Department of

IMF, *Determinants and Systemic Consequences of International Capital Flows,* International Monetary Fund, 1991, p. 6.

[3] According to the Bank for International Settlements, 1992, reported in George Anders, "The powers behind currency," in the *Globe and Mail* (Toronto), September 18, 1992.

[4] See the *Balance of Payments Yearbook* for 1991, Table C-12.

[5] See Paul Einzig, *The History of Foreign Exchange,* London, St. Martin, 1964, chapters 1–6.

6 We draw from Fernand Braudel's Volume III. *The Perspective of the World* describes the city-states. Volume I, *The Structures of Everyday Life,* notes that in the thirteenth century, English grain increased in price by 15% for every 80 km of overland travel.

7 See IMF, *World Economic Outlook 1992*, p. 49.

8 Dennis Mueller, discussing Gary Becker's paper, "A theory of competition among pressure groups for political influence," *Quarterly Journal of Economics,* August 1983, states, "Groups whose interests have public good or externality attributes are more likely to be successful than those seeking pure redistribution." (Mueller, "The growth of government," pp. 132–133). One could say that groups seeking the aid of the government are more successful if they make some claim to legitimacy.

Part I

International
Trade

Chapter 1 showed that freer trade has almost always been associated with periods of world-wide economic growth, and that trade has grown more than the economy, becoming a much larger share of national income in almost every country. Chapters 2 and 3 look at why increased trade raises national incomes.

Chapter 2 begins the examination with an exposition of the theory of comparative advantage, demonstrating why it remains the bedrock for analysis of the benefits of trade, and why we normally expect trade to improve welfare. Chapter 3 moves beyond the basic theory, asking why it is that some countries gain advantages in producing one kind of product. These questions are of particular interest because modern trade is often automobiles for automobiles, or photographic film for film, not products that are very different like the "wine or cloth" distinction favored in the principles books.

Chapters 4 and 5 examine barriers to trade that the state creates, examining their nature, their costs, and how they redistribute income. Chapter 6 turns its attention to policy, examining the history of trade policy and some of the reasons for continued protectionist policies. Finally, it takes on the arguments for greater protection, one by one, showing their limitations and the strength of the standard trade theory.

Chapter 7 reflects again on the question of price distortions, examining unfair trade practices and providing further tests for the standard theory. Chapter 8 examines some of the newer arguments for protection or export subsidies—strategic trade policies, in which the state systematically subsidizes and provides other advantages to specific industries. Finally, Chapter 9 discusses at length the problems and issues of regional economic integration, and whether or not it improves world welfare.

Chapter 2

The Theory of
Comparative Advantage

OBJECTIVES

Overall Objective: To explain the well-accepted and still powerful proof of the benefits of international trade known as the theory of comparative advantage.

MORE SPECIFICALLY:

- To demonstrate the theory of comparative advantage in numerical and diagrammatic ways.
- To show why becoming more productive may not affect comparative advantage.
- To use supply and demand diagrams to discuss the gains from trade, identifying some gainers and losers.
- To modify some of the key assumptions about the number of products and transport costs.

As noted in the first chapter, the creation of a national border running across a region should not change the economic rationale for trade. If Vienna traded with Budapest before Austria-Hungary was broken up, or if St. Paul traded with Winnipeg before there was significant control or taxes along the forty-ninth parallel, the economic gains should still be there afterwards. Yet somehow the advantages of trade we assume to exist domestically must be argued again in an international setting. Adam Smith pointed this out in the *Wealth of Nations*, following his discussion of the obvious gain that occurs when a shoemaker sells shoes to a tailor from whom he buys his clothes.

> *What is prudence in the conduct of every private family can scarce be folly in that of a great kingdom. If a foreign country can supply us with a commodity cheaper than we ourselves can make it, better buy it of them with some part of the produce of our own industry employed in a way in which we have some advantage.*[1]

It remained for the great English economist David Ricardo (1772–1823) in his *Principles of Political Economy and Taxation* of 1817 to develop a more elaborate theory of the advantages of trade, known as the *theory of comparative advantage*. This chapter presents that theory, albeit in modern dress. It shows the gains from international trade in both the Ricardian general equilibrium, where the functioning of an entire economy is analyzed with production possibilities and indifference curves, and the Marshallian partial equilibrium, which works through demand and supply curves to analyze a single good. In the process of doing so, the chapter develops the modern theory of comparative advantage. Subsequent chapters examine more deeply why certain trading patterns develop and the vast political, tax, and legal machinery that has arisen to block trade.

■ *RICARDO AND HIS MODEL*

Ricardo was one of history's greatest economists. He was also one of the richest, making a large fortune on the London stock exchange within 30 years of his birth. Public spirited, he used part of his wealth to buy a seat in Parliament, in which he served with distinction. His new theory of comparative advantage eventually moved British economic policy radically away from the old mercantilist idea that one country's gains from trade were another country's loss. In a relatively short period of time, the mercantilist belief that limiting imports and maximizing foreign exchange receipts were good goals in foreign trade was replaced by a broad new concept that liberal trading rules would best promote the public welfare. For nearly a century thereafter, Britain had the most open trade policy of any industrial nation.

For his model, Ricardo used wine and cloth produced in England and Portugal to make his famous examples. These were contentious topics in his day. The Methuen Treaty of 1703 had in fact reduced British tariffs on wine and Portuguese tariffs on cloth, the two products in which the countries were relatively inefficient, and this had provoked a long and bitter controversy.[2] The modern reader might think one of the product choices not apt. It is impossible to produce wine in England, one might say. But it *is* possible! English wines were indeed bottled from grapes grown along the warm southern coast in Ricardo's time, and a little is produced even today, with output boosted by the price support of the European Community's Common Agricultural Policy. The main reason we do not simply duplicate Ricardo's presentation is not the rarity of good English wine, but the fact that Ricardo used the labor theory of value to measure costs of production (the costs being only the man-hours of labor employed to make the products). Later economists considered also the value of land and capital, and turned Ricardo's argument into one based on opportunity cost. That is the approach we follow.

THE GAINS FROM TRADE IN GENERAL EQUILIBRIUM

To begin, let us follow Ricardo in postulating a world of two countries (plausible enough) and (implausible, but absolutely essential for a two-dimensional diagram with any clarity) two products. The products in this 2×2 analysis are wheat and cloth, the nations Agricola (the wheat producer, naturally) and Fabrica (the cloth producer). We will also assume that competition is perfect, with all relevant costs known and any idled resources quickly reemployed at their next-highest opportunity costs. This model encompasses only real flows of goods, and it does not incorporate factor flows such as international lending, or the holding of deposits abroad, or the movement of labor from one country to another. Because there are no capital flows, trade must therefore balance, with exports always equaling imports. At this stage we do not consider transport costs or any barriers to trade such as tariffs or quotas. We do not specify the type of economic system—whether this is market driven, socialist planned, or simply a computer game with the reader as Grand Coordinator. Furthermore, the present model has no dynamic effects such as changing tastes or production abilities. Each of these assumptions will be relaxed in turn during the course of the next few chapters. After completing that process, we will find that some of the conclusions stemming from Ricardo's model are altered in detail, but that the fundamental strength remains.

Begin with Table 2.1, which has the possible production combinations for two goods available to each nation, assuming *autarky*, a word meaning no trade between the nations. (The word *autarky* should not be confused with its homonym, *autarchy*, which refers to autocratic or dictatorial rule.) The table shows, among other things, that Fabrica can at any volume of production get 15 more bolts of cloth in return for giving up 30 bushels of wheat; that is, if it wishes to increase its wheat production from 30 to 60, it must decrease cloth production from 60 to 45. Agricola can at any point get 30 more bushels of wheat by giving up 10 bolts of cloth. Because of these production tradeoffs, we can conclude that in Fabrica the price of 30 bushels of wheat is 15 bolts of cloth, or half a bolt of cloth per bushel of wheat. Similarly, the price of 15 bolts of cloth is 30 bushels of wheat, or two bushels of wheat for a bolt of cloth. In Agricola, however, prices are different. The price of 30 bushels of wheat is 10 bolts of cloth, or one third of a bolt for a bushel. The price of 10 bolts of cloth is 30 bushels, or three bushels for a bolt.

Now begin trade between the two nations. Fabrica can buy its wheat in Agricola for one third of a bolt—one sixth of a bolt cheaper than if it produced the wheat itself. Agricola can buy one bolt of cloth in Fabrica for two bushels of

Table 2.1 Production possibilities for Fabrica and Agricola

Fabrica		Agricola	
Wheat (bushels)	Cloth (bolts)	Wheat (bushels)	Cloth (bolts)
150	0	240	0
120	15	180	20
90	30	120	40
60	45	60	60
30	60	30	70
0	75	0	80

wheat, one less bushel than it would have cost to buy the wheat at home. If Agricola specialized completely in wheat, it could produce 240 bushels; if Fabrica specialized completely in cloth, it could produce 75 bolts. No other combination will give so high a total "world" output of wheat and cloth—try it and see. Surely the Great Coordinator, in allocating resources, would want Agricola producing wheat and Fabrica producing cloth.

Suppose further that Agricola and Fabrica have the same population, wealth, and capital stocks. Agricola, however, can produce more of *either* wheat or cloth than Fabrica. Because the same amount of resources (land, labor, and capital) can produce more in Agricola, we can say that Agricola has a higher *productivity* than Fabrica. Agricola can make either a bushel of wheat or a bolt of cloth with fewer resources than Fabrica. In Ricardo's language, Agricola has an *absolute advantage* in both products. **An absolute advantage is said to exist when a country uses fewer resources to produce a product than does another country.**

The absolute advantage does not prevent trade, however. Agricola still has to contend with the fact that its opportunity cost for making an extra bolt of cloth is three bushels of wheat, while Fabrica's is only two bushels of wheat. The trade that springs up between Agricola and Fabrica is determined by *comparative advantage*—that is, the ratio of the tradeoffs within one country compared to the ratio in the other country. We compare costs, not productivity. The cost in Agricola is not the number of man-hours, quantity of land used, and value of capital engaged, but the cloth those resources could have produced. Agricola may very well have higher productivity, but that means that the wheat sacrificed to produce cloth is greater. Costs, which are always opportunity costs, are higher. Any nation may be capable of making quite efficiently any number of the things it imports, but only at a sacrifice if it is able to make other products even more efficiently. **A comparative advantage is said to exist when one country can produce a product at lower cost in terms of opportunities foregone than can another country.**

■ *THE BILLY ROSE STORY*

Charles P. Kindleberger of MIT unearthed a remarkable example of the common sense of comparative advantage. A famous and wealthy impresario of stage and screen in the 1940s, Billy Rose was also a world-class typist and stenographer with many awards to his credit. He would thus have encountered enormous difficulty in hiring a secretary who could work nearly as well as he himself could. Still he hired secretaries because even though he was the world's best at the job, he could still earn much more in an hour spent manipulating his stage and screen empire than he could in typing.

Frequently economic pundits intone that a nation must "increase its productivity" to improve its trading position. False. A nation of beavers and a

Table 2.2   **Production possibilities after a productivity change**

Fabrica		Agricola	
Wheat (bushels)	Cloth (bolts)	Wheat (bushels)	Cloth (bolts)
300	0	120	0
240	30	90	10
180	60	60	20
120	90	30	30
60	120	15	35
0	150	0	40

nation of goof-offs have ample reason to trade, and neither the industry of the beavers nor the lethargy of the goof-offs will change the trading pattern. Suppose that Fabrica is taken over by an efficiency-minded government, while Agricolan industry and farming suffer major efficiency losses, as a new spirit of fun-loving and leisure-mindedness infects the population. Productivity doubles in Fabrica and falls to half of its old levels in Agricola. Do trade patterns change? Interestingly, no. Table 2.2 shows that Fabrica can now produce double the amount it could previously make, 180 bushels of wheat and 60 bolts of cloth for example. Remarkably, however, the ratio of the tradeoff of wheat to cloth in more productive Fabrica is still the same: An extra two bushels of wheat must be sacrificed to get an extra bolt of cloth. Agricola, in spite of its now-lower productivity, still has a 3:1 tradeoff ratio. While clearly Fabrica is far better off than it was before, it will not overwhelm Agricola with trade. Agricola undoubtedly has fewer goods and services to enjoy, but trade will still leave it better off than it would be under autarky.

COMPARATIVE ADVANTAGE WITH PRODUCTION POSSIBILITIES CURVES

The data from Table 2.1 produce the solid lines in Figs. 2.1a, 2.1b, and 2.1c. The lines are what most students know as production possibilities curves (PPCs), though they are often called production frontiers and occasionally transformation curves. The difference between what is drawn in most texts and ours is that our PPCs are not curved, but are straight lines. Thus no matter how specialized or generalized each nation is, the tradeoff of wheat for cloth will be the same. This temporary expedient, consistent with Ricardo's illustration, will soon be relaxed. Figure 2.1a shows the production possibilities curve of Fabrica, 2.1b the PPC of Agricola, while 2.1c shows the two curves on the same diagram. We can see immediately that the two curves have different slopes, which is to say they represent different prices. The slopes indicate the price of cloth in terms of wheat, 1:2 in Fabrica and 1:3 in Agricola. Where the curves are located, that is, where they intercept the axes, depends on productivity. If we wished to repre-

Figure 2.1 Figure 2.1a incorporates the data in Tables 2.1 and 2.2 for Fabrica into production possibility curves. If productivity doubles for both wheat and cloth, the slope of the schedule does not change, and therefore the price of one product in terms of the other does not change. Figure 2.1b does the same for Agricola, showing the same thing. Figure 2.1c presents the two original schedules, showing that Agricola can produce either more cloth or more wheat than Fabrica, but that it is still to its advantage not to produce cloth.

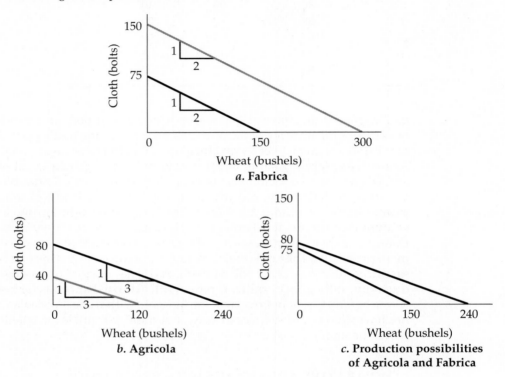

sent Fabrica after it became a nation of beavers, we would just move the production possibilities curve outward, as suggested by the lighter curve on Fig. 2.1a. To show Agricola becoming a nation of goof-offs, we would move its PPC inward, as represented by the lighter curve on Agricola's diagram.

The simple diagram cannot answer many questions we have about trade. It suggests that Agricola would specialize entirely in wheat, and Fabrica in cloth, but it does not provide enough information to tell just how much each nation would keep for its own use or how much welfare would improve. To begin that analysis, we turn to our more normal production possibilities curve, which is bowed, as in Fig. 2.2. Such production possibilities curves represent increasing costs—that is, the more wheat a nation wants, the more cloth it will have to sacrifice to get it; the more cloth it wants, the more wheat it will sacrifice. The

Figure 2.2 The introduction of increasing costs produces production possibility curves that are concave to the point of origin. The slope at a combination of wheat and cloth the community wants is represented by the line at the point *e*.

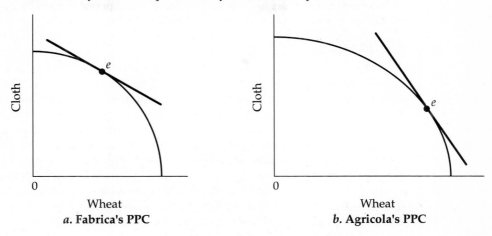

a. **Fabrica's PPC**   *b.* **Agricola's PPC**

assumptions are more realistic and consistent with normal partial equilibrium analysis (demand and supply), where supply curves slope upward, meaning that greater and greater opportunity costs are being incurred as production increases. An unbent production possibilities curve suggests a perfectly elastic supply curve for either of the two goods in question.

The problem with using a bowed PPC is that we have a great number of slopes to choose from, ranging from the nearly horizontal to the nearly vertical. To determine what is traded and what gains there might be, we have to know where on the PPC the nation would produce under autarky—what mix of the two products is the one it wants. We could initially just mark the mix desired, as with the points labeled *e* on each of the PPCs in Figs. 2.2a and 2.2b. At those points the price ratio in the economy can be represented by a straight line drawn tangent to the PPC at *e*. The slope of that line shows the cost ratio between wheat and cloth, that is, the amount of cloth that must be traded off to get more wheat and vice versa. Under competitive conditions, the cost ratio must also be the price ratio.

As long as the two points *e* are on the PPCs at places where the slopes are different, there is an incentive to trade, just as with the unbent PPCs of Fig. 2.1. The lines tangent to the PPCs of Figs. 2.2a and 2.2b at point *e* show the slope of the PPCs at *e*. Clearly, Fabrica has a great desire for cloth, Agricola for wheat, so the attempt to specialize that much has caused the price of cloth to be expensive in Fabrica and the price of wheat to be high in Agricola. Note that it is not just the difference in the set of production possibilities here, but the location of points like *e* on the production possibilities curve that causes the differences in cost structures.

ADDING INDIFFERENCE CURVES

Production possibilities curves define the range of combinations of goods available to the economy. The reason price and production settle at any given point, however, depends on community preferences. We can show this with *community indifference curves.* Some readers will have encountered indifference curves before, others not, since they are often an optional topic in introductory courses. An *individual* indifference curve marks out all the combinations of goods that are equally satisfactory to an individual. In Fig. 2.3, for instance, the indifference curves I, I_1, and I_2 mark out various combinations of wheat and cloth the individual would prefer. Each curve identifies combinations at which the person would be equally well off. Let us take wheat a little more broadly to mean food, and cloth to mean clothing. Then imagine a person thinking: "Well, given various sets of possible combinations of the two things, both of which I want, what is my own personal tradeoff between the two? Clearly I need both to eat and to be clothed, and I need some kind of balance between the two. I'll take more clothing in exchange for less food to a point, but I will demand more and more clothing to compensate because I'll have to eat poorer quality and less tasty food, and eventually, I'll start to get hungry. An extra shirt isn't going to be worth as much to me as a good meal. Similarly, I'll take more food for clothing, but as my wardrobe wears out I'll be willing to sacrifice more of my good meals in order to get some decent clothes."

This means that the individual's indifference curve has a bowed shape convex to the point of origin (that is, the "cave" opens away from the origin), because the person requires more and more of one good to compensate for additional losses of the other good. Any point on the same indifference curve is

Figure 2.3 **Adding indifference curves to the PPC.** Community indifference curves allow a statement of the amount the community would prefer of the two goods. A point where the production possibilities curve just touches the highest possible indifference curve gives the optimal point of production.

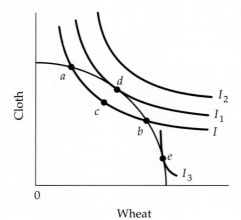

considered a point at which the individual is indifferent between the various combinations of goods shown along the curve. Moreover, an individual's welfare is increased if he can move to a higher indifference curve (I to I_1), since that means more of *both* goods.

A *community* indifference curve reflects the community's preference and can, with some welfare reservations noted below, be viewed as the summation of individuals' indifference curves. The indifference curve I in Fig. 2.3 indicates one possible set of combinations of wheat and cloth that would leave the community indifferent. Note, however, that points a, b, and c would be inferior to production at point d, which lies on the highest attainable indifference curve I_1.

An indifference curve marks out combinations that would leave the community indifferent at some given level of satisfaction. If we consider another level of satisfaction, we can suppose the community should have a new set of combinations that would leave the community indifferent. This allows us to draw an indifference curve for *any* level of satisfaction. Figure 2.3's I_1 represents a higher level of satisfaction than shown by curve I, and is an indifference curve that the nation can reach. The country would be even better off, being able to have more of both goods, if it could produce enough to reach I_2, but it cannot do so.

With any given output, the community is best off producing where the production possibilities curve and the indifference curve are tangent, just touching each other. As we have seen, I_1 is the highest curve the nation can reach, and it can only reach that curve if it produces at point d. Any other production combination would put the nation on a curve lying under I_1.[*] If the community has a different set of preferences, as for example the greater desire for wheat shown by indifference curve I_3, then it would produce a different combination of goods shown by point e.

■ *WELFARE LIMITATIONS OF COMMUNITY INDIFFERENCE CURVES*

Economists do a little dance around community indifference curves. It is no problem to say that an indifference curve represents a community's set of preferences or that given certain production possibilities, the point of production is that which the community prefers. Where we get into trouble is in handling the tradeoffs between individuals. Economic welfare theory itself says only that we can be sure that welfare is improved when an individual moves to a higher

---

[*] Those with a background in intermediate micro theory will recognize that this is the point where the marginal costs of the production of either product equal their marginal utilities or $MC_a/MC_b = P_a/P_b = MU_a/MU_b$. The terms "marginal rate of substitution in production" and "marginal rate of substitution in consumption" are often used instead of marginal cost and marginal utility. The equation fulfills the condition known as Pareto Optimality, named after the Italian economist Vilfredo Pareto (1848–1923). Given an initial distribution of income, this is the best welfare situation that can emerge.

indifference curve. Summing the curves for more than one individual presents difficulties.

Consider Fig. 2.4, on which we have summed two indifference curves, one for Abel and the other for Baker. This is supposed to show the combinations of cloth and wheat that would leave the community equally well off. But a problem occurs when the community is able to obtain a greater quantity of both goods. Suppose the community can now reach a point such as C' on I'_{a+b} instead of C on I_{a+b}. We cannot be certain whether there has been a welfare gain or not, because we do not know whether some redistribution of goods has occurred between Abel and Baker. Abel may have been an exporter who gained from free trade, while Baker, who was making something that was in competition with imports, lost from free trade. While the community may gain, this may be because the Abels have gained more than the Bakers lost.

Figure 2.4 The problem posed by community indifference curves

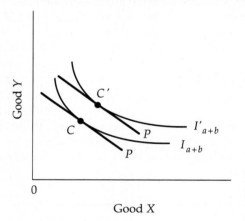

Economists cannot prove an unambiguous gain in this case because economics has no way to make welfare comparisons between persons. A large gain to Abel cannot be proven to offset even a small loss for Baker. Baker may weep and thrash about with the loss of a few shirts while Abel would be only mildly pleased by a whole packet of new goods. If we could put a utility meter on their heads to measure relative satisfaction and dissatisfaction, Baker's unhappiness would overwhelm Abel's increased pleasure.

Welfare economists attempt to cope with the problem of interpersonal welfare by employing the *compensation principle*. This principle states that if the gainers can gain enough to compensate the losers, actually do make these payments, and still have something left over, then there is an unambiguous gain to society as a whole. (It is normally assumed that the compensation would be undertaken through the political process, involving taxes and subsidies. It might, however, under some circumstances be arranged privately.) Suppose the Abels realized that the Bakers would resist any opening of trade and bought them all out at voluntary free-market prices and then closed them down or shifted their production to their next best alternative. We would then know the gain would be unambiguous.

Be wary. An argument that says economists are not sure every increase in trade improves welfare does not mean that trade should be restricted unless there is compensation. A dash of skepticism should not provoke violent protectionist reaction. In the wider scope of economic growth, the compensation question is only a minor issue. Like most other decisions, trade decisions are taken with uncertain information and uncertain consequences, and are to a considerable extent judgment calls. Economists are rarely going to judge that the lack of compensation overwhelms the beneficial effects of additional trade.

After all, nations do not operate solely on the basis of unambiguous tradeoffs. In the continual economic readjustment to technological and market changes, many people are displaced without compensation, and in practice we make many ambiguous decisions about what increases welfare. Certainly in numerous small-group situations, individuals take losses so that others may gain (or get their gains in psychological satisfaction). In a well-functioning body politic, some groups of people also take losses with a sense that the nation is the better for it. Every new product, every managerial reorganization, every change in production technology can mean layoffs and bankruptcies. Government-built highways bypass small towns, government-funded construction changes shopping and living patterns, all creating losses for some businesses and gains for others with no compensation paid. Indeed, if we were to assure ourselves that all economic gainers fully compensated all losers, we probably would make very few gains.

Now with two sets of production possibilities curves and two sets of indifference curves, we can analyze several ways in which trade between nations would improve welfare.

THE MODEL SHOWING SIMILAR TASTES BUT DIFFERENT PRODUCTION POSSIBILITIES

Let us suppose we have two nations with the same tastes, but different production patterns. Figure 2.5 shows both Agricola and Fabrica possessing the same set of indifference curves, but different production possibilities curves. Because the production possibilities differ, however, Agricola and Fabrica have different prices. Wheat is relatively expensive to produce in Fabrica, and cloth is relatively cheap; consumers respond by consuming more cloth than wheat, at point w. The price in Fabrica is indicated by the slope of the tangent line P_fP_f. In Agricola, cloth is expensive to produce, and wheat is cheap; consumers choose to consume at point x. The price in Agricola is indicated by the tangent line P_aP_a.

Now suppose we open trade between the two nations and pick the price at which we find the maximum benefits. There being no transport costs or trade barriers, a single equilibrium price ratio (called the *equilibrium terms of trade*) will result, so that the price line must have an identical slope in the two countries.

Figure 2.5 **Fabrica and Agricola before trade: same indifference curves, different production possibilities curves.** Fabrica and Agricola have identical sets of indifference curves, but do not produce the same mixture of wheat and cloth because their production possibility curves are different. Fabrica consumes at w and Agricola at x.

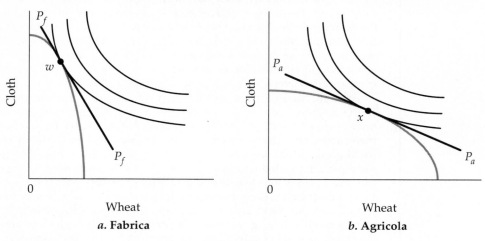

a. Fabrica   b. Agricola

Furthermore, the exports of a product from one country must equal the imports of that product into the other country.

With a little experimentation, we can determine whether an equilibrium price has been reached. Say we have chosen the price represented by the lines $Q_f A$ on Fig. 2.6a and BQ_a on Fig. 2.6b. Both these lines have the same slope, meaning that both nations pay the same price for goods. But they satisfy other conditions as well. At that price, Fabrica will produce at Q_f, but consume at point A, on an indifference curve that is *beyond* its production possibilities curve. It can do this because it *imports* M_f of wheat from Agricola and *exports* X_f to Agricola. These exports and imports form a triangle, the base of which is the trade in wheat (the product on the horizontal axis), the height of which is the trade in cloth (the product on the vertical axis), and the hypotenuse of which is the price line indicating the price ratio that occurs after trade has taken place. Because Fabrica is an *importer* of wheat, the line showing imports extends beyond the production possibilities curve; Fabrica on its own could not make wheat beyond its production possibilities curve.

Agricola also shows a move to a higher indifference curve at point B. In its case, it is cloth that is imported, so the vertical of the triangle extends beyond the PPC. It is wheat that is exported. We have arranged the diagram so that Agricola's exports match exactly Fabrica's imports and Fabrica's exports match Agricola's imports. That is, $M_f = X_a$ and $X_f = M_a$ at the equilibrium terms of trade. If this were not the case, then we would not have an equilibrium situation and whatever good was in surplus would continue to fall in price against the

Figure 2.6 **Fabrica and Agricola after trade, showing gains: same indifference curves, different production possibilities curves.** After trade, Fabrica produces cloth at Q_f, exports X_f of cloth, while importing M_f of wheat. It thus moves out to an indifference curve beyond its autarkal reach. A similar process occurs in Agricola with X_a wheat exported and M_a cloth imported. Note that the side of the triangle that represents the exported good must lie entirely within the production possibility curve, and the lines for the traded good extend outside it.

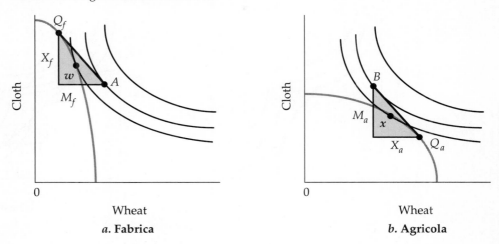

a. **Fabrica** *b.* **Agricola**

scarcer commodity. The gain to trade is represented by the move to the higher indifference curves. As is typical of situations with differing production possibilities curves, each nation becomes more specialized in what it produces, but less specialized in what it consumes.

THE MODEL SHOWING SIMILAR PRODUCTION POSSIBILITIES BUT DIFFERENT TASTES

Now change the model around and assume that the production possibilities curves are the same, but that tastes are dissimilar so that the indifference curves vary. Figure 2.7 shows this situation, with Fabrica and Agricola having the same PPC, but with Agricola wanting much more cloth (at point w) and Fabrica wanting much more wheat (at point x). Before trade the price ratios, as shown by the price lines, are different, so trade can take place. The price, as usual, will be between the two that exist. We have chosen a price, AQF, that will yield two identical triangles and be tangent to the production possibilities curve and an indifference curve from both countries. We find that both nations' output becomes less specialized, with production at Q. Neither nation has to suffer the increasing costs it was experiencing to produce the mix of cloth and wheat it wanted. Consumption, however, has become more specialized, with the foppish Agricolans buying plenty of clothing and the hungry Fabricans eating more food.

Figure 2.7 **Fabrica and Agricola after trade, showing gains: same production possibilities, dissimilar indifference curves.** With similar production possibility curves, but different tastes, a gain from trade is still possible. Before trade, Fabrica is producing at *x* to satisfy its great desire for wheat, while Agricola is at *w* so it can have more cloth. Trade allows more specialized consumption and less specialized production, as both nations move to point *Q* to produce.

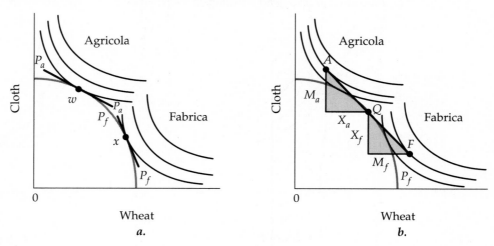

The obvious problem in handling the production possibilities and indifference curve diagrams such as those in Figs. 2.6 and 2.7 above is finding triangles that have just the right size and slope to fit the curves in both countries. The basic principle is simple. Find the market-clearing price, where the imports of a given good by one country are equal to the exports of the same good by the other country. Yet it takes imagination and a keen eye to draw the triangles correctly. Another tool, called the *offer curve,* is visually easier and gives us another way to examine the equilibrium in a two-country, two-commodity setting. Offer curves are explored in an appendix to this chapter.

THE GAINS FROM TRADE COME FROM TWO DIFFERENT SOURCES

The gains from trade, shown by a movement to a higher indifference curve, can be divided into two parts: the gain from trading at the world price rather than the old home price under autarky, and the gain from specialization as production is altered. Figure 2.8 shows a nation that in autarky would produce at A, with relative prices shown as P_aP_a. If this nation began to participate in world trade but did not shift its own production pattern, it could move out to wherever the world price is tangent to the highest indifference curve that can be reached. In this case, the world price is represented by the slope of P_wP_w, and it touches indifference curve I_2. The move to I_2 is accordingly the gain from the lower world prices for its imports and higher world prices for its exports.

Figure 2.8 **Gains from trade.** P_a (autarkal price) shows the price and production before trade. P_w (world price) shows what happens if the country can buy and sell at world prices, but does not specialize in production. P_{w_2}, also the world price ratio, touches point B showing that gains are increased when the country is able to shift its production into more cloth making.

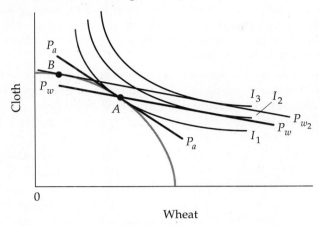

A further gain is, however, likely, as the nation specializes in the good in which it has a comparative advantage. When production shifts to point *B*, which is the equilibrium where prices and costs are equal with the world price P_wP_w tangent to its production possibilities curve, it can reach a higher indifference curve I_3. Therefore the distance between I_2 and I_3 is the gain from altering production.

SOME CONCLUSIONS FROM THE 2 × 2 ANALYSIS

1. Increased foreign trade is in a country's economic self-interest. While there are often political reasons for increased trade, that is icing on the cake. There is great unanimity among economists on this point—in a paper published in 1992, fully 93.5% of the economists surveyed in a large random sample agreed with the proposition that "tariffs and import quotas usually reduce general economic welfare." That was the highest level of agreement in the 40-question survey, tied with the 93.5% concurring that "a ceiling on rents reduces the quantity and quality of housing available."[*] Contrast this una-

---

[*] Richard M. Alston, J.R. Kearl, and Michael B. Vaughan, "Is there a consensus among economists in the 1990s?" *American Economic Review*, Vol. 82, No. 2, May 1992, p. 204. It is fair to add, however, that some slippage has occurred over the years. A survey of the members of the American Economics Association published in 1979 showed that 97% of the membership agreed that interference with trade by tariffs and import quotas reduced the general welfare. See J.R. Kearl et al., "A confusion of economists?" *American Economic Review*, Vol. 69, No. 2, 1979, p. 30.

nimity among economists with the statement by the chairman of the USX Corporation (largest U.S. steelmaker) that the theory of comparative advantage is a "combination of rhetoric, smoke, and mirrors."[3] Many business-people and politicians have yet to be convinced.

2. Trade increases output and hence consumption. Once two nations enter into trade, the same total quantity of labor, capital, and land is able to produce a greater output of goods because the two countries can move toward specialization in what they do best.

3. Gains are mutual. Both countries that enter into trade improve their welfare, such that one nation's gains are not at another nation's expense. Thus the theory of comparative advantage states that both sides gain from trade, though note it does does *not* say whether A gains more than B, or B more than A.

4. There is no basic difference, in economic terms, between the gains to specialization and trade that occur between firms or individuals domestically and those that occur internationally.

5. It is comparative, not absolute, advantage that determines the gains from and the direction of trade. When one nation has higher productivity than another—that is, any given combination of land, labor, and capital will produce more of any good than the same combination will in another nation—there is just as much reason to trade as when productivity is the same.

6. A small country trading with a large country stands to gain more than the larger one does. The big country's prices will be far less affected by the opening of trade than the little country's because the smaller country's trade is only a tiny percentage of the market. The doubling of the sales of Jamaican footwear in the United States or Peruvian cotton in Europe is unlikely to change U.S. or European prices much, if any. This means that the small nation takes most of the gain from trade, while there is little change in the larger country.

THE GAINS FROM TRADE IN PARTIAL EQUILIBRIUM

The general equilibrium conclusions can be usefully compared to the results in partial equilibrium using only the tools of supply and demand, with which welfare changes can be viewed by means of the alteration in consumer and producer surplus. Such a model is much simpler, because we look only at one good at a time—the simultaneous changes that occur in general equilibrium cannot be shown directly when looking at the supply and demand for just one good. Yet the partial equilibrium analysis has many uses, and conclusions drawn from it reinforce rather than contradict the judgments arrived at in general equilibrium.

THE GAINS FROM IMPORTING   Figure 2.9a shows the demand and supply in Hibernia for strawberries. The supply curve slopes upward, implying increasing costs, and the demand curve downward, implying decreasing marginal utility, consistent with our general equilibrium assumptions. Assume, to begin, that Hibernia is in autarky. With no trade, the market clears at a price of P_e and a volume of Q_2. With trade, however, Hibernia can purchase strawberries from other countries for price P_m. At P_m the quantity consumed is Q_3 and the quantity produced is only Q_1. Is Hibernia better off importing strawberries?

Consumers certainly are. The buyers of Q_2 were willing to pay the price P_e for their berries but can now buy them for P_m; their benefit is the rectangle formed by the rectangle A and the triangles B and C, essentially $P_m P_e$ times $0Q_2$. Their *consumer surplus*—the difference between what they pay and what the good is worth to them, which is the area above the price and below the demand curve—has increased. The increase is the difference between what they were previously willing to pay and what they *actually* pay for it. (A good example of a consumer surplus would be the benefit received when customers have already decided to buy an item and then find it is on sale. They were clearly willing to pay the regular price but obtain it for the sale price. The difference is the change in their consumer surplus.)

The buyers of the strawberries from Q_2 to Q_3 are not equally better off, however. The woman buying the extra quart of berries just to the right of Q_2 would not have bought that quart at price P_e before—she would have needed a few cents off for encouragement. Since she has more than just a few cents off, her benefit is almost as high as the buyers to the left of Q_2. The man just to the left of Q_3 would not, however, have bought the strawberries if they had been the least

Figure 2.9 **The gains from trade in partial equilibrium.** P_e is the price on autarkal equilibrium, P_m the world price for the import, and P_x the world price for the export. Each of the lettered areas is important to understand the benefits (and some of the difficulties) of trade.

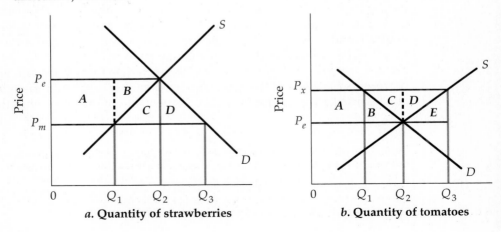

a. **Quantity of strawberries**   *b.* **Quantity of tomatoes**

bit more costly; indeed, his decision to buy was very painful as he struggled in his classical economic mind to compare the benefit of strawberries with all the other possible things he could do with the money spent on the berries. His added benefit from the lower price was therefore very small. We thus consider the increase in consumer surplus for consumers between Q_2 and Q_3 to be the triangle D, which reflects this declining value. The total consumer surplus gained is therefore the area $A+B+C+D$.

Producers of strawberries have, of course, lost, but they are not put out of work. The supply curve sketches the opportunity costs of the strawberry producers in alternative occupations (or the land and capital in alternative uses). A supply curve, after all, represents costs, and costs are always opportunity costs. Producers from 0 to Q_1 simply stay in the strawberry business.* Their loss, or change in producer surplus, is the area A. The producers from Q_1 to Q_2, however, suffer less of a loss because they are able to do other things. The farmer just to the left of Q_2 was thinking about producing another crop anyway: So close were his calculations that a penny less per quart on strawberries would have driven him to rhubarb production. His loss would be very little. The farmer down just to the right of Q_1, however, only found alternative crops or other occupations sensible when the price of strawberries fell to near P_m. His loss is nearly the entire distance between P_e and P_m. The change in producers' surplus, then, is the area $A+B$. The gain for the economy from importing the strawberries is the gain in consumers' surplus $A+B+C+D$ less the loss in producers' surplus $A+B$. The consumers' gain outweighs the producers' loss, leaving the triangles $C+D$ as the net gain.

THE GAINS FROM EXPORTING   The analysis is not yet complete, because we still must consider the new export, in this case tomatoes; their foreign price will be above the autarkal (no-trade) equilibrium point, as in Fig. 2.9b. As prices rise from P_e to P_x the quantity produced rises from Q_2 to Q_3, while the quantity demanded falls to Q_1. This allows exports of Q_1Q_3. Using the same analysis employed for the decline in price, we see that consumers are worse off, many paying higher prices (rectangle A) and a number shifting to other less satisfactory purchases (triangle B). Producers, however, gain back all of rectangle A, and triangles B and C, which is the added revenue for the same amount of production they had before (rectangle A and triangle B are from Hibernia's consumers, triangle C from the rest of the world). The rectangle formed by Triangles D and E represents the value of the expanded production Q_2Q_3. Only triangle D, however, is a true gain, because triangle E is the value of the goods that the resources

---

* We cannot tell if these were the most efficient producers or if costs have fallen in the strawberry business as some producers have exited. If we assume that all strawberry producers are identical— a normal assumption under pure competition—then we would have to assume that each producer had a mixture of excellent and mediocre land, and the decline in production was because each producer cut back on its less-good land, or turned land over from strawberries to a crop such as rhubarb that it would be best at producing, given the lower strawberry prices.

producing Q_2Q_3 could have made in domestic sales. Like the diagram in Fig. 2.9a, we have a producers' surplus ($A+B+C+D$) and a consumers' surplus ($A+B$). This time, however, the consumers' surplus is smaller than the producers' surplus, but it is the consumers' surplus that declines and the producers' that rises. The net gain from exporting is thus $C+D$.

CONCLUSIONS   The conclusion from the partial equilibrium analysis reinforces what we found in general equilibrium: For society, trade involves overall gains. For imports of strawberries, the gain to consumers outweighs the loss to producers. For exports of tomatoes, the gain to producers outweighs the loss to consumers. There is a net gain both from importing and from exporting. This powerful conclusion has an obvious corollary: Reducing trade by means of barriers will reduce a country's welfare.

Now consider the question of compensation. If both sets of producers and consumers are the same (that is, the same farms switch from strawberries to tomatoes, and the same consumers switch from tomatoes to strawberries), then an improvement in welfare takes place. If, however, there are different farmers and different consumers, then there is at least a case that welfare has not improved unless the tomato farmers transfer income to the strawberry farmers and the strawberry eaters compensate the tomato eaters.

As in general equilibrium analysis, the compensation principle discussed in the box titled "Welfare Limitations of Community Indifference Curves" is necessary to prove that trade results in an overall net gain in welfare.

RELAXING THE ASSUMPTIONS

The basic analysis of comparative advantage in a two-country, two-commodity model has now been completed. This is the point at which we begin to relax, one by one, the restrictive assumptions that have thus far been operative.

MANY PRODUCTS, MANY COUNTRIES

The fundamental conclusions of a two-country, two-commodity model survive when the model expands to include many countries and many goods.[4] In the higher mathematics of a multicountry, multicommodity model explored in graduate-level texts, there emerges a *chain of comparative advantage*, each country having a list, as it were, of all potential exportables and importables. At or near the upper end of the list are goods whose factor endowments, demand, and/or technological differences combine to give a comparative advantage so great in terms of relative costs that the country is sure to be an exporter of those commodities. At the other end of the list are goods whose comparative disadvantage is so great that the country is certain to be an importer of these goods. In the center of the list is a grey area where costs are so similar between countries, or transport costs are so high, that there is little or no push to export or import a good. The dividing line between what is exported and what is imported will be a function wholly of relative costs and prices.

DYNAMIC EFFECTS

The model of comparative advantage as viewed thus far in the chapter has been a static one, with no dynamic effects such as changing production possibilities or changing tastes. At this point we relax the assumption of static conditions and consider a number of dynamic effects that can alter comparative advantage.

SCALE AND SPECIALIZATION   For certain goods, and in certain conditions elaborated more fully in the following chapter, increasing production may lower costs. If there are major economies of scale for production, or if a high degree of specialization brings with it substantial cost savings, the economy may not face increasing costs. Specialization in rice, for instance, may bring some economies of scale, but more importantly will bring with it specialized traders, chemical companies, seed companies, agricultural extension agents, and even irrigation and water-control activities that will lower the cost of producing rice.

CHANGING FACTOR ENDOWMENTS   Factor endowments change. Sometimes the situation is obvious, as when a raw material source gives out or diseases hit important crops. Indeed, some countries have had periods in which major exports rose and then nearly disappeared, reflecting enormous changes in comparative advantage. Peru, for instance, exported gold and silver in colonial times; guano, a fertilizer consisting of bird droppings, in the early nineteenth century; and later nitrates, until they were seized by the Chileans in 1878. Each product dominated and squeezed out other exports, but then collapsed unexpectedly. Ivory was once the major export from West Africa's Ivory Coast, but the elephants gave out, and that now-misnamed country today exports mostly cocoa and coffee.

In newly industrializing countries, the stock of capital grows in relation to the labor force. As these nations manage to reinvest 25% or 30% of their GNPs into their economies, boosting net investment rates sometimes to over 20%, wages rise relative to the returns on capital. As a result, labor-intensive exports no longer have comparative advantages over capital-intensive exports. Japan began this century exporting labor-intensive goods, but by the 1960s was exporting mostly capital- (or technology-) intensive products. Similarly, both the United States and Germany were primarily agricultural exporters in the mid-nineteenth century, but by the end of that century were increasingly exporters of more capital-intensive manufactures.

Trade may be the vehicle for the changes in the factor endowments. For example, contact with foreigners may result in favorable effects on entrepreneurial behavior and methods. Imports might allow new markets to be identified and developed, so that risks of entering these markets are reduced for domestic producers. The potential for copying the imports themselves, or the technology through which they were produced, might be large.[5]

CHANGING TASTES   Tastes change frequently, leading to changes in trading patterns. We could show a simple change of tastes by altering the location of the indifference curve, relative to the production possibilities curve; and in partial equilibrium, by changing the location of the demand curve. An example might be the increasing taste for fish in the United States, spurred by health concerns about red meat and the general move toward lighter foods. The taste change has caused American fish imports from Canada to rise sharply. Japan was once the world's major exporter of silk, but as high fashion moved away from silk the Japanese moved toward products in greater demand. (The share of silk in Japan's textile and clothing exports was 99% in 1880–1882, still 88% in 1900–1902, down to 62% in 1924–1926, and only 4% in 1953–1955.[6]

Sometimes the taste change is a result of trade itself. Ragnar Nurkse (1907–1959) hypothesized a *demonstration effect,* wherein consumers in less developed countries acquired new tastes as they were exposed to a wide range of goods through international trade. The result was that changing taste caused a change in the chain of comparative advantage as the indifference curves moved. Some South American countries shifted from domestic foods such as corn to wheat and rice, from domestic meats to beef. Virtually the entire Third World has changed from native dress to more European clothes, often even when the clothing is quite uncomfortable in the local climate. Even the sins of the developed world such as tobacco smoking and overuse of infant formula have spread extensively to the Third World.

CONCLUSION   In each of the cases discussed in this section, the dynamic changes in supply (PPCs) and demand (indifference curves) are likely to result in a new equilibrium terms of trade. That is to say, dynamic changes can yield new price ratios, and can thus alter comparative advantage.

TRANSPORT COSTS AND THE MODELS

Throughout this chapter, the analysis has proceeded as if there were no transportation costs or other special costs of trade, and that international exchange thus equalized the prices of traded commodities between the trading countries. That is sufficiently unrealistic to require some adjustment. We develop in this final section a model that is useful for handling not only transport costs, but tariffs, export taxes, and other special costs of trade as well.

It is easiest to show the effect of transport costs in partial equilibrium, looking at the supply and demand for just one product. Return to our consideration of strawberry imports. In Fig. 2.10, we use back-to-back diagrams, as if we have flipped over the one on the left. Demand and supply appear to run the wrong way, but since the horizontal axis starts at zero in the center and increases as it goes to the left, *D* and *S* are actually correct. The importer is on the left and the

Figure 2.10 **Transport costs and trade.** Prices in an importing and an exporting country differ by the transportation costs between them, being higher in the importer and lower in the exporter.

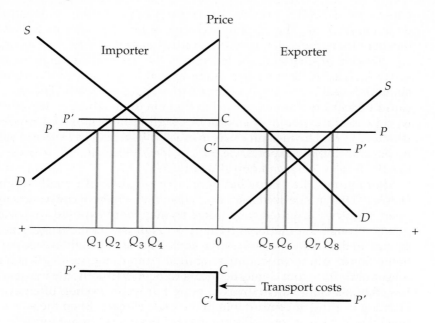

exporter on the right, showing that the economies establish different prices for strawberries in autarky. We can show trade without any transportation costs simply by finding a level of exports that happens to equal the imports of the partner country—that is, where Q_1Q_4 on the left diagram, the imports, equals Q_5Q_8 on the right diagram. We then bring the price line across from the left to the right half of the diagram. Equilibrium comes about when $Q_1Q_4 = Q_5Q_8$, which is at P.

To allow for transportation costs we put a crook into the price line, to indicate that there is a difference between the costs when the good leaves one nation and what its costs are when it arrives at the other. That crook in the curve, equal to the transportation cost, causes adjustments in both diagrams. We have, in essence, to fit a vertical distance like that on the bottom of Fig. 2.10 into the D and S diagrams such that the quantities exported and imported are equal. If the same level of exports were produced, the importer would not buy them all at the higher price with transportation costs included. If the importers tried to import the same amount, the exporters could not afford to produce that amount and pay the transportation cost. The result is that the price settles at some intermediate point, where imports and exports equal each other and the transportation cost is covered, as indicated by the Q_2Q_3 and Q_6Q_7 of Fig. 2.10. Note in particular that if transport cost exceeds the original price difference between the importer and exporter, then no trade will occur.

NATURAL PROTECTION AND LOCATION THEORY   An industry that has higher costs than a foreign industry but whose product faces high transportation costs is said to be naturally protected. A vast number of service jobs, from haircutting to medicine to legal advice, are protected by the considerable cost, relative to the value of the service, of transportation. Many of us who have lived in the Third World would love to have a hidden door opening to our old Third World homes or offices, not just to enjoy the sights and flavors, but so we could sneak out for haircuts, watch repairs, or dining at a fraction of our industrial world prices. Some products such as cement, gravel, bottled water, and beer are heavy relative to their value, so transport is relatively expensive. Some products are difficult to ship—natural gas when no pipeline is feasible, as from Algeria to the United States—and that also means a much higher price. Some are perishable, and are thus sold only as premium products. Apples and peaches do get to Southeast Asia and rambutans and mangosteens (to say nothing of the fabled durian, which smells like coal tar and is said to taste like heaven) are sold in North America. But as with imported beers, what is commonplace at home is at its destination a luxury provided at a luxury price.

With transport costs present, the location of industry as predicted by the model of comparative advantage may be modified by natural protection, which helps to explain both the existence and the siting of the affected industry, and why some goods and services are simply not traded at all. Such modifications of comparative advantage are the subject of location theory.

Transport costs can be important in deciding where to locate an industry. There are three possible cases: (1) supply-oriented industry, (2) market-oriented industry, and (3) footloose industry. In the first two of these cases transport costs influence the degree of comparative advantage. In the third case they do not.

SUPPLY-ORIENTED INDUSTRY   Supply-oriented industries must, because of transport costs, be located near raw materials or fuel. Typical examples are those raw material inputs that lose weight in processing. The ores of zinc or copper, for example, contain much waste material, and gold and platinum even more. They lose considerable weight in the refining of the metal. It is thus more economical to refine near the site of the mine than to ship heavy, useless waste material. Large-scale fuel consumption can mean economies in producing at or near a source of fuel. This is most true of fuels that are hard to ship, applying in particular to coal, at least historically. Coal was a tremendous attraction for industry, as seen in the German Ruhr, Polish Silesia, the English Midlands, and the region around Pittsburgh in the United States. Aluminum refining, which is done by passing a strong electric current through the dissolved concentrate, is inevitably close to good sources of electric, often hydroelectric, power. Agricultural commodities requiring immediate preservation or grading are also supply oriented. Tobacco must be hung for curing within a few hours of being picked; tea should be processed within eight hours, and many frozen and canned fruits and vegetables have only a few hours or days before their quality begins to decline. Grains, on the other hand, do not need to be processed particularly quickly.

Rural Thailand, for instance, has very little in the way of rice processing, but considerable tobacco, pineapple, vegetable, and fruit processing.

In other cases there are economies of assortment, where sorting and grading is best done before goods are shipped many miles. Sorting prevents certain grades or qualities from being shipped to inappropriate locations. Some mines, as those of highland Peru, produce ores heavy in several minerals—lead, zinc, silver, and perhaps antimony may all be jumbled together—and the ultimate destination of each of those elements is quite different, so it is cheapest to separate them out near the mines. Tobacco and coffee come in many grades in any one nation, but each of their ultimate markets only wants some of those grades. There is no sense in shipping a tar-laden, heavy-nicotine leaf to the United States when other peoples are dying for it. National (indeed regional) tastes in coffees differ considerably, and the beans from any one estate must be sorted out before being shipped.

MARKET-ORIENTED INDUSTRY   The cost of transport requires some commodities to be produced near the market. Perishable goods such as bread, milk, fresh corn on the cob, and asparagus may survive some long trips, but lose considerable value in so doing. Services, of course, are heavily market oriented. It is impossible to import a haircut. Any product that gains weight or bulk in processing will tend to be market oriented, such as beer and soft drinks, which, being mostly water, are invariably locally produced, with tiny portions of the market provided by imports. In addition, products that have to be changed for each local or national market tend to be produced closer to those markets. Tobacco may be cured near the farm and sorted near the port, but it is assembled and made into cigarettes near its final market. Coffee receives its initial processing as well as its grading at its source, but the difference in national tastes are such that the final blending of the beans and roasting take place close to the market.

FOOTLOOSE INDUSTRY   Transport costs are not so important with footloose industries, which can locate at the source of supply, at the market, or in between. Generally such industries produce products that neither lose nor gain weight in processing. Textiles provide a good example: They can be made near the source of the cotton and then be shipped to the market, or the cotton can be shipped to textile mills near the market. Either way, the transport cost is about the same. Many electronic goods can be shipped about for assembly, often with different parts of the operation being done in different countries. Relative to their value, computers and high-tech electronic equipment are very light. The whole of the world's semiconductor production, for instance, would fit into just 10 Boeing 747s.[7] Indeed, the declining transportation costs of the postwar period have meant that locational factors are less and less important in the siting of an industry.

Figure 2.11, taken from the work of E.M. Hoover, shows how to sum the procurement costs of obtaining raw materials and the distribution costs associated with shipping the final product.[8] Procurement costs, shown by a dashed line, are highest at the market, lowest near the source of supply. Distribution costs for the

Figure 2.11 **Location of production and transport cost.** The procurement costs of obtaining raw materials and the distribution costs associated with shipping the final product can be summed to obtain the total transport costs at any given geographical position. The good shown in the figure is supply oriented.

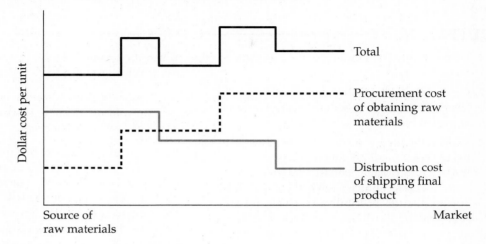

final product, shown by a shaded line, are highest at the source of the raw materials, lowest at the market. When added vertically, the two together indicate the total cost of transport, seen in Fig. 2.11. In the case shown the transport cost is lowest when production of the good is undertaken at the source of raw materials supply. This particular good is therefore supply oriented.

CONCLUSION

This chapter has presented the standard trade theory of comparative advantage, with its long heritage and powerful conclusions. An economist of 40 years ago might reasonably have considered the subject to be a settled one. In the next chapter, however, we shall see that controversy has arisen and continues on the question of what gives a country a comparative advantage and what causes it to change. These aspects of trade theory are among the more contentious in economics.

VOCABULARY AND CONCEPTS

Absolute advantage

Autarky

Chain of comparative advantage

Comparative advantage

Compensation principle

Consumer surplus

General equilibrium analysis

Indifference curve

Market-oriented industry

Natural protection

Partial equilibrium analysis

Producer surplus

Factor endowments
Footloose industry
Gains from trade

Production possibility curve
Productivity
Supply-oriented industry

QUESTIONS

1. Demonstrate, using numbers only, Ricardo's theory of comparative advantage.

2. Construct a table in which one country has an absolute advantage in both products, yet trade still takes place.

3. Explain the theory of comparative advantage using Figs. 2.5 and 2.6. Identify the gains from trade. Try the same exercise, drawing a diagram for each country freehand, using different production possibilities curves and the same pattern of indifference curves. Be careful about what part of the triangle remains entirely inside the production possibilities curve and what part extends outside it (the most common error on tests). Technically, the triangles should be the same size (or else one country would be exporting more than the other imports); see how close you can come. (This takes a keen eye, patience, and some experimentation.)

4. Explain, drawing on Fig. 2.7, what the gain from trade is and what occurs on that figure. Now try drawing a similar diagram freehand. (You will find it easier than the previous one.)

5. Why does a small country usually benefit more than a large country in a trading relationship? Show with a diagram.

6. Trade theory uses community indifference curves, yet uses them with caution. Why does it (a) use them and (b) take care in so doing?

7. A guru spoke: "There is no international competition; there is only domestic competition." (He is partially right, and right where most people do not think about it.) What did he mean?

8. Given the theory of trade, is it reasonable to ask which side won a trade negotiation?

9. Thus spake the guru: "A nation of beavers will gain no trading advantage over a nation of goof-offs." What did he mean?

10. Both your authors believe that increasing productivity is good for the economy. Both believe that an industry that increases its productivity more than others will move up on the chain of comparative advantage. Neither believes that increasing productivity will improve a country's trade balance. Explain.

11. Sometimes demand and supply diagrams explain better the gains from trade. Show what would happen if two nations entered into trade, using demand and supply diagrams for both the importer and the exporter.

12. Explain, using diagrams like Figs. 2.9a and 2.9b, the gain from trade. Point to the consumer surplus, the producer surplus, and the triangles that show the gain from trade.

13. Explain the distribution of gains and losses from trade, using Figs. 2.9a and 2.9b.

14. What are the dynamic effects of trade, and why might they be more important than the comparative statics we use in this chapter's models?

15. What is meant by *natural protection*? Show how transportation costs affect the amount of trade and the extent of reallocation of resources.

16. Distinguish supply-oriented, market-oriented, and footloose industries, giving an example of each.

NOTES

1 Adam Smith, *The Wealth of Nations*, London, 1776 [Cannan Edition, Random House, 1937], p. 424.

2 See Peter B. Kenen, *The International Economy*, Englewood Cliffs, N.J., Prentice Hall, 1985, pp. 5–6.

3 *Wall Street Journal*, June 14, 1989.

4 For more advanced treatment of the 2 × 2 model that confirms its strength, see W.J. Ethier, "Higher dimensional issues in trade theory," in Ronald W. Jones and Peter B. Kenen, eds., *Handbook of International Economics*, Vol. 1, Amsterdam, Elsevier, 1984, p. 181.

5 See W.M. Corden, *Trade Policy and Economic Welfare*, Oxford, Oxford University Press, 1974, pp. 327–329.

6 Young-Il Park and Kym Anderson, "The rise and demise of textiles and clothing in economic development: The case of Japan," *Economic Development and Cultural Change*, Vol. 39, No. 3, April 1991, pp. 531–548.

7 *The Economist*, February 16, 1985.

8 See Edgar M. Hoover, *The Location of Economic Activity*, New York, McGraw-Hill, 1963, p. 39. The diagram is simplified in our text.

Appendix 2.1

OFFER CURVES

Offer curves, invented before the turn of the century by two British economists, Alfred Marshall and Francis Edgeworth, give an alternative way to find the size and shape of the triangles of trade developed in this chapter in Figs. 2.6 and 2.7.

In the body of the chapter, all price ratios were presented as in Fig. 2.12, where a line runs from axis to axis showing a ratio such as 10 cloth to 20 wheat. Exactly the same ratio can be shown, however, as in Fig. 2.13, running out from the point of origin. This, too, shows the quantity of cloth (10) that will be exchanged for a quantity of wheat (20). This, too, is thus a price ratio.

FABRICA'S OFFER CURVE   Let us use price ratios drawn in this second way to construct an offer curve showing the amount of cloth Fabrica is willing to give up (export) in exchange for imports of wheat from Agricola. This curve will show simultaneously the supply and demand for the two commodities entering into trade. Assume that trade opens between Fabrica and Agricola. If prices do not change from their initial level, say 10:10, or 1:1, then it will make no difference to Fabrican consumers whether they buy their unit of wheat for one of cloth at home or abroad. So only a little trade is likely to spring up, as at *A* in Fig. 2.14.

If prices change, however, more trade will develop. We do not need to consider a price movement in Fabrica in the direction of, say, 1:0.5, because that would mean cloth had become cheaper and wheat more expensive after trade. Who in Fabrica would give up *more* Fabrican cloth in exchange for Agricolan wheat than the quantity of cloth that must be given up for wheat in Fabrica *without* international trade? A reduced price of wheat, and an increased price of cloth, say to a ratio of 1:1.3, will, however, cause Fabrica to desire more trade, as at point *B*. There, a larger quantity of cloth will be offered in exchange for a larger quantity of wheat.

Because at point *B* more wheat is available than before, the Fabricans will offer less cloth per unit of wheat. In other words, a doubling of wheat imports

---

Figures 2.12 and 2.13 **Two ways of expressing a price ratio**

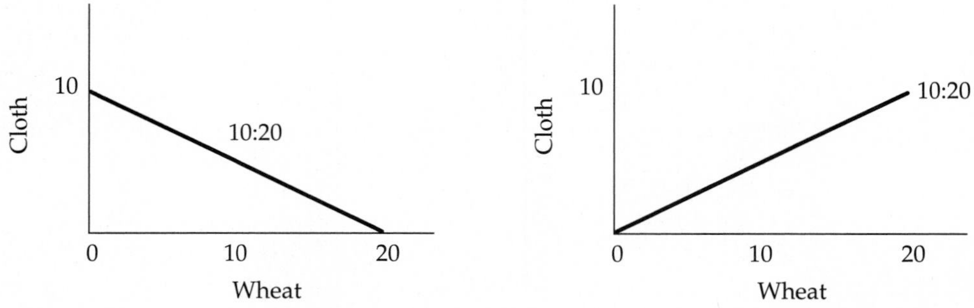

52

Figure 2.14 **Constructing Fabrica's offer curve**

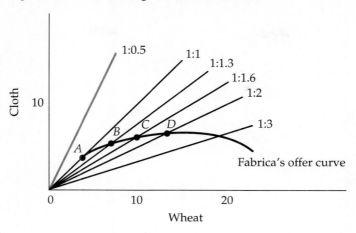

will less than double exports of cloth. At the even more favorable price ratio of 1:1.6, Fabrica at point *C* gives up more cloth to get more wheat, but not quite so much per unit as it was willing to give up before. The twin reasons for this are (1) Fabrica wants wheat less, and (2) each unit of cloth is now more valuable because some of it is exported.

If the price ratio were to change further, say to 1:1.7 or 1:1.8, with cloth more expensive and wheat cheaper, the same process would occur. More cloth would be given up for more wheat, though again not so much per unit. Finally, say at a price ratio of 1:2, Fabrica will not give up *any more cloth at all* for wheat, no matter how much more wheat could be obtained in further trade. (See point *D*.) The offer curve may even bend back far to the right in the diagram, as huge stocks of wheat lead to unwanted supplies and problems of storage, while consumers refuse to reduce their cloth consumption any further. Fabrica would then take more wheat only if it had to give up less cloth.

AGRICOLA'S OFFER CURVE Now we turn to Agricola's offer curve. Agricola's price ratio before trade was 1:3, with one unit of cloth exchanging for three units of wheat, as in Fig. 2.15. Agricola would be willing to undertake a little trade with Fabrica even if the price ratio stays unchanged, as at *A* in the figure. Fabrica would certainly have preferred to obtain four, five, or six wheat for one cloth, but Agricola would not trade with Fabrica at those prices because home-produced cloth is cheaper than that.

Thus with trade, the price line swings counterclockwise. At a higher price for wheat and a lower price for cloth, Agricola will be eager for more trade. See how at point *B*, at a price ratio of 1:2, Agricola is willing to exchange more wheat for

Figure 2.15 **Constructing Agricola's offer curve**

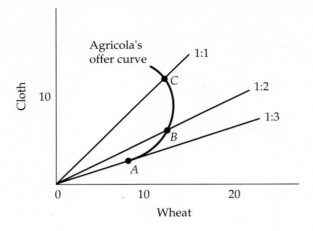

imported cloth. The analysis is the same as that for Fabrica in the last figure, except that the Agricolan offer curve swings around in the opposite direction.

The final step is to put both offer curves, one for Fabrica and another for Agricola, in the same figure (see Fig. 2.16). Notice that the two offer curves cross at point *P*. This crossing is important. Only there, at a price ratio shown by the line running from the origin through *P*, will Agricola want to export just the amount of wheat that Fabrica wants to import, as read along the *x-* (horizontal) axis. Also at a price 0*P*, and *only* there, will Agricola want to import just the amount of cloth that Fabrica wants to export. The price 0*P* is thus called the *equilibrium terms of trade,* and at that price the value of Fabrican imports equals

Figure 2.16 **The equilibrium terms of trade**

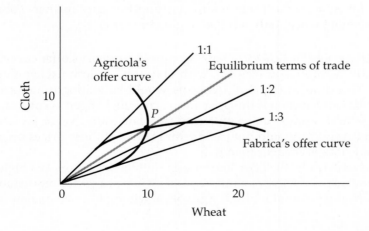

the value of Agricolan exports. Both in turn are equal to the value of Agricolan imports and Fabrican exports. A country's exports exchange for an equal value of imports at the equilibrium terms of trade.

The connection between the offer curves developed here and the diagrams using production possibilities and indifference curves presented in the body of the chapter is reasonably straightforward. The offer curves define the size and shape of the triangles that determine the gains from trade. The reading on the y-axis identifies the amount of cloth traded by both countries, and is thus the height of the triangles. The reading on the x-axis reveals the length of the triangles. The price ratio is the slope (though it must be reversed) of the hypotenuse of the triangles. If we draw carefully, all will work out well.

Chapter 3

The Sources of Comparative Advantage

Overall Objective: To understand what determines which goods are exported and which are imported.

MORE SPECIFICALLY:

- To develop an ability to explain and manipulate the factor-proportions (Heckscher-Ohlin) model verbally and in diagram form.

- To examine factor-price equalization.

- To explain how the Leontief Paradox and intraindustrial trade have challenged factor-proportions theory.

- To build more dynamic models based on decreasing costs.

- To develop an understanding of the role of demand in shaping what goods develop comparative advantages.

- To incorporate the role of managerial and governmental choice in contingent and dynamic trade models.

Comparative advantage explains why trade brings gains. It does not, however, in itself explain why countries' production possibilities curves have different shapes, and therefore why comparative advantage should be in one good rather than another. It is a satisfactory explanation of the gains from trade, but it does not predict precisely what patterns of exchange will emerge from trade.

Ricardo thought natural differences were a major explanation of the patterns of comparative advantage as, for example, when Portugal's sun and soil favored wine production while the sheep runs of England favored woolen cloth. It is not hard to find natural differences of the Ricardian sort when dealing with goods heavily dependent upon climate and other natural resources. Natural advantage, however, has a much more difficult time explaining why Sweden exports Volvos and imports Volkswagens or why the United States exports glass-fiber cable and imports radios. If we are to develop some sense of what is likely to be traded and a more specific understanding of the gains from trade, we have to move beyond simple comparative advantage to explore why such advantages exist.

To do so, this chapter first examines the by-now classic factor-proportions approach, which is quite satisfactory for working with many standard products or broad industrial groupings. The problem is that a factor-proportions approach does not handle very well a large share of modern trade, which tends to be among relatively similar industrial countries exporting and importing goods within the same industry. The balance of the chapter explores the newer theoretical and more dynamic models that can better explain this trade.

FACTOR PROPORTIONS: THE HECKSCHER-OHLIN MODEL

In the 1920s and 1930s the Swedish economists Eli Heckscher and Bertil Ohlin expanded the Ricardian view of natural advantage to one based upon differing quantities and qualities of the factors of production. The *Heckscher-Ohlin* (H-O) *model* and the many factor-proportions models that are its offspring typically focus on only land, labor, and capital, and most often on just labor and capital. Sometimes, however, they also incorporate additional factors such as human capital, technology, or entrepreneurship to provide an explanation of phenomena that otherwise do not seem readily explicable.

Basically, the Heckscher-Ohlin idea is that nations export goods that use their most abundant factor intensively, and they import goods that use their scarce factor intensively. The country with much labor and little capital will find that labor is comparatively cheap and capital is comparatively expensive. It will export goods that contain much labor relative to capital, and import goods that contain much capital relative to labor. In the Heckscher-Ohlin model, a country's factor proportions determine and predict both what it will export and what it will import. (In large part because of this discovery, Ohlin shared the 1977 Nobel Prize in economics. Active in politics, he led the Swedish Liberal Party for over 20 years.)

EXPLORING THE HECKSCHER-OHLIN MODEL WITH THE TOOLS OF MICROECONOMICS

The observation is at base relatively simple. It can be explored more thoroughly by using a tool of microeconomic theory, production isoquants. The production isoquants (labeled *PI*) in Fig. 3.1 are the starting point. The quantity of capital is shown on the vertical axis, and the quantity of labor is on the horizontal. The isoquant PI_{100} shows that 100 units of some good can be produced with various factor combinations. The 100 units might be produced with lots of labor (L_2) and only a little capital (K_1), as at point *a*, or with much less labor (L_1) and much more capital (K_2), as at point *b*. Another isoquant could be drawn to show a higher level of output, say 125 units, as with PI_{125}. A lower isoquant such as PI_{75}

Figure 3.1 **Goods can usually be produced with various factor combinations.** PI_{100} shows the different combinations of capital and labor that will produce 100 units of some good, and PI_{125} the combinations that will produce 125 units. The lines P_1 and P_2 represent two different prices of labor in terms of capital. With much labor exchanging for little capital (P_1), the country will produce at point *a*; with more expensive labor and cheaper capital, the country will produce at point *b*.

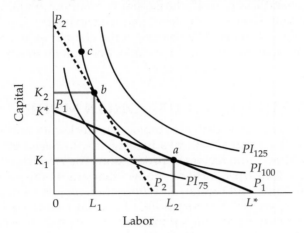

could be drawn to show 75 units of output. *Any* different level of output would be indicated by other isoquants drawn in the intermediate space.

The convex-to-the-origin shape of the production isoquants reflects the standard micro argument of diminishing returns to a factor. If much capital is already being used to produce the 100 units, as at *b*, then it is difficult to substitute yet more capital for labor. See that to produce 100 units at point *c*, a great deal more capital had to be used because the labor force was already small.

Whether producers will choose to utilize considerable labor and little capital, or vice versa, will depend on the relative prices of capital and labor. The line P_1P_1 in Fig. 3.1 is a *price line;* it shows the relative price of labor and capital. It is derived as follows: Say a given amount is available for hiring factors. If the entire amount were devoted to hiring labor, a quantity of labor L^* could be obtained. If the entire amount were devoted to acquiring capital, a quantity of capital K^* could be obtained. Here labor is cheap and capital is expensive, because the same amount of money would bring lots of labor L^* but much less capital K^*. Any combination of labor and capital along P_1P_1 is also obtainable for the fixed sum of money.

In Fig. 3.1, a price line P_1P_1 will cause the product to be produced with L_2 labor and K_1 capital, as shown by the point at *a*. With the affordable combinations of labor and capital along P_1P_1, producers could not reach a higher output quantity such as 125. Not enough labor and capital are available to permit that.

An output of 75 would not be satisfactory, however, as it is possible with the available factors to reach 100 units of output at isoquant PI_{100}.

What if labor were, however, much more expensive, and capital much cheaper, as shown along price line P_2P_2? In that case production would be undertaken at point b, with more capital used (K_2) than labor (L_1). Again no higher isoquant than PI_{100} can be reached, and no lower one would be tolerated.

In the case shown in Fig. 3.1, the good can be made either in a labor-intensive manner, with a high ratio of labor to capital as at a, or in a capital-intensive way, with a high ratio of capital to labor as at b. Indeed, most goods can be produced either in a labor-intensive manner or a capital-intensive manner. The Asian farmer walks for hours behind a bullock and simple plow to break the ground, spends yet more hours on back-bending labor to plant and weed by hand, at harvest swings a sickle, and follows that with hand-threshing to get the crop ready for storage. An American farmer prepares the soil with a $125,000 tractor pulling gang plows and then discs; attaches specialized implements for the planting, fertilizing, and weeding; watches the harvesting being done by giant combine-harvesters hired for the purpose; and then transfers the harvested crop to large trucks for the move to the local grain elevator. Very few people are involved per unit of output, compared to many in Asia.

Just looking at Fig. 3.1 does not, however, make it apparent which country will have the comparative advantage in producing the product. If labor is cheap enough, then labor-intensive production might win out in world markets. If capital is the cheap enough, world markets might be captured by capital-intensive producers. The good shown is not one that *intrinsically* requires more labor than capital or vice versa.

The Heckscher-Ohlin model comes into its own when we consider goods that intrinsically require labor-intensive or capital-intensive production. Figure 3.2 shows two different products from the textile and clothing industry. The set of isoquants labeled *PIK* (*K* for capital intensive) shows various levels of output for standard, machine-made synthetic fabric such as polyester. The production of this item is intrinsically capital intensive; that is, shifts between labor and capital can be made, but only within limits. A substantial amount of machinery and chemical apparatus are needed to obtain polyester shirts no matter how cheap labor might be. That is why the *PIK* isoquants for different quantities of polyester all cluster nearer to the vertical (capital) axis. The capital requirements always exceed the labor requirements even though some shifting between the two factors is possible.

Now consider the set of isoquants labeled *PIL* (*L* for labor intensive) in Fig. 3.2. Perhaps these represent fancy hand-sewn rodeo shirts. The production of these shirts is intrinsically labor intensive. Again, shifts between labor and capital can be made, but the shifting has to be within limits. So much hand sewing is needed to obtain rodeo shirts that no matter how cheap capital might be, a large amount of labor time has to be devoted to producing the good. Thus the *PIL* isoquants for different quantities of rodeo shirts all cluster nearer to the horizontal

Figure 3.2 **Isoquants showing capital-intensive and labor-intensive production.**
Rodeo shirts require a great deal of hand labor, and polyester shirts require a great deal
of capital, so the isoquants that show expanding production lie in quite different paths.
While it is possible to make rodeo shirts in more or less capital-intensive manners, both
P_1 and P_2 being tangent to some rodeo shirt isoquant, they are more labor intensive
than polyester shirts. A country with lots of capital and a P_2 price ratio will therefore
specialize in polyester shirts, producing at b, and the labor-rich country with a P_1 price
ratio will produce rodeo shirts, producing at a.

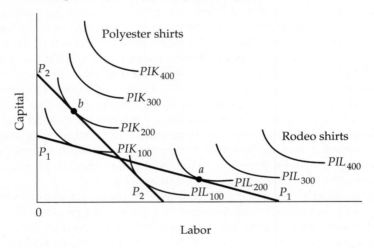

(labor) axis. The labor requirements always exceed the capital requirements,
and that intrinsic property does not change even though some shifting between
capital and labor is possible.

Assume that the country shown in the figure would always prefer to reach
an isoquant with a greater number (200 rather than 100) whether the product is
polyester shirts or rodeo shirts. If a country had large amounts of labor relative
to capital, then its labor would be relatively cheap, as indicated by the price
line P_1P_1. The figure shows—and it accords completely with intuition—that
with labor cheap it would be advantageous to produce the item that requires relatively more labor than capital—the rodeo shirts, at point a.

If on the other hand that same country had been relatively well-endowed
with capital, but labor was scarce, then its capital would be comparatively cheap
and its labor expensive, as shown by price line P_2P_2. In this case it would be
advantageous to produce the good—polyester shirts, as at point b—that requires
relatively more capital than labor.

FACTOR PROPORTIONS DETERMINE COMPARATIVE ADVANTAGE
IN THE HECKSCHER-OHLIN ANALYSIS

The Heckscher-Ohlin model suggests that comparative advantage will tend to be
determined by factor proportions. The consequences for international trade are

substantial. The capital-rich country will tend to *export* products that require proportionally large amounts of capital (that is, *capital-intensive* products). It will *import* products that require proportionally large amounts of labor (that is, *labor-intensive* products).

In the H-O approach, the price system sends signals concerning factor proportions that then mold international trade. In high-wage countries, it would be foolish to try to produce products that require large inputs of costly labor when such products can be imported from cheap-labor countries. Doing so frees costly labor for more productive uses in exporting industries, and in services where import competition cannot occur. In cheap-labor countries, however, it would be equally foolish to use scarce, expensive capital to produce products that can be more efficiently produced in countries where capital is cheap. For one thing, not enough capital is available to allow everyone to find jobs producing capital-intensive items. For another, the resulting output would be high in cost and unsellable abroad. Better to produce labor-intensive items with the cheap labor, export some of them, and import the goods that require much capital.

THE RYBCZYNSKI THEOREM: CHANGES IN FACTOR PROPORTIONS ALTER COMPARATIVE ADVANTAGE   It follows that an *increase* in the quantity of one factor of production (say capital) relative to the other factors (say labor) changes comparative advantage in favor of products that use the increasing factor intensively. The cheaper capital will cause a country's comparative advantage to shift to goods the production of which is basically capital intensive, such as the polyester in Fig. 3.2. The new advantage will cause the output of these capital-intensive export products to rise, while at the same time causing the domestic output of the labor-intensive goods to fall as imports of these goods increase. This is called the *Rybczynski Theorem,* after T.M. Rybczynski of City University, London, who first formulated this corollary to the Heckscher-Ohlin model.

Thus as a country accumulates more capital, and wages rise relative to capital costs, one expects exports and imports to reflect the change. For example, Japan's textile and clothing industry contributed 51% of all Japanese exports, 1900–1909, 38% in 1950–1959, but just 4% in 1980–1987. The British data reflect the same trend: Textile and clothing exports were 38% of all British exports in 1900–1919, when that industry was still Britain's largest. The proportion was down to 11% in 1950–1959, and 4% in 1980–1988. In both countries, the part of the industry comprising labor-intensive finished textiles and standard clothing was the first to decline, while the capital-intensive synthetic fiber and fabric producers may not decline at all, or only later.

FACTOR-PRICE EQUALIZATION

The import of labor-intensive items into economies where labor is expensive and items that are capital intensive into economies where capital is expensive can possibly have a dramatic outcome. If such a pattern of trade continues, then the ratio of labor costs to capital costs will tend to come together internationally.

Wages will rise relative to capital in the labor-abundant countries and fall in the scarce-labor countries in a process called *factor-price equalization.*

Start with a country where labor is scarce and capital is abundant, such as the United States. As imported labor-intensive products flow in, labor is released for other uses. This labor is absorbed in the more capital-intensive industries and in areas not subject to competition in foreign trade, but there is nonetheless downward pressure on wages. Meanwhile exports of capital-intensive products raise the demand for capital, the returns to which increase.

Conversely, in the cheap-labor country (say Mexico) the exports of labor-intensive items raise the demand for labor and thus put an upward pressure on wages. Imports of capital-intensive items have the opposite effect, reducing the returns to scarce and expensive capital. As the price of labor falls relative to capital in the United States and rises in Mexico, the economic structure of the two areas begins to bear a closer resemblance.

International trade's tendency to move factor prices toward equality is strictly limited, however. The actual likelihood of a full equalization occurring is remote, and the conditions under which it could occur are very restrictive.[1] For one thing, transport costs make many products and most services nontradable, so in most countries the pressure toward equalization is felt only by a minority of industries. For another, many trade barriers still exist even where goods are tradable, lessening competition in the industries involved and further reducing the movement toward equalization. Finally, as international trade increases efficiency and raises incomes (the prediction of the last chapter), people will want to consume more services. This tendency will provide considerably more employment in services, and at rising wages too in the long run, because it is difficult to raise productivity in most services that are labor intensive. These are major reasons why despite years of increasing trade, the share of U.S. income going for employee compensation has changed very little. In the European Community, labor income has converged, rising faster in the poorer members than in the richer, but it has not fallen even in the richest.[2] Thus the assumption that real wages will actually be lowered in an absolute sense is unrealistic.

It must, however, be realized that because international trade does tend to reduce the returns to the scarce factor and increase the returns to the abundant factor, then lower wages could occur in given labor-intensive industries because of the imports. Recent evidence indicates that U.S. trade with labor-intensive countries (the LDCs) raises the demand for skilled labor in the United States because of exports but increases the effective supply of unskilled labor due to imports. One study indicates that about 15% to 25% of the 11 percentage-point rise in the earnings gap between high school and college graduates 1980–1985 was due to the increased U.S. trade deficit.[3] This puts a premium on smoothly working labor markets, on government full-employment policies, on improving education, and on public assistance in retraining the otherwise unemployable. In an expensive-labor country the outlook for the illiterate, those who cannot do basic math, and the unskilled is generally bleak, as the world has plenty of people willing to do the work that requires nothing more at a fraction of the wages that U.S. workers believe are their due. These important topics are explored in subsequent chapters.

Because trade raises the returns to the cheap factor, it substitutes to some extent for the free migration of labor and unhindered movement of capital. This has some interesting implications:

1. Groups that oppose immigration because of its effect on wages will also tend to oppose free trade. American labor unions, prosperous in a land of scarce labor, have never welcomed extensive immigration. The attempt to dam up the inflow of Mexican labor across the Rio Grande, even if it succeeds, will not help less-skilled American labor much if the Mexican labor goes to work on the Mexican side of the border producing labor-intensive goods for the U.S. market.

2. Groups that are owners of capital in capital-scarce lands—the wealthy classes of many Third World nations—oppose free importation of capital because that will depress their returns. They must also oppose the free importation of capital-intensive goods, for that will have the same effect. Again, the conclusion that the returns to capital will fall for economies as a whole is more difficult to document than is the conclusion that it will fall in certain industries subject to the competition of capital-intensive imports.

EMPIRICAL EVIDENCE

A number of cross-country studies of international trade have been reasonably consistent with the Heckscher-Ohlin model. That by Bowen, Leamer, and Sveikauskas shows H-O receiving some empirical support in the exports and imports of Britain, France, Germany, and Japan.[4] Furthermore, the Heckscher-Ohlin model tends to hold strongly for less developed countries. Low-income nations appear to export similar labor-intensive manufactured products, the likes of which are not relatively so important in the exports of high-income countries.[5] The objection is sometimes made that Heckscher-Ohlin theory would seem to require that trade between rich and poor countries be huge in volume, whereas it is not. The LDCs have the cheapest labor, and the developed countries have the cheapest capital, but trade between them is actually only 19% of world trade. In rebuttal, we must note that trade barriers are very high in the LDCs, while considerable protection also exists in the developed countries against products from the LDCs.[6]

A very large body of evidence exists, however, on the other side. Generally, a substantial amount of international trade, including especially much U.S. trade, *does not* appear to conform to Heckscher-Ohlin predictions, and the proportion is growing. That is the major concern of much of the remainder of the chapter.

TWO CHALLENGES TO THE HECKSCHER-OHLIN MODEL

The problem with the Heckscher-Ohlin model is that in spite of its logical appeal and its ability to account for some of the world's trade, its explanatory power has proved to be limited. Much of international trade, and an increasing proportion at that, has stubbornly refused to pattern itself along the lines predicted by the theory. As we see in this section, countries rich in capital often export labor-intensive goods, and most trade is between countries with similar factor proportions. Furthermore, much intraindustrial trade takes place in goods produced by the same industry, as when cars exported from Germany to Sweden pass cars exported from Sweden to Germany. For example, intraindustrial trade in automobiles and parts between the United States and Canada, which have similar factor proportions, is very large. The trade in these items alone exceeds all trade between the United States and Mexico in all classes of goods, even though U.S. and Mexican factor proportions are very different.

We begin by examining two major challenges to the Heckscher-Ohlin factor proportions model: Leontief's Paradox and intraindustrial trade. Then we consider several alternative models that are now attracting considerable attention.

THE LEONTIEF PARADOX

It was almost dogma among economists that in the United States labor was the relatively scarce and expensive factor, while capital was the relatively abundant and cheap factor. The Heckscher-Ohlin model would therefore predict that U.S. exports would be capital intensive, while its imports would be labor intensive. The first sophisticated statistical test of that model (in 1954) did not, however, support that prediction. Indeed, it suggested the theory might be wrong.

Wassily Leontief was a Harvard professor, a pioneer in econometrics, and the winner of the 1973 Nobel Prize in Economics. Using the year 1947 as his base, Leontief compared the labor intensity of U.S. export industries with the labor intensity of U.S. imports. (Lacking good foreign data, he used the labor intensities of goods in the United States that competed with imports as the proxies for foreign labor intensities.) His results were surprising: For every man-year of labor, U.S. exports contained $14,010 of capital (a 1:14 ratio), but to produce the imports domestically, each man-year of labor would require $18,180 worth of capital (a 1:18 ratio). Exports were less capital intensive than imports! This was hardly what Leontief expected or what the Heckscher-Ohlin model predicted.

The findings created quite a stir among trade theorists, and came to be known as the *Leontief Paradox*. Economists could be forgiven for some initial skepticism, even given the eminence of its author. But the literature on the subject within a few years would have filled a good-sized bookcase, with the paradox persisting stubbornly in the data. It appeared again in U.S. data for 1951 and 1962, as analyzed by Leontief himself in 1956 and in Robert Baldwin's study of 1971; and it has been confirmed by the work of other scholars as well.[7]

The Heckscher-Ohlin model still survives because it works well for many other countries, particularly the less developed ones, and because there is some evidence (especially that of Stern and Maskus in 1981) suggesting that the paradox may have disappeared in the 1970s. For all that, the long survival of the Leontief Paradox in the U.S. trade data poses a major challenge for the Heckscher-Ohlin model.

INTRAFACTORAL AND INTRAINDUSTRIAL TRADE

The debates over the Leontief Paradox had already shaken the confidence with which economists viewed the Heckscher-Ohlin model of trade when additional remarkable evidence arose, presenting a further challenge to that model. In the 1950s observers began to note an unexpected pattern of trade not common before. Much exporting and importing was taking place among nations that seemed rather similar in their factor proportions and demand conditions. The pattern is quite clear today. Labor-scarce countries trade far more with other labor-scarce countries than the Heckscher-Ohlin theory would anticipate. Industrial countries buy only about 19% of their imports from less developed countries—down from 29% in 1980. The 12 most industrialized countries do about two thirds of their trade with one another. Trade in the old European Free Trade Association, which included very diverse countries such as Ireland, Iceland, Portugal, and Denmark, never expanded like that of the original European Economic Community, whose economies were far more similar to one another. Trade between the United States and Canada, both of which have high labor costs, is about four times the value of U.S.–Mexican trade, despite Mexico's cheap labor. In short, a considerable amount of international trade involves countries whose factor proportions cause them to specialize in capital-intensive goods trading with other countries whose factor proportions also lead to capital-intensive production.

Detailed studies of the issue added to the perplexity. Vast amounts of trade taking place among industrial nations turned out to be intraindustrial, meaning within the same industry. Research by Herbert Grubel and P.J. Lloyd revealed that much of the trade of the main industrial countries in 1967 was intraindustrial.[8] As one example, the value of French exports of photographic supplies was within 2% of its imports of the same supplies. This is closer than usual, but such figures are not that rare. A substantial portion of the *growth* of trade in recent years has also been intraindustrial. Not only does most trade take place between nations similar in factor proportions, but most of that trade is actually within the same industry! The trade is not only intraindustrial, but intrafactoral, involving like nations trading with like. How could this kind of trade be explained by the Heckscher-Ohlin model?

THE INDEX OF INTRAINDUSTRIAL TRADE   Let us start with the figures. It is now common to employ an index of intraindustrial trade in a form originally suggested by Bela Balassa:

(Eq. 3.1) $$\text{IIT} = 1.0 - \frac{|X - M|}{X + M}$$

Here IIT is the index of intraindustrial trade. The highest possible number, 1, would occur when exports (X) equaled imports (M) within that industry.

Say $X = 10$ and $M = 10$. In that case

(Eq. 3.2) $$\frac{X - M}{X + M} = \frac{0}{20} = 0 \text{ and therefore IIT} = 1.0 - 0 = 1.$$

The index of intraindustrial trade is thus 1 when exports and imports are equal in that industry.

The lowest number, 0, will occur when there is no intraindustrial trade. Say $X = 0$. In that case:

(Eq. 3.3) $\dfrac{X - M}{X + M} = \dfrac{10}{10} = 1$, and therefore IIT $= 1.0 - 1 = 0$.

$X - M$ is expressed as an absolute value, without regard to sign; hence the lines are drawn around it in the original expression so the figure will not turn out to be negative.

The index of intraindustrial trade for 10 industrial countries, only 0.36 in 1959 and 0.48 in 1967, had reached 0.60 by 1985 and is now probably somewhat over that figure.[9] The index is as high as 0.81 in Britain and 0.80 in France; it is 0.59 for the United States. It is much lower for Japan, only about half the rich-country average, because that country imports above-average quantities of natural resources, is resource poor, and has a distribution system that has been rather difficult for foreign firms to penetrate; and there are other reasons we shall have to examine. The less developed countries, which often export a high proportion of agricultural commodities and minerals and maintain high barriers to imported manufactured goods engage in little intraindustrial trade. The index numbers for them are usually very low, often under 0.10, and sometimes as low as 0.04 (Sri Lanka) or even 0.02 (Nigeria, Philippines), though the figures are higher for newly industrializing countries such as Korea and Malaysia.

EXPLAINING THE LEONTIEF PARADOX

Thus the two major challenges to Heckscher-Ohlin theory are the Leontief Paradox and the existence of intraindustrial trade. Several orthodox explanations (that is, consistent with the Heckscher-Ohlin thesis and the neoclassical tradition) have been offered in explanation of both challenges.

We begin with the Leontief Paradox, that the United States appears to export goods that are labor intensive and import goods that are capital intensive. Here each of the orthodox explanations appears to contribute something, though not much, to a resolution of this knotty problem. One such explanation involves U.S. trade barriers. What if the United States' tariffs and other barriers are relatively high on labor-intensive products, so that the United States imports relatively less of these? Imports of these products would be artificially reduced, which would make it appear that factor proportions were less important in determining trade flows. The evidence on this issue is mixed, but some studies do point to this explanation.

Perhaps the importance of U.S. imports of natural resources, which are capital intensive, contributes to resolving the paradox. Jaroslav Vanek did indeed find that U.S. exports embody only about half as much natural resource content as is the case for U.S. imports, representing a shift from an earlier period when *exports* were resource intensive.[10]

HUMAN CAPITAL AND TECHNOLOGY EXPLANATIONS

Leontief himself believed the explanation lay in the effectiveness of labor, as enhanced by the presence of human capital. The American level of education was for many years higher than that of all other countries, meaning that U.S. labor may have been more productive. In addition, the education of U.S. managers was considerably greater than that of foreign managers. Education is a form of capital in that it involves a saving from current consumption to improve productivity later on. Wealthy nations have the ability, in essence, to "save" the labor of millions of secondary school and university students who would otherwise be engaged in contributing to the GNP. Human capital formation can come not only from formal education, but also from on-the-job training, health care, and nutrition, all serving to raise the quality of labor and management. Hence high-quality labor is more akin to capital than it is to labor per se. The problem with adding human capital, however, is that it is difficult to measure. The labor is qualitatively different, and some education is more consumption than production, much being rather a waste. Nonetheless, the human capital argument does salvage to some extent the Heckscher-Ohlin theory.

We can also consider technology a factor of production. Like human capital, it alters the relation of land and labor. Unlike human capital, which makes labor more productive, technology could make land, labor, or capital, or some combination of all three, more productive. Like human capital, technology is to some extent the result of past investment in research, and may be a form of capital. One can then explain a particular pattern of industrial trade by pointing out that, say, the United States is exporting sophisticated telecommunications equipment, while it imports unsophisticated radios and television sets. Or we can assert that the Leontief Paradox may be caused by American technology, making labor relatively more productive than capital. (We should recognize, however, that the opposite is also possible—technology could make capital more productive than labor.)

Studies do indeed show that U.S. exports are correlated by industry to the proportion of the labor force employed in highly skilled categories, and also by the amount of investment directed toward research and development (R&D). *Technology* is an awkward concept, however, difficult to work with statistically and conceptually. R&D can be measured, of course, but it is not clear whether the expenditure on R&D can be directly correlated to technical advances. Technology, unlike land, labor, and capital, is dynamic and not innate, as technological gaps appear and disappear. Factor-proportions models that embody technology and technical change are thus likely to be more complicated and less sure in their prediction.

EXAMPLES OF TECHNOLOGY ALTERING COMPARATIVE ADVANTAGE   The semiconductor (microchip) provides an intriguing example of capital substituting for labor as a result of technical change. This tiny artifact allowed many types of electrical circuits to be miniaturized and inserted by mechanical means.

It replaced the large circuit boards of wires and transistors that required labor-intensive assembly. Suddenly, low-labor-cost countries lost their advantage in production and assembly of a wide range of electronic goods. By 1983, for instance, Hong Kong's cost advantage in electronics assembly had fallen from 66% to only 8% below U.S. costs.[11] There are many similar instances; recent changes sketched below have allowed many firms to see their manufacturing labor costs fall to figures between 5% and 15% of total production costs. This is a key statistic: If wages are below 15% of all production costs then wage differentials would have to be very high—say as much as 50%—to overcome the various costs of importing the product, such as transport, communications, travel for executives, insurance, and finance.[12] As a result, some Japanese TV producers have recently been pulling their operations out of South Korea and back to Nippon; GE has closed some of its Southeast Asian offshore factories and switched its foreign buying to Japanese producers; and other pull-backs have affected the garment and auto industries. Later in the chapter we turn to a further discussion of managerial and technological developments that have increased the ability of capital, and the human capital of skilled labor and good management, to substitute for labor.

Another example of the power of technology to affect comparative advantage appears in the data for exports from the newly industrializing countries, including Korea, Taiwan, Malaysia, Thailand, and several others. The original advantage of these countries was in goods manufactured by cheap labor—82% of their manufactured exports to the industrial countries in 1964 were categorized as low technology and only 2% were high technology. As their incomes grew, the skills of their labor forces improved, and wages rose, these countries became technically more sophisticated. By 1985 the proportion of their exports described as low technology had fallen to 53%, and the high technology component had risen to 25%.[13]

EXPLAINING INTRAINDUSTRIAL TRADE

Orthodox explanations have also been advanced in the case of the other major challenge to the Heckscher-Ohlin theory, the existence of intraindustrial trade. The basic problem is whether factor proportions can explain intraindustrial trade.

STATISTICAL PROBLEMS   Traditional approaches based on factor proportions can certainly be the reason for some intraindustrial trade. The statistics may hide deep factor differences. We think of an industry as being a group of firms making similar products, technologically related to one another. Sometimes, however, the firms making up an industry may have quite different input requirements. Examples might include furniture made of wood or steel, or fabric made of wool or artificial fiber. United States intraindustrial trade in floor coverings, for instance, is often very close to 1—but it is vinyl flooring that is exported and Oriental carpets that are imported. Such trade may be intraindustrial, but it may also be based on factor differences and consistent with Heckscher-Ohlin principles.

Though this serves as a partial explanation, it cannot explain *increasing* intraindustrial trade. We must look further.

TRANSPORTATION COSTS   Where products are homogeneous, such as copper, aluminum, red no. 1 wheat, or cement, it is easy to see that transport costs could be one reason for such exchange. The transport costs give rise to border trade. If Canada needs fertilizer in Alberta and has a surplus in Quebec, it is certainly not going to haul it 2500 miles to get it there. Far better to import it to Alberta from Montana, and export it from Quebec to the eastern United States.* The U.S. trade in oil, imported to the East Coast and exported from the Southwest, is a similar case; Canada does the same by exporting oil from the prairie provinces and importing it to the Atlantic provinces.**

Similarly, storage can be a reason for intraindustrial trade in standardized homogeneous goods. If it is cheaper to trade a product than to store it, as with perishables that have different growing seasons in two different countries, then exports will occur in one season and imports in another. Often this is a north-south trade between the hemispheres. Such trade can occur in an east-west direction as well, as when electricity is generated and transmitted over high tension lines to areas where the load is at its peak, the flow reversed a few hours later as use peaks in the first area.

DIFFERING FACTOR PROPORTIONS BY STAGE OF MANUFACTURE   Another form of intraindustrial trade occurs in the sending of semifinished goods to low-wage countries for assembly or preparation, and their reimportation as finished products. Trade of this kind, with the developed country as exporter of component and importer of final product, depends on transport costs being low enough as a proportion of the value of a given item to stand both the outward and the inward shipment. It includes some unlikely cases. For example, Haiti takes the cores of baseballs exported from the United States, sews their covers on, and flies them back—95% of U.S. baseballs follow this route. Elsewhere, Southeast Asia, Mexico, and the West Indies take semifinished clothes, gloves, and leather luggage and sew them together for reexport. There are many other examples, as discussed in the accompanying box. Imports of this type to the United States rose about 20% per year, 1966–1979. Currently the most important segments of this trade are apparel and electronic goods.[14]

---

* In 1990, Canada's national news network reported with some degree of horror that Canadians were exporting live cattle to the United States and simultaneously importing beef. The fact that the cattle were exported from Alberta and slaughtered to feed American Westerners, while the beef was imported 2000 miles away in Quebec, only appeared later in the story.

** The rhetoric of energy independence has, however, led to some strange aberrations. Alaskan oil must by U.S. law go entirely to the lower 48, despite the greater ease of shipping it to Japan, and the Canadians built a very expensive pipeline to move their western oil to Ontario and Quebec.

■ *EXPORT OF SEMIFINISHED GOODS FOR PROCESSING*
   OR ASSEMBLY

Over 20 American companies have located their data processing in the Caribbean, about half in Barbados and with other important centers in the Dominican Republic and Jamaica. Some countries in Southeast Asia, India, and even China also participate. They take data tapes flown from the United States for keypunching; sometimes they obtain the data via satellite. This new industry is supported mostly by airlines, hotels, credit card companies, and car rental agencies. The pioneer firm was American Airlines. The workers are mostly women, who sit behind keyboards with video-display terminals. Mexico gets loose ammunition from the United States, puts it into magazines, and then re-exports it. Taiwan, Korea, Mexico, Thailand, and India work on auto components from and for developed countries. The semiconductors, valves, and tuners for a wide variety of electronic equipment are manufactured in Hong Kong, Singapore, Taiwan, Mexico, and elsewhere.

Such trade is clearly consistent with the Heckscher-Ohlin model and is based on factor costs, the capital:labor ratio in particular. Multinational firms foster a fair proportion of this trade, especially in electronics, but they are by no means the only conduit through which this type of processing takes place. If the economic pressure is strong enough, the market is quite capable of arranging deals by subcontracting, as is typical in apparel. Whether by market or by administrative decision of multinational firms, the basic cost pressures created by differing factor proportions determine what is produced where. Thus we have another example of trade that is intraindustrial, but quite different in factor proportions. The remarkable development of such trade has been assisted by the willingness of rich countries to apply their tariffs only to the value added abroad, rather than to the value of the complete product when the finished goods are reexported back to where they started their journey. In the United States, numerous bills have been introduced in congress to repeal these provisions, so far without success.

CONTINUING THE SEARCH

Statistical problems, transportation problems, and differences by stage of manufacture surely explain some intraindustrial trade, just as the invocation of human capital and technology may explain some of the Leontief Paradox. A great many economists, however, believe that *they do not explain enough of it*.

WHY TRADE ARISES AMONG SIMILAR COUNTRIES

The search for further explanations of trade among countries with similar factor proportions has been dominated by two groups of arguments suggesting that *specialization brings decreasing costs.* Models analyzing why costs decrease include: (1) learning by doing, in which previous experience leads to lower costs, and (2) extensions of the well-accepted logic of scale economies based on specialization. As the remainder of the chapter demonstrates, the decreasing cost based on specialization is a principal source of comparative advantage in modern trade.

In some aspects the Heckscher-Ohlin factor-proportions model is quite compatible with decreasing-cost models, in both general and partial equilibrium. Yet most of the decreasing cost models are quite different from the H-O formulation in that they are *indeterminate and contingent.* That is, several outcomes are possible depending on the industries in which countries originally specialize, and comparative advantage can be established partly by that original selection. Our task in the remainder of the chapter is to discuss several such decreasing-cost models. Interestingly, we shall find some reason to believe that much of the trade arising because of specialization and decreasing costs is not as disruptive as trade that arises because of Heckscher-Ohlin conditions.

ECONOMIES OF SCALE AND DECREASING COSTS

Explanations that provide alternatives to the Heckscher-Ohlin factor-proportions approach invoke some form of scale economies that lead to decreasing costs. Such models usually involve a considerable degree of choice and indeterminacy, with comparative advantage established *because* costs decrease as a nation becomes more specialized.

DECREASING COSTS IN GENERAL EQUILIBRIUM   We begin with an overall view of the gains from specialization. Picture two identical countries in autarky, but with decreasing costs. Figure 3.3 shows these countries' production possibilities with decreasing costs. Their identical PPCs showing the tradeoff between Good 1 and Good 2 are convex to the point of origin. While the PPCs of Chapter 2 showed goods that were very different in manufacture and use, these production possibilities curves take two goods that are similar. The two goods could actually just be variations of one another, like station wagons and sedans, or they could be quite different but both incorporate advanced technology, such as glass-fiber cable and cellular telephones, or memory chips and integrated circuits. The production possibilities curves indicate that the more of either good the nation makes, the *fewer* of the other good it gives up. In the absence of trade, however, neither country can specialize because the structure of demand is such that people want about the same amount of each good, shown by their identical map of indifference curves I_1 and I_2. Both countries are originally consuming at point Z, which involves quantity W of Good 1 and quantity X of Good 2.

As Fig. 3.3 shows, in a decreasing-cost situation specialization brings lower costs. The three triangles in the figure all have the same height ($AB=CD=EF$). Their bases narrow, however, as the country becomes more specialized. (See how $FG>DE>BC$.) That means that producing the same amount of Good 1

Figure 3.3 **A decreasing-cost model.** In a decreasing-cost model, the production possibility curve is convex to the point of origin. An economy moving from *A* to *C* to *E* to *G* gives up the same amount of Good 1, but gets ever-larger amounts of Good 2. Trade would lead to complete specialization with one country at *G* and the other at *H*.

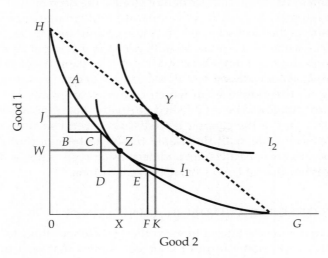

requires the sacrifice of less and less of Good 2 the *more* specialized the country becomes. In autarky, the countries produce and consume at point *Z*, and while Good 1 would be cheaper to make at a more specialized point, consumers would not buy it because the falling production of Good 2 would drive up its price, and vice versa. If both countries could specialize, one producing all of Good 1 and the other all of Good 2 (a "corner" solution), then they could enter into trade with each other. In the figure, the country producing at *H* could export *HJ* of Good 1 in return for imports of *JY* of Good 2; the country producing at *G* could export *GK* of Good 2 in return for imports of *KY* of Good 2. Each country could consume at point *Y*. Both would be much better off, now touching indifference curve *I₂*.

It is noteworthy that when trade opens, prices do not signal to firms which way they should move. Once movement starts, however, the first country to specialize in a good will find it has a growing comparative advantage in that good. It will move to the corner indicating complete specialization in that good. The other nation will move to the opposite corner. The gains from trade will be *ZY* in both countries.

A decreasing-cost model in this form suggests a major issue in modern trade theory: What might cause the movement toward specialization to occur in the first place? That question recurs for the balance of the chapter.

LEARNING BY DOING AND DECREASING COSTS

One way to analyze decreasing costs as output increases is to consider learning by doing. Learning curve analysis (LCA) is a means for doing so. LCA is a recent development, originally applied in management economics within a single country, but it can also show how the experience from greater output lowers costs, thereby possibly establishing a comparative advantage. LCA relates the increasing skills of labor and improved efficiency in production not to investment in education and research, which are assumed to be constant, but to the total quantity of products of any given type produced over time.[15]

Historically, the first indication that labor productivity could be systematically increased by cumulative work experience appeared at the Horndal steelworks in Sweden. This plant was built in 1835–1836 and then maintained in an unchanged physical condition for the next 15 years, with the labor force also unchanged in size. Yet output rose anyway by about 2% per year! The phenomenon came to be known as the "Horndal effect."[16]

In the 1920s, analysts noted an interesting pattern in the rate of labor's ability to learn. The man-hours spent on manufacturing a given product tended to fall by some regular percentage every time production doubled. Suppose a shipyard found that it took 10,000 man-hours to produce the first tugboat it made, and then discovered with the second tugboat that it took only 8000 man-hours. From these two points management could project that the fourth tugboat would take only 6400 man-hours, the eighth 5120 man-hours, and so on, with man-hours falling by 20% for each doubling of production. Sketched out on a diagram, we get a learning curve, as in Fig. 3.4.

See how as firms and workers accumulate experience in making a product, the costs of doing so fall in a predictable manner. Every time the firm manages to double its production, costs tend to decline by about the same percentage. Figure 3.4 shows a fall of 20% for every doubling of production.

Figure 3.4 **A learning curve.** As a firm's experience increases, its labor usage per unit of output falls, often by a predictable rate. In this diagram, labor hours are falling by 20% each time the firm manages to double its historical production.

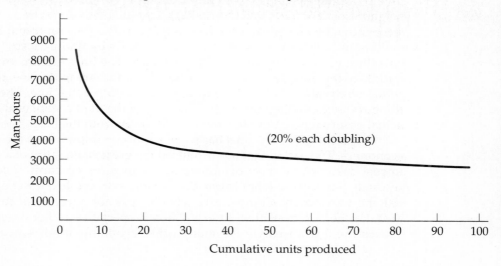

World War II provided major examples of learning curves in practice, with convincing evidence for their existence in airframe production, Liberty Ship construction, and destroyer output, among others. For example, excellent data are available for the labor time expended in the construction of large numbers of Sumner and Gearing class destroyers at Maine's Bath Iron Works between 1943 and 1945. These ships were virtually identical; no important alterations in the capital stock were made in this period; and the shipyard's employment did not grow. Yet between the first ships and the last, man-hours expended per ship fell by 52.3%, a result that could only be due to the effect of learning by doing.[17] The figure is, of course, a wartime one, when the motive to learn was boosted by the life-or-death nature of the struggle. Even so, it is very impressive.

There is reason to believe that not only labor costs, but capital and management costs also decline according to cumulative experience. The amount of technical innovation, scale changes, improvements implemented at the shop floor, and so forth, apparently correlate more closely with total production experience than to either elapsed time or even research expenditure. Such changes are of course affected by higher spending on R&D, or good management, but production experience, with normal expenditures on those other factors, is arguably the most important variable. The statistical and research techniques involved are still not completely accepted, but results are startling.

Figure 3.5 shows a number of learning curves the Boston Consulting Group, pioneers in this analysis, constructed from data gathered on various U.S. industries. The vertical axis is not labor, but total costs per unit, deflated by an appropriate price index. These curves are sometimes called *experience curves* to distinguish them from *learning curves*, which consider only labor's hours or costs. In this case, the addition of different technology would also be a factor in the change. Both the axes are in logarithmic scales such that a straight line shows a percentage change in costs compared to a percentage change in historical production—that is, a consistent percentage change (like 20%) for the same volume percentage change (100% or a doubling) will produce a straight line, the height being 20% and the width 100%, rather than the curved line of Fig. 3.4. The steeper the line, the greater the learning effect. The dots represent actual observations and the lines the statistical model, made by finding a straight line that cuts through the minimum vertical distances. The lines are drawn through the middle of the dots, so to speak. The closer the dots are to the line, the closer the actual observation to the statistical model—which is the line. The remarkable thing about these diagrams is the closeness of the fit of a statistical model to the actual observations. Very few dots are far away from the lines.[18]

The learning curve model has some important implications for international economics: The nation that has produced the greatest quantity of a good has the lowest cost, not because of unusual expenditures on capital, education, or research, but because it has learned to use its labor, and to a lesser extent its capital, more efficiently. Comparative advantage is not a given, but something created. It is not low costs that cause a nation to specialize; rather the specialization causes the low costs. Unlike many other economic models, learning curve

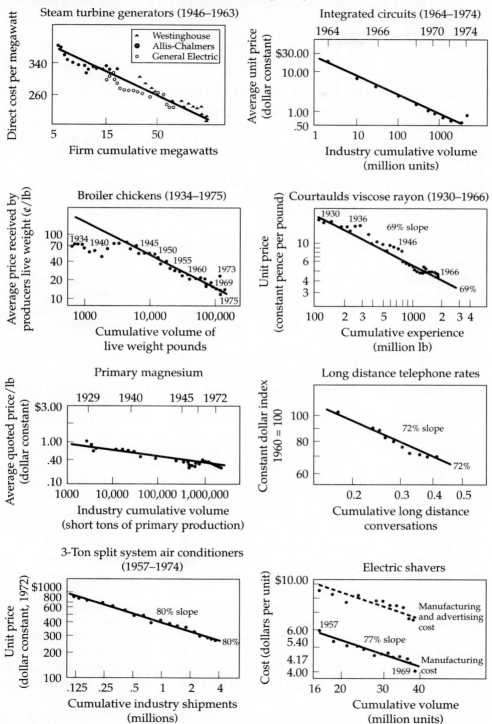

Figure 3.5 **Some sample experience curves.** Experience curves include not only labor, but other costs as well. Here is evidence of such a phenomenon, shown on log-log scales, where the straight lines indicate a regular percentage decline in costs based on the percentage change in cumulative production. The dots are actual data points. *Source: The Boston Consulting Group, Inc.*

models are not reversible. While a plant that must reduce its size to adjust to a smaller market will suffer diseconomies of scale, reduced output will not cancel the experience workers have already gained.

■ *TRADE BARRIERS CAN INHIBIT LEARNING*

An automobile industry was established in India in the late 1940s. One of the firms was founded at the same time that Toyota was founded in Japan. In the late 1970s, India was still producing more cars than Korea. Unfortunately, the stagnant industry showed little sign that cumulative learning was much of an advantage to it. The drive to learn is obviously lessened in the presence of high protection against foreign competition, a monopoly position at home, and lack of incentives to do anything but sit back and rake in profits.[19] The learning advantages are thus probably less for poor countries with high trade barriers and numerous monopolies.

COMBINING MODELS: PIONEERS AND LATE ENTRANTS   Comparing one world with identical countries entering into trade with another world where countries have very different costs is a neat pedagogical device, but a combination of both is actually more likely. Countries with small innate cost disparities would often tend to trade heavily in goods where cost differences are largely created by the advantages of learning. Where the innate gap between the cost of labor and capital is high, however, even large learning effects might not overcome the cost differences, and the predictions of the Heckscher-Ohlin model would prevail.

To illustrate this, assume there are two nations, a pioneer that first started the production of a labor-intensive product and a late-entry nation that starts production at a subsequent period. Further assume that the late entrant's costs are lower (its economic development is occurring after that of the pioneer). Since the product is labor intensive, the late entrant's lower labor costs should give it a comparative advantage. Because the late entrant is inexperienced, however, it cannot initially compete. Figure 3.6 shows this with two learning curves. E_p represents the learning curve of the pioneering nation, while E_l represents that of the late entrant. Curve E_l lies below E_p, indicating that at any point at which two nations have the same experience, the late entrant's costs would be lower. The late entrant's innate cost differences allow it to achieve a lower cost with less experience than the pioneering nation.

The intriguing aspect of this model is that the pioneering nation can keep the gap between it and the late entrant only so long as it can continue to double its production as fast as the latter. But it becomes increasingly difficult for the pioneering nation to continue doubling its production because the base grows so large. Consider how long it would take General Motors, Toyota, or Volkswagen to produce the quantity of cars equal to the entirety of its production since its found-

Figure 3.6 **Learning curves for a pioneer and a late entrant.** A nation pioneering a product whose costs are E_p can keep ahead of late entrants with lower cost structures only so long as it can keep expanding its production. If the pioneer moves from *a* to *b* at the same time the late entrant moves from *c* to *d*, both countries expanding production by 20,000 units, it will cease to have any advantage.

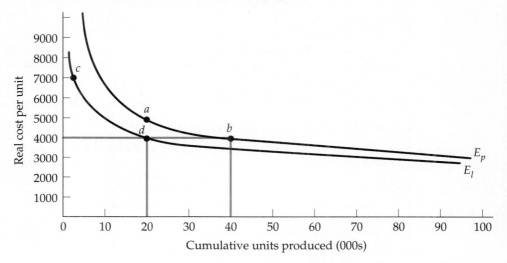

ing. Accordingly, the rate of cost decline in the pioneer slows, while the late entrant's costs fall rapidly. Return to Fig. 3.6 and suppose the pioneering nation is at point *a* on curve E_p when the late entrant (using some borrowed technology) starts at point *c* on its curve. Both nations now raise their sales by equal amounts of the product, say 20,000 units. The pioneering nation's new sales move it down its learning curve from *a* to *b*. For the same sales, however, the late entrant has moved from *c* to *d*. Unfortunately for the pioneer, point *b* and point *d* reflect the same cost of production. Comparative advantage and factor proportions thus appear to reassert themselves once the technological head start is overcome.

How, you might ask, could the late entrant ever move down its learning curve if the pioneer keeps ahead? It would not have any sales if the leading country always had the lower price. A competitive market would, however, support the late entrant if financiers had the knowledge that it would eventually displace the pioneer. They would then agree to finance, through loans or very low dividends, the late entrant until it caught up to the pioneer, using as their rationale the future earnings of the late entrant. To be sure, knowledge is not perfect, nor is the financial market, so this may not happen. But it could and does some of the time. In a situation of imperfect competition, the pioneering nation may also be producing at low costs, but not selling at low costs because its firms had some degree of monopoly control. If these firms fail to observe or respond to the new entrant, as American automobile firms failed to respond to the invasion of Europeans and Japanese in the small and luxury car markets, the new entrant can get a good start. From these considerations it appears likely that late entrants with more suitable factor endowments in the production of some particular good will eventually catch up to the pioneering nation.

It is possible that either pioneer or latecomer will find expected cost reductions cut short, so that the advantages of learning by doing are lost. An early freezing of work rules by trade unions, such as occurred in Great Britain, is a case in point and can stop the process by making impossible the reorganizations and shifts in tasks that learning allows. A resistance to skill acquisition on the job or a noncooperative workforce can substantially erode the advantages of experience.

■ *A PENALTY FOR TAKING THE LEAD?*

There may be a penalty for taking the lead that the pioneer has to bear. High-cost capital equipment that takes a long time to depreciate may eventually become obsolete and hence a drawback to the pioneering nation. Britain's industrial revolution in the first half of the nineteenth century saddled it with an inadequate railway system compared to the later networks of the United States and Germany. In order to negotiate the sharp curves of the system, British boxcars were (and are) small, with limited carrying capacity. Given the economic development along the rail lines, buying property to rectify the situation would now be extremely expensive. Similarly, the British iron and steel industry was trapped for many years by its heavy investment in Bessemer converters, at a time when Germany had gone on to the more efficient open-hearth method for steelmaking. (Then, after the Second World War, the United States and Britain were still stuck with their open-hearth systems while their bombing had done a splendid job of depreciating the German and Japanese mills, which were replaced with more modern facilities.) It is true, as economists point out, that sunk costs should ordinarily have no bearing on future investment decisions. To some extent, however, in practice they do. For one example, large costs may be associated with dismantling the old plant. For another, a heavy burden of outstanding loans on the now-outmoded capital may still have to be repaid, which may weaken the financial performance of firms and mean that they may have to face higher interest rates on subsequent loans. Finally, investment is risky and there may thus be a bias toward the status quo. All may represent penalties borne by the pioneer.[20]

The existence of learning curves does not disprove the Heckscher-Ohlin model, but adds to it. Learning is a form of information, and simple equilibrium models with a classical base assume that producers have all relevant information. Used judiciously and in the correct, presumably long-run, context, models incorporating this assumption are highly useful. We know, of course, that nations and companies do not have the same knowledge and that some production and marketing skills are exceedingly difficult to transfer. If we want to ask questions with the realistic assumption that production knowledge is imperfect, then learning curves make fascinating tools for so doing. If we wish to assert that factor proportions still hold in the abstract or in the long run, we can also do that.

THE MICROECONOMICS OF SPECIALIZATION AND DECREASING COST

The general idea is that trade among nations with similar factor proportions can occur because of scale economies that result in decreasing costs. The greater learning by doing as scale expands is one possible explanation. Another explanation involves a more traditional view of decreasing costs, as recently modified by advances in the study of specialization. The conventional microeconomic notion of what actually generates scale economies has focused on *plant-size economies of scale,* wherein costs fall as plants expand in size. Larger plants might allow greater division of labor, more specialized equipment and processes, assembly line techniques, fuel savings, and the like. *Firm economies of scale,* in which a single company may have many plants but through its coordinative mechanism manages to keep its costs lower than smaller single-plant firms, have also received attention.

In a more significant departure from the neoclassical tradition, *industry economies of scale* or *economies of agglomeration* may exist as great numbers of plants in a single industry cluster in certain areas. In the United States, for instance, there are regional concentrations of microchip plants in California's Silicon Valley, or of robotic equipment along Michigan's Route 94 west of Detroit. The clustering occurs because of the need for a pool of specialized labor, specialized inputs and services such as machine shops, technical advisors, and so forth—the infrastructure of an industry. In smaller nations, an excessive diversity could prevent the growth of such specialized infrastructure and accordingly of the lower costs that go with it.

PLANT-SIZE ECONOMIES We normally represent plant-size economies of scale with a long-run average cost curve. Typically (or probably) such curves are more or less U-shaped, with a long flat bottom, meaning that beyond a certain minimum amount, the minimum efficient scale or MES, costs per unit stay about the same over quite a range of plant sizes. They begin to rise again with very large plants, at the maximum efficient scale or MxES. Automobile assembly plants, for instance, may reach minimum efficient scale somewhere between 150,000 and 200,000 units a year, and have fairly constant costs through 300,000 or 400,000 units. In a small market, a firm might have to build a plant at suboptimal size. If it tried to build a plant at MES, but supply the small market, it would be operating it so far under capacity that it would be a very high-cost operation indeed.

Figure 3.7 **Plant economies of scale.** A firm operating on a short-run average cost curve that is less than minimum efficient scale (SRAC^1) will have higher costs than one operating on an efficient scale SRAC, such as SRAC^2, providing the latter has a market large enough to absorb its production. LRACs typically have rather long flat bottoms, with a minimum efficient scale (MES) and a maximum efficient scale (MxES).

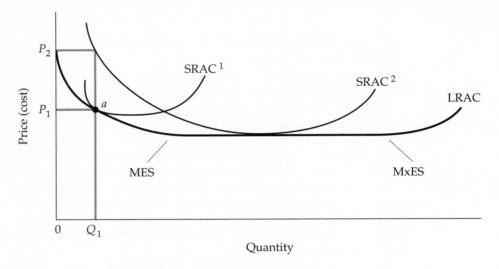

Figure 3.7 shows a long-run average cost curve and two short-run AC curves, which would apply to the firm once it built a plant. The firm building the sub-MES plant (SRAC^1) can operate at point *a*, with quantity Q_1 and price P_1, while the firm building at MES (SRAC^2) would be unable to sell more than Q_1 and, unable to spread its fixed costs over much volume, would thereby face very high costs, at P_2.

Typically, processing plants utilizing large amounts of heat have high MESs. Industrial gases (oxygen, chlorine, ethylene), petroleum refining, petrochemicals, milk processing, beer brewing, fruit and vegetable canning, sugar refining, paper making, fabrication of metal tubes and pipes, manufacture of cosmetics and perfume, glass making, and soap making are all among the industries with very high MESs. Gas and oil pipelines together with satellite and glass-fiber communication systems have perhaps the highest MESs of all.[*] Next come what can be called the metal-bashing industries, particularly those with continuous production lines such as motor vehicles and appliances. Below that are industries that

---

[*] One reason is that pipes and storage tanks do not have to be twice as big to carry twice the capacity. Compare a pipe that is 10 feet wide with one that is five feet wide. The formula for the area of a circle, which is key to the carrying capacity, is πr^2; the 10-foot wide pipe has an area of $\pi 5^2$ or about 79 sq. feet; the five-foot pipe has an area of just under 20 sq. feet. Also larger plants use little more labor and are better at conserving energy. It is said that a petrochemical plant producing 400,000 tons of ethylene a year costs only about 50% more, and uses only about 15% more labor, than one producing 200,000 tons.

are batch processors, although these are general rules of thumb, not economic precepts.[*]

Empirical evidence on the matter is not entirely conclusive. Joe S. Bain's 1950s work on U.S. and European data suggested that scale economies were overrated. Bain felt that most major countries had domestic markets large enough to support several plants of optimal size in most industries. Studies of Western Europe's plant sizes before the integration of the European Community also suggested they were about the same size as U.S. plants, which were presumably built to scale. It followed that integration would not increase scale economies by that much.

Bain's figures led to the conclusion that most major countries can support several plants of optimal size in most industries, both light and heavy; the very existence of multiplant firms demonstrated that. Further research in the 1970s by F.M. Scherer and others working with him confirmed the broad thrust of Bain's pioneering efforts.[21] Studies of specific industries do indicate that scale economies are not as important as might be expected in such industries as computers, diesel engines, generators, machine tools, rubber goods, shoes, and fish canning. To the extent that Bain, Scherer, and others are correct, the explanatory power of plant-size economies of scale is reduced.

In general, however, it appears that scale economies have been becoming *more* important in both exporting and import-competing industries.[22] It is especially clear that for countries with inadequate domestic markets, the diseconomies of small plant size can deliver a crucial cost penalty. The Australian petrochemical industry, for instance, has been operating at twice the cost of world-scale chemical plants, being both terribly under scale and, because of overly optimistic market forecasts, under capacity.[23] Many Canadian petrochemical operations, and a number of other industries, are seriously under scale and costly to operate—not because Canada's market is not big enough, but because transportation costs are much too great between market centers, which are mostly strung out along the U.S. border.

In such circumstances the achievement of plant-size scale economies through international trade can be critically important, and can outweigh other considerations. Belgium's industry specializes in auto parts and some machinery inputs, Denmark's in furniture, the Netherlands' in electrical equipment, Luxembourg's in steel, Sweden's in telecommunications, and Switzerland's in drugs and watches. In each case, without the scale economies made possible by trade, exporting these items would be difficult if not impossible. The same consideration affects the newly industrializing countries (NICs) of the Third World. Virtually *every* major manufactured good produced in Singapore or Hong Kong would be impossibly costly if it were not for the scale provided by the world

---

[*] Changes over time in plant economies have been noted as technology is standardized or altered. Thus in color TVs, MES in the early 1960s was observed to be about 50,000 sets a year, whereas by the late 1970s MES had risen to about 2 million. In steel, the old integrated steel mills had to produce about 2 million tons to reach MES; new mills reach MES with about half-a-million tons.

market. For these countries it is unarguable that high trade barriers to their exports will damage their welfare by inflicting scale diseconomies.

■ *SCALE PROBLEMS IN UNEXPECTED PLACES*

Inability to realize economies of scale can discourage trade in unusual ways. It is not worthwhile to produce a textbook in international economics specifically for the Canadian or Australian markets. Typically, only the large introductory courses have books adjusted to national circumstances; a Canadian or New Zealand student studying international economics, industrial organization, or even plain old intermediate theory, finds more discussion of the United States or Britain than is remotely necessary. Even newspaper comic strips need wide markets to be successful—and there are relatively few the United States uses from abroad. *Andy Capp* and *Fred Basset* (British), and *For Better or for Worse* (Canadian) are among this tiny group.

INDUSTRY ECONOMIES   Industry economies of scale may be more significant than plant scale economies. Each firm may face a normal long-run average cost curve, $LRAC^1$ in Fig. 3.8 for example, but as more firms enter the industry, this curve begins to shift downward, say to $LRAC^2$ and $LRAC^3$, as the essential industrial infrastructure comes into existence. The successful specialized industries of Belgium, Luxembourg, the Netherlands, Denmark, Sweden, and Switzerland are dependent not only on plant-size scale economies, as already discussed, but on industrial scale economies as well. An industrial strategy that encourages new plants simply because they meet existing MESs, yet are unrelated to other plants in the region, may never build the industrial infrastructure required to lower costs.

In Fig. 3.8, $LRAC_I$ represents the declining long-run average cost of the industry. A *firm's* LRAC (1, 2, and 3) represents that firm's long-run cost structure at some given industry output. As industry output increases, the firm finds that it faces lower costs. $LRAC_I$ slopes downward because as individual firms expand, they create benefits for other firms (externalities). They do so by enlarging the pool of skilled labor and management, supporting local universities and community colleges, and creating markets for a plethora of specialized suppliers and services.

SEGMENTED MARKETS AS AN EXPLANATION FOR TRADE

The demand and supply diagram all students learn in the first year has a horizontal axis labeled "cars" or "bushels of wheat" or, more abstractly, "widgets." The goods have to be identical, or the differences between them clearly quantifiable, for the model to work, and that simplification is enormously useful.

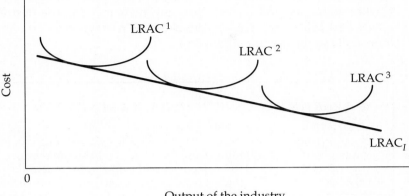

Figure 3.8 **Industry economies of scale.** Long-run average costs may fall when a number of firms operate in the same area due to economics of agglomeration. Thus the industry's LRAC (LRAC$_I$) slopes downward.

Most goods in the economy are not identical, however, and we do not want them to be identical either. Students' clothing may not fit the more rotund bodies of many of their instructors, and many students and teachers would feel foolish or stuffy in the other group's outfits.

The degree of difference is in essence a compromise between the economies of mass production and the rather specific needs of the consumers. In the Third World, inexpensive labor often allows individual tailoring, but the capital-intensive techniques of the developed world have, at least until recently, favored a great degree of standardization—whether it be clothing, cars, or breakfast cereal. We buy standardized clothes because of price. Unless we are very wealthy, we do not have our own tailors to match our sizes and shapes precisely. The market makes its own compromises—sport shirts come in four adult sizes, long-sleeved dress shirts in over 30. Consumers buy a good that is somewhat less than perfect because its price compensates—Oreo cookies may not be as good as Mom's, but Mom's are far more expensive, in that she would have to take a day off from work, while Oreos can be bought in a bag at the supermarket. The shirt may be a little long in the sleeve or a little tight at the waist, but the buyer saves a few dollars that can be used to buy something else.

Increasingly, however, consumers everywhere (in developed countries at any rate) have shown that their demand shifts away from standardized products as their incomes rise. When the affluence of these consumers increases, they become less interested in the saving on price alone, and more anxious to acquire a product that accurately meets their own tastes and needs. Rather than saving $75 on a washing machine to spend elsewhere, they buy a machine with extra washing cycles. Firms accommodate them to get their business. Since each consumer is somewhat different, the firm produces a line of goods with various features to serve various groups of customers—which, evidence indicates, is easier to accomplish when production is capital rather than labor intensive.[24] Complete personal customization is impossible, but the firm can divide its market into market segments, and manufacture products meeting the desires of each segment. This procedure, usually described as market segmentation, is discussed more fully in the accompanying box.

■ *A FURTHER LOOK AT MARKET SEGMENTATION*

Marketers sometimes distinguish between a segmentation based on market characteristics such as age, gender, income, lifestyle—young/old, black/white, yuppie/retired, ad infinitum—and those that are based on product characteristics—15-, 25-, 50-, 75-, 110-horsepower outboards, or the amount of chocolate in cakes and cookies. The product preferences for each motor or cake fall rather randomly across any market segment; and the purchase is determined by the function the goods are to perform.

Inevitably market segmentation adds to costs, but produces benefits consumers want. Hence even under highly competitive conditions, one could expect a considerable degree of market segmentation as firms try to answer the economic question of what to produce.

Under oligopolistic situations there may be rather more market segmentation because firms fear to engage in price wars. If Coke fights with Pepsi through a price cut, Pepsi can match it tomorrow, but if Coke comes out with a new flavor (say diet cherry), Pepsi would take months or longer to produce a competitive drink. Often the market is just not responsive enough to price cuts to make them worthwhile. If *Better Homes and Gardens* lowers its price, it is unlikely to gain customers from *House Beautiful.* Under such conditions firms speak of "deepening their market" and move toward a greater effort to identify market segments and produce goods specifically designed for each. In extreme cases there may be little redesign and merely an assertion that the product is for a particular group, as in a man's deodorant, a woman's laxative, a blue-collar beer. As a result, there is no inexpensive brand X but only more expensive customized products.[25]

Market segments do not necessarily follow national borders. Not all Americans like big cars and all Europeans small ones. Not all Frenchmen love French cars. Blue jeans and jean jackets are popular worldwide, particularly among young people, and their design does not change at the borders. What this means is that companies are able to plan and design for a world market involving a niche for some particular product variety. No single national market can support the BMW or the Volvo—there are not enough buyers in any one market. But the world as a whole makes the market large enough. Even textbooks, particularly those for the upper levels, benefit enormously from world market sales and are increasingly designed (like this one) with those sales in mind.

"IN-FIRM" DISECONOMIES OF MULTIPLE MODELS   Even when a firm can produce locally in multiple models, it is likely to find that its costs rise as the models proliferate. First are the additional costs that occur within a firm that decides to multiply its models. A major example involves the additional pre-production costs for market research, design, prototypes, and testing. Before a company decides to come up with a new model of car, a new textbook, or a new deodorant, it must identify a need or desire, often through market research. It must design a product and build prototypes. Finally, formally or informally it must test-market the product, often at considerable expense. A new automobile model, for instance, could easily cost $100 million before the first car is sold. If the company expects to sell only 200,000 units of that model (the output of one assembly plant for one year), those costs are $500 per car. A new textbook requires the labor of one or two authors, several editors, and another set of critical readers before it is edited or the type is set—and that can easily be $10 or more per book. Four-megabyte DRAM (dynamic random-access memory) computer chips probably cost about $2 billion before even one was sold.[26]

Additional costs will be incurred for advertising and the provision of information, as it will be necessary to bring each different model to the attention of the public. Furthermore, inventory costs will rise greatly as models proliferate. With numerous models, it will be necessary for a firm to increase its holding of parts and components, which will not be fully interchangeable. More finished items must be held in inventory as well, because consumers must be able to see examples of the product at stores or showrooms. Much of the inventory of finished items will not be sold for months, and some of it might not be sold at all.

Finally, if the product is a durable, then providing service for it will be more difficult if there are multiple models. Repair people will need more varied training, and diagnostic equipment will have to be more complex. A more complicated stock of spare replacement parts will also be necessary.

Each of the cases discussed above involves the firm with an increased burden of decision making associated with the proliferation of models. Whether to introduce an additional model will involve weighing the costs against the benefits of marketing that new model. This burden on management is another extra cost of production.

"IN-PLANT" DISECONOMIES OF MULTIPLE MODELS   In addition to the costs affecting an entire firm, there is another set of costs involving the actual production within a plant.[27] The introduction of new models into a production line, with no deletion of any of the existing models, increases the costs of all products in that line. More specifically, these in-plant costs involve:

1. *Changeover time.* Down time is the period when a machine or factory is being changed over for new production runs, idling machinery and manpower.

One Australian factory, for instance, reported that the set-up time on a machine was eight hours. The machine was used for two hours to turn out a supply of parts that would last many months, and was then reset for something else. The American parent firm, with its larger market, used the same machine for weeks after the set-up.[28] The cost of the changeover must fall on the products involved.

2. *Equipment usage rates.* Specialized dies and machinery are needed for each of the different models. Many of these must be left idle while other products are run, giving low usage rates. When the accountants go over the figures, they find that they must assign higher per-product costs as they divide the cost of the machine by the products it produces.

3. *Automation and the use of specialized equipment.* Many kinds of specialized equipment are justified only with high volumes of particular items. To quote an Australian manager:

> *Where we use a two- or three-cavity die, the U.K. company uses a twenty-four cavity die... And where we have a machine on which we do five different processes consecutively, stripping down the machine between each process, the U.K. company does the five processes simultaneously on one machine—but their machine costs about £400,000.*

And another Australian:

> *Where we use an ordinary turret lathe, the U.K. company uses a multistation loading lathe, and the U.S. company uses a twelve-spindle machine which performs twelve operations simultaneously.[29]*

Automation is only economical for longer production runs. Workers can be taught to switch tasks, but the machine that replaces them has a more limited range. If there are many different models to turn out, the process cannot be extensively automated, so labor costs must be higher.

4. *Labor's learning curve.* The repetition of tasks leads to a decline in labor costs, as we indicated previously, but if there are many models, the repetition is lessened and much of the learning is foregone.

Computer-aided design and managerial changes are making it easier to produce multiple models within a single plant, but multiple models are still more costly to produce than a few standard ones. According to the rule of thumb adopted by the Boston Consulting Group, reducing product-line variety by half cuts costs on average by 17%; reducing variety again by half yields another cost saving averaging 13%.[30] Studies in Canada have suggested that automobile companies saved 10% to 15% of their costs by orienting their production toward the U.S. market as well as the Canadian one.

Trade in market-segmented goods carries with it the same kind of convex production possibilities curve we showed in Fig. 3.7 for plant-size scale effects. Whatever the country decides to specialize in is cheaper than the product it decides not to specialize in. The effects of factor proportions are just too small to have much of an influence compared with the returns to specialization.

FACTORIES FOCUSED AND FLEXIBLE

Firms that solve the problem of bringing a wide variety of models to their customers while yet controlling costs have an obvious edge. At the same time, firms' solutions to the problems have significant international implications. Firms are following one of two paths: (1) toward more specialized plants—*focused factories,* and (2) toward plants that can change very quickly and inexpensively from producing one model to producing another—*flexible factories.*

FOCUSED FACTORIES   If firms can limit the variety of their product lines, producing in focused factories for one or a few of the ever-increasing number of market segments or niches, they can reap substantial in-plant economies. In each separate national market, such segments are often not large enough to allow scale economies. The result is likely to be more intraindustrial trade because different but related products will often be made in different countries. Typically a multinational firm may decide to produce all of a given product line in one plant, which happens to be located in one country, and all of another line of products in a second plant, which happens to be in a second country. Even a domestic company might decide to "source" part of its product line from an independent firm in another country. Shoe and fastener companies have been doing this for years. For example, a fastener firm in Rockford, Illinois, has for some time imported the standard nuts and bolts of its product line from various foreign companies, while utilizing its own production facilities for high-tech aerospace work. (Note how this contributes to the Leontief Paradox because the work the firm maintains at home is far more labor and technology intensive than the items it imports.)

Focused factories possess an inherent disadvantage. As market segmentation increases and as changes in consumer tastes occur more rapidly, a focused factory may find itself running up against growth constraints because its product variety is too limited and its response to taste changes too slow. Hence the development of the flexible factory, with the ability to produce multiple models without the many costs associated with doing so. The aim is to offer customized products priced as close as possible to mass-produced goods.

FLEXIBLE FACTORIES   A major technical change making the flexible factory possible has been the introduction of computer-assisted design and manufacture (CAD/CAM), also called computer-integrated manufacturing (CIM), based on the microelectronics revolution.[31] The new technology consists of computerized design of prototypes, automatic insertion devices such as programmable robots, very large scale integration, and automated, programmable assembly.

Design by means of math models rather than by means of mockups gives a major head start on both testing and tooling. It has allowed designers to work alongside manufacturing engineers in a variety of industries in a parallel rather than a sequential process. At the very least it allows for rapid transmission of information to and from suppliers rather than waiting for blueprints to arrive in the mail. Computer assistance has made possible a reduction in time expended on design activity by as much as 25% to 33%, and sometimes even more. Lockheed, for example, has reduced the time spent on manufacture and design of sheet metal parts from an average of 52 days to 2 days.[32] As a result, consumer demand for quality improvements can be met much more quickly than before.

It used to be common for a new model car or computer to sit in the product development stage for several years. Nowadays, however, world-class Japanese automakers plan for a development cycle of only three-and-a-half years for a new model; other automakers with a five-year cycle are at a disadvantage. This development, in essence reflecting a general shortening of product life, puts a premium on management and organization flexibility to cope with rapid changes in product markets, and conversely implies that narrow and sluggish bureaucracies will pay a greater penalty than formerly.

Production is also different in a flexible factory. The ease with which the programmable machines can be shifted among product varieties sharply cuts the down time associated with low-volume batch production. A dozen different models can come out of the same production line without any increase in labor or idled machinery. In a computerized factory, round-the-clock operation needs to be interrupted for only a few minutes to reprogram the tools to produce another model. Computerized numerically controlled (CNC) tools cut or shape according to programmable instructions, directed from central computer workstations, with programmed robotic movement of inputs. Flexible factories often run for 24 hours a day. They *must* do so to spread their overhead of costly machinery, engineers, and programmers.

■ *EXAMPLES OF OPERATIONS IN FLEXIBLE FACTORIES*

At the new Volkswagen plant in Wolfsburg, Germany, it now takes very little time and effort to switch from Golfs to Jettas. To make pilot 1989 test cars, GM engineers set the machinery after work ceased on Friday afternoon, turned out the test cars, then reset to the 1988 model for Monday morning. Honda's Accord has been updated on the line in a single day. A plant of the Allen-Bradley Company making electric controls can switch among its 725 products and varieties in an average time of six seconds.

Even more major retooling is facilitated by the new computerized robotics. When Nissan retools for a new body assembly, its costs are now only about a third of their old level, and the time taken to finish the job has been reduced from about 11 months to about four.[33]

Computers can also help control the flow of components and finished goods to cut inventory size and costs, thereby lowering the costs of producing multiple products, and the amount of working capital involved. The Japanese pioneered what is known as just-in-time (JIT) delivery. The JIT system is largely an inventory control method. It reduces inventories dramatically, as much as 90%, because the firms do not make products until they are needed, nor do the suppliers make the components until just before use. Hence the name *just-in-time*, implying that there is little inventory, often eight hours or less of major parts, semifinished, or finished goods. (The just-in-time system may be combined with computer-controlled robotics, as when preassembled and pretested modules held in closely monitored inventory are fitted into products by programmed insertion devices.)

Another possible implication of the just-in-time system is tying suppliers more closely to producers and therefore limiting the geographic or cultural scope of the suppliers. The ability to work closely with a producer or supplier, or the technical knowledge needed to fulfill the demands (on time) of a producer, has a considerable value. Often this value is far greater than the price savings offered by a foreign supplier. It may, for instance, be cheaper to order 50,000 automobile mufflers from Korea, but the cost of holding them in inventory, of waste of mufflers that are not used because of a change in consumer demand, and the slowness of a distant firm's response to changes needed may overcome any cost advantage.[34] A closely related supplier can often respond within one to three days, rather than taking two weeks or more to do so. That supplier can often be persuaded to originate new ideas, introduce better quality controls, suggest improved manufacturing methods, and allow the buyer to inspect operations and demand changes almost as if it were a subsidiary. In any case fewer suppliers tend to give more consistency in quality.

■ *JUST-IN-TIME INVENTORY MANAGEMENT IN THE UNITED STATES*

Just-in-time inventory management has been adopted by many U.S. firms, but the effect thus far remains limited. In automaking, for example, inventories of raw materials, work in progress, and finished stock still amount to 20.4% of total sales, compared to 4.7% in Japan.[35] Many ostensible users of just-in-time techniques have done nothing more than move inventory to nearby warehouses or shift it to suppliers without reducing it. In Japan, there has been much more cooperation between suppliers and users of parts, with long-term contracts often lasting for the lifetime of a model.

Finally, the interchange of electronic data can be used to improve coordination between customers' orders, distribution, and manufacture. In the late 1970s, Toyota could make a car in two days, but needed two to four weeks from a customer's signature on the dotted line to allow for transmission of an order, scheduling of manufacture, manufacture itself, and delivery of the car to the customer. With computers allowing better coordination, by 1987 this time period had been reduced to only eight days. In clothing, Benetton maintains inventories of undyed sweaters, shirts, and scarves, scans its computer orders every night, and decides on the colors for the next day's production. It used to take months. Orders for the electric controls of the Allen-Bradley Company can be filled the day after they are received.

In effect, computers give the flexible factory the ability to deliver both volume and variety. Management does not make goods or their components until it senses a real need for them, and then it makes and delivers them quickly.[36] Production is shifted closer to the market, and capital costs are lowered.

■ *FURTHER RAMIFICATIONS OF FLEXIBLE FACTORIES*

The flexible factory concept extends much further than computerization. Factories are reorganized in flexible workstations and are planned to avoid machinery that is only efficient with vast production runs of identical items. Labor rules are more pliable, as is the individual worker, who must possess greater abilities to deal with many tasks.[37] Under these conditions, workers may be able to decide collectively on their own schedules and sometimes even job assignments. With several sorts of skills needed to keep a computerized production process up and running, rewards for broader knowledge and abilities will presumably increase. In some flexible factories this has gone to the point of abolishing job titles and specific job descriptions; a premium is put on education, and pay is based on the number of skills mastered. One of the best known of the new applications is Volvo's creation of self-managing work groups, in which cooperation and informality are emphasized. In Volvo factories, cars are not assembled on the long-traditional production line, but at fixed positions. In some plants elsewhere the goal is to have every worker capable of operating the system; in others, each worker engaged in patrolling the assembly line has a switch that can stop the line.

Yet more benefits can be expected in the future. Improvements in health and safety are very likely, since welding, spray painting, lifting, and loading can be entirely mechanized. Many flexible factories have already found absenteeism reduced, sometimes sharply. A surge in useful employee suggestions for improvements in operation is another result already seen in practice. The adaptability of the new plants, with workers able to undertake many tasks and paid accordingly, opens a prospect of considerably more teamwork, group interaction, and commitment in the labor force. These predictions may prove to be overly optimistic, but some promise for the future is undoubtedly there.

The range of innovations that comprise the flexible factory concept has been called by some lean manufacturing, and by others the *Toyota production system*, from the company most associated with it at an early stage. Many other major users of the concept are Japanese as well, including prominently Sony, Hitachi, Toshiba, Honda, Sharp, and NEC. The combination of CAD/CAM, computerized robotics, just-in-time inventory management and close relations with suppliers, careful quality control, and employee decision making on the factory floor certainly emphasizes human capital and technology as a source of comparative advantage. More than that, however, it emphasizes the role of time. Fast response to consumer demand through rapid introduction of innovations to a wide range of product varieties is a central factor.[38] Observers note the importance of introducing all of these features at the same time rather than one by one. Because their effect is cumulative, it may not even be profitable to introduce just one or two of the innovations separately.[39]

Flexible factories, in contrast to focused factories, dispense with the need to import additional products from other countries to fill out a product line. The goods they produce have a comparative advantage partly because of the technology embodied in these factories, and partly because of skilled labor and management employed in them. These are consistent with a Heckscher-Ohlin factor approach. Partly, however, their output has a comparative advantage because of scale arguments. These plants develop the ability to overcome in-plant diseconomies involved in producing many models, while at the same time realizing the traditional scale economies from large operations. If they generate new trade, it will be because the companies have lowered the costs of the products they produce. Any technological lead already taken by the pioneers would likely be enhanced. Intraindustry or intrafirm trade may slow, but intrafactoral trade would not, with trade continuing to rise among the developed nations. A perception of gains to be obtained from intrafactoral trade underlay the trade pact between the United States and Canada on automobile exports signed in 1965. Similar perceptions have also been important in the development of the European Common Market.

WHAT COULD TRIGGER THE DIRECTION OF SPECIALIZATION?

THE PROBLEM Consider once again the decreasing cost (convex) production possibilities curve of Fig. 3.3. Economies of scale, decreasing costs due to economies of agglomeration, experience effects, in-plant economies when goods are produced specifically for segmented goods in focused factories, and flexible factories insofar as they yield scale economies all fit into the pattern of production possibilities curves convex to the origin. One implication of convex PPCs is that the market does not command the direction of specialization. Two identical countries could start out, both at the midpoints of their production possibilities curves; they would therefore have the same prices and, according to theory, would not trade. Yet a slight movement in one direction or the other would initiate a rapid movement toward complete specialization. With imperfect knowledge, this could occur even if potential gains were greater in a different pattern of specialization. Figure 3.9 shows two countries with the same prices, but rather different potentials.

We begin with both nations producing at an unspecialized level—*a* for the left nation, *A* for the right one. The slopes of the curves are the same at those points and match a set of prices. If the left nation begins to move toward *b*,

Figure 3.9 **Indeterminacy and optimization.** Given convex production possibilities curves and insufficient knowledge of the potential cost structure, countries could specialize toward either corner. This would be suboptimal if the right-hand country specialized at *C* and the left-hand one at *b*.

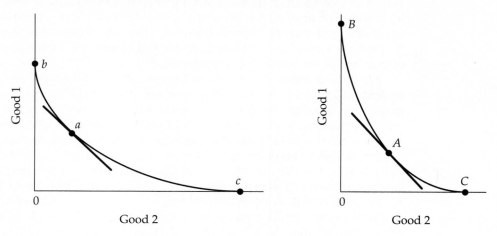

prices will force the right nation to move toward *C*, and specialization will end up there, not at the preferable points *c* and *B*.

No one, of course, can see the curve because it is a figment, albeit useful, of economists' imagination, so they would not know which way to go. Once the countries move off their midpoints, they will specialize, and once they start to move toward a corner, they will continue to do so, whether or not it is that corner that gives the largest gain. With a normal concave production possibilities curve, countries moving in the wrong direction would soon find their prices rising and would be forced to move toward the correct corner in a specialization that would be less than complete. With convex PPCs, a movement in either direction represents a gain to countries engaged in trade, but the size of the gain will be smaller should the initial price signals begin movement in the less-optimal direction.

The last few pages have suggested that a push toward specializing will bring lower costs and create a comparative advantage. When the road is once taken, the alternative road will never be tried. What then pushes a nation to one side or another? We suggest several models, all of which feature a degree of indeterminacy and contingency.

DEMAND AS A DETERMINANT OF COSTS: LINDER'S MODEL OF INVENTION AND DEVELOPMENT

Suppose a nation sits on an inwardly curved (convex) production possibilities curve. What is likely to give it a push in one direction or another? One possibility is domestic demand. The country that has a considerable domestic demand for a product will begin to make more of it, thus sliding down its learning curve.

The increased production represents a move along its production possibilities curve as well. The price differentials that would accordingly spring up will drive each nation toward the corner in which its initial domestic demand was highest.

The Swedish economist Staffan Burenstam Linder has a more elaborate and subtle explanation of the role of demand in creating comparative advantage. His model examines how goods are invented and how their use expands, rather than looking at initial cost differentials among products whose use is already widespread.[40] New product inventions and introductions, Linder held, are closely tied to differing national tastes and income levels, which thus become major determinants of trade.

To come up with an invention or innovation, one must perceive a need, have an inspiration, and then work and rework that initial idea to fit the market. Often this means not only making the product, but informing people about it and rendering it acceptable to them. Hence the key factor in determining where production begins is not the cost of the good, but the market for it. Only by working closely with the market can one invent and develop a good. Inventions and innovations thus occur in a quality range that appeals to and is profitable in a given national market. Tibor Scitovsky and Shlomo Maitel have done pioneering work on the boundaries between economics and psychology in attempts to explain the establishment of different tastes in different national markets, but such work is still in its infancy.[41]

Sometimes the reasons seem clear enough. The cold Swedish climate provided the right environmental breeding ground for Swedish stoves; long distances led to large American cars; a dispersed population fostered Canadian strength in telecommunications. Pronounced inequalities in British incomes just before and after World War I were surely a major reason for the initial development and success of autos such as the Jaguar, the Bentley, and the Rolls-Royce. Other cases are harder to explain—British preference for heavier beers or bourbon's popularity in the United States. We may not know why the nation's particular tastes begin, but its consequence is that it lowers the cost of producing whatever it is the nation prefers. The demand causes the cost to fall, which in turn generates the comparative advantage.

Whatever the explanations, as inventions are developed for national markets, consumers in other nations with similar needs discover the new products. Trade arises between nations with similar tastes and similar factor proportions, not the reverse. The sewing machine was invented and developed in the United States, but early exports were all to Britain, particularly the textile centers at Glasgow. Indeed, Singer built a plant in the area in 1868. Textile-making machinery moved in the other direction, from Britain to the United States, as did thread production. The Model T Ford, the cigarette, the vacuum cleaner (still known as a Hoover in England), and the elevator (or lift) all moved from the United States to Britain. Aspirin moved from Germany to Britain and the United States.

As Linder notes, the reason products like the vacuum cleaner or the washing machine spread was because the countries had similar economic structures.

Both Britain and the United States had high incomes, increasing labor costs, declining availability of servants, and rising mass markets (larger, albeit, in the States than in Britain). They therefore wanted each other's goods. Trade with Third World countries, interestingly, also follows much the same pattern, with the bulk of the industrial nations' consumer goods going to the rather narrow but wealthy urban sectors. The spread from the home market to an overseas market is likely to be most rapid when foreign buyers are price insensitive due to the product's unique characteristics. In that event the exporter can build up experience while maintaining a good return on investment. Cases in point are the premium prices U.S. consumers are willing to pay for BMW and Mercedes automobiles. Other examples are the prices that IBM used to be able to charge for its computers and Kodak for its film.

Linder goes on to point out another curious phenomenon: The importing country is the most logical next entrant into the export market. This is particularly true if that country has a large market for the good. Typically, domestic production follows imports. As experience is gained and domestic adjustments are made, exports often ensue as cost levels similar to the original exporter's are reached and new variants of the product are created.

Although Linder's ideas are useful ones and logically sound, it has been difficult to test them empirically. The avidity with which large manufacturing firms have recently been setting up research centers in their overseas markets provides circumstantial evidence that national tastes develop differently and are important for commercial success. Some direct support has emerged from data based on Swedish trade, for which the models were originally formulated. The testing has had less success elsewhere. One complicating factor has been that countries very similar in incomes and class structures (and thus with similar market segments) are often located quite close together, and the lower transportation costs make it difficult to identify Linder-type developments.[42] Like most of the modern trade models, Linder's depends on knowledge imperfections (on the parts of both the producer and the consumer). Unlike most, it gives primacy to the role of demand, which determines not only what is consumed, but ultimately the cost of what is produced. While it may not be able to predict exactly what product might be produced, it narrows the constraints by better identifying the contingent factors.

MANAGERIAL CHOICE: A VISIBLE HAND

Consider the situation of a firm producing many differentiated goods in several countries. It knows that it can cut costs by perhaps 20% if it moves to focused factories, but it is unclear that any country is going to have a sustained advantage over another in producing the goods. So it takes existing factories and personnel and cuts down the variety of goods they produce. While the companies may make some studies of different costs, the decision is in most cases quite arbitrary as to which plant is to produce what. The point is not to find what the nation is good at, but simply to specialize, for that in turn will yield a cost advantage. When Chrysler decided to make its Caravans in Windsor, Ontario, it made Canada the low-cost producer. Nowhere else could an extra Caravan be made with the sacrifice of fewer other automobiles. Again, the decision is contingent on Canada having automobile plants, a workforce capable of making cars, and a supportive infrastructure, but the choice of models is not *determined* by those factors.

As we shall see in Chapter 8, governments may also take a role in deciding the direction of specialization. Your authors are not overly optimistic about such approaches. They worry that governments' decisions will be too slow or too laden with political objectives, and so will fail to take into account the constraints already imposed by history and by what is happening elsewhere. Both firms and governments must also be aware that although there are many possible paths to success, success is not random but is contingent on what has gone before.

PRODUCT LIFE CYCLES AS INFLUENCING SPECIALIZATION

Both the Linder and the learning curve approaches to why specialization occurs lay a foundation (or certainly are consistent with) a more elaborate analysis based on life cycles of products and industries. Product life cycle analysis is a common tool among managerial strategists and provides a dynamic to trade analysis that some economists find appealing.[43]

Basically, a PLC model sketches the relationship of a product's sales per year to its age. Figure 3.10 shows the PLC of a typical successful product.

In the figure, time (unspecified) is on the horizontal axis while sales per period is on the vertical. The pattern of sales growth divides into four basic periods—introductory, growth, maturity, and decline—although different writers have subdivided these further. The typical product has an introductory period of uncertain length, sometimes many years, sometimes only a few months, in which sales are low. Following that is a period in which growth is quite rapid, then a long period of stable sales, and eventually a decline. These periods are closely related to changes in demand and supply conditions.

1. On the demand side, consumers have to learn how to use the product and what its benefits are. (We are again operating without all relevant knowledge.) At the same time, other goods and services that are part of the same usage system undergo development. The automobile had a small market when there were few paved roads, gasoline stations were scarce, and mechanics were hard to find. The consumers were a group called "pioneers" or "early adopters," who could fix their own tires, crank their own engines, and put up with impassable roads. When personal computers first came out, operators had to do their own programming, programs themselves were scarce, and repair people were hard to find. The benefits of owning one were uncertain, particularly in the highly important word-processing areas. Only people who had already had experience with computers in offices, or teenagers with a mathematical and mechanical bent and plenty of spare time to learn computer programming, were interested in purchasing them.

Figure 3.10 **A product life cycle.** A typical successful product goes through a life cycle, its sales slow at first, increasing rapidly, then leveling off, and eventually declining.

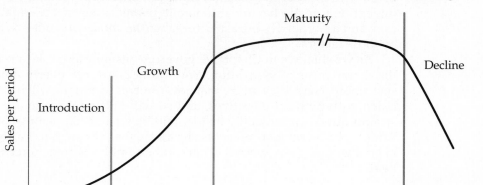

As the product becomes more standardized, more reliable, and more beneficial, sales expand rapidly. Again, in the case of the personal computer, the machines became user friendly, the number of available programs expanded almost bewilderingly, and the benefits became much clearer to a large number of people. It is a common process. Sixty years earlier the automobile had become more user friendly with the addition of the electric starter, closed cabs, and pneumatic tires; roads were paved, and gasoline and repairs became easily available, leading to a rapid increase in automobile sales.

Once a product becomes widely accepted, its sales growth rate falls. All the people who have the skills to use the product or who appreciate its benefit (and can afford it) have it. While there may be some marginal buyers who would find some use for the good and some benighted individuals who still have not really been exposed to the good's possible benefits, the majority has. Sales thus become limited to upgrading and replacement markets. This is the mature phase. Finally, the good is no longer even needed; or it may not die completely, maintaining some tiny residual market, as do black and white TVs and chewing tobacco.

2. On the technological side, costs tend to fall throughout the life of a product. When there are both rapid consumer acceptance and a steep experience curve, the two factors reinforce each other. The additional production lowers costs, and the lower costs open up new markets, further increasing production. Products that have had slow acceptance and long introductory periods, such as the electric typewriter, which was first produced in the 1920s but did not become standard until the 1960s, fail to benefit from the rapidly declining costs that production experience provides.

3. Competitive patterns also change as a product matures. Early on, there are many competitors, often with competing technologies (the electric, gasoline, and steam car; the 33-RPM and 45-RPM record, the Apple and IBM formats, VHS and Beta videotape formats). As the growth period moves on, the technology for making the product becomes more standardized, and the buyers move toward the standardized forms, both because of price and because the support systems are there. For example, the number of VHS-format movies soon grew to be overwhelmingly larger than those for Beta, and the production of new Beta machines was suspended in 1988. There tends to be a shake-out in the industry, with only a few successful firms remaining, or those remaining shifting to the standardized operations. Well into the mature phase technology becomes diffused, allowing the growth of some new firms, often foreign, as we described in the learning curve discussion. The onslaught of automobile imports into North America occurred because the technology to make the product was widely diffused, while the particular gains from additional production experience were small.

The first attempt to relate PLC models to international trade came from Louis Wells and Raymond Vernon of the Harvard Business School.[44] The Wells-Vernon model provides a thought-provoking historical analysis of U.S. trade. For many years the United States had the highest per-capita income in the world, and with that high income came the introduction of many new consumer goods plus a great quantity of new capital goods. United States consumers saw the first widespread use of the refrigerator, the radio, the clothes washer, and then later televisions and dishwashers. Initially, export sales of these products were small because few foreign consumers could afford them. Thereafter, as incomes rose abroad, export markets grew. We show this as a product life cycle first involving production for the home market only, and then involving exports, which begin at a later time period. (See the uppermost curve in Fig. 3.11.)

As foreign markets grew, however, foreign producers were tempted to compete, first with production for local consumers, and then for export. The process was feasible because the technology was more widely available and the technological lead of U.S. firms was shrinking, as our learning curve models showed. Though the foreign production may have been initially more expensive, trade barriers, transportation costs, and local preferences served to protect the foreign producers. American manufacturers at this stage also moved their production facilities abroad to be close to the expanding market—if they had not done so already. Note in Fig. 3.11 how home production in the top part of the diagram levels off as production picks up in the imitator countries. Finally, production *falls* in the home country.

To this point, the Wells-Vernon model is not controversial. The difficulty comes in the next step. Wells and Vernon go on to suggest that following the competitive phase both at home and abroad, the foreign producer now has the advantage. Why? Because the technological gap has been closed or is at least small, but foreign wages and incomes are still below the American, such that in

Figure 3.11 **Product life cycles in home and foreign markets.** It may be that the product life cycle is connected with the location of production, the pioneer country tending to sell at home during the introductory stage, then to export during growth, then to produce abroad, and finally to import in the declining stage. The PLC in other countries begins later, but has the same shape; it begins with importing and ends in exporting.

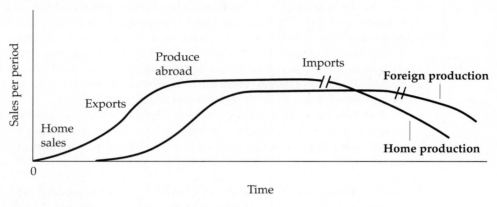

the mature stage the foreign country will export and the United States will import. As we noted in our discussion of the learning curve, this is a distinct possibility and may explain why the United States imports radios, televisions, and automobiles.

The problem with the Wells-Vernon theory is that there is very little supporting evidence that the pioneer nation becomes a net importer in the mature phase and loses its early advantages so completely. United States intraindustrial trade in road motor vehicles was at 94% in both 1967 and 1975. The supposedly embattled telecommunications industry did surprisingly well, with intraindustrial trade running 85% of total trade. Hence even in an area where penetration is fairly significant, exports continued strong. On a micro level, Georges Leroy's detailed study of five multinational manufacturers examined the development of several hundred products and failed to find a single instance of the sequence described by Wells—invention at home, production at home followed by export, production abroad, and then exports back home. Where there are products sent back to the home nation, they almost always embody considerable foreign technology, or else the firms have gone abroad to begin export back home without developing the local market at all.[45]

The reasons for the difficulty with the Wells-Vernon model may stem at least partially from changes in world economic conditions. Both the technology and wage gaps among Europe, Japan, and the United States are closing—in some nations wages are at par with or higher than American wages, although this depends crucially on the value of the dollar in the foreign exchange market at any particular moment. The United States is less and less the sole pioneer. Americans drive on radial tires, manage four-cylinder engines, ride ten-speed bikes, watch VCRs, shave with double-blade razors and use disposable lighters, all of which were developed outside the United States. Increasingly U.S. firms have bought out foreign firms for their knowledge, and vice versa. Leroy's study, for instance, showed extensive exchange of products and know-how between foreign and domestic sources of information within the same firm.

The mature stage of the PLC, rather than being a stage of importation, appears to be a stage of interpenetration. New variations on old products, such as razor blades, detergents, or car models, increase the amount of segmentation. Trade at this point becomes a matter not so much of technology, but of specialized production and consumption of goods. Managerial choice, constrained of course by past experience and various innate costs, may be the key factor in determining the direction of specialization.

For all the controversy, life cycle models do correctly emphasize the role of human capital and knowledge in giving a *temporary* comparative advantage. The original location of an industry may be explained by the existence of pioneering firms in initial home markets, whose patent protection and learning by doing that moves them down their learning curves gives them an advantage. Maturation of the industry eventually occurs as technology settles down, as imitation grows more important, and as learning by doing becomes less significant. The normal Heckscher-Ohlin predictions based on factor proportions then take over, and comparative advantage swings toward countries with the most appropriate factor proportions.

DISLOCATION AND INTRAINDUSTRIAL TRADE

The process of intraindustrial specialization involves much less dislocation than we would expect from the older trade theory. In that theory, if Portuguese wine replaces English cloth, that is too bad for the English producers, who must find other work. If foreign cane sugar replaces domestic sugar beets in Europe and North America, the farmers will have to find something else to plant, or go out of business. Under classical theory, trade is supposed to shift resources out of the weak industry into the strong, but it does this by driving the weaker industry to the wall. That does not happen, however, with intraindustrial trade: Canada and the United States still have an automobile business, and while imports have certainly penetrated both markets, that penetration has surely been slowed by the lower costs of production arising from the automobile pact. After 30 years of trade in Europe, no country has lost its automobile industry. This industrial survival is not because the companies are being nice or politically astute or because, in the case of the U.S.-Canadian pact, of stipulations on employment. It is because there are no particularly strong factor-proportions pressures that will force the automobile industry into one nation.

The consequences for labor are considerable. Suppose there are 10,000 workers in textiles and freer trade forces clothing prices lower and electronics prices higher, such that somehow 10,000 workers must be shifted out of clothing and another 10,000 into electronics. That is a major dislocation, involving a devaluation of job skills in textiles, movement to other regions, and lowered pay for some—even if all people are reemployed. With intraindustrial specialization, however, the only change is in the workers lost due to the increased efficiency. If the automobile industry manages to increase productivity by 10%, it will need 10% less labor. One thousand people, not 10,000, are displaced and have to find new work. The remaining 9000 would stay just where they were working before. In fact, the 10% reduction might be small enough to be covered by natural turnover and some early retirements.

Because intraindustrial trade causes less dislocation, it is politically more acceptable. The old models of international trade are thus not only inappropriate for a great deal of modern trade but are politically dangerous. Displacement, even if it is for the greater good, is not politically popular. The most liberal-minded and economically sophisticated senators or members of parliament are going to defend their constituencies' interest if they are threatened. Arguing that specialization will take place within the industry may be not only more realistic, but politically more astute.

CONCLUSION

Thirty years ago a text could view comparative advantage as based on factor-proportions theory. That still remains a fundamental idea. But the thrust of trade in the latter twentieth century has been in directions awkwardly handled by a simple factor-proportions approach. Indeterminate and contingent models with decreasing costs may serve as a better basis for understanding modern patterns of international trade. Such models are still consistent with the existence of comparative advantage. They simply offer a different explanation of what determines it.

VOCABULARY AND CONCEPTS

Capital intensive
Contingent models
Decreasing-cost models
Economies of agglomeration
Economies of scale
Experience curves
Factor proportions
Factor-price equalization
Focused and flexible factories
Heckscher-Ohlin theory
Human capital explanation
In-firm diseconomies
Indeterminacy and optimization
Indeterminate models
Intrafactoral trade

Intraindustrial trade
Isoquant
Labor intensive
Learning curves
Learning by doing
Leontief Paradox
Linder model
Natural differences
Pioneers and late entrants
Product life cycles
Rybczynski Theorem
Segmented markets
Technology explanation
Wells-Vernon

QUESTIONS

1. Explain in words the Heckscher-Ohlin theory of factor proportions, indicating what its essential assumptions are.

2. Since virtually all goods can be made in capital-intensive or labor-intensive ways, how can we decide if a good is capital or labor intensive?

3. Apply the Rybczynski Theorem to Japanese trade. What do you think will happen as Korea's workers get shorter hours and more pay?

4. Use factor-proportions theory to suggest what the effect might be on U.S. trading patterns of large numbers of Latin American immigrants.

5. What explanations have been offered for the Leontief Paradox? Which ones appeal to you the most? Why?

6. What is intraindustrial trade? How is it measured? Why is there so much trade of that sort when our factor-proportions theory suggests otherwise?

7. What are the implications of a production possibilities curve that is convex to the point of origin (that is, bends inward)? In what sense would it be an appropriate model to apply to many kinds of international trade?

8. Most economic models assume that costs rise with specialization, yet costs could fall. What might cause them to do so?

9. Explain the importance of scale economies in trade between industrial nations. Is it normally plant scale that is of such importance?

10. Explain what learning curves (or experience) curves are. What evidence is there for their existence? What do they imply for specialization?

11. "The advantages of experience may be temporary if other nations, with lower cost structures for producing the particular good in question, can gain equal experience." Demonstrate and discuss.

12. If factor proportions are highly important, we would expect that most trade would be between dissimilar nations. Is it? (Explain.)

13. What is the role of market demand in determining what goods are traded in decreasing cost situations?

14. Why would a nation demanding many different models of products be likely to benefit from international trade?

15. "When production possibilities curves are convex, we cannot view managers as responding automatically to prices. They create their own comparative advantages. What we trade is to a considerable extent determined by conscious choice, not the invisible hand." Explain.

16. Does the idea that specialization creates its own comparative advantage increase the value of national industrial policies in modern Western economies?

17. What do you believe are the policy implications of using models that are indeterminate and contingent?

18. Adjustments to an increase in intraindustrial trade involve considerably less dislocation of labor than do cross-industrial adjustments. Why?

19. Linder's model, despite the difficulty in demonstrating some of it, has considerable appeal as an explanation of trade among industrial nations. Why?

20. The product life cycle model combines elements of both cost and demand, but at least in its Wells-Vernon form it has not been a particularly good predictor of trade patterns. Why?

NOTES

1 See Paul A. Samuelson, "International trade and the equalization of factor prices," *Economic Journal,* June 1948, and "International factor-price equalization once again," *Economic Journal,* June 1949. There is a good survey in the various editions of Bo Södersten, *International Economics,* New York.

2 Dan Ben-David, "Equalizing exchange: A study of the effects of trade liberalization," NBER Working Paper No. 3706, 1991.

3 Adrian Wood, "How much does trade with the South affect workers in the North?" *World Bank Research Observer,* Vol. 6, No. 1, January 1991, p. 26; George Borjas, Richard Freeman, and Lawrence Katz, "On the labor market effects of immigration and trade," NBER Working Paper No. 3761, 1991.

4 Harry P. Bowen, Edward E. Leamer, and Leo Sveikauskas, "Multicountry, multifactor tests of the factor-abundance theory," *American Economic Review,* Vol. 77, No. 5, December 1987, pp. 791–809. The testing was accomplished by estimating the proportion of each country's factor supplies to the total world supply of that factor, and then calculating factor embodiments in exports. The authors used 1967 data.

5 The study by Bowen et al. showed Brazil, Hong Kong, Mexico, and the Philippines conforming much more to H-O predictions than did the developed countries. Other evidence for the less developed countries is reviewed in Jan S. Hogendorn, *Economic Development,* New York, HarperCollins, 2d ed., 1992, Chapter 13.

6 James R. Markusen and Randall M. Wigle, "Explaining the volume of North–South trade," *Economic Journal,* Vol. 100, No. 403, December 1990, pp. 1206–1215, present evidence that high protection explains the low levels of trade between the LDCs and the developed countries, which is consistent with a Heckscher-Ohlin view.

7 See A.V. Deardorff, "Testing trade theories," in Ronald W. Jones and Peter B. Kenen, eds., *Handbook of International Economics,* Vol. 1, Amsterdam, Elsevier, 1984, pp. 480–485; and Bowen, Leamer, and Sveikauskas, "Multicountry, multifactor tests of the factor-abundance theory."

8 Herbert G. Grubel and P.J. Lloyd, *Intra-Industry Trade,* New York, Wiley, 1975.

9 The early figures are from Grubel and Lloyd, *Intra-Industry Trade.* For the 1985 figure (covering 11 countries) see Margaret Kelly, Naheed Kirmani, Miranda Xafa, Clemens Boonekamp, and Peter Winglee, *Issues and Developments in International Trade Policy,* IMF Occasional Paper No. 63, Washington, D.C., 1988, p. 9. The U.S., British, and French figures, and some of the LDC figures are from O. Havrylyshyn and E. Civan, "Intra industry trade among developing countries," *Journal of Development Economics,* Vol. 18, 1985, p. 260. The great rise since 1958 in the IIT for the members of the European Community is noted by André Sapir,

"Regional integration in Europe," *Economic Journal,* Vol. 102, No. 415, November 1992, p. 1496. Also see David Greenaway and Chris Milner, "On the measurement of intra-industrial trade," *Economic Journal,* Vol. 93, December 1983, pp. 900–908.

10 Jaroslav Vanek, *The Natural Resource Content of Foreign Trade 1870–1955,* Cambridge, Mass., MIT Press, 1963.

11 See *The Economist,* April 11, 1987.

12 The labor cost figures are from the special article, "High technology," in *The Economist,* August 23, 1986, p. S15. We have also used this article elsewhere in this chapter.

13 *The Newly Industrializing Countries: Challenges and Opportunities for OECD Industries,* Paris, OECD, 1988, p. 24.

14 See Hubert Schmitz, "Industrialization strategies in less developed countries: Some lessons of historical experience," *Journal of Development Studies,* Vol. 21, No. 1, October 1984, pp. 10–11. A volume devoted to overseas assembly activities is Joseph Grunwald and Kenneth Flamm, *The Global Factory: Foreign Assembly in International Trade,* Washington, D.C., Brookings, 1985.

15 Formal economic literature contains elements of learning curves and decreasing costs in the work of Armen Alchian and Jack Hershleifer, although they tend to treat decreasing costs as a special case rather than the normal case. See Armen Alchian, "Costs and outputs," in Moses Abramowitz et al., eds., *The Allocation of Economic Resources,* Stanford, Stanford University Press, 1959, pp. 23–40; and Jack Hershleifer, "The firm's cost function: A successful reconstruction?" *Journal of Business,* Vol. 35, No. 3, July 1962, pp. 235–254.

16 For the Horndal effect see Paul A. David, *Technical Choice, Innovation, and Economic Growth,* Cambridge, Books on Demand, 1975, p. 174, citing the original work of E. Lundberg, *Produktivitet och Rantabilitet,* Stockholm, 1961, pp. 129–133.

17 Henry A. Gemery and Jan S. Hogendorn, "The microeconomic bases of short-run learning curves: Destroyer production in World War II," in Gregory T. Mills and Hugh Rockoff, *The Sinews of War: The Economics of World War II,* Ames, Iowa, Iowa St. U. Press, 1993.

18 The charts are from Derek F. Abell and John S. Hammond, *Strategic Market Planning,* Englewood Cliffs, Prentice Hall, N.J., 1979, pp. 110–111. Their source is the Boston Consulting Group. The strange pattern among broiler chickens reflects the development of broilers as a separate breed from roasters and egg-layers in the 1940s. Abell and Hammond's Chapter 3 is an excellent discussion of learning and experience curves.

19 T.N. Srinivasan, "Comment on 'The noncompetitive theory of international trade and trade policy,' by Helpman," *Proceedings of the World Bank Annual*

Conference on Development Economics 1989, pp. 217–221, World Bank.

20 For the case that sunk costs do matter in ways that standard theory suggests should not matter, see William J. Baumol, "Toward a newer economics: The future lies ahead," *Economic Journal,* Vol. 101, No. 104, January 1991, p. 6.

21 The pioneering work was Joe S. Bain, *Barriers to New Competition,* Cambridge, Mass., Kelley, 1956. The later research of F.M. Scherer et al. is in *The Economics of Multi-Plant Operation: An International Comparisons Study,* Cambridge, Mass., Harvard University Press, 1975. It is surveyed together with the work of Leonard Weiss and C. F. Pratten in Scherer's *Industrial Market Structure and Economic Performance,* Chicago, Houghton Mifflin, 2d ed., 1980, pp. 91–98.

22 Farhang Niroomand and W. Charles Sawyer, "The extent of scale economies in U.S. foreign trade," *Journal of World Trade,* Vol. 23, No. 6, December 1989, pp. 137–146.

23 T.G. Parry, "Plant size, capacity utilization, and economic efficiency: Investment in the Australian chemical industry," *The Economic Record,* Vol. 50, June 1974, pp. 218–244.

24 See Jeffrey E. Bergstrand, "The Heckscher-Ohlin-Samuelson model, the Linder hypothesis and the determinants of bilateral intra-industry trade," *Economic Journal,* Vol. 100, No. 403, December 1990, pp. 1216–1229.

25 Surprisingly little work has been done on the optimal number of products per firm. See Kelvin Lancaster, "Socially optimal product differentiation," *American Economic Review,* September 1975, pp. 567–585. Lancaster demonstrates that under monopolistically competitive conditions there will be more than an optimal number of models produced. Also see F.M. Scherer, "The welfare economics of product variety: An application to the ready-to-eat cereals industry," *Journal of Industrial Economics,* Vol. 28, No. 4, December 1979, pp. 113–134. Scherer discusses the costs of the large number of product introductions in the industry.

26 See *The Economist,* February 3, 1990.

27 See Wilson Brown, "Market segmentation and international competitiveness," *Nebraska Journal of Economics,* Summer 1972, pp. 333–348, for development of the list. Some of the ideas were drawn from Bela Balassa, *Trade Liberalization among Industrial Countries,* New York, 1967, Chapter 5.

28 Reported in Donald T. Brash, *American Investment in Australian Industry,* Cambridge, Mass., Harvard University Press, 1966, pp. 157–176.

29 Both quotations from Brash, *American Investment,* p. 158.

30 According to the BCG's George Stalk, Jr., "Time—the next source of comparative advantage," *Harvard Business Review,* Vol. 66, No. 4, July/August 1988, pp. 41–51.

31 See Stalk, "Time—the next source of comparative advantage"; Raphael Kaplinsky, "The international context for industrialization in the coming decade," *Journal of Development Studies,* Vol. 21, No. 1, 1984, p. 81, citing the work of J. Rada; Roy B. Helfgott, "America's third industrial revolution," *Challenge,* Vol. 29, No. 5, November-December 1986, pp. 41–46; and *The Economist,* March 2, 1985, p. S20, and August 23, 1986, p. S15.

32 Information on these advances can be found in the *Wall Street Journal* for February 23, 1988. The Lockheed example is from Paul Milgrom and John Roberts, "The economics of modern manufacturing: Technology, strategy, and organization," *American Economic Review,* Vol. 80, No. 3, June 1990, citing work of Otis Port and Warren Hausman.

33 For the examples, see Milgrom and Roberts, "The economics of modern manufacturing: Technology, strategy, and organization," citing work of Tracy O'Rourke, Thomas Moore, and Tom Peters; and also the sources cited in notes 35 and 36.

34 See, for instance, *The Economist,* April 25, 1987, p. 78. Mufflers tend to be highly specific for particular models of cars. They are often designed after all the other parts of the car are decided upon, more or less fitted into the car's undercarriage in spaces left over.

35 Boston Consulting Group data cited in *The Economist,* February 16, 1991.

36 See Richard J. Schonberger, *World Class Manufacturing,* New York, Free Press, 1986.

37 Helfgott, "America's third industrial revolution," was utilized here.

38 The role of time is not only emphasized by most of the new international trade models but in the work of the more innovative consulting firms as well. For example, the Boston Consulting Group is presently producing a Time-Based Competition Series. See, for example, No. 7 in the series, *The Time Elasticity of Profitability,* Boston, 1987.

39 Milgrom and Roberts, "The economics of modern manufacturing: Technology, strategy, and organization," citing work of Walter Kiechel and Ronald Henkoff.

40 Staffan Burenstam Linder, *An Essay on Trade and Transformation,* New York, Garland, 1961.

41 See Tibor Scitovsky, *The Joyless Economy,* London, Oxford University Press, 1976, and Shlomo Maital, *Minds, Markets, and Money,* New York, Basic Books, 1982.

42 The argument can be transposed: With transport costs low, exporting a good to a particular market segment located in a foreign country would be the more feasible. Alan Deardorff, "Testing trade theories," in Jones and Kenen, eds., *Handbook of International Economics,* Elsevier, Vol. 1, pp. 505–506, gives a skeptical view of Linder's ideas. An informative volume on this and other issues involving intraindustry trade is

Elhanan Helpman and Paul Krugman, *Market Structure and Foreign Trade: Increasing Returns, Imperfect Competition, and the International Economy,* Cambridge, Mass., MIT Press, 1985.

43 PLC analysis is explained in most marketing texts. A good advanced treatment of the subject is Chester A. Wasson, *Dynamic Competitive Strategy and Product Life Cycles,* Austin, Austin Press, 1978.

44 Louis Wells, Jr., "A product life cycle for international trade," *Journal of Marketing,* July 1968, pp. 1–6; Raymond Vernon, *Sovereignty at Bay,* New York, Basic Books, 1971.

45 Georges Leroy, *Multinational Product Strategy,* New York, Praeger, 1976.

Chapter 4

Tariffs, Quotas, and VERs

OBJECTIVES

Overall Objective: To convey the sense and reasoning that a barrier to trade not only causes economic inefficiency, but redistributes income, frequently in ways that are unfair and reward political rather than economic skills.

MORE SPECIFICALLY:

- To convey the numerous effects of a tariff on efficiency and income distribution.
- To show the importance of some institutional factors such as the type of tariff and its measurement.
- To introduce the idea of rent, and how tariffs and quotas produce rents.
- To compare import quotas to tariffs to show the greater difficulties that quotas create.
- To examine the burgeoning Voluntary Export Restraints and their effects.

All our analysis in the last two chapters has shown that the benefits arising from trade are considerable. Yet governments persist in indulging in numerous distortions to the free flow of trade despite ample demonstration, both theoretical and statistical, that by so doing they reduce the welfare of the whole. The very persistence of the distortions suggests deeply rooted political-economic factors, which we will touch upon in a later section. One of these political factors is ignorance—the public does not know how high the costs of protectionism are. At the minimum, we can help dispel some of that ignorance.

Broadly speaking, the distortions to trade fall into two groups: (1) those created by taxes, principally taxes on imports, called *tariffs,* but also taxes on exports, common in many less developed countries; and (2) those not related to taxes, including *nontariff barriers* or *NTBs* and many sorts of subsidies. NTBs include primarily the quantitative restrictions on imports known as *quotas,* the special type of quota known as a *voluntary export restraint* or *VER,* and a host of government regulations and laws that interfere (sometimes purposefully, sometimes incidentally) with the free flow of trade. This chapter explores the best-known distortions to trade: tariffs, quotas, and VERs. It investigates the nature of these barriers and presents the basic economic analysis. The next chapter goes on to consider a variety of other distortions, many of which have arisen only recently, and then the following two chapters examine the public policy implications of the analysis.

TARIFFS

Artificial barriers to trade seem as old as trade itself. An ancient caravan entering an Arab area had to offer a *ta'rif,* in Arabic merely a "notification," to be allowed entry; but since the notification of arrival also involved a tax, *ta'rif* came to mean a tax on trade. Still today in most Western languages tariff and its cognates generally mean a tax on imports, considered in the first part of the chapter, or on exports, addressed briefly in Appendix 1 at the chapter's end. (Occasionally the word *tariff* is also used simply to mean any tax.) Travelers to Hadrian's Wall, the Roman defense work running across the hills of northern England, find at almost every gate in the rampart the remains of a little room that once housed the tax collector, who imposed the tariff on goods moving into the Roman Empire. Today walls may be absent, but there are still gates and little houses for tax collectors at borders. Nothing appears more certain than borders and tariffs.

SPECIFIC AND *AD VALOREM* TARIFFS

Tariffs can be specific, defined as a flat rate such as $10 per pound, 5¢ a yard, $2 a pair. Or the tariff can be *ad valorem* (Latin for "on the value"), a percentage such as 10% or 20% of a good's value. A specific duty of $10 or an *ad valorem* duty of 20% would be equal on a good valued at $50; at other prices they would not be the same. Occasionally, some aspects of specific and *ad valorem* duties are combined into a compound tariff.* Specific duties are the traditional ones, and *ad valorem* the more modern. *Ad valorem* tariffs, for instance, hardly appeared in the U.S. customs lists before the 1960s, but today they are more common by far.

Each type of tariff has its own characteristics. Specific duties are easier to administer because imports do not have to be valued as they enter the country. All the customs official has to do is to decide which category an item is in and how much of it there is. Specific duties also provide more protection against price cutting. If textiles from Hong Kong cost 20¢ a yard and the duty is 5¢ a yard, or 25% *ad valorem,* then a big cut in the Hong Kong price, of say 10¢, means

---

* For example, the famous English *Corn Laws* against grain imports were specific duties on a sliding scale. Under the legislation of 1791, when grain brought 54 shillings in England, the tariff was only a nominal 6 pence; between 50 and 54 shillings the duty was higher at 2 shillings 6 pence; while under 50 shillings the duty amounted to a nearly prohibitive 24 shillings 3 pence. The tariff thus rose with any decrease in price. The modern variable levy of the European Community resembles the old Corn Laws: The duty on many agricultural imports is adjusted upward when price falls and downward when price rises so as to keep prices stable within the EC. This is called an *equalizing duty.*

that the specific duty remains at 5¢, now 50% *ad valorem.* Meanwhile an *ad valorem* tariff of 25% would fall to 2.5¢.

Specific duties also may be regressive, in that a low-priced version of a good will pay more tax as a percentage of the original price than a high-priced version of the same good. If poor consumers buy the low-priced variant, then they are taxed more heavily than the wealthy. Furthermore (though to economists this is a benefit, not a problem), specific duties lose their protective effect in inflations. If prices double, any given specific levy will be only half in *ad valorem* terms what it was before; indeed, about half of the decline in protection from the onset of the Great Depression to the early 1960s was the rise in prices while specific tariffs stayed unchanged.[1]

Ad valorem tariffs behave quite differently. They are not regressive (though they are not progressive), and there is no need to alter them as prices change. They are easier to apply to unique goods such as paintings, which may be of very high or very low value. The principal disadvantage of *ad valorem* tariffs is that customs officials have to place a value on each item entering the country. Rather than simply checking to see that the bill of lading describes what is being brought in, the officials must also assess whether the value given is correct. The information on the invoice or bill of lading may not be accurate, and the checking of such documentation is a nuisance to traders and customs officials alike. Facing *ad valorem* tariffs, importers try to keep their invoice values down, being anywhere from merely careful to outright dishonest.

It is possible that a customs official will assess a higher value than a good is worth, thus turning what looked like a low *ad valorem* tariff into one that is considerably higher. Indeed, sometimes governments have instructed customs officers to assess high. (The over- or undervaluation would, incidentally, find its way into the trade statistics, thus introducing an inaccuracy.) For many years, both the United States and Australia levied some tariffs on the *domestic selling price,* which because it included the tariff was higher than the imported price. These venomous ASPs (American or Australian selling prices) were finally done away with as the result of an international code on customs valuation. This code, established in 1981 and now signed by 34 members, has served to harmonize customs classifications around the world. Most countries use c.i.f. values of imports (cost, insurance, freight, that is, including the transportation costs, thus also taxing them). The United States and Canada are exceptions to this, using the f.o.b. values (free on board, that is, before transportation costs). Either system is permissible under the rules of the customs valuation code.

Worldwide, the UN estimates that lack of trained customs personnel able to make accurate assessments, arbitrary valuations, long delays, and outright dishonesty raise the costs of trade by about 10%. That has caused a number of less developed countries to establish what is called preshipment inspection. They contract with developed-country private firms that carry out inspecting and valuation when the good is *exported.* Other countries have found that computerizing their customs has reduced some of the transactions costs substantially.

CATEGORIZATION OF GOODS

A customs official has to decide which category an import falls into, and this is particularly important if as a result the tariff would differ greatly. They certainly *can* differ greatly—currently in the United States there are 8753 tariff lines, or categories of dutiable items, ranging from 1% *ad valorem* to 458%. Furthermore, the product might be a new one for which there is no existing category. The question of whether radar sets were measuring devices (highly protected) or radios (with little protection) tied up U.S. courts in a long legal battle. Traders are ever anxious to find opportunities (loopholes to their detractors) to have a product come in under a low tariff category when it seemingly is blocked by a higher tariff. The accompanying box contains some of the anecdotes that have surfaced concerning the categorization of goods. The stories are apparently endless, though their meaning, when we find one, is perhaps pathetic—that rules and tariffs, even when they are not major economic blockages, can cause such petty distortions. Economists have argued for many years that the stories would not arise if uniform *ad valorem* tariffs—the same on all categories of goods—were adopted. Great dissimilarities in rates obviously open up all-too-enticing opportunities for corrupt dealing between customs officials and importers.

■ *CAR OR TRUCK? MOUSE OR RAT? SOLDIER OR DOLL?*

In the 1960s, during the long-forgotten "Chicken War," the United States retaliated against European barriers to U.S. chicken exports by putting a 25% duty on small trucks, ten times the 2.5% duty on cars. (The small VW pickup, new at the time, was the main target.) A whole class of light utility vehicles and minivans sporting car-like features, including the Nissan Pathfinder, Subaru Brat, Suzuki Samurai, Toyota 4Runner, Mazda MPV, and GEO Tracker, thereupon sprang up to avoid the truck tariff.[2] In January 1989, the U.S. Customs Service slammed the loophole shut by classifying all these vehicles as trucks. Lobbying by importers resulted in a 1990 Treasury Department compromise: If it had four doors, or if it was a van with windows or doors on the sides and back and seats additional to the front one, it was a car; but if it had two doors, like the Nissan Pathfinder, it was a truck. That virtually stopped imports of two-door light utility vehicles. Then in 1993 Nissan won a suit in the U.S. Court of International Trade that, Cinderella-like, turned its Pathfinder back into a car.

A shipment of sewing kits, little bags containing needles and threads, was recently stopped by customs officials in Seattle, who insisted that the bags should be classified as luggage at nearly three times the duty. The importer involved had to plead his case in New York before this decision was reversed, but not before many orders were lost and much expense incurred. United States opera companies accustomed to importing their sets as duty-free works of art were recently told that they were instead utility items subject to duty ($24,000 in one case). United States customs raised the tariff on a shipment of 33,000 girls' ski jackets from 10.6% to 27.5% because the jackets had corduroy trim on the sleeves. That 2% of the material in the jacket changed it, according to customs, from "garments designed for rainwear, hunting, fishing, or similar uses" to "other girls' wearing apparel, not ornamented."[3]

In other cases, the rulings promote accommodation and subterfuge. The United States slammed tariffs on jogging shoes, defined as "footwear made of rubber and plastic." But if 50% or more of the shoe uppers were made of leather, the shoe would be categorized as a different type of footwear with a much lower tariff. Hence the introduction of spiffy leather stripes and trim on jogging shoes. A high tariff on jeans stitched with a decorative design hardly fazed one U.S. importer. He had the back pockets cut in two and stitched together again in what, however decorative the design, was clearly a functional stitch subject to a lower tariff. Digital watches, importers' lawyers argued, were not watch movements under the tariff, since they had no moving parts; they were instead "electrical articles not provided for elsewhere." That argument saved a tariff of 50¢ on a $3 item.

Of all the silly cases that have occurred, perhaps the winners are the long-tailed mice and G.I. Joe. United States duties on toys are high, but low on magic items and products used for jokes. A rodent with a short tail is surely a mouse and therefore a toy; if it has a long tail, it is surely a rat and therefore a joke. In a Darwinian survival of the fittest, the mice found in toy stores all have long tails and pay low duties. G.I. Joe (or his lawyers) proved less able at escaping the tariff. In 1989, that long-popular little fighting man was found in customs court to be a doll (12% duty) and not a model soldier (duty free).

NOMINAL AND EFFECTIVE TARIFFS

When considering a tariff, one normally thinks of the duty compared to the cost of the import; thus a $25 tax on a $100 item would be a 25% tariff. Economists refer to this as the *nominal tariff*, although perhaps a better term is *apparent tariff*. The words *nominal* or *apparent* hint that something is misleading in our everyday observations, and well they should. The actual amount of protection is measured by something called an *effective tariff*, a concept developed in the early 1960s, but not at all current among economists until well into the 1970s.[4] The effective rate compares the tariff to the value added in the country, not to the total value of the product.

One of the first expositions of the theory incorporated a most illustrative tale out of the annals of U.S. tariff history. The duty on strung pearls entering the United States was $50, back in the days when the string itself could be purchased in Greece for $100. This nominal duty of 50% was designed to protect the U.S. jewelry industry. Since pearl fishing was not protected, there was no tariff at all on raw pearls, or even on temporarily strung pearls, which, sized, holes bored, and threaded on a simple string, could be imported without paying any tariff. The cost of removing the pearls from their temporary string and rethreading them on a permanent string and clasp was about $1. No sane Greek exporter would therefore ever export strung pearls and pay a $50 tariff when he could arrange for the process to be done in the United States for $1. Effectively, the tariff on the strung pearls was $50 protecting $1 worth of labor, or 5000%![5]

The formula to figure the effective rate of protection is as follows:

(Eq. 4.1)
$$\frac{(y-b) - (x-a)}{x-a}$$

where x = the international price of the finished commodity, y = the domestic price of the finished commodity, including the tariff, a = the international price of the imported component, and b = the domestic price, including the tariff, of the imported component. (But note that several restrictive assumptions are embodied in the formula, and these are not easy to relax. It assumes producers do not substitute cheaper inputs for more expensive ones as tariffs are imposed, and it does not take into account any effect of quotas.[6])

For ease of calculation, say the nominal tariff on strung pearls is only $1; the cost of stringing $100 worth of raw pearls is also $1; and there is no duty on unstrung raw pearls. The price of strung pearls in the absence of a tariff would be $101. With a tariff of $1 (nominally about 1%), the price of strung pearls would be $101 + $1 = $102. Given these numbers, the *effective* tariff is:

(Eq. 4.2)
$$\frac{(102-100) - (101-100)}{101-100} = \frac{1}{1} = 100 \text{ percent}$$

It may look like a 1% tariff, but it is 100% protection for the value added.

In the vast majority of cases, the effective tariff is positive; that is, the more finished product pays the higher tariffs. Bela Balassa compared average nominal tariffs to average effective tariffs, based on rates before the last major round of tariff cuts. (Effective rates are difficult to calculate because of the need to gather extensive information on value added domestically, so studies often rely on older work.) Balassa's calculations showed effective rates 72% higher than nominal rates in the United States, 81% higher in Great Britain, 84% higher in Japan, and 54% higher in the (old) European Economic Community.

Recent tariff reductions have brought little or no improvement in the situation.[7] In the period 1980–1987, tariffs were cut further on raw materials (64% for all, 77% for the United States) than on manufactures (34% for all, 29% for the United States). Currently, the overall tariff rate for the industrial countries is approximately 0.3% on raw materials, 4% on semifinished manufactures, and 6.5% on finished manufactures.[8] Thus even with average nominal tariffs much lower than in the past, a significant degree of tariff escalation still exists.[*] Table 4.1 shows some of the current differences in tariff rates between raw and finished materials.

Because effective tariffs are so much higher on finished goods than they are on raw materials, economists speak of a phenomenon called *tariff escalation*. The

---

[*] The degree of escalation in the United States, the EC, and Japan is very similar. With the development of large econometric models in the rich countries, it has become possible to trace through more carefully the effects of any change in nominal tariffs. Thus the subject has gone somewhat out of fashion in those countries, though it remains a very important issue for the less developed countries as is discussed in the text. See Kenen, *The International Economy*, p. 184.

Table 4.1 **Nominal tariff rates on raw materials and finished products**

Product	Region		
	EC	Japan	U.S.
Green roasted coffee	5.0	0.0	0.0
Coffee extracts	18.0	17.5	0.0
Cocoa beans	3.0	0.0	0.0
Chocolate	27.0	27.4	6.5
Raw cotton	0.0	0.0	1.9
Cotton clothing	13.7	13.2	8.8
Bauxite	0.0	0.0	0.0
Wrought aluminum	9.7	11.7	2.9
Natural rubber	0.0	0.0	0.0
Rubber products	5.3	4.8	5.3
Hides and skins	0.0	0.0	0.0
Leather goods	11.7	11.0	14.4

greater the extent of processing, the greater the effective tariff. The tariff system is, in effect, rigged against the developing countries that wish to export more manufactures, or to export their primary products in a more finished form. Based on data from the 1970s, a United Nations study suggests that if the escalation could be removed, then the potential increase in the annual exports of 10 important commodities would be about one-and-a-half times the value of the unprocessed commodities themselves.[9] It certainly appears that the less developed countries have a legitimate complaint.

Occasionally the effective tariff is negative, meaning that the raw material inputs to production pay a higher tariff than the finished good. When inputs are subject to a tariff, then a product that uses these taxed inputs is at a relative disadvantage. That creates an incentive to do the processing abroad. A negative effective tariff on steel would, for example, mean that users of steel such as automakers would demand higher nominal protection for their own output to offset the negative effective protection on steel. In a related way, if a country's pollution control laws and charges penalize final output while imports of that product are not penalized, then the laws and charges are the equivalent of a negative effective tariff. Again, production abroad is encouraged.

ANALYSIS OF TARIFFS: THEIR EFFECTS

The analysis of tariffs may be undertaken with the supply and demand curves for one good in one country. Such partial-equilibrium supply and demand analysis allows for a considerable degree of insight into the benefits and costs of tariffs, and a number of other related questions concerning these trade barriers. To begin, take the explanations of the benefits of freer trade and modify them to show the harm caused by a tariff. In the simplest proposition, consider a tariff high enough to stop all trade, then just reverse the explanation of the benefits of trade given in Chapter 2's Fig. 2.9a. Rather than a tariff that leaves no imports, however, it is more realistic to show some imports remaining. This chapter's Fig. 4.1 is the key to the analysis. It shows a tariff high enough to restrict but not stop trade. In the absence of a tariff, the equilibrium price is P_w, with consumption of Q_4 made up partly from imports Q_1Q_4 and partly from domestic production Q_1. Figure 4.1's tariff raises the price from a world level of P_w to a domestic price P_d, which includes the value of the tariff.[*] We will assume that the change in tariff has no effect on the world price. In effect, the suppliers making up the world market will supply any quantity at a price P_w plus the tariff. The assumption is realistic when the importing country consumes only a small share of the world output of this product.

The resulting Fig. 4.1 has an appearance similar to Fig. 2.9, but it has acquired another rectangle—R, the revenue gained by the government. R is the amount of imports remaining after the tariff (Q_2Q_3) times the tariff (P_wP_d). We can now describe a number of the principal effects of the tariff in terms of the diagram.

---

[*] It is certainly conceivable that rather than leading to an increase in price, the tariff might lead instead to a decline in quality of the domestically produced good.

Figure 4.1 **Effect of a tariff in partial equilibrium.** P_w is the world price and P_d is the domestic price when a tariff is applied. When the tariff is applied, consumption drops from Q_4 to Q_3, production increases from Q_1 to Q_2, and imports fall from Q_1Q_4 to Q_2Q_3. The letters $A–K$ indicate areas that represent numerous welfare, revenue, and redistributive effects of the tariff.

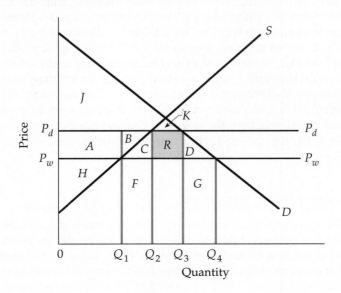

WELFARE AND REVENUE EFFECTS: PARTIAL EQUILIBRIUM

To build the explanation, take first the simple quantity effects of the tariff as seen along the horizontal axis, then the more complex ones.

1. *Production effect.* Domestic producers increase production from Q_1 to Q_2. (If there was no domestic output at all before the tariff, then any production caused by the high price would be from new producers entering the market.)

2. *Consumption effect.* With higher prices, consumers reduce purchases of the protected good from Q_4 to Q_3, buying less satisfactory substitutes or doing without the good altogether.

3. *Import effect.* Imports are reduced from Q_1Q_4 to Q_2Q_3. The consumer buys a greater quantity Q_1Q_2 domestically, replacing imports, and further reduces imports by Q_3Q_4.

   Now examine the more complex effects indicated by the triangles and rectangles.

4. *Revenue effect.* The rectangle R is the tariff revenue, found by multiplying the imports that remain after the tariff by the value of the tariff, or $(Q_2Q_3)(P_wP_d)$. For centuries tariffs were the major source of most countries' government revenue. In the United States, the first tariff of 1789 was a revenue tariff, and such revenue funded 90% to 95% of the U.S. budget until the 1850s. The figure was still 50% in 1900. (It is less than 1% at present, about $16 billion in 1991.) Even today tariff revenue is an important area of public finance in many less developed countries, especially in the poorer ones, where it can make up over 50% of all government revenue.

5. *Producers' subsidy effect.* The new revenue accruing to producers is $A+B+C+F$. Of this new revenue, the portion $C+F$ goes to paying the higher factor costs incurred because of the increased production. $A+B$, however, is not required to increase output; it is extra. $A+B$ can thus be looked at as equivalent to a subsidy to producers, transferred to them by consumers. This subsidy effect explains why an industry's low-cost firms, perhaps those that are better managed, or more efficient, or produce a more desirable differentiated product, may be as eager to obtain a tariff as are the high-cost firms being harmed by imports. The tariff acts as a windfall gain to them. (The waste of this subsidy effect might possibly be avoided by made-to-measure tariffs, carefully worded so as not to apply to the firms that would otherwise receive the windfall. But this would be possible only if the products were highly differentiated, and in any case the legal, political, and bureaucratic problems would probably be insurmountable.)

6. *Consumer tax equivalent.* With a tariff, additional costs must be paid by consumers, and these are the equivalent of a tax on consumption. These costs are found by multiplying the total amount purchased after the tariff (Q_3) by the higher price paid (P_wP_d). They total $A+B+C+R$. Consumers pay the entire bill: $A+B$ as a subsidy to producers over and above the costs of production, C

as the higher costs of the additional output, and R as revenue collected by the government.

The welfare changes caused by the tariff can also be traced. In partial equilibrium welfare changes can be explored by means of producer and consumer surplus, as follows:

7. *Producer surplus.* Producer surplus is the area above the supply curve but below the price. In Fig. 4.1 the original producer surplus is rectangle H, showing the amount paid to producers in excess of the actual marginal cost of producing the quantity Q_1. A tariff that raises the price from P_w to P_d raises producer surplus from an original area H to a new enlarged area $H+A+B$. Rectangle A plus triangle B shows the increase in producer surplus. (Say the good on the horizontal axis is corn. Rectangle A would be the added revenue accruing to the acres already in corn. B would be the revenue over and above resource costs accruing to the corn grown on land that was planted in soybeans before the tariff, but is now more valuable when planted in corn.)

8. *Consumer surplus.* The consumer surplus before the tariff was the entire area under the demand curve and above the price P_w, a triangle made up of $J+K+A+B+C+R+D$. When the tariff is imposed those consumers between Q_3 and Q_4 cease to buy while those between 0 and Q_3 continue to purchase the protected good but have to pay a higher price. The loss in consumer surplus is $A+B+C+R+D$.[*]

9. *The deadweight loss.* When a tariff is imposed, the gain in producer surplus and the gain to the government are not as large as the lost consumer surplus. See how producers gain $A+B$ (number 7 above), the government gains the revenue effect R, which we can assume is returned in the form of lower taxes (number 4 above), but consumers lose $A+B+C+R+D$ (number 8 above). The As, Bs, and Rs cancel one another, being both gains and losses, but there are two leftover areas of loss, triangle C and triangle D. This combined net loss is the deadweight loss effect of a tariff, occurring because the tariff harms consumers more than producers and government are helped.

The deadweight losses involved in these two triangles have different root causes. Area C is the producers' deadweight loss, an extra cost of producing the protected good. Consider a tariff on corn with land as the major input. The rectangle F represents the cost of the soybean land that is transferred into corn production, but that land cannot produce corn as efficiently as it could soybeans. C is the extra cost incurred when some land in soybeans has to be used for corn, and is thus a deadweight loss. Area D is consumers'

---

[*] In the presentation here, a tariff is placed atop an unchanged world price. Other variants are possible, however. The tariff may be in response to a fall in the world price, perhaps because one's own currency has appreciated, or because costs have declined abroad. In that case, the tariff offsets the losses that domestic producers would otherwise endure and the gains that would accrue to domestic consumers.

deadweight loss, reflecting their lost satisfaction as they shift away from the purchase of the newly protected good. Consumers between Q_3 and Q_4 shift to other, less desired goods, say from corn-based to wheat-based foods. Those near Q_4 suffer little loss, while those near Q_3 are almost ready to pay the higher import price, but in the end decide to buy the less satisfactory substitute.

■ *THE SIZE OF THE DEADWEIGHT LOSSES*

Note that the deadweight losses are not large in these diagrams, and probably not large in most economies. A rough estimate is not hard to make if you know the value of all sales of the protected good and the tariff on an *ad valorem* basis, and are willing to hazard a guess about the elasticities of demand and supply. Suppose a country is protecting shoes with a 10% tariff, sells a million dollars' worth of shoes, and shoes have a demand elasticity of 1. Assuming the shoes sell for $10 including a tariff of $1, then the height of triangle D will be 10% of the price. The width of triangle D will also be 10% because we have stated that the elasticity of demand is 1. Use the formula for elasticity, $\%\Delta Q / \%\Delta P = \epsilon$; if $\epsilon = 1$ and $\%\Delta P = .10$, $\%\Delta Q$ has to be .10 also. So if sales were 100,000 pairs, they would fall to 90,000. Triangle D is actually quite small: $.10 \times .10/2$ (the formula for a triangle's size) is .005, or just 0.5% of the value of all sales. Triangle C is drawn to look about the same, so we can guess that the deadweight losses amount to about 1% of sales—not the kind of thing to become incensed about. (Some have argued, however, that even a small loss is important because that loss, say 1%, occurs year after year. That means we should use the present value of 1% of domestic sales. One dollar at 5% interest for 20 years is worth $2.65.)

Certainly, one can pick different values for the size of the tariff and the elasticity involved, but even doubling them both yields only 8% for $C+D$. (The calculation is $.2 \times .4 / 2 = 4\%$ for each triangle.) For the vast majority of goods in industrial nations, such figures are unrealistically high. For example, Arnold Harberger's pioneering estimates for the United States showed deadweight losses of less than 1% of GNP. Several factors explain why $C+D$ is thought to be small. Most industrial nations have only a few tariffs in excess of 10%.[10] Most consumers continue to buy the imported good or its domestic substitute. Thus the shifts in production are only marginal, and the cost of that shift is also marginal. In our first statistical example, that using a tariff of 10%, the combined change in increased domestic production and decreased consumption is only 20%, the price change is just 10% of that, and only half the value of that sum is misallocation as measured by the triangles of deadweight loss $C+D$. It is also fair to say, however, that many industrial countries have quota restrictions that as we shall see below are likely to have a greater price effect. Furthermore, in less developed countries, the costs of tariffs and other protection can run much higher. Some recent estimates are: 7% of GNP in Brazil, 3% in Mexico, 6% in Pakistan, 4% in the Philippines, and 5% to 10% in Turkey. (The empirical studies on the subject are usually short run, however, and apply to rather broad product categories. Elasticities are expected to be higher in the long run and for narrower product categories, so deadweight losses would be higher also.)

THE PROBLEM OF THE REDISTRIBUTION EFFECT

Even if the size of the deadweight loss is relatively small, we still have an important *redistribution effect*, which is one of the least rational of all tax-subsidy schemes. Why should consumers of shoes or chickens be taxed in order to subsidize producers of those goods? If the government had levied a special income tax or a tailored property tax of the same amount on chicken consumers, and voted to use the revenue for a subsidy to producers of that product, it would be in serious trouble. Taxpayers would have two questions: (1) Why should the government subsidize a particular group in the economy? (2) Even given that the subsidy should be granted, why should consumers of the product be the ones to pay it?

For the present, we will accept that the community in its collective wisdom believes that a certain industry must be encouraged and will question only the way in which that encouragement is to be paid for. If a community were able to think through the issue, it might decide that any such subsidy should come from general revenues, where, at least, questions about fairness, collectibility, and economic distortions have already been asked. It is, unfortunately, often difficult to know the ultimate incidence of any tax, but it is likely that with a tariff the consumer of the good is the one who suffers, at least in the short to medium run. Many tariffs (and other import restrictions), particularly in the industrial nations, are almost undoubtedly *regressive* in their effect on incomes, taxing low-income people to support groups higher on the income ladder. This occurs because in industrial countries the heavily protected goods include food, clothing, and cars, situations analyzed at far greater length in succeeding chapters. The Federal Reserve Bank of New York has calculated that tariffs, quotas, and VERs on clothing, sugar, and autos were the equivalent of a 23% income tax surcharge on families earning below $10,000 per year. This compares to only a 3% tax equivalent for U.S. families earning over $60,000 per year. Alternative World Bank figures suggest that the tax equivalence of protection is 66% on people earning less than $8,000 per year, compared to 5% for those earning over $60,000.[11]

With large amounts of their income spent on heavily protected items, poorer consumers—who in any case may be least able to defend themselves from a tariff because they may lack the information, intellectual skills, and political power to do so—pay a disproportionate toll. Many less developed countries do have high tariffs on luxury goods, with Volvos and Mercedes paying tariffs equivalent to two or three times their cost at the ports, but they, too, often tend to have much in their tariff structure that is regressive.

Thoughtful readers might also ask whether the tariff taxes the people who benefit from it. Road and gasoline taxes, for instance, are designed to tax road users who gain from highway maintenance, and as a whole the tax does succeed in achieving that end and in that sense is fair. But a tariff on poultry does not tax those who benefit. Consumers of chicken, prevented from buying abroad more cheaply, appear to gain little from having a few more people employed in a rural area hundreds of miles away. While the community may have decided that it is a public good to have chicken farmers, such a benefit, however dubious, is enjoyed by all. Arguably the consumers of chicken should not be asked to pay a disproportionate share of the costs.

COST-RAISING EFFECTS

In the standard neoclassical diagram, the deadweight loss triangles are necessarily small and the costs of tariffs therefore low. In two types of situations, however, costs are greater than the little triangles *C* and *D*.

THE X-INEFFICIENCY EFFECT   The assumptions of our model to this point have been that all firms operate at their lowest costs, even when they are protected by a tariff. Presumably this occurs because sufficient competition remains to drive the poorly performing firms out of business, or to force executive changes to eliminate inefficient management. We know, however, from the works of management economists such as Herbert Simon, winner of the 1978 Nobel Prize in Economics, that managers develop goals quite separate from those of the businesses' owners and tend toward performances that are satisfactory rather than profit maximizing. In a protected environment, managers can generate returns satisfactory to their owners without performing optimally, and their owners remain unaware of potential greater returns. The economist Harvey Leibenstein has distinguished between a theoretically optimal performance level and the actual performance level, the latter inefficient to an unknown or *X* degree that he calls *X*-inefficiency. Leibenstein connects such *X*-inefficiency to the strength of oligopoly power, arguing that it is less likely under greater competition.[*]

The implications of the *X*-inefficiency argument for welfare are much greater than those of the deadweight loss. Protected firms can afford to be *X*-inefficient up to the value of the tariff, at which point they would suffer import competition. Under such a situation, costs rise to the level P_d in Fig. 4.1, so it is not just triangles *C* and *D*, but also areas *A* and *B* that are losses. In this case, the resources that *A* and *B* represent are drawn into the protected industry, but the output does not increase because of the inefficient way it is run. Suppose a country's corn is grown on farms run by overseers who note that with the higher prices of corn their owners' returns have risen, so they begin to add elegant accommodations to their houses, hire many relatives who do very little, and spend much more time on nonproductive activities. Costs could rise as far as the domestic price including the tariff, which would turn all of *A* and *B* into costs. On a gen-

---

[*] To make the argument properly, we need to show not only that competition is absent from the marketplace, but also that owners allow their managers to use their capital inefficiently and further that no corporate raider will enter to force management to operate efficiently. We are, in essence, requiring that ownership (or equity) markets be imperfect, as well as the goods markets of which Leibenstein speaks.

eral equilibrium diagram, X-inefficiency of this nature would appear as a shrinking inward of the production possibility frontier.

Nothing in the standard neoclassical theory of international trade says that industries at a comparative disadvantage are run inefficiently. Indeed, neoclassical theory assumes that all firms, given sufficient competition, are run efficiently. Those who have read the literature on protected industries are struck again and again at how inefficient many of these industries actually are. The discussions in the previous chapters of the automobile industry's adoption of many Japanese planning techniques demonstrate one of many examples of how international competition promotes not just resource reallocation, but more efficient (X-efficient, to use Leibenstein's term) use of resources where they are already employed. In the words of Mancur Olson, "tariffs can encourage, and free trade prevent, institutional sclerosis among manufacturers or any enterprises that have international competition."[12] Estimates of losses due to X-inefficiency in the United States run as high as 2% of GNP, higher than the deadweight loss.[13] Much X-inefficiency is not deadweight loss because the higher costs and organizational slack can often be seen as a gain to the managers and workers in the form of plush company cars and clubs, a quieter life, and so forth.

SPECIALIZATION EFFECTS   The specialization effects noted in the previous chapter, whether scale, industrial concentration, experience, or product specialization, all involve decreasing costs. In these models the more an industry specializes, the greater the decline in average costs. By preventing trade, tariffs in an importing country can block the attainment of plant and industrial scale, intraindustrial specialization, and the accumulation of experience in an exporter. That in effect keeps the potential decline in costs in the exporter from occurring. In such instances world price levels could have fallen, but because of the barriers they did not. We could then view P_w, the world price in Fig. 4.1, as higher than it needs to be.*

EFFECTS ON ECONOMIC GROWTH

In combination, several of the effects discussed thus far are likely to reduce the rate of economic growth. If efficiency declines because of protection, then more resources must be used per unit of output, and it is very likely that economic growth will decline. Growth will also presumably be reduced if domestic inputs that must be used because of the protection are lower in quality or higher in price. It might also be negatively affected by the reduction in innovation and diversion of entrepreneurial effort that goes on behind the trade barriers. If old-line manufacturing industries with a poor record of technical change obtain most of the protection, that too can have an adverse influence on growth.

---

* An additional complication with even larger losses inflicted on the community can be introduced. The failure to allow the potential trading partner to specialize will prevent the tariff-levying nation from specializing itself in an export product with declining costs, due either to retaliatory tariffs or insufficient incentive to trade.

F.M. Scherer has pointed out that firms that obtain trade barriers tend to make large cuts in their research and development expenditures.[14]

THE INCIDENCE OF TARIFFS: PASS-THROUGH, RENTS, LOBBYING

PASS-THROUGH   Tariffs on imports have a way of coming around to penalize exports in a so-called *pass-through effect*. There are two possible macroeconomic mechanisms, either or both of which can be at work.

1. As tariffs cause imports to fall, less foreign exchange is needed to purchase them and the demand for foreign currency declines. The domestic currency will thus rise in value on the foreign exchange market.[*] Exporters find that their foreign-currency earnings purchase less domestic currency and therefore they suffer. Looking back at Fig. 4.1, the reduction in spending on foreign exchange is equal to area $F+G$, which is the value at the world price P_w of the fall in imports $Q_1Q_2 + Q_3Q_4$. (Imports also are affected, becoming more attractive than before since the currency appreciation makes them appear cheaper. Even the initial effect of the tariff on imports can thus be eroded.) Econometric work for the United States indicates that a 15% across-the-board tariff would appreciate the dollar by 7%, cutting the initial improvement in the trade balance by one half.[15]

2. The pass-through effect is also felt as tariffs cause the price level to rise. Importers pass on their higher costs to buyers, and industrial buyers pass those costs on in the form of higher prices. For example, products using steel have risen in price following restrictions on the import of steel into many countries. To the extent that steel competes for factors of production with nontradable goods and services, then the tariff will raise the price of these as well. Consumers, hit directly or indirectly, include the inflationary price increases in their wage and salary demands. Everybody tries to pass the tax to someone else. The only group that is powerless to pass the costs on further are the exporters, who have to sell at world prices, and swallow those costs. In essence, a tax on imports becomes a tax on exports.[16] Studies cited by the World Bank indicate that for a wide range of developing countries, 43% to 95% of an increase in protection against imports is passed on to become a tax on exports. Studies in Australia suggest that protection that raises prices by 5% eventually raises labor costs by 4.4%. In this case, more than 80% of a tariff increase was converted into a tax on exports.[17] Although the effects might not be as obvious in a large nation like the United States, tariffs do tend to push up the price level.

The converse point, that inflation is moderated when trade is free, can be easily illustrated within a large national economy. In the period 1986–1988, unemployment in several states, including Massachusetts and New Jersey, was far

---

[*] This analysis applies if exchange rates are floating. If they are fixed, the fall in imports will affect the balance of trade by generating a trade surplus but will not change the exchange rate. If, however, the currency is revalued to eliminate the trade surplus (or foreigners devalue to eliminate their deficits, or both), the analysis is the same as under floating rates.

below the national average. Because of the free trade within national boundaries, however, inflation rates in these states with the major exception of housing costs were about the same as in the rest of the United States.

TARIFFS AND ECONOMIC RENT   One way to look at the losers and beneficiaries of the income redistribution that accompanies a tariff is with the concept of *economic rent.* Rent arises because factors are limited in supply. Take the example of the corn and soybean lands and assume that the supplies of labor and capital are perfectly elastic. In that case all the gains from a tariff will go to the owners of land, with the rent of the land producing corn rising with the tariff. In Fig. 4.1, the land already producing corn receives an increase in rent consisting of the rectangle *A*. That land that must be converted receives varying amounts of rent, depending on the difference between the return it generated with soybeans and the higher return it generates with corn. This amounts to triangle *B*.[*]

With higher values on corn land, farmers can presumably now sell that land for more money, charge tenants higher rents, or borrow more against the land. In their own costing, they should regard the *opportunity cost* of that land as higher by the amount of potential rent they could receive. As new farmers move in to replace the old ones, they pay a fully competitive value for the land, and thus stand to lose if the tariff disappears.[**] The winners are those who had the land when the tariff rose (unexpectedly). When farmers complain about losing protection, it does not mean that the farmers are presently benefiting from the rent, for they may well have borrowed on the higher value or bought the land with the expectation of the corn rent included. What it means is that farmers erred in their judgment of the land's value.

We can extend the concept of rent beyond land to any factor that has a vertical supply curve—in a relevant price range over a relevant period. A rent that is limited in time or limited to a certain range of prices is called a *quasi-rent.* Typical quasi-rents involved in trade are the wages and salaries employees receive that are in excess of what they could get outside the firm or industry in which they are working. Such quasi-rents may accrue in particular to people with industrially specialized skills or knowledge and to workers with seniority. Capital that is in fixed form (which is, in the short run, all of it) and not easily transferred to other uses (which is to say much of it), often earns considerably more than it could in its second-best use. A reduction in the price of that capital will thus not cause it to leave the industry. Owners of machinery, let us say of corn planting equipment, are not going to find it easy to convert the machines to other forms of capital, say,

---

[*] Technically, each acre of land, which has a vertical supply curve, receives the rent. If there were 1000 acres between Q_2 and Q_3 of Fig. 4.1, then the first acre converted would have a rent just short of the amount of the tariff and the last would have little rent at all.

[**] The naïve buyer would pay for the present value of the future corn crops, including the tariff. More sophisticated buyers might discount the value of the land if they believe that the tariff will fall.

to soybean planters (plausible) or to silos full of soybeans (impossible). These quasi-rent-takers also benefit from the tariff and suffer from its removal.

THE LOBBYING EFFECT   As tariffs, and more particularly, other import restrictions have surged to prominence once more, many firms have turned their energies from meeting the competition to lobbying for barriers against that competition. Gordon Tullock has argued that firms waste considerable amounts of their scarce resources in attempts to secure protection or to prevent others from obtaining it, and that these rent-seeking costs should also be included in an analysis of protection.[18] Figure 4.2 illustrates this idea with a *lobbying curve*. The curve starts at some positive tariff because the legislature may be willing to grant an industry a degree of protection even if it undertakes no lobbying at all. The cost of lobbying will rise as an industry receives a greater amount of protection. Next, we draw a benefit-from-the-tariff curve. This curve is assumed to rise, showing more and more benefits received by an industry until the tariff increases to the point that it prohibits imports altogether. Any further rise is an *excess tariff*, yielding no further benefits. The expectation is that the industry will expend funds for lobbying up to a tariff level T_2, at which point the marginal cost of bringing about an increase in the tariff is equal to the marginal benefit of the increase, thus maximizing the gains.

Figure 4.2 **Lobbying curve.** A firm or industry must make a rational decision as to how much effort to put into lobbying for a tariff. This figure pictures lobbying costs and the benefits of lobbying, and suggests that firms will stop pressing for higher tariffs when the cost of lobbying exceeds the probable benefit.

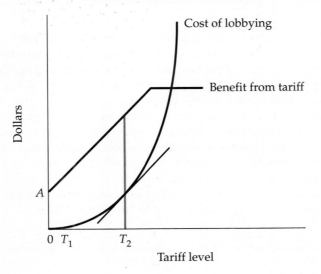

Such costs of lobbying used to be small by comparison with the size of international trade—they were probably less than $300 million per year for the United States in the early 1980s, only 0.1% of the total value of all U.S. trade. They appear to be rising rapidly, however, and are a diversion of resources away from other, presumably more socially useful, purposes.* Furthermore, those figures do not include any adverse political consequences abroad, nor do they reflect the damage that can rise from the harassment of trading partners as the legislature responds to the lobbying. Finally, lobbying may have to be undertaken by advocates of freer trade as well, either as a defense against protectionist interests, or to deflect their losses to others. When competitive lobbying by both producers and consumers becomes the norm, then the costs of this activity can increase greatly.[19]

■ *HOW HIGH COULD RENT-SEEKING COSTS BE?*

At worst the costs of rent-seeking and defending against losses could conceivably be as much as all of the producer surplus that might be gained ($A+B$) plus all of the consumer surplus that might be lost ($A+B+C+R+D$) in Fig. 4.1. But it is unlikely to be that high because consumers are hard to organize. Each individual consumer may lose only a little even though the community as a whole loses considerably. Thus consumers are not likely to devote as much to lobbying against trade barriers as producers do to lobbying for them. In any case, there is often a perception that the producer has the inside track. If a brother-in-law of the country's president owns a cement company, then that country's consumer lobby might reasonably decide there is little hope of reducing protection on cement. Jagdish Bhagwati calls this, aptly, the *brother-in-law theorem*.[20]

Once import restrictions are in place, lobbying may intensify because protected interests become vested. Farmers borrow against their more-valuable land, plants are built, professionals and retailers move to one-company towns, all garnering their share of the income generated from the rent. When the government considers lowering the tariff, the beneficiaries fight hard because their very livelihoods are at stake, and not, as it was in the beginning, just a bonus. Before becoming too sympathetic, however, remember that these people, like any other business, had to assess whether the economic conditions prevailing at the time of investment would continue, or perhaps whether they could keep lobbying the government to make them continue. If they erred, it was a business error, like those made by millions of other people who do not expect the government to ride to their rescue. (More on this at a later point.)

---

* The lobbying costs are not, however, deadweight losses because the revenues devoted to them are passed on to a wide range of recipients—the salaries of the lobbyists themselves, restaurant bills, advertising expenses, and the like.

THE TERMS-OF-TRADE EFFECT AND THE OPTIMAL TARIFF OR TAX

The terms of trade are the prices (in physical terms) at which nations exchange goods, for example the number of bushels of wheat for barrels of oil. A large nation trading with a small country can sometimes force the smaller one to lower its prices by reducing the demand for its exports. In essence, that may force the small country to pay all or part of the tariff the large one levies. This could then change the calculation of net benefits for the larger nation, which could count part of the tariff revenue as a real gain, not just an income transfer. We analyze this in partial equilibrium. (Appendix 4.2 shows the analysis in general equilibrium with offer curves.)

The terms-of-trade effect with demand and supply curves uses the same tools employed earlier for showing transportation costs. The price line connects two countries' prices, with a kink in it as in Fig. 2.10. If we say that the reason for the crook in the line is a tariff, not transportation costs, we can attribute all the changes in welfare to the tariff. Our Fig. 4.3 here is a similar one, differing only in showing the tariff revenue as a kink in the price line indicated by T. What happens in essence is that a tariff placed on a good by Fabrica causes adjustments in both countries, such that the Agricolan producers lower their price. In so doing, Agricolans lose less of their market in Fabrica, and we find a splitting of the effects of the tariff between the two countries, just as occurred with transportation costs.

Figure 4.3 **The terms-of-trade effect of a tariff.** Sometimes a tariff can force the exporter to lower prices. The model uses a kinked price curve in the same way as we handled transportation costs. The pattern of gains and losses is, however, rather more complicated, as the text explains.

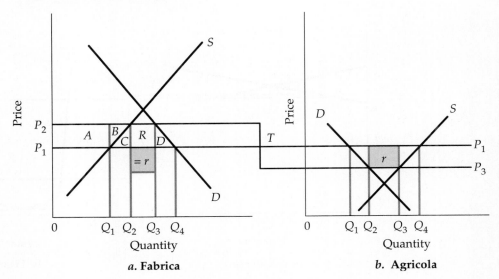

a. **Fabrica**   *b.* **Agricola**

An important difference remains: One nation gets all the revenue. The price Fabrican importers pay for wheat from Agricola, not including the tariff, has fallen from P_1 to P_3, so Fabrica receives revenue equivalent to the tariff times the new volume of imports, or $T \times (Q_2Q_3)$. Given the slopes in our diagrams, about half of the revenue comes from higher prices domestically (P_1P_2), and the other half from lower Agricolan prices (by P_1P_3). The loss to Agricola is rectangle r of Fig. 4.3b, equivalent to the small box under the rectangle R in Fig. 4.3a. Now, if the revenue Agricola pays to Fabrica exceeds Fabrica's loss from the tariff, that is if $r > C+D$, it would be to Fabrica's advantage to levy a tariff. Of course, it would not be to the world's advantage because Agricola is stuck paying the costs to offset Fabrica's deadweight losses.

The more inelastic are Agricola's curves and the more elastic Fabrica's, the greater Agricola's absorption of the costs of the tariffs. Suppose we consider two nations that are quite different in size—Colossa and Lillipute. Colossa's big, flexible market gives it very high elasticities of demand and supply, as shown in Fig. 4.4a, such that small changes in price call forth large changes in the quantity imported. Lillipute, however, has an economy based largely on the export of a primary product to Colossa. Domestic demand is a small percentage of Lillipute's production, while supply, particularly in the short run, is highly inelastic. Figure 4.4b shows that even at very low prices Lillipute would be exporting about the same amount as at high prices, and domestic consumption would increase very little.

Figure 4.4 **A large terms-of-trade-effect.** The terms-of-trade effect will be substantial if one country, normally a large one, has very elastic demand and supply curves and the other, a small one, has highly inelastic curves. The small country must swallow virtually all of the cost of the tariff.

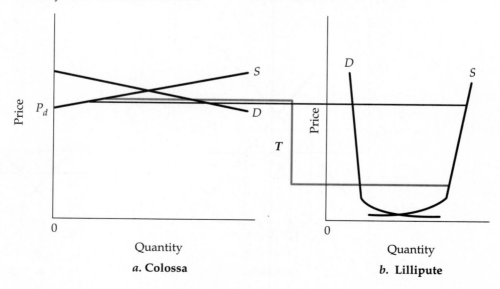

a. **Colossa**   *b.* **Lillipute**

In the situation just described, Lillipute ends up paying virtually all of the tariff. Lillipute has to sell to Colossa because it cannot cut back production nor divert much to the home market. What is more, it has to cut prices to sell because Colossa is very price sensitive and will quit purchasing from Lillipute, making the good itself or doing without, unless Lilliputian exporters absorb the cost of the tariff. In Fig. 4.4, the volume of products shipped from Lillipute to Colossa is almost unchanged. Indeed, the change is so small that it hardly affects the Colossan price at all and barely shows on Fig. 4.4a. (P_d presumably does rise a bit because the quantity imported into Colossa has fallen slightly.) Thus all but the smallest part of the tariff, T, is absorbed by Lillipute.

Such a situation would be typical of many small nations facing large developed countries, or groups of developed countries. Examples include Fiji's sugar exports to the European Community or the Dominican Republic's to the United States, New Zealand's lamb exports to Europe, or Sri Lanka's tea exports to Britain.

Some have argued that the terms-of-trade effect of a tariff on imports could be used as a policy. An importing nation could deliberately force down prices from the exporter in order to end up ahead. Indeed, if the shift in the terms of trade were great enough to offset the loss in trade volume, the importer *would* be in a better position. Presumably, then, a country could calculate an *optimum tariff* level for its welfare, wherein any greater rise in tariffs reduces a country's consumption by more than it gains from prices. The U.S. economy is so large that its optimum tariff would be relatively high, at least in the short run.[21] Such optimum tariffs, despite their technical validity, overlook the likelihood that one tariff to improve the terms of trade will beget another in retaliation. The risk of a trade war is high, understandably, because the gain in welfare to the country imposing the tariff is a loss in welfare to its victim. Economists who model possible strategies for a country facing a tariff imposed from abroad for such terms of trade purposes usually recommend a "tit-for-tat" strategy: a response identical to the opponent's move. Such retaliation might be called a *bargaining tariff*, which we shall consider again when we discuss negotiations for tariff reduction in Chapter 6.

Beyond retaliation, a further difficulty with using a terms-of-trade tariff or export tax as a weapon is that there is generally little practical knowledge concerning the elasticities of the export and import demand and supply curves, with politicians picking the numbers that suit what they want to do. Without exact knowledge of both short-run and long-run effects, the manipulation of tariffs or taxes to obtain a terms-of-trade effect is both senseless and dangerous. In fact there is little to indicate that the United States employs a terms-of-trade strategy to increase its welfare at the expense of other countries. For example, United States optimum tariff policy would presumably dictate high duties on primary product imports and stiff taxes on high-technology exports. Nothing of the sort is done. United States tariffs on primary product imports are especially low, and export tariffs are constitutionally prohibited.

QUOTAS AND THEIR ECONOMIC EFFECTS

A BRIEF DESCRIPTION

Quotas are protectionist devices closely related to tariffs. Rather than using taxes to limit imports, a government sets a limit to the quantity of the good that can be imported during the year. (Occasionally quotas are also placed on exports, a topic addressed in Appendix 4.1 at the end of the chapter.) The quota might be defined by volume (for example, 10,000 VCRs), or, less commonly, by value ($1 million worth of VCRs). Usually, the government issues licenses that must be presented upon importing the good.[*]

Quotas essentially were invented during the First World War; they had been very uncommon before that and were again little used in the 1920s. France resurrected them in 1930–1931 during the Great Depression, largely for protection of its farmers and for defense against low-price Japanese imports, which could not be excluded by high tariffs because of prior tariff agreements. By 1934, more than half the items on which France charged tariffs were subject also to the new quota limitations. These limits were strict, with many goods subject to quotas of less than half the quantities formerly imported. French actions were copied by others, including Nazi Germany, and by the end of the 1930s the situation had grown so serious that the term *free trade* came temporarily to mean trade that was unhindered by quotas, even though the tariffs paid might be quite high.

Vigorous and successful attempts were made by the industrial countries in the postwar period to end quotas on manufactured goods. They remain common in agriculture everywhere, however, as explored in Appendix 4.3, and in less developed countries they are frequently imposed on all sorts of commodities.

ANALYSIS OF QUOTAS

The diagram to show a quota is almost identical to the figure for a tariff. Indeed, we simply duplicate the earlier Fig. 4.1 as Fig. 4.5. The difference is that we will not levy a tariff and say instead that the amount Q_2Q_3 is the quota. The diagram still looks the same, though, because any time the quantity of a good is artificially restricted, its price rises. Because imports have fallen from the prequota Q_1Q_4 to Q_2Q_3, the price rises until the quantity demanded once again equals the quantity supplied, which is at Q_3. At that quantity the price is P_d. There is no tariff, but we disagree with the U. S. congressman who recently stated on national television that he would not support new tariffs because these were a tax, but he would support new quotas, since they would not raise prices. On the contrary, if you make something more scarce, its price goes up.

---

[*] Tariffs and quotas are sometimes combined in a measure called the *tariff quota*. Under this system, imports within a quota amount are subject to a low tariff, while further imports above the quota are subject to a high tariff.

Figure 4.5 **The revenue effect of a quota.** The diagram to describe a quota is identical to that used for a tariff, except that the revenue effect does not go to the government.

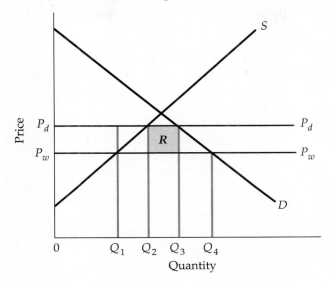

WHO GETS THE REVENUE EFFECT?   With the price at P_d because of the quota at Q_2Q_3, almost all the effects (on production, on consumption, the subsidy and consumer tax aspects, the welfare shifts and deadweight losses, the results for efficiency, the terms of trade, pass-through, and lobbying) are the same as they are for a tariff. The one exception is the revenue effect. No tariff is paid, so who gets the revenue shown by area R? The answer is seldom certain under a quota, but here are some possibilities.

1. The government could in effect obtain area R by holding an auction of the quotas. That would, in effect, be a type of tariff. Australia, New Zealand, India, Brazil, and some other South American countries have tried this method occasionally, but there is still a potential for difficulty if the bidders collude. The respected Institute for International Economics in Washington, D.C., has called for the auctioning of all U.S. quotas so that the public would obtain the revenue. Its estimate is that quota auctions would yield about $7 billion per year to the U.S. government.[22] (Importers usually decry auctions as "unethical," and often argue that their high overhead would allow fly-by-night competitors to underbid them at the auction.)

2. The license itself may become a source of political corruption. The officer in charge of deciding who gets the import license has, in essence, a piece of paper worth the difference between the world price and the domestic price, and will be sorely tempted to accept favors from those seeking the license, just as those who covet them will be sorely tempted to bribe the official. Corruption in the

granting of licenses is frequently a serious problem in Third World countries where the salaries are low and the potential gains high. In some nations, the corruption is institutionalized, and the government assigns posts in the office issuing the licenses as a reward to those whom it favors. (Ironically, however, a well-placed bribe might be much smaller in amount than the producer and consumer lobbying costs under a fair system presided over by honest officials—it is difficult for a crooked officer to take bids for bribes without being discovered.)

3. The U.S. experience has been that the importer gets a share of the quota for nothing and so garners the revenue effect. Note that the revenue is not necessary to stimulate the importers to make the effort; their effort would be the same with a tariff that yielded government revenue equal to rectangle *R*. It is hard to see why importers should have any special right to this form of subsidy. The case of the American quota restrictions on imported oil during the period 1954–1973 is the most notorious example. In those long-gone days, a barrel of oil could be purchased and landed on the East Coast of the United States for about $2. Oil interests, fearful of the flood of cheap Arab oil, persuaded President Eisenhower (and his next three successors) that the American oil industry could not survive at that price. So to "reduce American dependence on foreign oil," a quota on imports was declared under the Defense Act. This meant in effect that U.S. prices rose to about $3.25 a barrel. Oil companies were given import licenses according to 1953 import shares. Later, other companies, not importers, received licenses on the grounds that were it not for the quota, they would be operating abroad. Because not all recipients of a share in the quota actually used it, and because many companies wanted to import more oil than they had tickets for, a vigorous market grew up in spare licenses. The price, of course, was the difference between the domestic and international price, or $1.25. Americans today pay dearly for their earlier policy, which resulted in much heavier use of domestic supplies than would otherwise have been the case.

4. Foreigners may capture part of the revenue by raising export prices, which could occur if a foreign producer or exporting firm was a monopoly.[*] More commonly, foreigners capture the revenue when the quota is bargained with the foreign nation under the so-called voluntary export restraints discussed in the next major section.

QUOTAS ARE RIGID   Another reason why economists frown on quotas, and believe nations' leaders should also oppose them, involves their rigidity. (That is also an explanation as to why management and unions that are seeking protection prefer quotas to tariffs.)

Quotas are by their very nature fixed. They limit imports to a specific quantity no matter what the foreigner chooses to do about price. Compare Fig. 4.6a, showing a tariff, to Fig. 4.6b, which portrays a quota. Figure 4.6a shows demand

---

[*] The variations brought about in the presence of monopolies or oligopolies of producers of export goods, exporters of these goods, and importing firms, are detailed nicely by Bergsten et al., *Auction Quotas and United States Trade Policy*, Washington, DC, Institute for International Economics, 1987, Appendix A, pp. 185–203.

Figure 4.6 **Differing responses of tariff and quota to an increase in demand.** Under a tariff, an increase in demand for the product leaves the price unchanged (at P_d) and imports higher (from Q_1Q_2 to Q_1Q_3), but under a quota imports cannot rise above a quantity equal to Q_1Q_2, which is equal to Q_3Q_4, so prices must rise from P_d to P_d'.

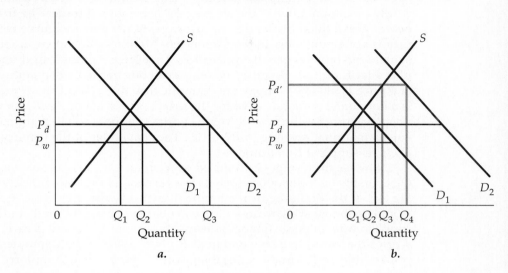

rising to D_2. Even though the tariff of P_wP_d still prevails, the quantity imported rises from Q_1Q_2 to Q_1Q_3. Given the ability of the world to keep supplying at P_w (we assume that the world supply curve is horizontal at price P_w), the price does not rise. Under quotas, however, the quantity of imports cannot increase when demand rises. Figure 4.6b shows the new level of imports, Q_3Q_4 as equal to the quota of Q_1Q_2; the rise in quantity sold has been entirely provided from domestic sources. As a consequence, the price rises to P_d'.

The same result occurs when the domestic supply curve shifts upward, due say to increased wages or a developing scarcity of raw materials. Under a tariff, imports would rise as domestic supply fell off, but under a quota, imports would not rise; the consequence would be an increase in price under a quota, while there would be no increase under a tariff. (The diagram is just a variation on Fig. 4.6a and 4.6b, and the reader is encouraged to sketch it.)

A third variation occurs if world prices decrease. Under a tariff, domestic prices will fall by the amount of the decline in world prices. Under a quota, the domestic price cannot fall, and the revenue effect, R, increases—it goes to whoever is fortunate enough to capture it. Domestic demand and supply conditions remain unchanged because imports are fixed. Thus those benefiting from protection prefer the certainty of quotas. It is far better for them if foreigners are unable to cut their prices in the face of a quota, as they can do with a tariff. It is also better for them that any consumer preference for imported goods cannot lead to a rise in imports.

QUOTAS ENHANCE MONOPOLY POWER   When additional competition is prevented by a quota, then any latent or real monopoly position can be exploited, and the stimulus to higher efficiency that stems from competition is lost. This case can be made diagrammatically.[23] Say that, as in Fig. 4.7, a domestic firm would be a monopoly in the absence of international trade. The firm's market power is exhibited by the downward slope of the demand curve facing it. This firm is not a monopoly in the presence of foreign trade, however, because consumers can buy imports at a price of P_t. That price P_t is the world trade price P_w plus a tariff of $P_w P_t$. Because customers can buy abroad any quantity they want at a price P_t, no one will pay the domestic firm more than that. Therefore $P_t MR_t$ is a horizontal demand curve for the firm's product, and $P_t MR_t$ is the marginal revenue curve for the firm as well. The firm produces where marginal cost (MC) equals marginal revenue (MR), or Q_t. The remainder of the country's demand, $Q_t Q_w$, is supplied from imports.

Now see the changes introduced by a quota. Let us establish a quota equal to $Q_t Q_w$ on the quantity of imports. At the very top of the demand curve, shown in Fig. 4.8, if the domestic firm attempted to charge the high price P_z, consumers would not buy it at all because the small quantity demanded at that price could be supplied from imports. Importers would buy at the low world price P_w and sell at a price that would always undercut P_z. Now what if the domestic firm cut its price a little, to P_y? In that case, there would still be enough imports to meet the entire demand because the horizontal distance over to the demand curve at P_y is just equal to the quantity allowed in under the quota. Any lower price, however,

---

Figure 4.7 **Trade polices monopoly power, even with a tariff.** Even with a tariff, a monopoly producer cannot charge more than the world price (P_w) plus the tariff, a price of P_t. The monopolist produces where $MC = MR$, which with MR a horizontal line at P_t gives a quantity of Q_t at price P_t. The monopolist is constrained by imports from charging any price higher than P_t.

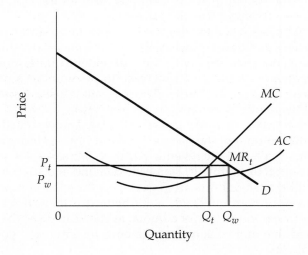

Figure 4.8 **With quotas potential monopoly power becomes real.** Under a quota, a monopolist need not fear a rise in imports above the existing level; this causes the *MR* curve to have a sharp downward slope as in MR_q and allows the monopolist to charge P_q, much higher than the P_t of Fig. 4.7.

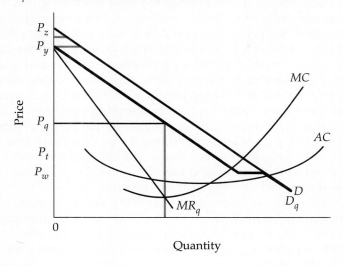

will mean a greater quantity is demanded but no more imports can get by the quota. In effect, starting at P_y the domestic demand curve is moved to the left by the amount of the quota. The leftward shift of the demand curve will continue down to the price level below which the importer cannot go, P_w. At any price below P_w, the domestic firm captures all the demand. The new demand curve shifted by the quota is D_q, shown as the heaviest line.

The end result is that if the same quantity of imports that flowed in under a tariff, Q_tQ_w on Fig. 4.7, is brought in under a quota, then consumers' welfare will be worsened. See how that is so. The new demand curve D_q on Fig. 4.8, shifted leftward by the amount of the quota, will have an associated marginal revenue curve, MR_q, located as microeconomics tells us halfway between the vertical axis and the demand curve at any price. We know that the profits of a firm are maximized where $MC = MR$. Thus the firm will maximize its profits with a price P_q far higher than it had been under a tariff (P_t). The associated reduction in output will presumably mean lower employment as well. The latent monopoly power, controlled under a tariff, was allowed to emerge into actual monopoly power when the tariff was converted into a quota. (The corollary of this is that converting quotas into equivalent tariffs would predictably have beneficial results for the public, though not, of course, for the firms receiving the protection.)[24]

Quotas thus encourage cost inflation by raising prices, and because costs increase, they also reduce the nation's ability to produce, having thus an adverse supply-side effect also.

QUOTAS PRESENT OPERATIONAL DIFFICULTIES   Quotas are difficult to administer and are very hard to allocate. If, for instance, a country decides to let in 1000 cameras a year, importers would rush to bring in the cameras at the beginning of the quota period to sell them at the high domestic price. The tiny U.S. peanut quota is administered in this way. Almost all foreign peanuts enter the country soon after the beginning of the fiscal year. To counter this seemingly irrational pattern, governments normally issue licenses, most often on the basis of past performance. If imports in 1993 were 10 million cameras and the government wants to cut that figure to 8 million in 1994, then it just issues an order that all firms importing cameras in 1994 can import 80% of their 1993 figure in that year. This method freezes the patterns of trade, lessening competition, and does not allow new and cheaper sources of supply to enter the market. Nonetheless it is very common. (One possibility for avoiding the problem is to save a part of the quota, say 10%, for new applicants. Even so, the old producers will have a vested position, and will be much more protected under the quota than they would have been under a tariff allowing in an equivalent quantity of imports.)

Furthermore, quotas beget quotas and become ever more complicated. United States quantity limitations on steel, for instance, encouraged foreign exporters to shift from supplying inexpensive cold rolled sheet to supplying specialty steels, which brings producers more revenue per ton. United States specialty steel producers had not pressed for a quota previously, because it was the big suppliers, with their ancient open hearths, who were being hurt by imports. When, however, the foreign producers moved upscale, the specialty producers were forced to demand quotas of their own. Textile manufacturers faced the same problem as foreign producers turned to supplying goods that had a high profit margin per item, areas that had traditionally been the industrial countries' strongest. The sugar quota has begotten quotas on syrups and on candies. Producers of these items, suffering from the higher costs of the protected sugar, find themselves undercut by imports that use cheap sugar. It is like trying to stem a flood tide: The force of the water is akin to the pressures wrought by comparative advantage; the quotas are sandbags thrown in its way, diverting the flow, saving a firm here or a group of jobs there, but passing the flood on to some other spot, which tries to find sandbags of its own.

When all these objections to quotas are combined with the many effects of the blockages of imports discussed in the tariff section, it seems clear enough that import quotas are inimical to the public interest.

VOLUNTARY EXPORT RESTRAINTS (VERS)

A *voluntary export restraint,* or VER, is a special kind of quota set on the export of a good to a given country. It is for all intents and purposes an import quota, except that it is at least technically administered by the exporter, and not all of the effects are exactly the same. VERs were scarcely used until the 1970s. About that time they came into sudden prominence, and have since become a major form of protection, presently affecting about 15% of world trade.[25]

■ *OTHER NAMES FOR VERS AND THEIR FIRST USE*

Sometimes VERs are called *voluntary restraint agreements,* VRAs, or *voluntary export restraint agreements,* VERAs, when the parties sign a formal agreement. Government-to-government agreements involving no industry participation in the bargaining and administration are sometimes called *orderly marketing arrangements,* or OMAs. In the United States, there is a legal distinction between OMAs and VERs, but the difference is unimportant both theoretically and practically.

The United States invented VERs in 1935–1936, when U.S. and Japanese producers negotiated limits on Japan's exports of cotton textiles to the United States. Apparently both governments consented to this private arrangement between producers. The argument has been made that the traditional Japanese practice of avoiding confrontation through compromise was reflected by this first VER.[26]

The somewhat unusual roots of voluntary export restraints lie in the legal systems and treaty obligations of industrial countries that have made other trade barriers harder to employ. The *General Agreement on Tariffs and Trade,* GATT, to which the United States and all other major Western industrial nations are signatories, has sponsored numerous tariff agreements that effectively prevent the raising of tariffs. Furthermore, with the exception of agricultural commodities and all imports to the less developed countries, GATT does not on the whole permit quotas for manufactured products. To avoid these constraints, protectionists have relied on persuading the exporting country *voluntarily* to limit its exports. Of course, an exporting country may well view this as a bad idea, but the importing nation can threaten to establish quotas or raise tariffs at a later date, even if that does mean breaking a treaty or other obligation. These are sovereign nations, after all, and cannot be sued (without their permission) in any court. No exporting country has yet called the Americans' or the Europeans' bluff, and no case involving a VER has ever been taken to GATT.

Politics contributed greatly to the rise of VERs. Internally, the U.S. legal system makes it difficult to impose quotas or tariffs without involving congress, something clearly intended by the Constitutional Fathers. If the administration were to go through congress, it would lose control over the policy, and action would be slower. With a VER, however, the administration can decide how much it will try to persuade the other nation to cut down exports.* Moreover, faced with a choice of dealing with a U.S. administration or the U.S. Congress, foreign nations would rather deal with the administration as the better of two bad choices because congress has the reputation of being the major source of protectionist sentiment.

---

* Such problems are less important in parliamentary systems, where policy coordination is usually better, but can occur when the government is a minority government, or when a prime minister wants to handle policy outside the normal legislative channels. There is nothing in a VER that would *require* the British Prime Minister to consult either with parliament or with the cabinet before finishing the negotiations.

From the exporter's point of view, some VERs are voluntary in name only, akin to the outlaw voluntarily putting up his hands when the sheriff is pointing a gun at him. Just as especially well-armed outlaws may not be pursued too far into the sagebrush, countries with a substantial capacity to retaliate are less likely to be challenged. VERs tend to discriminate against the poor and powerless. Other VERs may be welcomed by exporter and importer alike as a way to cartelize an industry with government permission and encouragement. A major advantage to the foreign exporter is that in both cases the revenue effect from the quota is usually distributed to the exporter, as explored in the next section. Government in the exporting country gains certainty, and possibly even some control over industry.

These considerations help to explain why VERs have proliferated worldwide. In textiles, the famous, or perhaps infamous, Multi-Fiber Arrangement controls textile and clothing exports from the less developed countries. World trade in steel is shot through with them, as is trade in automobiles and electronic goods. (All of these are discussed in this chapter's Appendix 4.3.) In mid-1988, 261 VERs were in place, about 80% of them negotiated government to government, while the rest are industry-with-government or industry-with-industry arrangements. Government-to-government VERs are by far the most common because their policing is usually more effective.[27]

■ *WHO IS HIT BY VERS?*

Of the 261 known VERs, 138 affected imports to the European Community, and 62 to the United States. The numbers do not include the hundreds of bilateral limits in the Multi-Fiber Arrangement. Japan has just 13, almost all involving various sorts of textiles from China, Korea, and Pakistan. About 75% of all VERs are aimed at less developed countries, Japan, and Eastern Europe. In 1984, 38% of Japan's exports to Europe and 32% to the United States were covered. The largest number were in textiles (72), agriculture (55), and steel (52). Other unknown VERs may exist, involving agreements between private industries or between a government in one country and an industry in another.[28]

ANALYSIS OF VERS

A VER has consequences identical to those of a quota with the exception of the revenue effect, which goes to the exporter. (Only if buyers in the importing country were monopsonistic would they be able to extract much of this revenue.) The most common outcome of negotiations is for the government in the exporting nation to agree to issue export licenses to its companies, as is done in Taiwan or Hong Kong. The revenue may accrue to private companies if the licenses to export are given away, as is most frequently true. After a VER with the United States covering automobiles, for instance, Japanese car exporters just raised the price of their cars to the higher American price (by some 13%–20%). The revenue may accrue to the exporters' government if it auctions off the licenses in a competitive market. If the bidding is rigged, the revenue will be shared in some proportion by government and producers.

In South Korea and Taiwan, the quota rights cannot be transferred. In Hong Kong they can be sold, and there are now over 1000 quota brokers who manage the transactions. The original recipients are allocated a share based on a formula tied to their export performance since the early 1960s, with a certain percentage reserved for newcomers. (Original holders must use at least 50% of their allocation and see to it that another 45% is used by others.) It is curious how a government like that of the United States, which lectures less developed countries on the importance of a free-enterprise economy, has fostered the growth of cartels and state control abroad to further American protectionism.

Because many VERs involve an element of market-sharing and collusion, exporting nations can certainly gain from them at the expense of the importers that imposed them. A gain can occur because the revenue obtained from the higher price charged, all of which is profit, may more than offset the profits lost because of the smaller volume allowed. Figure 4.9, yet another variation on our basic tariff diagram, shows how this can be so. The two rectangles labeled F and G represent the revenue lost to the exporter when complying with the VER—the old volume of exports, Q_1Q_4, minus the new volume Q_2Q_3 times the

Figure 4.9 **VER favoring exporter.** Under tariffs, R, the revenue effect goes to the government, while under a VER it goes to the foreign exporter. But the exporter loses sales revenue of $F+G$. If R is larger than $F+G$, the exporter is surely better off.

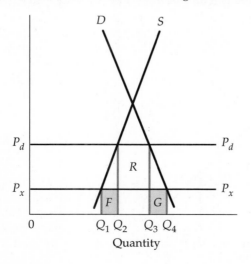

old price, P_x. The compensation for going along with a VER is the revenue rectangle, R. Michel Kostecki estimates that transfers of revenues associated with VERs totaled \$27 billion in 1984.[29] Here the capture of revenue from the higher price is greater than the loss in revenues because sales volume has declined; that is, $F+G < R$ as shown in the figure. There is an unambiguous gain to exporting firms, as well as to producers in the importing country. The profits of both can rise, with consumers footing the bill.

Even if the increase in price is a smaller portion of the export price, as in Fig. 4.10, it is still quite possible that the exporter will gain more profits than it loses. Here R is much smaller than $F+G$, but remember that R is pure gain while the revenues shown by areas F and G include all the exporter's production costs as well as profit. Under competitive conditions in world trade, the profit component of $F+G$ would be normal profit only, likely to be just a fraction of the total area involved. The addition to profits from the capture of R could easily exceed the loss of normal profit as total revenue declines.

Though calculating the gain or loss can be complex and even impossible because of inadequacies in data covering foreign firms, a general principle is clear. The outcome will depend on the elasticities involved. If, for instance, the United States negotiated a VER with Canada on nickel, it would surely be to Canada's great gain, since the U.S. supply of nickel is highly inelastic (there is none being mined) and the demand, because it is an ingredient in other products like stainless steel, is also highly inelastic. Prices would rise greatly, as in Fig. 4.9 rather than 4.10.

Figure 4.10 **Foreign firms might gain even when $F+G > R$.** If the demand and domestic supply for the import under a VER are more elastic than in Fig. 4.9, $F+G$ may exceed R. But the foreign exporter can still end up ahead, because R is pure gain while F and G include production costs.

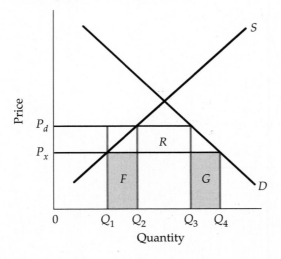

Even if a VER brings an exporting country profits sufficient to offset the loss as sales volume falls, losses of other kinds to that country may still ensue. Growth in exports will be curtailed, economies of scale and effects of learning will be lost, and the spur of competition from new firms challenging the old in export markets will diminish. On the other hand, it is conceivable that the revenues transferred to a restrained country because of a VER might be plowed back into investment and technical improvement, leaving that country in a better competitive position than before.

Still, the significant chance that exporters' profits will rise possesses undoubted allure. To some large extent, therefore, a VER creates interest groups abroad for its perpetuation. Firms that can rely on getting their piece of the quota may avoid vigorous price competition, may lose their competitive edge, and may instead work very hard on the lobbying or corruption involved in obtaining a large quota. When it is suggested that quotas be dropped, many of these firms may oppose that plan, in a sense because their comparative advantage has been in developing the connections needed to get the quotas. Smaller nations awarded an unusually large quota, for foreign policy reasons perhaps, might also end up supporting the VER in order to retain their artificially large share of the market.

Several other outcomes of a VER are possible or probable. As prices rise, the market share of exporting countries not included under the restraints is likely to increase. A terms-of-trade effect may occur, with world prices falling because exports are reduced. If that is so, an even greater incentive is created for other exporters not restrained under the VER to divert shipments to the export market where prices have risen. (In 1977, Japan was the source of 90% of U.S. imports of color TVs. A VER caused the Japanese share to fall by 1979 to 50%, but Korea and Taiwan increased their sales of TVs to take up the slack. These countries as well then had to be included in the restraint.) Exporters also may attempt to evade the VER by laundering their shipments through uncovered countries, which may be reasonably easy if the product concerned is homogeneous and its place of origin difficult to identify—cheap shoes and clothing, for example. Circumvention may also be possible if a nation facing a VER has plants in other countries from which the goods can be shipped without being subject to control. The more easily these can be started up, the less effective the VER will be. The European Community has recently been concerned that its VERs with Japan could be circumvented if the Japanese raise their exports to Europe from their U.S. plants.

■ *AN ADMINISTRATION MIGHT EVEN DESIRE A POROUS VER*

A Machiavellian might argue that a porous VER could give the appearance of protection to a congress or parliament and to the public, while actually approximating free trade conditions. In this reading the administration might advocate a VER as much to defuse protectionist pressure as to promote it. The administration could rightly claim that a VER had been negotiated, but could then be rather slow in adding new countries to it or rather lax in policing it. Prices would perhaps rise little if at all.

> Even a Machiavellian might on occasion be fooled, however. A VER that was set at the current level of imports could still result in higher prices if potential monopoly power were converted into actual monopoly power, as discussed in our earlier treatment of quotas.

For the importing country that imposed the VER in the first place, other features stand out. Because it is the outcome of negotiations, the VER is unlikely to provoke retaliation by the exporting nation. Offsetting this major advantage, however, is the expensive loss of the revenue effect, currently estimated to be about $5 billion in the United States.[30] Nothing comes back even from the income tax, as would happen if domestic firms protected by a quota garnered the revenue effect. When a foreign firm sells at a high price under a VER, it keeps the gains. Consumers may even face *higher* prices than they would under a regular quota, because the terms-of-trade effect will be reversed. (Foreign firms will be selling at a higher price, not at a lower one as might be true if they had to face a quota.)

This litany of adverse consequences explains why many economists believe that international surveillance and regulation of VERs should have the highest priority in trade negotiations. At the least, a reform that replaced VERs with tariffs or auctioned quotas would halt the hemorrhage of revenue to foreign countries. A requirement that the governments publish the amount of tariff revenue lost with a VER might also help.[*]

CONCLUSION

Tariffs, quotas, and VERs are the most familiar of the interferences with trade. The compass of the latter two has grown significantly in recent years to cover a

Table 4.2 **Share of sectoral imports affected by quotas and VERs, percent**

Product	USA	France	Japan
Textiles, apparel	68	43	17
Iron, steel	76	50	6
Autos	38	19	0
Agricultural commodities	18	48	50

Source: Margaret Kelly, Naheed Kirmani, Miranda Xafa, Clemens Boonekamp, and Peter Winglee, Issues and Developments in International Trade Policy, *IMF Occasional Paper No. 63, December, 1988, p. 122. The data apply to year end, 1986. The large Multi-Fiber Arrangement on textiles and clothing is included in the calculation. Note that these data show only the extent of imports covered, not the severity of the barrier.*

---

[*] A very new idea, a sort of mirror image to a VER, is a *voluntary import expansion*. Perhaps countries such as South Korea or Taiwan, with large trade surpluses, could be pressured "voluntarily" to raise their level of imports, thus diminishing their surpluses and increasing the exports of trading partners such as the EC or United States.

large and expanding share of international trade. In 1987, 23% of all developed-country imports were subject to them, up from 19% in 1981.[31] The Institute for International Economics in Washington, D.C., estimates that quotas and VERs now affect about 34% of the American market for manufactured goods, 32% of the French market, 20% of the German market, 10% of the Canadian, and 7% of the Japanese. In recent years, the increasing scope of these instruments has been notable in the United States, Canada, and the European Community (EC), in contrast to their reduced use in Japan. There are broad differences in the sectors affected, as shown in the accompanying Table 4.2.

Tariffs, quotas, and VERs are far from the only distortions to trade, however. Politicians have become increasingly innovative, finding other, less familiar means to interfere with trade flows. A wide variety of these other distortions are discussed in the next chapter.

VOCABULARY AND CONCEPTS

Ad valorem duty
Consumer surplus
Consumer tax equivalent
Consumption effect
Deadweight loss (consumer and producer)
Economic rent (from protection)
Export quotas
Export taxes
Import effect
Import quotas
Incidence of tariffs
Lobbying effect
Nominal and effective tariffs

Optimal tariff
Pass-through effect
Producer surplus
Producers' subsidy effect
Production effect
Redistribution effect
Revenue effect
Specialization effects
Specific duty
Tariffs
Terms-of-trade effect
Voluntary export restraints (VERs)
X-inefficiency effect

QUESTIONS

1. Explain what a tariff is, and distinguish *ad valorem* from specific duties. Which is harder to administer? Which is best for consumers?

2. "The arguments over categorization are ultimately very sad, as fine and often silly distinctions come to affect much that is serious and important." Comment.

3. "The decision as to where to manufacture or assemble a product is related not to the nominal tariff, but to the effective tariff." Explain what an effective tariff is and explain the statement.

4. How are effective tariffs measured?

5. Explain, using demand and supply curves, the gains and losses from instituting a tariff. Show the production effect, the consumption effect, the import effect, the change in consumer and producer's surpluses, the revenue effect, and the consumers' and producers' deadweight losses. Explain briefly the deadweight losses.

6. Deadweight losses probably are not very high. Explain why this is so.

7. Even if deadweight losses are not high, tariffs could cause a considerable loss in efficiency.

What other kinds of efficiency losses are there?

8. Even if deadweight losses are not high, we still have major questions about the redistribution effect and the party taxed. Explain why they are important.

9. "Ultimately, tariffs are paid by exporters." Explain.

10. What is the terms-of-trade effect? How is it related to the rather esoteric concept of an optimal tariff? Demonstrate with a diagram.

11. What is the nature of demand and supply between two countries that would cause a tariff to be absorbed by the exporting nation?

12. What is a rent, and how do tariffs produce it?

13. Demonstrate, using a diagram, that it is rational for producers to seek rents, and indicate at

what point they should stop paying to secure them.

14. Explain how the effects of a quota differ from those of a tariff.

15. Economists dislike quotas far more than tariffs. Discuss why, covering the issues of rent (from the revenue effect), rigidity, monopoly power, and administration.

16. Explain what VERs are and how they grew. How do they differ from quotas? Why are they so common these days?

17. Sometimes the exporter is eager to have a VER. Under what circumstances would this occur?

NOTES

[1] See D.D. Humphrey, *The U.S. and the Common Market,* New York, Praeger, 1964.

[2] See the *Wall Street Journal,* February 17 and 25, 1989.

[3] The sewing kit and opera set stories are from the *Wall Street Journal,* September 27, 1988. The tale of the girls' ski jackets is from James Bovard, "The customs services fickle philosophy," *Wall Street Journal,* July 31, 1991. Some of the following anecdotes were reported in the *Christian Science Monitor* for July 15, 1983.

[4] The history and analysis are covered thoroughly by W.M. Corden, *The Theory of Protection,* Oxford, Oxford University Press, 1971, pp. 35–40 and 245–249.

[5] The tale is from D.D. Humphrey, *The U.S. and the Common Market.*

[6] See Peter Kenen, *The International Economy,* Englewood Cliffs, N.J., Prentice Hall, 1985, pp. 183–184.

[7] For this statement see World Bank, *World Development Report, 1987,* Washington, D.C., 1987, p. 139.

[8] See C. Fred Bergsten and William R. Cline, "Trade policy in the 1980s: An overview," in William R. Cline, ed., *Trade Policy in the 1980s,* Washington, D.C., 1983, Institute for International Economics, p. 72. There is an analytical study by Stephen S. Golub and J.M. Finger, "The processing of primary commodities: Effects of developed-country tariff escalation and developing-country export taxation," *Journal of Political Economy,* Vol. 87, No. 3, 1979, pp. 559–577. More percentage rates of effective protection may be found in the World Bank's *World Development Report, 1986,* Washington,

D.C., 1986, p. 126, and in the 1987 Report, Washington, D.C., 1987, p. 138.

[9] Quoted in the Brandt Commission Report, *North-South: A Programme for Survival,* London, Pan Books, 1980, pp. 141–142.

[10] See *The Economist,* September 23, 1989.

[11] See "The consumer cost of U.S. trade restraints," *Federal Reserve Bank of New York Quarterly Review,* Vol. 10, No. 2, Summer 1985, pp. 1–12; and for the World Bank figures a citation in *The Economist,* September 13, 1986, p. 15.

[12] Mancur Olson, "The political economy of comparative growth rates," paper presented at the Cliometrics Conference, University of Chicago, May, 1978, p. 92. A recent volume that emphasizes the role of competition in promoting more productive and innovative business behavior is Michael Porter, *The Competitive Advantage of Nations,* New York, Free Press, 1990.

[13] One interesting test is reported by Walter Primeaux, "An assessment of X-efficiency gained through competition," *Review of Economics and Statistics,* Vol. 59, February 1977, pp. 105–108.

[14] F.M. Scherer, *International High-Technology Competition,* Cambridge, Mass., Harvard University Press, 1992. Some of the points in the paragraph are made by W. Max Corden, *Protection and Liberalization: A Review of Analytical Issues,* IMF Occasional Paper 54, Washington, D.C., International Monetary Fund, 1987, pp. 14–15. The negative effects of protection on eco-

nomic growth are explored further by Bernhard Heitger, "Import protection and export performance," *Weltwirtschaftliches Archiv,* Vol. 123.

15 See work of David Morrison reported in *The Economist,* January 31, 1987. The data apply to the year 1986.

16 See World Bank, *World Development Report, 1987,* p. 80.

17 See Kenneth Clements and Larry Sjaastad, *How Protection Taxes Exporters,* London, Trade Policy Research Centre, 1985, and the discussion of this work in *The Economist,* May 25, 1985, p. 69.

18 They are called *Tullock costs* by some economists. See Gordon Tullock, "The welfare costs of tariffs, monopolies, and theft," *Western Economic Journal,* Vol. 5, June 1967, pp. 224–232.

19 See John T. Wenders, "On perfect rent dissipation," *American Economic Review,* Vol. 77, No. 3, June 1987, pp. 456–459.

20 See Bhagwati's *Protectionism,* Cambridge, Mass., MIT Press, 1988, pp. 103–104. Other sources utilized for our analysis of rent-seeking are Robert E. Baldwin and T. Scott Thompson, "Responding to trade-distorting policies of other countries," *American Economic Review,* Vol. 74, No. 2, May 1984, pp. 271–276; Stephen P. Magee, William A. Brock, and Leslie Young, *Black Hole Tariffs and Endogenous Policy Theory: Political Economy in General Equilibrium,* Cambridge, Cambridge University Press, 1989; and Neil Vousden, *The Economics of Trade Protection,* Cambridge, Cambridge University Press, 1990.

21 The evidence is noted by W.M. Corden, *Trade Policy and Economic Welfare,* Oxford, Oxford University Press, 1974, pp. 182–184, citing Arnold Harberger, M.E. Kreinen, J.E. Floyd, Giorgio Basevia, and Franklin V. Walker.

22 See C. Fred Bergsten, Kimberly Ann Elliott, Jeffrey J. Schott, and Wendy E. Takacs, *Auction Quotas and United States Trade Policy,* Washington, D.C., Institute for International Economics, 1987. For a discussion of how

such auctions might work in the presence of monopoly power, see Wendy E. Takacs, "Economic aspects of quota license auctions," *Journal of World Trade,* Vol. 22, No. 6, December 1988, pp. 39–51.

23 This proof is provided in the appendices to various editions of the Lindert and Lindert and Kindleberger texts, *International Economics,* Homewood, Ill., Richard D. Irwin, Inc.

24 See W.M. Corden, *Trade Policy and Economic Welfare,* Oxford, Oxford University Press, 1974, pp. 202–203.

25 Michel M. Kostecki, "Marketing strategies and voluntary export restraints," *Journal of World Trade,* Vol. 25, No. 4, August 1991, pp. 87–99.

26 See Kent Jones, "Voluntary export restraint: Political economy, history and the role of the GATT," *Journal of World Trade,* Vol. 23, No. 3, June 1989, p. 129.

27 The total number of VERs is a GATT figure reported in Margaret Kelly, Naheed Kirmani, Miranda Xafa, Clemens Boonekamp, and Peter Winglee, *Issues and Developments in International Trade Policy,* IMF Occasional Paper No. 63, December 1988, International Monetary Fund, pp. 1–2. The percentage is from Kostecki, "Marketing strategies and voluntary export restraints."

28 For the numbers, see Clemens F.J. Boonekamp, "Voluntary export restraints," *Finance and Development,* Vol. 24, No. 4, December 1987, pp. 2–5. Boonekamp's analysis of VERs is also utilized at several subsequent points in the text.

29 For the Kostecki estimate see the Boonekamp article, "Voluntary export restraints."

30 The $5 billion estimate is from Robert E. Baldwin, "U.S. trade policy: Recent changes and future U.S. interests," *AEA Papers and Proceedings,* Vol. 79, No. 2, May 1989, p. 132.

31 Fuels are excluded from this calculation, the source of which is a 1988 study by UNCTAD. Imports of food are even more subject to NTBs, 38% of the total in 1987. See also World Bank, *World Development Report, 1988,* Washington, D.C., 1988, p. 16.

Appendix 4.1

EXPORT TAXES AND QUOTAS

These tools are less common than are tariffs or quotas on imports, but they are employed, especially in the less developed countries. Even complete prohibitions of exports have been enforced at certain times and places, a topic with a long and important history as explored in the accompanying box.

■ *EXPORT PROHIBITIONS HAVE A LONG AND IMPORTANT HISTORY*

Complete bans on export have a decided place in economic history. The fine word *sycophant*, "one who curries favor," has to do with the prohibition of all exports except olive oil by ancient Athens. In Greek *sykon phainein* means fig shower, one who curried favor by showing to officials the illegal exports of figs. Britain prohibited grain exports except under license from 1177 to 1394, and charged duties on exports from that latter year until the Corn Laws enacted by Charles II in 1663 established a different system favoring landowners. It also restricted machinery exports (so as to protect its technological lead) until 1842. The Ottoman Empire maintained for many years an entire prohibition of exports; its imports were paid for by cash transactions. Japan, as is well known, banned almost *all* contact with the outside world for over two centuries, from 1636. Trade was limited to a Dutch ship that touched annually at Nagasaki. The situation was little changed until after Commodore Perry's visits of 1853 and 1854.

EXPORT TAXES

Export taxes are a mirror image of tariffs on imports, and can also be analyzed by means of diagrams like Fig. 4.3a and 4.3b earlier in the chapter.

Say Agricola levies an export tax T on its wheat exports, as shown in Fig. 4.11b. Exports would fall from Q_1Q_4 to Q_2Q_3. The price per unit would fall in the exporter to P_3, but it would rise in Fabrica, the importer, to P_2. The export tariff T charged on exports Q_2Q_3 will yield Agricola's government a revenue of $r+R$. A portion of that revenue, box R, would come at the expense of consumers in Fabrica because import prices were forced up in that country. Agricola's welfare could conceivably rise because of the tax. Consider the welfare effects in that country: Because the price has fallen, producers lose surplus equal to $a+b+c+r+d$. Consumer surplus rises by $a+b$. The government collects export tax revenue of $r+R$. The two as, bs, and rs cancel one another, being both gains and losses. There is a deadweight loss of $c+d$, and a gain in government revenue of R. The export tax is advantageous for Agricola if the government revenue obtained at Fabrica's expense exceeds its own deadweight losses, that is, if $R > c+d$.

As with an import tariff, it is possible to calculate an optimum tax to improve the exporting country's terms of trade. The risks of retaliation are similar, unless

Figure 4.11 **The economic effects of an export tax.** By means of an export tax, an exporter may be able to force the importer to pay higher prices, thus shifting the terms of trade in its favor. The pattern of gains and losses is explained in the text.

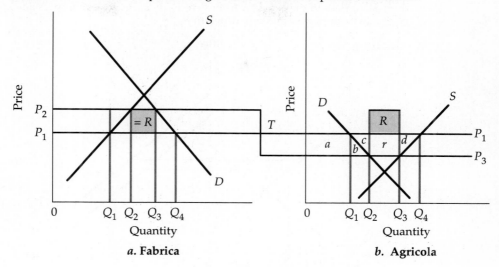

a. **Fabrica**   *b.* **Agricola**

a commodity is so important (oil, for example) that trading partners control their urge to hit back. Enormous gains, as all the world knows, followed from the export taxation employed by Saudi Arabia and other oil-producing states. Numerous other countries have employed export taxes, for example Ghana on cocoa, Chile on nitrates, Argentina on almost all its commodity exports, when they believe they have some ability to affect the terms of trade.

EXPORT QUOTAS

On occasion, quotas are extended to exports as well as imports. Just above we addressed the principle of export tariffs engineered for their terms-of-trade effect abroad. Export quotas can be imposed with the same end in view, as with OPEC. Another reason for export quotas is that for domestic political reasons a government may want to keep prices low for consumers at home. (Export embargoes on trade with rival nations are another matter, and are taken up in Chapter 8.)

An export quota to reduce domestic prices is shown in Fig. 4.12. Here, assume that government decides that rising world demand, seen on the right-hand side of the diagram as a movement from D_1 to D_2, has pulled the home price, shown on the Y axis, up to a level higher than desired. If export quotas are imposed, and these reduce the quantity exported from Q_1Q_4 to Q_2Q_3, then the market price will decline from P_h to P_l. Consumers gain, while producers lose.

One celebrated case involved the quota placed on U.S. exports of soybeans by President Nixon in the early 1970s. Though this quota lasted only three months, it wrecked America's reputation as a reliable supplier of that product,

Figure 4.12 **Export quotas to keep down domestic prices.** In a back-to-back diagram, the home market is on the left and the world on the right. A rise in world demand from D_1 to D_2 would have had the effect of raising exports from Q_2Q_3 to Q_1Q_4, and hence domestic prices in the exporter from P_l to P_h. If the exporter imposes an export quota of Q_2Q_3, domestic prices are kept down to P_l.

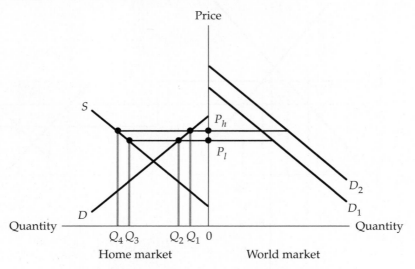

especially in Japan, which is a major importer. Brazil was the biggest gainer. The U.S. action gave Brazilian farmers the boost they needed, and soybeans became a major export of that country, the industry financed heavily by the Japanese. The United States has other restrictions on the export of oil from Alaska, refined petroleum (which runs up the U.S. trade deficit with Japan by an estimated $10–15 billion), and on timber from federal lands. The timber ban is intended to force Asia (mainly Japan and South Korea) to buy planks instead, though the main result has been a boom in log exports from countries such as Indonesia and about $1 billion added to the U.S. trade deficit. There are also procedures in place to control the export of scrap metal from the United States.

Other examples include long-standing controls on Thai rice exports to keep Thailand's rice price low, and temporary bans on the export of Indian tea and Brazilian rice, corn, and cotton. Ironically, soybeans were also covered for a time by a Brazilian ban, perhaps reflecting a lesson not learned from the U.S. experience. (The Brazilian restraints, associated with the inflation in that country, were lifted in 1988.[1]) There have even been attempts to get voluntary import restraint agreements, particularly in U.S. wood and wood-product exports to Japan.

---

[1] U.S. ITC, *Operation of the Trade Agreements Program, 40th Report,* 1988, p. 133 and *The Economist,* September 9, 1989.

Appendix 4.2

THE TERMS-OF-TRADE EFFECT IN GENERAL EQUILIBRIUM

To examine the terms-of-trade effect in a more general setting, it is convenient to use the offer curves developed in Chapter 2. Offer curves allow us to see clearly not only that a large country can affect the world price level, but also to examine the effects of the retaliation that may follow.

In Fig. 4.13, 0F is the offer curve for Fabrica under free trade conditions, while 0A is the offer curve for Agricola. The equilibrium terms of trade is 0E. If Fabrica puts a tariff on wheat imports, that will have the effect of moving (distorting) its original offer curve 0F. Why this is so can be seen at any point on the curve, such as X. Here Fabrica was formerly willing to trade 0W cloth for WX wheat. Now, however, Fabrica is willing to give up 0W cloth only if it obtains the greater quantity WY wheat, if XY wheat is collected by government as a tariff. Here the tariff rate is XY/WX, a rate that looks to be on the order of 33%. Point Y is one point on a new tariff-distorted offer curve 0F'.

We can find other new points in the same manner. Take any other position on the original Fabrican offer curve 0F, for example at X'. Then calculate X'Y'/W'X' = XY/WX. This and other such calculations yield a series of new points that lie on an offer curve 0F'. The new Fabrican offer curve's intersection with the Agricolan offer curve gives a new equilibrium terms of trade 0E'. The end result is that Fabrica finds its imported wheat is cheaper, and its exported cloth is more expensive, than was true before it imposed the tariff.

As is explained in the text, when a country can affect world prices, there is the possibility that it can improve its welfare by means of a tariff that shifts the terms of trade in its favor. (Note how at the new equilibrium Fabrica gives up

---

Figure 4.13 **A tariff shifts the terms of trade.** Because a tariff displaces the importing country's offer curve, it may be possible to shift the terms of trade in favor of that country (in the figure from 0E to 0E').

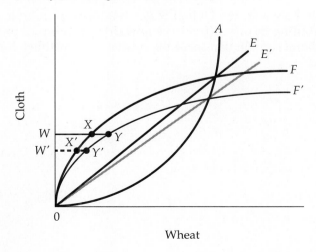

145

Figure 4.14 **A trade war shown with offer curves.** An attempt to move the terms of trade in one's favor may beget a retaliatory tariff, with the terms of trade much as before but with a substantial reduction in the overall level of trade.

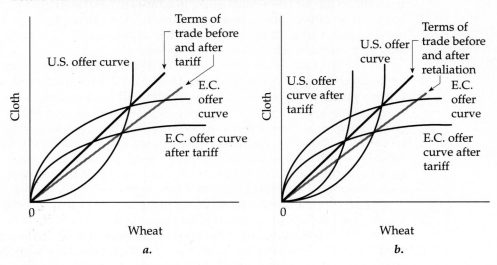

a.   b.

considerably less cloth to get only a little less wheat.) This gain in welfare is to Fabrica only, however, and is a loss of welfare to Agricola, which finds that its wheat buys less cloth than before. This is why Agricolan retaliation would be very likely, with Agricola raising its own tariffs to recapture the lost welfare.

The results of retaliation are shown in Fig. 4.14a and 4.14b. Take the case of an imaginary struggle between the United States and the EC. Figure 4.14a shows the EC's offer curve shifted downward as a tariff is imposed by the EC members against imports from the United States. This improves the EC's terms of trade, as shown.

In Fig. 4.14b, however, the United States retaliates, putting a tariff on EC cloth and thus shifting its own offer curve upward. The terms of trade return to their original relationship. In that sense the retaliation is justified, but total trade is much reduced.

Appendix 4.3

THE MOST IMPORTANT QUOTAS AND VERs

The major examples of quotas are in agriculture, while the major VERs involve predominately manufactured goods. Several cases are discussed in this appendix.

QUOTAS IN AGRICULTURE

The most important quotas are in agriculture. They are widespread because governments have to restrict imports if they want to boost prices for farmers by means of price-support programs. If governments did not restrict imports, they would flood in as a response to the high prices, overwhelming the governments' ability to assist farmers by purchasing commodities.[1]

Quotas to exclude imports are legal because of a GATT rules exemption covering their use in agriculture. The exemption dates from 1955, and was instigated by the United States which, unthinkingly, did not see the massive distortions to trade that would result.

THE CAP   The European Community uses quotas (as well as the variable levy, a tariff that rises when world prices fall) to restrict imports under its Common Agricultural Policy, or CAP. Behind the trade barriers, the EC pursues its purchases to maintain prices for its farmers at levels about 40% more than world prices. (In 1991, about 49% of farmers' incomes came from EC government programs.) Surpluses are the inevitable result of the government purchases. About a quarter of the EC's farm land produces nothing but these surplus commodities, called "mountains." The size of the mountains is shown in Table 4.3. The fact that the EC tries to be rid of these surpluses by exporting them at cheap prices has been very disruptive for world trade in agricultural commodities, as we shall see.

JAPANESE QUOTAS   Japan also subsidizes its farmers heavily (66% of their income in 1991) and in consequence protects its agriculture with quotas. Recently

---

[1]A good recent survey is Fred H. Sanderson, ed., *Agricultural Protection in the Industrialized World*, Resources for the Future, Washington, DC, 1990.

Table 4.3   **Size of EC surplus commodity "mountains" and wine "lake"**

Cereal grains	18 million metric tons (record high)
Beef	0.7 million metric tons (record high)
Butter	0.3 million metric tons
Milk powder	0.3 million metric tons
Wine	80 million liters

Source: EC Commission. The figures are for January, 1991. In recent years a combination of some CAP reforms, a U.S. drought, but mostly redoubled efforts to subsidize the export of the mountains brought large falls in some of the figures. Butter, for example, had been as high as 1.2 million metric tons in 1987, while wine was 740 million liters in 1988. There is also a "manure mountain" produced by the surplus livestock.

there were 22 categories of them, though that is down considerably from the 500 of the 1960s. Strict limits on sugar imports help to raise the domestic selling price to about five times the world price; meat is three times more expensive than world prices, and some cuts of steak sell in Japan for 10 times the price in U.S. supermarkets; wheat sells for nearly 11 times the world price. Rice presents the greatest problem. This is Japan's most important crop, as much for its political and emotional mystique as for its economics. Farmers receive eight to nine times the world price for this product, though consumers pay less (about six times) because of expensive rice subsidies. Rice imports are completely forbidden excepting small quantities used for rice flour, crackers, and the like. The usual reason given by Japanese politicians for the quotas, that an island nation is ensuring food security, seems to be widely accepted by the public. Yet the security argument is not very tenable. A war or boycott that cut off imported food would also presumably cut off imported petroleum-based fertilizers, without which Japanese agriculture could not feed the country. The alternative of stockpiling food against future emergencies is not practiced. Stockpiles of food could be purchased cheaply on world markets, and could be enlarged or diminished as the international situation dictated.

The argument is sometimes made that Japanese consumers prefer the taste of their own rice to the taste of imported rice. This is clearly not an argument in favor of quotas. If it is true, then quotas are not needed, and if it is false, then free trade would be an improvement for consumers.

U.S. QUOTAS   In the United States, government programs are not as important as they are in the EC and Japan, but in 1991 they still provided 30% of farmers' incomes. The share of U.S. imports covered by quotas and other quota-like barriers grew from 6% to 18% between the end of 1981 and the start of 1988. The quotas with the greatest effect are the extremely tight ones for cotton (including cotton waste and certain cotton products), peanuts, and dairy products (butter, milk, cheese), and the far more damaging one for sugar (including syrup and sugar-containing items). All protect a price-support program in one form or another.

The cotton quotas in force in the United States virtually exclude imports of upland cotton, which are limited to 28,000 bales, or about 0.002% of the market. Peanuts are a similar case. U.S. production is about 1.5 million metric tons a year. Domestic output is strictly controlled by its own quota, which is allocated by farm and supervised by (it seems a joke but it is not) federal inspectors acting as a "peanut police." The global quota for imports, established in 1953, is 775 metric tons, or about two imported peanuts per person per year. The tariff equivalent is about 90%. The 44,000 U.S. licensed growers, about one third of them absentees, profit greatly.

The butter and cheese quotas are also extremely restrictive. Possible producers face a quota limiting imports to about 0.06% of U.S. butter production, while cheese quotas range from 0.3% to 14% of U.S. production, depending on the type of cheese. Milk and cream imports are also limited, to 1.5 million gallons, a figure unchanged during the 1980s. These quotas allow in approximately one teaspoon of foreign ice cream per person and one pound of foreign cheese.

Table 4.4 Tariff equivalents of some U.S. agricultural quotas	
Butter	190%
American-type processed cheese	172%
Cheddar cheese	132%
Nonfat dry milk	142%

Source: U.S. International Trade Commission, based on data from 1986. There is also a beef VER with Australia and New Zealand, though it is not as restrictive as the quotas shown in the table.

Table 4.4 shows how high tariffs would have had to be to restrict imports as sharply as the quotas did.

The U.S. sugar quotas have the worst effect, because sugar cane can be grown efficiently in at least 100 countries, some of them very poor and whose alternatives for exporting other items are equally poor. Sugar protection costs these countries perhaps twice as much as the food aid they receive.

Though U.S. sugar protection is of long standing, the most recent quotas date from 1982. They are imposed by country and are based on historical performance. United States imports of five million tons in 1981 were immediately cut back to 2.8 million in 1982.

■ *DETAILS OF THE U.S. SUGAR QUOTA*

Though the sugar quota was originally announced as a temporary expedient, congress renewed them in 1985, at which time the U.S. International Trade Commission estimated that they were equivalent to a tariff of 233%. Since this renewal cut the direct subsidies paid to growers, it required even tighter quotas than before to maintain the U.S. sugar price, and in each of the four years to 1988, congress again slashed the amount of sugar allowed in. The quota cut in 1987 was 41% to about 1 million tons; the 1988 cut was 25% to just over 750,000 tons. United States imports in 1988, a quarter of the 1984 figure, were the lowest since 1875. Between 1985 and 1990, sugar was selling on world markets for between 3¢ and 15¢ per pound, depending mostly on the weather, but 21–33% lower because of the terms-of-trade effect of the U.S. protection.[1] The U.S. price, also paid for imports coming in under the quota, was 20.8¢ per pound. Even 3¢-per-pound sugar cannot beat a quota, and thus extreme price differentials are maintained. The disastrous result for exporters of sugar to the United States was a fall in their shipments by 70% from 1982–1987 and a collapse in their earnings from about $2 billion in 1981 to only $390 million in 1987.

The quotas represent a tremendous lobbying success for the 12,600 strongly united U.S. sugar producers. Clearly, numbers and their votes alone could hardly explain such success. Organization and regional influence can explain it,

---

[2] Brent Borrell and Ronald C. Duncan, "A Survey of the Costs of World Sugar Policies," *World Bank Research Observer*, Vol. 7, No. 2, July 1992, pp. 171–194. At one point the reduction in the world price caused by the U.S. sugar protection was estimated to be as much as 48%.

though—by occupation, sugar producers are the third-largest contributor of funds in American politics, behind only lawyers and doctors.[3] It is estimated that U.S. growers glean over $260,000 per grower from this system, with the biggest producers collecting the biggest benefits (an average of $1.6 million per producer in Florida). The only reason the country is not swamped with domestically produced sugar is that production costs are high. Meanwhile U.S. consumers during the 1980s paid approximately $2–3 billion more, or about $100 extra for a family of four, for their sugar. In 1991, the burden was equivalent to a 92% tax on sugar consumption.[4]

The imposition of the sugar quotas by country has the effect of freezing market shares and making it impossible for potential exporters to follow their comparative advantage. The damage to friendly economies can be as severe as if they were involved in a trade war. The Dominican Republic, for example, earned $330 million from its sugar exports to the United States in 1981, but only $65 million in 1987. St. Kitts-Nevis, a two-island country in the Caribbean, has seen half its labor force laid off because of the repeated reductions in its sugar quota. Yet a country with a share of the quota will obviously want to sell all that it is permitted to. Thus after Hurricane Hugo ruined its crop, St. Kitts-Nevis actually *imported* sugar so that it could be *exported* again to the United States. Guyana, with serious economic problems, has done the same.

In 1984 U.S. sugar producers charged that some sugar was slipping into the country by being included in other products, thus eroding the effect of the quota. The government agreed, and in 1985 it placed additional quotas (sometimes set at the zero level of imports) on sugar-based syrups, sweetened cocoa, pancake and flour mix, sauces, confections, and frozen pizzas(!). All contain sugar.

A GATT panel brought by Australia ruled the U.S. sugar quotas illegal in 1989. In a 1990 response the United States moved to a tariff-quota system, but the new system brought little real change. Any sugar imported above a national total of 1.725 million metric tons (the fiscal 1991 figure) is subject to high tariffs. The tariff is 16¢ per pound, far more than enough to exclude all imports above the quota, compared to 0.6¢ per pound on the amount under the quota. The U.S. sugar tariff was not bound, explaining why it could be raised. The quota allocations by country continued as before. If an outspoken statement may be permitted, the whole episode is scandalous, and sugar protection should be scrapped at once.

THE MAJOR VERs

The most prominent VERs cover trade in autos, steel, machine tools, and textiles and clothing.

THE AUTO VER   The United States negotiated an auto VER with Japan in 1981. It has been extended annually ever since, rising from an original 1.68 million Japanese cars per year to 2.3 million from 1985 to 1991, and then falling to 1.65 million per year for 1992 and 1993. Just as economic theory predicts, car prices rose in

---

[3] *The Economist*, December 12, 1992.

[4] *The Economist*, December 12, 1992.

the United States. A study published by the IMF estimated that the increase was $1650 (17%) between 1981 and 1984, with $620 of that due to the pure price effect of the VER. The study estimated that costs to consumers were $6.6 billion per year.[5] Of the $6.6 billion in increased cost to consumers, some large part flowed to the Japanese—estimates run from $750 million per year to $2.2 billion. A tariff, recall, would have prevented this loss of the revenue effect. Predictably the Japanese share of the market fell, from 22.6% in 1982 to 17.5% in 1984.

The Japanese reaction to the VER was interesting. They sought to maintain sales revenue not only by raising prices, but also by product upgrading, including higher power, heavier weight, air conditioning, and automatic transmissions. Thus the proportion of higher-price cars in the total of Japanese exports was greatly increased. Another response to the VER has been local production by the Japanese inside the trade barriers. (Local production also reduces transport costs, which was another reason for undertaking it.) Table 4.5 shows the location, ownership, and capacity of these plants, including the U.S./Japanese joint ventures called *transplants* in the industry's jargon.

Output of Japanese cars made in U.S. plants reached 14% of the U.S. market by 1990, compared to 18% coming in as imports. To the degree that the VER forced production in the United States that would not have occurred otherwise, the result is a decline in the efficiency of production.

An interesting aspect of the auto VER was that the U.S. government eventually ceased to demand its renewal, and the formal VER expired on March 31, 1985. But the Japanese announced that they would maintain export limits anyway, outside any agreement with the United States. Thus this one VER became

---

[5] Charles Collyns and Steven Dunaway, "The Cost of Trade Restraints," *IMF Staff Papers*, March 1987, pp. 150–175.

Table 4.5 **Japanese-owned or joint auto enterprises (ranked by capacity in 1991)**

Place	Launched	Participants	Annual production capacity
Marysville, Ohio	1982	Honda	360,000
Smyrna, Tennessee	1983	Nissan	250,000
Norman, Illinois	1988	Chrysler/Mitsubishi	240,000
Fremont, California	1984	GM/Toyota (Saturn)	240,000
Flat Rock, Michigan	1987	Mazda	240,000
Georgetown, Kentucky	1988	Toyota	218,000
East Liberty, Ohio	1989	Honda	150,000
Avon Lake, Ohio	1992	Ford/Nissan	135,000*
Lafayette, Indiana	1989	Isuzu/Subaru	120,000

Source: Ward's Automotive Yearbook, *1990 and 1992. *In 1993. In addition to engaging in joint ventures, U.S. companies now import cars built abroad and sell them under an American name. These are* captives *in the jargon.*

truly and uniquely voluntary. Economists suggested that the unilateral limits were continued first because that made good political sense in appeasing congressional protectionists, second because they could prop up the prices of Japanese cars and hence the profits made on them, and finally because swings in demand are dampened by the market guarantee.

Canada and Europe also have auto VERs with Japan. The results have been similar to those in the United States. Imports of larger, higher-priced Japanese cars have grown relative to smaller and cheaper ones. In Europe, the Japanese have moved toward production inside the protected market, with three plants in Britain and others elsewhere. Europe in an aggressive move has brought these plants under the VER. One question for Europe is what to do about exports to Europe of Japanese cars built in U.S. plants. The EC says these will not be included in the VER, but there is an obvious temptation to do so and that would be a cause for serious friction with the United States.

THE STEEL VER   The United States engineered a huge Voluntary Restraint Arrangement, as the steel VER was named, in 1982. Many types of steel were brought under the arrangement. Imports were cut sharply, from 26% of the U.S. market in 1984 to 18.2% in 1990. Eventually imports from about 30 countries were covered. Steel prices rose by 20–40%, causing distress to firms that used steel as an input. President Bush allowed the steel VER to expire in 1992, but the manufacturers responded with a major campaign to show that foreign steel was competing unfairly. They continued to urge the adoption of a new Multilateral Steel Agreement to limit imports. Europe has controlled imports of steel even more drastically, limiting them to 10% of consumption by means of a VER.

As a major steel user, the U.S. machine tool industry also pursued a successful strategy of lobbying for a VER. The machine tool VER of 1986, applying to Taiwan and Japan, was still in effect in 1993. It resulted in an initial rollback of imports from the two countries to their 1981 share of the market. James Bovard has called the machine tool restraints "America's most hare-brained trade barrier."[6] He notes that they forced Caterpillar Tractor, the second-largest U.S. exporter, to face several serious delays in obtaining the machine tools it needed for production. A major result of the VER has been a considerable increase of machine-tool production by Japanese transplant firms in the United States.

THE MULTI-FIBER ARRANGEMENT (MFA) IN TEXTILES AND CLOTHING   A mammoth global VER, the largest of them all, covering half of all world trade in textiles and clothing, is called the Multi-Fiber Arrangement (MFA). It is directed not at all countries, but only at the less developed ones and Japan. The effect is major because textiles and clothing make up 10% of world trade in manufactures, and a quarter of poor-country manufactured exports. In numerous poor countries, textiles and clothing together are the largest nonagricultural export and provider of employment. It appears that these countries have a healthy compar-

---

[6] *Wall Street Journal*, October 11, 1991.

ative advantage in the many lines of production where low labor costs are crucial and quick delivery is not important.

The MFA was first cobbled together in 1974, the name indicating that it applies to fiber made from cotton, wool, and synthetics. The fourth renewal of this arrangement, MFA IV, is due to expire on December 31, 1993, but it will probably be extended. A legal oddity, the MFA is outside GATT and contrary to its principles, but it has been negotiated under its auspices and is partly administered by it.

The MFA has now grown to a labyrinthine complexity of 69 clauses and some 20,000 annexes. It encompasses about 3000 bilateral quotas on different countries and products within the arrangement. For example, in 1991 the United States, with 147 different products subject to restraint, was involved in 38 bilateral agreements under the MFA, five more with countries outside the MFA framework, and quotas even for Guam and the Northern Marianas, which are U.S. territory. Recently the EC had about 400 quotas within 27 agreements. Nor is there respite in the smaller developed countries. Australia, Canada, and Scandinavia have relatively stringent protection as well, all involving bilateral agreements. Even the most liberal governments have joined in (excepting Japan, which enforces limits only against China, Korea, and Pakistan). The bilateral agreements freeze market shares, and unused quotas may not be transferred among countries. The enormous complexity creates uncertainties that undoubtedly have their worst effect on small suppliers with limited expertise and potential exporters who are discouraged.

Each agreement covers a wide range of individual products, with over 100 separate limits facing some countries. The MFA's mass of impenetrable detail means that even when imports would otherwise be permitted, great uncertainty faces exporters. As a flagrant example of what can happen, in 1987 a U.S. government computer error caused the publication of information stating that the quota on Chinese-made cotton coats was still open. When the error was discovered, the quota was immediately closed, and importers who acted on the incorrect information suffered serious loss when they had to renege on their contracts.

The effect on consumers is higher prices for clothing (doubled in the United States), curtains, bedding, towels, rugs, and so forth. The total bill in the mid-1980s was estimated to be $27 billion per year in the United States alone, equivalent to a 30% tariff.[7] The impact is regressive because these products take a higher proportion of the income of the poor. The worst effects are felt by the relatively powerless less-developed countries. It is believed that poor-country textile and clothing exports would be about twice as large if the MFA did not exist. (To be sure, the MFA looks better if one assumes that national protection would have been even worse without it.)

A tentative agreement to end the MFA over 10 years and move to free trade in textiles and clothing has been reached in the Uruguay Round of trade negotiations. Whether that agreement would actually be implemented was in doubt at the time of writing.

---

[7] See this book's Chapter 6, Table 6.4.

Chapter 5

Other Distortions to Trade

OBJECTIVES

Overall Objective: To demonstrate that it is not just tariffs, quotas, and VERs, but a broad array of laws, rules, subsidies, and institutions that distort trade, acting as barriers to the free import of goods and services and as stimulants to exporting.

MORE SPECIFICALLY:

- To show the techniques for measuring the distortions to trade.
- To identify and expound on these distortions—administrative protection; technical, health, safety, and environmental standards; subsidies on production, exports, and imports; border tax adjustments, and restrictions on trade in services.
- To convey a sense of the way in which firms use such laws for their own benefit.

Tariffs, quotas, and VERs are the most familiar of the distortions to trade. There are many others, however, including a wide variety of less familiar nontariff barriers to imports (NTBs), nontariff measures (NTMs, a wider term including administrative, health, safety, and environmental standards that may sometimes be used as barriers), as well as subsidies and taxes of various kinds that stimulate exports or discourage imports. Robert Baldwin's influential book written in 1970 noted the existence of hundreds of distortions of all kinds.[1] The current GATT publication, *Inventories of Non-Tariff Measures*, now attempts to catalogue them on an annual basis. They are becoming ever more visible as the average rate of tariffs drops through international negotiations.

THE EFFECTIVE RATE OF ASSISTANCE

Given the great diversity of all the various distortions to trade, a major task has been to find a method for obtaining some common denominator that allows comparisons to be made of their strength and incidence. Such attempts at measurement are relatively new, and complete agreement has not been reached on how best to carry them out. GATT is presently utilizing a method that calculates an effective rate of assistance on the individual goods in international trade.[2] The plan builds on the calculation of effective protection. It starts from the proposition that distortions to trade will affect either a price, or if a subsidy or similar measure is employed, a cost. Many distortions (the NTBs and NTMs) raise the prices of traded goods, just as do tariffs and quotas. Distortions with a subsidy element lower the prices of traded goods. Calculating an effective rate of assistance is tantamount to estimating the degree to which a barrier or subsidy changes prices.

Figure 5.1 below shows a typical calculation in the form of bar graphs. An investigator needs to know the world price of the item, the domestic price of the item including the estimated price-boosting effect of any trade distortion, the cost of inputs used to produce the item without inclusion of any subsidy element, and this same cost including any subsidy. The bar shown here on the left (Fig. 5.1a) presents no measurement problem. In this case there is no protection and no subsidy; the final price of $100 is made up of $60 in input costs and $40 of value added. The effective rate of assistance (ERA) is zero.

Figure 5.1b introduces a difference. One or more trade barriers are in place. A tariff equivalent has to be calculated. Here, because the price of the item has been raised by $20 to $120, the tariff equivalent is $20. The ERA can then be calculated. It is the total value added, including any trade distortion, minus the value added under free trade, expressed as a percentage of the value added under free trade. In the example, the total value added including the tariff equivalent of $20 is $40 + $20 = $60; while the value added under free trade, without

---

Figure 5.1 **Calculating the effective rate of assistance.** In part a, a firm pays $60 per unit for inputs and adds $40 of its own value, selling the good for $100 per unit, which is the world price. In part b, the firm has the same costs, but can sell the product for $120 because of some import restriction. The tariff equivalent of that restriction is $20. The effective rate of assistance is the tariff equivalent compared to the value added (under free trade): $(60 - 40)/40 = 50\%$.

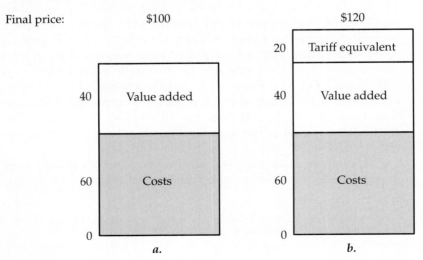

Figure 5.1 (continued) **Allowing for subsidies and input taxes in calculating the ERA.**
Figure 5.1c shows not only a higher price, but a subsidy of $10 per unit on the costs of
inputs. The ERA must accordingly compare both those items with the free-trade value
added: (70 − 40)/40 = 75%. Figure 5.1d shows domestic producers hampered by a tax
on inputs equivalent to $10 per unit, but aided by import restrictions equivalent to $20
per unit. ERA is thus (50 − 40)/40 = 25%.

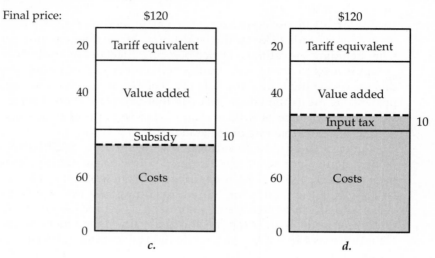

inclusion of the distortion, is $40. The ERA would thus be (60 − 40)/40 = 50%.
This method is related to the one we used to calculate the effective tariff on
strung pearls in the last chapter.

The next case (Fig. 5.1c) introduces greater complexity in the form of an
input subsidy, or some measure equivalent to a subsidy, that reduces input prices
by $10. We assume that measures with a tariff equivalent of $20 are still in place,
and that the final output is still sold for $120.[*] In this example, the ERA now
amounts to the value added including the effects of the distortions, here the free
trade value added plus the tariff equivalent plus the effect of the subsidy, all of
that expressed as a percentage of the free trade value added, or (70 − 40)/40 =
75%. Finally, Fig. 5.1d shows taxes, tariffs, or other NTBs on *inputs* giving a tariff
equivalent of $10, along with an unchanged output tariff equivalent of $20 and
final price of $120. In this case, the ERA is less; the producer is penalized by
the taxation of inputs. The total distortion is only $10; the complete calculation is
(50 − 40)/40 = 25%.

Through methods such as these, economists work to find acceptable ways to
assess the effects and intensities of distortions to trade. The method shown is not

---

[*] If the subsidy reduces the price of the final output, the example must be altered accordingly. We
leave it to the reader to work through such an example.

the only one available, but it is understandable and results in a single percentage figure that can be used to make comparisons.

Of the hundreds of different sorts of existing distortions to trade, many have little effect on trade flows and can therefore be safely ignored here. Some, however, are an important part of the international economic environment and warrant considerable description. Blessedly, with the exception of subsidies they do not require much additional economic analysis.

ADMINISTRATIVE PROTECTION

Around the world, most countries have adopted certain laws and regulations that one way or another serve to protect the domestic market against imports. In this section we examine a number of cases of administrative protection that do not appear to involve technical, health, safety, or environmental considerations (which cases we treat later in the chapter). Many of these measures can come very close to outright harassment of trading partners.

Perhaps most widespread and least objectionable of the administrative measures are the mark-of-origin requirements. Under these, imports must have a label announcing where the good was made, as in the familiar "Made in USA," "Made in Canada," "Made in the Republic of Korea," "Made in Singapore." These labels presumably give some useful information, but they are also presumably intended to stir patriotic feelings, allow citizens to bypass products from foreign parts, and promote the consumption of goods made at home. Certainly the very first such requirement, adopted by Britain in the 1890s, had this effect. It revealed a large amount of German imports and alarmed the British public, even though the imports were simply the counterpart of the very high level of British exports of the time. At the least, requiring an import to be printed or stamped with "Made in Spain," "Hecho en España," "Fabriqué en Espagne," and so on can increase the cost of goods substantially.

Many administrative regulations appear to serve clear protectionist purposes. France's administrative treatment of Japanese cars, in effect since 1977, shows the degree to which such policies can be carried. To limit the Japanese to a market share of 2% or less, the French government first altered the ceiling on permitted imports from yearly to monthly, making compliance more difficult. Next, the ministry in charge of issuing certificates of approval for new models started to delay issuance, including in the delay models to which the changes had only been cosmetic. Approval that formerly took two months slowed rapidly to six months or more; in effect customs had trapped thousands of Japanese cars on the docks by following the rules exactly. In the early 1980s, Canadian customs adopted the same general approach, checking every Japanese car at Vancouver in order to pry from the Japanese a "voluntary" agreement to limit exports. Another Canadian regulation concerns beer sales. Most provinces require that foreign beer be sold only in government-owned stores while Canadian beer can

also be sold in private retail outlets. The practice seems blatantly protectionist.*
More generally, soft drink containers must be of different sizes in different
provinces, and Quebec will not allow some products to be sold in nonmetric containers.

The Brazilians have also become adept at erecting administrative barriers.
Their Operation Tortoise was a slowdown by customs that very effectively
blocked imports through long delays at the ports. Taiwan has held up imports
while a large, often indeterminate, number of approvals are affixed to the shipping documents. Officials are said to show great zeal in ferreting out minor discrepancies in documents, which when found cause long delays.

Perhaps the most famous of all the cases of administrative protection was the
treatment meted out by the French to Japanese videocassette recorders, for reasons still in part uncertain but probably to force the hapless (but efficient)
Japanese exporters to agree to a VER. The French authorities ordered in 1982 that
all VCRs entering the Republic must come to the customs station at Poitiers,
near Tours. Poitiers' customs house is tiny, with a staff of four later enlarged to
eight. Of high significance, it has very few berths for ships—none, in fact,
because Poitiers is far inland! It does, however, have plenty of parking for the
bonded trucks in which the VCRs were transferred from the ports. At the same
time, the French announced that all documents covering trade had to be in
French (at the start of the 1980s, 37% were in English and German). All documentation was carefully examined, each container was opened, and serial numbers were checked. Some machines were taken apart to ascertain whether they
had in fact been built in Japan and not somewhere else. The instructions were
examined to ensure that they were in French. Some 64,000 VCRs had cleared customs per month before the new rules; that number fell to less than 10,000, with
the excess marooned for months in bonded warehouses at Poitiers.

The French government eventually lifted the Poitiers restrictions in exchange
for a tight VER and a decision by Japanese Victor to produce some machines in
France. (Elsewhere in Europe, outright quotas were used for the same end.) In
1985, as part of the VER, Japan was forced to accept a 28% reduction in its VCR
exports. Poitiers-type policies need not be implemented every day. Exporters are
likely to remember for a long time an impact as stunning as this was.

GOVERNMENT BUYING POLICIES

Many countries give limited or total preference to domestic producers where
government purchases are concerned.[3] Though it is difficult to gather informa-

---

* The United States took a case to GATT on the issue, and Canada received an adverse ruling in
1988. Canada agreed to halt the practice by the end of 1993, but, peeved, it made its own complaint
to GATT about the United States. It charged that U.S. state laws give excise tax breaks for instate
breweries, and that these instate breweries don't have to sell through wholesalers as is required in
most states for out-of-state beer. Canada won its case, and the U.S. federal government has agreed
to work with the states to eliminate the tax treatment problems. Tit-for-tat, as they say.

tion on such practices, they are pervasive. Federal and national governments, states (in the United States, Germany, Australia), provinces (in Canada, Italy), counties (in the United States, Great Britain), departments (in France), cities, wards, and even school boards frequently have rules that require preferential buying.* The procedures for announcing contracts, bidding, and finally drawing up agreements tend to favor insiders, mostly nationals, because the instructions are deliberately unclear, complex, and difficult for outsiders to follow. As noted in Chapter 1, the public sector of any modern economy is large, so the overall impact of preferential government buying has thus probably intensified greatly over the past two or three decades.

U.S. PREFERENCES   An excellent example of protection through the use of preferential buying policies is the U.S. federal government's Buy American Act dating from 1933. The present wording of the Buy American Act requires the federal government to place contracts with U.S. firms rather than with foreigners whenever the U.S. price does not exceed that of the import by more than 6%, or 12% in depressed areas of high unemployment, or 50% for goods purchased by the Department of Defense. Thus the lonely American visiting the Munich PX of an American army base finds California and New York wine in the heartland of Riesling and Rheinwein, and Budweiser instead of Lowenbrau. True, lots of Gallo and Bud would be there anyway as a matter of taste, but the Buy American Act requires it.

The Buy American Act was quietly extended by congress in 1982 for steel in U.S. highway and bridge construction and repair. This requirement is apparently worth about a million tons of steel annually for American industry. In 1985, congress ordered the TVA and other federal power agencies to let contracts for heavy-duty electrical equipment only within the United States, as long as the cost disadvantage in doing so was no greater than 25%. Also in 1985, congress required that purchases for the U.S. stockpile of strategic commodities be made when possible within the country. Finally, in 1988 the buying rules were altered to allow for retaliation against countries whose governments discriminate in their purchases.

A similar kind of law applies to ocean freight. The Ship American Act was applied first to military cargo in 1904. It has been widely extended, now requiring that three quarters of all U.S. government cargoes (foreign aid, subsidized grain, oil for the U.S. strategic reserve), and *all* military cargoes must go in U.S.-flag ships.[4] The charges on these shipments are roughly twice as much as on foreign-flag ships. The price per ton-mile for U.S.-flag tankers shipping oil for the U.S. Strategic Petroleum Reserve is about four times more than the charter price for tankers at international rates. Presently one third of the revenue of U.S. shipping companies exists only because of these ship-american provisions.

---

*Note that even if one were to track down every example of preferential legislation, the full magnitude of the problem would still not be exposed because officials and agencies frequently buy at home through habit even when not required to do so.

EUROPEAN PREFERENCES   Historically, government buying policies with a protective intent have also been very common, and even more sternly enforced, in Europe. For many years, few government contracts of any kind were put out to open bidding—on the order of only 2%, with only about half of the contracts won by foreign firms. Mostly governments and publicly owned firms have invited bids only from domestic concerns, or have invited contract offers just a short time before they were awarded. Very little information was provided with the offer, so that insiders had a distinct advantage in bidding. The problem has been especially severe in the less visible realm of local governments, school boards, and the like. A new EC rule imposed in 1992 requires government-owned telephone and electric companies to give a 3% price preference to EC suppliers of telecommunications and power generating equipment. The buying policies of the EC governments are estimated to have raised procurement costs (that is, subsidize) domestic firms by about 10%.[5]

JAPANESE PREFERENCES   In Japan, for decades *single tendering* was the rule, meaning that government would approach a single supplier with a contract proposal, there being no competitive bidding process. As late as 1983, several years after negotiations had been in progress to open up Japanese bidding to foreign firms, nearly 40% of government contracts were still single tenders.

The actions of the Japanese communications monopoly NTT (Nippon Telephone & Telegraph) are celebrated in this field and show the tangled complications that preferential treatment can involve. Only in 1981 were foreign firms allowed to bid for NTT contracts at all, but even so foreigners faced severe problems. Originally NTT released information on its technical requirements only in the Japanese language; sometimes the requirements were as thick as a five-inch book. The replies had to be in Japanese as well. Translating the documents was a lengthy and costly process. After a long period of foreign protest, these rules were eventually relaxed.

Japan resisted for several years the opening of its government market for supercomputers and satellites. That, too, was achieved after substantial U.S. pressure in 1990. These episodes reflect a pattern: Foreigners, particularly Americans, discover that a market is closed. Heavy pressure is brought on the Japanese government to open the market, usually involving threats of trade retaliation. The Japanese resist, and then give in, before the foreigners find another closed market to attack.

THE GATT PROCUREMENT CODE   A GATT code on government procurement, under negotiation for several years, went into effect in 1981. The signers of the code agreed to provide open procurement through competitive bidding for any government purchases valued above about $180,000, and at least 40 days' notice of the bidding.

A great deal of procurement is still, however, outside the code. Many countries have not agreed to it. Even for signatories, most individual government purchases are too small to qualify for inclusion. Thus when the code was implemented, it covered only about $32 billion worth of government purchases, out of a total world figure of about $130 billion.* Several countries have deliberately kept their contracts small so as to circumvent the regulations. France, for example, publicly announced that it would "buy French" in 14 sectors and thereupon broke up into small packages contracts whose value exceeded the GATT threshold. The Japanese have also split contracts into smaller units to avoid application of the code. To control such behavior, the United States advocates lowering the threshold amount to half its present level.

Several sorts of government purchases are explicitly excluded from the code. For example, certain EC government utilities such as post offices and telephones are not covered because of an earlier compromise. The United States wants to see them included. Other discussions are considering expanding the code to services, which are not now covered.

■ *THE STRUGGLE OVER PUBLIC CONSTRUCTION*

Another major exception to the code is construction, an issue on which the Japanese have been especially protective. The main problem was a rule that foreign firms had to have contracting experience in Japan to qualify as bidders, but because no contracts were ever issued to foreign firms, obtaining such experience was completely impossible. As a result not one U.S. company had won a major construction contract in Japan since the mid-1960s. The United States thereupon demanded that the contracting for new Japanese government projects, in particular the giant Kansai (Osaka) airport and the Haneda (Tokyo) airport extension, be opened to foreign contractors.

After long negotiations, the Japanese government in the end yielded somewhat, with major agreements in 1988 and 1991 naming the projects in which U.S. firms could participate (17 under the 1988 agreement, 23 more in 1991).[6] The requirement of previous Japanese experience was withdrawn in 1988. The dispute simmered on over private subcontractors that might not cooperate, but under the 1991 agreement the Japanese government promised to police bid-rigging (called *dango* and involving the clandestine rotation of winning bids) by private contractors. Though unofficial, such rigging does occur. There are now a dispute settlement mechanism and an annual review, showing considerable willingness by the Japanese to compromise. Yet many Japanese public works projects remain closed. In 1993, the struggle escalated once again, with Mickey Kantor, President Clinton's trade representative, threatening punitive measures unless Japan opened more of its construction to foreign firms. Japan spoke of retaliation. In general, large U.S. contracting firms do not want further sanctions because they are doing relatively well, and fear the retaliation, while small and medium-size firms do want them.

---

* U.S. government purchases covered by the code amounted to about $12 billion at the time of enactment, compared to $20 billion for the rest of the world. U.S. acceptance of the code's terms was qualified, with preferences staying on for defense contracts, for purchases from small and minority businesses, and for purchases from Japan where full Japanese compliance with the code has not yet occurred.

The United States has its own problem area, involving state, municipal, and private procurement, which is not covered by the code. A large number of U.S. states (37 in the mid-1980s) have their own Buy American laws. There is a suspicion that these laws are often not enforced very vigorously, but it is striking how few states are without them. That local governments do the same thing, or try to, was emphasized in 1992 by the action of the town of Greece, New York. Its local government achieved momentary fame when it patriotically chose a John Deere earth mover priced at $55,000 instead of a Komatsu at $40,000, only to discover that the Deere was made in Japan—except the motor, made in Des Moines—while the Komatsu was made in Illinois. The EC argues vigorously that governments below the U.S. federal level, especially the states, should be brought under the code. The EC also wants to include the U.S. "Baby Bell" phone companies, which are private but have a government-granted monopoly.

These questions heated up in February 1993, when the United States announced it would protest the new EC Buy European rules by barring European companies from U.S. government contracts for telecommunications and power generating equipment and some service contracts. It was another aggressive move by Mickey Kantor, the U.S. trade representative, a stronger move than Kantor's staff had recommended. The EC one day later threatened to retaliate by raising its preferences above the present 3%—5, 6, or 7% was mentioned. Clearly the GATT code had not yet brought peace to the area of government procurement.

LAWS REQUIRING PRIVATE FIRMS TO BUY NATIONAL

Occasionally even private firms are required to buy goods and services produced at home. In the United States the relatively obscure Jones Act of 1920 requires that all ships used in domestic trade (that is, in traffic between American ports) must be built in U.S. shipyards, manned by American crews, and owned and registered in the United States. Construction costs for U.S.-flag shipping are high, perhaps three times more than for ships built in a Japanese or Korean yard. Operating costs are even higher, with an American seaman's wage six times that of a Taiwanese, for example. Thus the Jones Act adds about $1 billion annually to U.S. transport costs, according to a 1986 estimate. Because of it, heavy goods that could be shipped to the West Coast, such as steel from Pennsylvania, cannot compete with Japanese or Korean steel, while West Coast lumber cannot compete with Canadian lumber in the U.S. Northeast. The allied Passenger Services Act of 1886 is a Jones Act for cruise ships, explaining why foreign cruise ships cannot take you from Bar Harbor to New York, and why Seattle has hardly any cruise ship traffic to Alaska while Vancouver in British Columbia has many sailings. United States maritime interests have been so generous in their support of these laws that "three of the past five chairmen of the House Merchant Marine Subcommittee have been indicted for criminal links to the maritime industry.... (A fourth chairman was indicted for other reasons.)"[7]

Legislation concerning *cabotage*, carriage within a nation's waters, is common around the world. For example, Australia has its own version of the Jones Act. Because of this, it costs more to ship a ton of freight from Melbourne to Fremantle than it does to ship the same ton from Melbourne to California!

In Canada another type of requirement can be found at the provincial level. Many provinces have their own Buy Provincial acts controlling private as well as public buyers. An oil company in Alberta cannot even have some items brought in from neighboring British Columbia and may have to restrict its hiring to provincial residents. Similarly, the province-owned telephone companies are required to give preference to local manufacturers, meaning that most provinces have a wire and cable producer. While restricting domestic trade, such laws also restrict international trade. (Barriers to interstate trade in the United States would, of course, be unconstitutional.)

DOMESTIC CONTENT LEGISLATION

Domestic (or local) content legislation requires a certain proportion of domestic inputs to be contained in imported products if a penalty is to be avoided. Worldwide, such laws are relatively common, even though they are illegal under Article III of GATT, which prohibits domestic content requirements. Among the several countries that apply them to automobile production are Australia, with an 85% requirement, South Africa 66%, the Scandinavian countries 60%, Mexico 36%, and Spain 55%. The EC has adopted domestic content requirements of 35–45% for many electronic products and for ball bearings; integrated circuits must be "diffused" (that is, given their memories) in Europe or heavy duties apply. Mexico's economy is widely affected by such laws. Many of the nearly 30 other countries with domestic content requirements are not industrialized, however, and the laws are usually not designed to protect a long-established industry.

In the United States, local content bills have received strong support from the United Auto Workers, and the AFL-CIO now (1993) agrees. Though none has been enacted, one passed the House in 1982 and again in 1983. That bill would have established a sliding scale. For the first 100,000 cars sold, the company making them would have to ensure that they were 10% American made, 20% for 200,000, and up to 90% for over 900,000 cars. When the Congressional Budget Office analyzed the effects of the proposed U.S. law, its predictions were doleful, suggesting large net losses for the U.S. economy.* In effect, the bill was a ploy by

---

* The CBO calculated that a gross gain of 100,000 jobs would result, 30,000 in the car industry plus 70,000 among supplier industries. But the CBO also calculated that the job gain would be more than offset by 173,000 jobs lost in exporting because of expected foreign retaliation, plus job losses of 7000 to 10,000 at the ports and at dealerships handling imports. Even were there to be no retaliation at all, the CBO calculated that the higher car prices resulting from the legislation, expected to be about 10% more, would mean each job created would cost the consuming public $196,000 per job per year, an extremely high figure.

domestic labor to import foreign entrepreneurs (who would be forced to establish domestic production to avoid the law) rather than foreign products.

The U.S. car producers, incidentally, have generally lobbied *against* domestic content legislation. Presumably they have done so because these laws would not protect them against foreign carmakers setting up inside the national market. Also, the carmakers have strong links abroad, with arrangements such as GM and Isuzu, GM and Toyota, Ford and Mazda, Chrysler and Mitsubishi, and the like, which lead to large-scale imports by the American companies. It must be admitted, however, that the effects of a local content law might be obtained even in the absence of actual legislation. The bullying over how many workers Japanese plants in the United States employ, or what proportion of U.S.-made parts they utilize, might in the end give the same effect.

Analytically, domestic content legislation would be expected to increase the demand for domestic inputs and raise the cost of the final output. It is not, however, easy to predict the overall outcome, and aside from the U.S. auto case, there have been few detailed studies. Pressure for such laws appears to be strongest when barriers to entry make the expansion of production difficult, for then economic rents are more likely to accrue to the firms and factors providing the local content.[8] Most economists, along with recent U.S. presidents, oppose the idea.

TECHNICAL, HEALTH, SAFETY, AND ENVIRONMENTAL STANDARDS

The imposition of standards to insure technical uniformity, a minimum degree of health and safety, and essential protection for the environment is reasonable public policy. Many such standards are obviously desirable in their own right: barriers to importing fruits, plants, and animals as a safeguard against the spread of disease; hygienic requirements in food production; and safety standards for vehicles and other machinery. Even though technical, health, and safety regulations are not border barriers, being enforced on all producers, not just foreigners, the anecdotal evidence is legion that they sometimes go further, toward bias against imports, or toward their complete exclusion. It is not always easy to separate a genuine public purpose from a protectionist intent.[9]

Even at their most justifiable, the standards are fully capable of distorting trade. Long-established differences in the threading of nuts (a metric or non-metric pitch, clockwise or counterclockwise rotation), pole instead of knife-type electrical connections, 110 volts or 220, steering wheels on the left rather than the right, and dissimilar railway gauges give rise to understandable, reasonable, but different national standards. Though innocent enough, such regulations are often quite inconvenient for exporters.

The problem is most serious in agriculture and forestry, where the outcome moves beyond inconvenience toward exclusion. The United Nations has noted that Latin American exports are subject to almost 400 U.S. trade barriers related to standards; about 100 similar Japanese barriers exist, along with some 300 erected by the EC. Many fruits, plants, woods, and meats are excluded. These regulations may sound wholly reasonable in their aim to prevent the spread of plant and animal diseases such as oak wilt or foot-and-mouth disease. But when the number of restrictions is so large, the suspicion grows that some of them are difficult to justify and mainly protective in intent. For example, outbreaks of foot-and-mouth disease in remote parts of Argentina have been followed by embargoes on meat imports from all areas of that country. The U.S. grading requirements for tomatoes may possibly make choice easier for consumers, but one effective result is to discriminate against tomatoes imported from Mexico. Mexican avocados are banned because they may carry the avocado seed weevil and seed moth. This sounds prudent, until it is learned that Mexican avocados are much cheaper and could be sent with complete safety—if only the law allowed it—to the lucrative market in the northeastern states.

The familiar U.S. and Canadian safety standards on automobiles (and also on tractors and electrical equipment), justifiable as they may be, effectively prevent the importation of many foreign makes and models. Bringing cars into conformity can be prohibitively expensive for companies whose North American markets are small. Even fuel efficiency standards can have a protective design. U.S. automakers want any such law to boost the required miles per gallon by the same percentage for all models. That would be hard for the Japanese to meet because their cars already are more fuel efficient. In turn the Japanese would prefer a miles-per-gallon target, which would be harder for American manufacturers to attain. Television is another area where standards problems are arising. The U.S. FCC recently ruled that the Japanese standards for high-definition television sets will not be approved by the United States because that would make obsolete many U.S. TVs. Standards issues can arise anywhere: In Switzerland, for example, the standard size for some kitchen appliances is five centimeters less than the standard in the rest of Europe. Prices for these small Swiss washers, dryers, and dishwashers are, not surprisingly given the diseconomies of scale, high, 45% above the European average.[10]

Table 5.1 presents some of the outstanding cases involving technical, health, and safety standards during recent years. (Many of these cases have now been solved, incidentally.) They are just the tip of the iceberg; thousands of similar measures never get any publicity.

It is not just the rich variety of such measures that gives economists, or in any case the authors, suspicions that some of the regulations are protectionist in intent. Frequent changes in the rules, and apparently tiny modifications that suddenly exclude imports, would seem to be a tell-tale.

Some of the disputes on technical, health, and safety matters involve complex questions that amount to more than sheer protectionism. The outstanding issues at present include who should make the decisions on health and safety, and the degree to which the decisions ought to be based on firm scientific evidence rather than public opinion. The next section outlines the scope of this debate, which is not at all settled.

Table 5.1   **Noteworthy recent uses of standards to block trade**

Product	Exported from	Exported to	Barrier	Comment
Poultry	United States	EC	Special chilling required	Most EC producers already used the required method; U.S. producers did not
Snails	Everywhere	France	Rigorous veterinary checks	Only one customs post with proper equipment in Jura region where the industry was located, and that one off the beaten track
Small lobsters	Canada	United States	Complete ban on imports	Said to promote conservation; implied Canadian incompetence to manage their lobster beds
Meat	World	United States	Closer inspection	Resulted in ban on imports from 14 countries, some in Europe where no charges of unsafe or unsanitary practice were made
Meat	United States	EC	Ban on wood in packing houses	No evidence that use of wood is unsafe
Meat	United States	EC	Ban on beef and pork imports	Poor hygiene claimed. U.S. said its standards were equivalent; bills in congress to ban EC meat
Meat	Canada	United States	Some states put embargo on pork	Dubious claim that Canadian hogs were fed with prohibited chemicals
Forklift trucks	Germany	France	Brake pedals must be on left, battery must be 60 volt	German forklifts had pedal on right and 50-volt battery
Scotch, bourbon	U.S., Britain	France	Advertising banned	No ban on cognac or wine ads
Light beer	Everywhere	Italy	Complete ban on sale	Protects wine industry
Hammers	Britain	Germany	Had to be stamped with maker's name	Justified because hammers are "dangerous goods"

Product	Exported from	Exported to	Barrier	Comment
Nonfizzy mineral water	Everywhere	Germany	Complete ban on sale	Germany argued that the bubbles in the fizzy kind (which German firms specialize in) kill bacteria
Margarine	Everywhere	Belgium	Royal decree that it be packaged as cubes	Imported margarine was packaged in sticks or as round balls
Cars	Everywhere	Japan	Mirrors had to be specially designed	Large expense for firms that sold only a few hundred cars in Japan
Telecom equipment	Everywhere	Japan	Strict standards for tying into local grid	Kept Nippon Telephone & Telegraph from buying imported equipment
Tennis balls	United States	Japan	Imports from Dunlop stopped	Safety concern about high pressure in cans
Metal bats	United States	Japan	Could not obtain safety certification	Dangerous to softball and baseball players

WHO MAKES THE DECISIONS? HOW STRONG MUST THE EVIDENCE BE?

The greatest acrimony on health and safety issues used to involve Japanese test procedures. Until 1983, the Japanese had a difficult test procedure for many goods, wherein imports had to be tested and shown to meet legal standards on a shipment-by-shipment basis. Though "type approval" was permitted for domestic production, it was not allowed for many imported goods. Even when it was, the approval had to be obtained again whenever a change in ownership (a merger in America, for example) occurred. The Japanese were also unwilling to accept foreign test data, insisting that the tests be done in Japan by the relevant domestic agency or trade group. That led to the exclusion of some imported cars until their mirrors were redesigned, and the ban on Dunlop tennis balls, metal baseball bats, and much telecommunications equipment, all noted in the table above. Many electrical appliances and drugs for animals could not be imported because foreign safety tests were unacceptable.

Eventually all these rules were liberalized, and the Japanese have made it possible to get type approval for far more goods. For some years, however, Japanese officials still had to visit a U.S. or other foreign plant for an inspection, and this was costly. Foreigners also feared leaks of privileged information about products or processes, hence the position taken by the United States that Japan should accept U.S. test data. Finally, in 1986, the Japanese yielded almost completely on this issue, agreeing that most U.S. factories could be visited by U.S. testing bodies, and also that U.S. test data could be used. Even though relations with the Japanese have improved on this issue, disputes on who should do the testing still plague trade relations. The United States would like to see changes in Japanese fire-safety codes, which often ban the use of wood, much of which is a U.S. export. United States-European Community disputes commonly erupt in this area.

SCIENCE VERSUS PUBLIC OPINION   The question of whether science should supersede public opinion has grown into a major dispute between the United States and the EC over the use of growth hormones.[11] GATT permits individual countries to enforce bans where there is a health risk, such as when pesticides are found in food. A question arises when a ban is not based on scientific evidence and acts to exclude imports.

As an opening salvo, in 1988 the EC banned the sale of meat treated with growth hormones. About four fifths of U.S. beef production is so treated, and the same hormones are utilized in every major meat-producing country outside of Europe. No scientific evidence exists to show that growth hormones do any harm at the doses employed, and the ban applies even if no traces of the hormone can be detected by scientific means. (In 1980, Italian farmers marketed meat with very high hormone concentrations that did cause a health problem. That is a major reason why European consumers now object to *all* hormones in meat.)

The EC would not agree to submit the dispute to an international panel of scientists, presumably because it believed it would not win—an international commission sponsored by the U.N.'s Food and Agricultural Organization had already recommended against any bans because no hazard exists, and EC scientific bodies have themselves reached the same conclusion. In the face of U.S. threats to retaliate against 30 types of food imported from Europe, the EC postponed application of the ban until January 1, 1989. On that date, however, the ban was actually imposed and U.S. retaliation followed immediately. The EC pledged to strike back, and the United States countered with a promise for yet further action.[*]

Rather horrified at the rapid escalation, the politicians held back, and at the time of this writing a compromise was being pursued. Several western states have said they would agree to certify meat as hormone free; EC inspectors would certify the feedlots (but that is going very slowly); the U.S. would relax its sanctions to the extent that its exports rise. A fundamental problem remains, however, because the compromise affects only so-called real meat, which makes up just 30% of U.S. meat exports to the EC. The large remainder of the market is offal, the heart, liver, tongue, brains, and so forth, which are much desired in Europe but not in the United States. This market is unaffected by the new developments.

Both sides in this case believe their position is the correct one. The United States claims that the action is nothing more than thinly veiled protectionism. It believes the issue is whether growth hormones are dangerous, and demands sound scientific evidence that this is the case. If the evidence is that they are *not* dangerous, then consumers can decide for themselves what sort of meat they want to buy. It claims that the EC's real concern is economic: that growth hormones will bring lower prices and thereby be costly for Europe's farm support programs. The EC insists that it is within its rights because its citizens dislike growth hormones. It believes the issue is whether a health standard that the public wants can be adopted if the rule does not discriminate against imports, and if it does not contravene any trade rules. It argues that GATT law does permit the regulation of processing. The EC suggests this is the same logic used by the United States when it adopted Prohibition in the 1920s, or by the many current national laws against heroin, cocaine, and marijuana.[**] It also points out that its other main suppliers (Argentina, Australia, Brazil, and New Zealand) have complied with the law. There the issue stands. Efforts to resolve this dispute have so far been unsuccessful.

---

[*] The amount of U.S. meat involved was about 12% of U.S. beef exports, worth $100 million per year. That was the total of EC exports on which the United States retaliated with 100% tariffs. The products hit with the retaliatory U.S. duties included canned hams, tomatoes, beef, instant coffee, and some wines and fruit juice. The EC threatened to counter against American canned corn, dried fruit, honey, and walnuts, together worth about $100 million, but has not yet done so. The further U.S. action in reply might include invoking a 1988 law that would allow the United States to prohibit meat imports from countries that ban U.S. meat where no health risk exists. The United States has also demanded proof that the EC prohibition is being fully enforced at home. Some European farmers are said to be illegally injecting their meat with black-market growth hormones prohibited under U.S. law.

[**] EC negotiators point out that the United States has laws against the importation of unbaked cheeses made from unpasteurized milk, but that *they* have never demanded proof from a scientific commission that such cheeses are dangerous.

All the cases discussed in this section reflect the unexpected difficulties that may lie in wait for an unwary exporter. Even when a solution is found, an exporter cannot know what the next barrier will be, or where it might arise. Indeed they *are* spreading, as developing countries begin to adopt their own rules, which are sometimes based on those enforced in their major developed-country trading partners. A GATT Standards Code was adopted in 1980. Reflecting the seriousness of this form of protection, that code has more members than any other (42), but even so it has done little to eliminate or even to control the problem. New GATT rules on testing, inspection, and certification are sorely needed.

TRADE BARRIERS BASED ON ENVIRONMENTAL CONCERNS

Trade barriers based on environmental concerns may seem like a new area for discussion, but actually they are not.[12] International treaties that exclude some imports for environmental reasons date back to the beginning of the century. A white phosphorous match import ban was agreed on in 1906 (the white phosphorus caused a loathsome occupational disease), while regulations against sealing and the hunting of sea otters date from 1911. Under GATT's Article XX, international agreements can "protect human, animal or plant life or health" so long as they are not a "disguised restriction on international trade" and the regulations apply to domestic producers as well as foreign ones. Examples of international action include the Convention on Trade in Endangered Species (CITES), which dates from 1975. CITES banned the trade in ivory, rhinoceros horn, rare turtle shells, and other animal products where extinction is an issue, and instituted a permit system for trade in endangered species. A 1986 treaty stopped commercial whaling. The Montreal Convention of 1987 prohibited imports of ozone-killing CFCs (chlorofluorocarbons), and from 1993 the import of products containing CFCs is excluded from countries that have not ratified the treaty. The Montreal Convention countries are now also considering a ban to take effect in 1995 on imports of goods produced with, though not containing, CFCs. A Basel Convention on movements of hazardous waste was signed in 1989, and came into force in 1992. That convention bans waste shipments to nonsignatory countries.

WHAT IF ONE COUNTRY TRIES TO IMPOSE ITS ENVIRONMENTAL LAWS ON ANOTHER?   The legal situation can become difficult when just one country tries to make other countries follow its own environmental bans. A July 1991 U.S. law banned the importation of fish from countries that allow large-scale driftnet fishing, then including France, Japan, Mexico, North and South Korea, Taiwan, Vanuatu, and Venezuela. Driftnet fishing for tuna kills dolphins and other marine life. The law was not being enforced until the Earth Island Institute of California won a court decision requiring the government to enforce it. Mexico thereupon objected and took a case to GATT. A GATT panel found in its favor, stating that "in principle it is not possible under GATT's rules to make access to one's own market dependent on the domestic environmental policies of the exporting country."[13] Environmentalists were outraged. (People are still free to organize boycotts of tuna, by the way.)*

POSSIBLE DANGERS FROM A GREENING OF TRADE LAW   More heat is certain to be generated on the question of trade barriers for environmental purposes. Many "Greens" appear to favor trade restrictions as a way to force other countries to support environmental agreements. For example, a ban on wood imported from countries that do not use sustainable logging practices would force them to do so, and halt the forest destruction that is a cause of global warming. Trade barriers also avoid the problem that arises when imports involving environmental harm reduce the profits of "clean" domestic firms and make it harder for them to conform to the law.

■ *THE POLLUTION-HAVEN HYPOTHESIS*

A pollution-haven hypothesis has arisen, suggesting that unless something is done dirty industries will move to poor countries. Their poverty will keep them from protecting their environment, which will give them a comparative advantage in industries that pollute. To stop this development, inhibiting their trade may appear easier politically than bribing them or working out international quotas would be.

Yet little hard data exist to show that poor countries are becoming a haven for polluting industries. The costs of controlling pollution in the rich countries have not been large enough to make much of a difference. Abatement costs have been only 0.5% of output on average for U.S. industries (1988), and 3% for the dirtiest industries, not enough to offset other factors such as labor costs. When multinational firms establish themselves in less developed countries, they often use the same technology as at home; that is cheaper than developing new technologies. In any case multinationals are not the biggest polluters. These are usually small companies. Furthermore, political and economic uncertainties in the LDCs have discouraged investment of all kinds. No significant movement of polluting industries to poor countries has set in as yet. Anecdotal evidence such as U.S. furniture makers moving to Mexico to avoid California's air quality laws, and other movements by asbestos, dye, and pesticide producers, seems quite limited at present. No doubt, however, potential does exist that polluting industries will move to more hospitable countries in order to escape environmental regulation.[14]

---

* The driftnet fishing law also bans imports from third countries that have bought the tuna from the country that did the fishing. Imports of tuna from Thailand have recently been banned under this provision. In March 1992, Mexico, Venezuela, and the United States agreed to a five-year moratorium on the use of purse nets in tuna fishing. Another U.S. law protects sea turtles from shrimp fishermen. About 80 countries face an embargo on their exports to the United States of several different fish products if they do not adopt turtle excluder devices on the nets carried by their trawlers. Japan, which imports considerable amounts of sea turtle shells, has been singled out for attention. Similar threats are being made against countries including Iceland and Norway that have indicated they might resume whaling. Under its new laws the United States would be compelled to impose a trade ban on fish imports from them, and perhaps on countries that import whale products from these two countries.

There is substantial danger that environmental clauses in trade laws could play into the hands of protectionists, ending up costing the public more than the benefits they deliver. Where are the limits in discriminating against a production process?[15] You could take action if the pollution impinges on your country, or on the oceans, or in the atmosphere, or wholly in another country (if, for example, the Central African Republic failed to preserve okapis and gorillas). What about when a process is polluting but no product is imported, as with electricity generation? Can you then use trade barriers against products that use electricity in their manufacture? Obviously, a great door could swing closed in world trade if the protectionists and environmentalists could persuade each other to ally on these issues. Environmentalists also are pushing for precautionary barriers against goods that *might* cause harm.

Several examples of blatant protectionism under the guise of saving the environment have already come to light. Ontario, for example, put a ten-cent environmental tax on aluminum beer cans (most imports from the United States are in cans), but exempted the bottles favored by Ontario's own breweries. Similarly Germany put a deposit on plastic bottles (often imported) but not the glass bottles preferred by Germany's own bottlers. Shopkeepers often did not want to go to the trouble of dealing with the imported plastics. (Under pressure this law was modified.) Germany is also considering laws that would require carmakers to recycle their cars when they are junked. Because of the logistics involved, recycling would be much harder on Japanese importers than it would be on EC producers. The Japanese would either have to shift their carmaking to Germany or ship their junk all the way back to Japan. The United States banned tuna imports from Canada in order to conserve the species, but somehow neglected to limit its own tuna catch. Not to be behindhand, Canada limited exports of herring and salmon, again for conservation, but failed to put limits on its own fishing industry. In both cases GATT found that the restrictions were not meant for conservation, but were protectionist. Thailand seemed to be taking a principled stand when it recently banned cigarette imports in the name of good health. A GATT panel called by the United States ruled against the Thais, however. Though, as GATT noted, imports can be banned for health reasons, Thailand was still permitting the sale of domestically produced cigarettes. The local manufacturer was being protected, not the lungs of consumers.

Clearly, a way must be found to make informed decisions on the reasonability of environmental measures, and to expose and defeat those environmental measures that are protectionism in disguise. As Arthur Dunkel, GATT's director-general, has stated, the world must guard "against the risk of the environment being kidnapped by trade protectionist interests."[16] For the most part, clear warnings on labels ("eco-labeling") ought to solve many issues. Yet there probably should be some scope for barriers in support of environmental treaties, just as trade sanctions are used for unacceptable political behavior, as we explore in Chapter 9. C. Fred Bergsten of the Institute for International Economics has suggested a nice compromise: a GATT environmental code under which countries could negotiate agreements like the driftnet fishing law. The idea seems an excellent one.

■ *LOWER TRADE BARRIERS MAY* IMPROVE *THE ENVIRONMENT*

There are reasons for hoping that lowering trade barriers may bring environmental improvement. Freer international trade means that less developed countries will be able to make and export more textiles, clothing, steel, and other manufactures whose trade is now controlled by barriers. These products are likely to cause less harm to nature than is caused by pesticides and clearcutting. Opening trade would also be expected to raise national incomes, and richer countries clearly both desire and can afford a cleaner environment. Some pollutant emissions, for example suspended particles, decrease as income rises at all levels of income. Others, including major ones such as sulfur dioxide and smoke, rise with income when income is low but then turn down at an income level of about $5000 per capita.[17] (Carbon dioxide and carbon monoxide emissions, among others, clearly *rise* as income grows, however, and must await a change in attitudes to bring them down.)

A major environmental improvement would likely follow freer trade in agriculture. The heavily protected farmers of Europe and Japan use extraordinary amounts of fertilizer in their agricultural production. Not nearly so much is needed to produce agricultural commodities in the countries that have the comparative advantage. Arguably, certain trade restrictions could be quite counterproductive. Say environmentalists succeed in banning timber imports to stop the clearing of rainforest land. But the ban may result in a reduction in the value of the forests, which settlers may proceed to clear at an even faster pace than before in order to farm—and perhaps export the resulting crops.

SUBSIDY AND TAX ISSUES

Subsidies interfere with free-market pricing and can introduce distortions to comparative advantage. They take several forms and require some additional analysis. Domestic tax systems can result in similar distortions, which are also discussed in this section.

SUBSIDIES TO PRODUCTION

If a nation decides that the public welfare requires the maintenance of an aircraft industry or a shoe industry, would it not be better just to subsidize it directly, rather than blocking imports of the product? Furthermore, if comparative advantage is influenced by economies of scale, industrial concentration, experience, and product specialization, then perhaps a government might conclude that subsidies as part of an industrial strategy will provide a head start. These propositions can be analyzed by means of the familiar tariff effect diagram, Fig. 4.1, modified here in Fig. 5.2 to show a subsidy.[18]

With no barriers to imports, goods enter the country at the world price P_w. Domestic production at that price is Q_1 while imports are Q_1Q_4. Now assume that the government pays a direct subsidy of P_wP_d per unit produced by domestic firms. In first-year economics, students learn that a sales-type *tax* shifts the supply curve vertically upward, because suppliers would continue to act as they did before the tax only if the full amount of the tax were paid to them in the form of higher prices. Conversely, a per-unit *subsidy* shifts the supply curve vertically downward, reflecting that a supplier would be willing to market a given amount of a good at the former price less the amount of the subsidy. Using this standard analysis, a subsidy equal to P_wP_d per unit would shift the supply curve in Fig. 5.2 from S to S_{SUB}.

This case has been designed so that the quantity of output rises because of the per-unit subsidy P_wP_d by exactly the same amount, from Q_1 to Q_2, as would have been true in the presence of a tariff P_wP_d. See how with a price of P_w domestic firms with their new supply curve S_{SUB} would produce a quantity Q_2. We can then compare the various costs of a subsidy to the costs of a tariff, given that domestic industry is stimulated to exactly the same degree. The total cost of

---

Figure 5.2 **A per-unit subsidy paid on production.** A direct subsidy amounting to the difference between S and S_{SUB} shifts the supply curve, leaving the domestic price at world price levels, avoiding both the revenue (R) effect and consumer deadweight loss effect (D).

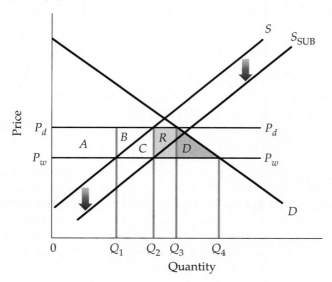

the subsidy is the subsidy per unit P_wP_d times the number of units, Q_2, which is equal to the area of the rectangle $A+B+C$. That, we recall, is just enough to cause producers to raise their output to Q_2 rather than remaining at Q_1; they respond just as if the price were P_d, even though it remains at P_w.

Because consumers continue to pay the price P_w, there is no tariff revenue generated (R) or consumer deadweight loss (D). The net loss for the economy is only triangle C, the producer deadweight loss. As taxpayers, consumers must pay $A+B+C$. If a tariff had been in place consumers would have paid $A+B+C+R$, but R represents revenue to the government so taxes could be lower or government services could be increased. Therefore, the main difference between a subsidy and a tariff is that the portion of consumer surplus shown by triangle D, lost under a tariff, is restored. If a quota were in place instead of a tariff, then the damage to society would be greater and to that extent more benefits would flow from using subsidies instead. With a quota the revenue effect R will usually go to the importers lucky enough to have a license to import. Consumers lose C, D, and R. If a VER is used rather than a quota, the outcome is more dramatic, and a subsidy therefore even more advantageous: C, D, and R continue to be losses, but in this case the revenue effect R will most likely be captured by the foreign exporters.

■ *A MADE-TO-MEASURE SUBSIDY COULD DECREASE COSTS*

The costs of a subsidy to the public might be less than we have indicated if government could figure out how to pay just triangle C as a subsidy, rather than $A+B+C$. Only the amount C is needed to produce the extra output; A and B have gone to raise the value of existing output. Such made-to-measure targeted subsidies are an interesting theoretical proposition, but very hard to put in place because old output is usually identical to new output. When oil prices soared in the 1970s, governments tried to pay different prices for "new oil" and "old oil," the idea being that the oil already discovered should not get the substantial rent created by OPEC's high prices. They soon found themselves in an administrative tangle, trying to separate out two oils the physical characteristics of which were identical.[*] Made-to-measure subsidies will always be difficult to administer, because to avoid payment on intramarginal units of output where the funds were not needed to stimulate production, governments would have to identify the new production and judge its costs with care.

The taxes to pay for the subsidy could certainly carry welfare costs of their own, as explained in the accompanying box, costs associated with the tax collection. One would not therefore want to insist that a given subsidy *must* carry

---

[*] The dual pricing was, moreover, a penalty for those who guessed right and secured the oil before the price went up, and a subsidy for those who guessed wrong, so its long-run wisdom is questionable.

fewer distortions than a tariff or a quota. The tax system currently in use would have to be examined with care to see if its distortions might not be larger than those carried by the protectionist tools. It is highly unlikely, however, that the tax systems of the United States, the EC, or Japan are nearly so distortionary as is trade protectionism.

■ *TAX COLLECTIONS CARRY WELFARE COSTS OF THEIR OWN*

An income tax with high marginal rates can, by reducing incentives, affect the amount of effort expended. A sales-type tax introduces distortions of its own, because the tax introduces a wedge between prices and costs. Consumers would be willing to pay for one additional unit of output more than the cost to society of producing that additional unit. In the 1960s and early 1970s, economists believed that the distortions caused by taxes were relatively modest, but later the pendulum swung far in the other direction. A common view of the 1980s was that taxes had large effects on economic behavior. The more recent view is that labor supply is *not* very sensitive to tax policy, and especially that moderate tax increases will not lead to a severe decline in work effort in any but the world's highest-tax countries, of which the United States is not one. In any case, there is a type of tax that theoretically can avoid these difficulties: the lump-sum progressive levy on income that tax experts suggest would eliminate the distortions that accompany standard income and sales-type taxes. Lump-sum progressive taxes have proved difficult to implement, however, both administratively and for political reasons.

The main reason economists favor subsidies over tariffs, quotas, and VERs is actually a different one: The subsidies are visible. The legislature and the press review the government's budget frequently. Both the incidence of taxes and the effects of subsidies come under consideration in a normal legislative process, however unsatisfactory it may seem. Tariffs, quotas, and VERs tend to escape scrutiny, however, perhaps for very long periods of time. In general economists do not approve of subsidies, but at least they are less damaging than tariffs and quotas as long as the tax system carries fewer distortions than does the protection (which is very likely). Even if the tax system is poorly constructed, the subsidies will receive much more frequent critical review, with therefore less danger that they will fossilize into permanent features.

In spite of the advantages of subsidies, politicians will often decide not to adopt them. The costs of the subsidy will be in the national budget, financed by an unpalatable tax increase or an unwelcome rise in the budget deficit, whereas the costs of a tariff or quota are not in the budget at all. Legislatures may thus shun subsidies, even though economists would note that the public very probably bears a *greater* burden with tariffs, but especially with quotas and VERs.

As we shall see in Chapter 7, when subsidies are paid they can give rise to considerable international controversy. Such payments on output that is then exported often violate the laws of the importing country, and the resulting penalties are legal under GATT's rules. There is widespread disagreement on just what does and does not constitute a subsidy. Included in these grey areas are regional development grants (Britain, France, Italy), tax holidays and concessions (France, Italy), accelerated depreciation (France, Germany, Japan, the United States), cheap loans (Germany, Italy, Japan), enhanced unemployment compensation for seasonal industries (Canada), and cheap government-controlled prices for natural resources (Canada, Mexico). An international consensus on the meaning of the word *subsidy* has yet to be attained.

SUBSIDIES ON EXPORTS ONLY

Instead of subsidies paid on production, a government could pay the subsidy on exports only. This strategy has quite different results, as seen in Fig. 5.3. Say a country has an advantage in the production of computers, so that exports Q_2Q_3 are occurring at a world price (P_w) that is slightly above the no-trade equilibrium price. Assume the country is a small one, so that the world demand for its exported computers is perfectly elastic, at a price P_w. What if the country now pays an export subsidy of $1000 on each computer produced? That would raise the amount received per unit by computer manufacturers to the price P_w plus the amount of the subsidy, or P_{w+SUB}.

Figure 5.3 **Analyzing an export subsidy.** A subsidy on exports only raises P_w to P_{w+SUB}. Consumers lose $A+B$, producers gain $A+B+C$, and the subsidy costs the government $B+C+D$. The result is a net loss of triangles $B+D$.

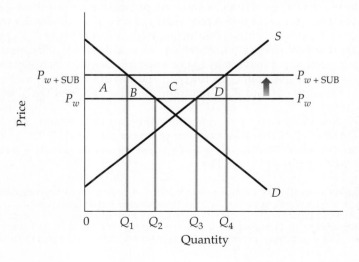

Suppliers will then raise the quantity they export from the old amount Q_2Q_3 to the new and higher Q_1Q_4. They will not sell at home for a price any less than $P_{w+\text{SUB}}$ per computer, because with world demand elastic, they could always earn that amount from their international sales. Since the domestic price will thus rise, domestic demand will decrease to Q_1.[*]

In welfare terms, there is a rise in producer surplus of $A+B+C$. Consumer surplus falls by $A+B$. The cost to the government is the amount of the subsidy on each unit (the distance from P_w to $P_{w+\text{SUB}}$) times the quantity exported (Q_1Q_4). This yields a rectangle $B+C+D$. Against the gain of $A+B+C$ there are losses of $A+B$ and $B+C+D$. Netting these reveals a loss to society of the triangles B and D. The area D is a loss because foreigners are obtaining the country's computers at a price below the social (resource) costs of producing them. The other triangle, B, can be seen first as lost consumer surplus because the price has risen; second as a rise in producer surplus; and third as part of the government subsidy, which is a cost. Thus two losses weigh in the balance against one gain, the net result being that triangle B is lost.

GATT's rules hold that subsidies paid on exports of manufactured goods are illegal for developed countries, and an importing country can countervail them with penalty duties when they are detected. They are commonly found in agriculture, however, and less developed countries have been able to employ export subsidies more freely.

The subject of subsidies to industry, either generally or on exports, has rapidly achieved new status as the possibilities for a strategic trade policy have been perceived and understood. That topic is considered in Chapter 7.

■ *IMPORT SUBSIDIES*

Subsidies on imports are also employed, particularly by less developed countries. Their effects are the opposite of subsidies on exports. In Fig. 5.4 we show a subsidy on rice imported into Penuristan. When the subsidy of P_wP_d per unit is paid, the domestic price falls to P_d, below the world price P_w. The quantity produced domestically is reduced by Q_1Q_2, while consumption increases from Q_3 to Q_4. Imports thus rise from Q_1Q_3 to Q_2Q_4. The cost of the subsidy to the government is the price per unit P_wP_d times the quantity imported Q_2Q_4, or the area $B+C+D+E+F$.

Now consider the welfare implications. Buyers gain consumer surplus equal to area $A+B+C+D+E$. Local farmers lose producer surplus $A+B$. The government loses $B+C+D+E+F$. Netting the gains against the losses reveals a deadweight loss consisting of the triangles $B+F$.

---

[*] In a free market, a backflow of imports would result, with foreigners reexporting computers acquired at price P_w and selling them in the country of origin for the higher price $P_{w+\text{SUB}}$. To prevent this backflow it will be necessary to erect barriers against their importation. It should also be noted that an export subsidy, by increasing the quantity of exports, could lead to a fall in price in importing countries. This would be an export subsidy's *terms-of-trade effect*, opposite to that of a tariff.

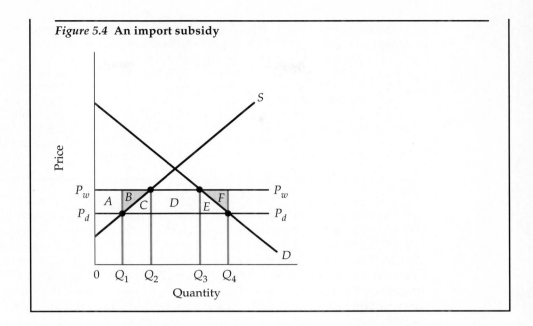

Figure 5.4 **An import subsidy**

SUBSIDIES ON EXPORT CREDIT

Export credit subsidies involve low-cost credit advances to the buyers of a country's exports. The major industrial countries all have agencies granting export credits to overseas buyers: Britain's Export Credit Guarantee Department, Germany's Hermes and Kreditanstalt für Wiederaufbau, France's Coface and Banque Française du Commerce Extérieur, Canada's Export Development Corporation, the Export-Import Bank of Japan, and the Export-Import (Exim) Bank of the United States.[19]

■ *HOW THE U.S. EXPORT-IMPORT BANK WORKS*

The U.S. Exim Bank provides a good illustration of how these agencies work in practice. The Bank was founded in 1934, intended, believe it or not, to finance trade between the United States and the USSR. That plan did not succeed because the Soviets made no use of the new institution. But the Exim Bank survived.

The Exim Bank does nothing to assist imports, and thus its name is a misnomer. Its main function is to borrow from the U.S. Treasury and then lend the proceeds to foreign buyers of U.S. exports, the loans limited to 65% of the value of the exports. Alternatively it will provide financial guarantees of up to 85% of the export's value. A study by the U.S. Treasury in the late 1970s estimated that two thirds of U.S. exports financed by the Exim Bank would probably not have been made without the financing, with a direct effect on perhaps 540,000 jobs. (The

U.S. Agriculture Department's Commodity Credit Corporation extends credits on exports of agricultural commodities by guaranteeing private bank loans.)

The Exim Bank, and all the foreign agencies as well, now also insure against the risk of nonpayment by buyers. Coverage has gradually risen over the years to reach 90% to 95% of the loss. It was once widely believed that government export insurance was justified because private insurance was expensive and limited in coverage. More recently, economists have argued that these gaps are not market failures, but instead reflect high risks and difficulties in identifying these risks on a worldwide basis. If so, then the government export insurance also represents an element of subsidy in addition to those already discussed.

The rate of interest paid to their countries' treasuries by most of these banks was for many years lower than the interest rate they charged borrowers. In the late 1970s, however, a credit war broke out among the major developed countries, and the rates charged became a major subsidy to buyers. There was a sixfold expansion of lending by the U.S. Exim Bank during the period 1977 to 1981. In general the lending rates of all the credit agencies were fixed at low figures appropriate to the first part of that time period. As world interest rates rose rapidly during the years 1979 to 1981, the element of subsidy contained in the loans soared from 14% to nearly 28%.[20]

At one point, the U.S. Exim Bank was borrowing from the Treasury at 12% and then lending to foreign buyers at 8.5%. For once, however, the major countries realized that concerted action was required. They established consensus rates for export credit in 1980. Though these have been revised several times (last in 1988), a consensus still survives except in the area of foreign aid, as noted in the accompanying box.

■ *THE CREDIT WAR CONTINUES IN FOREIGN AID*

The credit war still continues in the realm of foreign aid to less developed countries. It involves the practice of subsidizing the credit portion of aid when the credit is part of a package that also includes government grants of aid. These mixed credits, pushed most avidly by France, have recently grown to about one fifth of all medium- and long-term export credits to poor countries, $12–15 billion per year being advanced in mixed credits by the industrialized countries in 1989.[21] The United States strongly opposed the growth of mixed credits and has engaged in credit subsidies of its own to force further negotiations.

The wisdom of ever subsidizing export credits at all is debatable. When a subsidy is involved, that means transferring income from industrial-country taxpayers (not necessarily rich) to buyers (not necessarily poor) in foreign countries, and to the domestic exporters who benefit from the subsidies. Even when part of a foreign aid package, the subsidized credits do not seem an optimal way to deliver aid to the poor portion of an LDC's population. In the U.S. government at present, the belief seems to be that the United States must maintain a program of export credits in order to negotiate it away.

BORDER-TAX ADJUSTMENTS

Nontariff distortions to trade can be a complex topic, and no part of it more so than the complicated question of border tax adjustments. Such adjustments have been an important area of dispute in recent years. The dispute is the result of a GATT rule, dating from early in the organization's history, that depends on the belief that indirect taxes are shifted forward fully to final users of a product in the form of higher costs and prices for that product.[*] GATT thought at the time that if Country A levied a 10% indirect tax, then this 10% would figure in the final price of the good. If Country B, its trading partner, did not have large indirect taxes, then Country B would be unjustly favored.

GATT therefore tried to establish competition on an equal footing in the country where exports were to be sold, no matter what the differing rates of indirect taxes were. To accomplish this, countries were permitted to give tax rebates at the border on their exports, and to charge a special compensatory tax of the same amount on imports. Thus the distorting effect of the indirect tax would, in the theory of the time, be eliminated. Meanwhile GATT, again following then-current economic theory, assumed that income and profits taxes were not passed on to final buyers, being absorbed instead by the seller. Thus the GATT rules did not permit a border tax adjustment on these types of taxes.

From the 1960s much of the world began to adopt a system of indirect taxes called VAT, for value added tax. Recently 64 countries have adopted a VAT, including almost all of Europe and the whole of the EC, Japan, and Canada, where it is called the goods and services tax, or GST. In the major countries they range from Japan's 3% to Sweden's 25%; VATs typically collect 12–30% of a country's total revenue. Only the United States, Australia, and Switzerland among the world's industrial countries do not have one.

A VAT is an indirect tax calculated only on the value added by the firm being taxed. This is determined by subtracting the money value of purchases from other firms from the money value of sales, the sum equaling the value added. It is usually charged by taxing all sales and then rebating the tax paid earlier on all purchases. Say $2100 in VAT has been charged on a $15,000 German car. This $2100 under GATT rules can be rebated at the border when the car is exported. For symmetry, imports of similarly valued cars are subject to the same amount of VAT. Or if imported U.S. steel is used in the manufacture of the German car, VAT can also be charged on the imported steel. The end result is

---

[*] Direct taxes are those on income and profits. Indirect taxes are on purchases. Typical indirect taxes are sales taxes, value-added taxes (VAT), and excise taxes.

that the price of exports is free of indirect tax, and the price of imports is equalized with domestic production.

Government and private firms in countries without a VAT have long opposed the GATT rules on border tax adjustments. The tax rebate on exports has been called an unfair subsidy; the imposition of the VAT on imports has been called an unfair form of tariff.[*]

The economics of the issue are interesting. If GATT is correct in arguing that indirect VAT-type taxes are passed on to final consumers in the price charged, while income taxes are borne by the producer, then the rebate of VAT is logical and fair. If, however, VAT-type taxes are not fully passed on to the consumer, and are partly absorbed by manufacturers—which appears to be the prevailing opinion in most economics textbooks—then rebates of VAT do indeed discriminate in favor of countries employing that type of tax. Also, if corporate income and profits taxes *are* in part passed on to consumers and are not wholly absorbed by the manufacturer of the exports, then the VAT rebate again discriminates in favor of the countries employing it. Traditional theory has held that profits taxes are not passed on, but numerous economists have argued otherwise in recent years. Administered markup pricing, with taxes considered a cost and made part of the markup, may result in the corporation tax being transferred through prices to the final consumer. Some economists emphasize that both indirect and direct taxes are largely passed on in this manner.[22] If so, the GATT ruling is indeed unfair, discriminating in favor of countries with the VAT, and against countries such as the United States that rely heavily on income and profits taxes.

The whole debate on border tax rebates can be viewed in another way, as an example of producer bias. The principle used to justify the rebate of indirect taxes is never mentioned for subsidies. When domestic production is subsidized, imports are never eligible to receive them, nor do manufacturers have to rebate production subsidies at the border when goods are exported. Logic would seem to compel such treatment, but there would be no advantage in this for producers, and so this extension to the practice is not made.

From broader macroeconomic or general equilibrium points of view, the debate is less important. Macroeconomics tells us that through the price or exchange rate mechanisms trade will tend to balance (capital movements aside). Stated flatly and unsubtly, a country paying a 10% bonus to all exports and charging a 10% tax on all imports would see its currency appreciate by 10%, or its price level rise by 10%, or some combination thereof. A $10 ham exported with a $1 bonus would either cause the price level to rise to $11 or mean that the foreign exchange that used to buy $10 now buys only $9. Whether the taxes are passed on is not a problem in the long run for an economy as a whole. The mix of products exported and imported might, however, change considerably because

---

[*] Everyone agrees, incidentally, that there is no justification within this GATT rule for rebating *more* than the initial amount of the tax. Brazil used such a scheme of over-rebates, of 11%, but this was obviously tantamount to an outright subsidy, and in the face of heavy international pressure a phaseout was begun in 1984.

labor-intensive or technology-intensive goods paying more direct taxes will not be subsidized, while material-intensive ones, with higher indirect taxes, would be. The firms that are disadvantaged will cry foul, while those that reap an advantage will keep very quiet. Empirically, a recent IMF study shows VAT rebates have encouraged exporting much more in some countries than in others, with Korea on the high side, the EC on the low.[23]

PROTECTION IN SERVICES

Services, the invisibles that include banking, transport, travel, and insurance, amount to almost a quarter of world trade, and are growing steadily as a percentage of domestic economic activity, having now reached over 60% of developed-country GDP and about two thirds of all employment.[24] The growth rate of services in international trade was, however, no greater during the years 1968–1983 (11.25%) than was the growth of visible trade in goods; service trade, estimated at about $560 billion in 1989, is still only about 20% of the trade in goods.* This relatively mediocre performance was due to the multitude of non-tariff barriers to trade in services, barriers that are often little known. Only in 1982 were GATT members even asked to submit a comprehensive report on what their attitude was toward services; these reports have been made by a relatively small number of countries. In defense of some of the protective measures, there is no doubt that politicians often consider services to be quite intrusive from a cultural and political point of view, and few people anywhere would agree to have them completely in foreign hands. Radio, television, domestic airlines, and the telephone system are cases in point, with foreign operation seldom permitted, even in the United States.

Other services, however, are kept off limits to foreigners even though free trade would appear to give cheaper access to information processing, professional services, finance, and technology. For example, foreign insurance, banking, data processing, and computer hardware and software are sometimes excluded, even when foreigners have an obviously large comparative advantage in them. Brazil jealously guards its information and technology sectors; major international disputes have erupted around its protectionist measures against telephone switching, computers, and software from the United States and elsewhere.

Among the services where protectionism is currently most common are the following:

(a) Insurance. Numerous countries have laws directed against foreign insurance. A few nations (India for one) do not allow any underwriting of any kind. Life insurance seldom crosses national boundaries. Germany and France are especially strict, and EC insurance standards are not expected to be

---

* The trade in services appears larger when the services delivered abroad by subsidiaries of domestic firms are taken into account. Foreign subsidiaries of U.S. parent firms provide services almost 50% greater in value than the direct service exports of U.S. firms (1982 data).

standardized until the next century. Norway has not licensed a foreign insurer for over 40 years; all exports from and imports to Italy, Mexico, and nine other countries must have insurance from domestic underwriters. (A good question is what happens when such countries trade with one another.) Only South Korean companies are allowed to issue several types of insurance (including life and fire) in that nation. About two dozen countries, including Sweden and Kuwait, allow foreigners to write coverage only if the type of insurance the foreigner is providing is not available locally. Domestic insurance requirements are said at least to double the transport and insurance costs on about half of all imports into the world's less developed countries.

(b) Banking. Laws that discriminate against foreign banks are commonplace. In Japan, new entrants from abroad are prohibited from going into retail banking. Canadian law limits the proportion of foreign shareholding in that country's banks to 25%. In Taiwan, foreign banks are prohibited outside Taipei and Kaohsiung, and are excluded from the credit card business.

(c) Shipping. Liner codes fix market share and rates. These plus other laws often require that your country's exports must go in your ships. Australia's law mandates that 40% must do so. In Japan, the traditional ship-Japanese practice is a custom rather than a law, but Japanese ships nevertheless carry over 50% of Japanese exports even though in recent years they have charged some 35% more than market rates. The U.S. ship-American provisions and Jones Act have already been reviewed earlier in this chapter. Even stationary objects at sea or on the shore share in the endemic maritime protectionism. Britain prohibits foreigners from the design and construction of oil drilling platforms. Taiwan will not allow foreign ownership of container facilities at the ports.

(d) Airlines. The need to allocate landing slots at busy airports gives a convenient way to discriminate against foreign-flag carriers. International routes are strictly controlled by this device, with landing rights carefully hoarded to be traded off from time to time with another country to gain one's own access to that country's airports. Air travelers may pay extortionately for their passage when competition is reduced or eliminated by these means.

(e) Professional services (accounting, legal services, and so forth). There is considerable discrimination. In France, foreign accounting firms are prohibited from bidding on official contracts. Accountants practicing their skills in Brazil must possess a Brazilian degree. In Argentina, Mexico, Peru, and Venezuela local accountants must supervise foreign auditors. No foreign lawyers have been permitted to practice in Japan since 1955. Canada not only fails to recognize numerous *foreign* professional qualifications but also must endure the considerable discrimination of one province against another.

(f) TV, advertising, and films. Britain limits foreign TV programs to 14% of air time. A new EC television directive approved in 1989, not legally binding but likely to be followed, reserves a majority of TV time for European-made programs and films. France wanted strict, binding quotas of below 40% for foreign material. In Canada, Argentina, and Australia, broadcasts of commercials of foreign origin are restricted on the television or radio, while Italy requires local actors and film crews for commercials. Korea prohibits foreign investment in advertising. In Brazil prints of color feature films must be processed in that country if shown there. Taiwan limits imports of foreign films to six copies each. It can certainly be argued that such rules do protect the national culture, but just as surely they also protect the local advertising and film industries.

(g) Computers. In Germany, all companies that use computers must do some of their data processing there. All data processing done by banks located in Canada must be carried out in that country. Similar laws or data-flow restrictions exist in Japan and several other countries. The result is that companies such as American Express cannot completely centralize their processing of travelers' checks and credit cards, nor (under a law being drafted by Japan) can IBM or AT&T own more than 20% of the circuits that process as well as transmit data.

The GATT-sponsored trade talks, called the Uruguay Round, are considering protection against services, spurred on by the United States, which is the largest exporter.[*] The United States has proposed a General Agreement on Trade in Services (GATS) to cover all service trade unless specific exclusions are written in. The GATS proposal has proved contentious, with strong opposition especially from Brazil and India.[**] Even some major developed countries, in particular the EC members, want a service agreement to apply only to an explicit list of services and not to all. Due to the opposition, the service talks are being kept technically separate from the trade talks, even though both are being held simultaneously in Geneva. The opponents have yet to appreciate fully that concessions in this area could be exchanged for freer trade in manufactured goods and agricultural commodities. One hopes that the LDCs will come to understand that if they wish to capture the world's low-wage manufacturing, because that is where their comparative advantage lies, then they ought to allow countries with a comparative advantage in services to trade these. Eventually more persuasive to such countries might be the argument that poor services such as banking and telephones can clearly damage the prospects for exporting manufactured goods. At the same time, it is fair to say that developed-country governments have not generally been very sympathetic toward measures for maintaining cultural independence. A greater degree of tolerance, for example in attitudes toward TV and radio regulation, would increase the chances for a compromise settlement.

---

[*] The United States held 11% of the world total of service exports, or $56 billion, in 1987. France was close in second place at $53 billion. Japan was well back at $28 billion.

[**] Some LDCs, however, have become important exporters of services. South Korea, Singapore, Hong Kong, and Mexico are all in the world's top 20. They do not side with most of the other LDCs.

One intractable problem with any reform is that freer trade in services will require more foreign staff. The increases in immigration, even if temporary, may be troublesome. Would Korean construction workers be very welcome in Britain or the United States? Probably not, even though the exchange of labor-intensive services for capital-intensive services makes just as much sense as the similar trade in goods, and would enhance welfare. All in all, an agreement on trade in services has been difficult to achieve, and an end to the negotiations is not yet in sight.

CONCLUSION

As Chapter 1 noted, the very existence of nation-states with their various laws, regulations, and taxes creates the field of international economics. Nowhere is this clearer than in the observation of nontariff barriers and subsidies. As these in all their rich and sometimes rather opaque forms have come to take precedence over the traditional tariffs, a developing pattern of policy has become apparent.[25] (1) Trade distortions have become considerably less open, less visible, and less easy to quantify. (2) They have generally become more subject to administrative discretion, and less like firm rules. (3) They have included a great deal more discrimination against individual countries or groups of countries, so representing a retreat from multilateralism and equal treatment. (4) More and more the distortions to trade have been on a sectoral basis rather than representing a coherent national policy. The barriers and subsidies spread from industry to industry according to the balance of political power, perhaps first to agriculture, then to textiles and clothing, then steel, then autos, then computers and microchips. The lack of openness, the discretionary nature, the discrimination, and the absence of firm knowledge of what industry will be next are inhibiting for trade because they increase risk.

In all this we are dealing with governments' policies toward trade. Every government is conscious, at least to some extent, that its various laws affect its commerce with foreign countries. The struggle to achieve reasonably integrated and consistent approaches toward these laws is one of the most difficult tasks facing a modern government. It is to this subject that we turn in the following chapter.

VOCABULARY AND CONCEPTS

Administrative protection

Border tax adjustments

Buy American Act

Domestic content legislation

ERA (effective rate of assistance)

Exim Bank

Export credit subsidies

Export trading companies

GATT Procurement Code

Government buying policies

NTBs, NTMs

Ship American Act

Single tendering
Subsidies to exports
Subsidies to imports
Subsidies to production

Technical, health, safety, and
environmental standards
VAT

QUESTIONS

1. What is a nontariff barrier? Why have they become more important in recent years?

2. How are NTBs measured? What is the difference between a tariff equivalent and an effective rate of assistance? How does the ERA compare with an effective tariff?

3. How can government buying policies inhibit trade? Give examples from the United States, Canada, and Japan. What kinds of international controls exist to cover such problems?

4. Subsidies in general are superior to tariffs and quotas, but not as common. Explain why they are superior, and why they are not used so much.

5. What differences are there in the analysis of subsidies to production, to exports, and to imports?

6. What are subsidies on export credit? Why are such subsidies used so much? What kinds of international agreements restrict their use?

7. The balance of economic opinion is that the rebate at the border of direct taxes on exports

and the collection of such taxes on imports does not distort trade as much as might appear. Why? Explain the issues.

8. "The reason foreign firms have trouble getting government contracts is that they don't produce local votes." True in part, but what are other reasons for the difficulties?

9. "A nation has a sovereign right to protect its citizens against what they consider to be unhealthy food, regardless of whether it interferes with trade." Comment.

10. "Health, technical, safety, and environmental regulations are a necessary function of national governments; applying to domestic producers and importers alike, they cannot possibly be considered import barriers." True, false, or misleading?

11. Under what circumstances do you feel a country should restrict imports because of the environmental damage their manufacture causes?

12. The United States has been pressing heavily for freer trade in services. Is trade in services really so restricted?

NOTES

[1] See Robert E. Baldwin, *Nontariff Distortions of International Trade*, Washington, D.C., Brookings Institution, 1970.

[2] For a survey of empirical methods, see Sam Laird and Alexander Yeats, *Quantitative Methods for Trade-Barrier Analysis*, New York, New York University Press, 1990. The example used is from *The Economist*, March 5, 1988.

[3] Much of the information in this section is from the annual issues of the U.S. International Trade Commission (ITC), *Operation of the Trade Agreements Program*.

[4] Neela Mukherjee, "Multilateral negotiations and trade barriers in service trade: a case study of U.S. shipping services," *Journal of World Trade*, Vol. 26, No. 6, October 1992, p. 52.

[5] Cited in Jacques Pelkmans, "Liberalization of product markets in the European Community," in Herbert Giersch, ed., *Free Trade in the World Economy: Towards an*

Opening of Markets, Boulder, Colo., Westview Press, 1987.

[6] *Wall Street Journal,* June 3, 1991; *International Economic Review,* October, 1991.

[7] James Bovard, "Torpedo shipping protectionism," *Wall Street Journal,* November 26, 1991.

[8] See Stanislaw Wellisz and Ronald Findlay, "The state and the invisible hand," *World Bank Research Observer,* Vol. 3, No. 1, January 1988, pp. 59–80.

[9] For details, see recent issues of the U.S. ITC, *Operation of the Trade Agreements Program;* and the coverage in *The Economist.*

[10] *The Economist,* November 28, 1992.

[11] Materials from this section are from recent issues of the *International Economic Review* and U.S. ITC, *Operation of the Trade Agreements Program,* annual.

[12] Material in this section is drawn from Steve Charnovitz, "Exploring the Environmental Exceptions in GATT Article XX," *Journal of World Trade,* Vol. 25, No. 5, October 1991, pp. 37–55, and Kym Anderson and Richard Blockhurst, eds., *The Greening of World Trade Issues,* Ann Arbor, University of Michigan Press, 1992.

[13] *Wall Street Journal,* February 12, 1992.

[14] Material in the box is from Maureen L. Cropper and Wallace E. Oates, "Environmental economics: A survey," in *Journal of Economic Literature,* Vol. 30, June 1992, pp. 675–740; Hilary F. French, "Reconciling Trade and the Environment," in Lester R. Brown et al., *State of the World 1993,* New York, W. W. Norton & Co., Inc., 1993; H. Jeffrey Leonard, *Pollution and the Struggle for the World Product,* Cambridge, Cambridge University Press, 1988; and World Bank, *World Development Report 1992,* p. 67.

[15] These questions are asked in the special section on the environment in *The Economist,* May 30, 1992.

[16] *Wall Street Journal,* February 12, 1992.

[17] Gene Grossman and Alan Krueger, "Environmental Impacts of a North American Free Trade Area," NBER Working Paper No. 3914, 1992.

[18] How to diagram production subsidies, and export subsidies as well, is discussed by Erna van Duren, "An economic analysis of countervailing duties," *Journal of World Trade,* Vol. 25, No. 1, February 1991, pp. 91–105.

[19] This section relies in particular on all recent editions of the U.S. ITC, *Operation of the Trade Agreements Program* and the coverage in the *International Economic Review.*

[20] See William R. Cline, ed., *Trade Policy in the 1980s,* Washington, D.C., Institute for International Economics, 1983, p. 332.

[21] *South,* June 1990.

[22] For a full theoretical discussion of these issues, see Marian Krzyzaniak and Richard A. Musgrave, *The Shifting of the Corporation Income Tax,* Baltimore, Johns Hopkins University Press, 1963.

[23] See Alan A. Tait, ed., *Value-Added Tax: Administrative and Policy Issues,* IMF Occasional Paper No. 88, International Monetary Fund, 1992.

[24] Material in this section is from Irving Kravis and Robert Lipsey, "Production and Trade in Services by U.S. Multinational Firms," NBER Working Paper No. 2615, 1988; World Bank, *World Development Report, 1987,* p. 164, and "Trade in Services," *Research News,* Vol. 8, No. 2, June 1988, pp. 1–2; A.F. Ewing, "Why Freer Trade in Services Is in the Interest of Developing Countries," *Journal of World Trade Law,* Vol. 19, No. 2, 1985, pp. 147–169; and the coverage in *The Economist, South,* and U.S. ITC, *Operation of the Trade Agreements Program.*

[25] See W.M. Corden, *The Revival of Protection,* Group of 30 Occasional Paper No. 14, 1984.

Chapter 6

The Political Economy of Trade Barriers

OBJECTIVES

Overall Objective: To set the present context of trade policy by exploring its history and some of its political economy, and by scrutinizing the litany of arguments for restricting trade.

MORE SPECIFICALLY:

- To develop through historical discussion an understanding of American trade policy, the forces that drive it, and why American legislation is so important to any progress in trade discussions.
- To understand the purposes of and role of GATT.
- To identify the key issues facing world trade negotiators.
- To show why it is that despite protectionism's lack of economic sense, protectionist interests are so powerful.
- To appreciate the arguments for protection and the specific rebuttals concerning

    preference for domestic production as a personal value,
    preserving jobs and easing dislocation,
    preventing foreign sweatshops,
    reducing the trade deficit,
    trade barriers as devices for bargaining,
    developing infant industries,
    keeping up the national defense.

Trade barriers almost always arise out of public policy. Tariffs, quotas, VERs, and other measures come about because governments conceive them, impose them, and enforce them. The debate on whether to raise or lower the barriers is a central feature of the day-to-day activity of national executives and legislatures around the world, continuing a centuries-old tradition of prominence for policies on international trade. Costs and benefits rain out from these decisions, sometimes as a gentle shower, sometimes in thunderous storm. This chapter considers the relationship between public policy and trade barriers.

A SHORT HISTORY OF TRADE POLICY

Tracing the history of public policy toward trade barriers, even if briefly, is a useful exercise because over and over, countries have returned to the same issues, and often enough have made the same mistakes. Knowledge of past trade policies can lead to more informed policy choices in the future.

Tariffs were originally designed for revenue, with little thought being given to their protective effects. The United States, for example, used a modest tariff of 5% as its earliest and almost its only source of revenue.* Other sources of revenue proved difficult to generate. George Washington's administration had to face a Whiskey Rebellion when it tried to tax the domestic output of that product.

Only in the late eighteenth and early nineteenth centuries were the protective effects of tariffs recognized and employed. In England, the repeal of the Corn Laws (the English called grain "corn" in those days) was based on the recognition that farming interests were being protected and industry was being discriminated against by these tariffs on imported grain. In the United States, Alexander Hamilton, the first Secretary of the Treasury, recommended protective tariffs to develop infant industries. Use of these infant-industry tariffs raised the U.S. tariff rate to an average 12.5% at the outbreak of the War of 1812, and to about double that after the war.

The South depended on imported goods, however, and managed to block really substantial protective tariffs favored by the North until the Civil War—with one exception, the short-lived Tariff of Abominations of 1828. This high tariff so angered the South that one state (South Carolina) threatened to secede, forcing a new tariff law a scant four years later. At the time of the Civil War, the Confederate States of America continued the South's traditional opposition to the protective tariff by making it unconstitutional to protect any specific industry with a tariff.

The ascendancy of northern manufacturing interests after the Civil War ushered in a long period of high tariffs. With the Tariff of 1897, protection reached an average level of 57%. Across the Atlantic, German industrialists and economists were successfully advocating the protection of infant industries by tariffs, asking how Germany could ever develop industries in the face of floods of low-priced British manufactures. Thus by the end of the nineteenth century, the use of the protective tariff was well established.

---

* Under the U.S. Articles of Confederation, even tariff revenue was unavailable because unanimous agreement of the states was necessary for major legislation to be adopted. Two attempts were made, but opposition from Rhode Island in 1781 and New York in 1783 caused tariff initiatives to fail. Under Article 2 of the U.S. Constitution, congress received the power to regulate and tax trade.

The First World War gave tariffs an additional boost. Britain, which had had virtually free trade since the 1840s, turned to tariffs as a means to finance its skyrocketing war costs. The United States, which in 1913 had lowered its tariffs (to 29%), found that World War I had stimulated new, burgeoning industries in chemicals and pharmaceuticals. When it ended, these war babies demanded protection against imports, and in 1921 the Republicans, long the high-tariff party, were back in office and ready to help.

The world began to slide into greater protectionism. In the United States a curious bargain was struck in congress. American agriculture had changed much during the war years; high prices due to European demand and increased mechanization had expanded output greatly. As European agriculture began to recover, there was a sharp drop in grain prices, causing severe dislocation. To aid the farmers, congress first increased duties on agricultural imports. This was, however, a futile task because there were so few imports anyway. The tariffs were largely "excess tariffs." Figure 6.1 shows the United States with low wheat imports; the world price P_w is barely below the nontrade equilibrium price of P_{nt}. A tariff of P_wP_t cannot improve the price of agricultural goods beyond P_{nt}. Moreover, there is no revenue once imports fall to zero at P_{nt}. Hence the part of the tariff $P_{nt}P_t$ that lies above the equilibrium point is an excess tariff.

Farm states received their largely useless protection in 1921; the next year the manufacturing interests claimed their part of the bargain, and the farm bloc voted for high duties on manufactured goods, the so-called Fordney-McCumber Tariff named after its legislative sponsors. Unfortunately for the farmers, the high tariffs on manufacturing were not excess tariffs and thus had a large impact

Figure 6.1 **An excess tariff.** Like consecutive life sentences, a high tariff is not necessarily more effective than a moderate one. Once the tariff is high enough to exclude all imports (P_{nt}), anything higher is an excess tariff.

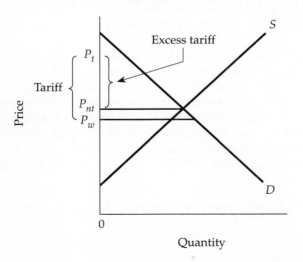

on price. The farmers had traded something for nothing. In Europe, revenue tariffs of the war years turned into protective tariffs. Fear of competitive devaluations (a justified fear in many cases) and a rise in economic isolationism encouraged more protectionist tariff policies. In Canada, protectionist interests grew stronger as well.

By the end of the 1920s many people of foresight felt that the tariff situation was out of hand. Some farm senators realized that in fact tariffs were not doing them any good. Surely the time had come to lower them. There was, however, no mechanism for negotiating reductions. American tariff policy was securely in the hands of congress; the president could promise a nation that the legislature would be asked to cut tariffs, but the legislators would not necessarily go along. It was not like a parliament, which would always agree to the cabinet's wishes or force a new election through a no-confidence vote.

President Hoover asked congress in April of 1929 for a revision of the tariff, seemingly to decrease manufacturing duties somewhat and to increase agricultural ones. The world waited for that decline in manufacturing tariffs. The House of Representatives, in which revenue bills must always be introduced first, voted through a bill sponsored by Representative Willis C. Hawley of Oregon with higher agricultural tariffs and more moderate manufacturing protection. But month after month in the Senate, where the rules on amendments were looser, new tariffs were tacked on under the leadership of the archconservative Reed Smoot of Utah. Eventually they totaled 800 items in all fields, at rates that averaged 59.1%, the highest ever in the United States and nearly twice the 1913 figure.[*] These developments were the less defensible since the United States was running a balance of trade *surplus* at the time.

Meanwhile the Great Depression had begun, but Hoover suggested no changes in the Smoot-Hawley legislation.[**] In March 1930, after many months of congressional logrolling, the bill went to the White House. Just over a thousand economists, a great majority of the membership of the American Economics Association, sent the president a statement that the bill not only would fail to help agriculture but would certainly invite retaliation by foreign governments on American exports.

To the dismay of the thousand and to the shock of world leaders, who had been hoping to stimulate their economies by exporting more to the United States, President Hoover signed the bill. The psychological effect was immediate and immense, further weakening business confidence abroad. The precise evil results predicted for the bill came to pass. Many of the tariffs were excess tariffs in that only part of the increase was enough to halt all trade; the remainder accomplished nothing except to anger foreigners. Twelve large trading countries retaliated almost at once with their own heavy tariffs. Spain, for example, put a

---

[*] In another sense, tariffs had been higher during the nineteenth century because there were fewer duty-free imports.

[**] By tradition the first name on a bill is its chief sponsor in the originating house of the legislature. Thus "Hawley-Smoot" would be the correct name. Senator Smoot was a commanding figure, however, and so "Smoot-Hawley" was and remains the more familiar term.

prohibitive duty on autos; the Swiss public boycotted American products; Italy announced it would buy no more from the United States than the United States did from Italy; Canada hit 125 U.S. export items with higher tariffs.

Trade spiraled downward. The total imports of 75 countries had been almost $3 billion per month at the start of the year 1929. They fell below $2 billion in June, 1930; below $1 billion in July, 1931, and fetched up at about half a billion dollars in March, 1933.[1] In volume terms, the total exports of the United States declined more than those of any other major nation and were only 53% of their 1929 volume in the year 1932. (Note that the volume of trade fell less than did its value because prices also declined. The price reductions in themselves served to increase trade barriers, however, because most tariffs of the time, including those under Smoot-Hawley, were specific rather than *ad valorem*.) Although much of the collapse in trade can be laid to the income effects of the Great Depression, even the income effects were related to trade because of the psychological impact of Smoot-Hawley on world investment. This was surely America's second "Tariff of Abominations."

■ *REVISIONIST VIEWS OF THE SMOOT-HAWLEY TARIFF*

Central though the Smoot-Hawley Tariff has been considered to be by economists who study the Great Depression, it is possible to exaggerate its importance, and a revisionist scholarship has appeared. The new duties covered only about a third of all imports, and the duty increases in percentage terms were somewhat smaller than they had been in 1922's Fordney-McCumber Tariff.[2] It has even been argued that the tariff, by cutting imports, increased the incentive to invest in American industries, though that interpretation neglects the negative effect on investment because exports were cut. In spite of the revisionism, no one doubts that Smoot-Hawley, coming as it did just at the onset of the Depression, gave rise to bitter hostility and had a stunning psychological impact. One portentous political result was soon apparent in Japan: The 23 percentage-point rise in the average tariff on Japanese goods undercut the liberals in the Japanese government and led to the supremacy of militaristic nationalism. The major lesson from Smoot-Hawley is that trade wars provoked by protection can cause a meltdown of world trade, that reductions in trade can make depressions much worse, and that the political results can be doleful.

A TURN IN TRADE POLICY

When the Roosevelt Administration assumed office in 1933, after an election that saw both Senator Smoot and Representative Hawley defeated by large majorities, it took rapid though belated steps to undo the harm. The result was the Reciprocal Trade Agreements Act of 1934, which has formed the basis for all subsequent American trade policy. With the RTA Act, the United States began a process that, where tariffs are concerned, has not ceased.

Several key parts of the act still survive:

1. The word *reciprocal* pointed to a main feature. Tariff cuts were made by the United States only in return for tariff cuts by trading partners. During its long life, the RTA Act was renewed 11 times, and eventually it covered 54 countries. The idea that mutual concessions would generate double gains, with increased imports benefiting consumers while increased exports benefited producers, was and remains a powerful one. Reciprocity also has an appearance of fairness, with each side appearing to give up something. The principle of reciprocity is still central to trade negotiations.

2. Congress gave the president *prior* authorization to cut tariffs on an item-by-item basis. This provision avoided the earlier problem of the executive branch being unable to negotiate for fear that congress would not agree. The principle was continued under the trade acts of 1962, 1974, and 1988; the president retained the power to negotiate tariff reductions in a big package. The Smoot-Hawley tariff was thus the last time in U.S. history that congress initiated an entire trade bill without delegating its power to the president. The situation did not develop so favorably in the European Community (EC, or European Common Market), where for a long time each member nation bargained separately, with no central authority authorized to carry out trade negotiations. In recent years, however, the negotiations have been undertaken collectively by the EC.

3. All tariff concessions were to be made on a nondiscriminatory basis. If the United States cut a tariff to one nation, it would cut them to all. This provision is known in diplomatic language as the *most favored nation* clause, or MFN. Even in 1934, it was a very old principle of tariff legislation. It had developed initially in Europe in the fifteenth and sixteenth centuries, and had become common in trade pacts because no country wanted to be left behind. The first treaty ever signed by the United States, with France in 1778, embodied the principle of conditional MFN treatment—the United States guaranteed MFN treatment for France if France guaranteed the same thing to the United States.

   For a brief period early in this century the United States departed from this tradition, but the provisions proved unworkable.[*] The problems of defining and enforcing separate tariffs for each of the thousands of product classifications were compounded greatly by multiplying all these by the number of countries in the world. Hence the 1922 (Fordney-McCumber) tariff reestablished the MFN principle that was retained in the RTA.

---

[*] Weaseling out of MFN commitments is an old tradition. The most famous dodge of all times was the German tariff of 1905 on cattle. The Germans wanted to give Switzerland a discriminatory rate without affecting the rate given to other countries. Hence this wording was adopted: The [favorable] tariff shall apply to dappled mountain cattle or brown cattle "reared at a spot at least 300 meters above sea level, and which have at least one month's grazing each year at a spot at least 800 meters above sea level."

A major exception from MFN treatment is permitted under the rules for free trade areas, customs unions, and common markets such as the European Community, which can lower tariffs among themselves without granting the same privilege to outsiders.

A second exception to the MFN provision is political in nature, made after World War II when the Communist bloc refused to enter into negotiations on tariffs. Rather than grant the Communists something for nothing, the United States and some other countries exempted them from the new tariff levels. Tariffs levied today on some remaining parts of what was the USSR and a few other Communist countries (Belarus, Cambodia, Cuba, Laos, North Korea, Romania, Vietnam) are the old Smoot-Hawley rates. Russia and Ukraine received MFN treatment in 1992, joining Poland, which got it in 1974, Hungary in 1978, and Czechoslovakia and Bulgaria in 1990. China has had MFN status as well, since 1980, but under U.S. law its eligibility must be reviewed every year. (Annual reviews also are required for Albania and Bulgaria.)

A final and more recent exception to MFN treatment is the Generalized System of Preferences, or GSP, which allows for duty-free entry of many goods from the less developed countries. Crucially for modern trade, however, MFN does not apply to VERs and other nontariff barriers. The rapid rise of these barriers has spelled trouble both for the Third World and for small manufacturing countries, neither of which have much bargaining power to retaliate against discriminatory practices. See the accompanying box for further details.

■ *THE GSP FOR LESS DEVELOPED COUNTRIES*

Since the 1970s the less developed countries (LDCs) have been granted special tariff preferences by the developed countries. Many of the former Communist countries have recently been made eligible for the same treatment. This generalized system of preferences (GSP) is constantly held up as a major concession by the rich nations to the poor ones. The EC first offered GSP in 1971; the United States in 1976. A form of GSP is now run by some 27 industrial and other rich countries. In 1990, about 4150 products from 130 countries were covered.

By boosting the returns on exports from the LDCs, the GSP certainly increased trade and thereby has probably contributed to faster economic growth. In general, however, GSP has been a disappointment. All the GSPs have time limits; they are not permanent, and renewal always involves a battle. The rich countries unilaterally reserved the right to remove the preferences and have frequently done so. For example the United States has always excluded textiles, clothing, shoes, and some electronic goods and steel, all of which are products of interest in the LDCs. Other exclusions apply when imports rise over certain trigger levels. Furthermore, under the U.S. law the president is permitted to graduate a country when it reaches an income level of $8500 per capita. (This seems reasonable.

When it becomes rich, a country deserves more normal treatment and full incorporation into the regular trading system.) Yet in 1989, when the United States
abruptly removed the GSP preferences for Taiwan, Korea, Hong Kong, and
Singapore, it was an administrative decision distinct from these rules. None of
these Asian Tigers had an income level near $8500 at that time.

Probably the great attention devoted to GSP has been a mistake. It gives the
developed countries a sense that they are generous, and it convinces the LDCs
they have received a concession. But making the LDCs full partners in world
trade and proceeding with general tariff cuts would have been even better. In that
case, the many exceptions and limits would not have been possible because most
favored nation treatment would have applied.

PROGRESS IN CUTTING TARIFFS

Progress in implementing reciprocal tariff cuts was slow at first. In 1934, the
world was so mired in the Great Depression that tariff cuts were hardly enough
to stimulate much export-led growth anywhere. World War II followed, imposing its own restrictions on trade, so that most of the major negotiations came in
the postwar period. By 1962, however, in the presence of 54 reciprocal agreements with other countries, the average tariff level in the United States had fall-
en from a 1934 figure of about 53¢ per dollar to only 11¢. About half of the fall
was due to the RTA negotiations. The other half was due to the fact that most
U.S. tariffs at the time were specific duties, such as "10¢ per widget." As noted in
Chapter 4, inflation will lessen the impact of any specific duty, and the inflation
that occurred in those years was about as effective as trade negotiations in bringing down the level of tariffs.[3]

THE GENERAL AGREEMENT ON TARIFFS AND TRADE (GATT)

The most important development in tariff policy after World War II was the
formation of an organization called the General Agreement on Tariffs and Trade
(GATT).[4] GATT deserves far more recognition than it receives from the general
public, for it has been a powerful force in furthering the goal of tariff reduction
and in encouraging trade.

GATT had an unusual origin. In 1944 at the Bretton Woods Conference in
New Hampshire, it was decided to establish an International Trade
Organization (ITO) to accompany the International Monetary Fund and the
World Bank that were established at the same time. The ITO was intended to
liberalize protection once World War II had ended. A charter signed at Havana,
Cuba, in 1947 formulated rules for the ITO, and the organization was to have
real teeth to enforce those rules. Unlike the other organizations created by
Bretton Woods, however, the ITO failed to gain approval, largely because the
U.S. Congress did not ratify the Havana Charter. Congress withheld its consent

for several reasons, but mostly because of fear that other countries would not abide by the various rules of the ITO.

An agency had already been established, however, to set the ITO on its way. This Interim Committee of the ITO was authorized by an administrative working agreement called the General Agreement on Tariffs and Trade. GATT thus did not require U.S. congressional ratification. Attempts were later made in congress to ratify it, but these have never succeeded. GATT nonetheless remained in existence because the need for it was seen and appreciated. Its small and elite staff numbers only about 350, compared to the 6000 or so employed by the World Bank. Its headquarters are in Geneva, Switzerland, and its present director-general is a Swiss, Arthur Dunkel. To this day GATT personnel carry identity cards and Swiss work permits that bear the name Interim Committee of the ITO. The GATT budget of some $40 million, contributed by its members in proportion to their share of world trade, is about the smallest of any international agency of significance.

GATT'S INFLUENCE ON WORLD TRADE   The half-in-jest assertion that GATT is the General Agreement to Talk and Talk is quite wrong. That organization is one of the few forces opposing the special interests in international trade, and negotiations under its auspices give the opportunity to repulse the lobbyists for these special interests by attractive trade-offs. GATT has had substantial influence on the development of world trade, as might be expected from the fact that the original 23 member nations have now grown to 111 (in mid-1993). There are also about 30 associated countries, most of them newly independent LDCs, that follow GATT rules and are extended the benefits of membership. Nearly 90% of world trade is conducted among the member nations. As noted in the box below, several major oil producers are not members; if oil is excluded, the proportion covered is even higher.

■ *THE GATT MEMBERSHIP*

GATT's membership is wide. Included among the GATT members are former Communist countries such as the Czech Republic, Slovakia, Hungary, Poland, and Romania. Numerous states of the former USSR want to join. China has observer status and has applied to reverse its 1950 resignation. Mexico, the most important of the Western nonmembers, changed course in 1986 after a debate of 40 years and took up membership. Countries that still do not belong, in addition to those mentioned above, are a few remaining Communist countries such as Vietnam and North Korea, and certain others mainly in North Africa, the Middle East, and Latin America. These include some major energy exporters: Algeria,[†] Iran, Iraq, Libya, and Saudi Arabia; and a group of Latin American nations including Ecuador, Honduras,[†] Paraguay, and Panama. (The countries marked with a dagger have applied for admission.)

On joining, GATT members agree to a number of rules, but significantly GATT has no power whatsoever to enforce these rules. Enforcement lies in the hands of the members, who are empowered to retaliate against a wrongdoer. Among the GATT rules are the following:

(a) Where tariffs, quotas, licenses, and so forth exist, the most favored nation principle will be extended to all members. The countries denied MFN treatment are not GATT members, although in general discrimination against nonmembers is not very common. As already noted, allowable exceptions to MFN treatment are the reduced tariffs for less developed countries under the GSP program and the permission to members of customs unions to lower tariffs among themselves. The legality of customs unions under GATT is important and these unions are the subject of a separate chapter (9) later in the book.

(b) Quotas are prohibited by GATT, with two major exceptions. First, less developed countries are permitted to use them for temporary defense of their balance of payments. Because of this Article XVIIIb of the GATT agreement, many LDCs still use this device. Often the rule is abused: Of the 4000 temporary quotas imposed by Brazil in 1975, about 1000 were still in existence in 1990; South Korea still employs quotas even though its balance of payments has been in surplus for some years now. A second exception to the rule against quotas is in agriculture. Countries that have price support programs are permitted to impose quotas against agricultural imports. Because of this clause, GATT has had little effect on farming, as we saw in Chapter 4. It should be noted that even where quotas are strictly illegal by the GATT rules, the prohibition against them is violated often enough.

(c) Members agree to consult on trade problems at meetings of the GATT Council of Representatives, and to submit their disputes to GATT panels. As Table 6.1 shows, these panels have recently been proliferating as trade disputes have intensified and as countries have become more willing to use this method.

Before 1987, two or three panel decisions per year had been the usual total; 52 panels had given a ruling between the time of GATT's foundation in the late 1940s to mid-1986. Under new dispute settlement rules adopted in 1989, the

Table 6.1   **GATT panels, 1983–1988**

1983	2	1986	2
1984	3	1987	8
1985	4	1988	17

Source: Jagdish Bhagwati, The World Trading System at Risk, *Princeton, 1991, calculated from pp. 115–125.*

empaneling process has been speeded up. Consultations take place within thirty days of a request, followed by sixty days for consultations, and six months for panel deliberations and a decision.

A good many GATT panels have been successful in healing trade disputes. We have already noted some of these, including the U.S. and EC case against the protectionist behavior of Canadian provincial liquor boards, which set high prices on imports (the decision went against Canada); and the U.S. complaint against Thailand's ban on imported cigarettes that led to a panel decision against the Thais. In 1986, the United States imposed a customs user fee, collected on an *ad valorem* basis at 0.17%, to assist in financing the customs service. Complaints to GATT by Canada and the EC held that collecting the fee on an *ad valorem* basis did not reflect the cost of the service and that it would raise more than customs spends. A GATT panel found against the United States, and in 1990 congress revised the fee, establishing a minimum and a maximum. Another complaint brought by the EC, Canada, and Mexico in 1987 challenged the U.S. policy of financing Superfund environmental protection by means of a discriminatory tax on petroleum of 8.2¢ per barrel for domestic oil and 11.7¢ on imported oil. GATT panels recommended an end to both these U.S. practices, and congress in 1989 adopted a single rate for both imported and domestic oil.

The successes have certainly been limited, however. Many major areas of friction never make it to GATT, as when a voluntary restraint is negotiated. For example, in the 1980s at a time when GATT-refereed agreements covered about $2 billion in trade, approximately $60 billion of trade was restricted without reference to GATT. Other disputes continue to fester even after a GATT ruling, because the ruling may be ignored. GATT panels are not binding if a party does not accept a judgment. If a country refuses to accept an adverse ruling, the only recourse is for the injured nation to retaliate legally. This right is obviously not of much use to a small country with little economic clout. The lack of any power to enforce decisions by applying sanctions has been an embarrassing one.

Indeed, there are numerous examples of panel decisions being flouted. The EC did so in a case of protection against citrus fruits imports, with a decision favorable to the United States ignored by the EC. That caused the Pasta War when the United States retaliated with tariffs against EC pasta. A panel's 1977 finding that the EC's subsidies for sugar exports were harming Australia and Brazil and should be changed has not affected EC policy. Another case involved EC subsidies on oilseeds. Oilseeds include sunflower seed, soybeans, and rapeseed, which are pressed for their oil. The EC was paying subsidies of nearly three times the world market price to oilseed processors to compensate them for buying the expensive EC product. U.S. oilseeds exports to the EC fell from 11.9 million metric tons in 1982 to 6.4 million in 1990. A GATT panel found against the EC in 1990. The EC proposed to shift the subsidy away from processors to oilseeds farmers. The United States said the subsidy would still be two times the world price, so overproduction would continue. Another GATT panel found against the

EC's reform in 1992, but once again the EC refused to abide by the ruling. This dispute was a dangerous one, with announcements of U.S. penalty duties and EC retaliation against them. A compromise was finally arrived at in 1993.

The United States has also ignored GATT rulings. The American Selling Price (ASP) case involved a few U.S. tariffs charged not on the foreigner's price, but on the American selling price of competing products. This, of course, led to much higher duties. ASP did not disappear until many years after GATT had found this type of tariff illegal. A case pressed by many countries against the U.S. sugar quotas discussed in Chapter 4 went against the United States in 1989, but the result was inconsequential: the quotas were replaced by tariff-quotas in 1990, with little effective change.

For a long time, political sensitivity inhibited GATT's ability to search for violations of its rules and publish the information. This has now changed, and since 1989 a Trade Policy Review Mechanism has been in place. Member countries now make reports to GATT on their existing barriers, after which GATT issues a commentary. The first reports and comments, in 1989, covered Australia, Morocco, and the United States. The GATT comments on the U.S. report singled out unilateral retaliation outside the GATT rules, with protection in sugar, dairy products, other agricultural products, textiles, clothing, steel, machine tools, autos, glass, and semiconductors all receiving specific attention. The report on the EC was issued in April 1991, the tenth in the series. *The Economist* stated that the first nine were relatively "genial and uncontroversial" while this tenth on the EC was "openly critical."[5] It underlined that the EC's political institutions are still too weak to resist the pressure for trade barriers of individual states and industries.

THE GATT ROUNDS OF TRADE NEGOTIATIONS   GATT's most impressive activity has been its sponsorship of conferences or rounds of multilateral trade negotiation. Seven such rounds have already taken place, and another is currently in progress. Negotiations have been held at Geneva in 1947; at Annecy, France, in 1949; at Torquay, England, in 1950–1951; at Geneva in 1956 and again in 1960–1962 (the Dillon Round) and in 1962–1967 (the Kennedy Round). The Kennedy Round cut tariffs some 35%, to an average *ad valorem* level of 10.3%, and became fully effective on January 1, 1972.

This was followed by the biggest of all the rounds to that time, the Tokyo Round of Multilateral Trade Negotiations, or MTN, of 1975–1979. Nearly 100 countries participated in the Tokyo Round, so named because it was decided on at a foreign ministers' meeting in Tokyo in 1973. (It was originally known as the Nixon Round, but a new name was needed in a hurry.) The negotiations actually took place at Geneva, not Tokyo. The Tokyo Round tariff reductions were phased in gradually, becoming fully effective on January 1, 1987. The major industrial countries cut their tariffs by about a third in trade-weighted terms, as shown in Table 6.2.[6]

The weighted average for all U.S. tariffs was 4.4% in 1988, slightly below the EC's 4.7% but well above Japan's 2.8%. The low, almost insignificant, nature of

Table 6.2 **Average tariffs before and after Tokyo Round (percent of value of imports) and depth of cut (percent)**

	Pre-Tokyo	Eight years after	Depth of cut, %
All industry	7.1	4.7	34
Raw materials	0.8	0.3	64
Semimanufactures	5.7	4.0	30
Finished manufactures	9.8	6.5	34
Agricultural products	11.7	11.0	7

modern tariffs as a barrier to trade has, however, been partly spoiled by the rise of many other sorts of obstacles. Some of these were described in Chapter 5; others will be addressed later in this chapter and in the next.

Many of the tariff reductions (well over 90% of those applying to industrial goods in the most important trading nations, all in the United States, 99% in the EC, 97% in Japan) were bound in an agreement not to increase them unilaterally. These bindings are, however, sometimes broken as part of trade disputes.

The most disappointing of the Tokyo Round's results was in agriculture, where the tariff cuts covered less than one third of total agricultural trade. Far fewer agricultural tariffs were bound, especially by Japan and the EC. Another disappointment is that tariff peaks still exist, rising above the relatively low duties on most products. The average rate may be low, but the peaks can distort trade significantly in the sectors where they apply. For example, a third of the EC's tariffs and a sixth of U.S. and Japanese tariffs are still above 10%, with textiles, clothing, shoes, and petrochemicals frequent beneficiaries. A further cause for regret was continuing high tariffs in the less developed countries, reaching an average in South Asia of 77%, 55% in Brazil, and 30% or more in Colombia, Ghana, Mexico, Thailand, Tunisia, Venezuela, and Zaire among others. The average in a 20-country sample of LDCs is 25.5%.[7] Most of the LDCs have bound only one fifth to one fourth of their tariffs.

The first six GATT rounds had focused almost entirely on tariff reduction, but the Tokyo Round was much broader in scope, with several codes of understanding signed in areas of major controversy. There is now a Customs Valuation Code to regularize valuation for tariff purposes, and a Standards Code to prevent unnecessary obstacles imposed by means of rules and appeal procedures. A Government Procurement Code attempted to open up government purchases, while a Subsidies and Countervailing Duties Code tried to bring the problem of subsidies for exports under control. Several of these have already been discussed; several will be returned to later. A Safeguards Code was, however, stillborn. There is as yet no agreement on the degree to which a country can impose temporary protection to rescue an industry harmed by tariff cuts. The EC argues strongly for selective safeguards that can be applied to the trade of individual countries. Many GATT members, and probably most economists, believe that such discrimination would be a significant backward step.

THE URUGUAY ROUND

During the early 1980s there was a long debate on the desirability of a new GATT round of trade talks. The most enthusiastic supporters were the United States, which wanted to control the problems in agriculture, services, and high-tech products, and Japan, which wanted to put a rein on the rapidly growing worldwide protection against its manufactured goods. At Punta del Este, Uruguay, the GATT membership in 1986 finally agreed to a new Uruguay Round of negotiations that began in 1987. The Uruguay Round is by far the broadest ever undertaken, with many aspects of international trade being considered that have never before been taken up in a GATT round. At one time 15 separate groups of negotiations were underway. The issues are very much interlinked, with progress in one area contingent on progress in others, which is why the membership must achieve a big package deal. By contrast to the earlier GATT rounds, this one has been surrounded by much less secrecy and has been conducted by much bigger delegations. The major Uruguay Round meeting held at Brussels in December 1990 could count over 300 official representatives from the United States alone, with another 600 or so industry and congressional observers and lobbyists in the U.S. entourage.

THE U.S. NEED FOR NEW TRADE LAWS FOR GATT ROUNDS   Alone among the major industrial countries, the U.S. congress must pass implementing legislation to give the president the power to negotiate in any new GATT round, just as it has in every round dating back to 1947. The trade bills granting this power also become a vehicle for other trade strategies, including those of protectionist interests. These enabling bills thus become landmarks of high importance, as discussed in the accompanying box.

■ *U.S. TRADE LAW IN RECENT YEARS*

The Trade Expansion Act of 1962 was the legislation passed to allow the United States to negotiate in the Kennedy Round. Under it, the president was authorized to cut any U.S. tariff by 50%. There was an escape clause whereby industries claiming harm could obtain some relief. The relief could be a reimposition of protection, as had also been true under the Reciprocal Trade Agreements. For the first time, however, there were also provisions for adjustment assistance in the form of federal aid to firms and workers that could show that injury had resulted from the tariff cuts.

The Trade Reform Act of 1974 enabled the United States to enter the Tokyo Round negotiations. This time the president received the authority to reduce tariffs by 60% on most items over a 10-year period. The ability of congress to obstruct an agreement was sharply limited by giving that body only 60 legislative days to veto the presidential action with an up or down vote. Adjustment assistance was liberalized.

A new act was needed to allow the United States to negotiate in the Uruguay Round, but its birth was long and difficult, finally taking place in 1988 only after a struggle to exclude clauses that would have protected numerous specific industries, a presidential veto, and a resubmission of altered legislation. Passage of a new trade bill always generates a frenzy of lobbying activity by special interests.

When the 1988 Omnibus Trade Act finally passed, it was over 1000 pages long, had been worked on by 199 members of 17 Senate reconciliation committees to bring the House and Senate versions into agreement, and resulted in a 3000-page conference report. ("There are two things," ran the quip, "that you don't want to see being made: sausages and trade law.") The act allowed 90-day fast-track, no-amendment consideration of the Uruguay Round results if these results were submitted to congress before May 31, 1991. A two-year extension was provided for unless congress blocked it by majority vote, and extension proved to be necessary when the 1991 deadline was reached without an agreement yet in sight. Attempts to block the extension failed, but the fast-track provisions expired anyway on June 1, 1993. President Clinton called for further fast-track legislation, which was being considered by congress at the time of writing.

Among the clauses of importance in the 1988 act is one that gives the president the power to negotiate a further tariff reduction of up to 50%. Others changed various rules on unfair trade practices, which we shall consider in the next chapter. Yet another is leading to the enlargement of the commercial staffs at U.S. embassies abroad, which staffs strikingly number only about 10% those of Japan. All in all, the consensus among economists was that in spite of some questionable areas the act was considerably less protectionist than had been expected.

The difficulties of pushing through new legislation for every GATT round has highlighted the lack of a centralized government agency for trade matters in the United States. Some have proposed the creation of a new Department of International Trade and Industry, a DITI to match the famous Japanese ministry of the same name (MITI). It is certainly true that trade policy has never had a proper home in the executive branch; to 1962, the negotiations were undertaken by the Department of State, while presently the duties are shared by the Department of Commerce, the U.S. International Trade Commission, and the president's special trade representative. It is also true that this fragmented approach means that U.S. policy usually reacts to complaints, unlike MITI's activism in Japan. But the Reagan Administration, originally strong in support of a new DITI, did not push the plan, mostly because congress insisted on some provisions the administration did not wish to accept. Though the proposal is likely to surface again, it was not included in the 1988 bill.

THE TENTATIVE AGREEMENT THUS FAR   Some Uruguay Round agreements have already been tentatively established, while other questions are still undecided.[8] Decisions made on subjects already addressed in this book are taken up here, while provisions in other areas are taken up as these areas are reached later in the book.

Tariffs   Tariffs will be cut again, with a target figure for the decrease of 33%. There is still a debate between the U.S. idea of reducing the tariffs on many nonsensitive products to zero or almost zero in order to get the decrease, and the counteroffer of many countries to impose an across-the-board cut. Tariffs on tropical products not grown in the developed countries will probably be abandoned. It is fair to say, however, that tariffs have already faded in importance as protective barriers, and getting rid of *all* remaining tariffs in the 18 major industrialized countries would probably increase their trade by no more than about 4% to 5%.[9] There are still remaining problems: tariff escalation against processed commodities, discussed in Chapter 4 and harmful to the LDCs; and the existence of tariff peaks and the high rates in the LDCs noted earlier in this chapter.

Quotas, VERs, and Other Nontariff Barriers   The Institute for International Economics estimates that if the industrial countries eliminated their NTBs, world trade would expand by $330 billion, or about 47% beyond the present level of trade in the covered items.[10] The Uruguay Round would phase out quotas and VERs, with special attention to reducing the heavy protection in textiles, clothing, and agricultural commodities. All would be subjected to *tariffication*—that is, tariffs would be substituted for quotas. (These industries are discussed in this book's Chapter 4.) Note that converting quotas to their tariff equivalents, even if no lowering were undertaken, would immediately increase government revenue, some of which could be used to aid workers and firms harmed by imports.

Trade-Related Investment Measures (TRIMs)   Various discriminatory practices applied to foreign firms, such as domestic content laws and trade balancing requirements in which the firms are required to export in order to import, would be prohibited, with a five-year phaseout period for the less developed countries. Export requirements for foreign firms, which are common in less developed countries, would still be permitted. Most industrial countries want to ban these practices, while Brazil, Egypt, India, and the Philippines have led the opposition. A much-needed item, an agreement to limit or eliminate the bidding over tax holidays and reductions used to lure production from one country to another, has not been achieved as yet.

Services   The negotiation of a General Agreement on Trade in Services (GATS) continues. Most favored nation treatment would be applied to barrier reduction in services. India has been the leading opponent of liberalizing this trade, and has proved to be a dogged negotiator. It has avidly protected its telephone industry. France is challenging the EC's right to negotiate on its behalf. A major stumbling block to an agreement is the United States' unwillingness to abandon maritime protection, which has led the EC to withdraw concessions in the audiovisual sector. The services negotiations will probably have to be extended for a considerable period (the EC suggests until 1997).

Government Procurement Negotiations are proceeding outside the Uruguay Round. Agreement has been reached to expand the code to include the European government-dominated utilities in energy, telecommunications, and transportation sectors that were excluded in the Tokyo Round. What to do about U.S. utilities, which are private, is still up in the air.

Dispute Settlement GATT panel reports would be accepted in 60 days unless they were rejected by consensus of the GATT Council members. Appeal will be permitted to a new body established for the purpose. If a country loses an appeal against a GATT panel report and still does not adhere to the report, retaliation will be permitted within 30 days by the injured party. Cross-retaliation among sectors will be allowed subject to controls. The possibility of cross-retaliation, say against cars because of a problem with agricultural commodities, would add a considerable amount of power to a GATT ruling.

A New Administering Organization A Multilateral Trade Organization (MTO) will be established to oversee the GATT agreements, the general agreement on services, dispute settlement, and all the other specific agreements. The extreme fragmentation brought on by all the GATT codes will receive some much-needed coordination. The new MTO could take action by majority vote, but that question is being left until the Uruguay Round is concluded. The MTO is not as radical as the interesting Canadian proposal to abolish GATT and replace it with a new organization akin to the Bretton Woods idea that failed to win approval after World War II.

The stakes are high, as Table 6.3 shows. If the aims of the Uruguay Round in reducing trade barriers can be achieved, there is a potential for a remarkable increase in world trade by about one-sixth.

Scheduled to last five years, this eighth GATT round has been difficult and its outcome is even yet uncertain. The round was to have been concluded in the five-day period of December 3–7, 1990, but the deadline was missed. So were year-end deadlines in 1991 and 1992. In 1993 the negotiations still remained stalled on the issue of agriculture.

THE ROUND STALLED BY AGRICULTURAL SUBSIDY ISSUES

The basic problem is overproduction of agricultural commodities due to price support programs. As already discussed in Chapter 4, high price supports have led to massive accumulations of surplus commodities, especially the EC's mountains.[11] The EC has struggled to be rid of these huge unwanted surpluses. Schemes abound for their use. For example, about one-third of all table wine production is presently being turned into industrial alcohol. Butter is being used for axle grease, in soap, in paint, and as a processed cooking oil. On occasion the butter has been fed to cows which then, of course, produce more butter. Some has simply been thrown away, and some has been donated as aid.

Table 6.3 **Major issues in the Uruguay Round (amounts in billion U.S. dollars)**

Issue	Amount of trade involved	Estimated trade expansion from complete liberalization
Protection by product type		
Goods	2500	400
Services	500	50
By type of protection		
Tariffs	2000	140
Nontariff barriers	700	330
Protection by sector		
Natural resource products	130	small
Textiles and clothing	160	50
Tropical products	40	2
Agriculture	330	100

Source: The Economist, *September 22, 1990, citing Gary Clyde Hufbauer.*

For the most part, though, the EC's chosen method for dealing with these surpluses has been to unload them on world markets for whatever price they will bear. These sales are of course at a loss; the loss constituting an export subsidy. GATT rules allow such subsidies as long as they do not lead to the acquisition of "more than an equitable share of world trade." The EC has largely ignored this qualifying clause, with the result that the EC, without a comparative advantage in agriculture, has been since 1986 the world's largest exporter of farm commodities. By 1988 its share of world farm exports had reached 36%. The EC had been a net importer of sugar, dairy products, and beef as late as 1974. Now it is the world's largest exporter of sugar, dairy products, poultry, eggs, and veal; vies with Argentina for the number-two position as a beef exporter; and is number three in wheat. The subsidized exports are sold in foreign markets in competition with domestic production and the exports of other countries. The prices received by local farmers in the countries that import the EC's surplus, and by other exporters that face the new competition from the EC, are forced down, and both groups lose market share. This, of course, is damage in addition to that caused from the lost markets in the EC itself, where imports are sharply restricted by trade barriers.

In reply to the EC tactics, the United States meets the price, that is, also subsidizes exports to keep its markets. The U.S. decision to retaliate with its own subsidies, though perhaps understandable, made the situation worse for the innocent bystanders (especially Argentina, Canada, Australia, New Zealand,

and Uruguay) that are damaged even more than before, and that cannot afford to follow this expensive tactic. A long battle developed, with the United States and numerous other supporters of freeing trade in agriculture highly critical of the EC's reluctance to change its policies. The basic demand of the free traders was that support for agriculture be decoupled from production and that the export subsidies be stopped.

In an attempt to referee the dispute and bring the Uruguay Round to a conclusion, GATT's Secretary-General Dunkel made a series of take-it-or-leave-it proposals in early 1992. After months of debate, during which the EC's chief agricultural negotiator resigned because a high EC official warned him that he had exceeded his powers in seeking a settlement, a great compromise was finally reached on November 20, 1992. It embraced most of the Dunkel proposals. The EC agreed to reduce the volume of its subsidized exports by 21% from a 1986–1990 base over six years, less than the 24% of the Dunkel draft but still a substantial figure. U.S. negotiators agreed not to count direct payment to farmers as production subsidies to be assessed against the 21% reduction in subsidized exports. The way seemed clear for the EC to cut back on its price supports and move to a new system of direct income payments less directly connected to production. (U.S. deficiency payments to farmers would not be counted as subsidies either.)

Hope was high for an imminent conclusion to the Uruguay Round. But then the situation began to unravel. France, which is the world's second-largest exporter of food, second only to the United States, objected to the compromise. Its government demanded that barriers to agricultural trade be raised or established in areas where they do not now exist (rebalancing) to make up for concessions under the agreement, and it challenged the EC's right to have gone so far with the compromise. It is easy to see why the French government was reluctant to accept the deal: French farmers can be amazingly militant. They sprayed manure on roads and politicians, burned foreign sheep alive, and dumped dirt and planted crops in crucial places such as the Champs Elysées in Paris. At the time of writing the new French government of Premier Edouard Balladur was calling for renegotiation of the farm agreement. Japan, which could bring enormous pressure on the EC to change its agricultural policies and conclude the Uruguay Round, remained content to sit on the sidelines because of its policy of excluding foreign rice. The Uruguay Round remained stalled.

Because of the delay, once-settled issues began to open up again, with squabbles particularly on tariffs, textile protection, and intellectual property. None of the agreements already struck can be considered as final until the whole package deal is completed. Undoubtedly somewhat disgusted, Arthur Dunkel, the GATT Director-General who has had so much to do with expediting the negotiations, announced his retirement. (Peter Sutherland of Ireland will be Dunkel's successor.) When and whether the Uruguay Round will be concluded is still up in the air, though politicians were once again aiming for an end-of-the-year (1993) completion date. All that could be said with certainty was that whatever the outcome, the Uruguay Round is a major turning point for GATT and for world trade.

WHY DO COUNTRIES PERSIST IN PROTECTIONISM? THE POLITICAL BASE OF TRADE BARRIERS

The argument underlying the theory of comparative advantage is very strong, as Chapter 2 demonstrated. Tariffs, quotas, and other nontariff barriers to trade lead to a less efficient use of the factors of production, so argued Chapter 4, with resulting restrictions on consumption and choice. Yet many people support trade barriers, and we must ask why they do so. The answers explored below are fourfold. (1) Most people do not understand trade theory and are largely unaware of the ways in which they are being hurt. (2) Those who might be hurt, or fancy themselves as being hurt, may be rational in seeking protection. (3) Politically strong industries, particularly those with a regional base, are able to use the state's powers to their own benefit, yet pass their actions off as legitimate by appeals to national interest. (4) A varied group of arguments exists under which some barriers to trade can be considered more or less legitimate and valuable tools. The traditional case is examined in this chapter. Newer arguments justifying trade barriers on the grounds of unfair foreign practices and strategic necessity are considered and critiqued in Chapters 7 and 8.

ON THE UNDERSTANDING OF THEORY

However elegant, the theory of trade is not particularly accessible to the average citizen. J.Q. Public recognizes taxes as a burden and is reasonably astute when it comes to tax and expenditure issues, but J.Q. is quite at a loss when the government increases the cost of goods without taxing them. (Recall the American congressman noted in Chapter 4 who said that quotas would not raise prices.) For that matter, even extremely well-informed citizens with training in economics will often have difficulty in estimating the actual effect on prices of some given barrier to trade.

As we have seen, protection raises the price of a product on the domestic market such that additional income goes directly from buyer to producer. Imagine the public outcry if congress voted a tax of $100 on every family of four to be paid to 12,000 U.S. sugar growers. Yet in effect that is exactly what has been done by means of trade barriers, with hardly a peep from the public.

Trade theory, moreover, cannot absolutely say that freer trade will improve welfare because of the difficulty of measuring welfare effects. Advocates of free trade are in the difficult position of having to defend their case against any conceivable objection, often theoretical ones with no empirical content. The theory, too, is rather vague on how displaced resources are going to be reemployed. However strong and however practical, no theory can give the certainty some citizens demand—and that applies to biology, geology, and physics as well.

"What you have is a theory," sneers the speaker. "What I have is 10,000 unemployed workers."

In essence, the level of economic knowledge is not sufficiently advanced. Politicians will listen to economists only if the voters are listening as well, but too often, deafness reigns.

ELEMENTS OF POLITICAL ECONOMY

The political case for protection is almost always stronger than the case for freer trade because the benefits of freer trade are spread thinly across the entire population, while the drawbacks are concentrated heavily on a narrow segment. J.Q. Public is not going to fight hard over a tariff that adds an extra $1 on a pair of shoes. Even if he recognizes that trade barriers do involve a cost for him, he has to figure out how to influence the governmental process, and do that for less than the few dollars each year it will cost him in higher shoe prices. The shoe companies and employees have their invested capital and their jobs at stake; particularly in areas where one-industry towns prevail, the local banks and shopkeepers find their interests affected also. Because they stand to lose major amounts of money, the narrowly based industries organize effective political actions. Which industries can best organize to do so is examined in the box on the following page.

What happens, of course, is that 100 or 1000 cases come up, each with the same pattern, until J.Q. Public finds himself paying hundreds or even thousands of dollars; he has been nickeled and dimed to death, to use the vernacular. At no point was it ever worthwhile to fight, yet the accumulated process has caused serious economic damage.

When a move toward trade barriers is made that harms a group with some political power, it is less likely to be successful. Manufacturers of machinery may be able to out-lobby the ball-bearing industry if the latter demands barriers; the damage to them is immediate and obvious. Computer manufacturers may eventually prevail when microchip makers demand protection; here too the consequences are obvious. All too often, however, the harm is so spread out among the consuming public that neither the political will nor ability to resist is sufficiently great.

An out-and-out appeal to transfer income from a large majority to a minority is unlikely in itself to be successful. Normally it must be glossed over with some appeal to legitimacy—protecting national workers, the evils of foreign sweatshops, national defense, and so forth. The smallness of the loss combined with the psychic pleasure of supporting national workers or striking a blow against foreign sweatshops may be enough to quiet opposition. One of the reasons we hear so much of fairness and level playing fields in the discussion of tariffs is to give a sense of legitimacy to what otherwise would appear to be a strictly economic, money-grabbing activity.[12]

■ VOTING PRESSURES TO BRING TRADE BARRIERS

Modeling by economists has attempted to identify which interest groups can bring the greatest pressure on legislatures. There is a significant statistical fit linking the presence of protection with the size of an industry's labor force, with the share of imports in an industry's markets, and with declines in these markets. Some models, for example that of Richard Caves, link the size of trade barriers to voting strength, which is in turn tied to the labor-output ratio in an industry and its geographical dispersion. Generally, the greater the number of workers involved and the wider the spread of an industry, the more successful it is in obtaining protection. Governments typically work hardest to avoid harm to the largest numbers. Models embodying these assumptions often predict the height of trade barriers reasonably well, though there are as yet many unanswered questions.[13]

Robert E. Baldwin posits that a legislator will be more likely to vote for protectionist positions (1) the higher the percentage of voters in a constituency working in industries threatened by imports, and the larger their campaign contributions; (2) the lower the percentage of voters who work in industries producing goods for export or in industries that use protected goods as inputs, and the smaller their contributions; (3) the more protectionist is the legislator's political party and the chief executive; (4) if there is no damaging political tradeoff in a bill; and (5) the fairer the protection appears, for example if it aids low-income workers with low skills rather than the privileged, or if it retaliates against blatantly unfair foreign trading practices.[14]

The idea that protection often adheres to the industries with the largest number of workers connects nicely to the factor-proportions arguments of Chapter 3. Recall that trade brings a higher return to the factors of production that are relatively abundant, that is, the ones that produce what is exported, and a lower return to the scarce factors of production producing what is imported. The industries clamoring for protection because they face intense foreign competition may most likely be the industries employing intensively the country's scarce factor of production. Imports will then be injurious to that scarce factor. The tariffs that protect a labor-intensive industry when a country's scarce factor is labor will raise the return to labor and lower it for land and capital. This argument, propounded by Wolfgang Stolper and Paul Samuelson and named after them the Stolper-Samuelson theorem, is that protection benefits the scarce factor at the expense of the abundant one.

The long and short of it is that sectoral interests often determine trade policy, and sectoral interest may well not be the same as national interest. Furthermore, national interest may not correspond with international or global interest. Would that these all coincided. That they often do not is the stuff of political economy.

ON RENTS

Both the labor and the capital in a protected industry benefit from the trade barriers. Both now have more security, and higher revenues that can be divided between them.

As Chapter 4 showed, the increased producer surplus is in some senses a rent. But note that the principal benefactors are usually those who hold the resources when protection is established, particularly if they acquired the resources before the possibility of the trade barriers was anticipated; it is they who collected the windfall. Take the case of the U.S. establishment of quotas on imported oil (in 1954), which effectively kept domestic oil prices one-third higher than international prices. We would expect that the price in all oil-producing lands would increase. Domestic oil refineries, producing a higher-priced product, would also rise in value.

The risks of doing business will decrease as foreign competition is lessened. Lenders to the newly protected industry, who previously had demanded higher interest rates, will reduce their rates as the risks decline. Similarly, employees may previously have been nervous about committing themselves to an uncertain future. They thus demanded a compensating wages or benefits package, but with the quota they find themselves more secure. Those already employed continue to enjoy higher-than-market wages. Only the previous riskiness brought this boon, but the employees do not rush to refund their extra pay.

Some economists believe that the original owners walk off with the rent and subsequent owners buy at market prices. In this case the original owners would sell off their properties to investors who may be unaware of the importance of protection in keeping industry revenues high and risks low. That view assumes that the investors and workers coming into a protected industry are naïve, unwittingly taking the risk that the protective measures will disappear. Surely, however, investors, and hopefully employees, are not so naïve when they commit themselves to other risky projects, for example opening a business in a small mining town, developing a pharmaceutical drug that is not yet approved and may never be, or going to work on a distant pipeline project. *Any* investment or employment decision must take into account the possibility that the firm or industry will have a limited life.

The logical conclusion is that no compensation need be paid to losers when trade restrictions are removed. *If* investors and employees had enough information to calculate, however notionally, the risks of being in a protected industry, then they have *already been paid* enough to fold their tents and steal away when the trade barriers vanish. If they failed to act on information, they are stupid. If information was available and they failed to get it, they are lazy. If information was not even remotely available, then they are merely unlucky.

With this theoretical (and philosophical) background, we turn to examine the common arguments for protection.

THE ARGUMENTS FOR TRADE BARRIERS

The arguments favoring trade barriers are highly diverse, and run the gamut from the intensely theoretical to popular folklore. The remainder of this chapter covers the traditional arguments, all of which have been around for most of this century at least. Chapter 7 moves on to consider how the traditional arguments have broadened to include legal restrictions against a number of so-called unfair trade practices. Finally, Chapter 8 takes up the new case for the strategic management of trade.

DOMESTIC PRODUCTION AS A "GOOD"

Many people think of domestic production as being a kind of public good. Like a flag, a currency, a national symbol, and a world-champion sporting team or figure, having a domestic steel industry or producing one's own sugar or defending jobs against foreign attack confers some kind of psychic pleasure.

Certainly many public opinion polls indicate that people are increasingly attracted to protectionist policies. Whereas polling data in the mid-1970s found only a quarter of Americans surveyed favored keeping foreign-made goods out of the country, that figure was up to 40% in answer to the same question in 1980 and over 50% in the mid-1980s. According to pollster Daniel Yankelovich, over 70% of those polled in the United States can be depended on to say they favor trade barriers to protect American jobs.[15] All this must be taken with a grain of salt: If higher prices, less choice, and retaliation by foreign countries are included in the questions, the favorable opinion of trade barriers drops radically, to 26–28% support according to Yankelovich.

Nonetheless many people do appear to have a "tribal" preference for products made at home. Data to this effect are available. In 1985, 22% of Americans polled said they purposely sought out U.S.-made goods, while by 1989 that number had reached 39%.[16]

■ *DISTURBING PSYCHOLOGICAL FACTORS APPEAR IN SOME POLLS*

The answers to certain polling questions seem especially meaningful, suggesting that disturbing psychological factors must be at work. Recent polling data indicate that the public's preference for barriers to save American jobs is about 10 percentage points higher when imports from Japan are mentioned as the cause of the job loss rather than just imports in general. Over 80% of the U.S. population would prefer slower growth in both Japan and the United States to faster growth in both countries, if with the faster growth Japan were to take an economic lead.[17] One gathers that the majority would be even larger if the comparison were between slow growth in both countries, but relatively faster in the United States, versus fast growth, but with Japan ahead. An experiment conducted at Harvard University lends further credence to the idea that psychology is at work. In annual surveys, a large minority of a professor's classes prefer a hypothetical situation where the U.S. economy would grow by 5% and Japan's economy by 8%, to a situation where the United States would grow by 10% and Japan by 20%.[18] This must be largely due to psychology rather than economics. The reasoning must include a fear of losing first place, jealousy of the good foreign performance, and perhaps some element of racism.

Economists have tended to view personal preferences as none of their business as long as they are voluntary, with their attitude much the same as toward the lawyer who cuts his or her own firewood because that activity is viewed as recreation. The high opportunity costs can be seen as balanced by the high perceived benefits of exercise in the out-of-doors. Thus discriminatory decisions to buy American, buy British, or buy Japanese, when voluntary ones based on tastes have usually been thought to be off limits to policy. Economists in their role as policy advisors do not have to accept a prejudice against foreign goods (or foreigners themselves) as a given, however. They can treat it as the product of ignorance that should be excised by education, exhortation to do otherwise for the national good, and government promotion policies, perhaps even including import subsidies.

The view held by many economists that voluntary individual choices should be respected loses its innocence when governments by means of trade barriers *impose* a prejudice against foreign goods on their citizens. There is a grey area between individual choice and imposed barriers, however. For example, the Korean government apparently encouraged buy-Korean thinking, and the Japan Federation of Cement Users Cooperatives, with government looking on, advised members not to use imported cement. The Korean case was a serious one: During much of 1990 an anti-import campaign was being waged, and though Korean newspapers reported it as a grassroots protest against conspicuous consumerism, it seemed to be sponsored by the government.[19] Alertness is called for when "free choice" is actually a government protectionist policy in disguise.

■ *REMEMBER THAT BUYING AT HOME MAY NOT BE SO EASY*

In Chapter 5 we saw how the town government of Greece, New York, in buying the John Deere rather than the Komatsu managed to buy the foreign machine rather than the domestic one. Private citizens intent on buying at home face the same difficulty, and tracing some examples serves to remind us how complex the web of commerce has become. Nowadays, the Ford Escort contains parts from 15 different nations and a Honda, Mazda, or Toyota sold in the United States is likely to be U.S.-made in a Japanese-owned factory.

Consider a particular case: the buyer of a $10,000 Pontiac LeMans from General Motors, so proud of his decision to buy American that he has just pasted that American-flag sticker on the rear window. That buyer has unknowingly engaged in a considerable number of international transactions. Here is how Robert Reich traces them.[20]

Of the $10,000 paid to GM, about $3000 goes to South Korea for routine labor and assembly operations, $1850 goes to Japan for advanced components (engines, transaxles, and electronics), $700 to . . . Germany for styling and design engineering, $400 to Taiwan, Singapore, and Japan for small components, $250 to Britain for advertising and marketing services, and about $50 to Ireland and Barbados for data processing. The rest—less than $4000—goes to strategists in Detroit, lawyers and bankers in New York, lobbyists in Washington, insurance

> *and health care workers all over the country, and to General Motors shareholders all over the world. The proud new owner of the Pontiac is not aware of having bought so much from overseas, of course.*
>
> Indeed, the globalization of firms challenges many common stereotypes.

THE LOSS OF JOBS

The models of trade the book has presented to this point do not explicitly treat unemployment. An industry in an industrial country that is under pressure due to low wages abroad is in fact under attack due to high wages at home. If its labor force did not have other opportunities for employment (or for comfortable leisure), workers could not demand the high wages. That is the fundamental insight of comparative advantage. If capital did not have other uses, it would not be so expensive, and the same is true of land. But not every displaced worker has another opportunity. Some, with very poor alternative occupations, receive high wages nonetheless. Wages are set to attract the *marginal* worker,[*] and usually that point forms the basis for the wage structure, with increments for seniority and additional skills. The increments for seniority are at least partially means for attracting workers on the margin, who come because they have a future in the company. If a plant closes, those workers who are young and better educated, and who had been attracted to their jobs by wages slightly above those elsewhere, will find nearly equivalent work. Some, when driven into the market for a job search, may even find *better* work. Other workers will find rather poorer substitutes, and yet others, particularly the older and less skilled, may find nothing at all.

Our trade models handle this situation poorly because they assume—or apparently assume—a full employment situation in which all released resources can be reemployed. If, however, some resources are never reemployed, or must be employed in residual low-productivity occupations, then the loss for the economy can be substantially greater. It was thinking of this sort that led Walter Mondale during the 1984 presidential campaign to ask "What do we want our kids to do? Sweep up around Japanese computers?"

Recent empirical research does indeed lend some support to the position that reemployment may be difficult for some factors displaced by trade. The problem appears greatest for low-skilled, blue-collar workers. A late-1980s study suggests that if U.S. imports rise $10 billion and U.S. exports do the same, that balanced change would result in 179,000 workers losing their jobs because of the imports while 193,000 new jobs would be created in exporting.[21] But the jobs lost would mostly be in blue-collar manufacturing while the gains would largely be in the service sector—professional, managerial, marketing, and clerical. Whether the

---

[*] *Marginal* in its economic meaning, not in the sense that the worker is marginally needed, but in the sense that the worker is the one most likely to find a job somewhere else.

individuals who lose the blue-collar jobs are the ones who could fill the service jobs is a troublesome question and open to doubt.

Is this the Achilles' heel of trade theory? Since that theory is an enduring one, we should investigate more closely.

1. If we can show that the motivation of the older workers was economically rational, taken with adequate knowledge of risk, we may conclude that the economy has already paid them their full compensation. Suppose that workers were informed that their firm might close in the next decade. Indeed, we might even suppose the odds were known. The youngest workers would, of course, leave, and the oldest workers would stay. The middle-aged workers would have to calculate their switching costs of finding other employment—perhaps a lower wage, retraining, moving, or a longer commute—against the value of staying on. If they stay, then they have taken their loss at that point.

2. Keeping workers employed through ensuring that the plants stay open is an expensive proposition. If the government tries to keep the plant open, it finds that the plant still needs the younger workers and needs regular infusions of capital, such that the cost per job saved, particularly per job saved *of those who would not find another job*, is normally very high. As the next section shows, in the United States such costs run from around $30,000 to about $1 million *per job per year*. In these cases, the figures are averaged over *all* additional employment, not just those who would otherwise be unemployed, a figure rather difficult to derive. Notional or not, the number who would remain jobless is unlikely to be more than one third of the workers, so the cost of keeping those jobs could be triple the figures cited above.

THE HIGH COST OF RETAINING JOBS THROUGH PROTECTION   Whatever the cost to the individuals who would lose jobs except for the trade barriers, protection as a method for keeping them employed is much more costly for society. That is so because those who could find other work stay employed in their old jobs producing high-price products, and because new capital that could be more productively employed elsewhere is attracted into the protected industry. Studies by economists in this area often present cost estimates so high that on first reading they appear to be misprints. They are not misprints.

Economists have made a number of studies, principally in the United States and usually on an industry-by-industry basis, that examine the cost of one job saved for one year through protection. The first of these studies to achieve wide attention was carried out in the early 1980s at Washington University, St. Louis. More recently, a major research project was published by the Institute for International Economics in Washington, D.C. Its authors, Gary Hufbauer, Diane Berliner, and Kimberly Elliott, brought together numerous estimates of protection costs in various U.S. industries.[22]

Table 6.4 summarizes the data. To interpret Table 6.4, select a protected product. The table includes ten of the 31 in the Hufbauer-Berliner-Elliott study. Column A shows the import value for the product in the year in which the

Table 6.4 **The high cost of saving jobs through protection**

	A Import value ($ billion)	B Tariff or tariff equivalent (%)	C Resulting price increase (%)	D Resulting cost to consumer ($ billion)	E Resulting increase in employment	F Cost per job saved ($)	G Gain to foreigners ($ billion)
1. Textiles and apparel	16.50 (1984)	30.0	24.0	27.0	640,000	42,000	1.8
2. Carbon steel	10.21 (1984)	30.0	12.0	6.8	9000	750,000	2.0
3. Autos	29.26 (1984)	11.0	4.4	5.8	55,000	105,000	2.2
4. Benzenoid chemicals	2.70 (1984)	15.0	4.5	2.7	300	1,000,000+	neg.
5. Color TVs	1.54 (1982)	15.0	6.0	.4	1000	420,000	.1
6. Rubber footwear	.33 (1983)	42.0	21.0	.2	7800	30,000	neg.
7. Nonrubber footwear	2.48 (1981)	18.5	5.5	.7	12,700	55,000	.2
8. Sugar	1.26 (1984)	30.0	30.0	.9	15,300	60,000	.4
9. Dairy products	.59 (1983)	80.0	40.0	5.5	25,000	220,000	.3
10. Petroleum	7.86 (1973)	96.0	96.0	6.9	43,000	160,000	2.0

Source: The summaries of the Hufbauer-Berliner-Elliott results reported in Gary Hufbauer and Howard Rosen, Trade Policy for Troubled Industries, Washington, D.C., 1986, pp. 7–9, 20–21. Note that for three of these products, protection is not currently in place, it having been removed from nonrubber footwear in 1981, from television sets in 1982, and from petroleum in 1973.

Column A shows the import value for the product in the year in which the industry was analyzed.

Column B shows the level of tariff, if tariffs are the protectionist device in use, or the *tariff equivalent* if quotas or voluntary export restraints are the device. Tariff equivalents, as noted in the last chapter, are the predicted rates of tariff that would have reduced imports by exactly the amount that the quota or voluntary restraint did reduce them.

Column C shows an estimate of the resulting price increase, incorporating information on the elasticity of demand and supply. A $1 tariff will not increase prices by $1 if foreign producers cut their price. In the list of ten products, only sugar and petroleum show a situation in which the foreign producer was able to pass on the entirety of the tariff to the domestic market as a price increase.

Column D shows the annual extra cost to consumers from the protection. This is obtained by multiplying the price increase times the annual consumption of the protected product from both imports and domestic production (basically *A+B+C+R* of Fig. 4.1). The results are shown in column D and range up to a high of $27 billion per year in textiles. The total present cost to consumers for the 31 industries in the Hufbauer-Rosen study is $53 billion. Much of this represents a transfer of income to producers, but part of it is an efficiency loss to the economy, the so-called deadweight loss of Chapter 4. (Some of the cost is a transfer to foreign producers of the revenue effect, as for example in a VER. Column G shows the amounts involved.)

Column E shows the estimates of the induced increases in employment caused by the higher domestic output resulting from protection. Note that the numbers are relatively small, being greatest in textiles and apparel (640,000) but ranging down to only 9000 for carbon steel, 1000 for color televisions, and 300 for benzenoid chemicals. These estimates of jobs saved do not include management and supervisory personnel, nor jobs retained in allied industries (machine tools or tires used in car production, for example). But neither do they include any effect from the higher costs in industries using the protected product as an input, such as the construction industry, which uses structural steel. Thus the estimates of jobs saved shown in the table are probably an exaggeration for the economy as a whole.

Finally, Column F shows the annual consumer cost of the protection divided by the induced increase in employment caused by the protection, thus arriving at the annual cost to the consuming public per job saved in the industry. These results usually come as a shock to those unaware of how large the costs are. In all cases, the figures are well above average wages in the industry concerned. Some of the figures are stratospheric, such as $105,000 per year per job saved in the automobile industry, $220,000 in the dairy industry, $420,000 in color televisions, $750,000 in carbon steel, and over $1 million in benzenoid chemicals. Even the very lowest of the figures, $30,000 annually for a job saved in rubber footwear, is more than double the actual wages paid per production worker in that industry. This does not appear to be a very good bargain. The figures drive home the point that maintaining jobs by means of protection is an expensive proposition.[*] Other costs of protection that are more general in nature, such as the adverse effects on management efficiency, reduced scale economies, less learning, sluggishness in adopting new techniques, and slower growth, are ignored in this analysis. (On the other side of the coin, adjustment costs involved in transferring workers out of these industries if they were *not* protected are also ignored. But these adjustment costs are short run, whereas the costs of protection are continuous.)

Ironically, the ability of protection to save jobs over time is poor. This is because of economic responses on the part of both consumers and producers. On the demand side, higher prices lead consumers to search for substitutes, and after some initial expansion in the domestic share of the market, a portion of the gains is lost. (This represents the old Marshallian rule that demand becomes more elastic in the long run.) On the supply side, the cause of the job loss is likely to be factor substitution. Labor, especially less-skilled labor, is relatively an expensive factor in the United States. Whatever the market price of the finished product, protection or no, management will see advantages in shifting factor proportions away from the expensive factor when it is possible to do so. The higher profits after protection may even be the catalyst for this decision. Thus capital and technology substitute for labor in the industries where labor is an important share of costs, and thus even during a period of protection, employment in the protected industry is likely to fall anyway. It did in fact fall in all the cases shown here in Table 6.5.

---

[*] It should be pointed out that the range of estimates for the costs of protection in the United States is wide, often by as much as 50% or more from highest to lowest. See the range cited by Robert C. Feenstra, "How costly is protectionism?" *Journal of Economic Perspectives*, Vol. 6, No. 3, Summer 1992, p. 163. Though fewer studies have been made in other countries, the conclusion that protection is very expensive per job retained is apparently universal. For example, the World Bank's *World Development Report*, 1988, Washington, D.C., 1988, p. 16, notes that the preservation by protection of one job in Britain's auto industry costs consumers four times the average wage in that industry.

Table 6.5 Annual change in employment, percent		
Textiles, apparel	1980–84	−1.6
Carbon steel	1980–84	−10.4
Autos	1979–84	−4.5
Color TVs	1976–82	−3.7
Benzenoid chemicals	1978–84	−2.1
Rubber footwear	1975–83	−4.5
Nonrubber footwear	1975–82	−1.5
Sugar	1976–83	−2.7
Dairy products	1978–83	−0.6
Petroleum	1954–75	−2.7

Source: From Hufbauer, Berliner, and Elliott, as summarized in Hufbauer and Rosen (see Table 6.4), pp. 22–24.

Considering all 31 of the most important cases of protection studied by Hufbauer, Berliner, and Elliott, employment increased only in motorcycles and fishing, stayed the same in two other cases, and fell in the remaining 27.

Interestingly then, industries after being granted protection have on the whole continued to adjust to changed economic circumstances, at least where their labor force is concerned. In effect, even with the very high cost of the protection to consumers, many jobs were lost, no doubt at a slower rate than in a free market, but lost in large numbers nonetheless.

CHEAP LABOR AND FOREIGN SWEATSHOPS: THE FALLACIES OF THE LOW WAGES ARGUMENT

The aspect of employment loss from trade that generates the greatest concern with the general public, and that is a wellspring of protectionist sentiment, is the fear of competition from cheap or pauper labor abroad. Generations of managers, voters, and legislators have harbored this fear, which holds that a developed country's industry is at a disadvantage when competing against foreigners who pay very low wages to the workers they employ. (Essentially, both the Smoot-Hawley Tariff and its predecessor the Fordney-McCumber Tariff embodied this argument. Its designers in many cases attempted to craft a scientific tariff to equalize all costs of production between the United States and its trading partners. Had the U.S. government followed the law literally, there would have been no trade at all. In the 1920s the United States actually sent delegations abroad to try to assess foreign costs so as to recommend an equalizing tariff. Foreign governments and manufacturers were not, however, particularly receptive to these delegations.)

Undeniably there is a large differential between hourly wages paid in the United States and Western Europe, and wages paid in South Korea, Taiwan, Brazil, and other newly industrializing countries. Sometimes, even in a major industry such as steel or autos, the wage gap can be as much as eight or ten times, or even more. Recently labor costs in manufacturing averaged $1.57 per hour in Mexico, $1.49 in Brazil, $1.79 in Korea, $2.19 in Taiwan, and 29¢ in Sri Lanka, compared to about $14 in the United States.[23]

Proponents of the cheap labor argument use the data on low wages abroad to make two claims, both of which appear persuasive to much of the public. First, goods manufactured by the cheap labor will so undersell domestic output that domestic producers cannot compete; and second, that domestic firms will be motivated to transfer their operations overseas so they, too, can employ cheap labor. Unemployment mounts.

The case contains grave weaknesses, however, some of which can be clarified by the theory of comparative advantage, others of which can be addressed on political and pragmatic grounds. Consider first this question: If indeed cheap labor is all-powerful in the marketplace, then how is it possible that a rich country can *export* anything at all in competition with the low-wage rates? We have seen the answer in Chapters 2 and 3.

Even in a labor-intensive industry, the labor may be sufficiently productive so that the high productivity offsets the high wages. A simple example will show this: What if wages in some developed country's industry are six times higher per person per hour than they are in poor Poveria? If productivity in terms of output per worker in this rich country's industry is less than six times higher, then Poveria will have the advantage; but if productivity is *greater* than six times per worker, then the rich country will have the advantage. In short, a large wage gap may be offset by an even larger productivity gap. Productivity differences may be due to complementary physical capital, to superior education, training, and skill levels, to more advanced technology—but the reasons may be even more basic, as when the low-wage labor is illiterate, or malnourished, or sickly, or unused to factory methods. The observer must not miss that the low-wage workers of poor Poveria, or middle-income Singapore or South Korea, may themselves view with substantial alarm the competitive strength of countries where capital is relatively cheap, where technology is relatively more advanced, where the stock of natural resources is large, and where labor is well-educated and highly skilled.

All this explains why the United States, in spite of many trade concerns, is the world's largest exporter, and why Japan has survived two decades of rising wages, which are now well above those of some European countries, to remain the world's most successful example of growth through export. In this view, the low wages abroad are irrelevant for the gains from trade; the labor can be transferred to other uses. The damage done by low wages is not general but specific—the injury comes to labor-intensive industries, where not only is labor use important, but also labor costs are high relative to productivity. The lesson applies everywhere, not just in the United States or Europe. Japan's textile producers found in the 1970s that Japan's labor costs were high enough to make that industry uncompetitive. Many textile firms transferred their operations to Southeast Asia. Singapore has recently been concentrating on more technically advanced items rather than on the traditional labor-intensive production. Its rapidly rising wages have priced it out of the running for some goods; Singapore's loss has been a gain to Indonesia, the Philippines, Malaysia, and so forth.

In a developed country it is a dangerous game to protect the labor-intensive industries harmed by low wages abroad. Keeping out the labor-intensive products of foreigners is an open invitation for them to limit imports of the developed country's own capital-intensive or high-technology products. Such trade war strategies are no solution—though they could and probably would benefit the owners and workers in the rich countries' labor-intensive industries, and the higher-tech, more capital-intensive industries of the less developed countries.

Lastly, even in areas of employment where foreign labor is both less expensive and equally or more productive than rich-country labor in that same industry, it is remarkable to see how limited the damage would be. A very large amount of employment is in the service sector, naturally protected against imports. The protection takes the form of high transport costs; sometimes it is not

Table 6.6	U.S. employment by sectors, 1989, in millions
Construction	7.7
Transport, public utilities	8.1
Wholesale, retail trade	24.2
Finance, insurance, real estate	8.0
Other services	38.2
Government (federal, state, local)	5.6
Total	91.8

Source: Bureau of Statistics, U.S. Department of Labor.

possible to transport the product at all. Table 6.6 illustrates this rather effective insulation against foreign competition. In 1989, total U.S. employment outside of agriculture was 114.1 million. Of this total, those employed in the service jobs shown in the table were subject to very little competition from imports.

The table's 91.8 million makes up 80% of the 114 million total, and that 80% is substantially protected from foreign competition. This naturally protected service sector is actually expanding; the figure was a lower 78% in 1984 and 76% back in 1976. The reader might sensibly ask whether foreign firms could enter into construction, or foreign banks compete with U.S. banks, or foreign interests buy U.S. motels, insurance companies, airlines, or department stores. All are possible, and the United States is actively encouraging freer trade in services. But these events would not weaken the claim of natural protection, because the immigration laws alone would require that such firms hire mostly American workers and not foreigners. At worst, some high management or technical positions would be lost. The natural protection remains intact. (It is true that huge illegal flows of immigrants might alter this picture, but that case is a far different one from claiming protection because of cheap labor abroad.)

The only segment of the nonfarm labor force that does not benefit from natural protection, then, appears to be manufacturing. This remaining 22% of the labor force, however, includes those workers employed in industries that produce for export, a figure that is well above one third of manufacturing jobs.

A last development is somewhat ironic. In the United States, labor costs have been falling relative to a number of important trading partners, as is traced in the accompanying box. United States labor is now cheap compared to, say, German labor.

■ *U.S. LABOR IS NO LONGER THE WORLD'S MOST EXPENSIVE*

Labor costs in U.S. manufacturing are now relatively lower than they used to be, below the costs of a number of trading partners, as Table 6.7 shows.

Table 6.7   The U.S. labor-cost turnaround

	Hourly compensation 1985	Hourly compensation 1990	Unit labor cost, 1985–90
Britain	$6.19	$12.43	+10.8%
Canada	10.80	16.02	+7.9%
France	7.52	15.23	+11.0%
Germany	9.57	21.53	+15.6%
Italy	7.41	16.41	+14.3%
Japan	6.43	12.64	+10.3%
United States	13.01	14.77	−0.1%

Source: U.S. Labor Department data for hourly compensation in manufacturing and unit labor costs reported in the Wall Street Journal, *January 27, 1992.*

In short, protection against cheap labor is unnecessary as far as the vast majority of American jobs is concerned. Even if it were attempted, it would jeopardize the large export sector that would surely be retaliated against. It would not be possible to erect barriers against cheap foreign labor without other countries raising their own barriers against what they see as cheap physical and human capital, cheap natural resources, and high-tech advantages.

THE SWEATSHOP ARGUMENT   Sometimes the cheap labor argument is made in another way. It is highly immoral, some would say, to purchase imported goods made by sweatshop labor working under substandard conditions. This human-rights argument appears persuasive on first hearing, and it carries considerable influence, notably in the United States and Scandinavia. Several laws to protect against goods produced by child labor or in countries that discriminate against union labor have been enacted by the U.S. Congress.

Yet the humanitarianism of the argument may not be as charitable as it seems. The workers in Third World plants are there because they have considered that the balance of costs and benefits is more favorable than it is in other occupations. While by rich-country standards conditions may be bad, or even very bad, we must compare the situation in a Third World factory or farm producing for export with conditions elsewhere in the country, which are worse. If the market is operating reasonably, these people have chosen to work in whatever circumstances and at whatever wages they accept because to the best of their knowledge they cannot do better. Our great-grandmothers and great-grandfathers made much the same choice. If an importing country were to restrict trade because of labor's poor conditions or low pay, the demand for labor would fall in the low-wage country. Predictably this would either cause wages to decline still further in that country or would result in unemployment if wages did not fall. Such a strategy would presumably not reflect a humanitarian concern for sweated labor.[*] The harm caused to consumers in the protecting country must also be considered, along with the danger that humanitarian concerns will be manipulated by protectionist interests. These concerns point toward alternative policies such as encouraging the establishment of labor standards through organizations such as the U.N.'s International Labor Organization (ILO).

■ *RECENT U.S. ACTIONS AGAINST SWEATSHOP LABOR*

The U.S. program of tariff exemptions for less developed countries requires recipients to ensure "internationally recognized worker rights," including trade unions and "acceptable" conditions of work. The latter clause has been used to halt the repression of unions and improve sweatshop conditions. Romania, Nicaragua, and Paraguay were the first to go for these reasons, in 1987. Chile followed in 1988; Burma and the Central African Republic in 1989, Liberia in 1990. After policy changes, Paraguay, Chile, and the Central African Republic were reinstated. Numerous petitions to exclude other poor countries have been filed by the AFL-CIO and are in process.

A LEGITIMATE SIDE TO THE CHEAP LABOR ARGUMENT   For all the fallacies associated with the cheap labor argument, it does have a legitimate side. In developed countries, manufacturing jobs in industries with low skill requirements will be under heavy competitive pressure from cheap labor costs abroad, and workers in these industries may well be forced either to find new employment or to go on the dole. Much depends on (1) a full-employment macroeconomic policy, (2) the numbers of low-skill workers displaced, (3) their willingness to take jobs in other unthreatened sectors of the economy, and (4) whether these workers have enough general education to benefit from retraining. The advanced country that neglects the education of its young people and the retraining of its workers as the fortunes of industry ebb and flow is asking for trouble when trade brings economic change.

THE HEALTH CARE ARGUMENT

A recent argument has arisen that U.S. health care costs, much of which must be paid by firms to cover their employees' health insurance premiums, make these firms less competitive. Each U.S.-made automobile carries a $700 higher price tag, so it is said, because of the health expenditures of the carmaker. Yet this

---

[*] Sometimes the behavior of an exporting country's government can go beyond the usual bounds. China, for example, has been charged with exporting goods produced with forced labor in penitentiaries, labor camps, and reeducation centers. A U.S. law of 1930 forbids imports made by "convict, forced, or indentured labor."

position is not as persuasive as it seems. Consider that if the carmakers' health care costs have risen, then these higher costs may simply result in lower wages for the workers rather than a higher price for the car. In any case, if health care costs rise for domestic firms and these costs are passed on to the price of their output, then the exchange rate will be affected. The lower U.S. exports and higher imports will tend to depreciate the dollar, thus working to offset the cost increase.[24]

PROTECTION TO REDUCE THE TRADE DEFICIT

Many countries have acted as if they believe that trade barriers can cure a deficit in the balance of trade, using one or more of the measures discussed in the accompanying box. If imports exceed exports, so goes the argument, then erect barriers that will stem the tide of imports and lead the country back to balance.

■ *MEASURES TO IMPROVE THE BALANCE OF TRADE*

The British pioneered in the use of deposit advances against imports for this purpose, though there had been some earlier employment of the idea in less developed countries in the 1950s. The original British scheme of 1968 required importers to deposit with the Treasury an amount equal to half the value of their imports for six months at no interest. Such regulations spread rapidly, and in the 1970s well over a dozen countries had established import deposit schemes. These included Iceland, Israel, Italy, Greece, and Yugoslavia.

Similar in intent is the import surcharge, a flat percentage tax charged across the board on imports. In the United States, President Nixon's 15% import surcharge of 1971 was a well-known example. Many other countries have used the idea in recent years, and it was being discussed in the United States during the mid-1980s as a possible means to offset the strong dollar of that time. Across-the-board surcharges are like a one-sided depreciation of the currency in that all imports are made more expensive, but unlike a depreciation in that exports are discouraged—domestic output now appears relatively more profitable. Also unlike a depreciation, tariff revenue accrues to the government.[25]

The argument that protection will reduce the trade deficit contains a major fallacy, however, even assuming that foreign governments do not retaliate. The problem is basically macroeconomic, drawing on lessons from Chapter 2 that will also be enlarged on in the second half of the book. First, a balance of trade deficit is commonly caused by improper macroeconomic policies, such as the long-standing U.S. government budget deficit, that lead to high interest rates. The high rates appreciate the currency, discourage exports, and suck in imports. If in response government attempts to exclude imports to correct the trade deficit, then fewer dollars are put on the foreign exchange market, and the dollar appreciates further. More imports can therefore be purchased, and the appreciation tends to offset the protection. If foreign exchange rates are instead fixed, then stemming the flow of imports will divert demand to domestic production, raising prices and incomes. The higher prices make imports look more attractive after all, and the higher incomes will suck in imports as well. Protection to end a trade deficit is basically self-defeating; macroeconomic reform is the proper course of action.

PROTECTION AS A DEVICE FOR BARGAINING?

High protectionist barriers can be made to serve as a tradeoff for bargaining purposes. This, it is said, is a reason for having them. The argument is very similar to the debates surrounding disarmament. Once you are disarmed, you lose the means to bring pressure on some adversary, who may then be less likely to disarm than before. This argument is probably correct in principle, but there are also a number of points to consider.

(a) Little or no unilateral reduction in protection will then take place, just as little unilateral disarmament ever occurs. Since the argument often seems to be applied to some possible future bargain, the action taken at any present moment is limited, and the harm from the trade barriers outweighs the gains from the bargain.

(b) Nothing is wrong with large unilateral decreases in protection. It has been done before—Britain in the nineteenth century, the United States in the 1840s and again in 1913, Australia and New Zealand in the 1980s. The results are not as good as they would be if the rest of the world cut protection, but they do increase welfare. What is more, they might increase welfare far more than some small multilateral decline in the future, for which the bargaining tariff is preserved. To repeat vivid questions first asked in the nineteenth century, should a country put big rocks in its harbors because *other* countries have rocky coastlines? Is not the very existence of the foreign rocks punishment enough for the foreigners? Or to put the same question in a more modern form: If trade barriers do damage, then isn't the argument that we must have them for bargaining akin to saying that because other people are drug addicts, we must become drug addicts as well to show them how misguided they are? These questions are not only vivid, but fair.

(c) The argument is equally able to justify increasing protection, for that course will presumably enhance one's bargaining power. That could be very dangerous, however, in a world where retaliation is possible and trade wars can occur. Economists estimate that a full-blown trade war, if it were conducted with quotas and if it involved several rounds of retaliation, could reduce output in the United States and the EC by as much as 20%. Not only would exports decline, but the tendency toward higher prices would (assuming unchanged monetary policy), boost interest rates and depress output even outside the foreign trade sector.[26]

THE INFANT-INDUSTRY ARGUMENT

The infant-industry argument for protection celebrated its bicentennial in 1991. It is perhaps the most familiar of the arguments against free trade, propounded by Alexander Hamilton, George Washington's Secretary of the Treasury, in his *Report on Manufactures* of 1791. It was further developed by Germany's Friedrich List in his *Das nationale System der politischen Œkonomie* of 1841. Both Hamilton and List directed their arguments against the massive preeminence of British manufacturing during this period. They emphasized that when an industry is small in scale, new, and inexperienced, its products will naturally be expensive, and it may be unable to compete with a well-developed foreign industry. If the infant is protected, that will allow new firms to operate, to acquire the knowledge needed to train their labor and move down their learning curves, to accumulate capital (since capital markets may themselves be in their infancy), and to improve production processes. When these goals are attained, the infant-industry tariff can be removed, as it will no longer be necessary.

In technical terms, trade barriers to protect infant industries are expected temporarily to put a country on a lower indifference curve because imports are made more expensive, but in the expectation that eventually the production possibility curve will shift outward far enough to more than recover the lost ground. Crucial to the argument is that eventually the whole world gains—both the country that develops the infant and the rest of the world that imports products from it if the industry grows up to have a comparative advantage.

In recent history, infant-industry protection has been employed heavily by Japan; Canada and Australia were important supporters of the argument and still are to some extent. The theory is especially popular in less developed countries such as Brazil, South Korea, and Taiwan, all of which have used it with notable success. It has even been resurrected for autos, steel, or other industries where some pioneer nation has less modern equipment than do latecomers, or where an industry has become less competitive behind protective barriers. With the barriers now lower, the industry believes that if it were given a breathing space to adjust, it would again become competitive. (This last case might be called a pseudo-infant or senescent industry.) These arguments are nowadays often included in making the case for a strategic trade policy, a subject we consider in Chapter 8.

For many years, the infant-industry argument was recognized as an interference with free trade that could increase welfare. But there are also a number of serious problems with the position that must be considered.

(a) It is all too easy to extend infant-industry protection to firms that have little or no chance of ever growing up. The literature on development is legion with examples of steel mills, automobile assembly plants, and petrochemical complexes built in nations whose markets could not under any conceivable circumstances support such operations for many years to come. Import substitution as a development strategy has been much criticized in recent years because of the rather indiscriminate approach to choosing protected industries.

(b) Protection may be very hard to eliminate even if the infant grows up. The labor, management, and capital in the industry will lose if the protection is removed, no matter how successful the industry has become. The higher incomes earned by protected industries can finance a substantial amount of political activity to ensure that the trade barriers are retained.

(c) Those who bear the costs of infant-industry protection do not particularly benefit from it. Even if the protection is removed after an industry grows up, there has still been a cost paid by the country's consumers. Only if the industry eventually has sufficient earnings to repay consumers for their initial sacrifice can the protection be said to have succeeded. The repayment (presumably through the tax system) would have to be with interest, of course, because forgone interest would also figure in the real opportunity cost of the protection. It should be noted that any such repayment is rarely if ever made.

These three points taken together are called the "Mill-Bastable Test." John Stuart Mill emphasized that the protection must eventually be dispensed with for the argument to work, while Charles F. Bastable stressed that the costs must be paid back to justify the action.

(d) No need for protection exists if capital markets are working well. Entrepreneurs, realizing that with a few years of experience they could bring costs down to the levels of their international competitors, would finance a few years of money-losing operations. There is nothing strange in a new enterprise losing money in its initial years. Such new enterprises may be units of larger firms, receiving their financing through the parent firm. Others may finance themselves through sales of shares and a limited amount of bank credit. Basically, financiers need only to anticipate future earnings high enough to cover the cost of using capital for a number of years without a return.

Because an adequate capital market undercuts the need for infant-industry protection, believers in that case must therefore argue that the capital system is imperfect. Banks may be biased against new entrepreneurs and are reluctant to invest in human capital and technology, which make poor collateral. But that argument applies to any new entrepreneur: Why should the banks be prejudiced just against those who want to make substitutes for imports? Moreover, capital markets include not only banks, but involve the large internal capital markets of conglomerate firms and holding companies, stock markets, and bond markets. Firms that face competition from imports may be a special case only in the sense that they can appeal for infant-industry protection, whereas firms that face domestic competition cannot. Furthermore, their chances of obtaining barriers may be better than their chances for obtaining loans from the credit markets. If private investors make a mistake, they must suffer the consequences, but if government officials make a mistake, they lose other people's money.

In all this, perhaps a less costly alternative solution would be for government to reform capital markets and help disseminate information rather than resort to protection. Yet it must also be admitted that in some less developed countries, it may be cheaper and more effective to provide infant-industry protection than to reform the capital markets. Even an argument that is often abused may occasionally be correct.

(e) Finally, on both political and economic grounds many economists would prefer an infant-industry subsidy to protection. (John Stuart Mill himself eventually came around to this point of view.) A subsidy can achieve the same end without many of the adverse side effects—prices for consumers are lower and the market for the infant industry's goods will thus be wider. (The Bastable argument still applies, however. The infant industry should repay the taxpayer, say by paying a bounty to the government and thus cutting tax bills.) If protection has been by means of a quota, as in Fig. 6.2, rather than by means of a subsidy, the cost would be the greater amount consumers pay for the good, P_wP_qVR. But if a subsidy were used, the cost to the public, paid now by taxpayers rather than by consumers of the good, is seen to be the lower amount P_wP_qWN. (The difference between the cases is that with a subsidy, imports do not cost more.) Furthermore, because prices do

---

Figure 6.2 **The cost of infant-industry protection.** If a subsidy replaces import barriers for infant industries, it is less costly for the consumer, who can still buy at P_w, and thus has no loss in consumer surplus. As taxpayer, the consumer still must pay for the protection, income transfer, and producer surplus, but as taxpayer, the consumer is likely to demand many reviews of the expenditures.

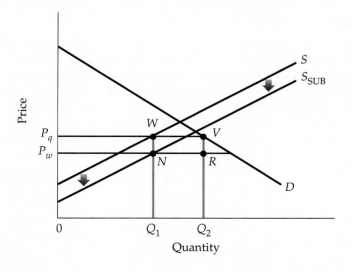

not rise there will be no loss in consumer surplus. Perhaps above all, a subsidy is likely to receive frequent review from the legislature, annually in the United States. In short, a subsidy is cheaper, and there is more chance that it will eventually be ended. Even then, a subsidy to infant industries may discriminate against the firms that export, attracting resources away from them and to the infants. It may be better to direct the subsidies toward education or infrastructure development, so as to keep incentives uniform throughout the economy.

THE NATIONAL DEFENSE ARGUMENT

It is said that protection must be made available to industries manufacturing such products as aircraft, firearms, ships, electronics, ocular glass, ball bearings, petroleum, and the like. If foreign competition were to ruin these industries, so the argument runs, a country would find its national defense compromised. The national defense argument dates back at least to Adam Smith and his *Wealth of Nations,* and it has always had a certain logical appeal. But there are also strong objections. As with infant industries, subsidies for this purpose are much to be preferred because a legislature can assess exactly how much is being spent and has an annual opportunity to reconsider its policies. A subsidy is presumably even more justified because defense is clearly the responsibility of all, not just the consumer of the protected good.

An annual review seems especially valuable because claims to protection based on defense can test credulity. Everyone wants to be considered valuable for national defense, and at various times and places, claims for protection on that ground have been made by the watch industry, by candlemakers (emergency lighting), by textile manufacturers (uniforms) and clothespin makers (*clean* uniforms), and by toothpick makers (good dental hygiene for the troops, of course). Japan, with its small defense establishment, has nonetheless used the argument as well, to prevent imports by Nippon Telephone & Telegraph of anything beyond small parts for communications satellites. Characteristic language for making the defense case was used by the president of the American Footwear Industry's trade association in 1984. He argued that:

> In the event of war or other national emergency, it is highly unlikely that the domestic footwear industry could provide sufficient footwear for the military and civilian population.... We won't be able to wait for ships to deliver shoes from Taiwan or Korea or Brazil or Eastern Europe.... Improper footwear can lead to needless casualties and turn sure victory into possible defeat.

Patriotism may not be solely the last refuge of the scoundrel, to paraphrase Dr. Samuel Johnson. In that refuge may also be found industries feeling the pinch of foreign competition.*

---

* "Why, a moral truth is a hollow tooth / Which must be propped with gold." Edgar Lee Masters, "Sexsmith the Dentist," from *Spoon River Anthology,* New York, Macmillan, 1914, 1963.

Even so, the argument once had some merit. Presumably it still does in some cases such as Israel's, where sudden boycotts could have an impact on small arms and ammunition supplies, tanks, aircraft, and the like. Similarly, some Middle Eastern members of OPEC are perhaps acting reasonably in using the defense argument to justify protection of domestic food production in expectation that food might someday be used as a weapon against them.

In the United States, the president can impose (or private firms can petition for) protection on the grounds that a product is necessary for the national security. Neither unfair foreign practices nor substantial injury from trade has to be shown. Used before 1986 only to allow oil import quotas, this clause has surfaced again. In that year the machine tool industry made sufficient progress with it so that the Reagan Administration negotiated a VER with Japan to limit imports. Efforts by the ball-bearing industry to obtain new trade barriers on the grounds of defense failed in 1988, and other attempts by petroleum producers, uranium refiners, and makers of plastic injection molding machinery to use the argument also failed, in 1989. The U.S. industrial gear makers are the most recent (1992) in the long line of producers to make the defense claim for protection. Furthermore, several new buy-American proposals concerning defense procurement have been before congress in recent years, and the Department of Defense ruled in 1988 that its contractors must buy only American-made ball bearings.

When a major country such as the United States bases part of its trade policy on the defense argument, logic is strained or trampled in most cases. It is hard to conceive of a modern war so serious that it halts international trade. Dependence on some vital imported item can certainly be worrisome, but if the item is available from a number of competing and geographically dispersed sources, the concern should presumably be reduced. This, together with some stockpiling of equipment and materials, should give adequate security. In any case, the greater interdependence fostered by open trade might encourage less violent solutions to political differences.

■ *RAPID CONVERSION TO MILITARY OUTPUT MAY BE POSSIBLE*

Modern countries such as the United States, the Soviet Union, and Germany showed during World War II that they were immensely able when it came to converting productive capacity from one use to another, or building new capacity, even under the most stringent wartime conditions. There were enormous successes, such as converting the U.S. auto industry to the production of tanks, trucks, and planes; the Russian rebuilding of its heavy industry east of the Urals when the German armies advanced up to Moscow; and the later thorough German program to rebuild and retool industry underground and in dispersed factories. All these took place in time periods of a year or less. Note that a war that blocked *imports* would also block exports, freeing vast quantities of productive factors for a war effort. Sample this passage from Norman Stone's *The Eastern Front, 1914–1917*.[27]

> *In September 1914, there was 40% unemployment in Nuremberg because the Franconian pencil-makers and pencil-sharpener-makers, who supplied the world, were deprived of markets. But the pool of skilled labor that this created, and still more, perhaps, the quantities of now unusable raw materials, were of utmost service to the war effort, and areas such as Franconia became important centers of the munitions industry overnight, and to everyone's surprise. It would be interesting to speculate how much less war-goods Germany would have produced if the British had allowed her to go on exporting.*
>
> In view of these efforts, most claims to the need for protection in the name of national defense appear rather pale.

PROTECTION AGAINST TEMPORARY DISRUPTION

Under GATT's controversial Article XIX, member countries are permitted to take temporary safeguard or escape clause action to guard against sudden disruption from imports.[28] Most countries' safeguard measures are essentially similar. In the United States, under Section 201 of the trade act (and hence called *Section 201 cases* in the jargon), the U.S. International Trade Commission is asked to make a finding that temporary protection is justified.* The president is then empowered to impose a tariff of not more than 50% *ad valorem* above the prior rate, impose a quota, negotiate a voluntary export restraint agreement, establish an adjustment assistance program, or take no action at all. If barriers are imposed, they are limited to a maximum period, including one extension, of eight years.

Before 1974, a firm claiming protection under the escape clause had to show that it was being injured by imports coming in because of a trade concession, and that these imports were the "major cause" (interpreted to mean the cause of over half) of the harm. Neither was easy to prove, and that explains why only nine cases of relief were granted under the escape clause in the period 1962 to 1974, out of 26 cases filed.

After 1974, proof that the imports were due to a trade concession was no longer required, and the words *substantial cause* replaced *major cause*. Under these looser rules, 50 cases were brought in 1975 to 1984, with the ITC recommending relief 29 times and the president granting it in 12 cases. This executive discretion to overturn an ITC recommendation has rankled protectionists, who tried but failed to include language in the 1988 trade bill to transfer control over the process away from the president and to make action mandatory. (Congress can by resolution require the president to act, though this power has never been used.)[29]

The ITC recommended use of the escape clause 14 times in 1976, but in the years since then its use has declined greatly. There have been only three cases

---

* The U.S. ITC dates from 1916. Its six members are appointed by the president to terms of nine years. According to law, not more than three members may come from the same political party, which means that the ITC often has members who are political independents.

of escape clause relief since 1983. One concerned the heavy motorcycles produced by Harley-Davidson. A rare declining tariff-quota was imposed in 1983.* Harley in an unprecedented move announced it did not need the last year of the five years of protection provided, and the tariff-quota was accordingly ended early in 1987, in what seemed an outstanding success for the escape clause.

The only other recent U.S. uses of the escape clause were in 1983 (protection for stainless steel and alloy tool steel, renewed in 1987, ended in 1990) and 1986 (tariffs on cedar shakes and shingles from Canada, now expired). No safeguards are in effect as of 1992, and only one investigation was made in 1989–1991 (on certain cameras, with no injury found to have occurred). Safeguard action is also rare elsewhere. Worldwide, 21 duties were in effect at the start of 1991, nine of them in the EC where it is usual to find two or so cases a year. In 1991, only two safeguard actions were taken (one by the EC and one by Austria).

The lack of importance is easy to explain. Discrimination is not permitted—under the GATT rules, safeguard duties apply on a most favored nation basis to all trading partners, including those with the power to retaliate. Also under the GATT rules, governments that take safeguard action must offer compensation in other areas, say by reducing a barrier elsewhere. Both reasons have kept governments from pursuing safeguards. From the point of view of U.S. private lobbyists, the standards of proof that an industry has been injured are high, the executive has wide discretion, protection does not necessarily result, and when it does its temporary nature is unattractive. The 1988 trade act introduced yet another obstacle: An industry granted relief is encouraged, though not absolutely required, to present a plan describing how it proposes to become competitive again. This does not appear very practical in industries with many small producers such as textiles or shoes.

In spite of the rarity of temporary safeguards against import surges, numerous economists believe that they are a reasonable policy response. Private capital markets would extend credit to injured firms if a surge of imports is believed to be temporary and the firm is expected to survive. But if the surge is of uncertain duration, and the firm's survival is in question, then safeguards may buy time for the firm to assess the situation and plan for adjustment, either by fighting back or running down. One explanation for the growth of protectionism has been the inadequacy of safeguards.

The area is being looked at again in the Uruguay Round, with several tentative agreements already reached to limit them to eight years, require compensation only after three years, and specify gradual easing of the barriers in all cases. The major question has been whether to allow selective (discriminatory) safeguards, including modulated safeguard quotas that vary by country, as the EC advocates. One liberal possibility is to employ only declining tariffs in combination with adjustment assistance, perhaps using the tariff revenue to fund the

---

* The quantity allowed in under the quota (15,000) paid no tariff; after that number a 45% duty was charged in the first year, declining in steps to 10% in the fifth year and zero in the year after that.

assistance. Another is to allow tariffs to be raised on just the portion of an industry in difficulty—small cars, for example, instead of all cars—which is not now permitted.

CONCLUSION

This chapter has discussed the traditional reasoning used to justify trade barriers. That reasoning in a few cases is convincing, though for the most part we have seen that protection inflicts costs on society greater than the benefits delivered to the firms and factors that shelter behind the walls.

The next chapter continues in this vein by examining the barriers that legislatures around the world have erected against a relatively new sort of economic crime, "unfair trade practices." What these practices are is now of central importance to international trade, and the attack on them through legislative and judicial action has become a major contributor to increased trade barriers.

VOCABULARY AND CONCEPTS

1988 Omnibus Trade Act
Customs Valuation Code
Excess tariff
GATT (General Agreement on
  Tariffs and Trade)
GATT panels
Infant industry
International Trade Organization (ITO)
Kennedy Round
MFN (most favored nation)
Mill-Bastable Test

Multilateral Trade Organization (MTO)
Reciprocal Trade Acts
Smoot-Hawley Tariff
Sweatshop argument
Tariffication
Tariffs for revenue
Tokyo Round
Trade Expansion Act
Trade Reform Act
Uruguay Round

QUESTIONS

1. "The United States had low tariffs only so long as strong export interests had influence and recognized how tariffs hurt them." Show, using evidence from American history.

2. What did the Smoot-Hawley Tariff show about congress and about the limitations of American legislation?

3. Why must the world always wait for the U.S. Congress to pass a trade bill in order to have trade negotiations?

4. A number of key features of American tariff policy today emerged in the Reciprocal Trade Act of 1934. What are they? In particular, how did the RTA handle the problem of congress having the last word?

5. What is the GATT and why was it formed?

6. State briefly the main features of the GATT agreement.

7. "GATT has no teeth, and the ITO would have been much superior." Debate, discussing the

strengths and weaknesses of GATT. Were countries willing to let it be stronger?

8. What was the Tokyo Round and what were its results?

9. What is the current U.S. trade act and what is its significance? How does it handle the problem of prior approval?

10. Given that economists have demonstrated time and time again the costs of protectionism, why does it persist? That is, what are the political-economic factors that drive its persistence?

11. Brown and Hogendorn argue that protection produces rents, but critical questions remain about who collects them. Explain.

12. It appears to be very expensive to maintain employment through restricting trade. Why? Give some examples and explain why it is so expensive.

13. In most cases, it would be cheaper to retire workers displaced by imports than to keep them working in protected industries. Why?

14. Frequently the extent of adjustment required due to trade liberalization is overestimated because the model people have in mind is one of interfactoral, rather than intrafactoral, competition (that is, inter-, rather than intraindustrial trade). Why should it make a difference? (See also Chapter 3.)

15. What are the arguments to support protection of infant industries? How well do they fit with ideas in Chapter 3? Why are Brown and Hogendorn leery of them?

16. "With well-functioning capital markets, no need exists for protection." Explain in the context of the infant-industry argument.

17. A footnote suggests that moral truths are hollow and used as glosses for underlying economic advantages. The comment is cynical, but at least partially right. Explain why.

18. Discuss critically the cheap labor and sweatshop arguments.

19. The national defense argument is terribly overused. Why?

20. What is the Mill-Bastable Test, and what is its current relevance?

21. There may be some reason for temporary protection, but even your authors disagree with each other on its merits. Why might that be so?

NOTES

[1] See the work of Charles P. Kindleberger, especially *The World in Depression, 1929–1939*, Berkeley, University of California Press, 1973.

[2] See Barry Eichengreen, "The political economy of the Smoot-Hawley tariff," NBER Working Paper No. 2001, August 1986.

[3] Don D. Humphrey, *The U.S. and the Common Market*, New York, Praeger, 1962.

[4] Some of the details in this section are from Margaret Kelly, Naheed Kirmani, Miranda Xafa, Clemens Boonekamp, and Peter Winglee, *Issues and Developments in International Trade Policy*, IMF Occasional Paper No. 63, International Monetary Fund, December 1988, p. 139; the recent issues of the U.S. ITC's *Operation of the Trade Agreements Program;* and the frequent articles in the *International Economic Review, The Economist,* and the *Wall Street Journal.*

[5] *The Economist,* April 20, 1991.

[6] For a thorough discussion of the Tokyo Round and tariffs, see Alan V. Deardorff and Robert M. Stern, "The economic effects of complete elimination of post-Tokyo Round tariffs," in William R. Cline, ed., *Trade Policy in the 1980s*, Washington, D.C., Institute for International Economics, 1983, pp. 674–676. The static gains from the Tokyo Round of trade talks appear to be surprisingly slight, though the dynamic gains are probably much larger. See R. E. Baldwin, "Trade policies in developed countries," in Ronald W. Jones and Peter B. Kenen, eds., *Handbook of International Economics*, Vol. 1, Amsterdam, Elsevier, 1984, pp. 586–588.

[7] See World Bank, *World Development Report 1991*, p. 98, and Kelly et al., *International Trade Policy*, IMF Occasional Paper No. 63, International Monetary Fund, December 1988, p. 130.

[8] *International Economic Review,* issues from February 1992, to March 1993. For analysis of many of the options, see Robert M. Stern, ed., *The Multilateral Trading System: Analysis and Options for Change,* Ann Arbor, University of Michigan Press, 1992.

[9] Alan V. Deardorff and Robert M. Stern, "Options for trade liberalization in the Uruguay Round negotiations," in Frank J. Macchiarola, ed., *International Trade: The Changing Role of the United States, Proceedings of the Academy of Political Science,* Vol. 37, No. 4, 1990, p. 19; Deardorff and Stern, "Economic effects," p. 708; Marcelo de Paiva Abreu, "Developing countries and the Uruguay Round of trade negotiations," *Proceedings of the World Bank Annual Conference on Development Economics 1989,* p. 27.

[10] Figures cited in *The Economist,* September 22, 1990.

[11] See Ulrich Koester and Malcolm D. Bale, "The Common Agricultural Policy," *World Bank Research Observer,* Vol. 5, No. 1, January 1990, pp. 95–121; Julius Rosenblatt, *The Common Agricultural Policy of the European Community: Principles and Consequences,* IMF Occasional Paper No. 62, November, 1988; Brian E. Hill, *Common Agricultural Policy: Past, Present, and Future,* London, 1984; Ian R. Bowler, *Agriculture under the Common Agricultural Policy: a Geography,* Manchester, Manchester University Press, 1985; Kelly et al., *International Trade Policy,* IMF Occasional Paper No. 63, 1988, p. 140; OECD, *National Policies and Agricultural Trade,* Paris, Organization for Economic Cooperation and Developments, 1987; Bernard M. Hoekman, "Agriculture and the Uruguay Round," *Journal of World Trade,* Vol. 23, No. 1, 1989, pp. 83–96; all recent issues of U.S. ITC, *Operation of the Trade Agreements Program;* numerous issues of the *International Economic Review,* especially September, 1991; and the constant coverage in *The Economist.*

[12] Interested students might start with the first three chapters of Bruno S. Frey, *International Political Economics,* Oxford, Blackwell Publishers, 1984.

[13] These types of models and their testing are discussed by Robert E. Baldwin, "Trade policies in developed countries," in Jones and Kenen, *Handbook of International Economics,* Vol. 1, pp. 573–582, and in Baldwin's *The Political Economy of U.S. Import Policy,* Cambridge, Mass., MIT Press, 1985.

[14] See Baldwin, *The Political Economy of U.S. Import Policy,* pp. 40–41.

[15] Daniel Yankelovich, "A widening expert/public opinion gap," *Challenge,* Vol. 35, No. 3, May/June 1992, p. 22.

[16] *Christian Science Monitor,* February 3, 1992.

[17] Wall Street Journal/NBC News polling data reported in the *Wall Street Journal,* 1990.

[18] Robert Reich, "We need a strategic trade policy," *Challenge,* Vol. 33, No. 4, July/August 1990, p. 41.

[19] *International Economic Review,* January, 1991.

[20] Robert Reich, "The myth of 'Made in the U.S.A.'," *Wall Street Journal,* July 5, 1991.

[21] According to modeling by Richard Belous and Andrew Wyckoff of the Conference Board and the U.S. Office of Technology Assessment, reported in the *Christian Science Monitor,* September 10, 1987.

[22] See Gary Clyde Hufbauer, Diane T. Berliner, and Kimberly Ann Elliott, *Trade Protection in the United States: 31 Case Studies,* Washington, D.C., Institute for International Economics, 1986. For the Washington University study, see Center for the Study of American Business Working Paper No. 80, and a version of this paper, Michael C. Munger, "The costs of protection," *Challenge,* Vol. 26, No. 6, January/February 1984, pp. 54–58.

[23] U.S. Labor Department data for 1987, except Sri Lanka, 1986.

[24] The argument is treated, skeptically, in Henry J. Aaron, *Serious and Unstable Condition: Financing America's Health Care,* Washington, D.C., Brookings Institution, 1991, pp. 95–101.

[25] See William R. Cline, "Macroeconomic influences on trade policy," *AEA Papers and Proceedings,* Vol. 79, No. 2, May 1989, pp. 126–127.

[26] See *The Economist,* January 31, 1987.

[27] New York, Scribner, 1975, p. 164.

[28] For this section we utilized all recent issues of U.S. ITC, *Operation of the Trade Agreements Program;* Kelly et al., *International Trade Policy,* IMF Occasional Paper No. 63, p. 36; P. Kleen, "The safeguard issue in the Uruguay Round—A comprehensive approach," *Journal of World Trade,* Vol. 23, No. 5, October 1989, pp. 73–85; and N. David Palmeter, "The antidumping emperor," *Journal of World Trade,* Vol. 22, No. 4, August 1988, p. 5.

[29] See Baldwin, *Political Economy of U.S. Import Policy,* pp. 35–36.

Chapter 7

Unfair Trade Practices

OBJECTIVES

Overall Objective: To examine closely unfair trade practices, demonstrating that it is the laws, not the practices, which are unfair.

MORE SPECIFICALLY:

- To define what dumping is and explain the laws, particularly the American law.
- To discuss the strength of the economic arguments against dumping.
- To explain the biases and arbitrariness that exist in American dumping and countervailing duty legislation and practice.
- To define what subsidies are and which ones can be countervailed, showing how American law expanded its definitions.
- To evaluate the more aggressive "crowbar" provisions of Section 301 of the U.S. trade act.

This chapter analyzes the emergence and central position of so-called unfair trade practices in modern international trade. With the decline in tariff rates resulting from the Tokyo Round, new significance has come to these once-obscure protective measures that allow tariffs to be imposed in special circumstances involving alleged unfairness. We shall see that the economic logic for banning these practices is weak. The most acceptable defense for them, prevention of predatory pricing, seldom has anything to do with the unfair practice laws. Yet from a political point of view the question of unfair trade practices is a burning one. If the people who are hurt by imports believe, and can convince others, that the source of the harm is an illegitimate tactic by foreigners—say sales at unfair low prices or government subsidies to the exporter—then they can gain political support for trade barriers even if these barriers are very costly for consumers.

The often-heard call for a level playing field is part of this appeal. The laws described below are pushed by a sense that it is unjust for people to be injured by the unfair practice. No matter that such practices are for the most part entirely legal when done by one's own firms within the country. When done by foreigners they just do not appear fair. That setting is perfect for protectionists, who, defending their own interests, are able to use fairness arguments to great effect. The balance of the chapter explores what these practices are and how the laws providing for trade barriers against imports involving them have become central to protectionist strategy.

The unfair practice laws are technical in nature. They include antidumping duties against what is called *dumping,* countervailing duties against foreign subsidies, and measures in response to violations of trade agreements. All of them treat foreign firms more harshly than domestic ones, providing an effective means at least to harass foreign competitors and at most to erect a significant barrier to imports. One of the practices, subsidies, has grown steadily in importance as countries have contemplated the adoption of strategic trade policies, considered in the next chapter.

Firms seeking barriers against imports have good reason to favor the unfair trade practice approach as compared to the safeguards discussed in the last chapter. In the United States, the president has no discretion to interfere with the laws that define such practices and impose a mandatory remedy. The U.S. government some years ago started publishing an annual accounting of foreigners' unfair practices, its "National Trade Estimate Report on Foreign Trade Barriers." Not to be overawed, the EC has countered with its own listing of unfair U.S. practices in an annual publication not only patterned after the U.S. original, but appearing only a few days later. GATT, in effect declaiming a plague on both their houses, has noted that a major reason for these laws is that they can be used in discriminatory fashion against single countries, and a major effect of them is their "trade-inhibiting uncertainty." Furthermore, the unfair trade practice laws do not allow matters of foreign policy or of harm to domestic consumers to be taken into account. No wonder they have become so popular among those who want to wall off world trade.

DUMPING

The first of the unfair trade practices is dumping, the idea that foreigners will unfairly undersell American firms and that penalties should be imposed to raise their prices to a fair level.[1] Few words in economics sound quite so horrid as dumping, and even those who do not know what it is could hardly be expected to defend anything apparently so nasty. The issue goes back to the late eighteenth century with concern that Britain's exporters would swamp the United States with cheap goods. Canada introduced the first antidumping law in 1904, reacting to the possibility of predatory tactics by U.S. firms—they might lower their prices, drive Canadian firms out of business, and then raise their prices in Canada to monopoly levels, so the argument went. The first U.S. legislation of 1916 was also aimed at predatory behavior.

Most economists would applaud hard treatment for actual predation, but the United States long ago, in the U.S. antidumping act of 1921, moved to a mechanical method aimed at less obviously damaging behavior by foreign firms. (The new U.S. interpretation of 1921 is said to have been designed to protect against imports of German chemicals after the Versailles treaty threatened Americans with increased imports as Germany attempted to pay war reparations.) Much of the behavior covered by the dumping laws actually penalizes foreigners for doing what honest and prudent domestic businesspeople do quite legally all the time. Their inherent bias is intensified because the importing country serves as prosecutor, judge, jury, and jailer.

Actually, the definition of what constitutes dumping under U.S. law has been greatly enlarged over the years, and as tariffs have declined, the concept has become ever more prominent. Dumping is now the chosen tool for protection in the United States and the EC whenever a case appears winnable, and the legal system that has developed around these laws is a bonanza for specialized counsel and their specialized economic consultants.

DUMPING CHARGES HAVE BECOME VERY COMMON

The use of laws against dumping has risen greatly in recent years. In the period 1981 to 1987, 1339 antidumping investigations were undertaken in Australia, Canada, the EC, and the United States, with 818 antidumping duties imposed as a result. In the slightly longer period 1979–1988, dumping duties made up 77% of all trade actions monitored by GATT. The United States brought 427 cases during this period; recently there have been between 50 and 65 U.S. cases per year, most directed against Japan and the EC. In 1990, about three quarters of the cases were successful, although even unsuccessful ones play a part in inhibiting imports, as we shall see. For the United States, at the start of 1992 216 products from 40 countries were affected.[2] Buyers of acrylic sweaters, aspirin, bicycles, cement, codfish, computers, computer disks, cooking utensils, flowers, martial arts uniforms, mirrors, photograph albums, radios, shingles, telephones, TVs, and 200 other products are purchasing something currently protected by a dumping order. Such orders can be very long lived, and quite a few date back to the 1970s.

In 1979–1988 the EC brought 406 dumping cases. About 50 cases annually are usual, many against Japan and South Korea. Canada is even more active, 128 cases in 1987, while Australia is the world leader, much criticized for its undisciplined use of a loosely worded law. Fifty-three countries had made dumping illegal by 1992; only eight had had such laws in 1980. Mexico and other developing countries, and Eastern European nations such as Poland and Hungary, have rapidly adopted laws of their own.[3] Japan also has a dumping law, but almost never uses it; its first major antidumping duties were levied in January 1993, against Chinese steelmaking materials.

THE RESULTS

When imposed, antidumping duties average about four times more than regular tariff rates. Data indicate that on average imports fall 18% in the first year after proceedings are initiated; and after three or four years import quantities are down by about 40%.[4] The results for *users* of a product are deemed quite irrelevant in determining how high the duties should be. It does not matter whether, as with cement, Florida's costs rose by $100 million a year; or whether antifriction bearings, which American exporters incorporate in their products, rose in cost 120 to 150% because of antidumping duties; or whether a 63% antidumping duty on flat panel computer screens proved prohibitive for companies that wanted to make laptop computers in the United States.[5]

THE PRIMARY DEFINITION OF DUMPING: EXPORT SALES BELOW THE HOME PRICE

Under the 1921 act, dumping is defined as sales in an export market at prices below those charged in the exporter's home market. If a Japanese firm that sells at home and also exports charges $100 in Japan and $90 in the United States for the same good, then that firm has dumped. In the early theory of dumping, that activity was thought to take three forms: sporadic, persistent, or predatory, each quite different from one another.

SPORADIC DUMPING   Sporadic dumping is sale abroad at prices below those charged at home because of some temporary overstock. It resembles the clearance sales held by department stores, and the loss-leader tactics used by firms to break into new markets. Because by definition the practice is not long lasting, it is seldom attacked under the antidumping statutes, which refer to dumping over an "extended time," in practice usually defined as six months. Henceforth we ignore it here.

PERSISTENT DUMPING   Persistent dumping is, as the name implies, the same practice carried on for a longer period. Even at the outset of our study, these laws exhibit analytical oddity. First, we notice that reverse dumping, as when Mercedes or BMW charges higher prices in its export markets than it does at home in Germany, is perfectly legal and done all the time. Second, economists would find it hard to agree that export sales below home price sales is such a bad thing. Take the extreme case where the exporter is a monopoly at home and a competitor in its export market. If costs are the same in the two markets, then the exporter will certainly want to dump. The damage, so one would think, is not the dumping in the export market, but the monopoly pricing that harms consumers in the *home* market.

Take an example: the recent minivan case. In 1991 the Big Three U.S. automakers charged Toyota and Mazda with dumping minivans. It is not surprising that the price in Japan is higher than in the United States: There is a near-monopoly situation in Japan because no competing U.S. van has its steering wheel on the right for the driving to the left that the Japanese do. Dumping was found, so the Japanese producers to avoid large penalties rapidly raised their prices. Now those Americans who still want to buy a Japanese van get to pay the same monopoly price the Japanese must pay.

Consider the problem as a technical one involving dissimilar demand in two markets. A profit-maximizing firm will have a motive to engage in dumping if the demand curve facing the firm is placed differently in these markets. The difference in shape, and hence in elasticity, may be due to variations in tastes, habits, national traits, levels of income, or degree of competition in the two markets. Trade does not equalize prices, perhaps because of monopoly power, or transport costs, or trade barriers.

In Fig. 7.1a and 7.1b, we see two different demand curves D_a and D_b facing Watanabe Electronics, a large Tokyo firm, with markets for its product in both Japan and the United States. The downward slope indicates that the firm has some degree of market power in each market. Each demand curve has an associated curve for marginal revenue, MR_a and MR_b. The marginal cost curves MC_a and MC_b are drawn on the assumption that marginal costs are the same in each market.

The managers of the firm must now decide what price to charge in each market. A moment's reflection will show that profits will be maximized (where $MC = MR$) if two different prices are charged. In Fig. 7.1a, which is Watanabe's home market, marginal cost equals marginal revenue ($MC_a = MR_a$) at a price P_a and quantity Q_a. This price is significantly higher than in Fig. 7.1b, the export market, where the profit-maximizing price is P_b (and the quantity is Q_b). In effect, a higher price is charged in the home market where demand is less elastic. Under GATT rules, as we have seen, this is dumping.

Figure 7.1 **Why a firm would want to charge a higher price at home than abroad.** A firm with two separate national markets can often maximize profits if it keeps the prices different. The MC curve is the same in all three diagrams, but the demand and MR curves differ. The firm maximizes profit in 7.1a at a price of P_a and in 7.1b at a price of P_b. If 7.1b represents the United States, then Americans pay a lower price, but the foreign exporter would be guilty of dumping. Forced to charge the same price in both markets, the firm combines demand curves as in 7.1c, and charges the same price in both markets, P_c.

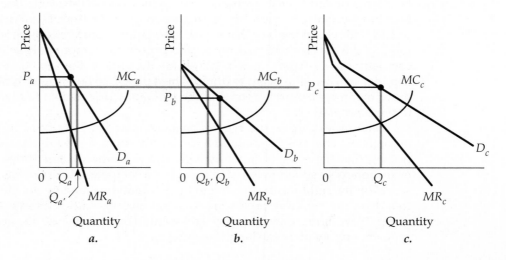

| a. | b. | c. |

Thus it is easy to appreciate why dumping is carried out—it is a profit-maximizing strategy. It is also understandable why many companies might choose to adopt an equal price strategy anyway. The exporter accused of dumping can avoid the charges by equalizing the prices in the two markets. The better part of valor may be a flat pricing strategy.

The results of a decision to charge the same price in the two markets is a bit curious, as seen in Fig. 7.1c. If Watanabe Electronics considers the combined demand in the two markets, the resulting demand curve D_c is the horizontal addition of D_a and D_b. Similarly, the combined marginal revenue curve MR_c is the horizontal addition of MR_a and MR_b. Given the unchanged marginal cost curve MC_c, the price charged in the combined market will be P_c because that price will maximize profits if the markets are treated as one. Look carefully at the diagrams: The result of eliminating dumping is a lower price in Watanabe's home market (Japan) and a higher price in the export market (the United States). The single price P_c would result in a quantity Q_c. Of this quantity, an increased amount (Q_a') will be sold in the home market, and a smaller quantity (Q_b') in the export market.[*]

Doubtless, the idea of charging a higher price at home than abroad in export markets does in these latter markets seem to violate the producers' sense of fair play. It is not usually explained why persistent dumping is thought to be so bad if a foreign firm is just matching a domestic competitor's price (a fully adequate defense for a *domestic* firm charged with price discrimination), or if it is charging more at home because it has a greater degree of monopoly power there. Is it sensible to claim that the importer too should pay higher monopoly prices for the product? Differential pricing among markets is *not* illegal if done by domestic firms. Senior citizens' and student discounts, lower prices for new magazine subscribers, brand name products sold for higher prices than the same unbranded product, loss leaders to get you into the store and to experience the product, are quite legal in *domestic* trade. Indeed, they are everyday business practice.

Furthermore, though the word *dumping* sounds very nasty indeed, the practice does benefit consumers by bringing lower prices. The thought crosses the economist's mind (though with little effect on the business community) that if a foreigner wants to charge us lower prices than are charged at home, then such generosity might even be welcomed! In Chapter 4, we saw that an import at a lower price brings net benefits to society because the gains to consumers from the import outweigh the loss to producers. If a country could gain in real income because of the sales of cheap dumped goods, it could presumably devote part of its gains to compensating losers and still be better off as a whole.

---

[*] The less developed countries benefited from a new rule included in the GATT Antidumping Code that resulted from the Tokyo Round. The code recognized that special conditions such as foreign exchange rate overvaluation and high marketing costs may mean that the home price in LDC markets may not be commercially realistic for calculating dumping. Under the code, prices in third-country export markets and cost of production plus a "reasonable amount for marketing costs and profit" now are the test of whether dumping is occurring.

But under present political conditions the abandonment of the antidumping laws, rather than being welcomed, would probably unleash yet more protectionist sentiment.

PREDATORY DUMPING   Predatory dumping is potentially much more serious, and most observers find it easy to recommend harsh treatment. This is akin to the domestic practice of carrying on a price war, cutting prices, perhaps to below marginal cost, with the intent of driving competitors out of the industry. The predator presumably then raises its prices to a higher level than formerly in order to extract monopoly returns. Such warlike tactics seldom if ever find much support, whether they are perpetrated by a firm in domestic operations or in foreign trade.

It is questionable, however, how common the practice is in international trade. Even domestically, its existence is dubious.[6] The problem is that once a potential monopolist drives out its competitors and establishes its monopoly price, new competitors reenter. A predatory firm would have to decide that the costs of driving existing competitors out of business can be made up by the high price charged between the time old competitors are driven out and new ones appear. That is a difficult case to prove either theoretically or historically. Furthermore, the predatory firm would have to have international, not just national, monopoly power in order to justify the tactic, or else imports would flow in as prices were raised. If in spite of all this the predator were to be successful, it would run into antitrust laws (with tough triple damage provisions in the United States) designed to combat predatory behavior.

Some authorities doubt whether a single authenticated instance exists of a predatory dumper acquiring monopoly power and then extracting monopoly rents.[7] According to dumping specialist N. David Palmeter, "In none of the 767 affirmative antidumping determinations reached by Australia, Canada, the EC, and the U.S. between 1980 and 1986 was predatory pricing remotely present."[8] The very concept of predatory pricing received a legal rebuff in 1986, when a U.S. Supreme Court decision in the antitrust case of *Matsushita Electric et al.* v. *Zenith* held that a predatory strategy is highly unlikely in the presence of substantial international competition. Also pointing to the rarity of predatory dumping, no one has ever won the treble damages available in American law in a private suit if predatory practice is proven.[9]

Many businesspeople nonetheless believe that predatory dumping does occur, and occasionally an academic case is made supporting their position. Some scholars have suggested that predation is not intended to drive competitors out of the industry, but merely to deter them from planned market expansion or new investment or new product development.[*] If judicious price cutting

---

[*] Some of the newer game-theory approaches suggest some situations in which modified predation might be useful. Even so, industrial organization specialists remain largely skeptical. For development of a game-theory model, see Jean Tirole, *The Theory of Industrial Organization,* Cambridge, Mass., MIT Press, 1989.

can lower a rival's profit expectations, one's own profits could be protected. There have been charges that Japanese dumping of the microchips used in computers has had a predatory intent and has caused cutbacks in the American industry. But as we shall see, the resulting higher prices of chips have attracted U.S. firms back into the industry. It is possible that scale economies in the monopoly that follows successful predatory dumping could, at least in theory, lead to cheaper output, and therefore lower prices, even in the presence of monopoly profits.

In any case there is absolutely no requirement under the dumping laws even to hint at predatory behavior. For example, dumping charges have actually been brought against foreign exporters that have held less than 1% of the market. It is plain that monopoly power is more likely to be furthered by dumping duties than by the risk of predatory tactics by foreigners. Notwithstanding all the above, however, if and when predatory practice is found it deserves attack on the ground that the results would distort world efficiency.

TRACING A DUMPING CASE UNDER U.S. LAW

Let us trace a dumping case under U.S. law. Keep in mind that if dumping is found, a penalty tariff equal to the dumping margin (the price difference between the exporter's home price and the price in the United States) will be placed on the exporter's goods.

The Charge   Dumping cases begin with a petition from several American firms to the Department of Commerce. A foreign country is named in the petition, with some basic evidence to back the charge. Nearly all dumping petitions are accepted. All foreign firms from that country now stand accused, even though only one or two firms might actually be guilty. Those firms that can afford to make a defense will want to contact an American law firm at this time, because as we shall see dumping is easy to prove under the present rules. The defense is likely to be expensive, with a routine antidumping investigation easily costing $100,000, enough to ruin a small exporting firm even if it is found not guilty.[10] A big case such as the one against foreign steel producers that ended with major duties against 19 countries in January 1993 can cost a foreign firm from half a million to three million dollars just for the American attorneys.

The cost and disruption to an innocent party can be great; even the very hint of a dumping charge can have a chilling effect and lead foreigners to raise their prices. Large corporations with significant budgets for a legal staff versed in these matters have come to see this aspect of the antidumping statutes as a useful means to harass their competition. It is surely no coincidence that J.M. Finger's research has revealed that big, concentrated industries are responsible for bringing the greater proportion of dumping complaints, but that these complaints succeed less frequently by comparison to complaints made by smaller firms. They still pursue the tactic, knowing that the growth of imports usually declines following a complaint.[11]

■ *WHAT IS AN AMERICAN FIRM?*

With the globalization of trade, dumping cases can be difficult. Under American law, only U.S. companies are eligible to bring charges. But what is a U.S. company? In case law, though not by statute, it is when half or more of a product is made in the United States. A Japanese firm's U.S. subsidiary, Brother Industries USA, makes portable electric typewriters in the United States. In 1993 it won a dumping case against Smith-Corona, a U.S. company that makes its typewriters in Singapore.

The Investigation   Department of Commerce practice is to investigate some firms, but not all, and then to assign the weighted average dumping margin for the firms investigated to the firms not investigated. A questionnaire is distributed to the chosen firms, allowing 30 calendar days for completion. It is in English, usually about 100 pages long, or 220 pages in the recent case against Norwegian fish farmers. (Imagine getting a 220-page questionnaire in *Norwegian* due in 30 days.) It demands data on home prices adjusted to from-the-factory value, U.S. retail prices, packaging, shipping, selling, and distribution costs, duties on inputs, U.S. duties, and value added in the United States. Price and cost data must be submitted in hard copy and computer-readable form.

If a reply is not received, or if the reply is found wanting, then "best information available" will be used. This is the original information supplied by the accusers, leading some to say it is actually the worst information available. In a sample of cases studied by Robert Baldwin and Michael Moore, when best information available is used the average dumping margin and therefore the penalty tariff is 67%, compared to 28% under the questionnaire method. No doubt some foreign firms fail to reply because they are guilty, but others do not do so because the requirements are onerous.

■ *THE ACRYLIC SWEATER CASE*

How a dumping charge is actually investigated can be illustrated with the acrylic sweater case.[12] Ninety million sweaters a year are (or used to be) imported into the United States from Hong Kong, Korea, and Taiwan. Four Hong Kong producers were investigated out of hundreds. One refused to cooperate, two were found not to be dumping, and one was found to be dumping. A 5.86% duty was imposed, followed immediately by the same duty on the hundreds of other Hong Kong sweater producers that were *not* investigated.

Hundreds of Taiwanese firms, some of them very small, were asked in this same investigation to fill out quickly a 100-page questionnaire. The average firm was asked to provide over 200,000 bits of information. In the end a 21.84% duty was imposed on the firms not investigated. The *regular* duty on acrylic sweaters is *already* 34%, and these sweaters are also subject to quotas estimated to be equivalent to additional duty of about 50%.

It is believed that the additional barriers will cut imports from these countries by almost half. Acrylic sweaters are bought by less affluent consumers, who thus find themselves protected by their government against the damage of low prices for the things they buy.

The Injury   The dumping laws require that American firms have to have been "materially injured" by the dumped imports or, following a 1984 amendment of the trade law, threatened with material injury. A finding to that effect must be made by the U.S. International Trade Commission. The EC has also shifted to a "threat of harm" interpretation. Though the injury test could be an important qualifier, the law is very weak. Another questionnaire is used, this one sent to American firms. Scientific sampling is not done, the information is not verified, and there is no external check on accuracy. Often it is enough to show a price-suppressing effect that keeps prices below the figure they might otherwise have reached. Of course *all* imports and all *domestic* competition tend to keep prices below what could have been reached. The argument that U.S. companies will need to adjust is basically an argument against all foreign trade, even if dumping is not involved, and against competition in general.

No account is taken of the injury to the public or to companies that use the imported product as an input. In 1992's case of laptop active matrix displays, the two U.S. firms bringing the charge were small and not capable of making what the big computer makers needed. The resulting 62.7% duty caused Apple Computer not to build a plant in Fountain, Colorado, but in Cork, Ireland, instead. IBM said it might build overseas, while Toshiba announced it would shut down its U.S. laptop plant and move it back to Japan.[13] In 1993, a case brought by a relatively small U.S. company located in Idaho, Micron Technologies, resulted in antidumping duties of up to 87% against Korean DRAM microchips. Because Korea is the second-biggest supplier of chips to the U.S. market, U.S. buyers such as Apple, IBM, AT&T, and Digital Equipment were up in arms over the higher costs they would incur. But the law, which takes no account of consumers of the product, had its way.

The Measurement   How the dumping is actually measured adds greatly to the impact of the laws, which are biased against foreign exporters to a considerable degree. Seven major biases exist under American law and procedural practice, all of which make it easier to find that dumping has occurred.

First bias: The Commerce Department takes the U.S. sale price for a product—say Brazilian orange juice. It subtracts from that U.S. price transport costs and tariffs, for these are not counted. For example, the United States has a 40%

tariff on orange juice, so 40% is subtracted from the U.S. sale price of Brazilian orange juice. It then compares the resulting adjusted U.S. price to Brazil's home market price. If the U.S. price is lower, dumping has occurred and importers of the juice are lawbreakers. It does not matter that with transport costs and tariffs Brazilian orange juice actually sells for much more in the United States than in Brazil. This is not considered.

Second bias: Say an investigation finds that during the period studied (usually six months) some foreign sales in the United States have been *above* the price in the home market. In assessing the dumping margin, any degree of pricing above home market prices is simply ignored, not counted with those sold at below U.S. prices.

Third bias: Say the Department of Commerce finds that some of the exporter's home market sales have been made at below the firm's cost of production. These low-price sales are also disregarded in determining whether dumping has occurred. Obviously this increases the probability of dumping.

Fourth bias: To find the dumping margin *individual* sales prices in the U.S. market are compared to the *average* foreign price over a six-month period. Thus if the foreigner sells at home and abroad at a high price for three months and a low price for three months, with the price always the same in the home market and the export market, then dumping has occurred.

Fifth bias: Dumping duties are imposed no matter how small the dumping margin is, down to a figure as tiny as 0.5%. This is called the *de minimis* rule. A duty this small is not, of course, a Smoot-Hawley tariff, but it does expose importers to an open-ended liability that may last for years, because far down the road, perhaps four or five or even 10 years in the future, the first temporary finding will become a permanent finding as Commerce goes back and completes a thorough transaction-by-transaction comparison. All that time importers have been paying a deposit to the government to import the goods. Perhaps the permanent finding will show lower dumping and some of the deposit will be returned. But perhaps it will show *greater* dumping, increasing the liability for imports made several years before, and with no theoretical upper limit. Even the mere charge is therefore damaging, as importers may not want to run the risk of dealing with a dumper. Thus very small preliminary duties can be a large barrier to trade because of the uncertainty they cause. This uncertainty may actually be the most pernicious result of the dumping laws, virtually forcing foreign exporters to overprice their products to avoid charges.

Sixth bias: Say you are a Japanese exporter. You know distribution costs in Japan are high (many more mom-and-pop stores than in the United States) but you also hope that these sales and distribution costs can be subtracted to get the price used in calculating dumping. Not so, however. Foreign firms can subtract sales and distribution costs only up to the amount of these costs in the U.S. market.

Seventh bias: With floating foreign exchange rates, if the rate changes but an exporter does not alter the price, then dumping has occurred. Say a good is priced at ¥200 in Japan and $1 in the United States, with the foreign exchange rate ¥200 = $1. Now say the dollar depreciates (yen appreciates) from ¥200 to ¥100 = $1. The good is priced at ¥200 in Japan, but that is now equal to $2. Unless the exporter immediately raises the dollar price in the export market to $2, whatever the consequences for market share, or consumer resistance to price change, or the menu costs of making a change, it is a case of dumping. Countries with volatile foreign exchange rates (Brazil, Argentina, Mexico) have indeed been much subject to dumping charges, and the Commerce Department is said to have solicited suits as the yen rose in the late 1980s. More specifically, a similar problem occurs when an exporting country has a seriously overvalued foreign exchange rate, its value kept artificially high by government exchange controls. Say Penuristan's penuri at 50 to 1 U.S. dollar is sharply overvalued, and that if there were a free market the exchange rate would be more like 100:1. Then if a Penuristan exporter sold an item in the United States at $1, and sold the same item at home for 100 penuris, it would be easy to prove dumping if the overvalued official rate were chosen to make the conversion. At the official rate, 100 penuris is $2, so the home price in the exporting country is higher than the price in the export market. In fact, official rates *are* used by the United States in making the comparison, even if the exporter was not able to obtain this rate at home and thus did not really dump.

The Antidumping Duty   After all this, if both injury and dumping are shown, the Department of Commerce then applies an antidumping duty equal to the amount of dumping. This duty stays in effect until the guilty firm shows it has stopped dumping. That can be done in either of two ways: by showing no sales at all for three years, or no dumping for two years at annual reviews. These cost some $50,000, so $100,000 would be the fee to show no dumping, a considerable expense for a small exporter.

THE SECONDARY DEFINITION OF DUMPING: SALES IN EXPORT MARKETS AT PRICES BELOW COST

What if you are an exporter with *low* prices at home compared to the United States, or perhaps with few or no sales at home, selling only in the United States and other export markets? It would seem that no dumping charge is then possible, but this is not correct. There is a secondary or cost definition of dumping, invented by the United States in 1974, adopted with little or no debate, and entering the laws of the other major countries by about 1980. If there are no home prices to work with, then a "fair" home price is constructed from data on cost and if an exporter sells below that price in the United States, then it is guilty of dumping. Under this cost definition, dumping occurs in the export market even if sales below constructed cost are occurring in the firm's home market as well.

The chances of dumping are greatly raised by the method used to construct the foreign exporter's cost. The cost definition basically used is full short-run average cost, including variable and fixed costs, with an extra 10% added on for administrative expenses, plus a fixed 8% profit margin added atop that. These added figures tend to raise the constructed cost of production in the home market, and give a high likelihood that your price will be below your cost. For example, the average rate of profit in the United States has in recent years been only 5% to 6%, and 13 of the 15 largest firms in the United States would not have been able to meet the 8% test themselves in 1989. Does an exporter have considerable research and development costs? Full recovery of R&D spending is usually assumed to be necessary over six months or at most a year, rather than the many years for products like airliners. No law forces domestic firms to earn an 8% profit, or incur 10% administrative expenses, or to recover R&D costs quickly. Behavior that is common for domestic firms in these circumstances is illegal if the firms are foreign ones attempting to export to the United States.

THE COST DEFINITION IS ESPECIALLY IMPORTANT IN A RECESSION   This cost definition is a powerful weapon in a recession. First-year economics courses for decades have covered the shutdown rule, the idea that it would not make sense to shut down your firm unless prices fall below average variable costs. Many firms make losses in a recession, sometimes billion-dollar losses, but of course they continue to produce because that minimizes their loss. But under the dumping laws a foreign exporting firm is not permitted to sell below cost. Say a country, like Japan, has a tradition of lifetime employment, keeping labor employed rather than laying it off in a recession. Then labor becomes a fixed cost and in a recession dumping is easier to show. All this helps to explain why the number of cases soars in a recession. Firms not only *want* trade barriers then, but dumping is easier to prove.[*]

THE COST DEFINITION AND NONMARKET (COMMUNIST) COUNTRIES   The cost definition of dumping is more difficult when the dumping charge is against a centrally planned economy, so there are no market prices by which the cost of production can be determined. It might be thought that because market prices are not used, dumping charges on the cost definition would not be possible. But this underestimates the ingenuity of the law's administrators, who have found a way.

The first method used by the Department of Commerce to establish costs was to examine the price of a like product in a comparable economy. Cooperation of a producer of the like product had to be obtained, however, and that dried up when the data furnished by a Finnish steel company in a 1982 case against steel from Romania was used in 1984 to prosecute the Finnish company. The Department of Commerce thereupon moved to a second method, reconstructing the costs of production from the costs of the factor inputs in similar market economies. For an example, consider the remarkable tale of the Polish golf carts.

---

[*] The problem can perhaps be exaggerated. D.G. Tarr's work, cited by R.E. Baldwin, "Trade policies in developed countries," in Jones and Kenen, *Handbook of International Economics*, Vol. 1, p. 606, turned up no evidence in the steel industry that cyclical dumping during recessions was being resorted to in the United States, the EC, and Japan.

Pezetel, the only Polish firm producing golf carts, was accused of dumping by selling below cost during a period that extended from 1975 to 1980. The Commerce Department reconstructed the Mielec, Poland, production cost of Pezetel by using Spanish costs as a proxy. Spain is not unlike Poland in some ways. At any rate the two countries are about the same size, they are both rather flat, and they are both rather poor, for what that is worth. The attempt was made to estimate what it would have cost to produce the carts if the Polish firm were transplanted to the plains of Castile. Then the cost in Spanish pesetas was converted to dollars to get the proxy for the American price. (Only a small amount of dumping was actually found, incidentally.)

For all the uncertainty in this method, its use against centrally planned economies became standard under the 1988 trade act. It has been employed in many recent actions against China, where production costs were established by estimating what they would have been if the product had been produced elsewhere. For Chinese paintbrushes, 27% dumping was found by using a Sri Lankan firm as the surrogate. In steel wire nails, Korea was the surrogate; in wax candles, it was Malaysia and the Republic of Guinea; for steel, Pakistan; for menthol, Paraguay; for porcelain-on-steel cooking ware, it was a weighted figure for Japan, Canada, Switzerland, Germany, the Netherlands, and France. Because labor costs in all these other countries are higher than China's, the results seem irrelevant and the method badly flawed. In any case, inefficiency in centrally planned economies may mean greater-than-usual factor use that when valued at market prices, might mean dumping would always exist if any exports at all were sold. In all this it should be noted that an accused country cannot know which surrogate will be selected and is not told until after the case begins.

OTHER REASONS FOR DUMPING

All would agree that predatory dumping, already discussed, is an exploitative tactic that should be kept out of bounds. Sometimes, however, other reasons for dumping may arise that are not predatory, but that still give rise to questions. In this section, the dumping would be both under the price definition and the cost definition.

DUMPING TO DECREASE A FIRM'S COSTS OF PRODUCTION   It is said that a foreign firm may benefit from dumping if it can restrict output in a protected home market and sell at high prices there. Then as a regular practice it might dump (that is, sell at a lower price in its export market) so as to move down its cost curve and perhaps its learning curve as well, which has the same effect. The lower costs could bring increased profits in the high-price home market. The tactic could pay as long as sales in the export market are made at a price equal to or above the firm's marginal cost, even if below its average total cost.

The logic of this latter case is explored in Fig. 7.2. In the diagram, the average cost of production is already covered at home in the domestic market, where the firm has some degree of monopoly power, buttressed perhaps by protection. The

Figure 7.2 **Profits may be enhanced by export sales at prices below average cost.** A firm could keep its monopoly price in the home market at P_m, but lower its costs from C_1 to C_2 by selling extra production of Q_mQ_x at marginal cost to an export market.

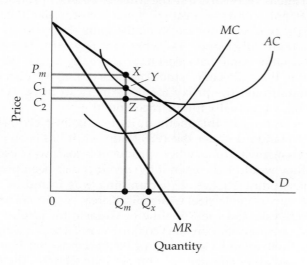

quantity produced is equal to Q_m; the price is P_m. Cost per unit is C_1. Profit is C_1P_mXY.

This firm has an opportunity available to it if it dumps in its export markets. What if the firm were to increase its output, say to Q_x, selling the increase Q_mQ_x in an export market? The firm might sell these exports at a price just high enough to cover the marginal cost of the additional output Q_mQ_x. Note that the increased output allows the firm to bring down its average costs from C_1 to C_2. That fall in average cost serves to raise profits in the protected home market by C_2C_1YZ.

In any price-discrimination situation, the discriminating firm must keep its markets apart; otherwise buyers in the cheap market will resell in the expensive one. Alternatively competing sellers in the cheap market will sell in the expensive one and also reap the value of the market separation; such competitive selling will move the markets toward a single price. Only if the discriminator's home market is protected against reimports or imports from the foreign market can the discrimination strategy succeed.

In such a situation there is certainly an argument that the *foreign* government should strengthen its antitrust laws and reduce its trade barriers so that its own consumers will benefit. The first-best solution would be for the importing country's government to encourage the exporter's government to make the exporter's home market competitive.

If this fails, the importing country can console itself in a number of ways. By receiving the dumped goods it is benefiting from the lower prices, and our standard model predicts that the benefits will outweigh the costs to producers harmed by the imports. The foreign exporter, rather than staying up its cost curve, is willing to move down it and share the benefits with consumers abroad. Predatory behavior is not occurring in this case.

Other arguments of illegitimate dumping are sometimes heard. Firms are said to cross-subsidize, say by pricing TV sets below cost and making it up by selling high-profit items to people who come into the TV shop. Firms are also said to dump *experience goods*, by charging low (forward or life cycle) prices for new types or models that consumers must become familiar with if the goods are to be sold. Later the firm will charge the regular price. Note, however, that although they do involve dumping these practices are quite familiar and legal for domestic firms. The test should clearly be, is the practice permitted for domestic firms? If the answer is yes, then a level playing field would seem to require the same treatment for foreign firms.

THE GROWING IMPORTANCE OF THE DUMPING LAWS

Use of these laws is growing fast: When the steel VER expired in 1991, U.S. companies launched a blizzard of antidumping charges, 70 in flat rolled steel alone. They won their case against 19 countries in January 1993, only to be hit immediately with heavy antidumping duties levied by Canada on U.S. steel exports. The U.S. auto industry is threatening suit against Japanese auto parts makers, having found a way to hit the Japanese carmakers that have built plants in the United States. (But plans to bring sweeping dumping charges against Japanese carmakers in general were apparently scrapped in February 1993, after intense criticism from the U.S. public.) The EC has adopted the U.S. definitions for dumping and added some new ones.

There seems little doubt that in recent years the antidumping laws have proved a useful tool for putting pressure both on foreign competitors and one's own government. The foreign competitor may react even to the mere filing of a dumping complaint by raising prices and restricting exports, if only to reduce the harassment. One's own government might be pushed to negotiate for a VER rather than contemplate a legal remedy that is very rigid, may provoke retaliation, and offers the president no discretion. The VER negotiated with Japan in semiconductors (microchips) during 1986 is a good example. Japanese microchip imports used in computers were due to be hit with antidumping duties of up to 120%, and both the United States and Japan preferred a VER to this result. This case is examined in detail in the next chapter.

NEW INTERPRETATIONS ARE SURFACING　　Recently new interpretations of dumping have surfaced. The rules, including those of the United States, have in the past said nothing about the dumping of components used as inputs in foreign-owned plants. The European Community decided in 1987 to attack such *input dumping*, extended its statutes to cover this practice, and has already brought a number of cases against Japanese companies with so-called screwdriver assembly plants in Europe. The new rule does not apply if the value of local content exceeds 40% of the final value of the good produced. (France enforces a stricter rule.)[14] A

GATT panel has been requested by Japan against these EC rules on dumping of parts and components, but the EC said it would not agree to a panel and that the matter would have to be settled in the Uruguay Round. Other large antidumping duties imposed by the EC in 1988 against Japanese VCRs were justified not on the grounds of harm to domestic industry, but instead because the dumping could eventually weaken profits in the electronics industry, which needs them to finance research leading to the next generation of consumer electronics. Finally, the EC is investigating a charge of predatory pricing by Korea's Hyundai Merchant Marine on cargo shipped from Europe to Australia—the first serious attempt to apply the dumping laws to services.

In the United States, congress has considered but has not passed laws to stop input dumping à la EC. A new U.S. interpretation did surface, however, in the 1988 trade act. Under that legislation, the antidumping laws were extended to cover imports from third countries that use the dumped components as inputs (diversionary input dumping, so-called). This, it is argued, will lower the price charged for the otherwise-innocent import. The U.S. government can request the third country to take steps, though as yet no enforcement powers have been established.

All the new EC and U.S. interpretations appear to be at odds with the GATT rules, and obviously the existing GATT dumping code (with 25 members in 1992) has been ineffective. As J. Michael Finger has observed, dumping is becoming anything you can persuade the government to act against, ordinary protection backed by good public relations.[15]

WHAT TO DO?

The subject of dumping is high on the agenda at the Uruguay Round. The need for progress is urgent because the antidumping rules have become a major new source of protectionist pressures. Many economists, including the authors, believe that the dumping laws should be abandoned as expensive and capricious barriers to trade that should be replaced by an even-handed competition policy applying to domestic and foreign firms alike. The Uruguay Round will not yield that much because of U.S., Canadian, Australian, and EC opposition, but the negotiators have tentatively agreed on substantial reforms. These include a large rise in the *de minimis* level, a phaseout of penalties after five years, a requirement that the biased use of averages be stopped, probably an end to the fixed percentages for profit and sales expenses in the cost definition, and perhaps ruling out dumping duties when sales are below average cost and market conditions make this reasonable. These would be great improvements. If the dumping laws cannot be scrapped in their entirety, the changes are a decent second-best approach.

SUBSIDIES

There is clearly a sense, strong among businesspeople, that subsidies abroad are unfair to domestic producers even though on a *national* basis the subsidy is like a gift to consumers. Most economists would surely agree that there is an element of distortion when exports caused by long-term production subsidies to firms *without* a comparative advantage harm domestic firms that *have* a comparative advantage. Subsidies have become much more prominent as strategic trade policies involving them are adopted by some countries. The question of subsidies is a difficult one, with the GATT rules less clear than U.S. law. Even the latter has some very fuzzy areas.

Unlike dumping action, which is aimed at firms, countervailing duties are aimed at countries that subsidize. A countervailing duty, which is a charge equal to the amount of the subsidy, is the remedy for this unfair trade practice. Almost all of them have been imposed by the United States, 281 from 1980 to 1986 compared to just seven in the EC where the law is not as broad and just one in Japan where it is virtually a dead letter. A few more cases have occurred in Canada and Australia. Many other countries, including Austria, Norway, Sweden, and Switzerland, have never imposed countervailing duties at all, without apparent harm be it said.[16]

In the United States the president has no discretion to interfere with the course of the law on the matter. That tends to increase the popularity of countervailing duties in the business community and also makes it possible to apply pressure on governments, perhaps leading toward a VER. The number of investigations and new countervailing duties imposed has undergone a massive increase. The United States initiated only 11 cases in 1970–1974, with duties imposed in 10 of these; but in the period 1980–1988 there were 389 cases, 59% against developed countries and the rest against LDCs. Strikingly, only five of the cases involved Japan compared to 177 involving the EC.[17] Sixty-six U.S. duties were in place at the start of 1992, some dating back to the 1970s. None were against imports from Japan.

DISTINGUISHING BETWEEN EXPORT SUBSIDIES AND PRODUCTION SUBSIDIES

We have already noted in Chapter 5 that explicit export subsidies are illegal, both to GATT and to the United States under U.S. laws dating back to 1897, and now mostly based on the Tariff Act of 1930. There are two exceptions. One is agriculture, where export subsidies are permitted if they do not result in an increased share of world trade for the country paying the subsidy. The other is export subsidies paid by less developed countries. The GATT code on subsidies signed after the Tokyo Round recognized that such subsidies are a legitimate tool of development and did not outlaw their use by these countries. Countervailing duties may be imposed against them, but only when material injury in the home market is shown. Injury in third markets elsewhere is not a sufficient cause to trigger a penalty under the code. The developing countries that signed the code agreed to phase out the subsidies when they are no longer needed for development or for competitive purposes. The fact that only 25 countries had signed the code by 1991 limits the benefits of this clause, however, and many U.S. subsidy cases (41% from 1980 to 1988 compared to just 18% in 1970–1974) continue to be brought against poor countries.

The situation is more tortuous when subsidies are paid on domestic production only, and not on exports. Arguably such domestic subsidies do cheapen production and make exports more likely. For example, British and French subsidies to the steel industry in the early 1980s are thought to have increased U.S. imports about 3%, and to have caused a resulting decrease of U.S. production of about 1%.[18] The GATT rules are not very clear, and national laws vary considerably. In the United States under a trade law amendment of 1922, the granting of domestic subsidies to a selected industry or group of industries can be "countervailed."

HOW IS A SUBSIDY COUNTERVAILED?

In the United States, the procedure for obtaining a countervailing duty is much like that for dumping. Private firms in an industry that is directly affected make the complaints. Self-initiation of a case by the Department of Commerce has been permitted since 1979, but that power is rarely used. Following the complaint, Commerce is responsible for determining whether a subsidy is being paid on exports or on production, and how large it is. (The Treasury had this task before 1979 but was much less interested in such questions.) The U.S. International Trade Commission must then determine whether there is material injury to U.S. firms. Until the Tokyo Round code on subsidies, duties were imposed even if no harm or injury was shown to have occurred—until that time the law had a very protectionist bias. In a major change under that code, the United States agreed to grant a material injury criterion, already mentioned when we discussed export subsidies, to the 25 signers of the code.

For the many nonsigners of the code, however, material injury still does not have to be shown. Where they are concerned, the law states broadly that any benefit from the subsidy can be countervailed. All that needs to be proved is that a subsidy exists, not that the subsidy has an effect on trade. To economists, the proper action would be to estimate the effect on exports of any given subsidy, as this is the degree to which the subsidy distorts trade. Doing so is easiest for export subsidies, more difficult for subsidies on domestic production. Estimating the trade-distorting effects of the latter would require that the domestic subsidy be converted to an equivalent export subsidy, and the effect on exports estimated. Under U.S. law, however, that is not necessary.

This situation means that even tiny subsidies may be countervailed, as low as 0.75% in a case involving Thailand. The duty itself was harmless enough, but the uncertainty and legal costs for the Thai defendants were not. After a countervailing duty is levied, it is reviewed administratively by the Department of Commerce every year and is lifted if the subsidy stops.

INTENT DOES NOT NEED TO BE CONSIDERED   Another aspect of the present laws is that no account needs to be taken of the intent of subsidies. Some are designed to allow the controlled running down of a declining industry. Say a subsidy is paid to a firm to persuade it to tear down one plant a year for three years and so put itself out of business. This subsidy is countervailable under U.S. law, although it is fair to say that outrageous action of this sort has been rare.

Other subsidies may be intended to compensate for government regulations such as above-market minimum wage laws, overvalued foreign exchange rates, or export taxes of various sorts. Consider what was done to Thailand by the United States in 1986. A countervailing duty was imposed against imports of rice from that country after various subsidies were found, including some price support, mortgage assistance, discounts to rice millers, and government assistance to cooperatives. But at the same time Thailand was collecting a large export tax that was over five times as high as the subsidy. (At the time the United States was paying large export subsidies to its own rice farmers. The U.S. program was transferring over $1 million per year to the average American grower, while the Thai program was transferring about $100 to the average Thai farmer per year before payment of the export tax.) Argentine wool growers were hit by a U.S. countervailing duty after a finding of a 6% subsidy, even though a 17% export tax was charged and even though U.S. wool growers get direct government payments that boosted the return to wool growing by about 50%.[19] To avoid such situations, Canada has proposed a new GATT rule that would allow countervailing duties only on the net difference between the subsidy in the exporting country and any subsidy given to that industry in the importer, but that reasonable change has not happened yet.[20]

Only subsidies that increase market share in export markets at the expense of other producers are a clear distortion to trade; the others can be considered as desirable corrections for market failure. Yet all production subsidies are treated alike under U.S. law.

THE GROWING LIST OF WHAT CAN BE COUNTERVAILED

A number of difficult issues have arisen concerning subsidies:

1. Are regional development subsidies to encourage development in poor areas countervailable? Yes, under U.S. law since 1973, when a Canadian subsidy to the Michelin tire company persuading it to build a plant off the beaten track was deemed sufficient to trigger a penalty. Until 1979 the foreigner was given a break. If the benefits of a subsidy were partly offsetting higher costs in the region being developed, they were ignored. Thus if a regional development subsidy of 15% of revenues is paid to a firm to establish in an underdeveloped area, and that raises the firm's transport costs by 5%, only the net of 10% was countervailable. Now, however, the whole 15% is subject to the penalty duty.

2. What about cheap access to a government-owned resource? For example, cheap oil made available from a government's national oil company might lead to lower prices than otherwise for Mexican manufactured goods or

Saudi Arabian petrochemicals. Other examples might include access to cheap water or other natural resource inputs. A major case has involved Canadian provinces, which own more than 90% of Canada's timber. Historically the provinces charged low prices (or stumpage fees) to Canadian timber companies for cutting rights on government land. Was this a countervailable subsidy? Yes, and a duty was levied by the United States in 1986.

■ *THE DEVELOPMENT OF THE UNPLEASANT CANADIAN TIMBER CASE*

This timber case with Canada has been thoroughly unpleasant. First Canada offered to assess a 15% surtax on its lumber exports in lieu of the countervailing duty until the provinces raised their prices for cutting rights. That way Canada would keep the revenue effect of nearly half a billion U.S. dollars. The Canadian government promised to return the tax revenue to the provinces from which the timber was exported. Canadians claimed that this issue had already been settled once before, in 1982–1983, but that U.S. views on what constitutes a subsidy thereafter changed. That aspect of the case shows that private interests can repeatedly file unfair practice charges, hoping for and sometimes obtaining a new interpretation. At the very least, forcing exporters to defend several times against the same charges will boost their expenses. According to Congressional Budget Office estimates, the settlement was expected to raise the cost of an average house constructed in the United States by $300.

Having been thus cooled down, the lumber dispute heated up once again in 1991, when Canada announced it intended to scrap its 15% tax on exports to the United States. In the four years since 1986 during which the tax had been in place, the Canadian share of the U.S. market had fallen from 33% to 26%. (During the period the Canadian dollar also appreciated, by 20%.) The Canadians thought this fall in their market share was punishment enough. In any case, the export tax has been withdrawn on a major share of lumber exports because some provinces had raised their stumpage charges, as was permitted under the agreement. The Canadian argument seemed strong, but congress called for immediate retaliation and the president's trade representative announced her opposition to the Canadian step. Action was initiated, unusually, by the administration itself; a 14.5% countervailing duty was levied in 1992. Americans wondered why their lumber prices were rising so sharply, the Canadian government reacted with anger, and the dispute returned to full boil.[21]

---

3. What about a related case where the subsidy is paid not on the product itself, but on some input? An example of such an upstream subsidy might be subsidized steel used by an unsubsidized automaker. Until 1984 countervailing duties were not applied, but under the U.S. trade act of that year, upstream subsidies were brought under the law, and an unsubsidized prod-

uct can now be penalized if some principal input is subsidized. The concept is not supported by GATT, however. When the United States applied a countervailing duty to U.S. imports of pork products from Canada, it claimed that Canadian government subsidies to farmers growing pigs passed through to the producers of pork products. Canada took the case to GATT, where a panel found that the U.S. duty was not justified.[22] The United States has proposed a change in the GATT rules to prevent shipment of subsidized parts and components to an importing country for assembly, or for assembly in a third country from these parts and components. The outcome of this particular issue was not certain at the time of writing.

4. What about a subsidy by a consortium of nations rather than by an individual country, for example the EC's Airbus program? Not countervailable by the United States until the 1988 trade law allowed action to be taken. We return to the Airbus dispute in the next chapter.

5. What if the subsidy is paid on an item that is leased rather than sold? Yes, sometimes now countervailable under the 1988 trade law, in which a clause backed by Boeing and McDonnell-Douglas made it possible to challenge leases that were equivalent to sales. Such leases are most common in the aircraft industry.

6. Are centrally planned Communist economies subject to countervailing duties on their exports? Not since a 1986 U.S. Court of Appeals decision. However, within months of a 1991 finding by the Department of Commerce in a separate dumping case that Chinese chrome-plated lug nuts were now being produced under market conditions rather than under planning, American firms brought charges of subsidization and sought countervailing duties.

7. What if the product subsidized by another country is not imported at all, with the effects felt only in third-country export markets or in the markets of the country paying the subsidy, so that the subsidy therefore harms one's exporting firms rather than firms that compete with subsidized imports? In that case countervailing duties would deliver no benefits. Under the GATT code, it is possible to bring complaints about the effects of subsidies in overseas markets to a GATT panel. The United States complained to GATT in 1988 about EC payments of subsidies to processors of EC-produced oilseeds. The panel found against the EC in 1989, declaring the subsidies an illegal method to get oilseed processors to use EC oilseeds. The EC has delayed reform in spite of the ruling, saying it would have to be part of the bargaining in the Uruguay Round. More generally, there has been talk of countervailing subsidies to offset the harm to exporters, but budget constraints are an obvious impediment to this course of action. The U.S. subsidies for export credit discussed in Chapter 5 were in large part an attempt to address this problem.

8. What about government assistance for a whole industry or group of industries, as when the Japanese Ministry of Trade and Industry subsidizes research and development expenditures, or when wage subsidies are paid in

Europe to promote employment? No, such links are too tenuous. As the United States decided in the Houdaille machine tool case, though the evidence of subsidies was persuasive, it proved hard to say what difference that made for the price of machine tools. No countervailing duty was permitted. (Houdaille obtained its protection anyway by making the national defense argument, as we have seen. A machine tool VER was negotiated with Japan in November 1986.)

THE CONCEPT OF GENERAL AVAILABILITY

These cases seem to have little enough in common. One element in them does appear to be agreed on, however, and is a provision in the GATT rules. It is understood that if a subsidy is "generally available" to all industries, then it will distort trade less than will a subsidy to a specific industry or group of industries. The reason is that a generally available subsidy, received by all, tends to appreciate the country's currency. The subsidy makes all exports cheaper to foreign buyers, meaning that the demand for the exporting country's currency will rise, thus pushing up the value of that currency. The appreciation will in turn mean that the country's exports appear more expensive than before to foreign buyers, thus reducing the initial effect of the subsidy. (This case is akin to the pass-through effect of an across-the-board tariff, which also appreciates the currency, as we saw in Chapter 4.) Imports benefiting from generally available subsidies are therefore less reasonable targets for countervailing duties than are imports produced by industries that receive specific subsidies. Since 1986, however, the United States has applied a new concept of "de facto specificity" when it finds a few dominant users of a widely available subsidy, and cases employing this definition have now been prosecuted.

THE FUTURE FOR SUBSIDIES IN INTERNATIONAL TRADE

Countries with large subsidy programs include Italy (3.43% of GNP), France (3.01%), Canada (2.48%), Britain (2.22%), and Germany (2.01%), though the percentages one sees reported are perhaps not always completely trustworthy because countries are reluctant to make themselves vulnerable to countervailing duty cases.[23] Norway, Ireland, and Sweden subsidize at double or triple these percentages. Of these countries, the growth in subsidies over the past decade has been most rapid in Canada. United States and Japanese subsidies are, however, much lower, at only 0.58% of GNP for the former and 1.15% for the latter. It should be noted that these figures do not include soft loans by government at low interest rates, tax concessions, or government purchase of stock, all of which raise the subsidy element, sometimes considerably (Italy to 16–17%, for example). If these were included, even the United States would seem open to the charge of subsidization because the U.S. government provides large amounts of research and development funding, mainly in defense-related activities but certainly affecting exports. The United States also has investment tax credits, R&D tax credits, and accelerated depreciation allowances in its tax laws (much reduced, though, in 1986). The value of these tax concessions during 1975–1987 was about two-and-a-half times that of the U.S. government's direct subsidies. The United States also maintains policies that provide cheap water, grazing land, and mineral rights in the West, and cheap food when deficiency payments to farmers reduce market prices.[*] These could be considered tantamount to subsidies. Similarly, Japan formerly made wide use of low-interest government loans in some sectors, and many countries still do so.

The United States wants to define a subsidy as any government action that delivers a benefit. That would include not only the grey areas discussed above, but such things as a favorable decision under antitrust law or government insurance against changes in foreign exchange rates. The EC and most other countries want to use a definition that covers only an actual transfer of resources from government. In none of these cases is it clear how the antisubsidy portions of trade law will evolve.

Subsidies and the countervailing duties against them have grown to become one of the most acrimonious issues in international trade. Several proposals for reform are current: Confine enforcement to GATT, rather than national governments; levy penalties for frivolous complaints; only allow the countervailing of serious subsidies. The tentative Uruguay Round agreement in this area as of late 1992 would prohibit export subsidies outside of agriculture and would establish a presumption that domestic subsidies greater than 5% of the export value of a good will have a damaging effect on trading partners. (Note that the *average* state subsidy to manufacturing in Italy is 6.0%, in Ireland 4.9%, in Greece 14.6%, and 3.5% in France.) The new rules would allow subsidies for regional development, for basic research up to 50% of total research costs, and for applied research up to 25% of total research costs. Subsidies for development, the construction of prototypes, and production could be countervailed.

From all the complications one salient point does emerge. The current heavy use of subsidies may to some significant extent interfere with comparative advantage. The subject is returned to in the next chapter, where we examine strategic trade policies involving subsidies.

OTHER UNFAIR TRADE PRACTICES

The unfair trade practice laws govern a wide range of other international transactions as well. Like the dumping and subsidy regulations, these laws have become more important as the average level of tariffs has fallen.

---

[*] In 1987, the first countervailing duty ever levied on an import from the United States was imposed by Canada, $1.05 per bushel on corn. The basis for the duty was that deficiency payments to U.S. corn farmers lowered the market price of corn and thus caused more imports to enter Canada. The United States has taken the issue to GATT.

INTELLECTUAL PROPERTY (SECTION 337)

Intellectual property, largely in the form of patents and copyrights, has extraordinary importance in such areas of trade as computer software, biotechnology, and pharmaceuticals. The U.S. International Trade Commission has estimated that the pirating of intellectual property cost U.S. firms $24 billion in 1986, while worldwide the trade in counterfeit goods is now estimated to have grown to 3–6% of world trade. Most of the purloining has occurred in the less developed countries.

Under Section 337 of the U.S. Tariff Act of 1930, goods can be excluded if they involve patent violations, false labeling, or infringement of copyrights and trademarks. Cases can be brought by means of a complaint to the International Trade Commission, or by the ITC on its own. There were 50 exclusion orders under Section 337 in effect at the start of 1992, mostly concerning patents. (A GATT panel found in 1989 that the U.S. procedure gave less favorable treatment to foreign firms than the U.S. courts did when the infringement was domestic. Thus far no U.S. action has been taken in response to the GATT finding.)

A major area of concern is how to handle violations when the resulting counterfeited item or technology does not involve imports. U.S. law allows barriers against other goods as retaliation, so-called cross-retaliation, but this is contrary to the current GATT rules. The U.S. argument is that if cross-retaliation is not permitted, very little leverage exists against those who steal intellectual property. Many countries, especially less developed ones against which most charges arise, fear that cross-retaliation is a very blunt weapon. By and large, however, the tentative Uruguay Round agreement has significantly tightened the rules, with patents safeguarded for 20 years, copyrights on sound recordings for 50 years, computer software obtaining the same status as literary works, and compulsory licensing procedures controlled. India has proved to be an especially tough negotiator, having managed to introduce a 10-year grace period for the less developed countries—meaning, for example, that India's pharmaceutical firms can go on producing counterfeit drugs for a significant amount of time.

THE CROWBAR: VIOLATION OF TRADE AGREEMENTS (SECTION 301)

Major attention has focused on laws that attempt to open up foreign markets closed to U.S. exports by attacking imports from the offending countries. Under Section 301 of the trade act of 1974 the president's trade representative is required to take action if a foreign government violates a trade agreement; the legislation gives discretionary authority to retaliate if a trade policy is judged to be unreasonable or discriminatory in excluding U.S. goods from a foreign market.[24] Such 301 actions have proven to be extremely contentious. They are noteworthy in that they deviate considerably from approved GATT procedures for settling disputes. They violate most favored nation agreements by discriminating among countries. They also usually impose high tariffs, with 100% *ad valorem* a common figure, thus violating undertakings to bind tariff rates. As such they are highly visible and controversial.

301 MECHANICS   Under Section 301, the president's trade representative may initiate action, or the process may begin by private petition. In 1989, two investigations were begun by private petition compared to seven initiated by the president. If the initiation is by means of private petition, the trade representative must decide within 45 days whether to start an investigation. Timetables are important in the 301 law. A finding on the necessity for action must be made within 18 months for a trade agreement breach, or 12 months for a practice not involving a trade agreement. If a finding for action is made, then steps must be taken within 30 days, or in 180 days if the trade representative determines that delay is desirable or substantial progress is being made. The action terminates automatically in four years, unless a case for extension is made.

USING THE CROWBAR   There were very few uses of Section 301 until 1986, with the president taking action only in two of 40 cases. Since then this part of trade law has become much more important, with 48 more investigations by the start of 1992. United States officials took to describing 301 actions as crowbars to open foreign markets. Among the major cases are those against Brazil's stringent protection of its computer and pharmaceuticals industries, South Korea's unwillingness to allow fire and life insurance policies to be written by foreign companies and its ban on beef, Taiwan's customs valuation procedures, the Thai cigarette ban, and Japanese protection against tobacco and citrus fruits. The Pasta War started as a Section 301 case involving EC barriers to U.S. citrus exports, and the initial move in the semiconductor (microchip) battle with Japan was also a 301 case. The EC's rules on meats and growth hormones are being attacked in this manner, and the disputes over new rules for U.S. agricultural exports when Spain and Portugal joined the EC also involved 301. Various foreign export subsidies, including EC oilseeds, are also being retaliated against under this section of the trade act. The 301 action brought against China is breathtakingly broad, in effect demanding that China change its Communist ways by dismantling its system of import licensing.[*]

    In some respects, the 301 approach has been a success. The United States does indeed have a great deal of leverage in trade negotiations because it is such a large importer. Often a country will prefer to yield in a trade dispute rather than to risk attack with the 301 crowbar, and in fact U.S. 301 action has been rare. Foreign counterretaliation has been even rarer, with just one case on record. Arguably it works best when it is not used, and is worth retaining for its

---

[*] There has also been just one Section 406 case, covering disruption by imports from Communist countries (petrochemicals from China). The 406 mechanism works much like the escape clause (Section 201), explaining the rarity of its use and why 301 law has more recently been used against China. Under yet another section, 307, the U.S. trade representative can impose duties or exclude imports found to have occurred because of export performance requirements in investment licenses. The first 307 case was brought against Taiwan in 1986.

deterrent effect. Yet all is obviously not well. The Super 301 episode examined in the accompanying box proved inflammatory and, politically, put the United States on the defensive. Furthermore, the 301 laws have strategic weaknesses, as are explored below.

■ *THE CONTROVERSIAL SUPER 301 PROVISIONS*

The 1988 trade bill contained new Super 301 provisions written by Richard Gephardt that proved even more controversial than 301 itself. Under Super 301, in effect in 1989 and 1990, a country's entire set of trade practices could be attacked. It required the president to compile a hit list of trade offenders, including both countries and "priority practices." The president's trade representative was required to negotiate with foreign countries to end the problems; success was to be judged not by elimination of the practice but by an increase in exports over three years. If no agreement could be reached, the trade representative had to decide whether to impose penalties.

As with the regular 301 law, Super 301 could also be initiated by private petition. The law required the president's trade representative to respond within 45 days. Indeed, the first use of a private Super 301 petition was by the U.S. Rice Millers' Association, which sought a finding that Japan unfairly restricted rice imports. This delicate issue, with serious implications for U.S. relations with Japan, had to be decided just 11 days before the 1988 election. (The trade representative surprised a great many people when he rejected the petition.)

On the initial 1989 listing of trade offenders were Japan (government procurement of satellites, exclusion of supercomputers, standards for wood products), Brazil (import bans), and India (insurance and investment rules). The responses of the indicted countries differed greatly. Japan made concessions on each of its named issues and was not designated again in 1990. Brazil also negotiated, and was excluded from the 1990 list. India failed to respond and *was* named again, the only country on the 1990 list. (Though India has been uncooperative, that country is also poor and is responsible for less than 1% of the U.S. trade deficit.) The EC, certainly a candidate for listing in many areas, announced that if this were done it would bring a GATT case and would retaliate immediately. Though the issues were all relatively minor, the Super 301 listing attracted worldwide attention, with congress treating this procedure as the centerpiece of its new toughness on trade.

The Super 301 provisions expired at the end of 1990. The charges against India were simply dropped. The expiration was greeted with a sigh of relief around the world. In the fall of 1991, Richard Gephardt introduced a successor that would require the president to frame an action plan against the countries named. In her recent book Laura Tyson, President Clinton's Chair of the Council of Economic Advisors, called for reinstatement of Super 301.[25] Whether congress will pass this new legislation—again being considered in 1993—will be a bellwether for U.S. trade policy.

A major problem with the 301 crowbars is now widely recognized. To some considerable extent the United States has ceased to discuss giving up its own barriers, and uses sheer economic power to force trading partners to remove barriers of their own. The tool does work to force open foreign markets, but the link between lower foreign trade barriers and lower U.S. barriers has been severed. "Might makes right" seems to be the apt description. Another difficulty is that the 301 approach when successful opens up foreign markets only to the United States, but not to others. These other innocent parties, many no doubt weaker and unable to bring their own leverage to bear, are left out.

In recent months the United States has used the 301 trade-reprisal process in a more restrained manner than had been true in 1989–1991. Still, many countries, especially the EC members, are demanding a U.S. abandonment of the 301 arrangement as part of a Uruguay Round settlement. The Bush Administration generally indicated a willingness to do so if strong GATT rules were adopted to replace 301. Some members of congress insist, however, that 301 be retained, and the Clinton Administration's policy on the matter is not yet clear. There for now the argument stands.

CONCLUSION

The laws concerning unfair trade practices are an appeal for a level playing field. Yet they possess substantial disadvantages. They diminish the flexibility with which governments address trade issues. Overly legalistic and overly rigid, discriminatory and creating great uncertainty, they focus on punishment rather than cooperation. In so doing they present private firms with excellent opportunities to harass their competition and bring pressure on their own governments. At best, this system of procedural protection tends to break down or be counterproductive in big cases against foreigners with substantial bargaining power, while biting sharply where retaliatory power is weak.

More broadly, these laws fail to take into account the entire playing field, instead looking only at a few sections of it. Our understanding of comparative advantage is that making one product (item A) artificially cheap, say by means of a subsidy, will make others artificially costly. Item A attracts factors of production from the manufacture of items B and C, driving up their production costs. If item A is an export item, then exports of it will rise, and if B and C are also imported, then imports of them will rise. If A is also imported, then the subsidy will cause less to be imported. If B and C are export items, then their export will be discouraged. For every producer abroad who competes with item A and squirms over the subsidy to A, there should be a foreign producer of item B who has less to fear from competition, and who may now even export B to the country that subsidizes A because the costs of the subsidy have put domestic producers of B at a disadvantage. The playing field has been dug down in some places by the subsidies, but bumps appear elsewhere. The favors granted to one set of producers act as a tax on another set. Overall, the field remains much more level than those concerned about unfair practices care to admit, but efficiency declines and energies are directed toward obtaining government favors.

Unfair trade practice legislation lies at the heart of modern protectionist strategies. Together with the more traditional approaches, these laws will certainly be utilized by firms seeking trade barriers against imports. The most that can be said for these laws is that they may serve as a useful deterrent against countries intent on employing strategic trade policies of the sort examined in the next chapter.[26] A thorough reexamination is overdue; whether the Uruguay Round will require reform is still to be decided.

VOCABULARY AND CONCEPTS

Countervail
The crowbar
De minimis clauses
Dumping
General availability
Injury
Intellectual property

Level playing field
Persistent dumping
Predatory dumping
Price discrimination
Section 301
Sporadic dumping

QUESTIONS

1. Examine what dumping is, using both the primary and secondary definitions.

2. Why might firms engage in dumping? Is there a difference between persistent dumping (for price discrimination reasons) and predatory dumping? Why should we object to persistent dumping? What evidence is there for predatory dumping?

3. Argue, using the American antidumping laws as a case in point, that what is most unfair about unfair trade practices is the law, not the practices.

4. When or why should we, as consumers, want to impose antidumping duties?

5. What improvements in dumping legislation will occur if the Uruguay Round discussions are successfully concluded?

6. "Anyone can sympathize with a company that has seen its market drop sharply because a foreign government is subsidizing exports. That does indeed seem unjust. But in practice it is usually quite the other way around, as the scope of what constitutes a subsidy or a countervailable subsidy expands from the obvious and conspicuous to the obscure and nebulous." Explain.

7. If subsidies and persistent dumping are so unfair, why don't countries ban them internally? After all, American states and Canadian provinces certainly subsidize some industries and penalize others, and firms often charge different prices in different areas.

8. Are crowbar provisions good or bad?

9. "A level playing field is an appealing, but deceptive image. Short of making all nations' laws exactly the same, there will always be bumps. What is important is to get on with the game, and to realize it is not the foreigner

whom our complaints hurt, but our fellow citizens." Explain.

10. Is the principal problem with unfair trade practice law its poor economics or its ultimate

unjustness? (Adam Smith was, after all, a professor of moral philosophy, so the question is economic.)

NOTES

[1] For this section we utilized John H. Jackson and Edwin A. Vermulst, eds., *Antidumping Law and Practice,* Ann Arbor, University of Michigan Press, 1989, especially essays by Alan V. Deardorff and Gary N. Horlick; Richard Boltuck and Robert E. Litan, eds., *Down in the Dumps,* Washington, D.C., Brookings Institution, 1991, especially the chapters by Tracy Murray and N. David Palmeter; J. Michael Finger and Tracy Murray, "Policing unfair imports: The United States example," *Journal of World Trade,* Vol. 24, No. 4, August 1990, pp. 39–53; J. Michael Finger, "Dumping and antidumping: The rhetoric and the reality of protection in industrial countries," *World Bank Research Observer,* Vol. 7, No. 2, July 1992, pp. 121–143; Jarl Hagelstam, "Some shortcomings of international anti-dumping provisions," *Journal of World Trade,* Vol. 25, No. 5, October 1991, pp. 99–110; Bernard M. Hoekman and Michael P. Leidy, "Dumping, antidumping and emergency protection," *Journal of World Trade,* Vol. 23, No. 5, October 1989, pp. 27–44; F. Lazar, "Antidumping rules following the Canada-United States free trade agreement," *Journal of World Trade,* Vol. 23, No. 5, October 1989, pp. 45–71; Phedon Nicolaides, "The competition effects of dumping," *Journal of World Trade,* Vol. 24, No. 5, October 1990, pp. 115–131; Ken Matsumoto and Grant Finlayson, "Dumping and antidumping: Growing problems in world trade," *Journal of World Trade,* Vol. 24, No. 4, August 1990, pp. 5–19; N. David Palmeter, "The impact of U.S. anti-dumping law on China-U.S. trade," *Journal of World Trade,* Vol. 23, No. 4, August 1989, pp. 5–14; James Bovard, "U.S. trade law strikes again," *The Margin,* Vol. 7, Fall 1991, pp. 74–75; and James Bovard, "The myth of fair trade," *Policy Analysis,* No. 164, November 1, 1991, pp. 2–8. Also see all recent editions of U.S. ITC, *Operation of the Trade Agreements Program.*

[2] U.S. ITC, *The Year in Trade 1991,* Washington, D.C., 1992, pp. 202–206.

[3] Malcolm D. Rowat, "Protectionist tilts in antidumping legislation of developed countries and the LDC response: Is the 'race to the bottom' inevitable?" *Journal of World Trade,* Vol. 24, No. 6, December 1990, pp. 1–29.

[4] Bernard M. Hoekman and Michael P. Leidy, "Dumping, antidumping, and emergency protection," *Journal of World Trade,* Vol. 23, No. 5, October 1989, pp. 33, 36, citing work of Patrick Messerlin.

[5] The examples are from Bovard, "The myth of fair trade."

[6] For an examination, see John McGee, "Predatory price cutting: The Standard Oil (N.J.) case," *Journal of Law and Economics,* 1958, pp. 137–169; Isaac R. Mark and L. Vernon Smith, "In search of predatory pricing," *Journal of Political Economy,* Vol. 93, April 1985, pp. 320–345; and Roland Koller, "The myth of predatory pricing: An empirical study," and Kenneth Elzinga, "Predatory pricing: The case of the gunpowder trust," both in Yale Brozen, ed., *The Competitive Economy: Selected Readings,* Morristown, N.J., General Learning Press, 1975.

[7] See David G. Tarr, "Does protection really protect?" *Regulation,* November/December 1985, pp. 29–34.

[8] Palmeter, "Antidumping emperor," *Journal of World Trade,* Vol. 22, No. 4, August 1988, p. 6.

[9] See Gary N. Horlick and Geoffrey D. Oliver, "Antidumping and countervailing duty law provisions of the Omnibus Trade and Competitiveness Act of 1988," *Journal of World Trade,* Vol. 23, No. 3, June 1989, pp. 5–49.

[10] IMF, *World Economic Outlook, 1988,* p. 93.

[11] Work of J.M. Finger cited by R.E. Baldwin, "Trade policies in developed countries," in Jones and Kenen, *Handbook of International Economics,* Vol. 1, p. 606.

[12] Details are from James Bovard, "The myth of fair trade," *Policy Analysis,* No. 164, November 1, 1991, pp. 2–8.

[13] *Wall Street Journal,* August 12, 1992.

[14] See *International Economic Review,* June, 1988, and Ivo Van Bael, "EEC anti-dumping law and procedure revisited," *Journal of World Trade,* Vol. 24, No. 2, April 1990, pp. 5–23.

[15] J. Michael Finger, "Dumping and antidumping: The rhetoric and the reality of protection in industrial countries," *World Bank Research Observer,* Vol. 7, No. 2, July 1992, pp. 135, 141.

[16] Information for this section is taken from Gary Clyde Hufbauer and Joanna Shelton Erb, *Subsidies in International Trade,* Washington, D.C., Institute for International Economics, 1984, especially Chapter 3; Kelly et al., *International Trade Policy,* IMF Occasional Paper No. 63, p. 130; Jagdish Bhagwati, *Protectionism,* Cambridge, Mass., MIT Press, 1988, pp. 52, 116; James Bovard, "The myth of fair trade," *Policy Analysis,* No. 164, November 1, 1991, pp. 9–11; N. David Palmeter, "Injury determination in antidumping and countervailing duty cases—A commentary on U.S. practice," *Journal of World Trade*

Law, Vol. 21, No. 2, 1987, pp. 123–161; and the coverage in U.S. ITC, *Operation of the Trade Agreements Program* and the *International Economic Review.*

[17] J. Michael Finger and Tracy Murray, "Policing unfair imports: The United States example," *Journal of World Trade,* Vol. 24, No. 4, August 1990, pp. 52–53. For the time limits applying to subsidy investigations, see p. 42.

[18] See the work of J. Mutti, cited in R.E. Baldwin, "Trade policies in developed countries," in Jones and Kenen, *Handbook of International Economics,* Vol. 1, p. 605.

[19] The rice and wool cases are from James Bovard, "The myth of fair trade," *Policy Analysis,* No. 164, November 1, 1991, pp. 9–10.

[20] U.S. ITC, *Operation of the Trade Agreements Program 1990,* p. 21.

[21] *International Economic Review,* October, 1991; *Wall Street Journal,* March 6, 1992.

[22] U.S. ITC, *Operation of the Trade Agreements Program 1990,* p. 112.

[23] The data are from 1985. A recent study is R. Ford and W. Suyker, "Industrial subsidies in the OECD economies," *OECD Working Paper No. 74,* 1990.

[24] A thorough 301 review is in each issue of U.S. ITC, *Operation of the Trade Agreements Program.* Also see Jagdish Bhagwati, "Explaining Section 301," Appendix IV of his *The World Trading System at Risk,* Princeton, Princeton University Press, 1991; Jagdish Bhagwati, "Departures from multilateralism: Regionalism and aggressive unilateralism," *Economic Journal,* Vol. 100, No. 403, December 1990, pp. 1304–1317; and Jagdish Bhagwati and Hugh T. Patrick, eds., *Aggressive Internationalism: America's 301 Trade Policy and the World Trading System,* Ann Arbor, University of Michigan Press, 1990.

[25] Laura D'Andrea Tyson, *Who's Bashing Whom? Trade Conflict in High-Technology Industries,* Washington, D.C., Institute for International Economics, 1992, p. 260.

[26] See Robert E. Baldwin and T. Scott Thompson, "Responding to trade-distorting policies of other countries," *American Economic Review,* Vol. 74, No. 2, May 1984, pp. 271–276.

Chapter 8

Strategic Trade Policy

OBJECTIVES

Overall Objective: To examine national trade policies as strategies in three areas: gaining certain competitive advantages through subsidizing chosen industries, furthering adjustment through extensive aid, and employing trade warfare.

MORE SPECIFICALLY:

- To evaluate whether strategic trade policy can be or is effective in a world of imperfect knowledge and externalities of learning, scale, or agglomeration.
- To understand the argument for subsidies to capture rents and its limitations.
- To consider the alternative of a sound policy favoring infrastructure, saving, and investment.
- To assess the effectiveness and wisdom of a vigorous trade adjustment strategy.
- To probe the effectiveness of trade sanctions in achieving political ends.

Much of trade policy is and has been largely piecemeal in nature, involving barriers and subsidies to make politically powerful industries more profitable, or keep beleaguered industries afloat, or allow governments to maintain high agricultural support prices. Beyond these essentially reactive approaches are national policies to establish and strengthen comparative advantage in certain areas at the expense of foreigners. The designs carry various names including *strategic trade policy, trade targeting, managed trade,* and *picking winners,* among others. (Managed trade can mean the same thing as strategic trade, but it is a broad term that often includes targets for exports to other countries and involves a "voluntary import expansion" by those countries.)

All these names describe some sort of collaboration and cooperation among businesses and governments to alter, more quickly than the market would, the existing pattern of comparative advantage. The tools for doing so usually involve a combination of subsidies and home-market protection by means of tariffs, quotas, VERs, and so forth to accelerate the development of some chosen industry. The subject has caused considerable stir among international economists, and represents a new intellectual challenge to the proponents of free trade.

Strategic trade policy contrasts with another and essentially different idea, national industrial policy. While some use the term to mean nothing more than the protection of existing industries, with perhaps some R&D subsidies thrown in, we will use a different definition. Industrial policy involves government participation in the effort to raise productivity generally and make a country's economy more competitive. It involves a broad range of educational reform, infrastructure improvement, research and development efforts, and policies to assist in transferring labor and capital out of declining industries.

Elements of strategic planning by governments date back to the nineteenth century, with Germany's long campaign to acquire and develop the technologies needed for new industries being the outstanding example. The stratagem has, however, come to be associated primarily with Japan since the 1950s, and later with South Korea, which has closely followed Japanese policy. An appendix to this chapter analyzes Japan's use of strategic trade policy. Many economists also believe that Taiwan, Brazil, and France stress these methods.[1] In the United States, economists who advocate a U.S. strategic trade policy have recently received considerable publicity.[2] Some Democrats have taken up the theme to suggest national measures to increase research and development expenditures and otherwise assist certain targeted industries. Republicans generally oppose. The ideas have also inspired considerable interest in the EC, where more than elsewhere they are being used to force foreign firms to invest in Europe if they want to sell there.

The economics of strategic trade policy involve new departures from the traditional trade debates explored in Chapter 7. Four main rationales, all relatively new, supposedly support strategic policies: imperfections in knowledge, the existence of external economies, the need to achieve learning and scale effects, and the capture of profits (rents) from foreign competitors in imperfect markets. We examine each of these arguments in turn.[3] Note that strategic policies can be defensive, to battle the trade barriers and export promotion of others, or offensive, involving an aggressive strategy to capture markets. This chapter looks closely at two cases of targeting so-called winners. The products involved are about as different as can be imagined: large commercial passenger aircraft subsidized by the EC, and the tiny semiconductors (microchips) at the heart of computers and much else of today's electronics that are said to be central to Japanese strategy.

IMPERFECT KNOWLEDGE: EXPORT TRADING COMPANIES AND GOVERNMENT INFORMATION SERVICES

The first of the strategic approaches to trade is relatively uncontroversial, designed to stimulate trade by improving knowledge about export markets. Numerous foreign countries, most of Europe and Japan for example, allow individual firms to band together in export trading companies financed by a parent bank, the company then marketing their products. Such companies are exempt from antitrust action. They have been particularly successful in Japan, where there are 8000 of them, called *sogo shosha* or "general trading companies." C. Itoh is the largest, followed by Sumitomo, Marubeni, Mitsui, and Mitsubishi in that order. The nine biggest of these companies are responsible for over half of Japan's total trade. They advise and manage in the areas of transport, marketing, finance, and distribution, breaking down knowledge barriers that might otherwise keep small firms out of exporting, and maintaining a far-flung Japanese presence around the world. As one of the attempts to improve U.S.-Japanese trade relations, there is now a move for the *sogo shosha* to make arrangements with small and medium U.S. companies.

The United States is far behind in such activities. Under the Export Trading Company Act of 1982, the old Glass-Steagall Act of 1932 that prohibited banks from engaging in trade was partially repealed. United States banks are now allowed to participate in foreign trade, with bank holding companies permitted to invest a maximum of 5% of their capital and surplus, not to exceed $10 million, in an export trading company (ETC). There are now some 60 of these ETCs. The U.S. design appears to resemble the Brazilian and South Korean arrangements most closely. Their particular value lies in persuading small firms to enter exporting. In the United States, it is estimated that 85% of exports of manufactured goods are produced by only 1% of the country's manufacturing firms, it being so difficult for small firms to obtain the advice and capital they need to enter foreign markets. The ETCs are intended to correct that problem.

One major criticism of the U.S. law is that it provides less flexibility and a far smaller financial base than the Japanese *sogo shosha* have. Furthermore, some argue that the emphasis on quick profits in the United States, together with the tight management control traditional in banking, has denied U.S. ETCs the fast flexibility combined with patience that is needed in this game. The U.S. Department of Justice has claimed that most ETCs have been formed to ensure against vertical antitrust suits. In any case, growth of the U.S. ETCs since 1982 has been slow, and they still account for only a small fraction of U.S. exports.[*]

GOVERNMENT TRADE PROMOTION: THE OUTSTANDING CASE OF JETRO

Governments also promote international trade by means of various agencies that deal in information. Although most countries have one or more agencies for doing so, the Japan External Trade Organization, JETRO, is by far the best known and most successful.[4] Dating from the 1950s, JETRO is modeled on a British original that lasted only a few years. It carries out general overseas market research, arranges participation in trade fairs and exhibitions, and does public relations work for Japan's trade as a whole. It also manages major programs to coordinate technical cooperation, joint research, and joint production. To the extent that trade promotion is a public good, this is useful and cost-effective. Originally JETRO was of special importance to small and medium-size exporting

---

[*] A few are impressively large, such as the ETC associated with the Chase Manhattan Bank which serves more than 200 companies. Some have been wound up, however, such as Sears World Trade and the General Electric ETC. A number of U.S. banks have also ended their efforts.

firms, but it is now a major promoter of *imports* as part of Japan's campaign to change its image of closed markets. It hosts "export to Japan" seminars, sponsors trade fairs and exhibits of its own, and maintains an ombudsman to whom foreign firms can complain about bad treatment. It supplies data on customs procedures and trade financing both in Japan and overseas, and now even trains interns from other countries, mostly less developed ones. Hong Kong, Korea, China, and other countries now have their own versions of JETRO.

EXTERNAL ECONOMIES

Remaining arguments for strategic trade are more controversial. The existence of external economies, or spillovers, is one such. If research and development (R&D) spending is the key to obtaining comparative advantage in a product, then the existence of external economies may mean that government subsidies to support the R&D are called for. A free market would lead to appropriate levels of private spending on this activity only if externalities did not exist or if they could be completely appropriated by the firm undertaking the expenditure. One illustration might involve a firm's willingness to pay. It may believe that the expensive R&D would soon become available to competitors if personnel with knowledge of it were hired away by those competitors. Another example might involve other firms disassembling and copying products embodying the new technology without otherwise paying for the R&D. The benefits might then be so reduced by this leakage of knowledge to others that the firm will not proceed with the R&D spending in the first place. A very similar argument is older and has been used to justify training subsidies: Skilled labor might be trained at great expense, but then the value of the training is lost to competitors who hire away the skilled labor at a wage that does not include a margin for the training costs.

Thus where R&D is a key to new comparative advantage, but diffusion of the resulting knowledge to others who did not pay cuts the benefits severely, it may make sense for government to subsidize the activity to offset the market failure. Conceivably a government subsidy could improve the whole world's welfare because new products might not become established, or processes adopted, if the R&D is not undertaken. The existence of distinct geographical concentrations of high-tech industries in a number of countries is advanced as evidence that a head start in R&D is important.

Though this argument for a strategic trade policy is persuasive within its bounds, it is also limited. One difficulty is that neither government nor firms are able to assess at the start which level of subsidization is optimal. Firms would presumably lobby for the maximum access to this open public trough. Another problem is that foreigners would still be able to appropriate the new knowledge as easily as before: In the end, a country's subsidies may do no more than establish a new comparative advantage somewhere abroad. An argument might actually be made that a country could improve its position in international trade by carrying on *less* R&D and appropriating what it needs from the countries with a comparative advantage in that activity. Finally, a substitute for subsidies might be to permit research consortia of a country's own producers, or even an international group, to pursue joint projects. In the United States, the antitrust laws would have to be further relaxed to allow more of this, even though some steps were taken from 1984 as discussed in the accompanying box. Such a relaxation might be as effective as a subsidy while being much less expensive for the public purse.[*]

■ *SOME JOINT RESEARCH EFFORTS ARE IN PROGRESS*

Dropping the antitrust penalties against firms that carry out joint research projects seems called for. A beginning was made with the National Cooperative Research Act of 1984. This act allows joint research ventures of a preproprietary nature, permitting firms to pool R&D resources and exempting them from the triple damages provisions of the antitrust laws. By 1989 there were 134 such joint ventures. One is USCAR (United States Council for Automotive Research), a Ford-GM-Chrysler project established in 1992 to carry out joint work on electric cars and electronics control programs, and to develop improved plastics and other composite materials for use in automobile bodies. These three automakers plus 14 oil companies established a joint research project on auto emissions and alternative fuels in 1989. Any joint activities in manufacturing and marketing remain prohibited, however. It is actually much easier for U.S. firms to collaborate with foreign ones than with each other.

REALIZING THE EFFECTS OF LEARNING AND SCALE

In Chapter 3, we analyzed the growing importance of learning and scale economies as explanations for changing comparative advantage. The country that appreciates these possibilities might decide that a small initial push provided by subsidies, or through protection of the domestic market against imports, might be the impetus for competitive strength in some new industry. This proposition is really an old one in a new guise—it is the infant industry argument in modern dress. Though the language is changed, and though the reasons why the infant needs support are altered to emphasize learning and less-

---

[*] A more theoretical argument has arisen concerning uncertainty. If some line of activity is especially subject to risk, then investment in that activity may be unduly discouraged unless it is subsidized. Newbery and Stiglitz argue that strategic intervention may be justified under these conditions. Dixit replies that incorporation of insurance markets in the Newbery-Stiglitz model would tilt the balance against government intervention. See D.M.G. Newbery and J. Stiglitz, "Pareto inferior trade," *Review of Economic Studies*, Vol. 51, No. 1, 1984, pp. 1–12, and A.K. Dixit, "Trade and insurance with moral hazard," *Journal of International Economics*, Vol. 23, 1987, pp. 201–220.

orthodox scale economies, the logic is the same. A dynamic exporting industry might grow out of the subsidies or protection.[*]

The usual objections apply. Why would the private capital markets not be able to see these possibilities as well as or better than government does, and why would it not make loans available? Such a "private subsidy," repaid with interest from the later profits of the firm receiving the loan, would meet the market test and avoid the burden on the government's budget. If protection is used rather than subsidies, then all the standard complaints surface. These complaints include higher costs for consumers and producers who use the protected product as an input, the losses of X-efficiency if firms lose the spur of competition, and the scale diseconomies if the domestic market for the new product is small. The targeting of some attractive industries, computers by Brazil, for example, while plausible on the surface, might simply reveal how important is local cooperation between computer designers and microchip makers, which are nonexistent in Brazil.

SEMICONDUCTORS (MICROCHIPS) AS AN EXAMPLE OF THESE ARGUMENTS

Semiconductors (microchips) stand out as an industry in which externalities, learning, and scale might justify a strategic trade policy. These tiny silicon wafers used in computers and many other electronic devices with a memory are said to be highly dependent on enormous R&D expenditure, with considerable technical spillovers. They are also believed to possess large learning and scale effects. If we sound skeptical, it is because the case is difficult to prove and the information needed for a full assessment of the arguments is, for proprietary reasons, unlikely to be available for a long time.

A number of economists have argued that protection of the Japanese market against the then-dominant American industry, together with government R&D subsidies, allowed that country to begin manufacturing its own 16K DRAM (meaning dynamic random access memory) chips, an activity that would not otherwise have been competitive, in the period 1979 to 1983.[5] The subsidies were not large, and the protection was removed in due course, but by then the Japanese industry had become firmly established. Another important factor was the encouragement given joint research in Japan, compared to the prohibition of joint research projects under U.S. antitrust law. By 1985 the big Japanese chip makers had taken to selling below average costs. Some said the tactic was predatory, while others claimed only that large investments in new factories had glutted the market and caused an overstock.

---

[*] Hardly ever noticed in the debates over this proposition is that *international* subsidies to promote learning and scale in countries that otherwise possess the most suitable factor proportions might be the best policy of all, with the world financing the resulting increase in global welfare. As is obvious, such proposals are at present utopian.

As a result of the Japanese successes, prices and profits began to fall, and American firms left the arena until by 1986 only two (Texas Instruments and Micron Technology) remained as sellers, plus a third, IBM, that makes its own chips but does not sell on the open market. Whether predatory or not, the Japanese strategy had clearly put pressure on producers in the United States.

The U.S. industry, unable to obtain its own subsidies, pushed for protection along several different routes. One of these, a dumping charge, led to the announcement of major antidumping duties of 120%. Before these were levied, they were overtaken in July 1986 by a VER that was the U.S. response to the Japanese strategy. This five-year VER went further toward cartelizing an industry than any other of the agreements in which those two countries have been involved. Under its terms, a fixed price minimum was maintained in the American market. The Japanese manufacturers also agreed to allow foreign firms a market share in Japan of 20% by 1991, compared to the 1986 figure of 9%, a prominent example of a managed trade export target.

Economists generally objected that cartelizing an industry would very likely create a scarcity and lead to higher prices for chips, with resulting windfall profits not just for the two remaining American firms, but for the Japanese industry as well. That is what transpired. Japan found that to boost prices, as required by the VER, it had to arrange a fall in exports to third countries as well as to the United States. It did so by imposing "voluntary" export controls according to the previous market share of its exporters. The output restraint, coupled with heavy demand from a healthy economy in 1988, led to serious consequences. As shortages developed, DRAM prices quadrupled. The resulting large profits led one U.S. firm, Motorola, to resume production, but it also led to much more R&D spending by Japanese firms, strengthening their new predominance in the industry.

The upshot of the semiconductor VER of 1986 was that chip prices increased in the United States and other foreign markets but did not do so in the Japanese market. All in all the whole episode seemed to demonstrate how *not* to respond to a trade strategy of others. The most memorable results were the damage to U.S. computer and software firms that had to pay higher prices for the chips they installed, and to U.S. consumers whose computers and other chip-using products cost more.

THE SEMICONDUCTOR STRUGGLE

The semiconductor struggle soon became one of the more complex of all the trade issues. The EC found the 1986 VER highly objectionable, because prices were raised there, too, and they complained to GATT. A GATT panel in 1988 found in favor of this EC complaint that the worldwide export restraints of the semiconductor VER were illegal under GATT rules, which bar export quotas. Japan responded by agreeing in 1989 not to control chip prices on exports to or production in third countries. The United States was thus the only market in which the penalty of higher prices was being paid; the agreement was effectively a tax on chip users imposed to aid a few chip makers.

The VER's guarantee of a 20% foreign market share in Japan caused endless trouble because for a long time that share failed to go above 13%. The Japanese claimed it was not actually a guarantee, but a target. Eventually competition arose from Korea, whose production was not covered by the VER. Korean sales rose 80% from 1988 to 1989, and its competition with Japan drove down the price of 1 MB DRAM chips to $10 at the start of 1990, 20–25% of their price before the competition intensified. By the start of 1993 Korea claimed 20% of the world market, most of that seized from the Japanese, and ranked second to Japan in the U.S. market.

Recently the United States has regained some momentum in the chip market, taking the lead in the development and production of advanced microprocessors; these processing chips are much more sophisticated and profitable than DRAMs. A number of joint development agreements have been made by U.S. and Japanese chip makers. The collaboration plus the better U.S. performance may have defused the U.S.-Japan microchip battle to a degree.

THE SECOND SEMICONDUCTOR AGREEMENT OF 1991   The first semiconductor VER expired July 31, 1991, lamented by few except the producers. It was succeeded by a new five-year agreement that took effect on the next day. In an important victory for good sense, the rules that kept semiconductor prices high in the United States were scrapped. Japanese chip makers agreed to collect and make available cost-of-production data to facilitate dumping charges if chips are sold below production costs. Another main feature is the reiteration of a 20% target for the foreign share of the Japanese market. Although it was decided that a target is not a guarantee, the arrangement still exemplifies another use of the managed trade approach to force open foreign markets by means of trade pressures. For the first time the 20% target for microchips was actually reached in the last quarter of 1992, increasing the probability that managed trade targets fixing market share would be established by the United States for other industries as well. Managed trade targets of this sort will clearly deepen government involvement both in the exporter and the importer, increasing the politicization of trade. They will also cartelize markets and, because they discriminate, will violate GATT rules.

STRATEGIC TRADE POLICY TO CAPTURE RENTS

The most intriguing of the grounds for a strategic trade policy is that governments could use subsidies to enable domestic firms to capture part or all of the economic rents being earned by imperfect competitors abroad. This argument is quite new and is attracting attention especially in the EC.

Assume that just *two firms* are the world's only manufacturers of some good. A capture of oligopolistic rents would be a possibility if a firm in country *A* finds a way to lower its production costs. It could then charge a lower price, and thus expand at the expense of a firm in country *B*, which would contract its operations as the demand for its output shrinks. The profits for the firm in country *A* rise, first, because of the fall in costs, and second, because its share of the market has increased. One way to push country *B*'s firm into this position would be for *A*'s government to pay a subsidy to the firm in *A*. That would be the equivalent of lowering the firm's costs and would start the process. *A*'s government would expect the profits earned by the home firm to be larger than the subsidies paid to start the ball rolling. (If this were *not* the case, the gambit would have failed.) The strategy when successful would ordinarily be predatory on *A*'s part, the gains to *A* coming at *B*'s expense.* The gains would be even greater if the subsidy allowed more learning and scale effects; but if learning and scale were important, then country *B* would conversely lose even more than otherwise.

To achieve its aims, the strategy would have to fulfill a number of conditions. (1) It would have to be credible. If the firm in *B* does not believe a subsidy will actually be paid after all, or will be paid only for a short time, it may not contract its output, and thus no capture of rents will result. (2) The subsidy ought not to be paid to firms in a highly competitive industry, for then there will be few foreign profits to capture. An industry with high capital requirements forming a substantial barrier to entry (aircraft?) would seem much better suited for the strategy. Similarly, subsidies paid to declining industries might just stave off foreign competitors for a time but result in no advances at their expense. (3) The best outcome for the strategy would be if foreign rivals had many other alternatives, for then foreign output would fall considerably as prices declined. It would also be most advantageous if the home firm moved rapidly down steep cost and learning curves as its output increased. (This implies in turn a disadvantage if any factor inputs are fixed or limited in supply because factor prices would rise as output increased.)

EUROPEAN AIRBUS SUBSIDIES AS AN EXAMPLE OF A RENT-CAPTURING STRATEGY   The Airbus consortium in the EC is apparently an excellent example of a rent-capturing strategy. The Airbus passenger aircraft, actually several different wide-bodied models, has received massive subsidies from European governments. There are no other European producers of wide-bodied commercial aircraft; no Japanese producers; and only McDonnell-Douglas in the United States remaining in the field alongside Boeing. If the Airbus subsidies could convince Boeing *not to produce* some new model, then Airbus might capture the economic rents that Boeing otherwise would have earned.

Paul Krugman of MIT illustrates this with a matrix of strategic possibilities, which we show as Fig. 8.1.[6]

---

* These gains would not necessarily accrue just to the owners and managers of the one firm and the factors employed there. Taxes could be used to distribute the gains to the public. It is conceivable that the fall in prices to consumers made possible by *A*'s subsidy, plus the rents captured from *B*, would in the long run sum to a greater amount than the cost of the subsidy and the rents lost to *B*. That would raise *world* welfare rather than welfare in country *A* alone. One would not want to count on that, however.

Figure 8.1 **A Krugman matrix of strategic possibilities**

Airbus

		p		n	
	P		−5		0
Boeing		−5		100	
	N		100		0
		0		0	

The letters p and P signify a decision has been made to go ahead with production by Airbus and Boeing respectively, while the letters n and N indicate no production will be undertaken by the two firms. In row P, Boeing will produce; in row N it will not. In column p Airbus will produce; in column n it will not. The lower left number in any quadrant is Boeing's profit; the upper right number is Airbus' profit.

Consider first the upper right quadrant. If Boeing produces a new model commercial aircraft, but Airbus does not, Boeing would expect to earn profits equal to 100 while Airbus would get nothing. The situation is reversed in the lower left: If Airbus proceeds while Boeing does not, the 100 goes to Airbus and Boeing gets the zero. If *neither* produces the new model aircraft, as in the lower right quadrant, *both* get a zero. If on the contrary *both* produce, then both will make losses (−5) as in the upper left quadrant.

Now alter this example so that the governments sponsoring Airbus make subsidies available, with an amount (+10) paid either on output or on export. In Fig. 8.2, we see that this decision changes the outcome. Now even if Boeing undertakes to produce in competition with Airbus, it will suffer a loss of −5 (upper left quadrant), whereas Airbus will make a *profit* of 5. Boeing, certain that Airbus will produce whatever it does, and equally certain that it will thus make a loss, may decide it has no hope in the long run of lasting out such a situation and may withdraw from the competition. If so, the Airbus subsidy of +10 has been well worth it to the governments concerned because we see in the lower left quadrant that Airbus captures all the rents, leaving it with 110, a fine return on the governments' money.

Recent studies have, however, not lent much empirical support to the concept of rent capture as a means to increase a country's welfare. Most of the studies on the issue show that losses from price distortion and X-inefficiency that accompany the subsidies usually outweigh the gains from the increased rents.[7] A calculation of the costs and benefits of the Boeing/Airbus struggle has been made by Richard Baldwin and Paul Krugman.[8] These authors claim that Europe lost somewhat (−$37 million) because the gain to consumers from cheaper aircraft was offset by the cost of the subsidy. The United States lost substantially (−$3.0 billion) because Boeing had to charge much lower prices because of the

Figure 8.2 **A strategic subsidy succeeds in capturing the market**

Airbus subsidies, more than offsetting the lower prices to consumers. The remainder of the world gained because of the lower prices ($1.8 billion). For the world as a whole, losses exceeded gains by $1.2 billion.

■ *DETAILS OF THE AIRBUS CASE*

The real-life events surrounding this case are, as usual, more convoluted than the model.[9] The market share for U.S. producers of large aircraft was 87% in 1980, but by 1989 that had declined to 64% in the face of the subsidized competition from Airbus. Boeing has a little over half the world market, McDonnell-Douglas about 17%, and Airbus the rest, its share having grown meteorically to about a third, which has made it the second-largest producer. Airbus Industrie is owned jointly by Aerospatiale of France (38%), the German firm Deutsche Aerospace that is now owned by Daimler-Benz (38%), British Aerospace (20%), and CASA of Spain (4%).

The amount of the subsidies is a closely guarded secret, but it is believed to have exceeded $13 billion since 1970, equivalent to perhaps 20% of product and development costs. If that amount had been borrowed on commercial terms, interest payments would have raised the figure to some $25 billion. In addition to cash, the grants are said to have taken other forms such as special landing rights at European airports for airlines purchasing the plane. The EC argued that the subsidies are actually long-term loans, but only tiny payments were being made and even these were not required if not enough planes were sold to cover the costs. (Defenders of this particular example of strategic trade make the point that the subsidies might have been fully repaid if the strategy had worked a little better.)

Another Airbus issue arose at the same time, the so-called dollar clause. The commercial aircraft market is conducted largely in U.S. dollars. The German government in 1988 announced a policy of government-financed exchange rate guarantees for Airbus sales until the year 2000. Thus if the U.S. dollar depreciated, as it was doing at the time, Airbus would receive assistance. The United States, claiming that this undercut adjustment by means of currency exchange rates, in 1991 called for a GATT panel on the issue, under the subsidies code. The panel found against Germany in 1992, and the scheme was suspended for the time being even though the Germans did not accept the ruling.

Airbus replied to the attacks with charges of its own that Boeing receives large indirect support from U.S. government military contracts and space research for NASA. Over $34 billion is claimed for the period 1976–1990, well above Airbus' own subsidies. Yet it seems an implausible argument. Aviation experts doubt whether military work has much carryover to civilian wide-body jets. If anything, where it exists the flow of technology may be in the other direction. Furthermore, the space subsidies are for basic research only and are freely available to all.

Convinced it was in the right, and vigorously supported by many economists, the United States searched for ways to take action.[*] It threatened antidumping duties, countervailing duties, and Section 301 action. The threats apparently had some effect, as the European governments involved agreed in 1988 to end production, sales, and marketing subsidies, but to retain them for research and development. With the recession after 1990 cutting aircraft sales and so intensifying the aggravation, negotiations continued. The EC proposed that in addition to halting the production subsidies, it would limit R&D subsidies to 45% compared to the average of about 75% that has been the case with Airbus models up to now (lower at 60% for the newest models, the A-330 and A-440). The United States demanded a limit of 25% on R&D subsidies and a commitment to repay the subsidies in 15 years on commercial terms.

A compromise was agreed on during July 1992 with an agreement to ignore past subsidies and to limit R&D subsidies on new models to 33%. Over $4 billion of Airbus' R&D subsidies will be repaid with interest by 1996. In turn the United States agreed to limit indirect (meaning military) subsidization of manufacturers' research to 4% of the value of each firm's annual sales. There is a dispute settlement mechanism. But when President Clinton spoke at Seattle's Boeing plant in February 1993—where large layoffs are taking place—he was scathing about the continuing subsidies on the existing Airbus models, and the U.S. government called for a reopening of the Airbus question. Whether the 1992 agreement would stick any better than previous compromises was thus open to question—but then perhaps it did not deserve to survive.

DEFENSE AGAINST PREDATORY SUBSIDIES

The discussion above was of predatory policies designed to seize rents at the expense of firms in other nations. For countries facing active policies of this sort, it is necessary to consider how to reply. A major aim for the victims would be to convince the perpetrator that a predatory strategy is dangerous and uncertain in its result.

A government could retaliate with its own subsidies to the firms harmed by the foreign strategy, or could impose protection against the subsidized product.

---

[*] It "seems outrageous because it is outrageous . . . raw commercial aggression . . . irresponsible and insulting." Robert Samuelson, *Newsweek,* July 8, 1991.

Controlled repetitive experiments utilizing the mathematical theory of games indicate that a tit-for-tat strategy may in fact be the most effective means of replying.[10] In this view, a clearly delineated announcement of plain and predictable steps that will be taken against a predatory strategy would have the greatest effect in discouraging such behavior. Tit-for-tat does not start a battle, requires a response to provocations, and in the end is forgiving of a country that abandons its original predatory plan. It never wins in the sense of capturing the rents of others, but it does encourage cooperation and general avoidance of conflict.

Intriguingly, this rule-based retaliation against subsidies, which we criticized in Chapter 7 as inflexible and dangerous, might be better than a discretionary policy because it would be a more dependable deterrent. The United States already has utilized tit-for-tat replies to a degree. Some uses of the countervailing duty laws against subsidies can be so seen, and are effective, though these duties do not affect subsidies that result in the seizure of markets in third countries. Further U.S. rejoinders to the strategic designs of others include the subsidies paid on agricultural exports and the cheap export credits made available by the U.S. Export-Import Bank. Replies do not have to be limited to the area of trade: A far wider arena offers itself. The retaliation might concern the defense umbrella, or the maintenance of foreign exchange rates (encouragement by the U.S. authorities of dollar depreciation, for example, which would make the subsidized foreign good appear more expensive to Americans). Removal of foreign aid is another possibility, while cultural, educational, and technical exchanges could also be pressed into service as bargaining chips. The possibilities are large. Yet even when defensive strategies to deter the predatory policies of others are logically sound, they must be handled with the utmost care to keep them from becoming the tools of special interests. It would be better by far to adopt a multilateral approach under GATT auspices. GATT rules to control aggressive strategic trade initiatives would seem clearly called for.

REASONS FOR REJECTING AN ACTIVIST POLICY

To this point in the discussion an active strategy to counter the predatory policies of others has been presented as a more or less reasonable use of deterrence. Yet many economists are nonetheless most reluctant to recommend such action. Their objections fall into one of two categories: The action would be incalculably costly, and it would be subject to political manipulation.

THE HIDDEN COSTS OF AN ACTIVE POLICY Opponents of an active strategy warn that governments are not competent to make the necessary choices because the knowledge of the hidden costs involved is far too limited. They point to the difficulty of even identifying above-normal profits in the first place: How to distinguish these from returns that compensate for risky past investments is not easy. They note the possibility that subsidies might attract other entrants into the *domestic* market, leading to open-ended expense for the government. What about the cost to domestic consumers if export subsidies divert production away from the home market, they ask. What about the rise in factor costs as greater production in the subsidized industry draws resources from other industries? Would not that raise costs in these other industries? Might not the budget deficits or higher taxes resulting from the subsidies be more damaging than any good that would flow from an active strategy? The unknown size of all of these is indeed a cause for queasiness.

THE POLITICAL DANGERS OF AN ACTIVE POLICY   Worse yet, claim the critics, an active policy runs a high risk of dangerous confrontation and political corruption. Why assume the subsidies would act as a deterrent, rather than assuming they would provoke a new type of trade war as foreigners reretaliate? That is, after all, the very warning that economists issue whenever they analyze the optimum tariff strategies discussed earlier. And what about the politics of the situation? Would not an active policy be a wedge for self-interest in the business community? Like a Moses leading his flock, any trade evangelist promising subsidies will at once have an enormous following among businesspeople. Does anyone believe that small industries would be more likely to get the subsidies than big ones or that American subsidiaries of foreign companies would be eligible? Does anyone doubt that on occasion a subsidy would be made available just before an election in some closely contested state or province, whether or not the industry involved fits the model very well? Arguably the politics of strategic trade intervention would cause supported industry to spread out across the country, thereby gaining political strength but avoiding the benefits of conglomeration that have accrued to Boston's Route 128, California's Silicon Valley, North Carolina's Golden Triangle, and so forth. With politicians holding the purse strings being major gainers from an active strategy, what is to control its size? And if a program *did* grow to large size, how would it be ended if it did not work as expected?

The problem thus amounts to comparing the benefits of successful deterrence to the costs, many hidden, of the same policy. The authors certainly cannot judge this issue: Information is far too limited at present to permit a conclusive answer. They do admit, however, to intense concern that these debates will be turned to serve the purposes of the self-interested.

INDUSTRIAL STRATEGY AS AN ALTERNATIVE: SAVING, INVESTMENT, AND INFRASTRUCTURE

Much of the debate on strategic trade policy tends to ignore steps that in the long run may be the most important of all. Providing adequate levels of saving and investment and repairing and improving a country's infrastructure are of primary importance in maintaining and increasing that country's productivity. Virtually all economists agree that changes in the productivity of the factors of production are central to improving competitiveness and hence levels of living. This section is necessarily brief, but it is also important: A country with slow productivity growth invites its politicians and workers to take protectionist action.

THE SLOWING OF PRODUCTIVITY GAINS AND THE DECLINE IN ECONOMIC GROWTH

Worrisomely, productivity growth after decades of steady increase has declined noticeably during the most recent quarter century, from 2.5% per year from 1950 to 1973 to only 1.0% from 1973 to 1984.[11] Though this decline is not directly associated with the subject of international trade, it is plain that countries with inadequate capital per worker, falling educational standards, and with decaying infrastructures of transport, communications, and other public utilities, force the private firms that utilize this infrastructure as an input to pay a penalty. The slowdown has affected other advanced countries as well, but the U.S. decline has been deeper and to a lower level than that of the others. This has the potential to change comparative advantage toward economic activity that will generate less income. Attention to the saving/investment problem and to appropriately chosen public investments may well do more, perhaps much more, for the economic well-being of these countries than will any strategy that focuses on international trade alone.

WHY HAS PRODUCTIVITY GROWTH SLOWED DOWN?

Though the reasons for the falling off in productivity growth are much debated, the following are probably the most important ones.

A DECLINE IN SAVING AND INVESTMENT AND A DECREASE IN THE GROWTH OF CAPITAL PER WORKER   A decrease in capital investment per worker has taken place, with U.S. domestic savings falling from 19% of GNP in the 1970s to only 13% in the late 1980s, and U.S. domestic investment slipping from 18% of GNP in 1970 to 14% in 1990. (The gap between domestic saving and investment was because of foreign investment in the United States.) The causes of the decline are complex. Suffice it to say that a country that invests less will have less capital per worker.[*]

Several policy measures could be used to reverse the damaging fall in net saving and investment. Decreasing the federal budget deficit would reduce the government's absorption of the country's saving, lower real interest rates, and therefore promote investment. Investment might also be stimulated by a tax credit that could be claimed on tax bills by firms undertaking new investment. Lowering the tax penalties on saving would also contribute to more saving, decreased interest rates, and therefore more investment. Reducing the income tax and adopting a value added tax would be one possibility. Another would be to raise the marginal rate of income tax and create a large deduction for saving.

---

[*] The situation for research and development expenditure is especially worrisome. In 1985–1989, the increase in U.S. civil R&D was slowest among the major developed countries (Japan, Germany, Britain, France). It actually declined in 1989–1991, while in other advanced countries it increased. That has led the Department of Commerce to state that the United States is dropping behind in leading-edge technologies.

THE DECAY OF THE PUBLIC INFRASTRUCTURE   The decline in U.S. investment had particular significance in the public sector, with noticeable decay in the
infrastructure of education and transport. Politics lies behind the neglect, with
revulsion during the Reagan Administration against "big government" and a
general unwillingness to pay taxes to support such activities. As a result, the
stock of public capital in the United States grew less than one fifth as much in the
1980s as it did in the 1950s. Public sector investment is very low by international
standards: U.S. net public investment as a percentage of GNP, 1.7% in 1967, is
currently less than 0.33%, compared to 1.5% in Canada, about 2% in Britain and
Italy, over 2% in France and Germany, and over 5% in Japan.

Growth theorists point to educational progress as the single most important
factor in the growth of real income per worker during the period after World
War II. Americans are, however, now used to hearing disturbing news about
their educational system, as noted in the accompanying box.

■ *EVIDENCE OF DECLINING EDUCATIONAL STANDARDS*

Standardized test scores of U.S. high school students fell from 958 verbal
plus math in 1967 to 903 in 1989. Over a quarter of the students in U.S. high
schools drop out. The *average* Japanese twelfth grader scores better than 95% of
American twelfth graders in math proficiency, and Japanese workers receive
considerably more mathematics and science training in school than do U.S.
workers. In separate tests of math skills and geographical knowledge, U.S. students were last among those of the major industrial countries. Two thirds of
the physics teachers in American high schools have never taken a college physics
course. When the National Association of Manufacturers surveyed 400 of its
member firms about the decline in educational quality, one third of the companies said they regularly reject applicants because they cannot read, and one
fourth reject them because of inability to communicate and use basic mathematics. A quarter of the companies admitted that they had been forced to cut
their entry-level standards, even though they realized that the lower standards
would reduce product quality. The NAM report concludes by stating that 60% of
the new jobs in the United States will require more than a high school diploma,
while 70% of the new entrants to the labor force will have less than that. The
NAM report speaks of damage to U.S. competitiveness in world markets, and of
the "seeds of a new underclass."

Reform is urgently needed. One possibility might be to establish appren-
ticeship programs in the schools, conducted jointly with local businesses and
emulating Germany's success. Raising teacher pay (now averaging about
$30,000) closer to Japanese and German standards (about $50,000) would help.
The money, much of which could come from cuts in the bloated educational
bureaucracy, would allow for a longer school year as in the countries the United
States competes with. A national proficiency examination would set some mea-

surable standards. Financial assistance for college paid in return for a year or two of national service seems an attractive idea. Perhaps a requirement that firms must spend 1.5% of their annual payroll on training, not unlike requirements in a number of European countries, would be helpful. (It might be noted that Taiwan and Korea are developing an education-based comparative advantage to a remarkable degree. For example, one in four of the students studying for a doctorate in the United States is from Taiwan.)

Education is not the only area of decline. The advancing and sometimes alarming disrepair of streets, highways, bridges, railroads, docks, dams, water and sewage systems, mass transit, airport facilities, and the like cause a penalty to be paid by the private firms that utilize this infrastructure as an input. Such firms will be less productive, and less competitive with producers in countries where the decay has not occurred. David Aschauer, a critic of infrastructure decline, asserts that the lower efficiency of the public sector causes the private sector to be less efficient as well. Trucks go slower and wear out faster on poor road surfaces, tracks and ties in poor repair keep speeds low on the railroads, and so forth. Aschauer estimates that if public investment had stayed at its level for 1953–1969, that during 1970–1988 the rate of return to private capital investment would have been higher by about 22%, while productivity in the private sector would have been greater by about half again.[12] Many economists argue that these numbers are exaggerated, but then there is a substantial margin for error.

Switching some spending away from the military, agricultural subsidies, and social security payments to those who are not needy would allow more spending on transport, communications, and education. The task confronting governments in countries where these public facilities are in decline would seem, perhaps obviously, to be their reconstruction rather than special attention to foreign trade strategies. If this requires higher taxes, then so be it—low taxes cannot adequately stimulate economic growth if saving is taxed as highly as consumption, and if the infrastructure is inadequate. In any case there is little evidence that mild tax increases would seriously erode the incentives to save and invest, and even more-than-mild increases would still leave U.S. income taxes below those of most other major countries.

We need only add that if economies following their comparative advantage are stronger economies—a position taken by the vast majority of economists— they will be better able to keep saving and investment at adequate levels and raise the tax revenues necessary for maintaining their public infrastructure.

TRADE ADJUSTMENT ASSISTANCE AS A STRATEGY

The strategies discussed thus far have been active ones designed to pick winners and seize rents, or reactive defensive ones to deter the policies of others, or reconstruction of the decaying infrastructure. At this point we take up a strategy very different in both its outlook and its implications: government adjustment assistance to help industries through the transitions that may be imposed on them by international trade.

One significant reason why protectionist pressures have intensified worldwide, and especially in the United States and EC, may be the insufficient attention given to programs of trade adjustment assistance.[13] To many, this is a missing link in modern trade policy. Any time imports flow into a country from new sources, they may dislocate labor. Whenever there are downward rigidities in real wages and prices, then markets will not adjust rapidly. Unemployment may develop in the affected industry along with excess capacity in plant and equipment that might be long lasting. The rigidities may even cause a country to end up exporting and importing the wrong things.[14] In such circumstances, proper trade adjustment assistance would be even more vital. The market will in time bring adjustments, as in Fig. 8.3, where an economy does adjust from X to Y even though it may dip temporarily below its production possibility curve before climbing back to it as the adjustment occurs. But the process may be slow and costly, the more so if information is imperfect, if transactions costs are high, and if the downward rigidities of prices and wages are long lasting.

THE SPECIFIC COSTS OF ADJUSTING TO TRADE FLOWS

In more detail, the costs to industry and its labor caused by trade take several forms. Perhaps the most important are likely to be the sudden obsolescence of specific skills and the loss of seniority. Figure 8.4's curve *EE* shows the normal path of earnings for industrial workers in a given industry, rising, though at a

---

Figure 8.3 **Adjustment may be costly.** If resources cannot be transferred easily from X to Y, the country may remain inside its production possibility curve for an extensive period.

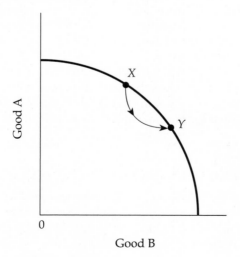

Figure 8.4 **Wages and opportunity costs over working life.** As workers age, they become tied to their industries, and their skills become more specialized. They earn more money, as the curve *EE* shows. Their ability to earn high pay elsewhere, however, usually declines, so *OO* shows falling opportunity cost.

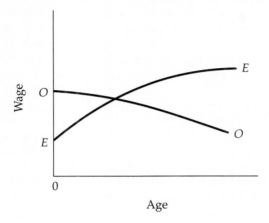

slowing rate, as age increases. Curve *OO*, the opportunity wage in the worker's next-best alternative occupation, behaves differently. It falls with age as opportunities diminish. (Though as shown, it might have started at a point higher than *EE* if young workers pick jobs partly because of future earnings prospects.) The gap between the two curves shows the sacrifice if trade results in loss of job. The gap will be greater yet if time and money have to be devoted to retraining and the acquisition of new skills.

The problem is more acute in the United States, where the newly unemployed may have trouble with transferring their pensions and health care insurance.[*] In *any* country they may have to make a geographical shift with possible high moving costs, take a capital loss on their housing, and suffer a breakup of family and social ties. (If the causes of the increased trade are of the factor-proportions, interindustrial type, then the newly unemployed workers may have to make greater shifts in occupation and location than is usual when unemployment occurs, because a whole industry may be affected rather than just a firm. If, as is more normal, the trade is intraindustrial, the adjustments need not be so severe.) The older the worker, the worse the loss, due to the likelihood that age brings more local ties, a greater stake in the pension plan, and higher seniority in a present job, but reduced opportunities in alternative occupations. In part, this will be due to age discrimination, and in part to the specific nature of the skills possessed by experienced workers. The costs will also be higher in smaller

---

[*] The United States is the only major industrial nation without government-provided health insurance. When workers or employees in that country lose their jobs, their options are either private insurance (at much higher rates) or no insurance at all. The costs of U.S. adjustment therefore exceed those of its major trading partners.

towns, because the local job pool and the local housing market will both be smaller, with more difficulty in finding alternative employment and a greater capital loss in selling one's house.

Worst of all for society as a whole, the concept of *hysteresis* in unemployment suggests that the longer a worker is out of a job, the more likely it is that the worker will *stay* jobless.[*] One may become an outsider whose commitment to work becomes suspect, and whose skills may be eroding due to lack of use. In effect, hysteresis means that high unemployment might remain high.

The greatest adverse impact for individual workers will be in beleaguered industries where wages for historical reasons are far above the national average. Perhaps the high wages are due to an earlier but now eroded productivity advantage, or perhaps to protection, with strong labor unions able to extract a share of the gains from the firms in the industry. In this case, there is every chance that alternative employment will be at a lower, and perhaps much lower, wage. In communities dependent on a single firm or industry, the damage will perhaps spread more widely, to merchants and anyone else selling goods and services to the now-distressed workers, and by means of decreased property tax collections from the damaged firm or industry to all owners of property who must make up the difference. For workers and communities, there is no easy way to insure against all this or to recover quickly. A stockholder can rapidly adjust share holdings to avoid or reduce losses, but for a worker or for a town, the problems are likely to be more intractable.

All these costs lead to a number of conclusions. First, a reduction in protection and a shift to freer trade are likely to be more acceptable politically if they are gradual. Letting attrition do the work is likely to be less painful than adjusting all at once. Second, these costs explain why multilateral tariff reductions are better than unilateral ones. When trading partners also cut their barriers, there will be a sharper stimulus for export industries to expand, thus reducing the dislocation costs. Finally, the costs will be reduced if the removal of protection comes during a period of economic growth and not in the middle of a recession when jobs are scarcer everywhere.

But the costs explain one more thing as well. Unlike the "normal" unemployed, those who lose their jobs because of the impact of imports are free to seek tariffs and quotas from congresses and parliaments. Those who stand to lose from the protection—consumers, foreign countries with a comparative advantage in some protected product, potential exporters to those foreign countries— are less well organized and carry less influence. In this view, a government program of trade adjustment assistance can compensate those with power to do harm, in effect buying them off and simultaneously acting as a caution signal that the aided industry is a declining one. The numbers of workers dislocated by imports are quite limited compared to the general run of the unemployed— perhaps only 5 to 10% or so in the United States—and thus a program aimed at

---

[*] The word *hysteresis* is taken from the physical sciences. It is used, for example, to describe the persistence for a time of an electromagnetic field even after the electricity is shut off. Edmund Phelps of Columbia University first applied the term to unemployment.

those impacted by trade would bring much less budgetary stress.[15] Lack of such a program spurs protection, as politicians note the employment losses in their home district. In turn the protection attracts new resources into the industry. The gains from trade are restricted.

POLICY IN THE UNITED STATES

In the absence of effective, wide-ranging trade adjustment assistance, the industries adversely affected by foreign trade understandably seek the protection of tariffs, quotas, and VERs as preferable to the not-so-tender treatment of the marketplace. If the benefits of free trade are to be preserved and defended, then a strong case can be made for a move toward more training for trade-impacted workers, who must be attracted and held even by generous cash allowances.

Many claim this is unrealistic in an era when the federal budget deficit has to be cut rather than increased. For most ordinary budget items, this logic would be correct. But the estimates from the Institute for International Economics that protection already costs American consumers well above $50 billion per year must be remembered. This figure is over 30 times what trade adjustment assistance has ever cost in the United States.[16] Further, an economy following its comparative advantage will be a richer economy, with increased tax collections that can help to finance adjustment assistance.

The clear implication of the cost-per-job-saved data presented in Chapter 6 is that workers could be paid large sums to be idle—their entire annual wage, for example—and if the protection were ended at the same time, the public would still realize substantial gains. The gains would of course be much greater if adjustment assistance were used to train workers and transfer them to productive employment. Those who argue the market will accomplish the transfers without government help overlook the logic of protection-seeking. Industries and workers will pursue trade barriers because it is profitable for them to do so, even if this makes no sense for the public as a whole. An effective program of trade adjustment assistance is thus a means to ensure that the gains from trade are preserved, and that new protectionist barriers are not erected. Yet up to the time of writing, the United States has never had an effective program.

■ *EARLIER U.S. EXPERIENCE WITH TRADE ADJUSTMENT ASSISTANCE*

The first introduction of adjustment assistance in the United States was in the Trade Expansion Act of 1962. The rules were liberalized in the Trade Reform Act of 1974. The key provision in the 1974 act was payment of 70% of the weekly wage for one year (but not over 100% of the average weekly wage in manufacturing) to workers displaced by imports from abroad. Relocation payments were 80% of expenses plus three weeks' wages; the job search allowance was up to $500. Workers were also eligible for federally funded retraining. The program of Trade Adjustment Assistance (TAA) attained great size, funded at about $1.5

billion in both fiscal years 1980 and 1981. But with deep budget cuts after the election of President Reagan, congress just managed to keep TAA alive, a shadow of its old self, its funding only 5% of its former figure. For a time in 1985–1986 it was even allowed to expire.

The decline of trade adjustment assistance was regrettable not because the old act was particularly well designed. Most of the money was spent for glorified unemployment compensation gleaned by very high-paid workers—auto and steel workers took 55% of the benefits, for example, much of this paid in the run-up to the 1980 elections when the program was nearly quadrupled in size. The benefits were paid in such a way, weekly and concurrent with regular unemployment compensation, that they had disincentive effects on finding another job. The counseling and training were laughable. According to Labor Department data, of the 1.3 million workers assisted by the program in 1977–1984, only 70,000 or 5% enrolled in retraining programs, only 28,000 (2%) completed the training, and only 4500 (0.3%) found jobs that utilized their new training. At the height of the program, 35% of the workers aided did not even know training was available! Most economists would agree that the old program involved far too much compensation and far too little adjustment. Few would defend this. Reform was overdue. But the virtual scrapping of trade adjustment assistance contributed to the kindling of protectionist fires.

Congress renewed trade adjustment assistance in 1986, but budgetary problems have brought sharp decline to the program. Cash benefits were $198 million in 1987, paid to 111,000 dislocated workers mostly in the shoe and apparel industries. Spending fell steadily, to $92 million in 1990, and President Bush's 1993 budget called for half that, or $42.3 million for benefits. To keep spending down, eligibility was cut by a new rule that imports must be a cause of unemployment "no less important than any other cause," instead of the old rule that it had to be "important." This rule, together with the small budget, meant that the United States had the developed world's least-developed program.

Training did eventually receive greater emphasis, reaching about a third of TAA's funding in 1991 and extending to 38% of the 53,000 workers who were eligible. This was well above the 9% who received training in 1987. But the training is focused on specific skills, and does not provide for general literacy and math upgrading, and in any case President Bush's 1993 budget called for an end to the retraining. In 1991, fewer than 1% received a job search allowance and only 1.4% got relocation allowances. Compare this experience to that of Sweden, the best example of a country using a highly activist retraining and relocation program. Sweden relies heavily on subsidies to employers to finance the training, spending almost 2% of GNP for its famous labor market policies that have a proven record of effectiveness in providing skills to the unemployed.

It would seem that the U.S. federal budget deficit would make a Swedish-style program virtually impossible at present, even allowing for the fact that the public already pays far more in the costs of protection than a greatly expanded program would cost. Yet it is actually quite feasible. If all U.S. nontariff barriers were converted to temporary tariffs, and if the tariff revenue were used for adjustment, then a major program could be funded with ease. The 1988 trade act, which is the present vehicle for trade adjustment assistance, did not do this. Thus the potential advances encompassed in that law (discussed in the box below) have not been realized because they could not be funded.

■ *TRADE ADJUSTMENT ASSISTANCE UNDER PRESENT LAW*

The 1988 trade act included much enlarged retraining, open to all workers whose plants had closed and not just those displaced by imports. To be eligible for cash assistance, for the first time workers *must* take the training or receive a waiver. Most of the training (80%) is organized by the states. A pilot project allows payment of earnings insurance to displaced workers, but only *after* they accept new employment. The payment will be a percentage of lost earnings; the percentage figure will decline gradually over time. The hope is that workers who receive the insurance payments will take jobs with initially lower pay, but with good chances for training and increasing seniority.

The act was to be funded by an across-the-board import fee of 0.15%, the first time that U.S. tariff revenue was ever to have been devoted to trade adjust-ment.[*] That caused a great deal of trouble, however, because a tariff increase would have broken U.S. commitments to bind tariffs at their present level. United States trading partners refused to accept this violation of GATT rules, even though from economists' point of view the cause was a good one. The 1988 trade act had ordered the president to implement the fee anyway, if after two years GATT had not made a rules change. In the end President Bush did not do so, which was permissible if he found that collecting the fee was against the national interest. Congress did not try to overturn the ruling. Proper financing for enlarged TAA has therefore never been provided, unfortunately, and because of the lack of funding the new program has not been fully implemented. (President Bush proposed a new five-year, $10 billion program for dislocated workers in 1992, with most of the money earmarked for training, but then he was defeated. The question is sure to be reopened by President Clinton.)

Even were major advances to be made, we query whether the new pro-grams would be adequate. Managerial, professional, administrative support, clerical, and other service jobs are clearly areas where employment gains will occur. Retraining steel or textile workers for these positions (writing computer

---

[*] At least once in the United States, under the National Wool Act of 1954, tariff revenue was trans-ferred directly to producers to persuade farmers to accept the lowered tariffs on wool that clothing manufacturers had lobbied for. Up to 70% of the (lower) duties were to be used to compensate farmers for the lessened amount of protection. The Roth-Moynihan Bill that did not pass in 1985 would have funded trade adjustment assistance with a 1% tariff on all imports, much larger than the 0.15% figure in the 1988 act.

programs, for example) is likely to encounter difficulties. A long look will have to be taken at the low-skilled unemployed, especially those raised in an environment where schools, learning, and skill acquisition have not been emphasized. Such workers may be exceptionally difficult to train. A broader focus on improved basic education may be needed, with perhaps massive remedial education and later retraining on a large scale, together with a vigorous full-employment policy. Wage subsidies paid by government to firms that hire displaced workers, or income supplements to those willing to retrain for service jobs, might eventually prove to be attractive. All of these suggestions have macroeconomic implications that would require careful management. One would surely not want to increase budget deficits under current conditions, even though it is worth pointing out that free trade and a productive, retrained labor force are an excellent prescription for controlling inflation.

EXPERIENCE OUTSIDE THE UNITED STATES

The question broadens into one of comparative economics. Is there something to be learned from the experience of others? A good case can be made that some aspects of Japanese adjustment to the pressures of trade have been especially successful. The flexibility within that country's economy is marked by a willingness to shift resources rapidly from declining industries to areas of increasing advantage. More declining industries exist in Japan than is generally appreciated, first because of the onset of high energy costs, second because of rising wages, and third because of the much-appreciated yen. Table 8.1 below shows the startling rise in import penetration into some Japanese markets between 1980 and 1987. Much of the competition has come from newly industrializing countries such as Korea, where wages on average are about one eighth of those of Japan.

Table 8.1   **Imports into Japan as a percentage of total consumption**

	1980	1987
Sheet steel	2.1	31.0
Cotton textiles	10.6	28.8
Outer clothing	20.8	46.3
Sewing machines	8.8	30.5
35mm cameras	7.7	46.6
Black and white TVs	1.5	54.4
Calculators	12.9	49.0
Radio-cassette players	4.6	47.5
Milling machines	15.4	41.9
Lathes	20.5	40.2

Source: MITI data, published in the Wall Street Journal, *July 20, 1988.*

Market forces are the prime instrument of change, but the Ministry of Trade and Industry (MITI) helps to smooth the transition. MITI is best known in the United States for its early and now partly mythical attempts to target export winners, as we examine in Appendix 8.1. It deserves to be far better known for its coordination of programs to buy up and scrap excess capacity in declining industries (some of which, it should be added, was necessary because MITI made the wrong choice in the first place).[17]

The Japanese have responded to what could be seen as a crisis in a measured way. First, the decision has been taken to run down several industries. By 1991, shipbuilding capacity had been reduced to 47% of its 1980 level, and in the same period the workforce in this industry was cut by a quarter. Thirty-six percent of ethylene capacity has been scrapped; 70% of aluminum capacity has been closed down. Further slimming is underway in the pulp and paper industry, while about one fourth of the Japanese blast furnaces for steel are slated for immediate closing. Much of the coal industry is being shut down as too expensive compared to foreign sources of supply, the action spurred by complaints from the steel industry. Many of the companies involved are attempting to diversify production into more profitable output, and to cut costs with more capital-intensive automated plant. Workers are being shifted to affiliates, and to subsidiary service companies, especially to cater to leisure activities. To facilitate the shifting, Japanese firms do considerable on-the-job training. In textiles and clothing, massive readjustment occurred earlier, much of it in the 1970s. A now-slimmer industry received some modernization subsidies for new plant and equipment; moved upstream into fast cycling of high value added items, bolstered by large R&D expenditure on CAD/CAM techniques; and invested heavily in overseas plants. In spite of the deep inroads made by imports, which have taken as much as 80% of the market in some lines such as knitwear, MITI resisted textile protection, and Japan has no textile import quotas (though it does have a handful of textile VERs).

In a further response, firms have transferred some of their operations to other countries on a large scale. Only 2% of the output of Japanese firms was produced abroad in 1983, when the transfer began in earnest. The figure was 5% in 1986 and was expected to hit 20% in 1992. Some of the output of these plants is being exported back to Japan, including even a portion of the output manufactured in the United States. (The growing international practice of transferring production to foreign branches to profit from cost differences and exchange-rate changes is explored in Chapter 19.)

Up to now, Japanese labor seems to have been more willing than the workers of the United States and the EC to shift among plants and among jobs. In part this is due to the willingness of Japanese companies with their lifetime employment tradition to cooperate, in part because unions are industry wide and do not defend particular crafts. For example, Japanese steel companies reduced their workforce by 13% in 1988, but this involved transfers to other jobs in affiliated firms and not unemployment. The many union-management joint consultation committees that promote knowledge-sharing, the good cooperation between firms and local governments, and the considerable amount of vocational training for new jobs carried on within firms all help. So far, so good—in spite of a serious recession in 1992–1993, Japan's unemployment remains the lowest of any major industrial country, a position it has held for over 20 years.

The high yen and the new competition from Korea and other newly industrializing countries will pose a stern test for this system. Up to now, big firms with a tradition of lifetime employment (30% of the economy or less) have been able to transfer workers to other divisions when reverses strike.* Even in that sector, however, some of the transfers have been nothing but makework schemes that push the unemployment on to others, as when a big firm establishes an in-house travel agency to employ its redundant workers, and stops giving business to its old travel agent. Transferring workers is not possible for the mass of small subcontractors that bear a greater burden of adjustment. In some spots such as Kyushu and Hokkaido unemployment is now abnormally high by Japanese standards. Further, there are sectors that Japan has not been willing to run down for political reasons, such as agriculture and to a more limited degree, apparel. In spite of all that, the record has been good. It remains to be seen if it will continue so.

A major lesson surrounding adjustments to trade is that some countries are much more willing than others to *disinvest* by closing low-productivity plant. For an efficient economy, it is as essential to disinvest as it is to invest, and Japan to this point has shown itself better able to bend with these forces of capitalism than have the United States and the EC, neither of which appears to be very good at accomplishing disinvestment. The implication is that capitalism is not being allowed to work; the problem on this reading is not so much industrial structure as it is human psychology. As yet this weakness has not been grappled with successfully. Many economists (but few politicians) would agree that the economy not afraid to run down its losers is the strong economy in the end. It is also the economy that does its share in promoting world growth and higher incomes for all.

TRADE SANCTIONS

Strategic trade can go well beyond the ideas discussed thus far, and in its broadest definition can include trade sanctions for political and military purposes.[18] Trade sanctions are usually carried out as another aspect to armed conflict, to

---

* Lifetime employment does not have as long a history in Japan as might be supposed. It came into being mostly in the 1950s and 1960s when labor was scarce, and companies considered that a stable labor force was a valuable asset. (Workers in that country receive more on-the-job training, much of it specific to the firm, than is true of the United States, so a mutual attachment of firms and workers is understandable.) The plan succeeded, with monthly turnover in Japan 0.9% of all workers compared to a U.S. figure of 3.5%. For an analysis, see Jacob Mincer and Yoshio Higuchi, "Wage structures and labor turnover in the United States and in Japan," NBER Working Paper No. 2306, 1987.

destabilize a foreign government during peacetime, to lower the military and economic capacity of a potential enemy, or to achieve some specific purpose such as the abandonment of racial discrimination (South Africa, Rhodesia) or poor environmental practices (whaling, killing of dolphins and sea turtles).

Obvious examples of trade sanctions accompanying military action are World Wars I and II. Earlier major cases include the British and French counter-moves of embargo and blockade during the Napoleonic Wars, Thomas Jefferson's embargo strategy that started in 1806 and lasted until the end of the War of 1812, and the federal blockade during the American Civil War.

In the twentieth century, sanctions have frequently been used as a peacetime strategy. They were employed 115 times between the start of World War I in 1914 and 1990, with a success rate, defined as a desired change in policy, of about 35%. Italy was treated to a League of Nations embargo on strategic goods to protest Mussolini's invasion of Ethiopia (unsuccessful); Japan was similarly served during its Chinese aggression (which backfired by increasing Japanese militancy); fascist Spain was so treated during part of the period when Generalissimo Franco was in power (with little practical effect). Recent examples include the U.S. trade embargoes of Castro's Cuba, Khomeini's Iran, Qadaffi's Libya, and Sandinista Nicaragua. Other outstanding cases include the American grain embargo and Pipeline War against the Soviet Union to protest the latter's Polish policies and its invasion of Afghanistan, and U.S. restrictions on trade with South Africa from 1986. OPEC's use of oil as a weapon in 1973 and 1979 is a well-known example.

The most famous recent case is the United Nations' embargo of trade with Iraq, a policy that started five months before the shooting began in January 1991 and that still continues at the time of writing. In mid-1992, the UN also voted a sweeping trade embargo of the remaining part of Yugoslavia (mostly Serbia) in connection with what it termed Serbia's aggression in Bosnia-Herzegovina. All trade including oil was banned except for food and humanitarian supplies. In addition, air links were broken and Serbian participation in international sports events was suspended.

JUDGING THE EFFECTIVENESS OF TRADE SANCTIONS

The net effectiveness of a sanctions strategy is the loss of income suffered by the "enemy" minus the loss of income to the imposer. The effect is greatest when one country identifies imports vital to the economy of another, hence inelastic in demand, that are either completely unavailable domestically or are inadequate in supply even when the enemy economy is at maximum output of these vital goods. Let us call these goods "impossible to supply," or ITS goods.

The counter-strategies open to the enemy will be either to buy the pro-scribed ITS goods from neutral countries (but no doubt at a higher price, so raising costs to the enemy), or possibly to buy illegally from the country or countries conducting the trade sanctions in laundered transactions through a neutral, or best of all, acquiring a patron who will take up the slack even if at high cost.

The potential for success in dealing with an enemy is highest in the following circumstances:

(a) When goals are modest. A small and powerless country as the enemy of a country important in international trade, and a single issue not of overwhelming concern to the enemy, offer the greatest chance of success.

(b) When the imports of the enemy economy contain a high proportion of ITS goods. Again, the smaller the enemy's economy, the more likely this will be.

(c) When a high proportion of world output of the ITS goods are produced by the country enforcing the trade embargo and its allies. Sanctions are especially effective if directed at a former friend that has no patron to bail it out.

(d) When there is a large terms-of-trade effect. Thus, if the enemy buys its ITS imports from neutrals, a substantial price rise will follow, and if the enemy diverts its exports to these neutrals, their price will fall sharply. It is also desirable that the expenses of transshipment (by means of blockade runners, smugglers, or launderers) raise the cost of imports considerably and reduce greatly the revenues from exports.

(e) When there is low slippage. The allies must maintain a united front, the blockade ought not to be leaky, laundering should be difficult, and smuggling hard. The Civil War in the United States is an excellent example of high slippage. Small, landlocked countries have special problems in arranging adequate slippage. When India blockaded Nepal in 1989 over a trade dispute, that Himalayan kingdom was immediately in serious trouble because India could easily police most points of entry. In 1986, South Africa's blockade forced little Lesotho (which it completely surrounds) to submit to its list of demands in just three weeks.

(f) When the time span of the action is short and the impact is large. Generally, the passage of time allows the enemy to adjust to the shortage by stockpiling, arranging more slippage, and adjusting production in the home country. A good example of a short, sharp strategy was President Jimmy Carter's prohibition of exports connected with the Moscow Olympic Games of 1980. The ban could not be overcome in the time available.

The only exception to the principle that time is on the enemy's side is if the enemy simply cannot adjust in a satisfactory way. Then the sanctions will pinch more, not less, the longer they last. But the benefits of more time to the enemy are usually clear. Consider first capital goods. A spare parts industry for embargoed capital goods can, and very often actually does, spring up. Even the imported capital goods themselves, not just the spare parts, can become domestic manufactures, though of course at some extra cost that might be very great. If primary product natural resources are embargoed, then domestic production can be increased by tapping old reserves more intensively, and by locating and developing new reserves. If that is not possible, then substitutes in supply can be obtained through research. United

States synthetic rubber after the fall of Southeast Asia in 1942, or German production of gasoline from coal in World War II, or Biafran backyard stills that converted petroleum to gasoline in the Nigerian Civil War, or even beet sugar, developed by Napoleon's chemists in response to the British blockade, are all good examples. Alternatively, production might be redesigned to minimize the use of an embargoed input, as in German economizing on ball-bearing use after the massive bombing of their ball-bearing capital, Schweinfurt, in 1943.

(g) It is a major advantage when the economic development of the enemy is at a low level. A poor, developing country is likely to suffer more heavily than a rich one for several of the reasons just cited: (1) Its imports will probably contain a high percentage of ITS goods. (2) There are likely to be more vital bottlenecks to the smooth running of the economy, including electricity, roads, railroads, and communications. (3) Foreign exchange shortages will often mean that a higher price has to be paid for laundering and for smuggled goods. If the enemy is not in a position to pay very large sums for ITS goods, then neutral sources of supply may be less sympathetic because their effort will be less profitable. (4) There is an inadequate technical base, making it difficult for local industries to substitute domestic capital goods for imported capital. (5) Often the demand for a poor country's primary product exports is likely to be inelastic. Diverting these products to neutrals will thus result in a significant fall in price. (6) Above all, a poor country is likely to be less flexible in reallocating its resources from one use to another.

(h) Lastly, it will be most advantageous when the costs of trade sanctions are low for the country pursuing the strategy. If this is not so, if for example harm to domestic producers and exporters becomes more and more apparent, then domestic political opposition will grow rapidly. The U.S. embargo before and during the War of 1812 was so damaging to the business community in New England that that region virtually dropped out of the war. As we shall see, the opposition of U.S. farmers to the grain embargo against the Soviet Union grew so formidable that the embargo had to be dropped.

In summary, the existence and control over ITS imports are crucial to a strategy of trade sanctions. Encouraging slippage and developing domestic substitutes are the counter-strategy. To make sanctions effective, it is essential either to bring into an alliance or to bring under control all major suppliers of vital ITS goods to the enemy. For that reason alone, embargoes by *one country* against another are likely to be ineffective.

RECENT EXAMPLES OF TRADE SANCTIONS

Major use has been made of trade sanctions in recent years. The most important cases involved the United Nations' embargo of Iraq, and the earlier U.S. response to the Soviet intervention in Afghanistan and the Soviet connivance in the suppression shortly thereafter of the Polish trade union Solidarity. The U.S. grain embargo and the Pipeline War were the result.

THE TRADE EMBARGO OF IRAQ   When Iraq invaded Kuwait in August 1990, the former already controlled about 10% of the world's proven reserves of crude oil. Conquered Kuwait added another 9.5%. Within a few hundred miles, lightly defended, lay the great Saudi Arabian oil fields containing 25% of the world's known oil. The frightening vision of a well-armed dictator close to obtaining nuclear weapons and moving to monopolize oil mobilized the United Nations to resist with a comprehensive trade embargo. Under UN auspices, sanctions were imposed on August 6, 1991, four days after the invasion of Kuwait. They applied both to exports (mostly oil) and imports from Iraq and Kuwait.

It was estimated that within five months Iraq's GNP had been cut in half, with most of the effect due to the 4 million barrels per day of lost oil exports.[19] This was reportedly the most damaging impact of any sanction of modern times. There was considerable danger that the tactic would recoil on oil-using countries, and oil prices did indeed soon hit a record high of over $40 per barrel. Prices dropped back considerably, however, to only a little over $20 in early 1991, as oil producers opposed to Iraq's action raised their production. In particular, Saudi Arabia increased its oil output by over half, from 5.4 million barrels per day to 8.2 million, between August and November 1990, so accounting for almost three quarters of the shortfall. Other countries including the United Arab Emirates, Nigeria, Iran, and Libya made up the remainder of the difference. Overall supply was not restricted and prices stayed well below what many observers had expected.

Iraq's loss of imports was painful but not fatal. The impact was lightened by the considerable leakages that took place across the Jordanian and Iranian frontiers. Saddam Hussein was fully prepared to use the suffering of his own people as a propaganda weapon. Supplies of food and medicine could be distributed in the loyal central areas of Iraq, and denied to the rebellious Kurds in the north and Shiites in the south.

Could the sanctions have made the shooting war unnecessary? The question is debatable. They have undoubtedly weakened the Iraqi economy. Yet, given the stunning military damage and infrastructure ruin that Saddam was willing to take before deciding to withdraw from Kuwait, and the lack of much impact on his policy after the war even with the embargo still in force, it seems unlikely that the embargo would have changed Iraqi policy in the short run. Detracting from this case, however, the shooting war probably rallied the Iraqi people to their embattled leader in a way continued sanctions would not have done. The sanctions are still in place at the time of writing in 1993, providing an extended test of whether they can in the end alter a country's policy of aggression.

THE U.S. GRAIN EMBARGO OF THE USSR   Soviet intervention in Afghanistan resulted in the grain embargo announced by President Carter in January 1980. It was not very effective, but it certainly commanded attention and provides lessons. The U.S. government believed that the grain embargo would be an effective use of sanctions because the USSR was suffering at the time from highly erratic grain production due to its underlying economic inefficiencies in agriculture.

The embargo was not a success, however. The figures in Table 8.2, covering the period July to June, show Soviet imports in the normal year 1979/80, and the embargo year 1980/81, in millions of metric tons.

There was certainly a large reduction in exports from the United States. Australia also agreed to limit its shipments, and so did the EC, which increased its exports only very slightly. But Canada, which also undertook to control the rise in its exports, still shipped enough to make a serious dent in the embargo policy. The main slippage came from Argentina, which did not participate in the embargo at all. Argentina almost made up for the entire shortfall all by itself. Slippage was found in other areas as well. There was a reduction in Soviet grain exports to Eastern Europe, which was mostly made up by rises in U.S. exports to those same countries.

The Soviets also tried to adjust with reorganization at home. Old rules and size restrictions limiting private farming were relaxed or dropped. Some adjustments were painful, as the Soviets substituted large amounts of home-grown wheat for the corn and soybeans that had made up the greatest share of the crops put under embargo. Wheat is an expensive way to fatten cattle; the weight of beef cattle dropped, and so did meat consumption.

Whether the embargo could have succeeded if left in place for a longer period of time was not to be tested. In the United States, farmers were incensed by the policy, and they applied enormous political pressure in an attempt to get it reversed. They succeeded: In April 1981, the newly elected President Reagan suddenly lifted the embargo.

A powerful mythology concerning this embargo still exists in the United States. Thousands of farmers believe that the downturn of American farming that set in during the 1980s can be traced directly to the shift in markets that occurred at the time the shipments were halted. This judgment does not appear to be credible. A 1986 study by the Department of Commerce claimed that the embargo caused little or no harm to U.S. farmers. United States agricultural exports actually *rose* in 1980, due to poor crop conditions in some other importers, to the

Table 8.2 **Soviet grain imports, by source (millions of metric tons)**

	1979/80	1980/81
United States	15.2	8.0
Australia	4.0	2.9
EC	0.9	1.5
Canada	3.4	6.8
Argentina	5.1	11.2
Others	1.8	3.6
Total	30.4	34.0

Source: U.S. Department of Agriculture data, cited by Lester R. Brown, "The U.S.-Soviet food connection," Challenge, *Vol. 25, No. 6, January/February 1983, p. 47.*

expansion of exports to Eastern Europe, and to enlarged grain shipments to China. The harm came later, from the strong dollar and large export subsidies paid by the Common Market countries.

THE PIPELINE WAR   The other trade sanctions strategy employed in response to the Afghanistan intervention (and the troubles in Poland) involved the large Siberian natural gas pipeline project. The Soviets needed imported equipment to build this line to the Western European gas grid. Contracts had been signed in 1981, after six years of talks. Important U.S. items included in the project were General Electric rotors and nozzles for turbines, and compressors from Dresser Technology. President Reagan embargoed the shipment of these items in December 1981.

At once a major loophole developed: A French nationalized firm, Alsthom-Atlantique, had a license to build the GE rotors, and moved to supply them to the USSR. President Reagan closed the loophole with a stern executive decree stating that European firms with an American controlling interest or firms that had a licensing agreement with U.S. firms were prohibited from delivering the listed products. The list was soon expanded to include oil and gas equipment even where contracts had already been signed. About seven subsidiaries and 13 licensees were affected by the regulations, which made them subject to a $100,000 fine per item shipped, or a prison term of 10 years for their executives. Such gross extraterritorial application of U.S. law incensed its allies.

The United States justified the approach with the argument that the pipeline left Europe too dependent on the Soviet Union for its natural gas. Europeans replied that North Sea gas gave them a safety valve. More to the point, they insisted that the gas purchase was their business anyway, and no one else's. The resumption of large U.S. grain sales to the Soviets right in the midst of the pipeline brouhaha added to the irritation of the Europeans, who quickly dusted off their long-standing laws forbidding a foreign government from dictating commercial policy to a national firm. The result in 1982 was a series of direct orders to such firms to ignore the American ban. Dresser-France thereupon went ahead with its shipment of compressors.

Checkmated, the United States in November 1982 abruptly lifted the sanctions. The episode was an excellent example of poor design in a trade sanctions strategy. The goals of the policy were unclear. The application of U.S. law against European manufacturing and engineering firms, retroactively and outside U.S. territory, seemed certain to be taken as a threat to national sovereignty, and so it was. Slippage proved far too large.

■ *COCOM*

Much more mild than the strategies involved in the grain embargo and the Pipeline War is the long-standing prohibition on the exports of strategic goods by NATO. For many years, since 1949, there has been a COCOM (Allied Coordinating Committee for Strategic Export Control), made up of all the NATO nations minus Spain and Iceland, plus Japan and Australia. This organization draws up rules for what constitutes strategic equipment banned for export. Unanimity is required for new rules; there are no enforcement powers and acquiescence is voluntary.

In the United States, administration of the COCOM rules is in the hands of the president, who actually has much more power to restrain exports, under the U.S. Export Administration Act, than he has to slow imports. (The president must be careful in the use of this power, however. The harm from halting exports can be both severe and very localized. A panel of the National Academy of Sciences suggests that the direct economic cost of lost sales when licenses are not granted is over $9 billion, involving 188,000 jobs.) A large amount of American trade with the USSR, as much as 40% in 1988, required an export license under the COCOM regulations.

With the breakup of the Communist bloc, the need for COCOM came into question. That organization is being maintained, but new strategic assessments have led to major reductions in the number of controlled items. A core list revision made in 1990 cut the number of controlled items by a third, and another reduction in 1991 reduced it by another half. The main areas still covered by COCOM are large mainframe computers and fiber-optic telecommunications equipment. Hungary was dropped from the COCOM list in May 1992, the first country to be exempted. Consultations between COCOM and the former Communist states are moving forward to see if streamlining of the licensing is now appropriate. No other former Communist states have yet been removed from the COCOM surveillance, however. The Czech Republic and Slovakia still export arms, while Poland and the countries that make up the old USSR face considerable political problems. They remain on the list. In addition, the United States unilaterally maintains a longer list of controlled items for countries that support international terrorism. The U.S. control measures are stricter and more labyrinthine than those of other countries.

Occasionally even staunch allies have received something like the COCOM treatment. In 1989, uproar in the U.S. Congress led President Bush to repudiate a Reagan Administration agreement to share technology with Japan for that country's advanced fighter aircraft (FSX) project. To be sure the fighter was to be based on the older U.S. F-16 whose design dates from the early 1970s; the United States would get improved composite wing technology and radar advances from Japan in return for its own technology; and the major U.S. aircraft producers (Boeing, General Dynamics, McDonnell-Douglas) actually favored the deal. Arguments such as these did not convince the congress, however, and the agreement had to be renegotiated with the understandably disturbed Japanese. By 1993, Japan's FSX had suffered cost overruns so great as to make it the most expensive fighter in its class, a main reason being the inability of the Japanese to acquire the U.S. computer software that allows dogfighting at acute angles. The episode seemed more a case of Japan-bashing than it was protection of valuable technology.

OTHER U.S. ATTEMPTS AT TRADE SANCTIONS

The United States has banned trade with several countries, the embargoes of long standing against Cambodia, Cuba, North Korea, and Vietnam and more recent in several other cases. The Cuban case shows how politicized such embargoes can be. Between 1963 and 1975, U.S. law prohibited not only U.S. firms, but also the foreign subsidiaries of these firms, from trading with Cuba. Foreign countries were not enthusiastic; some required subsidiaries operating within their borders to ignore the law, in a situation akin to the Pipeline War described above. To defuse the growing dispute, congress repealed the law. But then in 1992, mainly because of the political situation in south Florida, U.S. law was tightened to prohibit trade by foreign subsidiaries. The new law also prohibited ships from moving cargo to or from U.S. ports for six months after a call in Cuba. Britain rapidly issued a blocking order stating that Britain, not the United States, would determine whether British companies would trade with Cuba. Many other countries, including Canada and much of Latin America, protested that the move violated their sovereignty.[20] The U.S. embargo of Nicaragua to protest Sandinista rule, lifted when the Sandinistas suffered electoral defeat, also encountered opposition from U.S. allies. It had effects less severe than intended because many allies—much of Europe, Canada, Japan, South Korea, and Taiwan—did not join in and continued to trade with Nicaragua. The U.S. trade embargo against Vietnam dating from 1975 was in the process of being slowly lifted in 1991–1993, with food, clothing, and medical exports now permitted. The embargo of trade with Cambodia was repealed in 1992.

The U.S. embargoed crude oil imports from Libya from 1981, to little effect because Libyan oil has simply been sold elsewhere. All other trade with that country was banned at the start of 1986, but this had only a minuscule impact on the Libyan economy due to the small size of such trade. All trade with Iran was temporarily prohibited from October 1987, in the aftermath of the Iranian arms sale scandal. An embargo was directed at Haiti in 1991 over the ouster of President Aristide. This seemed a considerable backfire at the time of writing in 1993 because it hurt the Haitian economy badly and caused an exodus of refugee boat-people attempting to reach the United States, but without effect thus far on the military government of that impoverished country.

Embargoes directed against South Africa have been in effect in many countries. The United States in 1986 banned imports of iron, steel, coal, textiles, gold coins, agricultural products, and products produced by government-owned firms. Exports of crude oil and petroleum products were also forbidden, along with a variety of goods used by the South African government. In response to the sanctions, South Africa stockpiled crude oil, bauxite, and aircraft and computer parts, and has moved toward the establishment of a number of strategic industries (small arms, ammunition, tanks, aircraft, and the like). A complete trade embargo would probably have caused less damage to that country than it would to others of the same size and wealth for two reasons. First, the establishment of domestic industries had been deliberately planned to reduce the risk of a trade cutoff. With the exception of a few heavy industries including chemicals, transport and communications equipment, and some machinery, the country became less dependent on imports. Second, two of South Africa's major exports, diamonds and gold, could easily be marketed even in the case of a rather complete boycott. (Both are easy to transport, and hard to identify as distinctly South African.)

The risk-reduction strategy adopted by South Africa's leadership did to that extent succeed. (It points to the folly of making constant noise about possible embargoes without actually carrying them out—as noted earlier, time is usually on the side of the targeted country.) The strategy has been costly, however. Economists studying the problem suggest that it was a major cause of South Africa's very slow economic growth in recent years. One estimate is that South Africa's GNP is 20% to 35% lower than it could be because of the combination of the risk-reduction strategy and the effects of *apartheid*.[21] Furthermore, these costs will continue for a long time to come, even under President DeKlerk's liberalizing influence, because independence from imports has been built into the economic structure and cannot easily be reversed.

In recent years, the U.S. Congress has increasingly been inclined to adopt trade boycotts even when they are porous and accomplish little. They are an easy way to take the moral high ground, and if not too much trade is prevented ($2 billion in lost U.S. exports is a current estimate), they can be politically attractive. The whole process is selective in the extreme. For example, the United States never discouraged trade with the vicious dictatorships of Duvalier in Haiti, Idi Amin in Uganda, and dozens of others, nor does it do anything to suppress cigarette exports with their proven ability to kill their buyers.

The final part of this chapter has considered the cases where the trade winds blow cold. In the next chapter the breezes warm considerably as we turn to economic integration, customs unions, and common markets.

VOCABULARY AND CONCEPTS

Airbus	**Pipeline War**
COCOM	*Sogo sosha*
Industrial strategy	**Strategic trade policy**
JETRO	**Trade adjustment assistance**
Managed trade	**Trade sanctions**
MITI	

QUESTIONS

1. Explain the case for the government acting as a visible hand, choosing which industry to promote and thereby gaining scale or learning advantages.

2. Explain why Brown and Hogendorn remain skeptical of government's effectiveness, despite the theoretical considerations.

3. Potential externalities may remain internal. Explain how it is that firms continue to invent, have industrial economies of scale, and move down their learning curves domestically.

4. The rent-capture argument is on the surface a strong one, yet it is hard to find good examples. Why is that?

5. "Trade adjustment assistance is only a second-best choice. In some senses it is unfair, and in many ineffective." Explain what the statement means and comment on what a better choice might be.

6. There was considerable talk in Canada before the signing of the Free Trade Agreement that Canada would establish a trade adjustment system second to none, yet nothing has been done. Given the experience of the United States and other countries, what might be the problems in establishing a system, and why

might the government (and opposition for that matter) let it fall low in their priorities?

7. Does the United States have an adequate adjustment assistance program?

8. What is required for trade warfare to be successful?

9. Given the "Brown-Hogendorn Requirements" for successful trade warfare, would you say that the embargo against [whatever country we are now embargoing] will work? Why or why not.

10. The Russians left Afghanistan, but not because of the grain embargo. Why didn't it work?

NOTES

[1] See Dominick Salvatore, ed., *National Trade Policies*, New York, 1992, which is a description of the trade policies of 22 trading nations. Also see Gene M. Grossman, "Promoting new industrial activities: A survey of recent arguments and evidence," *OECD Economic Studies*, Spring 1990, Vol. 14, pp. 87–125.

[2] Examples of support for such a U.S. policy include Stephen S. Cohen and John Zysman, *Manufacturing Matters: The Myth of the Post-Industrial Economy*, New York, Basic Books, 1987; Robert Kuttner, *The End of Laissez-Faire: National Purpose and the Global Economy after the Cold War*, New York, Alfred A. Knopf, 1991; Robert Reich (now Secretary of Labor in the Clinton Administration), *The Work of Nations: Preparing Ourselves for 21st Century Capitalism*, New York, Alfred A. Knopf, 1991; Laura D'Andrea Tyson (now President Clinton's Chair of the Council of Economic Advisors), *Who's Bashing Whom? Trade Conflict in High-Technology Industries*, Washington, D.C., Institute for International Economics, 1992; and Laura D'Andrea Tyson, William T. Dickens, and John Zysman, *The Dynamics of Trade and Employment*, Cambridge, Mass., Harper Business, 1988.

[3] The first academic studies involving these arguments for strategic trade date from the early 1980s. James A. Brander and Barbara J. Spencer were early in this field, with their "Tariff protection and imperfect competition," in H. Kierzkowski, ed., *Monopolistic Competition and International Trade*, Oxford, Oxford University Press, 1984. A volume edited by Paul R. Krugman, *Strategic Trade Policy and the New International Economics*, Cambridge, Mass., MIT Press, 1986, is a good introduction. Essays by Brander, "Rationales for strategic trade and industrial policy" and Spencer, "What should trade policy target?" are included in the volume, as is a skeptical evaluation of the concept by Gene M. Grossman, "Strategic export promotion: A critique."

Also skeptical is Jagdish Bhagwati, *The World Trading System at Risk*, Princeton, Princeton University Press, 1991. An important recent work is Robert Z. Lawrence and Charles L. Schultze, eds., *An American Trade Strategy: Options for the 1990s*, Washington, D.C., Brookings Institution, 1990. Essays by Rudiger Dornbusch and Laura D'Andrea Tyson are favorably inclined toward managed trade; the view taken by Anne O. Krueger is different. The title of her essay is "Free trade is the best policy." Robert E. Baldwin agrees. He asks, "Are economists' traditional trade policy views still valid?" *Journal of Economic Literature*, Vol. 30, No. 2, June 1992, pp. 804–829, and his answer is basically "yes." Other useful volumes on the subject are Elhanan Helpman and Paul R. Krugman, *Market Structure and Foreign Trade*, Cambridge, Mass., MIT Press, 1985; these same authors' *Trade Policy and Market Structure*, Cambridge, Mass., MIT Press, 1989; and Robert M. Stern, ed., *U.S. Trade Policies in a Changing World Economy*, Cambridge, Mass., MIT Press, 1987 (see especially the essays by Paul Krugman, Alan Deardorff and Robert Stern, and Avinash Dixit). A technical approach is John McMillan, *Game Theory in International Economics*, New York, Harwood Academic Publishers, 1986. See also the coverage in *The Economist*.

[4] See Terutomo Ozawa and Mitsuaki Sato, "JETRO, Japan's adaptive innovation in the organization of trade," *Journal of World Trade*, Vol. 23, No. 4, August 1989, pp. 18–24.

[5] For details see Laura D'Andrea Tyson, *Who's Bashing Whom? Trade Conflict in High-Technology Industries*, Chapter 4; Michael G. Borrus, *Competing for Control: America's Stake in Microelectronics*, Cambridge, Mass., Harper Business, 1988; Kenneth Flamm, *Creating the Computer: Government, Industry, and High Technology*, Washington, D.C., Brookings Institution, 1988; Michel

M. Kostecki, "Electronics trade policies in the 1980s," *Journal of World Trade,* Vol. 23, No. 1, February 1989, pp. 17–35; and Michael Borrus, Laura D'Andrea Tyson, and John Zysman, "Creating advantage: How government policies shape international trade in the semiconductor industry," in Krugman, *Strategic Trade Policy.* Other sources for this section were the *International Economic Review,* March and April 1987 and October 1991; the *Wall Street Journal,* June 9, 1987, May 24 and June 12, 1989, and June 5, 1991; *The Economist,* February 27 and June 11, 1988, February 4 and March 18, 1989, and June 8, 1991; and recent issues of U.S. ITC, *Operation of the Trade Agreements Program.*

[6] The example is taken from Paul R. Krugman, "Is free trade passé?" *Economic Perspectives,* Vol. 1, No. 2, Fall 1987, pp. 131–144.

[7] Ten studies are surveyed by J. David Richardson, "Empirical research on trade liberalization with imperfect competition: A survey," *OECD Economic Studies,* No. 12, Spring 1989, pp. 8–44.

[8] Richard Baldwin and Paul Krugman, "Industrial policy and international competition in wide-bodied aircraft," in Richard Baldwin, ed., *Trade Policy Issues and Empirical Analysis,* Chicago, University of Chicago Press, 1988.

[9] See Tyson, *Who's Bashing Whom?* Chapter 5; *The Economist,* February 16, 1991, June 15, 1991; the *International Economic Review,* September, 1990, April, 1991, March, 1992; the *Wall Street Journal,* January 16, 1992; Kelly et al., *International Trade Policy,* IMF Occasional Paper No. 63, 1988, p. 187, and the recent editions of the U.S. ITC, *Operation of the Trade Agreements Program.*

[10] For the background to this research, which amounts to a type of prisoners' dilemma, see Thomas Schelling, *The Strategy of Conflict,* Cambridge, Mass., Harvard University Press, 1960, and Howard Raiffa, *The Art and Science of Negotiation,* Cambridge, Mass., Belknap Press, 1982. The experiments referred to in the text were conducted by Robert Axelrod. See the review of the work in J. David Richardson, "The new political economy of trade policy," in Krugman, *Strategic Trade Policy.*

[11] Angus Maddison, "Growth and slowdown in advanced capitalist economies," *Journal of Economic Literature,* Vol. 25, No. 2, June 1987, p. 650. The definition is labor productivity computed as GDP divided by hours worked.

[12] See David A. Aschauer, "Is public expenditure productive?" *Journal of Monetary Economics,* Vol. 23, March 1989, pp. 177–200, and the supporting case for more public-sector investment in Alicia H. Munnell, "Infrastructure investment and economic growth," *Journal of Economic Perspectives,* Vol. 6, No. 4, Fall 1992, pp. 189–198.

[13] In this section, in addition to the specific citations below we have depended on J.D. Richardson, "Trade adjustment assistance under the United States Trade Act of 1974: An analytical examination and worker survey," in Jagdish Bhagwati, ed., *Import Competition and Response,* Chicago, University of Chicago Press, 1982; J.D. Richardson, "Worker adjustment to U.S. international trade: Programs and prospects," in William R. Cline, ed., *Trade Policy in the 1980s,* Washington, D.C., Institute for International Economics, 1984, Robert E. Baldwin, *The Political Economy of U.S. Import Policy,* Cambridge, Mass., MIT Press, 1986; Baldwin's "Trade policy in developed countries," in Jones and Kenen, *Handbook of International Economics,* Vol. 1, pp. 593–595; and the most recent editions of the U.S. ITC, *Operation of the Trade Agreements Program.*

[14] See Richard Brecher, "Minimum wage rates and the pure theory of international trade," *Quarterly Journal of Economics,* Vol. 88, February 1974, pp. 98–116.

[15] A figure of 5% is cited by Charles F. Stone and Isabel V. Sawhill, "Trade's impact on U.S. jobs," *Challenge,* Vol. 30, No. 4, September/October 1987, pp. 12–18.

[16] See Gary Clyde Hufbauer, Diane T. Berliner, and Kimberly Ann Elliott, *Trade Protection in the United States: 31 Case Studies,* Washington, D.C., Institute for International Economics, 1986, and the summary in Gary Hufbauer and Howard Rosen, *Trade Policy for Troubled Industries,* Washington, D.C., Institute for International Economics, 1986, especially pp. 20–21.

[17] See Gregory B. Christainsen and Jan S. Hogendorn, "Japanese productivity: Adapting to changing comparative advantage in the face of lifetime employment commitments," *Quarterly Review of Economics and Business,* Vol. 23, No. 2, 1983, pp. 23–39; Shigeko M. Asher and Ken Inoue, "Industrial manpower development in Japan," *Finance and Development,* Vol. 22, No. 3, September 1985, pp. 23–26; and the frequent coverage in *The Economist* and the *Wall Street Journal.*

[18] For many details and points of analysis in this section we relied on H. Peter Gray and Roy E. Licklider, "International trade warfare: Economic and political strategic considerations," *European Journal of Political Economy,* Vol. 1, No. 4, 1985, pp. 563–583; Gary Clyde Hufbauer and Jeffrey J. Schott, *Economic Sanctions Reconsidered: History and Current Policy,* Washington, D.C., Institute for International Economics, 1984; and the same authors' *Economic Sanctions in Support of Foreign Policy Goals,* Washington, D.C., Institute for International Economics, 1983. A new study by Makio Miyagawa, *Do Economic Sanctions Work?,* New York, St. Martin's Press, 1993, analyzes over 30 cases.

[19] *Christian Science Monitor,* April 10, 1991.

[20] *International Economic Review,* December 1992.

[21] For an analysis of the South African embargo, see Charles M. Bucker, Trevor Bell, Haider Ali Khan, and Patricia S. Pollard, *The Impact of Sanctions on South Africa,* Washington, D.C., Investor Responsibility Research Center, Inc., 1990.

Appendix 8.1

A LOOK AT JAPANESE TRADE STRATEGY

Among all the world's countries, Japan is considered by the public and by many businesspeople to be the most effective user of a national strategy of restricting trade.[1] Great myths have grown up: Japan has erected impenetrable trade barriers; behind these barriers it develops an industry, takes over that industry world wide, then lifts the protection and moves on to take over yet another industry. This section considers the accuracy of the claims.

To a considerable degree, even the claim that Japan has an explicit national strategy is now a myth as well, but some truth does attach to it and once did so even more strongly. As Japan began to recover in the 1950s from World War II, its new and powerful Ministry of Trade and Industry (MITI) instituted a policy of encouraging industrial winners who could succeed in international trade. Who the winners would be was obvious enough at the time. Initially, very low labor costs provided the advantage. Later, scale-based development involving heavy capital investment could focus on industries easy to identify from sales trends in the United States and Western Europe. Loans at below-equilibrium rates were guided by the Ministry of Finance, which allocated scarce credit in this period to large firms in the favored sectors. MITI's advice was usually respected. It employed the best graduates of the best universities, and the bureaucrats who retired from the ministry at a relatively young age often obtained top posts in the very firms MITI was attempting to persuade.

Japan's internal markets were partly reserved for these firms, paving the way for their efforts in international trade, by a tight system of quotas that until 1960 covered about 60% of the country's imports. The higher prices paid by consumers—Japan's TVs sold for two and one-half times more in that country than the same Japanese sets sold in the United States, for example—served as a sort of tax to promote investment and development as the profits were reinvested. Cartelization was permitted, and favorable tax treatment was allowed, both stimulating profits that eventually financed massive marketing expenditures and heavy R&D spending. The R&D was supplemented by modest government

---

[1] There is a wealth of material on which to draw. Recent studies include: Mark Fruin, *The Japanese Enterprise System: Competitive Strategies and Cooperative Structures*, Oxford, Oxford University Press, 1992; Chalmers A. Johnson, *MITI and the Japanese Miracle: The Growth of Industrial Policy, 1925–1975*, Stanford, Stanford University Press, 1982; Paul Krugman, ed., *Trade With Japan: Has the Door Opened Wider?* Chicago, University of Chicago, 1991; Robert Z. Lawrence, "Efficient or Exclusionist? The Import Behavior of Japanese Corporate Groups," *Brookings Papers on Economic Activity*, Vol. 1, 1991, pp. 311-341; Edward J. Lincoln, *Japan's Unequal Trade*, Washington, D.C., Brookings Institution, 1990; D.I. Okimoto, *Between MITI and the Market: Japanese Industrial Policy for High Technology*, Stanford, Stanford University Press, 1989; Clyde Prestowitz, *Trading Places: How We Allowed Japan to Take the Lead*, New York, Basic Books, 1988; Laura D'Andrea Tyson, *Who's Bashing Whom? Trade Conflict in High-Technology Industries*, New York, Institute for International Economics, 1992; articles in the *Atlantic Monthly* by James Fallows, 1989; and numerous articles in *The Economist*, the *Wall Street Journal*, the *Christian Science Monitor*, the *New York Times*, and the *International Economic Review* together with all recent editions of the U.S. ITC, *Operation of the Trade Agreements Program*. A volume that claims relations over trade matters will deteriorate into real war is George Friedman and Meredith LeBard, *The Coming War with Japan*, New York, St. Martin's Press, 1991.

subsidies. For the moment technology was borrowed wholesale. The guidance is thought to have been important in the 1950s for steel and shipbuilding; in machine tools, some electronic goods, and perhaps autos in the 1960s; and for high-tech electronic goods in the 1970s. Japan's economic growth, as the whole world knows, set records.

It is, all in all, a pretty picture of a successful trade strategy, and it is probably even true that the strategy was partly responsible for the success. At the very least, as Kozo Yamamura notes, the importance of the strategy cannot be *disproved,* so giving encouragement to those who favor national trade strategies. As so often, however, the lessons are not really that clear, and the importance of the government's guidance is debatable. Japan with its educated and highly motivated labor, much of it available for industrialization because it was employed in low-productivity agriculture, its energetic and innovative managers, and its very high national rates of saving and investment, would surely have enjoyed rapid growth anyway, even if those first-rate MITI officials had never gone to college.[2]

As early as the 1970s, the government lost its ability to allocate loans as the private capital market grew, and as prosperous companies turned to internal self-financing. Administrative guidance receded as the firms' new prosperity allowed them to opt for more independence. The guidance and the cartelization were seen to deter the technical breakthroughs that come from the competitive, and even duplicative, R&D efforts made by adversaries. Obvious winners became much harder to pick, and experience showed several early choices had been quite poor. Autos were not high on the original list. The targeting of steel was probably a mistake. Steel had few external economies, its targeting did not result in much capture of foreigners' rents, and the profits realized in this industry were well below the Japanese average. Steel was rapidly overrun by Korean and other competition. Shipbuilding did well only for a relatively short time. The targeting of petrochemicals and aluminum was mistaken, with the energy crisis making it impossible for Japan to compete against countries with lower energy costs.

Though it is not easy to judge, it is probably fair to claim that Japanese trade strategy was well-designed to bring the country back from World War II and launch it into an era of high economic growth. That strategy is now much attenuated, however. Government still utilizes subsidies, directed toward several high-tech areas, including research into microchips, neural-network computers, superconductive materials, biotechnology, deep underground construction, hypersonic aircraft, and improved factory organization. The subsidies remain modest, however, and as a percent of GDP are only slightly higher than the U.S. figure, as we saw in Chapter 7. Probably more significant than the government money has been the encouragement of joint public-private research projects to promote technological advance in these areas. The government activities are

---

[2] Paraphrasing Kozo Yamamura, "Caveat Emptor: The Industrial Policy of Japan," in Paul R. Krugman, *Strategic Trade Policy and the New International Economics,* Cambridge, Mass., MIT Press, 1986; p. 201.

important, but they are also a far cry from the old policy of widespread targeting plus protection. The major developments of the 1970s and 1980s—competitive practices such as focusing on market segments to obtain in-plant scale economies, flexible factories utilizing CAD/CAM techniques and just-in-time production and delivery—had little to do with the government.

A striking change in Japanese trade policy is that the original high protection of industrial products through orthodox and explicit trade barriers has been dismantled. Claims otherwise are gross exaggerations. Japanese tariffs on manufactures and mining are not only lower (2.1% in 1987) than those of the United States (4.4%) and the EC (4.6%), but they have been so for some time. Antidumping duties and countervailing duties are virtually never used. Japan's nontariff barriers are also less restrictive than those of the United States and the EC, except in agriculture. The only remaining non-farm quota applies to coal. The few existing Japanese VERs (13 of them) almost all apply to textile imports from China, Korea, and Pakistan. Little more progress on tariffs and quotas is now possible outside of agriculture, because both are almost negligible, though farming remains heavily protected as we have already discussed.

Responding to criticism of its earlier protection, Japan initiated seven Action Programs on Imports to ease market access between 1981 and 1987. This was atypical in a world where impediments to trade are rising, not falling. Astonishingly the Export-Import Bank of Japan extends low-interest loans to importers, unheard of anywhere else, and in 1992, interest rates on these loans were cut. Japan runs the world's only system of import-credit insurance. In 1990, a new tax credit was established, with firms that raised their imports more than 10% able to claim 5% of the value as a reduction in taxes. Even on the level of molding public opinion, the government is active. Premiers exhort the Japanese people to purchase more imports to ward off foreign displeasure. MITI sponsors import promotion months and in direct talks with company presidents lobbies private firms to expand their imports. All have great symbolic significance, because many Japanese until only a few years ago *did* appear to treat imports as generally inferior. In response to the premier's call in 1985 for more willingness to import, a poll indicated that only 23% of those surveyed said they would cooperate.[3] As we shall see, however, this reluctance to buy imported goods has been breaking down.

The contrast with the usual stereotype could hardly be greater. Yet the perception of Japan as a protectionist nation survives and thrives. Basically, the public tends to equate trade protectionism with trade surpluses, and Japan in recent years has run a large trade surplus with the United States. Obviously, so runs the story, if you export a lot but hold down your imports, then you will have a trade surplus.

---

[3] See C. Michael Aho and Jonathan David Aronson, *Trade Talks*, New York, 1985, p. 84.

There are problems of plausibility with this story, however. First, we have seen in Chapters 2 and 4 that in the long run protection does not yield trade surpluses—it just reduces trade. Trade barriers hit exports as surely as they do imports, by means of the pass-through effects. The higher prices of imports feed through the price mechanism to raise the price of exports, too. Reduced Japanese imports also reduce the demand for the dollar, lowering (depreciating) its value and making it harder for Japan to export and easier for it to import.

The second problem with the idea that protectionism gives Japan a trade surplus is that although this could happen in the short run before the pass-throughs take effect, a very large surplus with the United States has been in place for a long time. A small bilateral surplus of $1.8 billion in 1975 had risen by 1980 to $9.9 billion, while by 1985 it was four times more. In 1987 the surplus amounted to $57 billion (out of a total U.S. trade deficit in that year of $158 billion), and it was still $49 billion in 1992 (59% of the total U.S. trade deficit of $83 billion). This Japanese trade surplus with the United States has been in existence for far too long to call it a short-run phenomenon. Even in the short run, economists who have studied the alleged unwillingness of the Japanese to import have estimated that a *total elimination* of all Japanese barriers would have the effect of reducing the trade surplus with the United States (and the rest of the world as well) by no more than about 10%.[4] The magnitude is about the same as the short-run *increase* in the surplus that would result if the United States opened its own markets more fully to Japanese exports.

There is a third problem with the view that trade barriers generate a trade surplus. Even if the argument were true, then the rising Japanese surplus of the late 1970s and most of the 1980s would presumably have required that Japanese trade barriers be rising. We have seen that this is not the case.

It is also fair to ask if Japan's import restrictions have the effect of limiting *all* trade with that country, not just U.S. trade. Some economists do indeed argue that Japan's imports are far lower, perhaps by 25% to 45%, than an economy of its stature should have, and that the index of intraindustrial trade (IIT, see Chapter 3) is also low. Japan's IIT for manufacturing in 1987 was 0.40 whereas the U.S. figure was 0.72.[5] The data are not certain, however, and other economists claim that Japan's trade is *not* that far out of line.[6] Gary Saxonhouse is a prominent critic of the low-imports charge. He claims that when proper account is taken of Japan's limited natural resources, scale economies, and product differentiation, Japan's imports are not abnormally low.

---

[4] Robert Z. Lawrence, "Imports in Japan: Closed Markets or Minds," *Brookings Papers on Economic Activity*, Vol. 2, 1987, pp. 537–538.

[5] Rudiger W. Dornbusch, "Policy Options for Freer Trade: The Case for Bilateralism," in Robert Z. Lawrence and Charles L. Schultze, eds., *An American Trade Strategy: Options for the 1990s*, Washington, D.C., Brookings Institution, 1990, p. 122.

[6] See Gary Saxonhouse, "Differentiated Products, Economies of Scale, and Access to the Japanese Market," in Robert C. Feenstra, ed., *Trade Policies for International Competitiveness*, Chicago, University of Chicago Press, 1989.

WHY THEN DOESN'T JAPAN IMPORT MORE FROM THE UNITED STATES?

What then are the major causes of the U.S.-Japanese trade imbalance? Several explanations are explored in this section.

SCARCITY OF NATURAL RESOURCES   One reason is structural, having to do with Japan's poverty in natural resources. Being resource-poor, that country must import huge quantities of raw materials, fuels, and food, which made up about three fourths of all imports as recently as the mid-1980s. These must be paid for by manufactured exports. In part that explains why Japan's ratio of manufactured goods imports to GNP is so low. This situation is changing: by 1987, over 40% of Japan's imports were manufactured goods; by 1990, the figure had reached 50%. But it still exerts an impact.

THE DISTRIBUTION SYSTEM   Another reason for Japan's low imports is that the country has a complex distribution system, with several more layers of suppliers (on average about four) than are encountered in Europe and the United States (about two). Approximately 80% of Japan's wholesale establishments employed fewer than 10 workers in 1985. These feed a huge number of small mom-and-pop stores, which in part are an employment system for retirees, often set up in their stores by their former employers. That has left Japan with a huge number of retail shops, 1.6 million compared to the 1.5 million of the United States with two times the population and 25 times the area. For a long time this fit with the tastes of Japanese housewives, who mostly walk to the shops daily, but distribution costs are raised substantially.

Further, Japanese law allows small shopkeepers some say in the granting of site permits for supermarkets. For a long time these permits often took six to seven years to acquire, and sometimes as much as 10, though recently that has been shortened to about three years. One result is that Japan's largest retailers account for a relatively small percentage of total retail sales. Because the large stores import proportionally much more than the small shops, imports are penalized. Furthermore, price-fixing is common, sales involving mark-downs are rare, coupons in newspapers are not legal, and many stores will stock only the goods of the manufacturers that set them up. Manufacturers' rebates, exceedingly generous credit advances to wholesalers and retailers, plus the right to return unsold goods to the manufacturer for a cash rebate, all contribute further to high distribution costs. In addition, sole import licenses have heretofore been legal under Japanese law. It appears that these practices are mostly responsible for the high retail price of goods in Japanese stores, prices that average almost half again more for a large market basket of goods and services than in the United States.

In these conditions a premium is put on long-term relations with suppliers. The system can be difficult for foreigners to break into, one reason why until quite recently only 5% of manufactured goods were imports. Entry can be difficult for the Japanese, too; in some years bankruptcies among firms have run six times higher than in the United States. This suggests that the distribution system is not designed as a trade barrier, as some would have it, but is simply an institutional fact of life.

Foreigners have long urged the Japanese government to take steps to improve the cumbersome distribution system, and that country has committed itself to a reform. In a major step taken in 1990, the government agreed on a large-store approval process that would take eighteen months at maximum. Japan's laws allowing resale price maintenance were repealed in 1992. The Japanese Fair Trade Commission has traditionally been ineffectual, but with American prodding it is obtaining new powers, increasing its fines, and acting with new vigor.

KEIRETSU RELATIONSHIPS Keiretsu means "system" in Japanese.[7] Vertical keiretsu relations involve a manufacturer in a close-knit network with suppliers. Such relationships are most important in autos, steel, and electronics, and include firms such as Hitachi, Toshiba, Nissan, Toyota, and Nippon Steel. In the auto firms, for example, 50% to 75% of a car's cost is now subcontracted. Under these conditions, cost conscious and effective suppliers are essential.[8] Some economists and many foreign businesspeople view the keiretsu form of organization as a virtual conspiracy to hold the market closed against imports. Recent work by Robert Lawrence does indicate that they hold down imports to a degree. Others say quality control, cooperative quality improvement, and smooth supply of components are all aided by a keiretsu relationship, so they make good business sense and develop comparative advantage. Evidence exists that manufacturers in vertical keiretsu have better export performance than firms that buy their inputs at arm's length. Furthermore, argue the critics of Lawrence's position, if comparative advantage is improved by a keiretsu arrangement with domestic suppliers, then it is understandable that inputs produced domestically will predominate over imports. In this view, countries lacking a network of mutually supporting, vertically related firms in close proximity to one another should go about encouraging their formation rather than harassing countries that have already achieved it. (U.S. antitrust authorities in 1992 announced that they might prosecute U.S. branches of Japanese firms for keiretsu behavior.)

MACROECONOMIC CONSIDERATIONS The items mentioned thus far contribute to an understanding of why Japan does not trade more—as we know, if the country would import more, it would export more as well. Explaining why

---

[7] For the keiretsu, see P.A. Geroski, "Vertical Relations Between Firms and Industrial Policy," *Economic Journal,* Vol. 102, No. 410, January 1992, pp. 138–147; the *International Economic Review,* June, 1991; and Robert Z. Lawrence, "Efficient or Exclusionist? The Import Behavior of Japanese Corporate Groups," *Brookings Papers,* 1991.

[8] George Stalk in *The Economist,* March 21, 1992. For analysis of the advantageous relationship between automobile producers and parts suppliers, see Michael J. Smitka, *Subcontracting in the Japanese Automotive Industry,* New York, Columbia University Press, 1991.

Japan has a trade *surplus* with the United States requires further analysis of consumption, saving, and investment, which will be undertaken in the second part of this book. Here we may briefly make the point that the Japanese export more than they import because they consume less and save more of their total output than is true of most other countries. For example, consumption in Japan is currently only 66% of GNP, and saving is 33%, whereas in the United States consumption is 87% of GNP and saving is 13%.[9] Because the Japanese spend less on everything, they import less as well. Why is this so? (1) Japan has a relatively low ratio of elderly to working-age population, so saving is higher and consumption lower than it would otherwise be. The social security system is not very advanced, thus encouraging saving to cover expenses after retirement, and the low standard retirement age of 55 and high life expectancy work in the same direction. (But the growing proportion of retired persons compared to the working-age population will cut into the savings ratio. This, combined with a probable rise in the retirement age to 60 or 65 and improvements in social security, will serve to reduce the proportion of saving to GNP.) (2) Land prices are much higher in Japan than in the United States. The mortgage market is poorly developed, and mortgages are not tax deductible. Down payments for homes usually range from 25% to 40% of the purchase price, compared to a U.S. figure of 10% to 30%. Thus the Japanese must save more if they want to buy a house. (3) In Japan savings have traditionally been untaxed or taxed very lightly. (4) Japan's lump-sum bonus system, under which bonuses are paid semiannually to employees, leads to larger average cash balances in bank accounts than would otherwise be true, and thus more savings.

Many of the problems discussed here were subject to U.S.-Japanese negotiations during 1989–1990 in the Structural Impediments Initiative talks. Though U.S. negotiators obviously wanted to focus on the Japanese impediments surveyed here, other topics such as the U.S. budget deficit and the U.S. tax structure that penalizes savings were also considered. In an agreement of 1990, the Japanese committed themselves to spend $2.8 trillion on public works between 1991 and 2000, to higher taxes on saving and interest income, to a land tax that was adopted in 1992, to more antitrust enforcement, to strengthened monitoring of keiretsu relations, and to a national cut in working hours to boost spending on leisure activities. Follow-up negotiations were agreed on, to be held during the next three years. Even at best, however, progress in reforming the Japanese economy will undoubtedly be slow as long as there is no strong consumer lobby, and as long as small businesses continue to be influential in politics.

It ought to be pointed out that something of a slippery slope is involved when differences in domestic economic policy are given the blame for a trade advantage. Japan has been making real accommodations, but what is Bangladesh to do if foreign critics begin to claim that labor is cheap there because its population control policies are inadequate and its economic policies are not efficient?

---

[9]Consumption is defined as private plus government; saving is gross domestic saving. The figures are for 1989. See World Bank, *World Development Report 1991*, p. 221.

Where is the line to be drawn on such issues?[10] An international forum where complaints of this sort could be considered would presumably be helpful, but no such forum presently exists.

THE JAPANESE RECESSION AND THE TRADE IMBALANCE

Japan was involved in a major recession in 1991–1993. Industrial production, retail sales, and wages were down sharply, all by about 5% in 1992. The recession partly undid the progress that Japan had made in reducing the size of its trade surplus with the United States.

Until the recession hit, Japan's imports had been surging. They had increased by about 100% in dollar value and by over 50% in volume between 1986 and 1991. That brought the Japanese level of imports per capita in 1990 to about $1,900, only slightly less than the U.S. figure of $2,050, although both figures are low by European and Canadian standards. (Germany imported $4,460 per person in that year, for example.) By 1990 the bilateral U.S. trade deficit with Japan had been cut to less than half its 1986 level. Consumer goods imports had grown especially fast, twice as fast in the period 1986–1989 than as projected by historical trends. Docks, airports, and warehousing were being overwhelmed by a flood of imports that some said was spectacular.[11] The import surge called into serious question older psychological explanations of low imports based on psyche and culture. Some of this resistance no doubt still survives, but the great surge of imports in 1986–1991 demonstrated that attitudes can change, or be made to change, as markets alter relative prices.

Unfortunately, the 1991–1993 Japanese recession, deepest since the 1970s, cooled off the purchases of imports considerably. Lower purchasing power meant fewer imports were purchased. The lower level of imports caused a rise in Japan's trade surplus with the United States, after years of decline. Table 8.3 shows the data.

Politically, the rise in the trade surplus was inopportune, first because the U.S. public tends to equate trade protectionism with trade surpluses, and second because 59% of the total U.S. trade deficit was with Japan. Amid the rising chorus of U.S. complaint, it availed the Japanese little to point out that their surplus with

---

[10] So asks Jagdish Bhagwati, "United States Trade Policy at the Crossroads," p. 459.

[11] See Robert Corker, "The Changing Nature of Japanese Trade," *Finance and Development*, Vol. 28, No. 2, June 1991, pp. 6–9.

Table 8.3 **Japan's trade surplus with the United States, 1988–1992**

1988	$53 billion	1991	$44 billion
1989	$49 billion	1992	$49 billion
1990	$43 billion		

Asia and Europe had increased by much more than it had with the United States, and that their surplus with southeast Asia was actually greater than with the United States.

Under heavy U.S. pressure, Japan in 1993 announced a $117 billion program of emergency public spending to stimulate the economy. The public works component, including highways, freight yards, airports, port facilities, tunnels, bridges, causeways, parks, sewers, office buildings, residential towers, and hospitals was planned not only to offset the recession's domestic impact but also to raise imports and provide some work for foreign contractors. The United States demanded even more such public spending, to 10% of GDP, but this demand was rejected. Japanese officials and voters looked at it as leading to too much deficit, debt, and possible inflation, and involving more-than-ordinary meddling in a domestic policy question.

ARE WESTERN FIRMS PARTLY RESPONSIBLE FOR THEIR POOR EXPORT PERFORMANCE?

Sometimes it appears that the responsibility for the relatively low level of exports to Japan lies with the foreign exporters rather than with any perceived Japanese intransigence. Autos make an excellent example. U.S. auto executives argue that the playing field is not level because of Japanese barriers to auto imports. But Japan, like Britain, drives on the left. Not until January 1993 did any U.S. car, truck, or van maker place the wheel on the right, where the Japanese need it to be. (The first U.S. company to move the wheel was Chrysler on its exported Jeep Cherokees. Ford indicates that it plans to do so around the end of 1993.) Wheel position is not the only problem, however. U.S. vehicles are on average larger than Japanese ones; many Japanese roads are narrow and so are parking spots. Garages are small. Japanese license plates will not fit in U.S. holders; U.S. makers do not offer retractable mirrors, needed to keep the mirrors from being knocked off in narrow passageways; speedometers are in miles per hour and not kilometers; and there is a notable lack of American dealerships, which are difficult to establish because of high land prices and low sales volumes. Chrysler has only 50 outlets, for example, about the same number that Rolls Royce has in the United States. Japanese consumers are known to be quality-conscious, and inadequate servicing was cited by 60% of potential Japanese customers in one survey. European carmakers have acted on most of these problems. For example, BMW has spent half a billion dollars to establish dealerships, and sales have increased six times since 1983. The charge that the low sales of American cars in Japan are proof of a tilted playing field do not seem serious.

Finally, far too few foreigners are able to read and speak Japanese, an obvious and substantial handicap in doing business. A recent study in the *New York Times* stated that a majority of American businesspeople in Japan did not speak the language, and only 7% were sufficiently skilled to read a newspaper. Even the entire elimination of protection will presumably have less effect than might be expected until change takes place in the attitudes of foreign sellers.

JAPAN'S TRADE STRATEGY: A SUMMARY

In short, the Japanese did indeed employ a national trade strategy involving both protectionism and subsidies, and it appears to have worked. But contrary to widespread perception, Japan's orthodox trade barriers are low, except in agriculture, and government subsidies are modest. These tools belong to Japan's past, an era of infant industries when winners were easy to pick, and they play a much less important role today when picking winners is not nearly so obvious. Thus the country most often cited for government activism in trade does not now provide very persuasive evidence of this case.

Japan still does run a major trade surplus with the United States. To be sure, whenever a country finds itself with a large balance of trade surplus and at the same time can claim rapid economic growth with low unemployment, which has been the norm in spite of the (presumably) temporary recession in 1991–1993, it should surely be forward in dismantling its remaining trade barriers. The lower barriers would help counter any inflationary tendency and would tend to reverse the surplus. It is in Japan's interest to raise its imports. But your authors recommend that foreign pressure to that end is better done internationally through negotiations than by means of bilateral threats.

Chapter 9

Economic Integration

OBJECTIVES

Overall Objective: To evaluate whether customs unions improve world welfare, or even the welfare of their participants, examining in theory and practice what leads to high benefits and what leads to high costs.

MORE SPECIFICALLY:

- To show what kinds of customs unions exist in theory, law, and actuality.
- To show what makes a customs union trade creating or trade diverting.
- To assess the economic effects of the European Community, the U.S.-Canada Free Trade Agreement, the North American Free Trade Agreement, and numerous arrangements involving Third World countries, exploring why they do or do not work.
- To look at free trade zones as partial moves toward freer trade.
- To examine the use of countertrade.

Economic integration is the process of joining together two or more countries into a closer economic union than each has with the rest of the world.[1] Typically, economic integration begins with an arrangement in which tariffs and nontariff barriers are abolished among the nations involved, but not with the rest of the world. Economic integration, however, can also involve freedom of resource movement, common economic policies, even a common money. Both in theory and in practice, integration raises economic questions that are sometimes less than obvious, but are of considerable importance.

INTEGRATION AMONG THE MARKET ECONOMIES

Economic integration is hardly new and has played an important role in the history of numerous nations. The U.S. Constitution of 1789 by abolishing the separate tariffs of the 13 states created an economic union out of those loosely federated entities. (Under the Articles of Confederation, which prevailed from the Revolution until 1789, New York had actually charged some tariffs on imports from Connecticut.) Austria eliminated internal barriers to trade in 1775, France in 1790. Sixty years before the French move to free trade within its own borders, there had been over 4000 internal tolls. In the nineteenth century came the German Zollverein (customs union) of 1834, which was an arrangement among many of the sovereign states that were only unified politically under Bismarck in 1871.

When GATT was established, a portentous decision was taken to allow preferential trading arrangements as one of only two permitted exceptions to the GATT rule that most favored nation treatment must be applied to tariffs. (The other exception is that tariffs can be lowered or abolished by rich countries in favor of poor ones.) But the right to give preferences under GATT rules was subject to two restrictions: (1) The agreement must not "on the whole" result in barriers that are more restrictive to outside exporters than the barriers that had existed before; and (2) Trade barriers must be eliminated on "substantially all trade" among the members of an agreement within "a reasonable length of time." The clear meaning of the second restriction is that though countries can *eliminate* their barriers against the other members, they *cannot* under the GATT rules cut them by less than 100% for more than a transitional period. Yet these rules have in practice not had much importance. The quoted passages, "on the whole," "substantially all," and "reasonable length of time," have provided wide latitude for arrangements to do much as they please, and GATT has never formally objected to a single agreement.[2]

FREE TRADE AREAS, CUSTOMS UNIONS, AND COMMON MARKETS

The differences in definitions employed by the economists who study economic integration are important. In a *free trade area,* the members eliminate their tariffs against one another, but maintain their own national protective barriers against outsiders. In Fig. 9.1a, each country has its own trade barriers, their strength indicated by the thickness of the circles. In 9.1b, a free trade area has been formed, with internal free trade but the same old barriers against the rest of the world. The members need supplementary regulations dealing with country of origin rules, or else goods will be shipped from the outside into the lowest-tariff nation, and then exported to members with higher tariffs. Such rules will ordinarily specify how much value must be added in the low-tariff country to qualify the good for onward shipment to other members at a zero rate. This, of course, creates economic inefficiencies by encouraging processing within the low-tariff country.

Formerly the best-known free trade area was the *European Free Trade Association,* or EFTA. It is now in the process of dismantling itself. The outstanding example at present is the U.S.-Canada Free Trade Agreement. Both cases are discussed later in the chapter.

A *customs union* is more ambitious. Instead of the differences in protection against outsiders that characterize a free trade area, a customs union has a common external tariff against goods entering any of the members from the outside. This is shown in Fig. 9.1c and 9.1d, where the three members that originally

---

Figure 9.1 **Forming a free trade area**

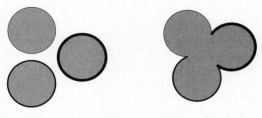

a. **Independent trade policy**   *b.* **Free trade area**

had different tariff structures have adopted a common external tariff that is approximately the average of the countries' rates before the union.

A *common market* is a customs union but carries the additional provision that capital and labor move freely within it. The *European Community*, EC, is justifiably the most famous of the common markets, involving a customs union with free trade among the members, and with workers and capital free to move, as when Italian workers take jobs in Germany and German capital flows to Italy.

Finally, *economic union* goes beyond a common market to include fixed exchange rates among the members' currencies and requirements for monetary and fiscal policies to support the stability of these rates. In addition, an economic union will usually involve coordinated public policies for the transfer of revenues from richer to poorer areas, for agricultural policy, and so on. Currently the EC is moving toward union, as we shall see.

THE GREAT DEBATE: TRADE CREATION OR TRADE DIVERSION

For many years, the general opinion was that any economic integration would be beneficial. Free trade was the optimum, and free trade areas and customs unions represented a movement toward free trade. Therefore the integration must

---

Figure 9.1 (continued) **A common external tariff distinguishes a customs union**

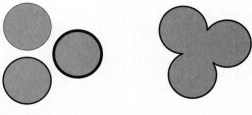

c. **Independent trade policy**   *d.* **Customs union**

increase welfare. Well into the twentieth century, there did not exist an adequate theory to explain the economic impact of integration. Few questioned the conclusion that it was a good thing, but in fact no one had made a rigorous study of the subject and the literature covering it was scant.

Then came a striking theoretical development, in 1950, when Jacob Viner showed in his book *The Customs Union Issue* that the standard opinion was not necessarily correct, and that under certain circumstances economic integration could result in a reduction of welfare. Viner's conclusion illustrates what came to be known as the paradox of the second best. This paradox, first put in print by Richard Lipsey and Kelvin J. Lancaster of the London School of Economics, states that although a first-best course of action *must* optimize welfare, the second-best course of action may *not* increase welfare (something like jumping 99% of the way across a canyon).

How can this be so? All along, people had assumed that integration would allow lower-priced imports from a trading partner to replace higher-priced domestic output, thus increasing welfare. Viner showed this could indeed be the case, as is demonstrated in modified form in Table 9.1. Case 1 presents the price of wheat in three countries, X, Y, and Z. To protect its domestic producers, X has a tariff of 200%. At that tariff, not even Z with its low production cost of $1 can compete in X with X's $2 wheat. Assuming constant production costs for the present, we can reasonably conclude that all of X's wheat is purchased at home.

Now let us forge a customs union with Y, and examine the change in prices as shown in Table 9.2. The union lowers Y's price to consumers in X, so that they shift their purchases to Y, leaving X's farmers to grow something else. Assuming full employment, X is clearly better off producing something else and importing wheat from Y, the low-cost producer.

Viner called this type of arrangement a "trade-creating customs union," and so it is, with trade in wheat replacing domestic production. Today we would speak of it as being a customs union that had only a trade creation effect. Of course X would have been even better off if Z had been included in the customs union, but the welfare of X is nevertheless improved, while the welfare of Z is unaffected.

Consider, however, that this case is only one possibility, and that the result would be very different if the level of the tariff is changed. In Tables 9.3 and 9.4, a 90% tariff is substituted for the 200% tariff.

Before the customs union, the cheapest wheat in X was that imported from Z, hence X's farmers did not grow wheat and Z enjoyed X's wheat market. With the signing of a customs union with Y, however, a curious thing occurs: Y's

Table 9.1 **No customs union, 200% tariff in X**

	In X	In Y	In Z
Cost of wheat	$2.00	$1.50	$1.00
Tariff in X	—	$3.00	$2.00
Price in X	$2.00	$4.50	$3.00

Table 9.2   After customs union, 200% tariff in X

	In X	In Y	In Z
Cost of wheat	$2.00	$1.50	$1.00
Tariff in X	—	—	$2.00
Price in X	$2.00	$1.50	$3.00

Table 9.3   No customs union, 90% tariff in X

	In X	In Y	In Z
Cost of wheat	$2.00	$1.50	$1.00
Tariff in X	—	$1.35	$0.90
Price in X	$2.00	$2.85	$1.90

Table 9.4   After customs union, 90% tariff in X

	In X	In Y	In Z
Cost of wheat	$2.00	$1.50	$1.00
Tariff in X	—	—	$0.90
Price in X	$2.00	$1.50	$1.90

price to X's consumers falls below Z's, so that X *diverts* its trade from Z, the lowest-cost supplier, to Y, a higher-cost supplier. People in X may think they are getting wheat more cheaply—the price for them is down 40¢ per bushel from the $1.90 they used to pay for imports from Z. But they have forgotten that their government was collecting 90¢ per bushel in tariff revenue, 50¢ of which is now lost and 40¢ of which goes to the consumer. The world has seen wheat that cost $1 supplanted by wheat that uses up $1.50 in resources. Viner called this a "trade-diverting customs union," in which trade has been diverted from a more efficient to a less efficient producer.

DIAGRAMMING TRADE CREATION AND TRADE DIVERSION

Later research concentrated on further explorations of trade creation and trade diversion.[3] Viner had focused attention on changes in production, but diagrammatical analysis soon made it apparent that the effects of a customs union could be more complex. We can use the partial equilibrium model of the gains from trade and harm from tariffs to explore this issue.

Figure 9.2 illustrates the customs union effect. It shows country X's demand and supply curves, and the price of wheat imported from Y and Z. Country X has increasing costs, as indicated by the positively sloped supply curve. For

Figure 9.2 **A trade-diverting customs union.** P_y is the price of the good from the partner country and P_z from the outsider. The gain from the customs union is $B+D$, the elimination of some deadweight loss. The loss to the customs union is the higher costs from producing in the partner country or E. Under the conditions of a great difference in cost between partner and outsider ($P_y > P_z$), a high tariff (P_z+T), and inelastic demand and supply curves, B and D are small and E is large.

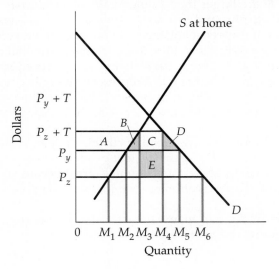

illustrative clarity, we endow Y and Z with constant costs. (Perhaps that is because they are large countries unaffected by trade with X, or perhaps it is just that the diagram gets very messy if we don't make this assumption.) P_z is the price of Z's wheat before a tariff, and P_y is Y's wheat price. The tariff, a specific duty amounting to T, can be added to both P_z and P_y, giving P_z+T and P_y+T.

With no tariff at all, M_1 is produced in country X, M_6 is consumed, and $M_1 M_6$ is imported. There will be no imports from Y, and in fact very little production in X. After the tariff, country Z with its price P_z+T is still the lowest-cost supplier. X's production expands to M_3 and its consumption declines to M_4, these being the usual effects of a tariff.

Now let us open a customs union between X and Y. The price of Y's wheat falls to P_y, below P_z+T, and trade is thus diverted to Y. The lower price and greater quantity traded lead to a gain in consumers' surplus, which is the triangular area above the price but below the demand curve. The triangle of consumers' surplus has expanded to an area larger by $A+B+C+D$, because the price has fallen and the quantity has increased.

But this is not an unadulterated gain for society. Country X's own domestic producers are harmed by the lower price; their producers' surplus is reduced by area A. Tariff revenue is also down. Country X had been collecting tariffs on its imports, but does so no longer on the imports from Y, its fellow member in the customs union. This lost tariff revenue is equal to areas $C+E$, which is found by multiplying the tariff T by the quantity of imports M_3M_4. C is redistributed to consumers, but not E, which must be used to pay Y's higher costs. In short, there is a welfare gain comprising $A+B+C+D$, and a welfare loss to society of $A+C+E$.

The net result is determined by comparing the little triangles B and D to the rectangle E. If B and D are larger than E, then gains in consumer surplus outweigh lost producers' surplus and lost tariff revenue. The customs union thus creates more trade than it diverts; it enhances welfare. But the reverse case, with E larger than $B+D$, shows reduced welfare in a customs union that is on balance trade diverting. In our Fig. 9.2, trade diversion obviously predominates, with $B+D$ smaller in size than area E. Rectangle E represents not only country X's loss, but world loss. It shows the additional resources used in producing wheat in Y; or, to use the numbers given earlier, the 50¢ per bushel additional cost for Y's wheat.

By contrast, Fig. 9.3 shows a trade-creating customs union. Again the gain in consumers' surplus is $A+B+C+D$. Again the lost producers' surplus is A; again tariff revenue falls by $C+E$. But here the net gain is great because triangles $B+D$ are far larger than area E. Trade creation predominates; trade diversion is minor; welfare is enhanced.

Make careful note of the two main characteristics of the figure that cause $B+D$ to exceed E, so giving rise to trade creation.

Figure 9.3 **A trade-creating customs union.** As in Fig. 9.2, the partner country has a price (cost) of P_y and the outside country P_z; the tariff is P_z+T. Because the demand and supply in the home country are highly elastic, and the fall in price large, B and D are large. Because there is not much difference between the price in country Y and country Z, E is small. The customs union creates more trade than it destroys.

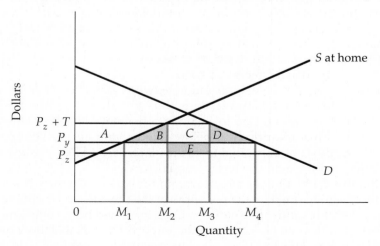

1. The supply and demand curves are highly elastic. The extra flatness of these elastic curves will, if price falls, cut domestic output sharply and also increase consumption greatly, thereby raising imports by a substantial amount. See in Fig. 9.3 how imports rise substantially after a customs union, from M_2M_3 to M_1M_4. The larger volume of trade increases consumer surplus. The flatter curves serve to raise the size of B and D.

2. The price in the home country X differs greatly from its partner in the customs union, Y; and at the same time the difference is small between the partner's price P_y and the price P_z in the lowest-cost nonmember in the outside world, Z. Note in Fig. 9.3 that Y's price is indeed close to Z's price, so that little trade diversion is possible.

TRADE CREATION CAN ALWAYS BE MADE TO PREDOMINATE In theory, countries participating in economic integration could manipulate their structure of tariffs, lowering them as necessary, to leave the total amount of their trade with nonmembers unchanged. In that case trade diversion would not occur and the integration, by eliminating all internal tariffs, would be unambiguously beneficial. This "Kemp-Wan proposition," named for its formulators, has unfortunately had little practical effect.[4] The problem is that countries engaging in integration hardly ever make an effort to adjust their external tariff to avoid trade diversion. Note that free trade areas would find it easiest to follow the Kemp-Wan logic, because *individual members* could decide to lower their own barriers to offset any trade diversion. The members of a customs union must have a common external tariff, and the entire membership would have to support its reduction. Furthermore, a customs union might require its most liberal members to *raise* their barriers to the common level, increasing the chances for trade diversion.

Trade creation may be restricted if VERs, antidumping duties, and the like, are retained on outsiders. This might be an especial problem if one or more members of the arrangement felt that harm from fellow members could be offset by stern restriction of imports from outsiders. More effective policing by GATT of such barriers could reduce the danger of trade diversion. GATT might even ban free trade areas and allow only customs unions, and then require that the members of a union must adopt a common tariff equal to the lowest in the union while keeping their tariffs bound at that level.[5] There is little likelihood that this intelligent suggestion will be adopted, however.

FURTHER CONCLUSIONS ON TRADE CREATION VERSUS TRADE DIVERSION

Important conclusions emerge from the analysis of trade creation and diversion. The first is that the larger the customs union, the less possible is trade diversion. This is reasonable because if all countries were to be in the same customs union there could be no trade diversion whatever. The unpleasant corollary, however, is that the larger the customs union, the greater the harm to those left outside it. Consider the circumstances of the last nation in the world left out of the World Economic Community. If this pariah is to trade at all, and is being underpriced because of competitors' tariff-free privileges, it will have to cut prices to absorb the tariff. (If it were country Z, for example, it would have to lower its price to be competitive with Y, thus absorbing most of the tariff.) This explains the urgency with which outsiders pursue membership in large arrangements: Greece, Spain, and Portugal in their successful negotiations to enter the EC; all the remaining EFTA members except Iceland deciding to apply for entry to the EC as well; Mexico's sudden desire to join the U.S.-Canada Free Trade Agreement, and so on. Even so, every successful joiner passes along the problem of being an outsider to the remaining nonmember nations, who now have to face a larger customs union than before.

A second theoretical conclusion is that the GATT rule requiring 100% elimination of trade barriers among member countries actually increases the danger of trade diversion. A permanent partial cut would deliver a smaller advantage to the member countries, so less trade would be diverted. In this view, the GATT rule is too strict.

Further conclusions are contained in the checklist at the end of the next section.

DYNAMIC EFFECTS OF ECONOMIC INTEGRATION

So far we have examined preferential arrangements only in terms of their static effects—as if the production possibilities curves of the member nations were unchanged by the integration. It is likely, however, that economic integration will also have *dynamic* effects that serve to push out the production possibilities curves of the members. The dynamic effects usually cited are in two categories, both of which would increase production possibilities.

(a) Competition effects. These include higher levels of investment, improved marketing, greater productive efficiency, and the spur to the adoption of new technologies.

(b) Scale effects. A larger market means that industries can realize scale economies not possible in a smaller market.

The dynamic effects of economic integration are often called on to buttress the arguments in favor of such action. As we see below in the discussion of the most successful examples of integration, there are a number of cases where dynamic effects have far outweighed any negative static effects from trade diversion, with impressive economic growth generated by the ultimately improving impact of competition and the development of scale economies. It would be odd indeed to complain about an arrangement that caused a diversion of 10% of trade if the selfsame union had produced sufficient economic growth to generate a doubling or tripling of total trade.

For example, the old pattern of multinational firms setting up national subsidiaries in the various markets of Europe changed considerably after the formation of the EC. Thereafter, it became standard practice for multinational firms to design and produce goods in one center for the entire Common Market, allowing for greater productive efficiency on a community-wide scale. All over the EC, other firms, formerly sheltered from the winds of trade, were forced to cut costs and become more efficient in both production and organization in order to maintain their market share and profit margin. Nicholas Owen's research suggests that dynamic effects based largely on scale economies resulted in an increment of some 3% to 6% of GDP for the original six members of the EC.[6]

Such arguments about integration's dynamics are, however, subject to certain difficulties: One must show that the customs union was *necessary* to have the dynamic consequences. All the results categorized under "competition effects" can be achieved with unilateral cuts in tariffs and NTBs. If a country wants the bracing wind of international competition, all it has to do is cut its import barriers. If every one of the present members had wanted more competition, they could have had it immediately if they had simply lowered their tariffs to all outsiders. Such a mutual lowering of tariffs to all nations would also have provided the opportunities for scale economies, albeit with more international competition. In the specific case of the EC's growth, one gets into treacherous statistical waters in ascribing the dynamism and growth of its members to the customs union itself. The nations were already growing in 1956 before the EC was formed; Sweden and Switzerland, outside the EC, grew just as rapidly. The authors are rather inclined to accept the dynamic arguments as being generally valid, but admit to uncertainty about attempts to quantify them. It is not at all clear by how much the growth induced by the economic integration expanded trade, nor is it easy to say if that extra boost to growth overcame the sometimes very substantial trade diversion that accompanied the EC's agricultural policies.

DYNAMIC EFFECTS ARE NOT NECESSARILY POSITIVE

Not all dynamic effects of economic integration are necessarily positive. Consider first the scale effects. What if economies of scale are important but external tariffs are high? With the now-larger market allowing for scale economies, new industries might become established behind the protective walls at costs low enough to capture markets from importers. Yet these producers would not have survived without the trade barriers. This is known as the trade suppression that might follow from economic integration, and will be most likely when the external barriers are steep. Then consider that economic integration may increase regional disparities within member countries. Say the new dynamism within a union has a more favorable effect in some members than in others. In many unions, cultural and linguistic barriers to migration prevent labor's easy movement from declining regions to more prosperous ones. Thus in the EC when Germany prospers but Greece does not, there is little movement of Greeks to Germany. In the United States, people who need jobs are far more likely to move from one state to another, explaining why unemployment rates are much more similar among the states than they are among the countries of Europe. (This is one of the reasons why the EC has adopted a compensating regional policy to counteract some of the negative dynamic effects of trade.)

THE LONG TERM: A COMMON CURRENCY

Perhaps the single most important dynamic advantage of economic integration may come in the long term if the members move to currency unification. The advantages of eventual monetary unification are wholly obvious, and the United States is often used as the best example. A single currency, the units of which are exactly equal and interchangeable, is highly desirable for safety and convenience. There then would be no necessity for foreign exchange transactions, or for maintaining numerous separate currencies and central banks. There would be no risk of fluctuations in rates, and no need for a forward market in currencies. Any American knows how advantageous it is that a dollar is a dollar in New York, in Chicago, and in Los Angeles. For example, travelers in the United States with $1000 in U.S. currency never need to exchange it at all, and incur no costs for commissions. But those same travelers in Europe with $1000 in U.S. currency, if they exchange their money in each of the 12 EC countries, would lose over half of it to commissions. (See Chapter 18.)

Trade in the world's customs unions and free trade areas would indeed be much more simple, convenient, and cheaper if the currencies were unified. But the goal of monetary union among the countries engaged in economic integration is still a long way in the future, with a few limited exceptions such as most of the island countries of the Caribbean. Even the EC, where the discussion has been intense for years, is still some distance away from currency unification. Keeping separate floating currencies is the proper prescription if countries wish to pursue independent fiscal and monetary policies for the fight against inflation and unemployment, and when they want to maintain an image of political independence. It will surprise the authors if the goal of a single currency is achieved in this century by any present integration arrangement.

A CHECKLIST OF CONDITIONS FOR WELFARE IMPROVEMENT

The following is a checklist of the static and dynamic conditions that will generally determine when a regional trade arrangement will be most successful in raising the welfare of its members.[7] Success will predictably be greatest when the following twelve conditions are met.

1. If the elasticity of demand in the member countries is high, a cut in the barriers against fellow members of the arrangement will lower price and cause a large increase in consumption. Much additional trade is generated. The result will be more positive the higher the duties were in the first place.

2. If the elasticity of supply in the member countries is high, production within the arrangement will rise rapidly to take the place of the former imports from nonmembers when a demand increase occurs because of the fall in tariffs.

3. If low-cost producers of any given good also belong to the arrangement, then there will be only a small sacrifice in shifting trade from nonmembers to members. It follows that the larger the area involved, the better for the participants, for then the chances are greater that low-cost producers will be among the membership, so lessening the trade diversion.

4. If countries already conduct a large proportion of their trade with one another before integration takes place among them, then there is bound to be little trade diversion when a union is created.

5. If the member countries import only a small percentage of their consumption, then diversion of trade to a higher-cost source within the arrangement will make little difference.

6. When countries forming an arrangement had very low tariffs to start with, or very high ones, the chances for trade diversion are lessened. When tariffs were very low, the diversion will be slight when they are dropped altogether. If they were very high, there was little trade to divert because the high tariffs suppressed it.

7. If in negotiating a customs union, the external tariff against outsiders is more or less an average of the previous rates existing in the member countries, then the dispersion of tariffs is likely to be reduced. This is an advantage. When very high and very low tariffs exist together, incentives become skewed toward and away from the industries concerned. A smaller variation in tariffs means comparative advantage has a greater chance to work.

8. If the union is so large that its external tariff can affect the world market for an imported item, then it may be able to manipulate the tariff to alter the terms of trade in its favor. If a large union results in a shift of members' demand away from nonmembers' exports, the nonmembers may have to cut their prices if they wish to continue exporting. The union might also be able to obtain a terms-of-trade effect with exports if export taxes are standardized. Note that in these situations any gain to the welfare of the membership is automatically a loss in welfare to outsiders.

9. Arrangements among countries with very different factor proportions will tend to stimulate trade along Heckscher-Ohlin lines. Countries will special-

ize and trade the items that have the right factor proportions. On the contrary, countries with similar factor proportions will see less trade creation when trade occurs because of Heckscher-Ohlin principles.

10. If trade is instead based on decreasing costs due to traditional scale economies, in-plant economies from specialization, learning curves, and the like, then much of it will be intraindustrial. In that case, the growth of trade will be greater when incomes are high and the integrated market is large.[8] Intraindustrial trade tends to be less disruptive for the economies of the members. There will be fewer cases of entire industries having to go out of business. (One reason why trade expanded in the original EC to a far greater degree than it did in EFTA is that the EC with its high average income levels and its large market could support substantially more intraindustrial trade.)

11. If the economic growth of the members is rapid, then adjustment to free trade within an arrangement will be easier. "A rising tide lifts all boats." Wealthy countries can afford regional development funds and trade adjustment assistance to cope with the temporary damage that may be caused by imports.

12. Outward-oriented economic policies in such areas as foreign exchange rates and government regulation give a greater chance that trade will increase as barriers are lowered. On the contrary, overvalued foreign exchange rates, price-fixing by strong vested interests, and corrupt governments can hinder the effectiveness of trade liberalization.

THE MAJOR EXAMPLES OF ECONOMIC INTEGRATION

Examples of economic integration under the GATT rules began to appear in the 1950s. Once rare, they have now proliferated, with 23 arrangements involving 119 countries in place in early 1992.[9] The fastest growth is occurring at the present time, with regional integration having achieved a sudden popularity in the 1990s—for reasons not always altogether laudable, as we shall see.

THE EUROPEAN COMMUNITY

The European Community, or EC, is the most famous example of modern integration, and that is where we shall begin. The connection between political and economic unity was not lost on the statesmen of Western Europe and America who sought to rebuild the Western world after the Second World War. These leaders did not want a divided Europe to continue. Rather they envisioned a Europe united politically, economically, and militarily, a Europe that would no longer fight with itself, but would be strong enough to resist the threats from the Soviet Union and from homegrown radicalism. The first and most practical step would be to create a customs union. Not only did a customs union make economic sense, it would force the countries into regular political consultation. Thus the creation of the European Economic Community, or EEC, in 1957 had more than economic purposes. Its economic behavior, and the tolerance of the United States toward some of its excesses, must be understood in this broader political context. A mixture of lofty ideals and hard economic and political realities can produce some unusual reactions.

The European Community—a name that implies a goal of ultimate political unity—has replaced the original name EEC or the more colloquial Common Market in the speech of those who share the goal, though the usage EEC still has a strong following, especially in Great Britain. The EC was founded in Rome in March of 1957 by six nations: France, West Germany, Italy, Belgium, the Netherlands, and Luxembourg. It was based partially on an earlier cooperative effort known as the Benelux union, a customs union among the last three nations named above. It was also based on experience gained in tariff-free trade in coal and steel in the ECSC, the European Coal and Steel Community. Tariffs on industrial goods were cut rapidly, and a common external tariff, somewhat lower than the weighted averages of the then-existing European tariffs, was attained in 1968. In contrast, agricultural policy developed slowly and painfully, and not until the mid-1960s did agricultural commodities flow freely.[*]

The Six became the Nine when Britain, Denmark, and Ireland joined in 1973. Greece made it the Ten in 1981, and the present figure of twelve was reached when Spain and Portugal were accepted for membership on January 1, 1986. The results were spectacular. Trade among the nations that now comprise the Twelve was only 34.5% of their total trade in 1960, but that figure had grown to 60.4% by 1990, making up over one fifth of all world trade. (Such statistics are a useful indicator of whether economic integration has worked to increase trade among the members. By this test, the EC's performance has been superb, far surpassing any other of the world's free trade areas and customs unions. Keep in mind, however, that an increase in intraregional trade is not necessarily the same as a welfare increase, because trade diversion may have occurred. Later in the chapter we shall cite the much lower figures for intraregional trade in other preferential arrangements.)

New members are in the offing. By 1992 Austria, Finland, Norway, Sweden, and Switzerland had all applied for membership or were close to it. Earlier applications from Cyprus, Malta, and Turkey are still outstanding. Even if all goes well, however, entry from this list is not likely to take place until 1995–1996 at the earliest.

A major move toward unified economic policies has been underway for some years. European Community ministers meeting in Brussels now fix farm prices and set the fishing rules for all the members. The EC Commission manages

---

[*] The external tariff raised German and Benelux barriers, because these countries originally had relatively low tariffs, and lowered the high French and Italian tariffs. The effect on outsiders was very different, depending on whether they traded more with the former four countries or the latter two.

antitrust policies, regulates aid to industries, and conducts much of the bargaining in international trade negotiations. A VAT has been adopted by all the members, and the rates are now closer to harmony than they once were. Great progress has been made in reducing nontariff barriers to trade among the members, including the difficult issues of health and safety standards, labeling, and administrative regulations. Even the size of trucks is now standardized, so that goods do not have to be transshipped or put into especially small vehicles to move from one nation to the other. Thus heavy European trucks have been causing annoyance in many of England's small towns. Although this may be a burden, there are many balancing benefits. NTB eliminations mean, for instance, that a lathe or radio made in England can be sold without modification in any of the member countries.

TRADE CREATION AND TRADE DIVERSION IN THE EUROPEAN COMMUNITY
The extent of the trade creation and trade diversion that resulted from the founding of the EC is a subject of considerable importance. In manufacturing, the model that emphasizes trade creation seems to fit the case best. European Community members have economies that are competitive with one another, so substitution among commodities is easy and demand curves are flat. Mass production techniques that allow large increases in output with little or no rise in costs lead to an elastic supply. Incomes are high and the market was large right from the start, so intraindustrial trade creation was vigorous, especially in chemicals, machinery, fuels, and transportation equipment. Trade diversion in industry was unlikely to be very important because many of the industries in the EC were already cost competitive with the rest of the world (meaning there would be no trade to divert) or were close to it (meaning only a small loss in diversion) at the time the market was established. This analysis suggests that trade-creation effects have dominated in manufacturing.

By contrast, agriculture in the EC appears to approach the heavy trade diversion model of Fig. 9.2 earlier in the chapter.[10] The members of the EC are not very similar in agricultural production. The British emphasize the raising of livestock, the French are more labor intensive than the Danes, the Mediterranean countries are uncompetitive with the north. In the main, the lowest-cost producer within the union is by no means the *world's* lowest-cost producer. This certainly applies to grains, dairy products, and meat. Demand is relatively inelastic for many agricultural commodities such as grain and meat. Supply is also inelastic in the short run, as production is difficult to increase or cut back during the life cycle of animals or during a crop year. Substantial trade diversion is thus likely, especially from the United States, Canada, New Zealand, Australia, and Argentina. The major impact in the EC appears to be felt by Britain and Germany, both of which formerly imported a great proportion of their food supplies from the cheapest sources overseas, and which now must import from high-cost sources within the Common Market.

A wide range of empirical estimates has appeared in the literature on the EC, generally supporting the conclusion that considerable trade creation has occurred in manufacturing and considerable trade diversion in agriculture. The overall balance between creation and diversion is still being debated; a recent survey by Richard Pomfret states that the empirical work on the overall outcome is not conclusive one way or the other.[11]

Some limited evidence also indicates that there has been a positive terms-of-trade effect for the EC as foreign suppliers had to cut prices because of the higher trade barriers that some members put in place when the common external tariff was adopted.

1992: **THE PLAN FOR FURTHER EC UNIFICATION**   The EC still has some considerable way to go before economic union is achieved. A single central bank and currency are still years away, and even exchange rates are free to vary within limits (under the European Monetary System). The EC's tax rates are not yet harmonized, with standard rates of value added tax ranging from 12% in Spain and Luxembourg to 22% in Denmark. (But a minimum rate of 15% is expected soon.) In addition, the EC had no commonality of VERs; recently France and Italy were limiting imports of well over 100 products each, while Germany was restricting only about 30. Many different NTBs concerning health and safety standards still exist. The EC's experience has certainly justified the belief that customs unions and free trade areas are easier to form than is an economic union.

In 1987, the EC agreed to set a target date of December 31, 1992, for the elimination of all remaining barriers.[12] Although the target was not hit, the term *1992* has become part of the language of those who study the EC. Among the many changes expected from *1992* are the following:

1. Border crossing simplification. The EC eliminated its customs checks at borders at the start of 1993. It is estimated that simplifying customs at these checkpoints will generate a one-time cost reduction of $10 billion and lead to $19 billion in new business.[13] One immediate result is that it has become harder to police the 6000 or so separate national quotas that still exist. For example, France, Italy, Portugal, Spain, and Britain all have their own VERs with Japan on cars. To enforce their limits these countries are now depending on the fact that cars are usually sold by exclusive dealerships that can be checked, and have to be licensed at government offices. Other separate quotas present a greater problem that may not be solvable; for these the EC will have to set limits as a unit.

2. The regulations on truck transport that prohibit foreign trucks from carrying goods from point to point within a country, and which now cause one third of all foreign trucks to travel empty on their return home, will disappear. That will reduce distribution costs by perhaps 10–15%.

3. Product health and safety standards are to be subjected to mutual recognition, and so will not be an internal barrier. This development will be significant for exporters to the EC. For example, goods allowed into Portugal will then be allowed into Germany as well, so exporters should benefit. The danger exists that EC-wide standards might be raised toward the toughest

existing ones; in that case Community standards would become more exclusionary. Furthermore, it is possible that individual members will be able to exclude imports from outside the EC. They could still come in "from Portugal," but if they do, then transport costs would be boosted.

4. Public procurement will be made more competitive among the members, with the EC Commission taking more control of this problem (but similar treatment will not be extended to outsiders unless required by the GATT code discussed in Chapter 5).

5. Financial services such as banking and insurance will be opened up to free trade, and professionals (lawyers, accountants, and so forth) will be able to practice anywhere within the Community. Value added tax is expected eventually to be standardized, possibly in two bands, one for necessities and the other for all remaining goods.

A number 6, large R&D and infrastructure subsidies that many businesspeople apparently believed would be part of *1992*, was not, however, included in the final plan.

These steps, and others taken at the same time, require that the member countries consider nearly 300 new laws, and most of these have now been passed. Yet the process has been slow, with some disputes still unresolved, and *1992* has fallen behind schedule. Fortunately for the EC, the deadline is extendable.

THE GAINS FROM *1992* The EC Commission's Cecchini Report of 1988 claimed that *1992* would deliver considerable benefits to the member countries. The report predicted a one-time boost to GDP spread over a number of years of 4.5% to 6%, a gain of 2 million new jobs, and prices within the Community lower by 6%.[14] Critics claimed these estimates were on the high side, and a section of the report using more conservative definitions suggested a gain of 2% of GDP and a million jobs. Findings in other research have been more conservative yet, usually below 2% of GDP—though of course even a small percentage represents a huge amount of money and is well worth having.[15] But another school of thought is more optimistic, emphasizing that savings and investment will rise because of the improved business climate, that greater competition will enhance efficiency, and that some new economies of agglomeration will occur. Possibly the long-run dynamic effects might be considerably more positive than the current research has predicted.

LOSSES FROM *1992*? Not everyone welcomes the prospect of *1992*. In Britain the Thatcher and Major governments have deplored the erosion of national sovereignty that they contend will occur. There is some danger that if *1992* proves more disruptive to the economies of the members than anticipated, or if income growth is less than predicted, then the result could be higher EC trade barriers.[16] The United States and Japan suspect that the EC might tighten its quotas in the process of standardizing them; might establish harmonized, but different and more protective, technical standards; might initiate new reciprocity rules; might base a new exclusion policy on its rules of origin. Any of these could potentially be trade diverting. If the EC's external trade barriers were increased under the *1992* program to the highest levels now obtaining, instead of being established at the EC average, then the cost to the rest of the world would be large, with a predicted decline in world GDP of over $100 billion.[17]

There is a point to be made on the other side of the issue as well. After the *1992* reforms, foreign multinational companies operating in the EC may actually have an advantage in competing with many EC firms because the foreign multinationals have been treating the EC as a unified market for a long time. Many firms inside the EC still do not do so.[18]

Economists studying the likelihood of trade diversion from *1992* predict that some will occur, but that it will probably be much smaller than the trade creation effects. For the United States, for example, the effect of gross trade creation from *1992* has been estimated at $6.4 billion, with net creation estimated to be about a third less at $4.4 billion because of the negative effects of the trade diversion.[19]

Whatever the outcome, the ferment surrounding *1992* further cements the position of the European Community as the world's most famous example of modern progress toward economic integration.

■ *EFTA, THE EUROPEAN FREE TRADE ASSOCIATION*

Formed in response to the better-known European Common Market in 1960, the European Free Trade Association grew to include Austria, Britain, Denmark, Finland, Iceland, Norway, Portugal, Sweden, and Switzerland (with Liechtenstein). Intraregional exports as a percentage of the total exports of the EFTA countries rose from 21.1% in 1960 to 28.2% in 1990. Over the years, however, EFTA has undergone a long process of breaking up. On January 1, 1973, two original members, Britain and Denmark, left that organization to join the EC; another, Portugal, was lost to the EC in 1986; and all the rest excepting Iceland have already or soon will apply for EC membership. EFTA administrative arrangements lacked the closeness and supranational authority characteristic of the EC. There was no need to decide on a common tariff, common agricultural policy, or common immigration laws.

Concern mounted among the six EFTA members as *1992* approached. The worry was that they would be left out. That gave the impetus for a new European Economic Area (EEA), which was negotiated between the EC and EFTA in 1991.[20] The EEA is actually an enhanced free trade area rather than a full customs union because separate EFTA national barriers against outsiders will be maintained. Internally it embodies free trade including services (though health and safety standards will still apply) and free movement of labor and capital. Qualifications for lawyers, accountants, and so forth will be generally recognized. The EC's economic legislation on antitrust, public procurement, subsidies, the environment, and other matters will have to be adopted by EFTA, but EFTA will not have decision-making power on new laws nor will it participate in rules enforcement. EFTA's role will involve consultation only. EFTA markets are often still small and dominated by a few firms, so the increased competition should yield dynamic efficiency gains.

Individual countries (18 of them) have to ratify the EEA agreement, a process that began in April 1992. Switzerland rejected it in a referendum in December 1992, which slowed down the process. When the ratifications are completed, the new union will control 46% of world trade. But the EEA is probably destined to have only a short life, because as already noted all the EFTA members except Iceland have either applied for or soon will apply for full EC membership. If that were granted, as it probably will be, then the late 1990s could see the complete disappearance of EFTA.

THE AUSTRALIA-NEW ZEALAND AGREEMENT (ANZCERTA)

A recent antipodal arrangement, the Australia-New Zealand Closer Economic Relations Trade Agreement (ANZCERTA), is important because of its comprehensiveness and its openness. Tariffs were completely eliminated in 1987, and all quota restrictions were removed in 1990. All subsidies on exports within the area have been abolished, as have antidumping rules. Technical, health, and safety standards are harmonized, and equal access has been given to government contracts. This is one of the few arrangements to liberalize its protection against outsiders at the same time that the internal barriers were being torn down. The chances of trade diversion are accordingly lessened. Intraregional exports as a percentage of the total exports of Australia and New Zealand rose from 5.7% in 1960 to 7.6% in 1990, admittedly still a very low figure.

The Australia-New Zealand agreement appears to be in part a response to fears that *1992* in the EC will cause further problems of access, to the U.S.-Canada Free Trade Agreement, and to the possibility that a Japanese trade area may be formed in the future. Several neighboring island-states may be included in ANZCERTA in the future.

THE U.S.-CANADA FREE TRADE AGREEMENT

Free trade between the United States and Canada is an old and contentious idea for economic integration. An agreement was actually reached in 1854, eliminating barriers against natural products. But the United States terminated it in 1866, partly out of pique against what it took to be too much British sympathy with the Confederate States in the Civil War, partly because high tariffs were politically back in fashion at that time. Another attempt to integrate was defeated in the U.S. Senate in 1874. In 1891 an election was lost in Canada by a government that supported free trade, and a replay took place in 1911 when the United States and Canada were set to sign a free trade agreement. (It was in itself not a treaty but an agreement to pass concurrent legislation allowing almost all goods free access to the other country.) The Canadians had dissolved parliament and were facing an election, with all signs favorable for the bill's passage.

But on the south side of the border, an overenthusiastic U.S. congressional leader suggested that the agreement would be the first step in annexing Canada. In a memorable campaign, Prime Minister Wilfrid Laurier's Liberal government was turned out of office; "no truck or trade with the Yankees" was the battle cry that carried the day for his opponents. the new government never passed the necessary legislation.

A later attempt by President Franklin D. Roosevelt and Canada's prime minister, Mackenzie King, foundered in the uncertainties of the Great Depression. The failure of these attempts diverted Canadian development policy back to a strategy of attracting American branch plant manufacturing through levying high tariffs. After the Second World War, Canada, like other developed nations, lowered its tariffs, but like Australia and New Zealand it cut them less than did the United States and Europe.[21]

■ *CLOSE CONNECTIONS ALREADY EXISTED BEFORE THE PACT*

Canada and the United States were already very closely linked when negotiations for the free trade agreement began. Even before the agreement, Canada sent more than three quarters of its merchandise exports to its southern neighbor, representing about 22.5% of Canadian GDP. On the U.S. side, imports from Canada in most years exceeded those from any other country. (Japan is always close, and in some years has held the first-place position.) Canada was the largest foreign supplier of natural gas to the United States, the second-largest of oil (Mexico is first), and a major source of electric power. Meanwhile about 70% of Canada's imports were from the United States, accounting for 21% of all U.S. exports, nearly twice as much as the number-two buyer of U.S. exports, Japan. Ontario alone imported more U.S. goods than did Germany, France, and Italy combined. Trade (exports plus imports) between Canada and the United States, at over $150 billion in 1988, was by far the largest bilateral trade in the world. U.S.-Japanese trade was in total under $120 billion. About three quarters of U.S. and Canadian trade (70% of U.S. exports to Canada and 80% of Canadian exports to the United States in 1988) already entered each other's markets duty free. For all that, Canada had rather high tariffs for a developed country, about double those of the United States, and a wide and growing range of nontariff barriers applied to imports into both countries.

The high level of already-existing trade meant that a U.S.-Canada FTA probably would not divert very much trade. Furthermore, the similar economic structure and high income levels of the two countries meant that intraindustrial trade should eventually expand significantly.[22] The signs were auspicious.

AGREEMENT REACHED IN 1987 Renewed negotiations for a free trade area between Canada and the United States began in 1986. Clearly the talks grew from doubts that the Uruguay Round of trade negotiations would ultimately be successful, and that a free trade arrangement would provide insurance against the development of exclusionary trading blocs abroad, such as the enlarged EC. After some cliff-hanging moments agreement came on October 3, 1987. In the previous month, the Canadians had walked out of the negotiations. They returned only on October 2, one day before the U.S. congressional grant of authority to negotiate a pact was to expire. Consensus was reached, melodramatically, at midnight the next day.[23] Formal signature by President Reagan and Prime Minister Mulroney came on January 2, 1988.

THE CANADIAN OPPOSITION   Emotions ran high in Canada. After Prime Minister Mulroney signed the treaty, the Canadian Senate in an unprecedented step blocked its ratification. That senate is not elected, and its honorific members, appointed by the prime minister whenever one of the 104 seats falls vacant, serve for life or until they retire. Never before had the senate refused its assent to a bill passed by parliament, but on U.S.-Canadian free trade, it did so. That led to a national election in November 1988, after a campaign that was focused principally on the trade issue.

The sources of the political opposition in Canada were varied. By region, the greatest aversion was in Ontario, which had the largest share of Canada's protected manufacturing. By political party, the Liberals (who might well have struck a similar agreement had they been in power) caved in to that party's nationalist left, now opposed free trade, and argued that any such development would be a U.S. victory. Other Canadian opposition to the agreement came from industries in which protection had traditionally been high, such as electronic goods, shoes, and publishing; most labor unions (often splitting from their employers); many intellectuals; and parts of the media including the *Toronto Star* and the Canadian Broadcasting Corporation.

The most-heard complaints among those who opposed the treaty were as follows: (1) Risk. Canada is almost as rich as the United States, so ran the argument. Why risk the dislocations that can accompany the small-country role in a free trade arrangement? (But then, as we have seen, the growth of protectionism is a risk, too, and the establishment of a free trade area served to avoid it.) (2) Canada gave up too much. The rules on dumping and subsidy were not strict enough; the guarantee on energy went too far. These are discussed below. (3) The treaty was a trap on cultural grounds. Canadian values would be altered unfavorably by the presence of giant American corporations and their increased advertising. Canada's liberal unemployment insurance, its public medical care programs, its special insurance arrangements, and much else would be jeopardized as illegal subsidies. (Unlikely, said most economists. These subsidies are "generally available," not easy to attack under the GATT rules, and not countervailable under current U.S. practice.) (4) Increased trade with the United States would aid the Americans in achieving some of their unworthy international aims, an argument representing an underlying current of anti-Americanism present in Canada since the War of 1812. (5) The Americans would abuse the agreement, which, considering the stance of U.S. law, jurisprudence, and administrative action, was a plausible argument.

The election was the most bitter in recent Canadian history. The Conservatives were victorious, but they garnered less than 50% of the popular vote, and their parliamentary majority fell from 63 seats to 21. That was sufficient to allow another parliamentary ratification, to persuade the senate to withdraw its objections, and to allow the agreement to go into effect as scheduled on January 1, 1989, but it was not nearly large enough to quiet the controversy. Many Canadians still believe that the best part of the U.S.-Canada FTA is that it can be easily abrogated—either country can withdraw from it by giving six months' notice.

PREDICTED GAINS TO CANADA FROM A FREE TRADE AGREEMENT For all the controversy, economists expected Canada to realize significant scale economies because the American market is ten times larger than the Canadian. The scale economies were expected to be proportionally greater for British Columbia, Alberta, Manitoba, and the Atlantic Provinces because the "Canadian customs union" up to the time of the FTA was a significant trade-diverter as far as these provinces were concerned. Canada also stood to benefit from the effects of greater competition. That country possesses an inefficient segment in its manufacturing. Firms often seek to satisfy broad market segments with a range of products beyond their ability to deliver efficiently, given the small size of the domestic Canadian market and its regional separation. They have done so because of the combination of import protection and restricted access to the large American market.

Some Canadian government studies have predicted large eventual efficiency gains sufficient to boost Canadian real GDP by 5% to 10%, though at the cost of substantial adjustments in the economy. Other studies are less optimistic, at least for the short term, predicting eventual GDP gains in the range of 2.5% to 3.5%. The difference in the results comes from two main causes. (1) A number of the studies take account of the productivity enhancement expected from increased competition, while others do not. (2) Some of them assume decreasing costs in industry, while others assume constant costs. Most scholars agree that the deadweight loss approach discussed in Chapter 4 yields quite small GDP gains of less than 1%. That the benefits are predicted to be much larger than this for Canada emphasizes that the gains from trade are openly understood to be not of the Ricardian, static variety but to increased dynamic efficiency. Even if the end result is not fully quantifiable, the gains from trade are likely to be impressive.

Another reason to expect rewards for Canada involves the small-country rule of Chapter 2. Recall that when trade is freed, one expects the prices in the trading partners to move furthest in the smallest country, which has less influence over the now-unified market. Thus the small country has the advantage of being able to trade at prices close to the large country's original prices, with the potential to glean the greater gains.

Finally, Canada was buying insurance. A growing wave of U.S. protectionism might eventually break over the Canadian economy, too, with damage that would be no less severe because it was unintended. Assertive congressional trade initiatives, or presidents less inclined toward free trade than Presidents Reagan and Bush, were both to be feared from the Canadian point of view. Squabbles over the definition of subsidies could be especially injurious because the regional development grants and cheap resource policies north of the border might eventually have called down the full force of U.S. countervailing duties. Given the transport situation, Canada's overseas trade alternatives looked to be a poor substitute. Even if the worst had *not* happened in their largest foreign market, Canadian firms would have faced difficulties in planning their long-term investment strategies when they were unable to predict what protective measure would be taken next along the frontier. From the Canadian point of view the time for an agreement seemed ripe. A progressive Conservative government was willing. Business interests seemed generally supportive, retaining their unhappy memory of 1973 when Britain joined the Common Market, leaving Canada on the outside. Tariffs were already much lower than in the past, so the necessary adjustments to free trade would not be wrenching. Finally, the expectation was that most of the growth in trade brought about by the agreement would be intraindustrial, so labor displacement would be even more limited.

PREDICTED GAINS TO THE UNITED STATES FROM A FREE TRADE AGREEMENT   For the United States, the advantages predicted were more limited—$1 billion to $3.5 billion, no greater than 1% of American GDP at the time—because the U.S. market was already more than adequate to promote economies of scale, and because it is the large country. Opposition in the United States was mostly concentrated among the lumber, fishing, and potato interests of Maine and the West Coast. These foes were overwhelmed in congress, which ratified the agreement by a wide margin during 1988.

CONTENT OF THE AGREEMENT   The 300-page agreement is for a free trade area, not a customs union. The different tariffs of the two countries stay in place against outsiders. The agreement was sweeping and its technical details were innovative. All tariffs are to be eliminated. Some went at once. Many others are being reduced by 20% of their original amount per year in each of the five years after the implementation of the agreement. Acceleration in these tariff reductions took place, with 400 tariffs eliminated faster than indicated by the original schedule. Finally, yet other tariffs—those on the most sensitive items, including steel, many agricultural commodities, processed fish, pleasure boats, textiles, and wood products—are falling by 10% of their original amount per year over 10 years. All tariffs are to be eliminated by 1998.[*] Virtually all quotas were elimi-

---

[*] Recall that tariffs are low already, but removal of even a 2% or 3% tariff may have a significant impact on *profits*. In any case, the tariff structure of both countries is such that effective protection is generally higher than nominal protection. For example, the United States has a 1.7% tariff on zinc ore but a 19% tariff on zinc alloy.

nated. To qualify for preferential treatment, it is agreed that goods must be of North American origin. Three ways are open to meet this test. First, a good can be wholly made in North America. Second, it can be sufficiently modified in the production process so that it becomes subject to a different tariff classification. Finally, as with autos, it qualifies if 50% of production costs are North American. Government contracts are open for bidding by nationals of both countries if they exceed a quite small figure of $25,000. The clauses freeing the trade in services are the most liberal in the world—there is little expectation that the Uruguay Round negotiations on services will transpire so well. Both governments promise not to impose restrictions on free trade in energy.

Canada promised to withdraw many transport subsidies, to scale back the postal subsidies that favor Canadian publishers, and to treat U.S. banks in the same way that Canadian banks are treated. The drastic *de facto* protection against American wines, kept out by limiting their sales in provincial liquor stores, was halted. Barriers against the import of used cars from the United States will eventually be dropped. The investment licensing threshold that required any U.S. investment of $5 million or more to undergo government scrutiny was raised by 30 times to $150 million.

Several exceptions are written into the agreement, some reasonable, some more than a trifle embarrassing. Transport, telecommunications, legal and medical services, and child care are excluded wholly or in part. Escape clause (safeguard) rules mostly remain intact. Free trade does not apply to Canadian fresh fish and poultry, beer, and logs produced in both countries. The Jones Act restricting shipping between American ports to U.S.-flag ships remains in force; so do the restrictive rules on trucking. The notorious U.S. sugar quota still applies. Most of these exceptions were the result of bargaining: If you keep the Jones Act, we won't let your trucks pick up and deliver in Canada. All these matters are treated outside the FTA, with several disputes having gone to GATT.

Much labor went into the construction of the mechanisms for settling disputes under the FTA. Disputes are taken up by a Canada-U.S. Trade Commission, which oversees the operation of the agreement and attempts to resolve problems. If the Commission cannot agree, controversies are submitted to binding arbitration by five-member dispute settlement panels, with two members chosen by each country and a fifth by the Commission or by the other four arbitrators. Though economists are generally uncertain as to how this binational tribunal and its attached arbitration panel will work out in the long term—only two of them had been called as of 1992, both on seafood—they consider that their very establishment was a major step for the United States to take.

An obvious loose end was the inability of the negotiators to settle the question of what antidumping and antisubsidy rules will apply. It proved impossible to come up with a satisfactory definition of a subsidy. Canada was adamant in not wanting to give up its long-standing regional development policies and its social assistance programs, while the United States was equally unwilling to ignore these. To obtain an agreement, it was necessary to finesse these questions, and separate negotiations still have to be carried out on these prickly issues.

Nonbinding arbitration panels attempt to resolve dumping and subsidy disputes. The dumping and subsidies dispute settlement process led to 28 cases, 18 of which were resolved unanimously or nearly so, in the first three years of the agreement.[24] Most of them concerned agricultural issues. Once an opinion has been issued, it is possible to appeal to an extraordinary challenge committee for a quasi-judicial decision. Each country appoints one judge, and these two select a third. An extraordinary challenge was made for the first time by the United States in the case of the striking down of a U.S. countervailing duty on pork. Canada said its exports were only 3% of the market, and could not harm U.S. producers. The United States lost and had to refund the duty collected on fresh pork imports since May 1989. For the time being the mechanism seems to have worked as planned.

THE ECONOMIC RESULTS OF THE U.S.-CANADA FTA   Not enough time has passed to make a judgment—recall that the reductions in trade barriers are being phased in—but some first results may be commented upon. A healthy increase in bilateral trade of 14% took place during the first three years of the agreement. Intraregional exports as a percentage of the total exports of the United States and Canada rose from 26.5% in 1960 to 34.0% in 1990. The rise in Canadian exports of manufactured goods to the United States was pronounced. On the U.S. side of the border, several cities, especially Buffalo, New York, were experiencing a new prosperity from the additional commercial activity.

Scholars believe that even before it was signed, the FTA had *already* had an effect on international corporate mergers and acquisition activity in Canada. A sharp increase occurred just before the FTA was signed, from $29 billion in 1986 to $68 billion in 1988. This is much greater than can be explained in the absence of the expected FTA.[25] Much adjustment had already taken place in anticipation of lower barriers to come. Some plants or firms with broad product lines and production on both sides of the border have been rationalized, with output concentrated at one spot instead of two or more. That has meant the shutdown of some plants, but it has also meant higher productivity and exports from those that remain open. A spurt of plant closings that coincided with the highest rates for the Canadian dollar, especially in Ontario, has now slowed.

The impact of free trade has actually been swamped by the effects of simultaneous recessions in the United States and Canada. The macroeconomic situation in Canada was a contributor to the slump, with tight money raising Canadian interest rates to real levels considerably above those of the United States, thus sharply increasing the value of the Canadian dollar for a considerable period. That exacerbated the Canadian recession and temporarily blunted the new incentives to export. Canadian unemployment in 1991–1993 was quite high, in the 10–11% range compared to about 8% at the time the agreement was signed. High interest rates, the appreciated Canadian dollar, and the contemporary economic slowdown in the United States probably had the main responsibility for the poor performance, and it is extremely difficult to isolate the effect of the FTA from those more powerful elements.

Yet Canadian opposition to the FTA is still vociferous. Job losses in any industry and at any location receive the closest scrutiny and, often enough, the FTA receives the blame even if the United States is losing jobs in the same industries. Public opinion polls currently report half to three quarters of the Canadian public opposed to the FTA, compared to under 10% opposed in the United States. When Prime Minister Mulroney resigned in February 1993, it was clear that, however unjustly, the FTA was part of his problem.

It seems fair to suggest that anything less than excellent Canadian economic performance will keep the Canadian opponents fully mobilized. Though there has been no investment boom in plant and equipment in Canada (as some had hoped), and though significant overall economic benefits do not seem obvious at present, your authors remain optimistic that Canada will gain in the long run.

A NORTH AMERICAN FREE TRADE AGREEMENT (NAFTA)

The movement to enlarge U.S.-Canada free trade to include Mexico in a North American Free Trade Agreement, or NAFTA, has been a remarkable development.[26] A NAFTA would create the world's largest single market in terms of population, comprising over 360 million people.

THE U.S. VIEW   Ronald Reagan supported North American free trade early in the 1980s, George Bush backed the plan since his run for president in 1988, and for the most part President Clinton has supported it as well. Although there would be relatively large consequences in the states of the Southwest, the overall effect on the U.S. economy (and Canada as well) would be limited.[27] Tariffs are already low and the Mexican economy is small. A NAFTA should stimulate Mexican income growth, which would result in a high multiplier effect on American exports. The Mexican marginal propensity to consume American goods is about .15, meaning that a $1 increase in Mexican income increases U.S. exports to Mexico by about 15¢. The overall effect according to a recent study by Hufbauer and Schott would be a swing of the U.S. trade balance further into surplus with Mexico, by about $7 billion per year.[28] Furthermore, growing Mexican prosperity would cause immigration to the United States to diminish, with estimates of the decline at about 200,000 people per year from the present million or so. (President Salinas called for a concurrent agreement on immigration to go along with the one on trade, which caused some negotiating difficulties.)

In the United States, the main opponents are U.S. labor unions (including the AFL-CIO), a significant portion of the Democratic party, Ross Perot, and conservatives led by Patrick Buchanan. The basis for the opposition in the United States is mostly connected with the existence of protected labor-intensive industries. These, understandably from their point of view, fear that U.S. firms will move to Mexico in search of the longer working hours (a six-day week is allowed), the less strict health and safety standards, and especially the low wages. In Mexican industry, labor costs averaging $2.17 per hour are far below the $15.45 average in the United States (1991 figures), and also well below the wages of the major Asian exporters such as South Korea, Taiwan, and Hong Kong. (The U.S. Free Trade agreement with Canada is not feared for this reason—labor costs in Canada are much the same as in the United States.) Job losses would be greatest in lower-tech segments of steel, textiles, and agriculture.

Debate has been fierce on the issue, with supporters pointing out that the low-wage U.S. jobs will be lost anyway, mostly to Asia if not to Mexico, and that perhaps twice as many U.S. jobs would be created from new exports (mainly of higher-tech products) than would be lost to new imports. Supporters also point to the favorable outcome in similar situations abroad: For example, in the enlarged EC, Germany and Portugal remain happy members of the union even though the wage gap is very large.[29] Undoubtedly, however, low-skill, low-paid U.S. labor would suffer somewhat, raising the need for trade adjustment assistance and better training overall.

Opponents in the United States also emphasize other negative aspects. Child labor, though against the law, is common in Mexico. Environmentalists decry Mexico's lower level of regulation, and it is quite true that enforcement is weaker in that country. The low standards of regulation will, it is said, cause U.S. factories to move to Mexico. These environmental questions have attracted substantial attention; the issue is explored further in the accompanying box. The opposition to the NAFTA can take comfort in the abrogation rules, which are the same as in the U.S.-Canada FTA: Countries can withdraw on only six months' notice.

■ ENVIRONMENTAL QUESTIONS IN THE NAFTA

Mexico has declared that it has no intention to become a dumping ground for pollutants. Its 1988 law has standards similar to those of the United States, and though enforcement is lax it has improved since 1990. Higher Mexican income will make it possible to enforce tougher laws. The danger with this "clean up later" approach, of course, is that the situation might get worse before it gets better, with deleterious effects on those who live north of the border. Bilateral negotiations on pollution control seem clearly called for; probably physical targets need to be set. Some environmentalists argue that NAFTA will give Mexico the right to challenge the strict U.S. regulations. While true, any challenge must be based on an absence of scientific evidence justifying a trade barrier. The draft does in fact allow countries to enact stricter standards if they are scientifically based, and states may do so as well. The burden of proof is on the challenger when a claim is made that a standard is not scientifically based. Process standards not reflected in the good itself (destruction of a wetland by filling, use of DDT, particulate emissions) are not addressed. Some of this would have entirely local consequences and can safely be left to Mexico, but some may have cross-border or global effects. Hence President Clinton's call for an environmental commission to be included in the NAFTA.

A recent NBER study is optimistic. It finds that a NAFTA would probably cause Mexico to produce less chemicals, rubber, and plastics, all "dirty" items, because that country does not have a comparative advantage in these products. Taking their place would be more agricultural production and labor-intensive manufacturing, both relatively cleaner. Some of the improvement would be offset by much larger production of electrical equipment in Mexico, which is dirty, but the net effect according to the NBER study would be a (rather small) decline in toxic emissions. The study suggests that the movement of some U.S. firms to Mexico, underway for some years now, has not included industries that are especially polluting. It identifies the causation as mainly associated with lower costs for unskilled labor. The authors note that pollution abatement costs for the average U.S. manufacturing firm are 1.4% of value added, far less than the difference made by lower labor costs for labor-intensive industries.[30]

A rather weak joint plan to clean up border areas was announced in 1992. It involves $800 million over 3 years, mostly for water cleanup.

THE MEXICAN VIEW In Mexico, there has been a striking turnabout in opinion toward a NAFTA. The idea would once have been unthinkable. Mexico was an intellectual center of so-called dependency theory—the belief that trade is an inadequate means to development, or even counterproductive—and politics reflected that fact. Free trade would make Mexico a "backwash" area, so it was argued, with little chance to break away from primary product exports, raw materials processing, and labor-intensive manufacturing. This belief lay behind numerous laws relating to domestic content. One such is the 1977 auto decree that allocates foreign exchange to firms according to the percentage of Mexican materials contained in the final product. Because of local content measures of this type, an extensive structure of subsidies paid to producers, many quotas, controls over capital movements, and other deviations from GATT, Mexico did not even join that organization until 1986. Even as late as 1987, former President de la Madrid stated that free trade with the United States was not a possibility. According to the conventional wisdom, the practical problems involved in dismantling Mexico's restrictive trade policies would mean at the least several years of negotiations and implementation that Mexican membership in a NAFTA would require.

The conventional wisdom was wrong. President Salinas threw strong support to the NAFTA and backed the support with major efforts to reform Mexican trade law. The change of mind certainly seems plausible. As a buyer of U.S. exports, Mexico ranks as the third most important, behind only Canada and Japan. As a provider of U.S. imports, Mexico is in fifth place. About 60% of Mexico's imports are from the United States; just under that figure (58%) of Mexican exports travel the opposite route. A NAFTA would act as a guarantee to Mexico that it would not be shut out of the large American market by some future rising tide of protectionism. Mexico would also stand to gain most from an arrangement because of the small-country rule. Roughly four times more jobs would be created there than in the United States, according to the recent study by Hufbauer and Schott.[31]

THE CANADIAN VIEW   Mexican-Canadian trade is small, only 5% of that between Mexico and the United States. Less than 0.5% of Canada's total exports go to Mexico compared to over 75% going to the United States, and any economic gains to Canada would be small, which explains the rather lukewarm Canadian reception to NAFTA. (Some Canadians fear that the auto plants currently located in that country may move south to Mexico if complete free trade is adopted.) From a political point of view the major advantage to Canadian membership may be the insurance that it will be a participant in rule making, such as determining what rules of origin will apply, and perhaps enlisting Mexico's help to reduce the unpredictability of U.S. trade law. Problems with Canadian membership include unwillingness to eliminate agricultural import quotas, unsureness about auto and textile rules, and unhappiness about opening up the Canadian film, book, and TV industries that have protected status under the U.S.-Canada FTA.

THE AGREEMENT DELAYED   Adoption of the NAFTA, which had seemed imminent, was delayed at the time of writing. The negotiators reached agreement in August 1992, and President Bush signed it in the following December. But President Clinton called for revisions on the environment, on job losses, and on import surges. When the NAFTA is submitted to congress, ratification will involve the same 90-day fast-track procedure as the GATT Uruguay Round negotiations.

   In the draft agreement so far, tariffs with Mexico will be phased out over 15 years, though about 50% will go at once. The period allowed is much longer than permitted in the U.S.-Canada FTA, where the final phaseout will occur on January 1, 1998. Major advances include a dispute settlement procedure and provision for panels in dumping and subsidy cases much like that of the U.S.-Canada agreement, the dropping of many Mexican restrictions on foreign delivery of services, and the elimination by the United States of its 25–35% tariffs on fresh fruits and vegetables. Rules of origin remain controversial. The domestic content (made in North America) rule for cars is 62.5%, superseding the lower 50% in the U.S.-Canada FTA. In textiles the rule of origin is more byzantine: The clothing must be sewed in North America from fabric made in North America from yarn made in North America.[32] Such rules will probably lead to trade diversion. There will be a sensitive list of products for which the elimination of barriers will be slower than for the rest. Textiles, glassware, citrus fruits, sugar, watches, footwear, luggage, and some steel and electronic products are on the U.S. list. There are agricultural safeguards permitting barriers to be reerected if imports reach some trigger level. Mexico will keep its state monopoly on exploration for oil.

   Unanswered as yet are whether barriers against outsiders will rise, and whether the United States will be willing to abide by the GATT rules in all aspects of NAFTA. Clearly, the agreement could be a model for future cases of wider economic integration, or it could be an excuse for other regional arrangements to raise their barriers as well.

■ *THE* MAQUILADORA *PROGRAM*

One area of progress toward U.S.-Mexican free trade already exists. Mexico from small beginnings in 1965 has made a major effort to establish a zone with special trade rules along the U.S. border.[33] The initial idea sprang from an attempt to do something about the high unemployment in border areas following the end of seasonal farm work. Originally a strip 12 miles deep was designated all along the border from Mexicali in Baja California to Matamoros opposite Brownsville, Texas. Later (from 1972) it became possible to obtain the same status in the interior, where labor is even cheaper. The inland activity subject to the special rules is only about one fifth what it is along the border, however. Under the scheme, Mexico's laws restricting foreigners to minority holdings do not apply, and the ownership of firms can be entirely expatriate. Duty-free access is permitted for imported raw materials and semifinished goods, as well as for the plants' equipment. Fifty percent of output must be exported, while the remaining 50% can be sold in Mexico.

Largely due to the substantial wage differential and the ability to import cheap American components duty free, business has boomed in the assembly plants. *Maquiladoras* they are named, from the toll that millers collected in Spanish colonial days for processing someone else's grain. About 2000 *maquilas*, as they are known for short, were operating on the Mexican side in 1991, up from virtually none in 1979. About 90% are U.S. owned. They employ half a million people, mostly women before 1982 in garments and electronics, now increasingly men (doubling to about 35% of the total in 1982–1988) in woodworking, plastics, and especially autos and auto parts, with GM now Mexico's largest single employer. The most important centers are Ciudad Juarez, Tijuana, and Nogales. The *maquilas* became Mexico's second-largest earner of foreign exchange in 1986, ranking behind only oil, and responsible for over 10% of the country's exports. They supplied 44% of Mexico's exports to the United States in 1987, compared to just 29% two years earlier.

Mexican criticism of the *maquiladoras* has been intense, even bitter. It is said that their simple assembly tasks and the preponderance of women in the workforce are clues to their low impact on the economy; that they purchase very few other inputs locally; that they pay low taxes and are footloose industries that would quickly move elsewhere if wages rose; and that they represent closer control of the Mexican economy by the *gringos* to the north. All the charges are true to some degree. Yet the *maquilas* pay wages 30% to 50% higher than in other Mexican industry, and their unwillingness to purchase local inputs is partly due to quality problems that will in time be solved.

The *maquiladoras* have their detractors in the United States. Just as unions and other opponents argue that a full free trade agreement with Mexico would take U.S. jobs, that health and safety regulations for labor would be avoided, and that the labor works long hours for low pay, they make the same arguments against the *maquilas*. All these charges are no doubt true, and the large depreciation of the peso since 1982 has been a major factor in persuading runaway American firms to move across the border, whence they export their products back to the United States. United States trade unions charge that about 300,000 jobs have been lost to the *maquiladoras*. Union objections have grown with the

> realization that the Japanese and Koreans are now investing in the border plants. Moves are afoot in congress to suspend the duty-free treatment of imports from the *maquilas.* Yet the pessimism is largely unwarranted. Rising Mexican income increases imports to that country and hence U.S. exports. A "number of important and rigorous studies" show that *maquiladoras* increase employment in the United States.[34]

ECONOMIC INTEGRATION WITH A RICH PATRON

Mexico is poor and the United States and Canada are rich. If and when a free trade area is forged among them, it would be another in a new trend toward economic integration between less developed countries (LDCs) and developed countries. Such action has a certain "colonial" pattern, as it usually ties the trade of the LDC partner tightly to the metropolitan economy of the "patron." Counting the aid, technical help, and defense umbrella that may accompany the deal, it can still be worth doing from the poor country's point of view. The oldest of these preferences are those advanced by the EC to the former colonies of its members, the African-Caribbean-Pacific (ACP) states. Lower tariffs and guaranteed access outside quota barriers and VERs are commonly granted to this group. (But the preferences to the ACP countries have had only limited benefits.[35] The margins are slim, trade diversion has predominated, monopsonistic European buyers have captured some of the preferences, and the poorest ACP states have not been flexible enough to take advantage of the arrangement.) The EC has many other regional agreements, with North African, Mediterranean, Middle Eastern, and Eastern European countries that involve bilateral preferences and not so much aid as the EC provides the ACP states.[36] For example, the EC's agreements with the former Communist countries of Eastern Europe are generally 10-year pacts to establish eventual free trade, but with major exceptions for textiles, agriculture, steel, and other sensitive products.

ENTERPRISE FOR THE AMERICAS   *Enterprise for the Americas* embodies the idea that NAFTA be extended to hemisphere size. Suggested by President Bush in 1990, this vast proposal for a free trade area has received considerable support from Latin America's political leaders. (Twenty years ago the idea would have been vilified by that region's leaders as Yankee imperialism.) Free trade agreements are expected to be negotiated bilaterally or multilaterally within a few years. Thirty-one agreements to talk about it were in effect in 1992, at which time only Cuba, Haiti, and Suriname were excluded.[37] The United States intends to negotiate a free trade agreement with Chile after NAFTA is completed. Because only about 13% of U.S. trade is currently with Latin America, there is presumably some significant chance of trade diversion.

THE CBERA   The United States already has three rich-poor arrangements, one with the Caribbean, one with Bolivia and Colombia, and one with Israel. A

Caribbean Basin Economic Recovery Act (CBERA) took effect January 1, 1984. The name *Caribbean Basin Initiative* (CBI) is also used. Originally subject to a time limit, it was renewed permanently in 1990.[38] The long time frame was thought to be important for planning investments. CBERA was the first U.S. preferential treatment for an entire geographical area. Its details are explored in the accompanying box. Canada has a similar arrangement with the Caribbean called *Caribcan.*

■ *CBERA DETAILS*

All Caribbean territories are included except Cuba and Suriname, which have not qualified for political reasons, and Anguilla, the Cayman Islands, and the Turks and Caicos islands, which have had tax disagreements with the United States. To acquire duty-free status, an article must be imported directly to the United States from a CBERA territory. Thirty-five percent of the import's appraised value has to be value added in one or more of the beneficiary countries. The duty-free treatment can be suspended entirely (a clause that was applied to Panama during the Noriega troubles and Nicaragua during Sandinista rule), or tariffs lower than MFN tariffs can be imposed under escape clause legislation.

All U.S. import quotas remain in force, including those on textiles and clothing, peanuts, cotton, and sugar, all of which could be important to the CBERA countries and all of which were discussed in Chapter 4. Sugar is especially important for some island countries, and any gains from the CBERA have to be weighed against the decline in their cane sugar production to a level only half the 1.5 million tons of 15 years ago. Furthermore, U.S. antidumping and countervailing duty legislation continues to apply, petroleum and petroleum products do not qualify for preferential treatment, and there is a clause carrying extra safeguards for perishable agricultural commodities.

The result of all the exclusions (nearly half of all U.S. imports by value from the CBERA countries are not eligible for duty-free treatment) is that the impact of the CBERA has been strictly limited. While not denying that eventual dynamic effects might develop, it is quite clear that the CBERA had been gutted by U.S. protectionist interests. The elimination of many tariffs does not compensate for the retention of quotas on the most important items.

THE ANDEAN TRADE PREFERENCE ACT (ATPA)   An *Andean Trade Preference Act* (ATPA) was passed by the U.S. Congress in 1992. It establishes a duty-free arrangement resembling the CBERA for Bolivia and Colombia. Congress also made Ecuador and Peru eligible for ATPA preferences, though the latter two have not yet been included. Much the same exclusions (quotas on textiles, clothing, sugar, and the like) and rules of origin apply as they do to the CBERA countries. ATPA is designed to compensate for the impact of the war on drugs on coca exports. The act will expire in 10 years, unlike CBERA, which is permanent.

THE U.S.-ISRAEL FREE TRADE AGREEMENT   The remaining U.S. preference agreement took effect in March 1985, when the United States and Israel agreed to eliminate all tariffs against one another in four stages over a ten-year period culminating in 1995.[39] The customs union with Israel might appear not very important on the world stage, but it was the first U.S. bilateral arrangement, and it removed virtually all tariff and nontariff barriers. (Escape clause safeguards, antidumping laws, the regulations against subsidies, and textile protection still apply.) The new union would appear to pose some threat of trade diversion for Israel, with more expensive U.S. exports substituting to some extent for what Israel could buy at cheaper world market prices. From the Israeli point of view, however, that problem is no doubt completely overshadowed by the further evidence of a strong political and economic alliance with the United States. Any costs of diversion are well offset by benefits in other forms, including aid and military support.

THE "COLONIAL" PATTERN OF THESE AGREEMENTS   All these agreements reveal an increasing tendency for rich patrons to cement their poor clients into trading blocs, all discriminating against one another, and with the client states becoming wedded to their privileges. There is some irony in the United States joining in that game, because intransigent opposition to the very similar imperial preferences of the British and French colonial days was a hallmark of U.S. foreign policy for three quarters of a century.[40] No single patron-client arrangement may have the capacity to do very much harm, but together, by making trade discrimination commonplace, they could harm world welfare. The ominous possibility of trade diversion is ever present. At the very least, the growing need to administer different trade laws applying to different countries will mean a more bloated bureaucracy than before and increased frictions over trade issues.

It should be noted that the U.S. agreements with the Caribbean countries and the EC arrangements with its former colonies are one-way. That is, the less developed countries involved did not have to extend reciprocal tariff cuts to the patrons, the United States and the EC. Thus there is a considerable chance for trade diversion in the poor countries.[41] The later arrangements (the United States and Canada with Mexico in NAFTA, the U.S.-sponsored Enterprise for the Americas, the EC with countries such as the Czech Republic, Slovakia, Hungary, and Poland that were not former colonies) all involve *reciprocal* preferences.

DANGERS OF REGIONAL INTEGRATION

Obviously the United States has embraced the regional integration of North and South America, and the recent moves to enlarge the EC indicate the same is true of Europe (and Africa, which is linked because of the old colonial ties). Further unions among major trading partners are being much discussed. Japan's MITI, for example, has commissioned a feasibility study of a possible U.S.-Japan Free Trade Area. If this regionalization continues for much longer, Japan would clearly envisage an Asian union, a "yen bloc" that might possibly include the East Asian countries and perhaps Australia and New Zealand as well. Taken together, all of this could represent a long step away from multilateral trade.

The danger inherent in the growth of regional integration arrangements is that substantial trade diversion is possible or even likely.[42] Much depends on whether the regional integration is accompanied by continued multilateral reductions in trade barriers against outsiders or whether it is not. Large and hostile regional free trade blocs peering at one another over forbidding external barriers hardly seems optimal. Trade wars are worse when the many rather than the few are involved, and the dangers would seem intensified in a three-bloc world. Furthermore, severe difficulties might face the small countries left out of a regional arrangement. This latter problem does have a solution: automatic entry for countries that want to join. But under U.S. law "only self-contained FTAs may qualify for 'fast-track' implementing provisions."[43]

THE DEBATE ON LARGE BLOCS   Recently a debate has sprung up on the issue of large trading blocs. It is generally agreed that trading blocs are less trade diverting if they are small, and also that there will be no diversion if one bloc grows so large as to encompass the entire world. Following this logic, a small number of very large blocs might cause the greatest amount of trade diversion. Two or three large blocs focused around Europe, the United States, and Japan—quite likely if the Uruguay Round were to collapse—might be the worst case.[44] Paul Krugman downplays the problem, arguing that arrangements among neighboring countries will usually be less trade diverting, because the natural protection of transport costs causes such countries to trade more with one another. "Natural zones" are less trade diverting because so much trade goes on among the neighbors anyway. In this reading, "unnatural" free trade areas (for example, the existing U.S.-Israel FTA and a possible U.S.-Korea arrangement) would be more likely to cause trade diversion.[45]

C. Fred Bergsten's view of the Krugman position is cautious. The effect of geographical propinquity has been diminished by reductions in transport and distribution costs, he notes. A great deal of trade is *not* among neighbors; trade diversion is the *goal* of numerous arrangements.[46] Many neighbors (in Africa, South Asia, and Latin America) trade little with one another in any case. It can be added that trade bargaining may become much harder when it is between large blocs. The countries within the blocs may have had a difficult time in coming to an internal decision among themselves, with so many carefully balanced compromises that there is little scope to change the position in negotiations with another bloc. A prime example is the agricultural policy of the EC. The internal negotiations leading to that policy have been so hard fought that there is virtually no room for give and take with foreigners—the arduous task of reaching an internal consensus would have to be done all over again. All these considerations point to multilateral free trade as much the best policy.

Admittedly, some of the talk on regional preferential arrangements probably contains an element of bluffing in order to propel forward the GATT negotiations. Yet no one can be sure whether the large regional blocs would be "halfway houses to global free trade or the battlements from which future trade wars will be fought."[47]

REGIONAL TRADE ARRANGEMENTS IN THE LDCs

Fifteen examples of economic integration including 70 countries existed in 1989 among the less developed countries, with more of them in Africa and Latin America than elsewhere.[48] Table 9.5 gives details of these south-south arrangements, both past and present ones.

Table 9.5   **Regional trade arrangements among less developed countries**

Key to the table

Short name (full name), year founded	Intraunion trade as % of total	
Members	(where available)	
Comments	1960	1990

AFRICA

East African Community, 1967

Kenya, Tanzania, Uganda

Defunct. At its inception perhaps the most widely discussed of all the efforts to form an economic arrangement outside of Europe. But intractable disputes arose, the Community disintegrated, and borders were closed.

CEEAC (Communauté Economique des Etats de l'Afrique Centrale), 1981

Burundi, Cameroon, Central African Republic, Chad, Congo, Equatorial Guinea, Gabon, Rwanda, São Tomé and Principe, Zaire

Name means Economic Community of Central African States. Little success.

CEAO (Communauté Economique de l'Afrique de l'Ouest), 1974

Benin, Burkina Faso, Côte d'Ivoire, Mali, Mauritania, Niger, Senegal

Name means Western African Economic Community. Reasonably good performance. A cut in nontariff barriers and an expansion of intraunion trade to 10% have taken place.

CEPGL (Communauté Economique Pays des Grands Lacs)	1.0%*	0.2%**

Burundi, Rwanda, Zaire

Name means Economic Community of the Great Lakes States. Has not yet been able to lower barriers.

ECOWAS (Economic Community of West African States), 1976	1.2%	5.5%

Benin, Burkina Faso, Cape Verde, Côte d'Ivoire, Gambia, Ghana, Guinea, Guinea-Bissau, Liberia, Mali, Mauritania, Niger, Nigeria, Senegal, Sierra Leone, Togo

Was scheduled to abolish all tariffs in 1989, but "progress negligible" and "virtual paralysis in the mutual reduction of trade barriers."[†] Very strict rules of origin are a hindrance. Problems have arisen because the former French colonies in ECOWAS (see the CEAO above) use the strictly managed CFA franc while other members (Ghana, Nigeria, Sierra Leone) have had much looser money management and rapid inflation.

(continued)

Table 9.5   **(continued)**

Also, the CEAO has trade rules not always compatible with those of ECOWAS. The influence of Nigeria grates on the smaller members.

MRU (Mano River Union), 1973	0.2%[*]	0.3%

Guinea, Liberia, Sierra Leone

The Mano River touches all three of these West African countries. Rendered ineffective by 1990s civil war in Liberia and 1992 coup in Sierra Leone.

PTA (Preferential Trading Arrangement), 1984	8.4%	8.5%

Burundi, Comoros, Djibouti, Ethiopia, Kenya, Lesotho, Malawi, Mauritius, Mozambique, Rwanda, Somalia, Swaziland, Tanzania, Uganda, Zambia, Zimbabwe

Full name is Preferential Trading Arrangement for Eastern and Southern African States. Aiming to eliminate tariffs and reduce NTBs by 2000. "Some progress in reducing tariffs."

SADCC (Southern African Development Coordination Council), 1980	2.4%	3.9%

Angola, Botswana, Lesotho, Malawi, Mozambique, Swaziland, Tanzania, Zaire, Zimbabwe

More concerned with growth projects than with reductions in trade barriers. Squabbles over its domestic content rules.

UDEAC (Union Douanière et Economique de l'Afrique Centrale), 1966	5.0%[*]	4.6%

Cameroon, Central African Republic, Chad, Congo, Equatorial Guinea, Gabon

Name means Central African Customs and Economic Union. One of the oldest of the world's attempts, small, still not properly organized. "Almost complete nonimplementation."

Lagos Plan of Action, 1980

All African countries

A move to construct a framework to facilitate an eventual African common market. No progress to report.

ASIA

ASEAN (Association of Southeast Asian Nations), 1967	20.7%[*]	18.6%

Brunei, Indonesia, Malaysia, the Philippines, Singapore, Thailand

Move to an Asian Free Trade Area (AFTA) within ASEAN agreed on only in 1993, to take 15 years. NTBs—of which there are many—are not addressed. Now only some 20% of intraregional trade is at preferential rates. Indonesia has high tariffs while Singapore's are virtually zero. Strict rules of origin to qualify for preferences (50% of a given product's value added must be local) limit the benefits yet further. ASEAN's attempts to establish joint ventures are proceeding very slowly, partly due to the

(continued)

Table 9.5   **(continued)**

---

opposition of Singapore, which does not approve of protection. Indonesia and the Philippines, the poorest members, are the least inclined to move rapidly. Brunei joined in 1984. 1991 announcement that Burma (Myanmar), Cambodia, Laos, and Vietnam would eventually be allowed to join.

LATIN AMERICA AND CARIBBEAN

CARICOM (Caribbean Community), 1973	4.5%	6.3%***

Antigua and Barbuda, Bahamas, Barbados, Belize, Dominica, Grenada, Guyana, Jamaica, Montserrat, St. Kitts-Nevis, St. Lucia, St. Vincent and the Grenadines, Trinidad and Tobago

An earlier West Indian Federation fell apart due to internal dissension. Many deadlines missed, FTA in effect 1991, common external tariff not yet adopted.

CACM (Central American Common Market), 1960	7.0%	14.8%

Costa Rica, El Salvador, Guatemala, Honduras, Nicaragua

Included allocation of industries. Rousing start, with about 95% of items traded having duty-free status by 1969 and intraunion trade reaching 26% of all trade. Trade diversion is believed to have outweighed trade creation, however, and considerable oligopolistic behavior instead of specialization and scale economies.[49] William R. Cline believes that nevertheless, other static and dynamic gains were sufficient to bring a net benefit— perhaps 3% of GDP for the CACM as a whole—in spite of the trade diversion.[50] The 1969 Soccer War between El Salvador and Honduras caused temporary breakup. Honduras withdrew in 1970, stopped trade with El Salvador, and reestablished duties with the rest. Costa Rica was expelled in 1972.[51] Revived from 1986, aiming first for a 20% ceiling on its (quite high) tariffs, free trade by the end of 1992, and a customs union by 1994. In 1991 the countries negotiated bilateral free trade accords with Mexico to be in place by 1996. Venezuela and CACM signed an agreement in 1991 for a free trade area by 1996. El Salvador and Guatemala now have bilateral free trade. Panama is now part of the talks.

LAFTA (Latin American Free Trade Area), 1961		

Argentina, Brazil, Bolivia, Chile, Colombia, Ecuador, Mexico, Paraguay, Peru, Uruguay, and Venezuela

Expired 1980. Tried but failed to eliminate tariffs in 10 years and to allocate industries among member countries. Some studies indicate significant trade diversion.[52]

LAIA (Latin American Integration Association), 1980	7.9%	10.6%

Same as LAFTA

Less-ambitious successor to LAFTA. Internal duties not yet eliminated. No common external tariff yet, though Argentina, Brazil, and Mexico have removed tariffs on many imports from other members. Relatively successful.

Andean Group, 1969	0.7%	4.6%

Bolivia, Ecuador, Colombia, Peru, Venezuela

Formed partly to escape from Brazil's influence. "Many postponements." Chile withdrew in 1976, and Peru temporarily in 1992. FTA in 1992 but only for Bolivia,

(continued)

Table 9.5 (continued)

Colombia, and Ecuador. Others supposed to join in 1993. A customs union is planned in 1994 and a common market in 1995. 75% of interregional trade is now duty free. Large static gains have been claimed, although some authorities state that these gains are exaggerated.[53]

Mercosur, 1991

Argentina, Brazil, Paraguay, Uruguay

Mercosul in Portuguese. Common market planned from January 1, 1995, with a low common external tariff of 5%, free movement of services, capital, and labor. Hindered by extreme differences in rates of inflation and in economic policy as well. Brazil and Argentina continue to exclude hundreds of items on which tariffs still exist.

Miscellaneous

Mexico, Colombia, and Venezuela plan to establish a free trade area in 1994. A Chile-Mexico FTA went into effect in 1991, and a Venezuela-Chile agreement in 1993 (to eliminate almost all tariffs by 1997). All may join with the United States in a FTA.

MIDDLE EAST

GCC (Gulf Cooperation Council), 1981	3.0%[*]	4.4%

Bahrain, Kuwait, Oman, Qatar, Saudi Arabia, United Arab Emirates

Tariffs abolished 1983. Common external tariff is now scheduled for 1993. Little accomplished because trade among the members is small.

Miscellaneous

Plans for an Arab Common Market and a Mahgreb (North African) Customs Union exist, but little progress has been made.

Source: De la Torre and Kelly, Regional Trade Arrangements, *pp. 20, 26–27, 30, 32; Fieleke, "One trading world, or many," pp. 4–5; David Greenaway and Chris Milner, "South-south trade: Theory, evidence, and policy,"* World Bank Research Observer, *Vol. 5, No. 1, January 1990, pp. 47–68; and* World Bank, *World Development Report 1991, p. 107. Some information is from "Market-integration and market-sharing schemes," in B.P. Menon,* Bridges Across the South, *New York, 1980, pp. 106–111, and Vaitsos, "Crisis in regional economic cooperation." The comments in quotes are from de la Torre and Kelly, pp. 26–27, except [†] which is from Fieleke, p. 9. The 1960 data are for the membership before the formation of the arrangement. [*]1970 figure. [**]1983 figure. [***]1987 figure.*

WHY ARRANGEMENTS AMONG THE LDCs USUALLY DO NOT PERFORM WELL

The major problem with most attempts at economic integration is that aside from the EC, EFTA, NAFTA, and ANZCERTA they have usually been pursued among less developed countries. That creates difficulties. Arrangements tend to be weakest when the level of industrialization is low, for then new industries do not spring up easily and when they do they are high in cost. The chances for trade diversion and monopoly creation are then increased. Frequently, regional arrangements among LDCs have quite high external barriers against outsiders, which increases these chances. Especially in Africa, "negligible trade creation has been the rule, rather than the exception."[54]

In almost every case, progress in poor-country arrangements has come easily at first, as the intraregional duties are lowered initially on goods that are not produced in any member country. When production already exists in one country but not the others, progress is not so simple. The country with the lead typically wants to eliminate trade barriers rapidly; the others obstruct in the hope that they can catch up; the advance slows. Perhaps more important than the political element, however, is that the economic characteristics of most LDCs do not favor the extensive intraindustrial (and intrafactoral) trade characteristic of developed nations.

A FURTHER LOOK AT THE PROBLEMS OF LDC ARRANGEMENTS: A REVISIT TO THE CHECKIST OF CONDITIONS   Unfortunately, even though most regional trading arrangements have been formed in the less developed countries, often these LDCs cannot meet many of the conditions already discussed in the checklist of conditions for welfare improvement earlier in the chapter.[55] The numbers below are the same as in the checklist, which can be referred to as needed. The comments in brackets indicate why the conditions may not be met by many LDC arrangements.

1. The elasticity of demand should be high, so that as internal barriers are lowered, trade will be created among the members. [LDC imports often contain a high proportion of essential inputs such as capital goods and oil. Demand may be quite inelastic.]

2. The elasticity of supply should be high, so that as tariffs fall among the members production will rise rapidly to take the place of imports from nonmembers. [A poor economy is an inflexible one; LDCs have more government controls over economic activity, an inadequate infrastructure of transport and communications, low levels of literacy, education, and so forth. Supply may be inelastic as a result.]

3. Low-cost producers should belong. [Especially in capital-intensive and high-technology manufacturing, LDCs are not the lowest-cost producers. Furthermore, LDC unions often have a rather limited membership.]

4. If countries already conduct a large proportion of their trade with one another, then diversion of trade to a higher-cost source within the union will make little difference. [Many LDCs carry on little trade with their neighbors. Transport to the developed industrial countries is often much easier.]

5. If the member countries import only a small percentage of their consumption, then diversion of trade to a higher-cost source within the arrangement will make little difference. [Some LDCs, including the smaller ones and minerals exporters, import a large share of their consumption.]

6. Tariffs in a middling range may leave the membership most vulnerable to trade diversion. [LDC tariffs are often in a middling range.]

7. The external tariff should be constructed to reduce the dispersion of tariffs. [LDCs' tariffs show great variation; LDC trade arrangements have often adopted high external barriers.]

8. A union if economically important may be able to exert a favorable terms-of-trade effect. [LDCs are often economically unimportant; their unions will seldom have this power.]

9. Very different factor proportions will stimulate trade along Heckscher-Ohlin lines. [The economic structure of the LDC members of a union is often quite similar, so trade creation on Heckscher-Ohlin lines does not occur.]

10. Growth in intraindustrial trade may make an arrangement less disruptive. [LDC trade is seldom intraindustrial. Their level of development and hence income is too low to permit trade creation along intraindustrial lines.]

11. Fast economic growth is advantageous. Wealthy countries can afford regional development funds and trade adjustment assistance. [Economic growth in numerous LDCs has been slow, especially in Africa but also in Latin America and South Asia. Regional development funds and trade adjustment assistance are often unaffordable.]

12. Outward-oriented economic policies will tend to stimulate trade. [Inward-oriented policies are common in the LDCs. Vested interests are strong; corruption may be rampant. LDCs tend to resist reductions in internal barriers; they know some parts of their small industrial base will suffer, but that government funds for adjustment will be limited or unavailable. Rules of origin are often very strict. Economies of scale frequently do not appear, largely due to an oligopolistic structure that includes market sharing and the fact that barriers have often not been reduced sufficiently to generate them.[56]]

THE LESSON FOR THE LDCS   The lesson is that policymakers must be especially alert to possible trade diversion when preference arrangements are made. None of the above is writ in stone. A strong commitment to free trade can work wonders, and even if static trade diversion predominates, an arrangement still might be worthwhile if the dynamic effects—economies of scale in intraunion sales, higher investment, improved marketing, a greater spur to productive efficiency, better management, technical change, an end run around proliferating NTBs in trading partners—are large enough to offset the trade diversion. The greater zeal for open trade in the LDCs, and the adherence to free trade arrangements by major players like Mexico, Brazil, and Argentina (in NAFTA and Mercosur) may in time begin to change the perception that LDC arrangements work poorly.

■ *FOREIGN TRADE ZONES: LITTLE BITS OF FREE TRADE*

If a nation cannot join in union with others and fears the effect of just removing tariffs, it has the option of making *part* of its country free of trade barriers. Under GATT rules it is perfectly proper to designate certain geographical areas as zones of free trade, even when the rest of the country is subject to normal tariffs, quotas, and VERs. These are called Foreign Trade Zones (FTZs), or alternatively Export Processing Zones.[57]

Such zones are much used everywhere, and have been for many years (the first one was established at Hamburg, Germany, in 1888).* Recently there were about 400 of them in 80 countries including Russia and China, with some 10% of global trade routed through them. They are "isolated, enclosed, and policed" areas, to use the language of the U.S. law, where a country's trade regulations mostly do not apply. If the goods are intended for sale in the country concerned, duties, quotas, and so forth, are levied only when the goods cross the boundary of the zone.

FTZs are allowed in the United States under an act of 1934. The first one was established at Staten Island in New York. For many years they were typically used for warehousing of goods in transit—imports later reexported—and for inspection, destruction of inferior goods, remarking, and repackaging. For example, it would be embarrassing to import 10,000 pairs of shoes, and then, having paid the duty, to find that 50 pairs were defective. Far better to import the shoes into an FTZ and examine the shipment there. No waste would occur when the shoes cross the zone's boundary; no duty will have to be paid on defects. But business was slow to develop. By 1970, there were still only eight U.S. zones, and turnover was only about $100 million in value. Manufacturing inside U.S. FTZs was authorized in 1950. In 1980 the law was again amended so that domestic processing costs incurred in the zones and profits earned there would be free of duty. Thus tariffs would apply only to the imported inputs. Finally, a 1982 amendment allowed the exclusion of overhead costs such as transport and insurance from dutiable value, further reducing the base value on which tariff is collected.

All customs ports of entry are eligible to have an FTZ, and subzones may be established elsewhere at the discretion of the U.S. Foreign Trade Zones Board, which administers the law. Typically a subzone surrounds a manufacturing plant. In 1988 there were 129 zones (including 60 subzones) and 78 more zone projects in the United States, compared to a total of just 27 in 1975. Most were approved in the 1980s. The only state currently without a zone or subzone is South Dakota.**

Their rate of growth has been a phenomenon: In 1988, items valued at $59 billion were shipped into the zones (76% of that from domestic sources) and items worth $72 billion were shipped out of them.[58] In these terms performance was over 90 times the level of 1975. Exports used to be the major activity, but now the domestic market is the preferred destination; 90% of the output manufactured in the zones is sold in the United States, and is thus subject to the trade regulations,

---

* Long before that a single ship had been given similar status by the Imperial Russian government. When Tsar Peter the Great opened the new port and capital city of St. Petersburg in 1701, he granted to the first foreign merchant vessel that arrived exemption from Russian tariffs for the rest of its life. Probably you will not be surprised to learn that this wooden ship proved to have an extraordinarily long career, lovingly maintained in good repair by its Dutch owners, keeping to the seas for nearly a century and, needless to say, calling often at Russian ports. See Fernand Braudel, *The Wheels of Commerce*, New York, Harper and Row, 1980, p. 241.

** Students researching the activities undertaken in the zones had best be alerted that their managers are tight lipped about them. (See the comment to that effect in the *Wall Street Journal*, September 30, 1987.) In Maine, author JSH could not persuade the manager of the Bangor zone (No. 58) to reveal the names of any of the firms operating there, even after explaining that all he wanted was some examples for an international economics textbook.

while 10% is exported. Approximately 165,000 people were employed in U.S. FTZs in 1987, compared to fewer than 12,000 in 1980.

The FTZs have a major advantage whenever components pay a higher duty than a finished product, which is called a reversed-cascading or inverted tariff structure. A firm can then import components, assemble the product in a zone, and then sell the product in the national market, so reducing its tariff liability. For a case in point, note that TV tubes imported from Taiwan are dutiable at 22%, but when zone-assembled in the set, they in effect pay a duty of only 11% because that is the tariff on complete televisions. Over two thirds of the firms responding to a 1987 survey of the U.S. International Trade Commission said they used the FTZs to lower their tariff bills when tariffs were higher on components than finished products.

Though the zones had virtually no adversaries for many years, in the 1980s the opposition to them grew intense. Protectionist interests have severely limited the use of FTZs by producers who use imported sugar or make bicycles or TVs. The Foreign Trade Zones Board in practice applies limits if it believes the inverted tariff structure causing components to have higher duties than finished products was intended by congress, but it does not do so when it believes that the situation has resulted from trade concessions and negotiations.

Many critics now claim that the absence of duties on imported components fuels U.S. imports. A proposal presently being considered by the Foreign Trade Zones Board is to disallow applications for FTZs that would cause a net increase in imports. The AFL-CIO has called for the *complete abolition* of the U.S. law, or, at minimum, repeal of the portion of it that permits manufacturing in the zones. It can be confidently predicted that such resistance to zones used by foreigners is likely to grow. Critics in the United States and other countries as well have also charged that liberalizing trade inside the zones may divert attention from illiberal policies outside the zones, a sweeping under the rug that could conceivably do more harm than good. The path to freer trade, even in the innocuous form of a foreign trade zone, here as elsewhere can be a rough one.

THE TRADE OF THE FORMER COMMUNIST COUNTRIES: COMECON AND COUNTERTRADE

There used to be some economic integration of the Communist bloc countries in the form of an organization known as COMECON, the Council for Mutual Economic Assistance.[59] It was also known by the initials CMEA. COMECON included the Soviet Union, six Communist countries of Eastern Europe (but not Albania and Yugoslavia), Mongolia, Cuba, and Vietnam. The wave of reform that swept over the old Soviet Union and Eastern Europe in 1989–1991 brought the death of COMECON and considerable *disintegration* of the trade of the former Communist countries.

Much of Eastern bloc's foreign trade was within COMECON, for example, over 60% of the USSR's. COMECON as a whole was responsible for a little under 10% of total world trade. Typically, the Soviet Union paid low prices for the other members' manufactured exports, in turn charging lower-than-market prices for its oil exports to these countries. The organization's main problem was always how to go about balancing trade. Central planning had been a major facet of all its members' economies, with foreign trade held subservient to the domestic goals of the central plan. Exports were thought of as production surplus to the needs of the plan, while imports were viewed as a means to avoid planning bottlenecks. Pricing was especially difficult because exchange rates were fixed by a planning agency rather than established by supply and demand on the world market. The currencies of the countries involved were not traded internationally. Thus they could not be used in the conduct of COMECON's trade, which became a matter of delicate negotiations, often at the ministerial level. Bilateral balancing within COMECON was the method used to determine the amount of trade. A ruble value was put on exports and imports, and at the end of the accounting period (at the longest every two years) a country that had not exported as much as it imported had to agree to export some additional goods.

The breakup of Communist rule brought the sudden demise of COMECON, which ceased operating on January 1, 1991. The former members agreed to adopt market pricing and to make payment in convertible currencies in place of bilateral balancing. Trade was now to be conducted in dollars and other hard currencies. The step proved to be premature, however. If the firms of the former Communist countries have to pay in hard currency, then given a choice they prefer to buy Western products. Furthermore, hard currencies were not sufficiently in supply to finance all the interregional trade that had been carried on by means of bilateral balancing. The hard currency rule was a major reason why commerce among the former COMECON members suffered a drastic fall. The 1991 trade statistics told a doleful tale.[60] Overall export volume fell 40.0% in Bulgaria, 10.7% in Czechoslovakia, 10.0% in Hungary (January–October), 1.5% in Poland, 29.7% in Romania, and 32.7% in the old USSR. Exports from the old USSR to Eastern Europe declined greatly: according to the IMF, by 35–45% to Hungary, 50–65% to Bulgaria, Czechoslovakia, and Romania, 75% to Poland. Meanwhile imports into the old USSR from these countries were down by over 40%. Numerous major firms in Eastern Europe were close to bankruptcy because of this loss of markets, raw materials, and energy supplies.

FINDING A WAY TO TRADE WITHOUT HARD CURRENCY: COUNTERTRADE

It began to grow on observers that the death of COMECON, in spite off all its irrationalities, had been ill timed. The destruction of export markets was not balanced by sufficiently rapid development of exports to the West. The quality problems, inefficient marketing, and lack of export financing were millstones. Disputes over prices, inexperience with foreign trade, disruption of long-term agreements, and preference for Western goods all contributed to the decline. So did East Germany's unification with West Germany, which reduced demand in that major market for the goods of its former COMECON partners. Above all, the shortage of hard convertible currencies stifled trade.

Methods had to be found if trade was not to collapse even more completely. Fortunately, other methods did already exist—barter and countertrade, long since utilized when the Communist countries had traded with Western countries. Pure barter had been a consistent resort ever since Communist governments were first instituted. A substantial amount of East-West trade, running at some 20–25% in the 1980s, was conducted this way. Included were deals such as wheat for petroleum and trucks for sugar; Pepsi took Soviet ships in exchange for its soft drinks; the USSR traded vodka for Latin American coffee.

In the 1970s, new types of East-West trade had developed, making barter methods seem old-fashioned. The new arrangements received the collective name *countertrade*.[61] Though several of the countertrade techniques originated in East-West trade, they soon spread far beyond those limits to include much trade of the less developed countries and even some of the trade carried on among the developed industrial nations. There are many variants, but all of them have in common the need for a good deal of bargaining. Included in the forms of countertrade are the following:

1. *Switch trading,* which is chain bartering. *A* barters with *B*; *B* barters with *C*; *C* barters with *A*, all as part of one transaction. The chain makes it feasible to effect a trade that might be impossible if only two countries were involved. To take an example, albeit a complicated one: The U.S. Caterpillar Company recently exported machinery to Venezuela, which as part of the arranged payment sent iron ore to Romania, which sent men's suits to Great Britain for cash, which was paid to Caterpillar.[62]

2. *Counterpurchase,* which is pure reciprocity. You buy from us in value terms what we buy from you. Often such agreements are expressed as a percentage: If country *A* sells $10 million in equipment to country *B*, then 80% counterpurchase would require country *A* to buy $8 million in other goods from country *B* over some time period, perhaps five years.

3. *Offset,* which requires the investment of a certain proportion of the value of an export deal in the importing country. Offset is extremely common, and may even predominate, in trade involving military equipment and civil aircraft. Clear cases in point are the use of Rolls-Royce engines in passenger aircraft sold to British airlines, and French-built Snecma engines in the Boeing AWACS aircraft sold to France.

4. *Buy back,* which is payment for a capital project or technical information by means of the product produced. For example, a license might be granted by a Western firm to an Eastern producer, along with technical help. The Eastern firm pays by shipping to the West a portion of the good manufactured under the license. Alternatively, a complete factory might be delivered by a Western company to the East, paid for by shipments of a portion of the goods manufactured in the factory. These buy-back arrangements came to be

very large, involving most importantly chemical deals between Germany and the Soviet Union.

Countertrade grew greatly in the 1980s, not just in East-West commerce (about 25% of the total) and intra-COMECON trade (about 40%), but globally. Some 20% of trade among the LDCs, 10% of trade between the developed countries and the LDCs, and even 2% of the trade among the developed countries themselves, was by means of this method.[63] In the early 1970s, only 15 countries had been involved in countertrade, but the number was nearly 90 in 1990, accounting for 8–10% of all world trade.[64] Both Eastern economies and developing countries had discovered that countertrade could be a means for breaking into new markets. Products difficult to sell independently might in a countertrade relationship find market access through the sales outlets of a multinational company. Perhaps in time the products will be accepted, and can be sold for cash.

The collapse of international trade in the former COMECON countries brought a major slowdown of countertrade in 1991, but after that the practice surged again. Western trading partners of Russia and other states of the former USSR demanded delivery of actual goods in return for their own exports; the republics of the old USSR rushed to conclude countertrade arrangements with one another; and the old COMECON partners were often using it as well. The former Soviet republics are extremely dependent on trade with one another, even more so than the COMECON states were. The interrepublic trade of all of them except Russia had been 78% or more, and even for Russia the figure had been 59%.[65] Switching to dollar payment was not possible because dollars are scarce and could not be found to finance all the trade among the republics that was once conducted in rubles. Often balances are kept in dollars or other hard currencies, with countertrade deficits and surpluses settled at the end of the year by whatever means the countries choose.

The methods involved are sufficiently complicated so that many large banks now have countertrade departments that specialize in providing the (expensive) consulting necessary to effect a transaction. The Japanese *sogo shosha* trading companies are adept at the practice and receive considerable help from the Japanese government. (The U.S. government does little, however, to assist its firms in learning about countertrade practices.) Even specialized journals are published on the subject, for example *Countertrade Outlook* and the *Countertrade and Barter Quarterly*. The specialized knowledge is certainly necessary, because countertrade hides prices. It is all too easy to fit in rakeoffs, kickbacks, and other forms of corruption difficult to detect in a price-less environment. The risk of nondelivery because a deal falls through is high, and insuring against that eventuality is expensive. A further obstacle is that countertrade often limits competition, because not every trading partner is willing to engage in it. Governments generally oppose it in principle (Russia even banned it for a few months in 1991) while accepting it in practice.

COMING OUT OF IT? THE CEFTA AND THE FUTURE   Some signs of improvement are now being seen. At the end of 1992 an agreement for a Central European Free Trade Area (CEFTA) was signed by the Czech Republic, Hungary, Poland, and Slovakia. These are the countries that have thus far made the greatest progress in redirecting their trade to the West.[*] Tariffs among the members are to be eliminated by the year 2001. All have already been given associate status with the EC, although their agricultural commodities remain excluded, their textiles for 10 years, and their steel for five years. Many imports into these Eastern countries (and Romania and Bulgaria as well) are now free of controls except for tariffs.

Undoubtedly a tremendous potential for trade expansion exists among the former COMECON countries, and among the republics of the old Soviet Union as well. When the expansion will happen is an open question.

CONCLUSION

The major result deriving from both theory and evidence is that economic integration may bring substantial benefits, but that it will not necessarily do so. A broad body of evidence points to static and dynamic advantages in a wide variety of settings. But the discovery of the trade diversion effect in the 1950s, followed by the EC's trade-diverting actions in agriculture, has made economists far more aware of the economic burdens that unions place on nonmembers and the costs that could be inflicted on the member populations. The poor performance of most LDC customs unions and the abject failure of COMECON reemphasize the lack of certainty that such unions are the best path to a more efficient world. Finally, the possibility that three great trading blocs will emerge to dominate world trade gives many economists cause for alarm. An outcome where integration leads to even more intense disputes than the present ones is alarming indeed.

---

[*] Poland's foreign trade is doing especially well. Its exports to the EC rose 60% in 1990 and 30% more in 1991, according to the *International Economic Review,* May 1992. It might be noted that China, never a member of COMECON, is doing well in international trade. U.S. trade with China is actually much greater than U.S. trade with Eastern Europe and the old Soviet Union. In 1991, U.S. exports to China were $6.2 billion out of $10.9 to all the Communist countries of the present or past, while U.S. imports from China were $18.9 billion out of $20.6 billion from the entire group. See U.S. ITC, *Trade Between the United States and China, the Former Soviet Union, Central and Eastern Europe, the Baltic Nations, and Other Selected Countries* for the first quarter of 1992, p. 3.

VOCABULARY AND CONCEPTS

ANZCERTA (Australia-New Zealand
  Economic Relations Trade Agreement)
ASEAN
Caribbean Basin Economic Recovery Act
  (CBERA)
Cecchini Report
COMECON
Common Market
Countertrade
Customs union
Economic union

European Community (EC)
European Free Trade Association (EFTA)
Free trade area
Maquiladoras
Mercousur
North American Free Trade Agreement (NAFTA)
Trade-creating customs union
Trade creation
Trade diversion
Trade-diverting customs union
U.S.-Canadian Free Trade Agreement

QUESTIONS

1. What is the difference between a free trade area and a customs union? An economic union? Use the example of the European Community after *1992* and the Free Trade Agreement between Canada and the United States to illustrate your points.

2. For the EC, what was the significance of December 31, 1992?

3. Explain, using simple (Viner-type) tables, the concept of trade diversion and trade creation.

4. Show, using diagrams, what causes a customs union to be trade diverting and what causes it to be trade creating.

5. In a customs union, under what circumstance will the importing nation be a net loser? Demonstrate. (Hint: Check the relation of $C+E$ to $B+D$.)

6. In what types of goods has the EC shown trade creation effects more than trade diversion? Vice versa? Why?

7. Why do customs unions seem to work less well among poor countries? Give examples and show what conditions lessen their chances for success.

8. The Free Trade Agreement between the United States and Canada is predicated upon dynamic gains to specialization resembling Chapter 3's discussions. Explain.

9. Static gains involving elimination of deadweight losses would hardly have been enough for Canada to enter a FTA with the United States. Why?

10. Explain and evaluate the pros and cons of the NAFTA agreement, including the environmental questions.

11. What might be the problems of world trade if the world becomes divided into large trading blocs?

12. "Like so much else, an FTZ is the product of a nation's rather peculiar laws." Explain why FTZs are formed. Supposing they remained legal, consider what kinds of changes in national laws would lead to fewer of them. (Don't concentrate on regulating FTZs. Think instead of why companies use them.)

13. What were the problems of COMECON? What functions did it perform that seem to be missing now in Eastern Europe?

14. "Countertrade is not a simple concept. It involves a variety of means for carrying out trade when hard currency is scarce." Discuss.

NOTES

[1] For a survey of the literature on economic integration, see Ali M. El-Agraa, *The Theory and Measurement of International Economic Integration*, New York, St. Martin's Press, 1989. Also see El-Agraa, ed., *International Economic Integration*, Basingstoke, 2d ed., Macmillan, 1988; Miroslav Jovanovic, *International Economic Integration*, New York, Routledge, 1992; and some of the essays in Robert E. Baldwin, ed., *Trade Policy Issues and Empirical Analysis*, Chicago, University of Chicago Press, 1988.

[2] Norman S. Fieleke, "One trading world, or many: The issue of regional trading blocs," *New England Economic Review*, May/June 1992, p. 6.

[3] For an analysis of the empirical measurement of trade creation versus trade diversion, see W.M. Corden, "The costs and consequences of protection: A survey of empirical work," in Peter B. Kenen, ed., *International Trade and Finance: Frontiers for Research*, Cambridge, Cambridge University Press, 1975, pp. 51–91.

[4] The Kemp-Wan proposition was advanced by M.C. Kemp and H. Wan, "An elementary proposition concerning the formation of customs unions," *Journal of International Economics*, Vol. 6, 1976, pp. 95–98.

[5] See Jagdish Bhagwati, *The World Trading System at Risk*, Princeton, Princeton University Press, 1991, p. 77.

[6] See Nicholas Owen, *Economies of Scale, Competitiveness and Trade Patterns in the European Community*, Oxford, 1983.

[7] See Augusto de la Torre and Margaret R. Kelly, *Regional Trade Arrangements*, IMF Occasional Paper No. 93, 1992; David Greenaway and Chris Milner, "South-south trade: theory, evidence, and policy," *World Bank Research Observer*, Vol. 5, No. 1, January 1990; Frank R. Gunter, "Customs union theory: Retrospect and prospect," in David Greenaway et al., eds., *Economic Aspects of Regional Trading Arrangements*, New York, New York University Press, 1989; Corsten Kowalczyk, "Welfare and customs unions," NBER Working Paper No. 3476, 1990; Jeffrey J. Schott, "Trading blocs and the world trading system," *The World Economy*, Vol. 14, No. 1, March 1991, pp. 1–17; Paul Wonnacott and Mark Lutz, "Is there a case for free trade areas?" in Jeffrey J. Schott, ed., *Free Trade Areas and U.S. Trade Policy*, Washington, D.C., Institute for International Economics, 1989; and Constantine V. Vaitsos, "Crisis in regional economic cooperation (integration) among developing countries: A survey," in Paul Streeten and Richard Jolly, eds., *Recent Issues in World Development*, Oxford, Pergamon, 1981, pp. 279–329.

[8] See Greenaway et al., *Economic Aspects of Regional Trading Arrangements*, for the connection between intraindustrial trade and the performance of integration arrangements.

[9] Fieleke, "One trading world, or many," p. 3.

[10] Empirical work emphasizing the trade diversion aspect is noted in El-Agraa, *The Economics of the European Community*, New York, St. Martin's Press, 1980; and the same author's "The European Community," in his *International Economic Integration*, New York, St. Martin's Press, 1982.

[11] See Richard Pomfret, *Unequal Trade: The Economics of Discriminatory International Trade Policies*, New York, Blackwell Publishers, 1988, especially p. 131 and the sources cited in this work. Another recent study citing many sources is L. Alan Winters and Anthony J. Venables, eds., *European Integration: Trade and Industry*, Cambridge, Cambridge University Press, 1991.

[12] Michael Emerson, Michel Aujean, Michel Catinat, Philippe Goybet, and Alexis Jacquemin, *The Economics of 1992: The EC Commission's Assessment of the Economic Effects of Completing the Internal Market*, Oxford, Oxford University Press, 1988; L. Alan Winters, "International trade and '1992': An overview," *European Economic Review*, Vol. 35, April 1991, pp. 367–377; and the special issue on 1992 of *The Economist*, June 8, 1991.

[13] *The Economist*, June 8, 1991.

[14] For a full accounting see Paolo Cecchini, *The European Challenge, 1992: The Benefits of a Single Market*, Aldershot, Ashgate Publishing Company, 1988. The percentages are estimates by Emerson et al., predicting total economic gains of 5.8–6.4% of GDP by microeconomic measurement techniques, and 3.2–5.7% of GDP using macroeconomic estimates.

[15] See Richard Baldwin, "Measurable dynamic gains from trade," *Journal of Political Economy*, Vol. 100, February 1992, pp. 162–174; Richard Baldwin, "The growth effects of 1992," *Economic Policy*, Vol. 4, No. 9, October 1989, pp. 248–281; Harry Flam, "Product markets and 1992: Full integration, large gains? *Journal of Economic Perspectives*, Vol. 6, No. 4, Fall 1992, especially pp. 24–27 with numerous sources cited there; and M. J. Peck, "Industrial organization and the gains from Europe 1992," Symposium of Europe 1992, *Brookings Papers on Economic Activity*, No. 2, 1989, pp. 277–299.

[16] Sven W. Arndt and Thomas D. Willett, "EC 1992 from a North American perspective," *Economic Journal*, Vol. 101, No. 409, November 1991, pp. 1567-1579; Gary Clyde Hufbauer, *Europe 1992: An American Perspective*, Washington, D.C., Brookings Institution, 1990.

[17] De la Torre and Kelly, *Regional Trade Arrangements*, Washington, D.C., International Monetary Fund, 1992, p. 2.

[18] See R. Lipsey, "American firms face Europe," NBER Working Paper No. 3293, 1990, and M.J. Peck, "Industrial organization and the gains from Europe 1992."

[19] For discussions of the economic effects of 1992 on the rest of the world, see Baldwin, "The growth effects of 1992"; A. Jacquemin and A. Sapir, *The European Internal Market: Trade and Competition*, Oxford, Oxford University

Press, 1989; André Sapir, "Europe 1992: The external trade implications," *International Economic Journal*, Vol. 6, No. 1, Spring 1992, p. 3; and Gary C. Hufbauer, "An overview," in Hufbauer's *Europe 1992: An American Perspective*, Washington, D.C., 1990, pp. 22–23.

[20] For the background see Richard Abrams et al., *The Impact of the European Community's Internal Markets on the EFTA*, IMF Occasional Paper No. 74, 1990.

[21] See C.P. Stacey, *Canada and the Age of Conflict*, Vol. 2, Toronto, University of Toronto Press, 1981, pp. 169–179.

[22] De la Torre and Kelly, *Regional Trade Arrangements*, p. 21.

[23] See the discussions in recent editions of the U.S. ITC, *Operation of the Trade Agreements Program*; Jane Sneddon Little, "At stake in the U.S.-Canada Free Trade Agreement: Modest gains or a significant setback," *New England Economic Review*, May/June 1988, pp. 3–20; John Whalley with Roderick Hill, eds., *Canada-United States Free Trade*, Toronto, University of Toronto Press, 1985; Paul Wonnacott, *The United States and Canada: The Quest for Free Trade: An Examination of Selected Issues*, Washington, D.C., Institute for International Economics, 1987; Kelly et al., *International Trade Policy*, IMF Occasional Paper No. 63, 1988, p. 12; and the coverage in *The Economist*, the *Wall Street Journal*, and the *Toronto Globe and Mail*.

[24] *International Economic Review*, April, 1992.

[25] De la Torre and Kelly, *Regional Trade Arrangements*, p. 24.

[26] For this section see Gary Clyde Hufbauer and Jeffrey J. Schott, *North American Free Trade: Issues and Recommendations*, Washington, D.C., 1992; and the same authors' *NAFTA: An Assessment*, Washington, D.C., Institute for International Economics, 1993; Nora Lustig, Barry P. Bosworth, and Robert Z. Lawrence, eds., *North American Free Trade: Assessing the Impact*, Washington, D.C., Brookings Institution, 1992; Drusilla K. Brown, Alan V. Deardorff, and Robert M. Stern, "North American integration," *Economic Journal*, Vol. 102, No. 415, November 1992, pp. 1507–1518; Sidney Weintraub, *U.S.-Mexican Industrial Integration: The Road to Free Trade*, Boulder, Westview Press, 1991; Philip Mirowski and Susan Helper, "*Maquiladoras:* Mexico's tiger by the tail," *Challenge*, Vol. 32, No. 3, May/June 1989, pp. 24–30; the coverage in *The Economist*, the *Wall Street Journal*, the *International Economic Review*; and all recent editions of the U.S. ITC, *Operation of the Trade Agreements Program*.

[27] The gains as measured in numerous studies are presented by Brown, Deardorff, and Stern, "North American integration," p. 1510.

[28] Hufbauer and Schott, *NAFTA: An Assessment*, p. 16.

[29] A point made by Rudiger Dornbusch, "It's time to open up trade with Mexico," *Challenge*, November/December 1990, p. 53.

[30] Gene Grossman and Alan Krueger, "Environmental impacts of a North American free trade agreement," NBER Working Paper No. 3914, 1992.

[31] Hufbauer and Schott, *North American Free Trade: Issues and Recommendations*.

[32] James Bovard, "NAFTA's protectionist bent," *Wall Street Journal*, July 31, 1992.

[33] Leslie Sklair, *Assembling for Development: The Maquila Industry in Mexico and the United States*, Boston, Unwin Hyman, 1989; *Wall Street Journal*, April 30, 1991.

[34] Nigel Harris, "Export Processing in Mexico," *Journal of Development Studies*, Vol. 27, No. 1, October 1990, p. 122.

[35] World Bank, *World Development Report, 1986*, Washington, D.C., 1986, p. 144.

[36] For an accounting of the EC's regional agreements, see André Sapir, "Regional integration in Europe," *Economic Journal*, Vol. 102, No. 415, November 1992, p. 1492.

[37] De la Torre and Kelly, *Regional Trade Arrangements*, p. 7; *The Economist*, May 23, 1992.

[38] For this section we have drawn on U.S. ITC, *Annual Report on the Impact of the Caribbean Basin Economic Recovery Act on U.S. Industries and Consumers*; Joseph and Gregory K. Schoepfle, "The impact of the Caribbean Basin Economic Recovery Act on Caribbean nations' exports and development," *Economic Development and Cultural Change*, Vol. 36, No. 4, July 1988, pp. 753–796; Peter D. Whitney, "The CBI: Important incentives for trade and investment," U.S. Department of State Current Policy No. 1065, April, 1988; Richard E. Feinberg and Richard Newfarmer, "The Caribbean Basin Initiative: Bold plan or empty promise," in Richard Newfarmer, ed., *From Gunboats to Diplomacy*, Baltimore, Johns Hopkins University Press, 1984; W. Charles Sawyer and Richard L. Sprinkle, "Caribbean Basin Recovery Act," *Journal of World Trade Law*, Vol. 18, No. 5, 1984, pp. 429–436; *International Economic Review*, April and September, 1989; all recent editions of the U.S. ITC, *Operation of the Trade Agreements Program*; articles in the *Wall Street Journal* and *Christian Science Monitor*; a special section in *The Economist*, August 6, 1988; and personal communications from the Latin America/Caribbean Business Development Center of the U.S. Department of Commerce.

[39] See Sidney Weintraub, "A U.S.-Israel free trade area," *Challenge*, Vol. 28, No. 3, 1985, pp. 47–50; and recent issues of U.S. ITC, *Operation of the Trade Agreements Program*.

[40] For a discussion, see Richard Pomfret, "The quiet shift in U.S. trade policy," *Challenge*, Vol. 27, No. 5, 1984, pp. 61–64.

[41] For this argument, see Paul Luyten, "Multilateralism versus preferential bilateralism: A European view," in Jeffrey J. Schott, ed., *Free Trade Areas and U.S. Trade Policy*, Washington, D.C., Institute for International Economics, 1989.

[42] For an exploration of the issues, see David Greenaway et al., eds., *Economic Aspects of Regional Trading Arrangements*, New York, 1989; Jeffrey J. Schott, "More free trade areas," in Jeffrey J. Schott, ed., *Free Trade Areas and U.S. Trade Policy*, Washington, D.C., 1989; C.

Michael Aho and Sylvia Ostry, "Regional trading blocs: Pragmatic or problematic policy?" in William Brock and Robert Hormats, eds., *The Global Economy*, New York, W.W. Norton & Co., 1990.

[43] Jeffrey J. Schott, "More free trade areas," p. 23.

[44] See Paul Krugman, "The move toward free trade zones," *Federal Reserve Bank of Kansas City Economic Review*, November/December 1991, p. 11.

[45] Krugman, "The move toward free trade zones," p. 13.

[46] C. Fred Bergsten, "Commentary: The move toward free trade zones," *Federal Reserve Bank of Kansas City Economic Review*, November/December 1991, pp. 27–35.

[47] Christian E. Petersen, "Trade conflict and resolution methodologies," *American Economic Review*, Vol. 82, No. 2, May 1992, p. 65.

[48] Greenaway and Milner, "South-south trade," p. 56.

[49] L. N. Willmore, "Trade creation, trade diversion and effective protection in the Central American common market," *Journal of Development Studies*, Vol. 12, 1976, pp. 396–414.

[50] William R. Cline, "Benefits and costs of economic integration in Central America," in W. Cline and C. Delgado, eds., *Economic Integration in Central America: A Study*, Washington, D.C., Brookings Institution, 1978.

[51] *International Economic Review*, April, 1991.

[52] De la Torre and Kelly, *Regional Trade Arrangements*, p. 37, citing R. George, Rolf J. Langhammer, and Dean Spinanger.

[53] De la Torre and Kelly, *Regional Trade Arrangements*, p. 37, citing K. Khazeh and D. Clark.

[54] De la Torre and Kelly, *Regional Trade Arrangements*, p. 37.

[55] We consulted especially Beverly Carl, *Economic Integration Among Developing Nations: Law and Policy*, New York, Greenwood Publishing Group, 1986, and Constantine V. Vaitsos, "Crisis in regional economic cooperation (integration) among developing countries: A survey," in Paul Streeten and Richard Jolly, eds., *Recent Issues in World Development*, Oxford, 1981, pp. 279–329.

[56] De la Torre and Kelly, *Regional Trade Arrangements*, p. 37.

[57] For surveys and analyses of the zones, see Peter G. Warr, "Export processing zones: The economics of enclave manufacturing," *World Bank Research Observer*, Vol. 4, No. 1, January 1989, pp. 65–88; Don P. Clark, "U.S. production in foreign-trade zones: Potential for reducing tariff liability," *Journal of World Trade*, Vol. 22, No. 6, December 1988, pp. 107–115; Walter H. Diamond and Dorothy B. Diamond, *Tax-Free Trade Zones of the World*, New York, Matthew Bender & Co., 1977, D.L.U. Jayawardena, "Free trade zones," *Journal of World Trade Law*, Vol. 17, No. 5, 1983, pp. 427–444; *International Economic Review*, August, 1989; and *South*, February 1989. The statistics on the U.S. zones are from the May 1988, data sheet in the *47th Annual Report of the Foreign Trade Zones Board* (these annual reports have fallen badly behind schedule because of funding problems).

[58] Information supplied by the Foreign Trade Zones Board.

[59] For the latest developments see the U.S. International Trade Commission's quarterly publication formerly entitled *Trade Between the United States and the Nonmarket Economy Countries*, and now in a vivid sign of the times renamed *Trade Between the United States and China, the Former Soviet Union, Central and Eastern Europe, the Baltic Nations, and Other Selected Countries*. Also see the annual surveys of the area in IMF, *World Economic Outlook*.

[60] *International Economic Review*, June 1991 and May 1992.

[61] We utilized Jack L. Hervey, "Countertrade — counterproductive?" Federal Reserve Bank of Chicago *Economic Perspectives*, January/February 1989, pp. 17-24; "Countertrade Reconsidered," *Finance and Development*, Vol. 24, No. 2, June 1987, pp. 46-49; the Group of 30, *Countertrade in the World Economy*, New York, 1986; Bart S. Fisher and Kathleen M. Harte, *Barter in the World Economy*, New York, 1985; and various issues of *The Economist*.

[62] Reported in *The Economist*, May 9, 1987.

[63] *International Economic Review*, August 1992.

[64] Grant T. Hammond, *Countertrade, Offsets and Barter in International Political Economy*, London, St. Martin's Press, 1990.

[65] IMF, *World Economic Outlook 1992*, p. 42. The figures are for 1987.

Part II

International Macroeconomics:
Saving, Growth, and Finance

AN OVERVIEW OF PART II

The aims of domestic macroeconomic policy are to keep prices stable, employment and production high, and provide a basis for long-term economic growth. Such goals may often be in conflict, and economists differ on the priority of the different aims and on the very mechanisms through which they work. Part II necessarily deals with some of those conflicts, but it also faces some special international twists to the questions.

1. Macroeconomic policy is also useful for keeping trade deficits and surpluses from growing too large. It is thus charged with a fourth task to add to its employment, price, and long-run growth objectives.

2. The maintenance of moderate trade *imbalances* (that is, acceptable deficits and surpluses) can make it easier to get on with the other three tasks.

3. Macroeconomic policies in one country spill over into other countries. What may be a perfectly adequate solution to a problem for one country may seriously complicate matters for other countries. As with trade policy, we must contemplate both the domestic effects and the entire international system in which the country operates.

The topics and their order in Part II are modeled after contemporary principles of economics texts: national income models, followed by aggregate demand and supply and Keynesian income models, followed in turn by financial analysis. In each case, the text modifies, deepens, or expands material developed in principles books to handle international matters. International economics, of course, has topics that do not occur domestically—the balance of payments, foreign exchange markets, and the nature of international economic cooperation—and these are integrated into the material.

Chapter 10

Saving, Investment, and the Trade Balance

OBJECTIVES

Overall Objective: To reveal the strength of the patterns of consumption, investment, and production in determining trade imbalances.

MORE SPECIFICALLY:

- To show the key national income formulas, particularly those dealing with the saving-investment and income-absorption gaps, such that the relation of trade imbalances to national income is clear.
- To understand that persistent and awkward trade imbalances are symptoms of other generally more deeply rooted problems associated with saving, investment, and growth.
- To explore the role of demographics and the role of the government in trade imbalances.
- To begin to establish an understanding of the functions of a trade imbalance.

Trade deficits and surpluses lie at the center of almost all international macroeconomic discussions. This chapter examines trade imbalances in the context of national income and expenditures, demonstrating the close connection between patterns of national saving and investment and emerging trade imbalances. It examines how deficits or surpluses arise using models that do not involve money, price levels, or exchange rates (which later chapters cover), laying a firm foundation for those later topics.

HOW CAN COUNTRIES HAVE TRADE IMBALANCES?

Popular wisdom suggests that the cure for trade imbalances is to manipulate exports and imports through taxes, subsidies, quotas, and like instruments. If the United States has a deficit, it must be because of other countries' devious machinations. Or, say the self-blamers, the lack of American productivity. Yet nothing we learned in the first chapters of this book suggests that productivity or trade manipulation, however greatly they may limit the *volume* of trade, alter the *balance* of trade. We must look elsewhere, starting with the most fundamental of questions: that of how any nation can develop a trade imbalance.

THE MARKET AT CASTORIA

Perhaps the best way to understand how a trade balance develops is to consider just two nations. Imagine a situation as in the beginnings of the North American fur trade. On a given market week in a place somewhat apart from their home countries, all the Fabricans and all the Castorians come to a marketplace, each with their packets of trade goods—the Fabricans carrying cloth and the Castorians beaver pelts for the trade. Unfortunately, the Castorian trapping has been poor, so compared with the previous year, the market has more cloth than pelts. We would expect the price of cloth in terms of pelts to fall, and for the market to clear. No packets of goods should be left in the marketplace at the end of the day—that is, the market *clears*. How, then, could there be a deficit or a surplus?[*]

Fabricans are, of course, unhappy about having to bring home fewer pelts. They could just pack up their cloth and return home, never offering some of their cloth on the market. But that would be difficult (that is, costly), so they offer the Castorians a deal: They will let the Castorians have all the cloth this year, in exchange for additional pelts *next year*. With expectations of better trapping, the Castorians agree. In addition, the Castorians recognize that they do not have to spend their efforts making cloth and can get down to the business of expanding traplines, placing more traps, and building larger canoes.

To put the agreements in writing, the Fabricans and the Castorians make pictures of beavers in an account book to show how many beaver skins are owed.

Now consider some observations based on the trading scenario.

1. The market clears in the sense that the marketplace is empty at the end of the day, but promises as well as goods have been exchanged. Fabrica has *lent* cloth to Castoria. We can now speak of Fabrica as having a trade surplus and Castoria a trade deficit.

2. Since prices were not flexible, the market cleared only with promises of more goods to be delivered at another time.

3. Castoria now has more goods available than it actually produced (measured by the prices it traded for). It brought a smaller harvest to the market, but went back with the same amount of cloth. It will therefore be able to use for consumption and investment more than it actually produced. The opposite is

---

[*] This is only slightly different from what actually went on in the early days of the fur trade in Canada. For convenience, we have chosen to make it more abstract and turn the North American groups into a country. We have also restricted trade to beaver pelts and cloth, rather than to the variety of trade goods the Europeans brought in, and the greater variety of things the Indians traded.

true of Fabrica, which produced some bundles of cloth that it counts in its national income as if they were sold, but for which it has not yet been paid. What Fabrica uses for investing and consuming is therefore less than its output.

4. Fabrica has *invested* the cloth that the Castorians are using. Fabricans have counted the value of that cloth as their income, but lacking pelts this year, they have not used the income for purchases; accordingly they have *saved* income equivalent to the value of the cloth they lent. They could have taken the cloth home and put it in storage, which would increase inventories, but instead they accepted a promise that Castoria would pay. Next year, the Fabricans expect to receive pelts for that cloth.

5. The Castorians have borrowed the cloth. They are able to spend more than they produced because more cloth is available than otherwise would have been, were the Fabricans to have packed it up and taken it home. Castorian consumption and investment are therefore higher than what people were paid to produce the pelts.

6. Over a longer period of time, the Castorians and Fabricans would not want their credits and debts to keep mounting, expecting that next year more furs would be available: That is, the market should still clear. If we were to combine two years and assume that the Fabricans and Castorians were correct in their assessment that the following year would be good for trapping, Castoria could repay Fabrica. To do so, some of its beaver pelts would be used to settle the old promise, and would not appear in this year's price-setting bargaining. Castoria would develop a trade surplus and Fabrica a trade deficit. For the two-year period, however, the market would clear completely.

The basic example may serve from time to time to bring us back to underlying realities: that (one-year) markets fail to clear only if the parties offer and accept debt obligations; that when those obligations occur, the borrowing nation has more goods and services on hand than it produced, and the lender faces the opposite situation; and that the lender's domestic saving must cover the goods lent abroad, and the borrower's domestic saving must fall short of the goods borrowed from abroad. We pursue these questions now in a more conventional and macroeconomic manner.

THE THREE IMBALANCES: IMPORTS-EXPORTS, SAVING-INVESTMENT, AND OUTPUT-ABSORPTION

WHAT A TRADE IMBALANCE MIGHT TELL US ABOUT SAVING AND INVESTMENT

From 1984 to 1990, the United States had a trade deficit (deficit of goods and services) of around $100 billion in each year, often 10% of exports and 1 to 2% of GNP. As the example of Castoria shows, moreover, the $100 billion tells us much about other numbers, far more hidden. While we see the number plainly before us, it is in a sense a shadow upon a screen, a product itself of other figures moving in the background. A trade deficit, like such a shadow, may be projected from several shifting figures more dimly perceived and understood.

If we understand some of the simple relationships the Castorian example showed, we can perceive much about some shapes behind the screen. And while we may not be able to marshal the statistical evidence to prove beyond doubt causal relationships, we can certainly find some good clues. Knowing the trade deficit of $100 billion, for instance, we can say that domestic investment exceeds domestic saving by $100 billion. Or we could say that what the United States used for consumption, government, and domestic investment, exceeds output Americans generated by $100 billion.

Was that an excess of investment? A shortfall of saving? If so, whose saving—government, household, or corporate? If it was a shortfall of saving, was it a prodigal consumption spree? We are not sure, but let us peek behind the screen to see how these relationships developed.

THE CONCEPT OF ABSORPTION

When statisticians add up national income figures, they cannot tell whether a given expenditure classified as consumption, investment, or government has been spent on imports or not.[1] An automobile, for instance, could be entirely of foreign manufacture or could have imported parts, or the very materials used in manufacture could be imported. Tracing such a thing would be impossible. So, after $C + I + G$ is totaled, imports are *subtracted* from that total. That, however, still leaves the expenditure foreigners made on exports uncounted; since those expenditures produced wages and profits, they must be counted. In essence, to handle the international aspects of national income accounting, exports are added to total output, but imports are subtracted from it. We therefore obtain a formula for GNP which is:

(Eq. 10.1) $$C + I + G + (X - M) = \text{GNP}^*$$

■ *GNP AND GDP*

The two key measures of an economy's total output are *gross national product* and *gross domestic product*. The two figures are normally within a percent or two of each other; for most of the statistics we use here, our choice of GNP does not make a great deal of difference to broader conclusions.

GNP does not count a group of payments made abroad known as factor payments as belonging to the nation of the recipient of those payments. GDP, in

---

* $X - M$ is put in parentheses simply to identify it; there is no mathematical reason to do so. In all our figures we include net factor payments as imports and net factor receipts as exports, so technically, we must use GNP in the formula.

contrast, counts the payments, which are generated domestically, as domestic. Chapter 11 has more details, but here we note that these items are largely interest payments such that heavily indebted countries find their GDPs are higher than their GNPs. Canada, for instance, pays nearly three percent of its GNP abroad (net of what it receives). GDP includes those payments because they represent production within Canada. GNP does not, so Canada's GNP is lower than its GDP. The United States, in contrast, receives more interest than it pays out; its GNP includes what it receives, but not what it pays, so its GNP is slightly higher than its GDP.

GDP shows what happens in a territory the nation controls, and therefore is a good gauge of the effectiveness of government policy. A country's net indebtedness, however, stands out more clearly when using GNP, which is why we use it in this chapter.

Rather than always speaking of consumption, domestic investment, and government consumption $(C + I + G)$ we use the shorthand word *absorption*. When absorption is larger than GNP (the nation is *absorbing* more than it produces), it has a trade deficit equal to that excess absorption. When it *absorbs* less than it produces, it has a trade surplus. That is:

(Eq. 10.2) $$GNP - (C + I + G) = (X - M)$$

In accounting terms, GNP is the total *output* of the economy, and that output is also the economy's total *income*. Conventionally, then, we use *income* and its symbol Y to represent GNP. This gives us:

(Eq. 10.3) $$Y - A = X - M$$

■ *IRISH ABSORPTION*

Ireland provides a particularly dramatic example of the income-absorption gap, as it ran some whopping trade deficits in the 1970s and early 1980s.

Figure 10.1 shows the relation of absorption to the trade deficit. Any part of $C + I + G$ that lies above the 100% line (which is 100% of the economy's output or GNP) must be supplied from a surplus of imports over exports, the part of the bar that is negative. So any amount of absorption that shows above the 100% line is matched by a trade deficit as the bar projects below the zero line. In 1979, for example, consumption was over 60% of GNP, $C + I$ was nearly 100%, and government consumption another 21%, bringing the total $C + I + G$ to 120% of AD. $X - M$, of course, was negative by 20%, bringing total AD down to 100%. Late in the decade, Ireland made considerable strides to improve its payments position, and as absorption fell, the trade deficit fell also.

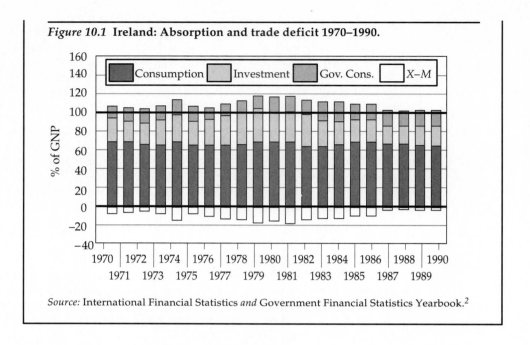

Figure 10.1 Ireland: Absorption and trade deficit 1970–1990.

Source: International Financial Statistics *and* Government Financial Statistics Yearbook.[2]

THE RELATIONSHIP OF $X - M$, $S - I$, AND $Y - A$ AS A FLOW DIAGRAM   We can capsulize the foregoing discussion with two flow diagrams. Given a fixed level of output, an increase in absorption due to increases in investment, consumption, or government spending leads to a worsening trade balance.

(FD 10.1) $$\overline{Y} - A\!\uparrow\; \rightarrow (X - M)\!\downarrow$$

If saving falls or investment rises, causing the saving-investment gap to increase, absorption must rise, and given a fixed income, the trade balance (X–M) must fall.

(FD 10.2) $$(S - I)\!\downarrow\; \rightarrow (\overline{Y} - A\!\uparrow)\!\downarrow\; \rightarrow (X - M)\!\downarrow$$

The opposite is true if the saving gap closes and absorption falls:

(FD 10.3) $$(S - I)\!\uparrow\; \rightarrow (\overline{Y} - A\!\downarrow)\!\uparrow\; \rightarrow (X - M)\!\uparrow$$

THE SAVING AND INVESTMENT APPROACH

SAVING AND INVESTMENT IN A CLOSED ECONOMY   The Irish example highlights the way in which a saving and investment approach can further our understanding of what has happened. Approach it more formally: Recall that the simplest national income accounting systems classify all goods and services produced as either consumption or investment—that is to say either used up during the year or set aside for future use. The measure of investment is gross fixed capital formation—which is all the new investments in such things as machinery, plant, housing, roads, or schools, whether built privately or publicly—plus any increase in inventory, known technically as change in stocks. Since to save something from one year to the next requires it to be in physical form, everything else produced in that year has to be consumed.[*]

The income spent on consumption and investment produces wages, salaries, interest, and profits, which in turn are *disposed of* as either consumption or saving. That is, households either use the income to buy goods or they don't use the income at all. This results in a simple accounting identity:

(Eq. 10.4) $$C + I = C + S$$

Since the consumption of goods and services produced equals in value the income spent on them, we can subtract C from both sides of the equation, getting

(Eq. 10.5) $$I = S$$

In this simple model, investment expenditures always equal saving.

EXPENDITURES AND SAVING AND THE BALANCE OF TRADE   The relation of the balance of trade to domestic saving and investment emerges when we add imports and exports to the equation. Expenditures on exports (X) come from outside the country and add income, resembling investment in their effect on demand. Exports include goods and services, with services including payments gained from investments abroad. Expenditures on imports (M) act domestically much like saving, and are withdrawn from the income stream.[**] Domestic households have the goods to use, but nobody domestically receives any income from them. The formula now has two added elements, X and M, such that

(Eq. 10.6) $$C + I + X = C + S + M$$

(Eq. 10.7) $$\text{or } I + X = S + M$$

With the added two variables, it is no longer true that domestic saving has to equal domestic investment. If, for instance, exports exceed imports, then saving will exceed investment.

The formula can be rearranged as follows:

(Eq. 10.8) $$X - M = S - I,$$

which is to say that exports exceed imports by the same amount that saving exceeds investment. A trade deficit equals the shortfall of saving; a trade surplus is the excess of saving.

Note that Castoria also experienced a situation in which its domestic use of resources (presumably for consumption and domestic investment) exceeded its production (by the amount of imported cloth). Fabrica undoubtedly saved more

---

[*] We recognize the difficult question of saving services, as in increased education, and students may check their other texts for the debates on how to handle that issue.

[**] The reader should be warned that it is customary to use M for imports as well as for money supply; the alternative is to use something like Z for imports, which is fine for formulas, but in practice it tends to throw some people more than having M occasionally mean something else. If the difference is not sufficiently clear from context, we refer to the money supply as MS.

than the surplus of cloth it exported, but it used all but the savings matching the cloth exports on various forms of domestic capital formation and inventories. (If it had brought cloth back from the trading market rather than lending it to the Castorians, it would have put the cloth in inventory, which would be a domestic investment.)

Economists sometimes refer to the shortfall of saving or the excess of saving over investment as the *saving gap*. We can compare the difference between saving and domestic investment with the difference between exports and imports—the *trade gap*. The following two charts express the saving gap as $I - S$, such that we produce a positive figure to describe the size of the gap and the trade gap as the usual $X - M$. First, examine the picture for the United States in Fig. 10.2.

The U.S. position in the 1980s contrasts with that of Japan, where total saving in recent years remained higher than domestic investment, yielding a saving gap with an excess of saving over domestic investment, as Fig 10.3 shows.

GOVERNMENT SAVING, INVESTMENT, AND CONSUMPTION

Often we lump government activities with private ones in our analysis, such that C includes government consumption, I includes government investment, and

Figure 10.2 **United States: Saving-investment gap and trade balance.** The U.S. trade deficit appears as the mirror image of the saving gap. The cause of this relationship is the accounting identity of $X–M$ with $S–I$. The diagram expresses the saving gap as $I–S$, such that any excess of investment over saving is reflected in an excess of imports over exports, as measured on $X–M$.[3]

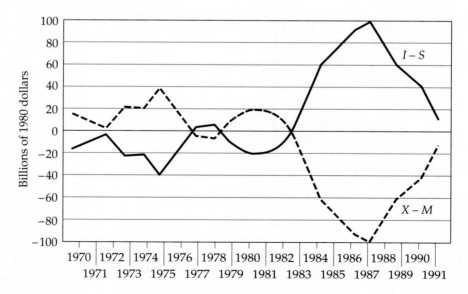

Figure 10.3 **Japan: Saving-investment gap and trade balance.** Japan's saving has remained higher than domestic investment, yielding a trade surplus.

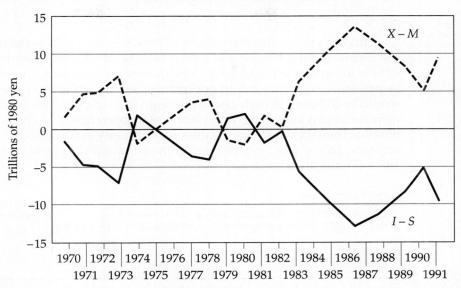

S includes government saving. Finer analysis can separate out the government's activities.

Adding government expenditures and taxation to the formula is straight-forward. G is government expenditure, which, like investment and exports, produces income. To conform to normal statistical categories, we consider only that part of government expenditure that is spent on consumption goods and services, and specify it as G_c. Government expenditures on investments, such as roads, bridges, and buildings (in the United States about 15% of all government expenditure) are included with I—gross fixed capital formation plus change in inventories. To specify that I includes both private and government investment, we will call it I_d for *domestic investment*.

T is government taxation and, like saving and imports, is a disposal of income.[*] Total domestic saving less taxes is now just private saving, which we label S_p.

(Eq. 10.9) $$I_d + X + G_c = S_p + M + T$$

---

[*] Neither G nor T includes government transfer payments: $10,000 in pension payments given to one person and taken from another is treated as if it were moved directly from the taxpayer to the recipient and does not appear as T or G. As the first chapter noted, the vast increase in government expenditure has not been on goods and services, but on transfers, so T, or the taxes net of transfers, is considerably lower than all government tax receipts (or R); just as G, government expenditures on goods and services, is much lower than gross government expenditures, including transfers (or E). In this case we are concerned only with taxes and government, net of transfers.

Government saving is $T - G_c$, tax revenues minus government consumption expenditures.[*] Combined with private saving we get:

(Eq. 10.10) $$X - M = S_p + S_g - I_d$$

This is a very useful relationship. While we see $X - M$ as the trade balance, the forms moving behind the screen may be of greater importance. A trade deficit, for instance, might arise from an increase in domestic investment, a fall in private saving, or a fall in government saving. Policy to reduce the deficit would be different in each case, as it might call for a decrease in investment, an increase in private saving, or an increase in government saving, or some combination thereof, but in no case does it call for any action directly on exports or imports. To see why, examine again the situation of Ireland in the 1970s and 1980s (Figure 10.4).

---

[*] Government investment, usually only a few percent of GNP, is normally not counted as part of the government's expenditures in figuring government saving. $T - G_c$ will therefore differ slightly from $T - G$ (all government expenditures), which is also the fiscal deficit.

Figure 10.4 **Ireland: Saving, investment, and balance of trade.** The huge Irish trade deficits occurred when both private and government saving fell in the early 1970s, while domestic investment rose. The Irish trade deficit reached 20% of GNP in 1979 as capital investment rose to 32% of GNP, and private saving declined. Government saving, already running between minus 8 and 10% of GNP, remained stable. Ireland recovered as private saving recovered somewhat and the government budget moved toward a (very modest) surplus, while investment fell from its dizzy heights.

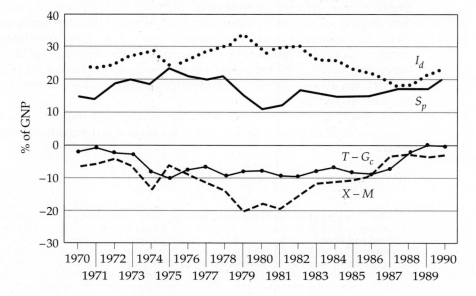

■ *KOREA REDUCES ITS TRADE DEFICIT*

For a contrast, see how Korea's sharp increase in saving in the 1980s turned a worrisome trade deficit into a thumping surplus.

Figure 10.5 **Korea: Domestic saving and investment.** As Korean income grew, domestic saving increased spectacularly, rising from about 17% of GNP in 1970 to 40% in 1988. Domestic investment also increased during the same period, but not as markedly. As domestic saving came to exceed domestic investment (in 1981), the trade balance swung sharply positive and the reliance on foreign saving ended. From 1981 to 1989 Korea was able to reduce its net indebtedness to almost zero.[*] From 1989 to 1990, saving declined a bit from its quite extraordinary peak, and domestic investment rose to an unprecedented level. The trade balance moved once again into deficit. This was textbook behavior for eliminating net foreign debt while keeping domestic investment high.

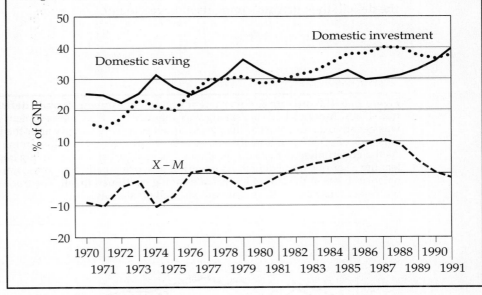

A DECLINE IN SAVING CAN CAUSE A TRADE DEFICIT

A trade imbalance generally has its roots in an imbalance between saving and investment or between income and absorption. Suppose we start the ball rolling

_____

[*] The diagram is in percentage of GNP terms. In real terms, 10% of GNP in 1988 was much larger than 10% in 1970, so the debt could be reduced dramatically.

by introducing a shock to $S - I$. We postulate a decline in saving (either government *or* private) *and* hold national income constant:

(FD 10.4) $$S{\downarrow} - \overline{I} \rightarrow (X - M){\downarrow}$$

Since a decline in S means an increase in C, then A, absorption, has also risen, so

(FD 10.5) $$\overline{Y} - A{\uparrow} \rightarrow (X - M){\downarrow}$$

THE UNITED STATES   A number of economists have cited the increasing government deficits as causing the severe balance of trade problems of the 1980s.[4] The basis for the argument is the relation of government deficits to the trade deficits. As Fig. 10.6 shows, in the 1970s U.S. private saving tended to offset government dissaving, leaving a small trade surplus. After 1980, however, private saving failed to rise to cover the increased government dissaving, producing the deficit; then private saving itself began to fall.

Figure 10.6 **U.S. private & government saving, investment, & trade deficit.** Until the mid-1980s, American private saving was about 20% of GNP. Government saving $(T - G_c)$ was negative during most of the period. It fell especially sharply after the Reagan tax cuts took effect. Notice how the slopes of $T - G_c$ and $X - M$ are close in the early 1980s. As the government deficits diminished in the late 1980s, private saving began to fall, leaving a serious trade deficit. As governments, principally state ones, improved their balance sheets in the late 1980s, private saving continued to fall. The trade deficit did not worsen because domestic investment also fell off sharply.

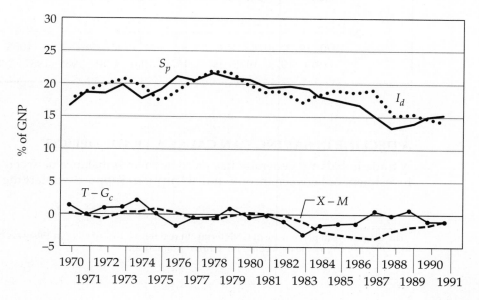

In the case of the United States, it appears until the late 1980s to have been principally government saving that has changed, as represented in a flow diagram.

(FD 10.6) $$(S_g\downarrow + \bar{S}_p - \bar{I})\downarrow \rightarrow (X - M)\downarrow$$

If the cut in taxes led to higher consumption, then

(FD 10.7) $$C\uparrow \rightarrow (\bar{Y} - A\uparrow) \rightarrow (X - M)\downarrow$$

TRADE IMBALANCES AND THEIR EFFECT ON $S - I$

To this point, we have been experimenting with the idea that it is powerful domestic factors that drive the trade balance. But however dramatic the analogy, $X - M$ is more than a shadow on a screen, and we have something to gain by shifting the scene, putting $X - M$ behind the screen and $S - I$ in front. Changes in $X - M$ also cause changes in $Y - A$ and $S - I$. How could $X - M$ influence $S - I$?

1. A decrease in the value of exports lowers income. As people try to maintain some semblance of their old spending levels, they decrease saving.

2. An increase in the price of imports, particularly of imports with inelastic demand curves such as food and fuels, may cause people to dig into savings so that they can buy both the imports and also the domestic goods they were accustomed to buying.

3. A decrease in the price of exports in itself may cause the government deficit to rise, either because

   a. total tax revenues are down, or more specifically,

   b. much tax revenue derives directly from exports.

4. Misapplied Keynesian methods (expanding an economy when in fact there was little voluntary unemployment) might be partially to blame for the deficit, although what we note under number 3 may suffice. If the government realizes that income has fallen and tries to stimulate the economy through fiscal means, and it does not respond, then the deficit will also rise.

One particularly clear example of the effect of trade prices on saving is that of Norway. With its large oil exports, the country, and particularly the country's budget, are heavily dependent on oil revenues. Figure 10.7 shows Norway's experience.

Take another step now to try to see what may lie yet deeper in the shadows. Given that saving seems such a key part of trade deficits, what drives it?

THE PROBLEM OF DOMESTIC SAVING: SOME MICRO ROOTS

THE DECLINE OF SAVING

The amount of saving is important in influencing both the trade balance and economic growth. Despite growing incomes, saving has declined as a percentage of

Figure 10.7 **Norway: Budget and trade balance.** The Norwegian government budget is closely tied to oil revenues. As a consequence, when oil revenues fell after the 1972–1974 oil crisis and again in the mid-1980s, both government saving and the trade balance fell together. When oil prices rose after 1978, the budget went into surplus, rising something like Kr 25 billion in three years. While the diagram on the surface shows that government saving and the trade balance are closely related, it is the trade balance that is highly important in determining government saving.

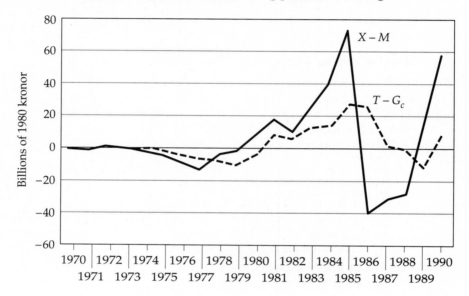

GNP in most major industrial countries, as shown in Fig. 10.8. The saving rates themselves may be quite slow to react to normal government fiscal and monetary policies, suggesting difficulties in countries' abilities to control both their rates of growth and their trade balances. If so, they impart a rigidity to the system that could have serious consequences.

As international economists, our principal concern with the large changes in saving is their effects not on economic growth, but on international adjustment. If governments could adjust their saving rates, they would not have to rely on manipulating investment levels to correct payments imbalances. To correct a trade deficit, would it not be better to increase saving rather than to decrease investment? If faced with an unnecessary surplus, would it not be better to increase consumption somewhat and enjoy life a bit?

A number of recent studies have struggled to understand what is occurring with saving. They seek to answer (1) What determines levels of saving? and (2) Can it be controlled, or at least tempered?

The answers that are emerging suggest that movements in saving levels are long-term ones, influenced by government policy, but slow in responding to

Figure 10.8[5] **Gross and net saving rates of industrial countries 1965–1987 (in percent of GNP)**

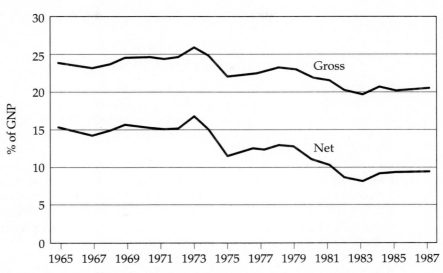

Source: *Organization for Economic Cooperation and Development,* National Accounts.

changed conditions. Governments have some room for maneuverability, but not a great deal.

We can look at the problem in two ways: by separating government saving (taxes minus government consumption or $T - G_c$) from private saving (S_p) or by looking at factors affecting both. Start by examining explicitly the role of government deficits.

GOVERNMENT SAVING AND TRADE DEFICITS: THE TWIN DEFICIT QUESTION

Government saving may play a vital role in national saving. Exactly what role it plays is in dispute, so we begin there.

THE DECLINE OF PUBLIC SAVING: BUDGETARY DEFICITS AND THE TRADE BALANCE   A common argument about public debt is that we owe it to ourselves, and it is therefore less serious a problem than if we owed it to outsiders. Most U.S. Treasury bills are indeed held by Americans. Even something like 80% of Canadian federal government debt is held by Canadians.[6] But who holds a bond is no more important than who pays a tax; taxes can be passed on and so can debt. If the government sells all its debt to its nationals, it still has to contend with one basic relationship: $X - M = S - I$. If we hold private saving equal to domestic investment and have a government deficit, we find that

(Eq. 10.11)
$$I_d + X - M = S_p + T - G$$
$$I_d = S_p$$
$$(X - M) = (T - G)$$

Thus, *the budget deficit equals the trade deficit!*

While the conjunction $S_p = I$ would be unusual, figures approximating it are not, and the lesson, in any case, need not be lost. Any change in $T - G$, given no change in S_p and I, will equal the *change* in $X - M$. Many critics of the Reagan Administration argued that in essence, the government deficits of those years *caused* the trade deficits, that the government borrowed private saving and spent it on government consumption. The Institute for International Economics' C. Fred Bergsten calls the budget and trade deficits *the twin deficits*, and argues that the elimination of the government deficit will make a major contribution toward eliminating the trade deficit.[7] We saw the twin deficits appear in Fig. 10.6 as the United States entered the 1980s.

In that figure, we could see that the increase in the federal government deficit after 1982 was closely linked to the increase in the trade deficit, particularly in the early years of the decade. The reduction of the deficit (combined federal, state, and local) in 1987 may have contributed to the small improvement in the trade balance.

If the budget deficit decreases domestic saving, then it helps create a trade deficit by widening the gap between I_d and S. Should this occur, it negates one of the standard defenses of an unbalanced budget—we owe all the debt to ourselves. The advantage of owing money to others in the same nation is that repayments are just transfers from one subset of people in the nation to another subset. Instead of Set 1 (taxpayers) getting the goods produced in the nation, Set 2 (bondholders) get the goods. The extent of the income redistribution is uncertain, because some individuals are in both sets, but the important factor is that the nation does still enjoy all the goods it produces. To reduce foreign debt, however, the nation must produce a trade surplus, saving more than it invests. There are accordingly real costs involved, regardless of the income distribution effects.

BARRO EFFECTS   We cannot conclude that a decline in government saving automatically leads to an increase in the trade deficit. This is because we do not know what impact the decline in government saving has on private saving or investment. For government saving to affect the trade balance, we need to hold Y, S_p (private saving), and I_d constant. If, however, a cut in taxes increased private saving, possibly by as much as the amount of the tax cut itself, then domestic saving would be unchanged.[*] Harvard's Robert Barro, among others,[8] argues that private and government saving tend to offset each other. His reasoning is

---

[*] The *permanent income hypothesis* arguments, as well as life cycle hypotheses, suggest that changes in government taxes or expenditures are offset by the private-sector reactions.

that when governments run deficits, taxpayers recognize that future taxes will be higher and increase their rate of saving to compensate. If, for instance, you planned on supplementing your Social Security with $20,000 a year in income, you might wish to set aside $300,000 (to yield 7.5% and leave your estate intact). If, however, you expected higher tax rates or that inflation would require a $30,000 supplement, you would save *more* as the government deficit rose (and less as it fell). While logical, the model will only work if citizens are both rational and well-informed, and while as economists we may assume the first, we cannot assume the second.

Barro's argument in a sense is not so much one of theory but one of behavior. Yes, rational, fully informed households will increase their saving to offset government dissaving resulting in little or no change in total domestic saving, *but* households are not always well informed and generally do not, or at least in some countries do not, so react. This may explain why the evidence for *Barro effects* so far is mixed. United States figures did not show strong support for any counterbalancing in the mid-1980s,[9] although the late 1980s provided some support as the declining government deficits were offset by declining personal saving.[10]

In contrast to the American, Canadian figures seem to substantiate Barro's thesis, with private saving rising as government saving falls, and falling as it rises. Canadian government deficits were larger on a percentage or per-capita basis than American deficits, yet because private saving was high, Canada was able to run a number of trade surpluses in the 1980s. Figure 10.9 shows the twin deficits for Canada.

Theory, policy, and statistics come together on this question. If private-sector saving behavior is sufficiently isolated (by lack of information, appreciation of the information, or ability to act) from public-sector deficits, then fiscal policy can cause or eliminate trade deficits. At first blush, the U.S. figures seem to confirm that assessment, while the Canadian ones do not. Yet, if it is the information and its assessment which are key, why should the Americans differ so much in their response from the Canadians? With all due respect to the True North Strong and Free, little suggests to either author that Canadians are more sophisticated about economic matters than Americans.[*]

More important, perhaps, than trying to demonstrate if Barro is right or not, is to keep in mind that private and government saving may not be independent. Barro is certainly right some of the time, and almost always to some degree. Most economists in policy positions would probably reject the more extreme position that private and government saving always (or in the long run) offset each other, and opt for some middle ground. The government deficits are, at least in some situations, the probable cause of trade deficits, but

---

[*] Clearly, other factors may also affect the statistical correlations. Our purpose here is not to apply exhaustive analysis, but to indicate general relationships. The IMF's Tamim Bayoumi in a recent paper figured that Barro effects might account for about 25% of an offset: That is, a $1 million increase in government deficit in many OECD countries was partially offset by a $250,000 rise in saving. See pp. 370–2 of his "Saving-investment correlation" in *IMF Staff Papers*, June 1990, pp. 360–387.

Figure 10.9 **Canada: A Barro effect?** Figure 10.9 tracks government saving on the left-hand axis, private saving on the right. The very good mirror images of the two pairs of lines show that movements of government and private saving tended to offset each other throughout the two decades shown. The correlations do not tell us whether the offsets occurred *because* people anticipated future expenditure, or whether some other factor affects government saving one way and private saving the opposite way.

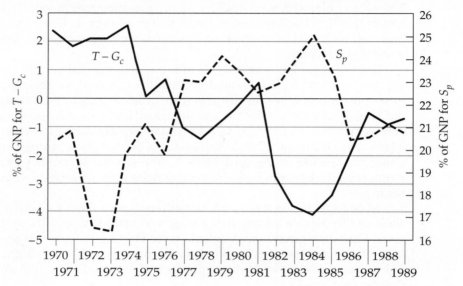

since it is uncertain in what situations that is true, the prescription just to cut the deficit is in itself simplistic. It may work and it may be, as Fred Bergsten argues for the Americans, "the only game in town," but its success is not assured.

We turn now to consider what it is that could be causing a general decline in saving—and if we do not fully accept Barro, we can call it the decline in private saving.

PRIVATE SAVING

Governments take the brunt of much complaining, but (1) private saving has also declined, and (2) it may have declined *even farther* if the government saving has not declined.[11] The decline in private saving, accordingly, commands close attention. The causes of the decline in (private) saving may be principally demographic, but other factors come to bear as well.

DEMOGRAPHIC CHANGE AND THE SAVING LIFE CYCLE HYPOTHESIS
Putting on rose-colored glasses for a moment, contemplate a plausible hypothesis: International trade imbalances may be nothing more (or less) than large intergenerational transfers, smoothing the consumption pattern of individuals and also of nations. Let us see why.

People tend to save most money in the years before retirement, when earnings are high but are expected to fall. They save the least in retirement, in the years before they work, and in their early working years. That, in essence, is the *life cycle hypothesis* of saving, useful in domestic macroeconomics. Its international implications are of great importance because it suggests that a country's saving (as a percentage of GNP) can be predicted by observing its demographic profile. Moreover, the same intergenerational patterns of the working-age people lending to the young and the old using up (or not increasing) their saving extends into the international sphere.

The 1980s' trade deficits of the United States and Canada, for instance, were the result of the large number of *baby boomers* (children born between 1946 and 1964) in the late school and early working years. As they move into their high earning and saving periods, North American saving is expected to rise. Western Europe and Japan, on the other hand, have relatively older populations, many of whom will be moving into retirement, and their saving is expected to fall. Given no sharp change in investment patterns, North America would then move into a trade surplus position. Table 10.1 illustrates the changes in *dependency ratio*—the number of under 15- and over 64-year-olds as a percentage of the 15–64-year-old population, historically and as projected.

The life cycle saving hypothesis suggests, then, that high-saving middle-aged people in Europe are lending resources to younger, lower-saving North Americans. When, however, the Europeans and Japanese turn older, they will save less while North Americans save more. North Americans will repay their debt and in the process all groups will enjoy a smoother pattern of consumption over their lives. What appears to be a spendthrift period in North America evens out with a thrifty one in the longer run.

OTHER CONSUMPTION-SMOOTHING DEVICES   Several other sources of declining saving are also at root devices to smooth income over a person's life.

1. One powerful force has been the cushion provided by Social Security, widespread unfunded[*] pension benefits, and various other advantages that have reduced the need for such high individual saving. (Japanese old-age benefits, for instance, are poor and may be related to that country's high saving rate.) Since such arrangements are not created by setting aside any after-tax income, they will require those working in the future to have lower after-tax incomes.[**]

2. Better financial markets, allowing easier borrowing (particularly for consumer and mortgage credit) and safer and higher-yielding investments may also have contributed to the decline in saving. The young people can borrow

---

[*] Funded pensions are those the employer creates by setting aside funds today and investing them in the capital market. Unfunded benefits are paid out of the employer's revenue when due.

[**] None of these elements are new enough to explain the sudden drop in saving in the recent decade. They may contribute, but in themselves they are not the cause of the problem. This applies to a number of the other factors as well.

Table 10.1   **Selected demographic variables, 1965–2025 (in percent).** If saving is highest in nations with lower dependency ratios, as most studies suggest it indeed is, then the trade deficits of the United States should turn into surpluses sometime in this decade. Canada's will turn, but a bit later. Japan and Western Europe should develop deficits. This clearly depends on domestic investment not rising sufficiently in North America (or falling in Europe and Japan) to overcome the rise in saving.[12]

				Projections			
Country	1965	1975	1985	1995	2005	2015	2025
	Population under 15/population 15–64						
United States	51	39	33	34	29	29	30
Japan	38	36	32	25	28	28	27
Germany, Federal Republic of	35	34	22	23	22	19	23
France	41	38	32	31	28	26	28
Italy	—	—	—	25	25	22	24
United Kingdom	36	37	29	31	31	31	31
Canada	57	41	32	30	27	25	28
	Population 65 and over/population 15–64						
United States	16	16	18	19	18	21	29
Japan	9	12	15	19	26	33	32
Germany, Federal Republic of	18	23	21	24	29	31	37
France	19	22	20	22	24	27	33
Italy	—	—	—	22	25	28	32
United Kingdom	19	22	23	23	22	24	28
Canada	13	13	15	18	19	25	34
	Overall dependency ratio						
United States	67	55	51	52	47	50	59
Japan	48	48	47	44	54	61	59
Germany, Federal Republic of	54	56	43	47	51	51	60
France	61	60	52	53	52	53	61
Italy[a]	52	54	45	47	50	50	55
United Kingdom	55	59	52	54	53	55	59
Canada	70	54	48	48	46	50	61

Sources: Organization for Economic Cooperation and Development, Labour Force Statistics, 1964–84, 1967–87; *and* OECD Secretariat, Directorate for Social Affairs, Manpower, and Education, Demographic Databank projections.

[a] *Fund staff estimates for 1965–1985.*

easily, balancing the consumer debt with the expectation of higher incomes in the future. The elderly can find high-yielding investments for their remaining nest eggs. The young of North America have been borrowing from the old of Europe and Japan.

OTHER INFLUENCES ON SAVING

Wealth Effects   A combination of influences, particularly the increased demand for housing (generated to a considerable degree by the baby boomers) and rising values of shares in the stock market, have meant that less saving was needed. Since people (and corporate pension funds) usually aim for a given target of wealth to hold, the increased values of their properties, land, and shares have lowered the need for saving.

Taxes Many countries have systematically discouraged private saving with their tax systems. Income from saving is taxed even when inflation has brought the real interest rates down to zero or even less. Inflation itself, by lowering real interest rates, may also have contributed to lower saving.[13] Corporate profits taxes reduce the amount corporations are able to put into retained earnings. Tightened restrictions on retirement funds (United States) or on tax-free interest on some kinds and amounts of saving (Canada) have also reduced the incentive to save.

In addition, many tax systems encourage debt over saving. In the United States, the United Kingdom, and a number of other countries, mortgage interest is tax deductible, as payments on consumer loans have been. If at the same time, interest on saving is taxed (even when it just holds even with inflation), why should anyone pay off a mortgage? Personal saving rates in Canada, which does not have such deductions for interest, are considerably higher than those in the United States, a fact that may be related to the tax system.

While *domestic* investment and *domestic* saving are often closely correlated, they need not be. *Total* investment and *total* saving, however, remain an accounting identity, something we explore, with some of its implications, in the next section.

TRADE IMBALANCES AS PROBLEMS AND SYMPTOMS

TRADE IMBALANCES, CAPITAL ACCUMULATION, AND GROWTH

Capital accumulation is an essential for economic growth over the long term. In the short term, a nation that has substantial unemployment and underutilized physical facilities can grow simply by using its existing facilities more—that is, by getting close to full employment. Even at full employment, a nation can grow through better use of the existing capital—a better use deriving from greater education levels, improved technology, wider markets, and/or greater specialization of production, to mention a few key elements. Still, at some point such gains are used up, and it would be an odd nation indeed that changed technology and education without increasing its capital base at the same time. Without the accumulation of physical capital to produce more goods and services—more transportation facilities, more machinery, more buildings, more communications facilities, *many of them embodying the new technology*—the other sources of economic growth would have far less effect.

Growth in this sense derives from the *domestic* capital base. But what about the saving a country has lent abroad? Of what use is that to it? It is indeed part of a nation's capital base. Unlike the domestic base, which is held in physical form, the foreign base is held in *financial* form, a topic we explore shortly.

DOMESTIC BASE

The domestic base of a nation's capital is the total accumulation of everything that has been made, saved, and not used (or depreciated). Statistically, it is the accumulated gross fixed capital formation, plus changes in inventories, minus depreciation. All the arguments about the definition of investment, therefore, also apply to the definition of capital.

Subtracting the rate of depreciation with gross investment shows net domestic investment:

(Eq. 10.12) $$I_d - Dp = NI_d$$

where Dp = depreciation (capital consumption) and

NI_d = net domestic investment

An important related concept is *net* national product, which has depreciation (often called *capital consumption allowance*) subtracted.

(Eq. 10.13) $$GNP - Dp = NNP$$

Occasionally under duress of war, revolution, famine, collapse of export prices, or other economic difficulties, nations fail to replace their capital stock, and national product begins to shrink. If I falls below Dp, the capital base of the economy will decline, and in subsequent years productivity—or at least that part contributed by the increase in capital—will fall.

FOREIGN CAPITAL BASE

An accumulation of foreign assets is also an important part of a nation's capital base. The investments made abroad produce interest and profit, which are part of the income stream. As Chapter 19, on multinational firms, explains, foreign investments are also closely connected to the full exploitation of the value of innovations, inventions, and other forms of *proprietary* knowledge, serving therefore to increase employment in various knowledge-producing or -processing jobs. If a particular firm or bank sees an opportunity to invest abroad at a higher interest rate (and the same risk) than it does domestically, that income will yield a larger income stream than it will if it were invested in domestic capital. A nation whose foreign investments decline sees a decline in its income and jobs just as much as does a nation whose own physical capital decreases.

Note that foreign investment can be in financial form and need not be in physical form like domestic investment. The introductory textbooks teach us that investment must be in physical form (or perhaps in human capital) to be counted as investment, not income transfers. Yet here we are treating strictly financial investments like physical investments.

For the nation, an accumulation of foreign assets fulfills the criterion needed to be an investment—goods set aside in one period that can be used in a subsequent period without having to devote new resources to their creation. A Canadian purchasing a bond in the United States does not increase North American investment one iota, but does increase *Canadian* investment; Canada can in any future year claim goods and services from the United States equal to that investment—and that is, from a national viewpoint, just as much an investment as inventory increases or machinery. The sale of the bond by the American has decreased U.S. claims on the rest of the world and is a form of international borrowing or disinvestment; in the future, Americans will have to provide the goods and services represented by that bond sale whenever the Canadians desire to cash in the bond.

Since the United States has not physically set anything aside on selling the bond, no North American investment has occurred; U.S. disinvestment matches Canadian investment, so the *net* effect on *world* investment is zero. If we add all the nations' investments and disinvestments together, we should come out with zero. No double counting should occur.

THE INTERPLAY OF DOMESTIC AND FOREIGN CAPITAL STOCKS

The only way a country can have a trade deficit is to go into debt or sell off existing foreign assets. Castorians went into debt when they agreed to deliver more pelts the next year; they could also have borrowed money from some other source in Fabrica to pay the traders. If in previous years they had accumulated credits or bought assets in Fabrica, they could turn them in. A country with a surplus has to place the surplus in some financial form. The Fabricans left their surplus as pictures of beavers, and extension of *commercial credit*, to be technical. In a more modern economy, they could have received money and invested that in bonds or physical assets in Castoria.[*]

To the extent that a nation draws down its stock of foreign assets or incurs additional foreign debt, its domestic investment is not *net* investment. A firm that reduces a sinking fund to build up its plant and equipment does not count the increased value of its plant as net new investment. In the same way, a country cannot count the increase in its domestic capital as net of whatever it has sold off or borrowed abroad to make those investments.

We can best show this by returning to our formula for national product.

(Eq. 10.14) $$GNP - Dp = NNP$$

---

[*] Students sometimes ask, "Can't they buy goods with it?" Of course, but if they buy goods they no longer have a surplus. Chapter 11 handles the more special problem of gifts. Fabrica could *give* away its surplus and be left with no investment.

Enlarging this to show the components of GNP, C, I, G, and $X - M$,

(Eq. 10.15) $C + I + G - Dp + (X - M) = \text{NNP}$

If imports exceed exports ($M > X$), then the stock of foreign investment is lowered. To pay for the deficit, the country must sell off foreign assets or borrow by selling its own assets to foreigners. The *net* foreign investment of the country accordingly falls. In this sense, a trade deficit is much the same as depreciation and has to be subtracted from the country's net investment. We can show this by stating the trade deficit as $M - X$, which produces a positive figure if imports exceed exports. Restating the formula, we get:

(Eq. 10.16) $C + I + G - Dp - (M - X) = \text{NNP}$

Unless I exceeds both Dp and $(M - X)$, the nation's capital base will shrink and its potential productivity in subsequent years is lowered.

IS A TRADE DEFICIT A BAD THING?

A trade deficit is not in itself good or bad. The country may be borrowing abroad to invest at home in investments that have much higher benefits. Or it may, as can be argued for the United States, wish to smooth consumption patterns over several decades and be willing and able to pay the cost of doing so. We thus have two questions, neither easy, to answer:

1. Is the deficit too costly such that the payments on the borrowings might be unsustainable? We will begin to address this in the next chapter.
2. Is the benefit, even where payments can be sustained, worth the cost?

    We turn to the second question now.

THE COST   Nations whose net foreign investment position is negative—that is, who owe more than they have invested abroad—usually have more interest and profits payments flowing out of the country than coming in. Expenditures that otherwise could have been made on domestic consumption, investment, or government are instead spent on the profits and interest payments required to pay for another year's use of other nations' saving. These count as imports of services, but certainly do not give as much satisfaction as imported capital goods or consumption goods. Economically, it may be quite reasonable to borrow considerable amounts from abroad if the investments those borrowings allow are sound and help build capacity in the domestic economy; in such cases the payments abroad are only a small portion of the net economic benefits. When, however, the borrowing from abroad is used for largely consumption purposes and investment does not rise, future payments for those borrowings must come from the same economic base as before. Some examples can illustrate these points.

Figure 10.10 **United States: Domestic, foreign, and net investment and depreciation.**
Real domestic investment, I_d (the top line) was under $600 billion for the entire period.
More troubling, while I_d remained stagnant, the United States was losing its foreign
assets and increasing its debt abroad. The trade deficit, $X - M$, represents the amount
the United States was borrowing or investing abroad; it turned negative in 1983 and
U.S. net assets abroad began to fall. Depreciation, high because of the large capital stock
in the United States, became larger as GNP rose. The bars are net investment, figured as
in Equation 10.15; net investment appears to be negative in recent years, even with the
improvement in the trade balance.[*]

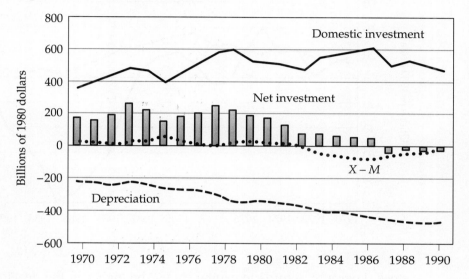

THE SITUATION OF THE UNITED STATES: BORROWING FOR CONSUMPTION
In the case of the United States, as shown in Fig. 10.10, there is no evidence that
its foreign borrowing in the 1980s built up the domestic capital stock. Rather, it
functioned as an intergenerational transfer of consumption between the United
States and the rest of the world. Net total investment figures for the United
States throughout the mid-1980s were low—under 4% between 1983 and 1987. In
chart form, the 1980s show a picture of declining U.S. net investment.

Accompanying the declining foreign asset base has been a decline in earnings from foreign investments, measured mostly in an item called *net factor payments from abroad*, which Fig. 10.11 shows.

THE CASE OF THAILAND: CHANGING THE PORTFOLIO It is fairly common
for a developing country to increase foreign debt to build up its domestic capital

---

[*] The amount of depreciation is a difficult figure to calculate, and your authors rather doubt net
investment has been negative. Despite such inaccuracy, a low net investment figure is an indicator
of problems.

392 *International Macroeconomics*

Figure 10.11 **United States: Trade deficit and net factor receipts.** U.S. income from foreign investments, the major component of its net factor receipts, ran well over 40 billion 1980 dollars in the early 1980s. As the trade deficit began in 1982, the United States started to run down its foreign assets and increase its foreign debt, causing the net factor receipts to fall. It seemed in the late 1980s that NFR would fall below zero, but as the size of the trade deficit declined, they began to rise again.[*]

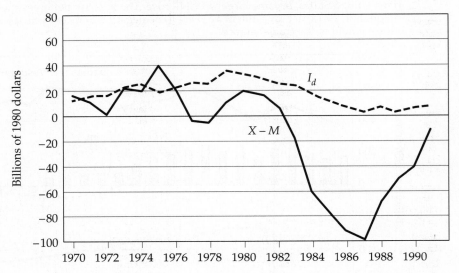

stock. Logically, returns to capital should be higher in the developing world than in the developed, so people in a developing nation can, judiciously of course, borrow from the developed world and invest at home at a higher return. So long as the nation can *service* the foreign debt by paying the interest and principal, the strategy can be successful. After all, the United States ran a trade deficit from its colonial beginnings until nearly the end of the nineteenth century, and was able to borrow easily throughout most of the period.

Such a strategy is plausible only if a nation's export receipts continue to grow enough to cover the accumulated debt. Figure 10.12 shows Thailand's investment patterns.

By reducing its foreign borrowings in the 1980s, Thailand also managed to stabilize its foreign debt payments, as shown in Fig. 10.13.

---

[*] How can returns increase if the United States is still borrowing more than it invests? Good question, with no obvious answer. Falling interest rates would mean lower debt payments to foreigners holding short-term U.S. assets, and the extensive American holdings in foreign direct investments could be increasing their dividends. Recent work suggests that the assets of U.S. companies abroad have been underestimated, since they are usually valued at cost rather than at putative market value, and the latter would be a better indicator of anticipated income streams. If so, profits abroad and reinvested earnings have also been underestimated. See Chapter 19.

Figure 10.12 **Thailand: Total and net investment, depreciation, and trade balance.**
Thailand's increase in domestic investment from 1974 to 1980 (top line) was closely
connected with increased foreign borrowing shown by the trade deficit ($X - M$), so net
investment remained at about the same level of just under 100 billion 1980 baht.
Thailand was clearly using the transfer from abroad to help it increase investment.
After 1980, however, Thailand's reliance on foreign saving lessened. Domestic
investment dipped only in 1982, then began to rise again, while the trade deficit fell to
nearly zero. Net investment rose steadily from 1983 onward, as more and more of the
gross fixed capital formation was generated from Thai saving. When foreign borrowing
became easier in the late 1980s, Thailand began to increase domestic investment again,
and redeveloped a trade deficit.

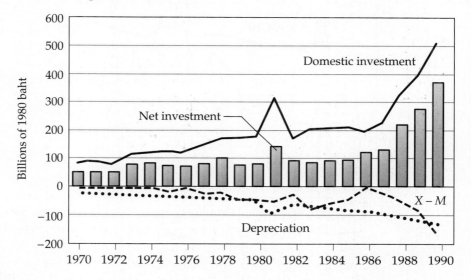

THE PROBLEMS FOR LENDERS So much for borrowers. What of lenders?
Whether the placing of additional saving abroad is a good or a bad thing depends
on the objectives of the country and its neighbors. With a given level of saving, the
choice between domestic and foreign investment is, in a sense, a *portfolio* choice,
with the nation deciding how many of its assets or debts it wishes to place at
home or abroad. Too much foreign investment can lead to a weak domestic economy, as has been argued for Britain in the last decades of the previous century
when *half of all British saving* was going abroad. The same argument has been
made for the Netherlands, as the expansive seventeenth century economy led into
a rentier eighteenth-century "Periwig" economy with vast sums invested in
British bonds.[14] Too little foreign investment, on the other hand, means forsaking
excellent foreign investment opportunities, the income from which will provide
foreign goods and services for years to come. And as Japan enters the mid-1990s
with sluggish demand at home and slowly growing markets, it, too, may begin to
question how much of its wealth it wants to place abroad.

Figure 10.13 **Thailand: Net factor payments as percent of GNP and exports.** Thailand can support its debt because its payments are moderate portions of its GNP and exports. Such payments have remained under 2% of GNP. Perhaps more important are net factor payments as a percent of exports, shown on the right-hand scale. NFP were negative (that is, they were net factor receipts) in 1970 and 1974, but they rose sharply in the 1970s, coming to near 8% by 1982. After that, however, they fell back to easily managed levels. One reason for the sharper decline against the right-hand scale is that exports were growing as a percentage of GNP.

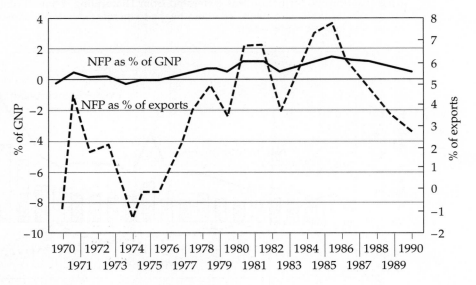

TOTAL INVESTMENT EQUALS TOTAL SAVING

A trade deficit measures the gap between domestic saving and domestic investment. When the United States has a $50 billion trade deficit, it means that foreign countries have saved $50 billion of income from goods they sold to the United States but did not collect on (much as the Fabricans did with the Castorians). Total domestic investment thus equals domestic saving plus foreign saving. To put it algebraically,

(Eq. 10.17) $$S_p + S_g + (X - M) = I_d$$

and $X - M = S_f$, where S_f = foreigners' saving, so

(Eq. 10.18) $$S_p + S_g + S_f = I_d.$$

Looking at the same issue from another angle, we could also say that total American investment was I_d *less* $(X - M)$. In this case, $X - M$ is foreigners' investments and must be subtracted, as in the examples above, from total American investment. We do not violate the basic equality of investment to saving.

THE INTERNATIONAL CAPITAL MARKET AND NATIONAL SAVING

It is surprising, given the differences in saving rates among countries, how small net transfers are—that is, how little trade imbalances count as a portion of income or saving. High-saving countries tend to invest heavily in their home markets, such that I_d and S_d are closely correlated.[15] In the late 1980s there was some shifting away from that pattern, typified perhaps by the lending between Japan and the United States, as shown in Fig. 10.14.

While overall domestic saving and investment are closely correlated, that is not so for private investment and gross capital formation (Fig. 10.15). Some IMF economists argue that private capital does indeed seek the highest yielding investments, but that government saving offsets the private movements.

This argument suggests that governments may either accidentally or deliberately keep their trade imbalances down. Where a country's private saving is high this could involve greater government investment or dissaving, and where saving is low, less government investment or more government saving.[16]

CONCLUSION

A principal thrust of this chapter has been to show the relationship of the saving-investment gap and the related absorption gap to trade imbalances—the *trade gap*, to give it a name. Patterns of causality are complex, but there is ample

---

Figure 10.14[17] **The United States and Japan: Gross national saving, domestic investment, and current account balance, 1965–1987 (in percent of GNP).** The United States and Japan, like most other OECD countries, saw saving and investment rise and fall closely together until the mid-1980s. After that period, gaps opened up, indicating increasing net foreign investment and borrowing. The current account balance, explained in the next chapter, is very close in size and meaning to the trade balance.

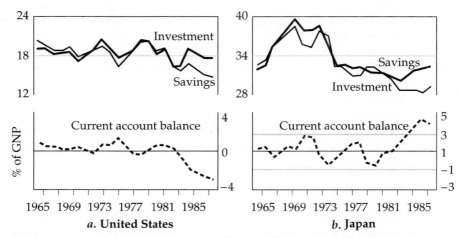

a. **United States**   *b.* **Japan**

Source: Aghevli et. al., "The Role of National Saving in the World Economy," Occasional Paper No. 67, IMF, March 1990.

Figure 10.15[18] **Saving and investment: Average values, 1965–1986 (as a ratio to GNP).**
The left panel shows total saving and investment as closely correlated. Investment as a
portion of GNP is on the vertical axis, and saving on the horizontal. Low savers are
clearly also low investors. The right-hand panel, however, shows considerably less
correlation when comparing private fixed investment with private saving.[19]

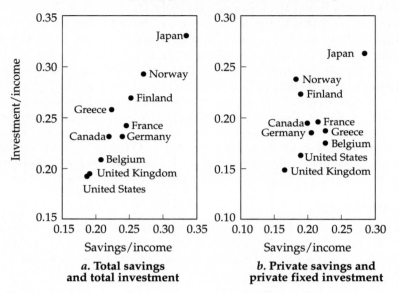

a. **Total savings
and total investment**

b. **Private savings and
private fixed investment**

evidence to suggest that it is frequently shocks to the domestic gaps that give rise
to the trade imbalances. If, indeed, trade imbalances emerge from deeply rooted
patterns of saving and investment, then *macroeconomic* policy may be singularly
ineffective in correcting them. Changes in tax structures, in controls over government expenditure, in incentives for private saving, or in encouragement of the
proper long-run level of investment may be what is required to eliminate trade
deficits or surpluses.

A second thrust of this chapter has been to indicate what the costs of trade
imbalances are, both to the trade-deficit and to the trade-surplus country. Is
their control in fact the *central question* or is their size *incidental* to other basically
more important economic goals such as high levels of employment, efficient
allocation of resources, and economic growth? We trust it becomes clear that the
pursuit of balanced trade for its own sake is neither fruitful nor wise. Countries
can live for generations with deficits or surpluses; the ultimate question is
whether in so doing they are in fact reaching some optimal level of growth and
employment.

A backward look is also instructive. Trade deficits do not arise because of
other countries' trade policies. Protectionism reduces the total amount of trade
and economic efficiency. Artificial boosting of trade may increase trade, but

reduces efficiency. Neither fundamentally affects the balance of trade. If a country absorbs more than it produces, it will have a deficit; if it produces more than it absorbs, it will have a surplus.

The following chapter takes up several of the questions we have raised in this one. In particular, it examines how a trade deficit is financed to show the cost of deficits—the interest costs of carrying debt. Moreover, it shows how one can use the balance of payments statement to develop far more precision and far greater insights into the international economic situation of any country.

VOCABULARY AND CONCEPTS

Absorption

Balance of trade

Barro effect

Capital accumulation

Consumption-smoothing device

Demographic change

Domestic capital base

Foreign capital base

GDP

GNP

Income-absorption gap

Life cycle hypothesis (and trade imbalances)

Output (income)

Savings-investment gap

Twin deficit question

Trade imbalance

QUESTIONS

1. $X - M$ is:

   a. the difference between exports and imports
   b. the difference between domestic saving and domestic investment
   c. the difference between production and absorption
   d. the foreign saving a nation uses or the saving it places abroad
   e. all of the above

   Why?

2. "If markets clear, then we can have no trade deficit." Explain.

3. Assume that the Castorians and the Fabricans trade together as described in the text's example, and that the Castorians fail to bring the usual number of beaver pelts to the market. To get the same number of trade goods, the Castorians agree to deliver next year an extra 2000 pelts and the Fabricans supply their usual number of trade goods.

   Explain the following:

   a. How this is a trade surplus or deficit?
   b. How does the market clear?
   c. Who can absorb more than they produce and who less?
   d. Who is using whose saving?
   e. Who has invested what in whom?

4. Why are imports subtracted from $C + I + G + X$? Why not just count the domestically made C, I, and G?

5. In the first year we learned that $S = I$, yet we can see here that S_d need not equal I_d. Why?

6. Korea's trade deficit declined sharply as growth and saving rose. The book describes the growth of the trade surplus, and its subsequent moderation, as "textbook behavior." What was peculiarly appropriate about it?

7. What is the twin deficits problem? What are the arguments for $T - G$ causing the decline in saving? What arguments are there against this?

8. What in the pattern of demographic change might give a Canadian or an American hope for turning around balance of payments deficits?

9. The foreign capital base is held in financial form. Is that consistent with other economic interpretations of investment?

10. Thailand, a developing country, has used foreign saving to cover about 17% of its gross fixed capital formation over the last two decades. In the late 1980s, it began to reduce its dependence on foreign saving. Explain, using algebra and referring to the graph on Thailand.

11. Despite vast improvements in international capital markets, countries that are high savers are high domestic investors, with only a bit flowing outside. What is the evidence for such a statement? Why might this be happening? Is it a new thing or something old?

12. One interpretation of the U.S. trade deficit is that it is a result of the Reagan tax cuts of 1982 which, as one wag put it, "raised the disposable incomes of all those who had not read Robert Barro and David Ricardo." Explain, showing the role of the decline in government saving, and what the Barro effect is.

13. Are trade deficits bad? Are trade surpluses good?

14. "Government deficits are no problem because we owe all the money to ourselves." The speaker either doesn't know his international economics or is a neo-Ricardian (a believer in Barro effects). Why?

15. Countries with trade surpluses are investors abroad. Is that always a good thing?

16. A recent newsletter from the Federal Reserve Bank of San Francisco reviews the improvement in the U.S. balance of trade in 1991 and concludes:

> The continued existence of U.S. trade deficits reflects an imbalance of national saving above investment [that is, I > S], not any fundamental decline in competitiveness. . . . But thinking that the U.S. is uncompetitive and "over the hill" can create undue attention for inappropriate short-term economic solutions such as greater protectionism, managed trade policy, or industrial targeting, particularly during the current period of macroeconomic stress.[*]

At root, do the problems of trade imbalances have much to do with trade policy? Are they problems of fiscal policy?

NOTES

[1] The concept of absorption goes back to Sidney S. Alexander, "Effects of a devaluation on a trade balance," *IMF Staff Papers*, 1952, pp. 263–278. By giving primacy to the domestic saving and investment patterns, the absorption approach fits in well with much of the current policy literature, and to some considerable extent our saving and investment model fits better into that framework than it does the Keynesian, which we expound in Chapter 12. See Thomas F. Dernburg, *Global Macroeconomics*, New York, Harper and Row, 1989, Chapter 9.

[2] All of the national income figures used in this chapter are derived from three readily available data sources: *International Financial Statistics, Government Financial Statistics Yearbook* (which gives figures on

consolidated government spending, particularly investment spending, which is rarely included as a separate item in the *IFS* statistics), and *National Accounts Statistics Yearbook*. The last is a good publication, but is normally years behind in the data it presents. It is, however, one of the few good sources for depreciation estimates.

[3] All figures in this chapter are based on national income accounts. The trade deficit as figured in such accounts often differs substantially from the figures given in balance-of-payments accounting. The System of National Accounts makes no attempt to reconcile balance-of-payments figures with national account figures.

[4] See, as a well-articulated statement of the position, the first five chapters of C. Fred Bergsten, *America in the*

---

[*] Reuven Glick, *FRBSF Weekly Letter*, Number 92013, March 27, 1992.

World Economy: A Strategy for the 1990s, Washington, D.C., Institute for International Economics, 1988.

[5] Bijan Aghevli, James M. Boughton, Peter J. Montiel, Delano Villanueva and Geoffrey Woglom, *The Role of National Saving in the World Economy,* IMF, March 1990.

[6] Far more of the provincial debt is held abroad.

[7] C. Fred Bergsten, *America in the World Economy,* Washington, D.C., Institute for International Economics, 1988, Chapter 5. An interesting set of essays on the issues, quite approachable for undergraduates, is in James M. Rock, ed., *Debt and the Twin Deficits Debate,* Mountain View, CA, Bristlecone Books, 1991.

[8] A recent discussion of the problem is Tamim Bayoumi, "Saving-investment correlations," *IMF Staff Papers,* June, 1990. See pp. 370–372, and bibliography.

[9] See Lawrence Summers and Chris Carroll, "Why is U.S. national saving so low?" *Brookings Papers on Economic Activity,* Vol. 2, 1987, pp. 607–635.

[10] See A. Lans Bovenberg and Owen Evans, *IMF Staff Papers,* September 1990.

[11] We rely on Aghevli et al, *The Role of National Saving.* See also Olli Pekka Lehmussaari, "Deregulation and consumption: Saving dynamics in the Nordic countries," *IMF Staff Papers,* March 1990 and A. Lans Bovenberg and Owen Evans, cited above. For general readers, a review of these and several other related articles is in the June 1990 issue of *Finance and Development.*

[12] The table and some of the discussion derive from Paul R. Masson and Ralph W. Tryon, "Macroeconomic effects of projected population aging in industrial countries," *IMF Staff Papers,* September 1990, pp. 453–490. The table is from page 457. Masson and Tryon also demonstrate several other macroeconomic effects (on the investment side) of the demographic trends that will also contribute to a shift toward North American trade surpluses.

[13] It is hard to be sure which way inflation works, since it increases uncertainty and may encourage saving.

[14] See C.R. Boxer, *The Dutch Seaborne Empire: 1600–1800,* New York, Alfred A. Knopf, 1965.

[15] The classic article is Martin Feldstein and Charles Horioka, "Domestic saving and international capital flows," *Economic Journal,* June 1980, pp. 314–329. Their findings have been confirmed consistently.

[16] Bayoumi rejects the ideas of endogeneity and blockage to international capital movements. Endogeneity, where wonderful investment opportunities would stimulate people to save, is plausible, but does not meet his statistical tests. The vigor of the international capital market demonstrates that it would be very hard for governments to keep capital at home (or out).

[17] From Aghevli, *The Role of National Saving...,* p. 15. Aghevli's source was the OECD.

[18] Bayoumi, p. 364.

[19] Bayoumi's measurements show a beta value of .97 for the left-hand panel and .58 for the right-hand panel. (The beta measures correlation, 1.0 being a perfect correlation.) See Bayoumi, p. 364.

Chapter 11

The Balance of Payments

OBJECTIVES

Overall Objective: To demonstrate how the figures on balance-of-payments accounts mesh with those for national income, giving a more precise description of the nature of current account surpluses or deficits, and of how surpluses were invested or how deficits were financed.

MORE SPECIFICALLY:

- To show the situations of several key countries.
- To demonstrate how to read a basic balance-of-payments statement, identifying the key accounts.
- To present the basic principles involved in constructing and understanding the accounts.
- To relate the figures on the balance of payments to national income accounts.

An ability to understand a balance-of-payments statement (BOPS) is as important to an international economist as reading a corporate account is to a financial analyst, or reading personal accounts is to a bank loan officer. It is key to being able to combine theoretical with statistical analyses, and contributes toward the always-difficult art of taking models that are general and fitting them to individual cases. What this chapter reveals is that no two countries are alike—that even two countries of the same size with the same trade deficit may face very different kinds of problems, with differing degrees of seriousness. We should not, after all, be surprised at that: Of three students in debt, one owing money to her parents, one to his bank with collateral to back it, and one to the guy with dark glasses who hangs around the poolhall, we might surmise that the last has the most trouble. Similarly, the nature of the international debt—and to some extent the cause of the debt—can vary immensely, as can the consequences of missing payments.

For anyone with a bent for accounting, or at least its theoretical side, the BOPS has its own fascination, if only for the crudity of its figures and the difficulties of its classification system. For those who just want to have the ability to find some concrete numbers to go with theory, BOPS is an essential tool.

WHAT A BALANCE-OF-PAYMENTS STATEMENT SHOWS

A BOPS shows, in brief:

1. The extent of a country's trade imbalance and in what categories (for instance, in physical goods, in tourism, in interest on debt) it had deficits or surpluses.

2. The extent to which a country went into additional debt or drew down foreign assets, or paid back debt or built up foreign assets.

3. The nature of the borrowing or investment that went on. This includes the specifics of private borrowing and lending and the various categories in which they occur.

4. The activities of monetary authorities—the central banks and the Federal Reserve.

In all, a careful examination of a BOPS can give a good sense of where international debt or credits were incurred, how debt was financed or credits invested, and what kinds of risks or advantages result from the particular patterns. We examine these points more closely.

BALANCE-OF-PAYMENTS ACCOUNTING

THE NATURE OF THE BALANCE OF PAYMENTS

Probably not one in a hundred economists, even those specializing in international economics, could explain every item on a payments statement, so students should not feel overwhelmed when they first view a real BOPS, with its great list of items.[1] The object of this chapter is to show how the balance-of-payments statement fits in with the discussions of national income in the previous chapter and to provide an introduction to using payments statements. The full significance of some of the material, particularly that under the monetary account section, will not emerge until later in the text, but it is important to develop a basic understanding of it at this point.

PAYMENTS AND CLAIMS

An imbalance of trade ($X > M$ or $X < M$, including services) always generates a claim by residents of one nation on residents of another. As Fabrica found when it traded with Castoria, it had not only a trade surplus but also a claim on Castoria at the end of trading. Because it did not use all it received from exports on imports, it held the surplus as a claim on Castoria. Similarly, any country in Fabrica's position holds its surplus as a claim on another nation's goods. It can do only three things with its surplus:

1. Invest it, in which case it keeps the claim.

2. Pay back debts accumulated abroad, thereby canceling a claim some other nation had on its future production.

3. Relinquish its claim by giving it to the residents of another country, or by having it taken away, as would occur if a company in another country defaulted on a loan.

A nation with a trade deficit has to explain how it managed to obtain the means to buy imports worth more than the goods and services it exported. It could have done so in only three ways:

1. It used previous savings it had abroad, selling off its holdings of foreign bonds, banking accounts, and the like, and reducing its stake in foreign companies.

2. It *borrowed* through selling foreign residents bonds, bills, bank accounts, shares in corporations, or the corporations themselves.

3. It managed to persuade foreign residents (or their governments) to give it extra goods or services, as, for instance, a form of economic or military aid.

WHAT IS SUPPOSED TO BALANCE

The principle behind any accounting balance statement is simple enough—the account must add up every payment that the nation received from the rest of the world, and show what it did with what it received. (An *accounting* is, at root, a *telling,* an explanation.) Payments from abroad are *receipts,* or *credits,* and arise from all the nation's income from exports of goods and services, all the money foreign residents invested in the country, and all the gifts from abroad it received. The *payments,* or *debits,* account traces how the nation disposed of those receipts. The nation would use its foreign exchange receipts to import, to invest abroad, to retire foreign debts, and to make gifts and other unilateral transfers. The receipts always equal the payments because the account just describes what happened to the receipts—or how they were *disposed of.* The whole explanation could be seen the other way, with the receipts (or credits) explaining where the nation got the foreign exchange to make the payments (debits).

An analogy to a household may be instructive: If the household has spent on consumption expenses more than it earned, it will discover that the difference between what it earned and what it consumed has been provided by income transfers from others—perhaps a scholarship or gift, a loan from a bank, or just credit received on a credit card. If the household has consumed less than it has earned and seeks to account for the difference, it can check for increases in its savings accounts, repaid loans, accumulations of cash in drawers and piggy banks, or gifts of cash to others. Even if it fails to find what happened to all the money it earned, it still is trying to *account* for it, and would have to note that it had an unexplained amount, known as an *error* or a *discrepancy.* Anyone who has tried to tote up a year's household expenses knows that it is almost always easier to figure out what was spent on living expenses than to trace through the complexities of borrowings (including credit cards charges not yet on the statement), repayments, investments, and drawing down of assets, and even money in sugarjars. The family knows it is ahead if it did not consume or give away what it earned, but just where the money is may be difficult to discover.

Balance-of-payments accounting is similar to the household example, particularly in the sense of it being rather more a set of estimates than a record of transactions. The nation adds up all it has taken in from exports of goods and services, subtracts what it has spent for imports of goods and services, then tries to figure out what made up the difference. It looks first at gifts and similar transactions where goods are given away with no claim taken in return, and these are typically fairly small (at most a few percent of GNP). Then it looks at investments. If it had a trade surplus and did not give away all of that, then it will have made investments abroad. (Even if it is simply a case where goods have been shipped in December and payment is received in January, the balance of payments would count the goods as exports and the money not received by the close of the year as short-term investments.) Nations with trade deficits and insufficient gifts to cover those find that they have borrowed, and they show a net inflow of foreign investment.

In practice, the accounting is far more complicated, partly because investment flows are so much larger than trade flows. Short-term money may be flowing in, long term out. Debts are being repaid, while others are building up. Money is borrowed to be reinvested abroad. The central bank may be accumulating foreign investments. When all capital movements are taken together, they will equal the net difference in the current account, but it never looks as simple as that.

THE STRUCTURE OF THE BALANCE OF PAYMENTS

The balance-of-payments statement for any nation has three principal divisions, usually complicated by a number of items that do not fit cleanly: (1) the current account, which is the trade balance plus or minus unrequited transfers; (2) the capital account, which is a record of all the nation's borrowing and investment, except that done by the monetary authorities; (3) the official or monetary account, which records the lending or borrowing done through the monetary authorities (central bank for most countries and Federal Reserve for the United States).

THE CURRENT ACCOUNT

The current account shows the *net* change in a nation's international investment position—that is, whether it has increased or decreased its *net* claims on foreign residents.[2] The current account is further subdivided into visible or merchandise trade, invisible or service trade (including *net factor payments* or *net factor receipts*), and an unrequited transfers account.

The *balance of trade in goods and services* shows the extent to which a country generates claims on another country. The *unrequited transfers* indicate the amount of these claims that were simply relinquished—that is, some kind of debt was generated in trade, but it was never claimed. Typical unrequited transfers are foreign aid, immigrants' remittances (money immigrants send back home to their families), or pension payments across borders, all cases where a claim is transferred without anything being received in return. Together, the two trade accounts and the unrequited transfer account make the *current account.* The *current account balance* must always equal the net change in the investment position.

THE TRADE ACCOUNTS   The current account balance indicates the change in net credit or debit position of the nation—the extent to which it built up net foreign assets or increased its net foreign debt. The balance on goods and services is the key to telling how much the country saved: It is the $X - M$ of the formula $X - M = S - I$ and thus reflects the difference between domestic saving and investment.

The *balance on goods and services* records the value of all imports and exports of goods and services. It, in turn, is usually divided into trade in goods, known as *visible* or *merchandise* trade, and trade in services, or *invisible trade.* The *trade balance* is a bit ambiguous. In many accounts, including those of the IMF, it is equivalent to trade in goods, not including services. The popular media often fail to distinguish the *balance on goods* from the *balance on goods and services* and mislead the public. Canada, for instance, rarely has a deficit on the merchandise trade account and never has a surplus on the services account, yet many Canadians think that Canada's merchandise surplus means it is exporting more than it is importing. In fact, the Canadian merchandise trade surplus has to be substantial to overcome the deficit in services.

Economists often use *trade balance* to mean *the balance on goods and services.* That is our practice in this book, and if we mean otherwise we specify *merchandise* trade balance. Alone, the *merchandise* or *visible* trade balance has almost no economic significance. Whether people earn income from goods or services, whether countries borrow to pay for goods or services, or whether it is the good or the service we enjoy in the act of consumption hardly affects theory. The usage of *trade balance* to mean *merchandise* trade balance, like many other phrases in economics, comes from nineteenth-century usage patterns, not from economic analysis.

Another trade account item requiring some explanation is the services referred to as income. These are the factor payments noted in the previous chapter. Recall that it is these payments that distinguish Gross National Product from Gross Domestic Product, and that they are, for most countries, largely payments for use of borrowed capital. These payments must be figured in the trade account because they pay for a service consumed by a producing firm (and thus are a factor payment), rather than one rendered directly to the purchaser (which would make them final services).

■ *HANDLING FACTOR PAYMENTS: AN EXAMPLE*

We may illustrate factor payments by looking at how the balance of payments handles the affairs of the hockey stars, Jacques and Jean Penalité from Baton Elevé, Quebec. Brother Jacques plays for the *New York Rangers*; although living in the United States during the season, he maintains his Canadian resident's status. Fans who watch him are consuming the services of the *Rangers*, their payments going as consumption expenditures. Jacques' income turns up in American GNP, figured from the factor side, as wages. Since his residence is in Baton Elevé, Quebec, his income is also a *factor payment abroad* or *income debit*, and is subtracted from GDP to figure GNP. Jean, the second brother, plays for the *Montreal Canadiens*; when he plays in New York, American expenditures go to the *Canadiens* and Jean's share would fall under the import of services, not factor income. Jean does the same as his *Ranger* brother, but the team is a Canadian team, and so his income would not, like the *Ranger* brother, turn up in U.S. *wages and salaries* on the factor side of GNP. Both brothers are foreigners rendering services, but they are categorized differently. Both types of payment, however, should be categorized as payments for the import of services.

Unrequited Transfers   The goods and services balance does not fully show the changes of a country's net investment (or borrowing) with the rest of the world. This is because it does not include *unrequited transfers*, which are transfers of income from one nation to another that do not involve purchases of goods or services or claims on the transferees.[*] Typical unrequited transfers are foreign aid, gifts, pension receipts, immigrants' remittances back to their families, and even defaulted debts. A particularly dramatic case is the payments the United States received from its allies for American expenditures on the Iraq invasion; these served to reduce the current account deficit to the lowest in years. Normally, unrequited transfers are well under 1% of GNP, but can be a significant part of net total investment, which is sometimes in itself under 3% of GNP.

Because of the unrequited transfers, a nation's foreign capital stock may not change by the same amount as implied by the formula $X - M = S - I$. In 1986 Thailand, for instance, had a trade deficit equivalent to 1.5% of GNP, but received unrequited transfers (in the form of foreign aid) of 0.5% of GNP, so its net foreign indebtedness rose by only two thirds of what the trade deficit alone

---

[*] Such transfers are no problem in our domestic models, which tend either to be one country or all the world, because we can cancel out all of them—if Peter gives Paul $10,000 and Paul invests it, then it is Paul's investment and Peter's income. The $10,000 goes down on the income side as Peter's and on the expenditure side as Paul's, and the national accounts balance. But if Peter lives in the United States and Paul in Canada, Canada would show $10,000 more in total expenditures (the investment) than it shows in earnings because no one in Canada earned that amount. Canadian statisticians cannot show Peter's income because it was not earned in Canada. It isn't a wage, interest, profit, or rent. To account for such payments, they must keep an item called unrequited transfers.

suggests. Trade-surplus nations that give foreign aid and run negative unrequited transfer accounts do not, of course, see their foreign investments rise by the full amount of their trade surpluses. Japan, for instance, in 1986 had a huge trade surplus equivalent to 5% of GNP, but gave away a tiny bit amounting to 0.1% of GNP, so it did not accumulate quite so many foreign assets as the trade surplus alone indicates.[3] $X - M$ still measures the transfer of saving, but one must figure in the unrequited transfers to determine net foreign investment. (The figure is usually a very small percentage of GNP.)

THE CAPITAL ACCOUNT AND MONETARY ACCOUNTS

THE CAPITAL ACCOUNT   In a sense, the remaining accounts explain how the current account deficit was financed—what combination of borrowing and selling of foreign assets allowed the nation to have a current account deficit. In the case of a surplus, the remaining accounts tell how the nation invested the surplus it received. A small part of that activity takes place through actions of the central bank (or Federal Reserve System in the United States), and that is under the *monetary account,* but the bulk of capital movement is carried on by private banks and firms, public corporations, or governmental units other than the central bank. These noncentral-bank transactions go under the capital account.

The capital account is usually divided into two parts: long term and short term. Long-term capital includes *portfolio investments* in bonds of longer maturities, corporate shares or stocks, and *direct investment*—which is the money that corporations put into firms they own in another country.

Short-term capital includes investments in treasury bills, commercial paper (short-term corporate debt), bank deposits, and commercial credit. It tends to be more volatile than long-term capital, and highly interest-rate sensitive.

THE MONETARY ACCOUNT   A country also holds foreign assets or incurs debts through its monetary authorities. The Federal Reserve or central banks hold foreign treasury bills and accounts in other central banks, and changes in their holdings are described under the official or monetary account. In the older, simpler times, when gold was an international money, the monetary account was the gold account and recorded how much gold had flowed into or out of the nation. As Chapter 13 explains, today central banks hold foreign exchange of other countries as reserves, so the account now records changes in those holdings, plus a number of other things the central banks have done. They hold most of these in the form of the other countries' treasury bills, and the rest as bank accounts in the other countries' central banks.

A central bank's sales of foreign exchange (or gold) are *receipts* on the balance of payments, even though they are *debits* on a nation's holdings of foreign assets. It is just like an individual who transfers money from a savings to a checking account; he or she will debit the savings, but credit the checking account. The Bank of Canada in 1988, for instance, bought US$7521 million of foreign assets, almost entirely foreign treasury bills. That is just as much a minus sign on the BOPS as if a Canadian resident had bought foreign treasury bills. It is, of course, a plus sign for the assets of the Bank of Canada, just as it would be a plus sign in the Canadian resident's foreign holdings, but we are looking at the BOPS, not the accumulated assets.

For nonaccountants, this can be disorienting: A plus on the balance-of-payments account occurs when the central bank's assets are falling, a minus when they are rising. (Just keep in mind the savings and checking account analogy; moving money from a checking to a savings account is a debit on the checking account.) Consider, too, that an inflow on the capital account occurs when foreign assets are depleted or borrowings made.

Points for Future Reference on the Monetary Account   Two items normally grouped with the monetary account are *counterpart items* and *liabilities constituting foreign authorities' reserves.* Very briefly:

1. The *counterpart items* occur when the value of the central bank's holdings of foreign exchange rises, due to a change in price of the foreign exchange.

2. *Liabilities constituting foreign authorities' reserves:* As we will see in later chapters, central banks hold their foreign exchange reserves largely in treasury bills of the industrial countries—principally U.S. dollars. When the Bank of England buys U.S. Treasury bills, it is an investment in the United States, and therefore an inflow to the United States. Because it is an action of a central bank, it is included in the official account.

OTHER DETAILS

EXCEPTIONAL FINANCING   Some activities are difficult to classify when they involve the central bank, which does not itself buy or sell foreign exchange, so its holdings are unchanged. The central bank, for instance, may negotiate a loan, but arrange for the loan to go to the government or even to private banks. Such activity could go under the monetary account, because it is so closely related to central bank actions. Often exceptional financing stands alone, under neither account, but since it does not in itself increase monetary reserves, and since we wish to keep our three-part division, we group it with the monetary account.

ERRORS AND OMISSIONS OR DISCREPANCIES   Because of the difficult nature of collecting balance-of-payments figures, recorded outflows and inflows almost never match closely. An *error* or *discrepancy* figure is entered to make up the difference. The discrepancy item in balance-of-payments statements is often so large that we must make some sense of it. As a rule of thumb, we consider most of a discrepancy as short-term capital. A more detailed look is in order.

Balance-of-payments accounting involves many estimates. It does not have the accuracy of a corporation account and is more akin to GNP estimation than to financial accounting. Tourism expenditure is difficult to assess. Undeclared or undervalued imports are tricky. Illegal or simply unrecorded movements of capital, including *flight* capital, are notoriously hard to figure. Trade in illegal substances, a major part of the earnings of some Third World countries, is also hard to count, since the dealers do not report regularly to government statisticians. It should not surprise people that the figures toted up for the payments side differ from those counted up on the receipts side.

Since one set of figures merely explains what was done with the other, in concept they have to equal. While corporate accountants might bury a few small discrepancies in *miscellaneous expenditures or receipts* to hide what they cannot find, balance-of-payments accountants do not expect to find every expenditure or payment. They just declare that there is a discrepancy, leave the figure that seems the most solid, and adjust the other. Very often the discrepancies are large—nearly $47 billion dollars for 1990 on the U.S. account. Sometimes, too, the discrepancy is larger than the trade deficits or surpluses, so the nation is not even sure if it has a surplus or a deficit.

Some clue as to what is in the discrepancy comes from the sensitivity of that figure to interest rates. A country with high interest rates finds that its discrepancy is positive: That is, its receipts appear to exceed its payments. When the interest rate falls, the discrepancy falls also.[*] This suggests that an important part of the untraced transactions is short-term capital funds. The sharp swings in the discrepancy, too, do not accompany legal, political, or consumption changes that would encourage or discourage smuggling. The best guess, then, is that the discrepancy, or at least most of it, is made up of unrecorded short-term capital movements.

Payments accounts often differ from the same statistics in national income accounts, alas. The 1989 American national income accounts show a much lower trade deficit than do balance-of-payments figures, and the difficulty of reconciling payments and national income figures is such that it is not done. Within the balance-of-payments system, it usually takes several years of reworking the numbers before statisticians are satisfied with the results.[**] (If occasionally some of the figures in this book do not jibe with others, we trust they originate in as-yet unreconciled accounts.)

Payments accounts may also differ between the organizations that collect and publish data. The Bank of Canada's data and the International Monetary Fund's data on the Canadian balance of payments differ considerably. Payments figures present some very tricky problems and a number of estimates, so perhaps this should not be surprising.

---

[*] Some countries that normally have negative discrepancies—that is, outflows appear larger than inflows—find that the discrepancy shrinks when their interest rates are high and rises when they are low.

[**] Using national income figures, the trade deficit is *exports of goods and services* plus *net factor receipts* minus *imports of goods and services.*

■ *DOUBLE-ENTRY ITEMS*

A number of entries on payments accounts do not involve any actual flow of funds, but are needed to keep reasonable track of the aggregates involved. In handling these, simultaneous credits and debits are entered in the account. Some important examples are:

1. Foreign aid given in kind, as for example, a shipment of $1 million worth of tractors sent from Canada to Jamaica. Canada has to count it because wages and profits have been paid in the making of the tractors, raising GDP. Canada would place $1 million as exports in the *receipts* or *credit* side of the ledger; this is necessary to figure national income and saving, since people were paid to make those tractors and their income turns up on the factor side of GNP. Exports on such a transaction would exceed imports by the full million dollars, so the entire amount must be part of saving. That possible claim on Jamaica, however, is relinquished, so accountants also place $1 million payment or debit in the unrequited transfers.

2. Reinvested profits of foreign corporations. *Often* reinvested earnings are included in direct investment—for example, the $10 million in profit *Global Enterprises* earns but reinvests in the country is added to direct investment receipts. The profits *Global* earned, however, go into *payments* under net factor income abroad. That way an outflow on the current account matches the inflow on the capital account. Not every nation, however, treats reinvested earnings in the same way; some simply do not count it at all, and since the two entries are the same, the overall balance is unaffected, even if the direct investment is understated. The treatment of reinvested earnings as a double entry is a recent practice the IMF encourages, used for the most part in the last decade.

SOME REAL-WORLD BALANCES OF PAYMENTS

THE U.S. BALANCE OF PAYMENTS

Table 11.1 shows in simplified form the structure of the U.S. balance of payments.

1. The balance of goods and services and income, equivalent theoretically to our $X - M$, is minus $57.52 billion (the lowest deficit since 1983). This, of course, is also equivalent to the difference between domestic saving and investment in the United States.[*]

---

[*] The actual match between balance-of-payments figures and national income figures is very poor. The sources of figures, the handling of items in inventory, and the counting itself are often very different, and normally done by different government departments. Governments do not attempt to *reconcile* national income figures with BOPS figures. So while we say that the balance on goods and services theoretically matches $X - M$, that does not mean that the statistics do, or even come particularly close.

Table 11.1   **The U.S. balance of payments, 1990 (in billions of U.S. dollars)**

Current account

Goods exported	388.71
Goods imported	−497.55
Balance on goods	−108.84
Services exported	132.02
Services imported	−112.35
Factor receipts	160.15
Factor payments	−128.5
Balance on goods, *services, and income*	−57.52
Unrequited transfers	−32.94
Balance on current account	**−90.46**

Capital account

Long-term capital	
Direct investment (net)	12.45
Portfolio (net)	−33
Other long term (net)	22.55
Balance on long-term capital	2
Short-term capital	11.19
Balance on capital account	**13.19**
Discrepancy	**47.46**
Balance to this point	**29.81**

Monetary account

Dollars held as reserves elsewhere	32.04
Change in reserves	−2.23
Balance on monetary account	**29.81**
Total balance	**0.00**

2. The U.S. increase in net indebtedness in 1990 was higher than the trade balance indicates because unrequited transfers were minus $32.94 billion. The United States secured, somehow, $57.52 billion to cover its trade deficit, and another $32.94 billion to cover what it gave away, for a total current account deficit of $90.46 billion. Where did it find that money?

3. The capital accounts tell most of the story. The United States borrowed a net of $2 billion on the long-term capital account. Direct investment and other long-term borrowings provided new sources of funds, but foreigners were

withdrawing money from stocks and bonds (portfolio investments), causing an outflow in that item.

Short-term capital inflows—purchases of Treasury bills or short-term corporate paper (securities), credits extended to buyers, bank deposits, to name a few—accounted for another $11.19 billion. The total capital account balance was $13.29, hardly sufficient to account for the $90.46 billion the country actually used.

4. The monetary account shows how the United States obtained a sizable chunk of the $90.46 billion: Foreign central banks purchased $32.04, an item called "Dollars held as reserves elsewhere" in Table 11.1, and "Liabilities constituting foreign authorities' reserves" in Table 11.2. (Later chapters explore why they did so.) At the same time, the United States purchased $2.23 billion of foreign currencies to hold as reserves, so the net amount was $29.81 billion. Note again that the debit on the balance of payments reflects an addition to U.S. foreign exchange reserves.

Still, the accountants were unable to explain the $90.46 billion. The capital inflow of $13.19 plus the monetary inflow of $29.81 equals only $43.00, less than half of the amount.

5. The only thing to do is to show the difference as a *discrepancy* or *errors and omissions*. The statisticians were pretty sure that they had the debits reasonably correct, so had to assume the United States received more than they could trace, and therefore they wrote in a discrepancy figure of $47.46 billion, a handsome error indeed. Over the next several years, they will continue to work at the figures and be able to reduce the size of such errors. The 1989 discrepancy figure, for instance, was listed as +$22.60 billion in 1990 and 1991, but in 1992 data, it was reduced to $2.43 billion.[*] Similarly, the 1990 data, nearly three years old at the time of the printing of this book, will be later modified.

A CLOSER LOOK   Table 11.2 shows an authentic U.S. balance of payments statement, as taken from the International Monetary Fund's *Balance of Payments Statistics Yearbook.* It is the single-page summary, and in the book is followed by several pages of even more detailed figures. Economists seeking to understand a country's international situation frequently go to this source, which is reliable and widely disseminated.

Note first that only one of the three accounts—current, capital, and monetary—is immediately obvious. Table 11.1 combined items B and C to figure the capital account, and items D, G, and H from Table 11.1 to derive the monetary account in Table 11.2.

---

[*] Roughly $14 billion of it was assigned to short-term capital, and another $9 billion went to the trade account, particularly in the calculation of factor items and reinvested earnings.

Table 11.2

Aggregated presentation: United States transactions data, 1984–1991 (in billions of U.S. dollars)

	Code	1984	1985	1986	1987	1988	1989	1990	1991
A. Current account, excl. group E	A..CA	−98.99	−122.25	−145.42	−160.20	−126.37	−101.20	−90.46	−3.69
Merchandise: exports f.o.b.	1 A . A 4	219.90	215.93	223.36	250.28	320.34	361.67	388.71	415.96
Agricultural products	1 A . A P	38.40	29.57	27.36	29.55	38.25	42.19	40.18	40.13
Other	1 A . A Q	181.50	186.36	196.00	220.73	282.09	319.48	348.53	375.83
Merchandise: imports f.o.b.	1 A . B 4	−332.41	−338.09	−368.41	−409.77	−447.31	−477.38	−497.55	−489.40
Petroleum and related products	1 A . B X	−57.32	−50.39	−34.39	−42.94	−39.63	−50.92	−62.30	−51.18
Other	1 A . B V	−257.09	−287.70	−334.02	−366.83	−407.68	−426.46	−435.25	−438.22
Trade balance	1 A . C 4	−112.51	−122.16	−145.05	−159.49	−126.97	−115.71	−108.84	−73.44
Services: credit	1 V . A 4	60.79	61.86	72.26	81.81	91.50	113.91	132.02	145.71
Services: debit	1 V . B 4	−62.11	−67.06	−73.20	−82.66	−89.06	−97.69	−112.35	−113.21
Income: credit	1 Q . A 4	98.66	88.35	88.34	99.71	121.63	153.88	160.15	143.25
Reinvested earnings	1 E 1 A 4	17.22	14.11	10.02	19.71	13.33	14.77	19.48	17.89
Other investment income	1 N . A X	75.73	68.16	70.95	70.82	97.32	125.93	124.08	107.44
Other	1 Q . A Y	5.71	6.08	7.37	9.18	10.98	13.18	16.59	17.92
Income: debit	1 Q . B 4	−71.21	−67.76	−71.88	−85.24	−108.42	−129.98	−128.50	−113.99
Reinvested earnings	1 E 1 B 4	−2.91	1.37	2.30	.86	−2.82	8.52	16.28	20.05
Other investment income	1 N . B X	−66.66	−67.51	−72.30	−83.79	−102.51	−134.87	−140.54	−128.92
Other	1 Q . B Y	−1.64	−1.62	−1.88	−2.31	−3.09	−3.63	−4.24	−5.12
Total: goods, services, and income	1 T . C 4	−86.38	−106.77	−129.53	−145.87	−111.32	−75.59	−57.52	−11.68
Private unrequited transfers	1 K . C 4	−1.77	−2.06	−1.86	−1.84	−1.76	−12.32	−12.39	−12.99
Total, excl. official unrequited transfers	1 U . C 4	−88.15	−108.83	−131.39	−147.71	−113.09	−87.91	−69.91	−24.67
Official unrequited transfers	1 H . C A	−10.84	−13.42	−14.03	−12.49	−13.29	−13.29	−20.55	20.98
Grants (excluding military)	1 H 1 B K	−8.68	−11.28	−11.87	−10.28	−10.74	−10.77	−21.86	−18.08
Other	1 H . C Y	−2.16	−2.14	−2.16	−2.21	−2.55	−2.52	1.31	39.06
B. Direct investment and other long-term capital, excl. groups E through G	9 Z 1 X A	29.94	78.32	81.86	−57.52	93.48	85.58	2.00	2.94
Direct investment	3 . . X A	13.97	5.86	15.39	27.10	41.54	38.87	12.45	−15.65
In United States	3 Y . X 4	25.55	19.03	34.08	58.14	59.42	67.87	45.14	11.50
Abroad	3 L . X 4	−11.58	−13.17	−18.69	−31.04	−17.88	−29.00	−32.69	−27.15
Portfolio investment	6 Z 1 X A	28.76	64.43	71.60	31.06	40.31	43.50	−33.00	5.44
Other long-term capital									
Resident official sector	4 Z 1 X A	−4.25	−.97	−.47	−1.26	1.05	2.43	3.70	6.45
Disbursements on loans extended	4 C 1 Y 4	−7.80	−5.90	−7.14	−4.85	−5.82	−3.93	−6.65	−10.11
Repayments on loans extended	4 C 1 W 4	4.07	4.30	5.65	7.19	9.92	6.29	10.36	16.04

Other	4 Z 1 X Y Code	1984	1985	1986	1987	1988	1989	1990	1991
		-.52	*.63*	*1.02*	*-3.60*	*-3.05*	*.07*	*-.01*	*.52*
Deposit money banks	5 Z 1 X A	-8.54	9.00	-4.66	.62	10.58	.78	18.85	6.70
Other sectors	8 Z 1 X A	...	...	...	...	...	...	...	...
Total, groups A plus B	B 1 . X A	-69.05	-43.93	-63.56	-102.68	-32.89	-15.62	-88.46	-.75
C. Other short-term capital, excl. groups E through G	9 Z 2 X A	42.58	29.86	13.92	52.54	5.75	30.12	11.19	-20.71
Resident official sector	4 Z 2 X A	1.57	-1.44	-.52	-1.96	-.15	1.80	3.77	-.71
Deposit money banks	5 Z 2 X A	27.54	24.30	26.76	45.88	5.49	10.91	-1.05	-14.81
Other sectors	8 Z 2 X A	13.47	7.00	-12.32	8.62	.41	17.41	8.47	-5.19
D. Net errors and omissions	. A . X 4	27.19	19.87	15.86	-6.72	-9.13	2.43	47.46	-1.12
Total, groups A through D	D 1 . X A	.72	5.80	-33.78	-56.86	-36.27	16.93	-29.81	-22.58
E. Exceptional financing	. Y . X B	—	—	—	—	—	—	—	—
Total, groups A through E	E 1 . X 4	.72	5.80	-33.78	-56.86	-36.27	16.93	-29.81	-22.58
F. Liabilities constituting foreign authorities' reserves	9 W . X 4	2.41	-1.96	33.46	47.72	40.19	8.34	32.04	16.82
Total, groups A through F	F 1 . X 4	3.13	3.84	-.32	-9.14	3.92	25.27	2.23	-5.76
G. Reserves	2 . . X 4	-3.13	-3.84	.32	9.14	-3.92	-25.27	-2.23	5.76
Monetary gold	2 A . X 4	—	.01	.01	—	—	.01	—	—
SDRs	2 B . X 4	-.98	-.90	-.25	-.51	.13	-.53	-.20	-.18
Reserve position in the Fund	2 C . X 4	-1.00	.91	1.50	2.07	1.02	.47	.66	-.37
Foreign exchange assets	2 D . X 4	-1.15	-3.86	-.94	7.58	-5.07	-25.22	-2.70	6.31
Other claims	2 E . X 4	—	—	—	—	—	—	—	—
Use of Fund credit and loans	2 Y . X 4	—	—	—	—	—	—	—	—
Memorandum items									
Total change in reserves	2 . . R 4	*-.97*	*-8.21*	*-5.11*	*2.58*	*-1.79*	*-26.81*	*-8.68*	*5.61*
of which: revaluations	2 . . B 4	*2.15*	*-4.37*	*-5.43*	*-6.56*	*2.13*	*-1.55*	*-6.45*	*-.15*

Source: Balance of Payments Statistics Yearbook, 1992. *The code numbers are used by the IMF for cross-referencing account information.*

Now note some interesting details from Table 11.2:

1. The factor income (Item A: income, credit) here is substantial—in 1991, 34% percent of merchandise exports and 20% of goods, services, and income. Indeed, the services and factor earnings make up 41% of all exports. The vast bulk of these factor receipts are for capital—interest and profits. The double-entry item, reinvested earnings, also appears. $17.89 billion of earnings of corporations that were reinvested abroad in 1991 turn up as an inflow on the current account. Although not shown specifically, they form the bulk of the $27.15 billion of direct investment outflow.

2. The last two major items under A show just how the unrequited transfers were divided between private and government. *Other* is probably mostly military.

3. The long-term capital account (B) shows considerably more detail on direct investment. One of the interesting things to note is how foreign direct investment in the United States rose sharply until 1989.

4. The short-term capital (Item C) gives further breakdowns. The official sector is the government. Most activity consists of holdings by *deposit banks*—which is to say commercial banks.

5. People often wonder whether illegal transactions cause the *error and omission* or *discrepancy* (D). Cocaine, marijuana, and heroin are, of course, difficult to handle as imports, but even at the inflated figures police give, they could not account for balance of payments errors of $36 and $27 billion. The United States has illegal exports as well as illegal imports—arms travel well when covered with wheat. Surely illegal trade is in the *discrepancy* figure, but the telling point is that it cannot account for the *swings* of tens of billions of dollars. The answer to the question of what explains the changes in the *discrepancy* item in the balance of payments is not illegal drugs—unless they have an odd proclivity to respond to interest rate differentials.

CANADA: CURRENT ACCOUNT DEFICITS AND LONG-TERM CAPITAL INFLOWS

Table 11.3 shows in an abbreviated form similar to that of Table 11.1 the payments situation of Canada in 1990. It shows that Canada, like the United States, had a substantial current account deficit, but that its composition was quite different. In contrast to the United States, Canada relied entirely on private capital markets to pay for its trade deficit. A few interesting points:

1. Canada normally has a merchandise trade surplus, but both its service and income (factor) accounts are in marked deficit. The US$29 billion of factor payments (Table 11.3) in the income debit item are almost entirely interest, profits, and other expenses associated with foreign ownership of

Table 11.3 **Canadian balance of payments 1990 (in millions of U.S. dollars)**

Current account

Goods exported	129075
Goods imported	−119894
Balance on goods	9181
Services exported	16285
Services imported	−26574
Factor receipts	8370
Factor payments	−29161
Balance on goods, services, and income	− 21899
Unrequited transfers	−66
Balance on current account	**−21965**

Capital account

Long-term capital	
Direct investment (net)	2978
Portfolio (net)	7931
Other long term (net)	2652
Balance on long-term capital	*13561*
Short-term capital	8800
Balance on capital account	**22361**
Discrepancy	**229**

Monetary account

Change in reserves	−625
Balance on monetary account	**−625**
Total balance	**0**

Canadian assets. In contrast, Canada's foreign investment (which is quite substantial) produced only $8370 million. If Canada does not have a large merchandise trade surplus, it cannot cover its income and service payments and must borrow to do so.

2. Table 11.3 shows Canada borrowed heavily long term ($13,561 million), and substantially short term ($8800 million). In 1988 and 1989, it was also a heavy borrower of long-term capital.

3. Table 11.3 also shows the balance on the capital account was such that it more than paid for the current account deficit. The difference was picked up by the monetary authorities, which bought foreign exchange to invest in foreign treasury bills.

JAPAN: A CURRENT ACCOUNT SURPLUS INVESTED IN FOREIGN STOCKS AND BONDS

Japan's payments account gains its importance because of Japan's share in the world's trade and its large recent surpluses. If we said that Japan had run large trade surpluses since the 1970s, that it was investing most of this in establishing its companies abroad, that it was not an important borrower on world capital markets, and that the Bank of Japan had accumulated large amounts of foreign exchange assets, a good many readers would sagely agree. But these would just be debating points: None of these statements is on the whole true.

The current account shows that large surpluses do not appear before the mid-1980s, and they are largely produced by a surplus in goods trade, while trade in services and income is more nearly balanced.

What has Japan done with the substantial trade surpluses of the late 1980s? How, in essence, has it held its claims on the rest of the world? Table 11.4 shows:

1. It has relinquished very little of those claims. Over the period 1982–1990, its unrequited transfers total only around US$20 billion, out of a trade surplus of over $440 billion—about 5%.

2. Direct investments made up about 207 billion US dollars out of a total trade surplus (1982–1990) of $533 billion—about 40%. Almost all the remainder has been in portfolio investments.

3. Japan borrowed short term from 1982–1990, only seeing an outflow in 1991. Just as an individual might borrow short term to make a long-term investment, the Japanese as a whole are borrowing short term and lending long term. Such a pattern is not all that rare—we can see it in Britain throughout most of the 1980s and in the United States in quite a number of years. Patterns of this nature often emerge in large banking centers as the banks accept short-term deposits from many nations and relend them long term. Because Japan borrows short term, its long-term investments can exceed its current account surplus.

4. Until 1986, very little of the surplus was held by the Bank of Japan. Recall that the U.S. account showed how the U.S. deficit was financed by private inflows until that year. Between 1986 and 1988, however, the Bank of Japan picked up increasing amounts of foreign exchange (that is, of U.S. dollar Treasury bills). From 1989 to 1991 the Bank was again selling foreign exchange.

READING PAYMENTS BALANCES: SUMMARY

The knowledgeable reading of a balance of payments has its rewards and gives insight into a country's economy. Each nation, sometimes each year, has its own characteristics that are impossible to summarize in a short space or by looking at some single figure. The BOPS does not reveal its secrets that easily. But it will reveal much and suggest many questions about an economy to the careful reader.

Table 11.4 Aggregated presentation: Japan transactions data, 1984–1991 *(in billions of U.S. dollars)*

	Code	1984	1985	1986	1987	1988	1989	1990	1991
A. Current account, excl. group E	A..CA	35.00	49.17	85.83	87.02	79.61	56.99	35.87	72.91
Merchandise: exports f.o.b.	1A.A4	168.29	174.02	205.59	224.62	259.77	269.55	280.35	306.58
Merchandise: imports f.o.b.	1A.B4	−124.03	−118.03	−112.77	−128.20	−164.77	−192.66	−216.77	−203.49
Trade balance	1A.C4	44.26	55.99	92.82	96.42	95.00	76.89	63.58	103.09
Services: credit	1V.A4	22.48	22.47	23.54	28.85	35.03	39.70	40.83	44.65
Shipment and other transportation	1P.A4	12.88	12.44	11.32	12.94	15.54	18.15	18.16	19.67
Travel	1D.A4	.97	1.14	1.46	2.09	2.89	3.15	3.59	3.44
Other	1V.AY	8.63	8.89	10.76	13.82	16.60	18.40	19.08	21.54
Services: debit	1V.B4	−32.80	−32.74	−35.45	−48.42	−63.53	−75.01	−81.97	−85.04
Shipment and other transportation	1P.B4	−15.92	−15.09	−13.85	−19.05	−22.98	−25.90	−27.65	−29.93
Travel	1D.B4	−4.61	−4.82	−7.23	−10.76	−18.67	−22.50	−24.93	−24.00
Other	1V.BY	−12.27	−12.83	−14.37	−18.61	−21.88	−26.61	−29.39	−31.11
Income: credit	1Q.A4	19.67	23.04	30.16	50.81	76.75	104.21	125.13	143.94
Income: debit	1Q.B4	−17.10	−17.94	−23.18	−36.96	−59.52	−84.52	−106.18	−121.24
Total: goods, services, and income	1T.C4	36.51	50.82	87.89	90.70	83.73	61.27	41.39	85.40
Private unrequited transfers	1K.C4	−.13	−.28	−.59	−.99	−1.12	−.99	−1.01	−.66
Total, excl. official unrequited transfers	1U.C4	36.38	50.54	87.30	89.71	82.61	50.28	40.38	84.74
Official unrequited transfers	1H.CA	−1.38	−1.37	−1.47	−2.69	−3.00	−3.29	−4.51	−11.84
B. Direct investment and other long-term capital, excl. groups E through G	9Z1XA	−50.01	−63.26	−132.08	−133.98	−117.09	−93.76	−53.08	31.39
Direct investment	3..XA	−5.97	−5.81	−14.25	−18.35	−34.73	−45.22	−46.29	−29.37
Portfolio investment	6Z1XA	−23.96	−41.75	−102.04	−91.33	−52.75	−32.53	−14.49	35.45
Gensaki transactions	6Y1XY	−.36	1.32	−.66	3.04	13.36	−3.77	−9.68	−4.21
Other	6.1XY	−23.60	−43.07	−101.38	−94.37	−66.11	−28.76	−4.81	39.66
Other long-term capital									
Resident official sector	4Z1XA	−3.44	−1.74	−2.73	−4.10	−6.91	−8.51	−10.41	−11.27
Deposit money banks	5Z1XA	−8.71	−7.66	−6.60	−9.69	−6.07	−4.90	−6.04	1.52
Other sectors	8Z1XA	−7.93	−6.30	−6.46	−10.51	−16.63	−2.60	24.15	35.06
Total, groups A plus B	B1.XA	−15.01	−14.09	−46.25	−46.96	−37.48	−36.77	−17.21	104.30

(continued)

Table 11.4 (continued)

	Code	1984	1985	1986	1987	1988	1989	1990	1991
C. Other short-term capital, excl. groups E through G	9 Z 2 X A	13.44	9.73	58.60	88.61	50.87	45.83	31.54	-103.24
Resident official sector	4 Z 2 X A	.79	1.33	1.28	-3.77	1.50	11.55	14.39	9.89
Deposit money banks	5 Z 2 X A	17.56	10.85	58.51	71.80	44.46	8.58	-13.66	-93.46
Assets	5 L 2 X 4	-5.77	-24.70	-81.56	-107.07	-147.47	-133.88	-56.01	37.86
Liabilities	5 Y 2 X 4	23.33	35.55	140.07	178.87	191.93	142.46	42.35	-131.32
Other sectors	8 Z 2 X A	-4.91	-2.45	-1.19	20.58	4.91	25.70	30.81	-19.67
D. Net errors and omissions	.A . X 4	3.69	3.78	2.49	-3.71	3.13	-21.82	-20.92	-7.68
Total, groups A through D	D 1 . X A	2.12	-.58	14.84	37.94	16.52	-12.76	-6.59	-6.63
E. Exceptional financing	. Y . X B	—	—	—	—	—	—	—	—
Total, groups A through E	E 1 . X 4	2.12	-.58	14.84	37.94	16.52	-12.76	-6.59	-6.63
F. Liabilities constituting foreign authorities' reserves	9 W . X 4	...	...	...	...	...	...	...	...
Total, groups A through F	F 1 . X 4	2.12	-.58	14.84	37.94	16.52	-12.76	-6.59	-6.63
G. Reserves	2 . . X 4	-2.12	.58	-14.84	-37.94	-16.52	12.76	6.59	6.63
Monetary gold	2 A . X 4	—	—	—	—	—	—	—	—
SDRs	2 B . X 4	-.12	.06	.14	.10	-.61	.42	-.38	.47
Reserve position in the Fund	2 C . X 4	-.07	.20	.14	-.07	-.57	-.31	-2.04	-1.68
Foreign exchange assets	2 D . X 4	-1.93	.33	-15.12	-37.97	-15.34	12.66	9.01	7.83
Other claims	2 E . X 4	—	—	—	—	—	—	—	—
Use of Fund credit and loans	2 Y . X 4	—	—	—	—	—	—	—	—
Memorandum items									
Total change in reserves	2 . . R 4	-1.83	-.29	-15.54	-38.72	-15.76	12.77	5.46	6.44
of which: revaluations	2 . . B 4	.29	-.87	-.70	-.78	.76	.01	-1.13	-.19
Conversion rates: yen per U.S. dollar	. . R F 4	237.52	238.54	168.52	144.64	128.15	137.96	144.79	134.71

Source: Balance of Payments Statistics Yearbook, 1992. *The code numbers are used by the IMF for cross-referencing account information.*

If an examination of a balance of payments leaves more questions than answers, that—provided the questions are good ones—is a worthy result in itself.

THE WORLD DEFICIT

It stands to reason that one country's trade deficit is another country's surplus, and that if we added together the trade account imbalances of every country, we would come out with a figure of zero. The same is true of the current account— what goes out of one nation must go into another. Given the necessarily rough way in which many payments components are estimated, it would not be surprising if the figure were a few billion dollars off one way or the other. The problem is that current account balances added together are *always* in deficit and by far more than random errors would be expected to produce. See Table 11.5.

Payments figures apparently overstate imports and understate exports. In turn, capital or error accounts would overstate the credits, implying more was borrowed than actually was. More detailed analysis shows that understatement is particularly true of services. While both goods and services have negative balances, goods accounts are reasonably close, always within 1.3% of each other, and generally closer. It is the invisibles accounts that are way off—10% is not unusual. The problems lie particularly in investment income. The cause appears to be that governments are better at counting the payments their citizens make than those they receive. That should not be surprising, since payments firms make can be subtracted from profits, while payments people and firms receive are subject to income taxes, so that there is incentive to hide the receipts, but not the payments. Moreover, it is difficult to hide physical imports, but not difficult to hide payments for services.

The IMF has had a special team working on the problem of the world discrepancy and in 1991 began publishing estimates of where the errors occur. The

Table 11.5 World current account discrepancies

Year	Current account (billion $)	Imports of goods and services (billion $)	Exports of goods and services (billion $)	% discrepancy between world imports and exports of goods and services
1985	−75	2928	2853	2.6
1986	−60	2885	2825	2.1
1987	−45	3292	3247	1.4
1988	−53	3908	3855	1.4
1989	−79	4333	4254	1.8
1990	−112	5025	4913	2.2
1991	−91	5170	5079	1.8

Source: Derived from Balance of Payments Statistics Yearbook, *Vol. 43, Part 2, 1992, pp. 27–28.*

principal errors lie with reinvested earnings and investment income; the IMF could trace about $53 billion of those items that were either underestimated as receipts or overestimated as payments. Canada, for example, might have estimated a payment in these items of $1 billion to the United States, yet the United States only estimated a receipt of $900 million from Canada. The other item was in *official unrequited transfers* which, despite their coming from governments, were overestimated by the payers and underestimated by the receivers.[4] With these adjustments, the IMF was able to reduce the world deficit by about 20% of its initial figure. Other problems exist in the counting of imports, usually done quite carefully because they pay tariffs, and exports (often counted more casually), and in figuring shipping charges. The IMF's estimates do not make corrections for each country, but are able to assess the size of the discrepancies for the world as a whole.

The problem with wrong figures is that they make things look worse than they are and may encourage nations to try to correct current account deficits they do not have. The United States and Canada, for instance, regularly find that they both have trade deficits with each other, and they have a special committee to reconcile the two accounts. It would not do to have each nation trying to cut imports from the other on the grounds that each had a trade deficit. The need for timely information is important for policy, but policy makers should take balance-of-payments information with several grains of salt, and use it judiciously.

CONCLUSION

The balance-of-payments statement is an important source of statistics for international economists. The current account figures show how domestic imbalances of saving and investment have been reflected in the flows of goods and services, modified slightly by unrequited transfers. The other parts of the payments statement show the results of a myriad of financial transactions that serve, net, to indicate the nature of a country's debt or foreign investments. We see not only that $I > S$, but also just how the borrowing was done to allow those extra resources to enter the country. If $S > I$, then we can see how the country placed its savings abroad.

When we come to face the question of whether a given trade imbalance is good or bad, we do not look just at its size, but also at the nature of the financial assets and liabilities it generated. If we look at a trade deficit, the balance-of-payments statement allows us to see the various categories of borrowings: short term, long term, private, government, or central bank. That information helps make a judgment on the *soundness* of the financing. Similarly, a country with a trade surplus will generate assets abroad, some of which may be quite vital and promising; others, like large amounts of low-yielding foreign treasury bills, look rather unpromising as long-run investments.

The analysis in Chapters 10 and 11, particularly the algebraic and statistical parts, has been static—that is, it has examined each year at year end, much like a photograph. All the equations balance and all the accounts balance at that particular moment. But, like the economist who slipped on a banana and remained in equilibrium all the way down,[*] where an economy is at a given moment may be less important than where it ends up. Chapters 12–15 impart more of a dynamic to the situation, focusing on longer-run and more stable forms of equilibrium.

VOCABULARY AND CONCEPTS

Capital account

Counterpart items

Current account

Direct investments

Discrepancies (errors)

Double-entry item

Exceptional financing

Factor payments

Factor receipts

Goods and services account

Invisibles (Invisible trade)

Long-term capital

Merchandise trade

Official account

Portfolio investments

Short-term capital

Unrequited transfers

Visibles (Visible trade)

QUESTIONS

1. Read a balance of payments of one or another country, answering such questions as:

    a. the relation of domestic saving to investment

    b. whether foreign borrowing (or investment) is greater than or less than the trade deficit

    c. if the country has a current account deficit, how it managed to import more than it exported. If it has a surplus, what did it do with its surplus funds?

    d. come up with a quick "balance" showing the movements of capital—where the inflows were and where the outflows were

    e. identify the movement of funds into or out of reserves

    f. if given multiple years, spot trends

    g. if the country is a large debtor or creditor, identify, if possible, the item showing the debt service, or at least composed mostly of debt service payments

2. Explain the principal divisions of a balance-of-payments account. Why does the account always balance?

3. Why do some nations' payments balances have such large errors and omissions? Can illegal shipments of drugs and arms account for such errors?

4. Many countries make policy on the basis of their latest balance-of-payments statistics, particularly their trade deficits. People who have worked with such figures, however, are likely to furrow their brows and raise a cautionary finger. Why?

5. A trade surplus is a claim on another country. What can the surplus country do with that claim?

6. Author WBB lives in Canada. When he receives a royalty payment for sales of this book, under what category will it appear on

---

[*] "You just have to make the intervals short enough, and make your calculations quickly," he explained as he lay on the sidewalk, still maintaining that no good economist ever loses his equilibrium. "It is just that some equilibria last longer than others."

the U.S. BOPS? He has a book with another publisher, published in Toronto; how will his royalties fit on that book if sold in the United States? What if the U.S. branch of his Canadian publisher publishes the book and pays the royalties to the Canadian branch? If you are confused or just frustrated at making fine lines, does that suggest why net factor payments are really services? Does it offer some reason why GNP might be a better measure than GDP?

7. When did the U.S. trade deficit begin? Pick one year (not 1987 or 1989) and trace through the main accounts to see how the United States paid for the extra imports it made.

NOTES

[1] If you have a project that involves an intimate knowledge of many of the statement's items, you may want to use *Balance of Payments Manual* (4th ed.), New York, International Monetary Fund, 1977.

[2] Payments forms report many figures *net*—the account shows only the difference between the payments and the credits. Sometimes this is a convenience, and the gross figures are published on more detailed accounts; the entry for private unrequited transfers (gifts, immigrants' remittances, and pensions) provides an example. Sometimes, the gross figures are not known, but net figures can be inferred from end-of-period balances. Trillions of dollars' worth of foreign exchange credits and debits, for instance, move through commercial bank balances, but their net change over the year is usually in the low billions. The *net* figure is far easier to find and more important to report. To make a humble analogy to household accounting, the household can infer what it took in during a garage sale by subtracting what it had in the till at the beginning from what is left in the end.

[3] The formula for figuring a nation's net investment position, then, must include unrequited transfers.

$$I_d = S_p + (T - G_c) + (M - X) + U$$

where U = the unrequited transfers from foreigners.

[4] See Vol. II of the 1990 *Balance of Payments Statistics Yearbook*, pp. 4–6.

Chapter 12

Income, Price Levels, and Trade Imbalances

OBJECTIVES

Overall Objective: To introduce dynamic models using the national income concepts of Chapters 10 and 11 to relate price level and income changes to the trade balance.

MORE SPECIFICALLY:

- To explain the basis on which economists differ in their opinions on the way in which changes in aggregate demand affect income and prices, and how to represent those differences in *AD* and *AS* diagrams.

- To show how changes in exports and imports affect the aggregate demand and supply model.

- To demonstrate how to handle income effects through injections and leakages models.

- To present the foreign repercussion effect.

- To demonstrate that income adjustments alone are probably not sufficient or even desirable to correct trade imbalances.

- To consider how shifts to aggregate supply affect the trade balance, price level, and output.

National economies continually adjust to international changes. Sometimes, as Chapters 10 and 11 have shown, the adjustment is slow, and large trade imbalances emerge, and at times governments use macroeconomic policies to try to influence the kind of adjustment. They may, for instance, try to lessen a trade deficit or moderate a surplus. Or they may try to improve employment and output, and must have a sense of what might happen to their trade and capital balances.

This chapter begins to explore the complex interrelationships of output, price levels, and trade and capital balances. To do so in all its fullness, the text eventually has to consider two kinds of price effects—price level changes and exchange rate changes. At present, it keeps the exchange rate changes in the background and deals with the more familiar macroeconomic models of aggregate supply and demand and the Keynesian income models.

INCOME AND PRICE LEVEL EFFECTS: BASIC CONSIDERATIONS

Many key adjustment mechanisms work differently depending upon whether changes in aggregate demand affect real output or prices. If they affect output, they have income effects; if they affect prices, they have price level effects. And of course, they may affect both prices and output. A closer look is in order.

KEYNESIAN AND CONTEMPORARY MODELS

Macroeconomics deals with the questions of income or price level effects through use of aggregate demand and supply models. The basic models in contention are the *Keynesian model* and one that goes by various names, the *Neoclassical model,* the *Friedman-Phelps* model, or the name we choose to use, the *Contemporary model.* Both Keynesian and Contemporary models illustrate their points using aggregate demand and supply curves, as in Figs. 12.1 and 12.2 with the price level on the vertical axis and real GDP (or output) on the horizontal. Both models agree that aggregate demand is downward sloping and on the factors that shift the aggregate demand curve, so we can begin there.

If the price level falls, people consume more. One way to understand why this occurs is to consider that all savings that people hold denominated in money (that is, savings accounts, checking accounts, cash, bonds, corporate paper, and short-term bills) will now buy more goods and services. People need not save as much as they previously anticipated and therefore will spend more. The opposite occurs when the price level rises: People must save more to keep their real wealth from falling.[*] A second way to understand *AD*'s slope is to view how people hold money: If prices rise, they must hold more money to cover their weekly transactions, and that cash is not available for investment purposes, so investment falls. The aggregate demand curve shifts when the sum of its components changes.

Aggregate demand is $C + I + G + (X - M)$. If *at any given price level* consumption rises, and investment, government, and the trade balance (sometimes called *net exports*) do not change, or do not fully offset the increase in consumption, then *AD* shifts to the right. Using a flow diagram:

(FD 12.1) $$C{\uparrow} + I + G + (X - M) \rightarrow AD{\uparrow}$$

---

[*] Another explanation is that as prices fall, people need less money for transactions purposes; they therefore try to move out of holding cash and into holding some other form of wealth, whether it be increased financial assets (causing interest rates to fall and investment to rise) or increased real assets, such as housing or consumer durables. The opposite occurs when prices rise, as people must shift their assets into money.

If one of the factors falls in value, then *AD* shifts to the left. Suppose, for instance, that a poor harvest led to a sharp increase in imported foods, then imports would rise, causing *X − M* to fall, and causing *AD* to fall. In addition, lower farm incomes would cause consumption to fall. To wit:

(FD 12.2) $C{\downarrow} + I + G + (X - M{\uparrow}){\downarrow} \rightarrow AD{\downarrow}$

Where the Keynesian and Contemporary models differ is in the nature of aggregate supply. The Keynesian model holds that the level of employment is critical. At low levels of employment, an expansion of *AD* will induce an increase in output without any significant rise in prices. At almost-full employment, prices will rise and output expand as *AD* rises. At full employment, there will be only price effects. The Contemporary model differs in that it suggests that the basic or natural rate of employment is determined by the choice between work and leisure, and in the long run only changes in real wages will alter that choice. The long-run *natural* rate of unemployment is therefore fixed, and any effects that come from aggregate demand changes are short run. If, in the short run, aggregate demand rises, prices will also rise. Normally, however, prices rise faster than wages. Employers, seeing a higher value for their sales, add more employees, and the new employees, slow to realize that prices are rising and real wages are falling, agree to work for them. Figures 12.1 and 12.2 show the two models.

Figure 12.1 **The Keynesian model.** Under Keynesian assumptions, few people are voluntarily unemployed. Markets fail to clear because prices of both goods and labor are rigid. In recessions, most workers would gladly go back to work at existing wages, so there is no reason to think an increase in aggregate demand is going to increase prices. An expansion of aggregate demand from *AD* to AD_1 would increase output from 0*a* to 0*b*, but the price level would not rise. An expansion from AD_1 to AD_2 would increase output from 0*b* to 0*c*, but would also raise prices. An expansion from AD_2 to AD_3 would raise prices only.

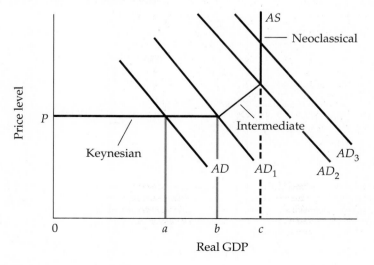

Summarized in flow diagrams, we would say that a positive shock to aggregate demand under Keynesian conditions causes income (output) to rise, and negative shocks cause the opposite.

(FD 12.3) $AD\uparrow \rightarrow Y\uparrow$ or $AD\downarrow \rightarrow Y\downarrow$

At full employment, however, a positive shock would lead to inflation as in part (a) of FD 12.4 below. In a period of inflation, a negative shock to *AD* would lead to a decline in price levels, as in (b) in FD 12.4 below.

(FD 12.4)   (a) $AD\uparrow \rightarrow P\uparrow$ and (b) $AD\downarrow \rightarrow P\downarrow$

THE HYBRID MODEL

For expositional purposes, we choose to use a *Hybrid model*, as shown in Fig. 12.3. The Contemporary model depends on inflation to induce greater output. But it is conceivable that Keynesian price rigidity could dominate in the short run. Many people who were previously working or who are working fewer than their normal hours will be induced back to work or to work more at the same wages or salaries in the short run. In the longer run, however, people working more than their rewards justify will leave the workforce. Professor Grunge is not going to resign when, to meet a flood of new students, he is pressured into taking on a fourth preparation (for a modest bonus). Art Mack is not going to complain or raise his prices right away if his trucking jobs increase by 25%, and Frieda

Figure 12.2 **The Contemporary model.** The effect of an increase in aggregate demand in the short run is to increase employment, as indicated by the positively sloped short-run *AS* curve. As AD_1 rises to AD_2, prices rise to P_2 and output expands to Y_2. In the long run, the level of employment and thus of output is independent of the price level; therefore output returns to its older level of Y_1, but at a price level of P_3.

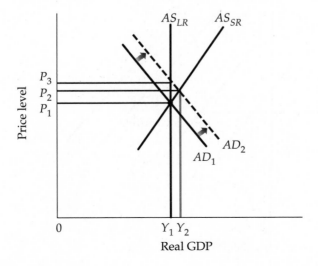

Longaur is not going to leave her factory job to take more care of the kids or aging parents when her hours increase from 30 to 40 a week. After a year or two of doing so, however, they may be sorely tempted to an early retirement or may voluntarily leave the workforce for several years (a stop-out). People may work more at the same rates, but not indefinitely. In such a situation, the short-run *AS* curve would be horizontal, rather than upward sloping as in the Contemporary model.

Whether or not we accept the general applicability of the arguments above, the Hybrid model is quite useful expositionally, because it separates income and price effects clearly, however tangled they may be in the real world. The skeptical can look at what happens to the horizontal part of the curve and figure the modifications that would occur if it were sloped upward. Or should they wonder if a long-run curve were really relevant in a particular situation, they could tentatively dismiss those particular consequences.

A flow diagram would show two paths leading from a shock to aggregate demand, the short run (the top one in the diagram) leading to an increase in output, the long run only to inflation.

(FD 12.5) $AD\!\uparrow \rightarrow \begin{array}{l} \rightarrow \overline{P}, Y\!\uparrow \\ \\ \rightarrow P\!\uparrow, \overline{Y} \end{array}$

Figure 12.3 **The Hybrid model.** The Hybrid model assumes that in the short run, output can rise beyond the full-employment point (as defined by people's willingness to exchange work for real income). The short-run *AS* curve (AS_{sr}) is thus flat over the range of output considered. The long-run curve, AS_{lr}, however, is vertical. If, for instance, aggregate demand were to rise from AD_1 to AD_2, output would expand in the short run to $0b$. Given that the rate of employment is determined, however, by the real goods and services wages can produce, output will eventually return to AS_{lr}. When it does so, the price level will rise to P_2.

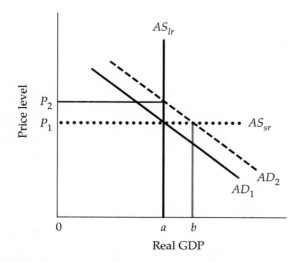

INCOME EFFECTS: THE INJECTIONS AND LEAKAGES MODEL

We leave many of the details of price effects for later to concentrate upon those changes that shift *AD*, which produce real income effects. For the bulk of the discussion below, we will assume a horizontal *AS* curve, either because the economy is operating in the short run or because it is below full employment. We will, for the time being, hold the *AS* curve from moving. This allows a closer examination of the nature of shifts in *AD*.

Most introductory textbooks use the $C + I + G$ model in which income is on one axis and expenditure on the other. Because of our strong interest in saving and investment and various expositional requirements, we eschew the venerable 45° line in favor of the *injections and leakages* (I&L) model. Figure 12.4 shows the I&L model. The model takes one of Chapter 10's basic equations, $I + X + G = S + M + T$, and relates it to the level of national income. Injections ($I + X + G$) describe the source of income, while leakages ($S + M + T$) indicate its disposal. In most normal models, the injections show little or no change as income levels change, while the leakages are directly related to the income level.

To begin, assume that our economy is closed or autarkic and government is subsumed under consumption and saving, so investment must equal saving. That is: $C + I = C + S$, so $I = S$.

We can relate saving to income such that saving rises as income, here shown as real GDP, rises, much as introductory books showed consumption rising with income. Figure 12.4 shows this relationship. Saving is zero at a national income of $200 million. People are so poor that they have nothing left over for saving. At even lower levels of income, they dig into past saving, so the S curve can go below zero. Saving rises by $1 million for every $4 million increase in income—a *marginal propensity to save* of 0.25. (An MPS of 0.25 means that the marginal propensity to consume is 0.75, but we do not at this point look directly at the consumption schedule.) Figure 12.4 represents investment as a horizontal line, labeled I_1, at $200 million. This means that, whatever the income level, investment is $200 million—completely exogenous. The only level of national income that can satisfy equilibrium for an economy, given the saving and investment schedules, is $1000 million ($1 billion). At higher levels of income, saving would exceed investment, and at lower levels, investment would exceed saving.

Now, suppose that investment rises by $100 million to $300 million, represented by the horizontal line I_1. The only level of national income at which saving equals investment is $1.4 billion. It is easy to see the multiplier in I&L diagrams—the *rise* of 100 over the *run* of 400 is the slope of the curve, and that very slope also defines the 1:4 ratio that establishes the multiplier. Thus the rise in income that came from the increase in investment of $100 million (from $200 million to $300 million) shows up as a horizontal distance of $400 million (from $1 billion to $1.4 billion).

The I&L model has a number of advantages. In contrast to the *AS/AD* model, it shows the multiplier effect. Instead of just shifting *AD* to the right, as we do with the *AS/AD* model, we get a more precise idea of how far *AD* shifts. It

Figure 12.4 **Saving and investment in an injections and leakages diagram.** *S* represents the saving schedule, with a slope of .25. I_1 is the original level of investment. Together the two lines produce a national income of $1 billion. If investment rises by $100 million, national income rises by $400 million to $1.4 billion.

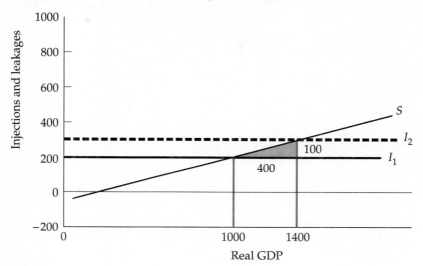

is, moreover, easier to see the multiplier on an I&L model than on the expenditure-income (*C* + *I* + *G*) model. Just look at the slope of the saving curve, for that determines how far injections must rise to produce any given income change. Algebraically, the rise in income, or the *income multiplier* (indicated by the symbol *k*), is 1/MPS; in this case 1/.25 = 4.

EXPORT AND IMPORT SCHEDULES

The same tools serve to integrate exports and imports into a dynamic income model. Imports, like saving, rise with income. A richer country can afford more of them. Exports, like investment, are largely determined by exogenous factors and normally have horizontal schedules. Now imagine an economy with no saving and investment and no government: The only determinant of changes in national income would be trade.[*] The formula for national income would be *C* + *X* = *C* + *M*, which reduces to *X* = *M*. Exports would have to equal imports because those are the only leakages and injections we allow. A rise in exports would increase national income, and therefore consumption, until the addi-

---

[*] Technically, it would be impossible to have an economy with no saving, but a temporary suspension of disbelief, a helpful characteristic of good economics students, gives a quick insight into the model.

tional income leaked out as imports. Figure 12.5 shows a diagram similar to that of Fig. 12.4, but with the vertical axis measuring imports and exports.

The formula for the income multiplier likewise parallels that of the model with saving, only in this case, instead of MPS, we use the marginal propensity to import, or MPM. In this case the multiplier is: $1/MPM = k$. Here, it is $1/.25 = 4$. The formula for the change in income produced by the change in the injection (the change in exports) is:

(Eq. 12.1) $$\Delta Y = \Delta X \times 1/MPM$$

It is conventional and convenient to show exports, like investment, as an exogenous variable, insensitive to income changes. Many nations do indeed find that their exports are dependent on the demand in world markets or on demand in neighboring countries. Malaysia's exports of rubber or Saudi Arabia's exports of oil are not influenced by the level of income in those countries—although they certainly help determine the level of income. In developed countries where the product exported is also consumed at home, depressed domestic markets often encourage producers to seek export markets, while buoyant home markets encourage them to neglect the export markets. In such situations, the export schedule might slope downward. Normally, however, we keep to the

Figure 12.5 **Imports and exports on an injections and leakages diagram.** This figure parallels Fig. 12.4. Exports are at $250 million ($X_1$) and then rise to $350 million ($X_2$). Imports are zero where there is no income and rise again at a pace of 1:4 or .25. (Imports, unlike saving, cannot be negative. We may dig into past saving, but we can't send imports back.) Since this model does not allow saving, if exports rise to $300 million, income will rise to $1.4 billion. At that income, imports are $300 million, equal to the new level of exports.

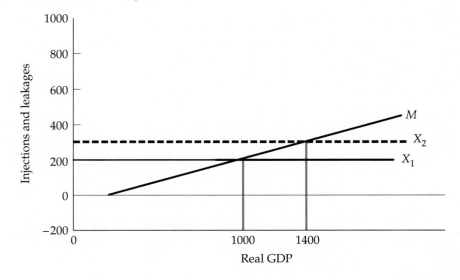

convention of a horizontal curve unless there is some specific point or situation requiring a downward-sloping curve.

COMBINING *S*, *I*, *X*, AND *M* SCHEDULES

It is artificial to consider an economy without saving and investment, so put them back into the picture, developing an income-determined model using all four schedules—*S*, *M*, *I*, and *X*, combining the two injections to make *I* + *X* and the two leakages to make *S* + *M*. It is easy enough to handle *X* and *I*—they are both injections of income into the economy, independent of the level of national income. Figure 12.6 shows the combination. The horizontal lines are added to each other. Imports and saving are leakages from the system. Because one sloped line is being added to another, the combined slope is greater. (It is just like putting a triangular block on top of another triangular block.)

Note that the multiplier is now lower. A marginal propensity to save (MPS) of .25 and a marginal propensity to import (MPM) of .25 would yield a *combined marginal propensity* (CMP) of .25 + .25, which is .5; the multiplier is calculated as 1 divided by the combined leakages: $1/(.25 + .25) = 2$. Algebraically: $1/(\text{MPS} + \text{MPM}) = k$. More concisely, we could combine MPS and MPM as above and state the formula as $k = 1/\text{CMP}$.

Figure 12.6 **Combined injections and leakages *S* + *M* and *I* + *X*.** The two horizontal schedules for injections, *I* at 200 and *X* at 250, together form *I* + *X* at 450. The two leakages, which at zero income are −50 and 0, each rise at a slope of .25. The *combined leakage* schedule, *S* + *M*, rises at a slope of .5. Equilibrium occurs where *S* + *M* = *I* + *X*, which in this case is $1 billion.

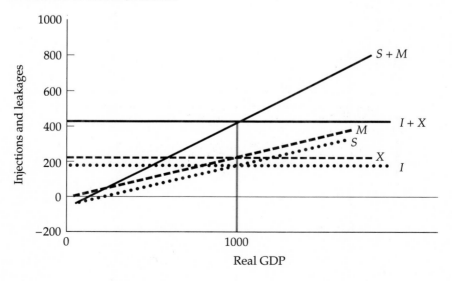

One advantage of the $S + M = I + X$ diagram is that it shows the differences between the way imports increase and the way saving increases. Figure 12.7 shows a rise in investment and exports of $100 million, using the same schedules as before. The higher injections cause income to rise by $200 million ($2/1 \times 100 = 200$), but imports would rise only by $50 million.

In a formula:

(Eq. 12.2)

$$\Delta(I + X) \times (1/\text{MPS} + \text{MPM}) = \Delta Y$$

$$\Delta Y \times \text{MPM} = \Delta M$$

The flow diagram does not quantify, but we can note the quantities derived from the diagram and formulas as subscripts.

(FD 12.6)

$$(I + X)\uparrow_{100} \to Y\uparrow_{200} \to (S\uparrow_{50} + M\uparrow_{50})$$

The same kind of problem emerges if imports are restricted by tariffs. Figure 12.8 shows how a tariff forces imports to decline as a percentage of GNP. M shifts to M_1 (a vertical distance of $100 million), and $S + M$ falls to $S + M_1$. That change increases national income by $200 million. The price effect of higher tariffs, which caused M to fall, is partially overcome by the income effect. While the country has succeeded in lowering imports by $50 million, it still is far short of its mark of a $100 million reduction.

Figure 12.7 **An increase in injections produces additional saving and imports.** The shift from $I + X_1$ to $I + X_2$ causes the equilibrium level of national income to rise to $1.2 billion. As injections increase, $50 million of them leak into saving and $50 million leak into imports. The small triangle shows how much imports rise when income rises by $200 million.

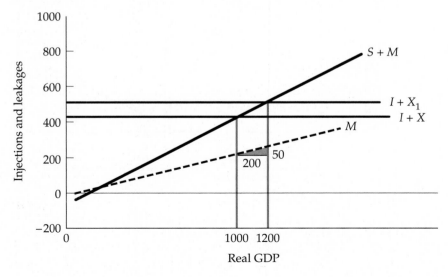

Figure 12.8 **A tariff increases income and partially decreases imports.** An increase in tariffs shifts the import schedule to M_1, which lies $100 million under M. The combined leakage shifts from $S + M$ to $S + M_1$, also $100 million. The increase in domestic expenditures causes income to rise by $200 million to $1.2 billion. The rise in income of $200 million has an income effect on imports, causing them to rise by $50 million (MPM = .25). Thus imports at an income of $1000 million are $250 million, and at an income of $1200 million, they are $200 million.

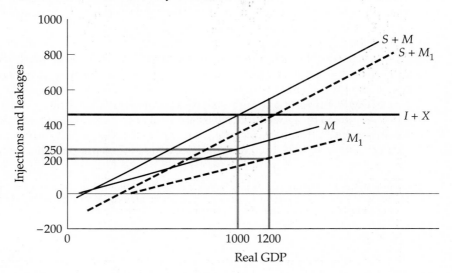

Algebraically, the change in imports is as follows:

$$\Delta M = \Delta I \times 1/CMP \times MPM$$

(Eq. 12.3)   or $\Delta M = 100 \times (1/.5) \times .25$

$$50 = 100 \times 2 \times .25$$

A flow diagram also shows this sequence, using the decline in imports as a shock and the quantification from the example above. (Remember, the *decline* in leakages increases aggregate demand and income.)

(FD 12.7) $(\bar{S} - M\!\downarrow_{100})\!\uparrow_{100} \rightarrow Y\!\uparrow_{200} \rightarrow S\!\uparrow_{50}, M\!\uparrow_{50}$

ADDING GOVERNMENT—*G* AND *T*

All six components of injections and leakages can be combined on one diagram to give a more complete picture. We can be more explicit about government by drawing schedules for G and T. Like investment and exports, government expenditure is largely exogenous; it will not go up or down as income changes within the year. (Clearly government expenditure is related to expectations of revenues, conditioned by previous incomes, but shortfalls of revenue or surpluses *within the year* caused by changes in national income do not alter budgets very much.) *G*, the schedule representing government expenditures, is therefore horizontal. Taxes as a whole rise with income. Sales and value-added taxes rise at the same rate as expenditure. Income and profits taxes tend to rise even faster, because they are often progressive, increasing in proportion to income as income rises. The result is that *T* slopes upward, like *M* and *S*. The combined leakage curve—*S* + *M* + *T*—would slope up even more steeply than *S* + *M*, as in Fig. 12.9.[*]

Low multipliers are more typical than unusual. Although many of our introductory textbooks often deal in multipliers of 3 and 4, a quick glance at the spending patterns in most nations suggests that their multipliers are much lower. Just try a back-of-the-envelope calculation for Canada, using the formula $k = 1/\text{CMP}$. Imports average nearly 30% of GNP and probably have marginal rates similar to or above that. Taxes are well above a 25% marginal rate, and only saving is likely to be below the marginal rates suggested in our diagram. But even if saving is 15%, the combined leakage is .7, with a multiplier of 1.4.

---

[*] Those students with intermediate macroeconomic background will recognize that one cannot simply add *T* to *S* + *M* because the very act of taxation may cause *S* to shift downward. We can do so, however, if we assume that the *S* + *M* curve is an after-tax curve.

Figure 12.9 **All injections and leakages** $S + M + T$ **and** $I + X + G$. The big combination yields higher injections, but an even smaller multiplier. The diagram has taxes rising at $1 for every $4 in income. The three leakages added together give a combined leakage of .75. The multiplier is thus much reduced—$1/.75 = 1.33$. Algebraically: $k = 1/\text{CMP}$, but in this case CMP includes not only imports and saving, but taxes (defined as the portion of additional income taken out as government revenue) as well.

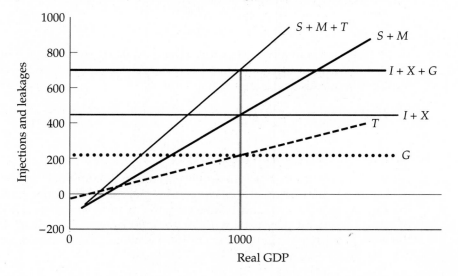

THE FOREIGN REPERCUSSION EFFECT

Analysis to this point has been of just one nation. Any income put into saving or imports cannot be respent. But imports produce income in another country, and that other country will have income effects, and presumably increased imports. We can represent this foreign respending effect, known as the *foreign repercussion effect,* with a simple two-country model. In our diagram exports are unrelated to the country's income, and we don't propose to change that. But one country's imports are another's exports, so if Country 1 increases its income and imports, we will have to establish a new level of exports for a second country. And the second country will then import more from the first, and its imports are the first country's new exports, so we will have to raise the first country's $I + X$. And this process can repeat itself. To keep matters simple, assume we have only two countries and that both are identical to the model country we have been using.

Country 1 initiates change, raising investment by $100 million to $550 million. The injection of $100 million produces a rise in national income of $200 million. As income rises, half of the new income leaks into saving and the other half into imports. Figure 12.10 illustrates the process through looking at the country that begins the economic expansion.

Country 1's imports are Country 2's exports. So Country 2 finds its $I + X$ rising by $50 million. Figure 12.11 shows that for Country 2.

Figure 12.10 **Foreign repercussion effect: Country 1.** The three horizontal lines are all $I + X$ at various stages, with the final stage represented by $I + X + X_r$, the X_r indicating all the remaining repercussions. In the first instance, Country 1 sees $I + X$ rise by $100 million from the line marked $I + X$ to the first thin line above it. With that change income rises to $1.2 billion. Country 1's imports rise by $50 million (.25 × 200), as shown by the little triangle and the number 50 on the import schedule.

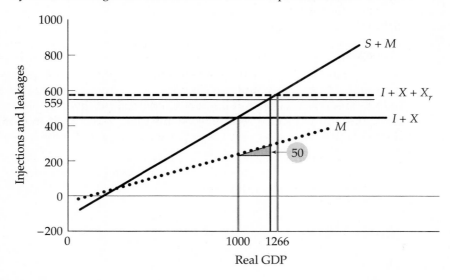

Figure 12.11 **Foreign repercussion effect: Country 2.** Country 2's increased exports cause $I + X$ to rise $50 million (shown by the thin line above it), and income to expand by $100 million to $1.1 billion. That rise in income also produces an increase in imports of $25 million (.25 × 100), as shown by the line labeled 25 on the import curve.

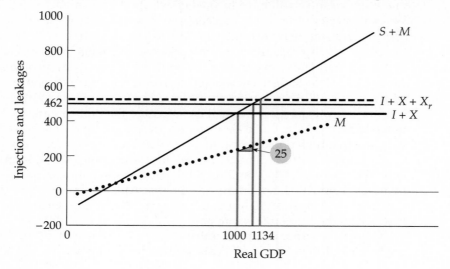

The next effect is on Fig. 12.10, where we can see the $I + X$ schedule rise by $25 million, the middle of the horizontal lines. In turn, Country 1's imports rise by $12.5 million (not shown). Country 2's income rises again by its new exports of $12.5 million times the multiplier (12.5 × 2 = 25), and again, it imports some more from Country 1. Round upon round follows, but they get very small. The top horizontal line on both diagrams indicates the total effect.

The full impact of this foreign trade multiplier, with foreign repercussions included, carries an impressive formula, which we footnote.[*] In our example, the formula is less complicated because both countries have identical curves. The total increase in output is $400 million ($266 million in Country 1 and $134 million in Country 2) just as if it were one country without any imports. The gain, however, is not equal between the countries. Country 1 sees investment rise by $100 million, and the first round of the foreign repercussion effect gives it another $25 million, the second round gives it $6.25 million, the third round $1.56 million, each round falling by 75%. The pattern occurs because each round sees the expenditure fall by

---

[*] The multiplier for Country A when repercussions in Country B are considered is:

(1) For an autonomous change in exports

$$\Delta Y = \Delta X \times \frac{1}{MPS_a + MSP_b + MPM_b(MPS_a/MPS_b)}$$

(2) For an autonomous change in investment

$$\Delta Y = \Delta I \times \frac{1 + (MPM_b/MPS_b)}{MPS_a + MPM_a + MPM_b(MPS_a/MPS_b)}$$

half (100 to 50 to 25). In final equilibrium, Country 1 has new injections of $133 million, of which $100 million came from the original new investment and $33 million from the foreign repercussion effects, for a total injection of $559 million. Its national income has risen by $267 million (2 × $133 million) to $1.267 billion. Country 2 achieves an income of $1.134 billion; the $134 million increase arose from the additional $67 million in export injections. Country 1's trade balance worsens against Country 2's, as its imports rise by $66.5 million (.25 × $266 million) and its exports by $33.50 million.

As a flow diagram, we can picture the foreign repercussion effect as follows. (The subscript 1 refers to the country in which the initial shock takes place, and subscript 2 refers to the trading partner.)

(FD 12.8)

$$Y_1\uparrow \rightarrow M_1\uparrow \begin{array}{c} \\ \end{array}$$
$$ X_2\uparrow \rightarrow Y_2\uparrow \rightarrow M_2 \quad X_1 \rightarrow Y_1\uparrow \rightarrow M_1\uparrow$$
$$\text{etc., etc.}$$

■ *CANADA'S FOREIGN REPERCUSSION EFFECT*

The example above is quite restrictive, with only two countries, and obviously much oversimplified. Sometimes, however, some basic figuring will establish the statistical parameters of an argument. Take the case of Canada and the United States.

Suppose Canada has a MPM of .3, which is realistic. We know it imports 70% of its imported goods and services from the United States. Suppose the United States has an MPM of .1, which may be a bit low. One third of U.S. imports come from Canada. Now: Canada raises income by $1 million. That leads to a $300,000 increase in imports, $210,000 of those from the United States. The United States in turn would import about $21,000 more in goods, spending about $7000 in Canada. The rest of the world would spend less in Canada, although its propensities to import would be higher, so a bit more might trickle back to Canada. In any case Canada would be lucky to get more than $30,000 of respending from that $300,000 leakage.

The process doesn't end there, because the extra $30,000 spent in Canada would lead to about $9000 more in Canadian imports. And some of the additional imports made by the United States and other countries would stimulate somewhat more spending. The leakage is so high, however, that subsequent rounds will be small. It is a little like throwing a rock in a lake and watching the ripples spread not only from the rock but from the drops of water it throws off into the water. They become smaller and smaller until eventually they cannot be seen any more.

FACTORS UNDERLYING THE IMPORT SCHEDULE

It is not possible to go to the library and look up an MPM—any more than it is to find an MPC or a demand curve. For the most part, these are models to encourage thinking and questioning, but they can, within some limits, be made statistical and be used to establish the probable magnitude of a reaction.[*] The best clue to the import function's slope is the composition of imports themselves, particularly if viewed in conjunction with the domestic economy's ability to produce import substitutes. Clues to the response of imports to income changes emerge from examining the types of goods imported.

1. Income-sensitive consumer goods: Imports often tend to be goods that are more in demand when people's incomes rise—that is, they are *income elastic*. Typical American imports of this kind are electronic goods and medium-priced automobiles. Third World nations often find that imports of meat, sugar, and wheat soar as income rises, particularly if the response of domestic agriculture to the changes in demand is slow.

   Conversely, if a nation's consumer imports tend to be largely staple foods or if they are generally considered inferior to domestically produced goods, then people are not going to spend a great deal of their new income on imports. Americans used to prefer American-made automobiles and still prefer the more stylish brands of domestic clothing, and such tastes may account for the rather shallow slope of the import function America had during the 1950s. As foreign producers have been able to produce goods more to the taste and quality demanded by American consumers—moving upscale, so to speak—the American marginal propensity to import has become higher. (It makes a reasonable postulate, anyway.)

2. Fuels and raw materials: Some imports are essential to fuel the economy. American imports of petroleum, for instance, vary directly with the use of energy, and the use of energy in turn increases whenever the economy grows. Since petroleum represents a major part of U.S. imports and since domestic stocks do not respond quickly to changes in demand, virtually all of the increase in oil consumption must be provided through imports. Similarly, but in not so marked a fashion, imports of minerals and metals used in manufacturing rise and fall in response to the level of economic activity.

3. Some goods respond more sharply at the beginning of economic boom cycles—it is as if the import schedule tips up for a year or so as the business cycle turns up. These include:

   a. Industrial goods in short supply: Often as domestic tool and machinery companies reach capacity, they are forced to quote longer periods of delay before filling orders. In response, their regular buyers abandon them in favor of foreign suppliers who promise a quicker even if sometimes more costly delivery. This also occurs with industrial raw materials like steel, aluminum, and chemicals.

   b. Inventories: In periods when there is a sharp recovery, there is often a sudden increase in demand for inventories of raw and semifinished mate-

---

[*] It is difficult to distinguish price from income effects statistically and to handle situations in which suppliers shorten or lengthen the order queue rather than increasing prices.

rials. The inventory problem is particularly serious for Japan and Great Britain, which rely heavily on imported materials to feed their factories. The sudden increase in inventories of raw materials, although generally short in duration, can send the import figures skyrocketing and put a lot of pressure on the home currency in the foreign exchange market. This creates a ticklish situation in which the government is tempted to quash the economic recovery in order to defend the currency.

A concept sometimes used to figure the response of imports to income changes is the *income elasticity of imports.* Resembling all other income elasticities, it is the *percentage change of imports* divided by the *percentage change of income* ($\%\Delta M/\%\Delta Y$). It can be calculated in a crude way simply by comparing real income changes to real import changes, but that fails to isolate other possible influences, particularly that of price. A more sophisticated regression model, which tries to control for the influence of changing price, is sometimes used. Recall from Chapter 1 that imports have been rising as a percentage of GNP for many years; part of this, particularly in the nineteenth century, reflects price elasticity, but the data also suggest an income elasticity of imports greater than 1.

Another way to approach the question is through a computer-modeled income-output matrix, which traces the input requirements of every industry. One could, for instance, find that an increase in income normally led to a rise in output of automobiles, which needed greater inputs of steel, tires, aluminum, and so on, and then see what the higher needs would be for each of those industries. With a model in place, the computer will crank out the effects on the supplying industries, including imports, for a variety of assumptions about end-production.

NATIONAL INCOME AND THE BALANCE OF TRADE

THE TRADE AND SAVING GAP DIAGRAM   Chapter 10 dealt with the trade and $S - I$ gaps as single points derived from historical data. The assumption that both gaps are partially determined by income levels presents a way to imagine alternative scenarios from the single one that happened. *If* income were higher, what *might* the trade deficit have been? The diagram is a variation on the I&L diagram.

Take the formula that equates national saving with the balance of trade, $S - I = X - M$, and examine it through the leakage and injections model to get the relationship between income and the trade and investment-saving gaps. X, a constant, less M, a term that rises as income rises, gives us $X - M$, which slopes downward. $S - I$, a schedule of the saving gap at various incomes, has the opposite pattern, with the constant being subtracted from the rising S schedule, and therefore the $S - I$ rises.

The same data we used to build the I&L diagram serves to build the trade and saving gap diagrams. Figure 12.12 is the equivalent of Fig. 12.6, highlighting, however, the relationship of the trade and investment-saving gaps to the level of income.

Figure 12.12 **Trade and saving gap approach:** $S-I = X-M$. The curves $S - I$ and $X - M$ incorporate the same data we used earlier to establish the basic national income at $1 billion. Those initial figures were designed to have imports equal exports at the equilibrium level of national income. $S - I$ equals $X - M$ at an income of $1 billion, which is also the point at which exports happen to equal imports. If, however, investment increases or saving decreases by $100 million, national income will rise. The new equilibrium would be at $1.2 billion, and at that income the trade balance would be negative (–$50 billion). The trade deficit shows as the difference between the crossing point of the two curves and zero; in this case the trade deficit at the new equilibrium is –$50 million. This, of course, is also the saving gap.

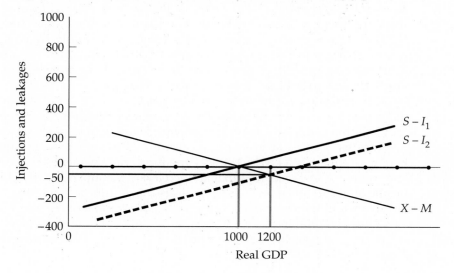

Any upward movement in the schedule $X - M$ due to a rise in exports or a fall in imports—the diagram conveniently does not ask us to specify which—will raise the level of national income. Similarly, any downward movement in the schedule $S - I$ due to a fall in saving or a rise in investment will also raise the equilibrium level of national income, moving it to the right on our diagrams. Note also, however, that the resulting trade balance changes are not so large as the initial change.

Figure 12.13 shows once again the case of the higher tariff that discourages imports.

Diagrams such as these can easily handle cases where exports are not autonomous, but are instead related to the level of income. Such a relationship would, as mentioned earlier, be a negative one, with exports falling as income increases. As new domestic orders flow to firms, management tends to pay less attention to export markets; when domestic sales are dwindling, the search for foreign sales intensifies. This phenomenon is particularly marked with capital-intensive goods where a high and steady volume of production is necessary, for example, petrochemicals and steel. Where this is the case the schedule for X has a downward slope as income increases, and so $X - M$ must decline more sharply than otherwise. The result is that any change (higher I, lower X, and so

Figure 12.13 **A higher tariff partially restrains M: $S-I = X-M$.** A decrease in imports causes $X - M$ to rise (remember, it is subtracting a rising figure, M, from a constant, X). Income rises, as in our other diagrams, to $1.2 billion. At first, it would seem that imports would decrease by $100 million (as they would if income remained at $1 billion). But income rises, and with it imports also rise (by $50 million). The new equilibrium level of income has a positive balance of trade.

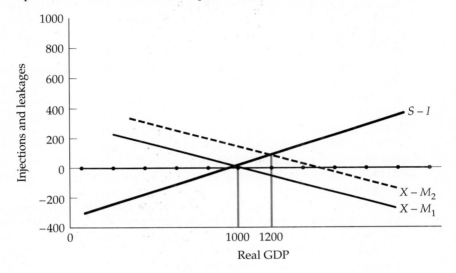

on) will have a greater effect on the balance of trade and a lesser effect on national income than appear in our standard diagram.

The trade and saving gap diagram also helps to visualize the relationship of a change in the trade surplus to saving. Suppose the country exports more, or receives higher prices for its exports. $X - M$ shifts downward and income increases, and as income increases, saving also increases. Summarized as a flow diagram:

(FD 12.9) $$(X - M)\uparrow \rightarrow Y\uparrow \rightarrow (\bar{I} - S\uparrow)\downarrow$$

Using the same diagram, consider what happens when a decline in saving shifts $S - I$ downward. At any given level of income, $S - I$ is lower, and as it moves along the $X - M$ schedule, imports rise.

(FD 12.10) $$(S\downarrow - \bar{I})\downarrow \rightarrow (\bar{X} - M\uparrow)\downarrow$$

POLICY IMPLICATIONS

The policy implications stemming from the theory outlined here are important. *The balance of trade can be adjusted by changes in national income.* Assume that the United States has a balance of trade deficit and wishes to correct it. Several policy alternatives involving income are available and can be used to attempt a cure for the situation. First, as shown in Fig. 12.14, the country might raise the level of saving (including both private saving, S_p, and government saving, $T - G_c$), causing $S - I$ to rise from $S - I_1$ to $S - I_2$. $S - I_2$ crosses $X - M$ at 0, so the trade deficit would fall to zero. Alternatively, it could lower the level of investment to shift $S - I$.

The chief problem involved in this sort of adjustment is readily apparent. Income falls from Y_3 to Y_2. Recession works to cure an international imbalance. Unfortunately, however, the fall in national income will be politically most unwelcome, and hardly optimal policy. (It is only likely to be used when there is danger of the economy overheating or if there are major price effects accompanying the income effects—in which case we are talking about price rather than income effects.) Countries with a low MPM, and hence a relatively flat schedule for $X - M$ (for example, the United States) would have to reduce national income considerably to be rid of any balance-of-trade deficit, while those like the Netherlands, with a high MPM, could achieve adjustment with a much smaller change in income. The converse is also true: The United States with its low MPM can stimulate its economy within broad limits and suffer less significant balance-of-trade effects than most countries. In the Netherlands, by contrast, any fiscal or monetary policy that raises I or reduces S would have a very high leakage into imports.

Changes in income arising from sources other than international transactions, whether desired or not, can create their own sets of trade balance problems. An autonomous change in saving or investment rates or changes in fiscal policy can have unwanted effects on the balance of payments. Take the case of Japan in 1992. As the country entered its worst recession in over a decade,

---

Figure 12.14 Shifts in $S-I$ produce changes in $X-M$ through income effects. The three $S - I$ schedules represent possible configurations of saving and investment. As $S - I$ shifts upward against a stable $X - M$ schedule, the balance of trade improves from $-a$ to 0 to b, but income falls from Y_3 to Y_2 to Y_1. If $S - I$ shifts downward, the balance of trade worsens.

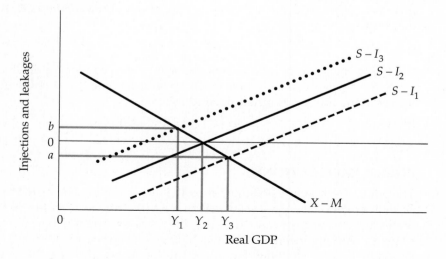

imports fell off sharply, and its current account surplus rose from less than US$40 billion to $119 billion. A diagramatic representation would look like Fig. 12.14. $X - M$ did not shift because nothing occurred to change the relationship of exports or imports to any given level of income.[1] This would be like a movement from $S - I_2$ to $S - I_3$, except that in this case the trade balance was already positive to begin with. (An accurate representation would add an $S - I_4$ still farther to the left.) While American politicians continued to bash Japan's trade policy, the surplus was a sign of major Japanese economic difficulties, which its leaders did not in the least want, not some clever trade maneuver.

■ COULD INCOME INCREASES IN JAPAN AND GERMANY HAVE ENDED THE U.S. TRADE DEFICIT?

It is possible, using the tools we have developed to this point, to examine more closely America's proposed moves for Germany and other trade-surplus countries more closely. We can come up with back-of-the-envelope estimates fairly readily. We cavalierly assume that for either Japan or Germany any rise in income will increase imports by one third of that amount (MPM of .33), and of that increase in imports, .25 will be spent in the United States. (Both estimates are probably far too high, particularly the MPM of .33 for Japan.) This means a $12 billion rise in income will produce $4 billion worth of imports, only $1 billion of which will be spent in the United States. For each billion dollars' worth of reduction in the U.S. trade deficit, Germany, with a GNP of $883 billion in 1988, would have to increase its GNP by 1.36%. Japan, with a larger GNP, would have to expand it by 0.57%, a little over half a percent. The U.S. balance-of-trade deficit in 1988 was around $130 billion; even if Japan and Germany expanded their incomes by 10% above their otherwise projected levels, the help for the United States would not be great. Specifically, a German increase of 10% yields $7.35 billion, and a Japanese increase of 10% yields $17.54 billion, not much of a dent in what was then a $130 billion deficit.

Using more sophisticated econometric modeling, MIT's Paul Krugman and Columbia's Richard E. Baldwin have calculated that if the whole rest of the world increased their income by 5%, the resulting increase in U.S. exports would not come near to eliminating the U.S. deficit problem.[2]

MIXED PRICE AND INCOME EFFECTS: A RECIPE FOR CONFLICT

To this point we have dealt principally with income, not price effects. But an income effect in one country could be a price effect in another. A country expanding its economy will import more, but its trading partners may not want the additional exports if they contribute to their own inflation.

In the 1980s, the United States acted much like Country 1 in the foreign repercussion example. As the Reagan tax cut expanded consumption, American imports grew enormously. Some countries (like Canada) had been reluctant to expand their own economies for fear of developing a trade deficit; now they could safely do so and welcomed any income effects from expanded exports; indeed they might have given their economies an added push by following expansionary fiscal or monetary policies. Other countries, however, felt any expansion of exports would be inflationary—either because they considered themselves in a situation where the long-run *AS* curve was indeed vertical, or because they felt they were very close to full employment. German economists in particular were disturbed, since they did not want inflation and knew their real wages were quite rigid.

SHIFTS IN AGGREGATE SUPPLY: MORE PRICE EFFECTS

To this point, we have held aggregate supply unchanged. *AS* can shift, however. What happens if it shifts and why might it do so?

SHOCKS TO THE SHORT-RUN *AS* CURVE

A short-run *AS* curve carries certain implicit *institutional* assumptions about the nature of wage settlement, of bargaining, or of price setting. If output falls when *AD* falls, it is not because of economic necessity, since the economy can produce just as much as it did before and apparently wants to produce it. It is just that nominal wages and prices cannot fall quickly enough when aggregate demand declines sharply. Similarly, a movement in the horizontal *AS* curve comes about because of institutional factors. Wage increases in one sector may be immediately followed by so-called equity raises in other sectors. AS_{sr} would move upward. So long as the long-run *AS* curve does not shift, however, the government could allow a rise in *AD* and thereby return to full employment levels, albeit at a higher price level. Using the Hybrid model, Fig. 12.15 illustrates this. If the short-run *AS* shifts from AS_{sr_1} to AS_{sr_2}, then income will fall to $0a$ and prices rise to P_2. If, however, aggregate demand rises from AD_1 to AD_2, then output will be restored at $0b$, even though the price level is higher.

In an international context, the short-run *AS* curve *might* rise if import prices rise. Take a classic *cost-push* inflation. As Chapter 16 discusses at greater length, a fall in the value of a country's currency, by raising the cost of imports and the value of exports, *may* trigger a general rise in prices. If such a thing happens, the path to improving the balance of trade would become far more twisted, as the price increase may cause unemployment (the fall of output from $0b$ to $0a$ in Fig. 12.15). In this figure, the government has managed to get the country's currency to fall in value, but that fall has triggered an unanticipated rise in short-run aggregate supply, a process discussed at more length in Chapter 16. The market cannot clear at the higher prices, given the level of *AD*, leading to cutbacks in output. The curves to begin with were AS_{lr_1} (long-run *AS*), AS_{sr_1} (short-run *AS*) and AD_1. With the shift to AS_{sr_2}, prices rise to P_2 and employment falls, causing output to fall to $0a$. That is an *income effect*.

Figure 12.15 **Shifts in *AD* and short-run *AS*.** Cost-push factors drive the general price level upward from AS_{sr_1} to AS_{sr_2}, despite there being no change in the economy's potential output. As a result *AD* at AD_1 cannot support full employment, but only a real GDP level of 0*a*. The government can therefore expand *AD* to AD_2 to achieve an output and employment level of 0*b*.

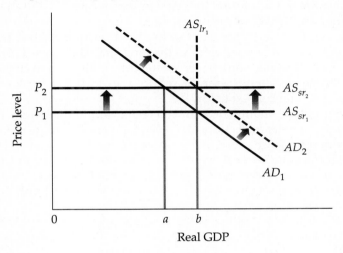

We know from the discussion above that the *income effect* will improve the balance of payments. The price effect, however, has been wiped out by the unanticipated movement of the *AS* curve. The government can restore full employment by expanding aggregate demand to AD_2, but that brings the country back to the beginning of the path, not the end. The government's credibility is lower and the price level higher.

In 1991, some Canadian economists feared such a scenario. They worried lest the Bank of Canada decide that the Canadian dollar should be lower in value, to correct the large trade deficit. If the Canadian dollar fell, from US$0.87 to around US$0.75, or 15%, domestic prices might rise by 15%. Since there would be insufficient domestic demand for the market to clear at those prices, either prices would have to fall again (which would be unlikely) or there would be unemployment. To battle the unemployment, the federal and provincial governments might increase demand, causing the price level to rise 15%. *Exchange rate effects* would counter *price level effects*, and the trade surplus would not improve. The country would again be at square one, but with a higher price level.

Late in 1992 the Canadian dollar did indeed fall as far down as US$0.72 (before recovering to about US$0.80 in March 1993). But short-run aggregate supply did not appear to shift, and the low rates of inflation of the preceding few years continued. Mired in recession, merchants and their suppliers were unable to raise prices, and workers were unable to muster support for higher wages. The economists' worst fears were not realized.

SHOCKS TO THE LONG-RUN *AS* CURVE

An inward movement of the *long-run AS* curve indicates a decline in potential output. Even if people are fully employed, they cannot produce the same output. Such a situation could come about because of a decline in productivity that might come after war or natural disaster. In such a case, raising *AD* would raise prices further and leave output unchanged. Figure 12.16 shows that the price level would rise to P_3 if *AD* were to rise to AD_2. This happens because there is no way to expand output beyond AS_{lr_2} in the long run. The rewards for working in real terms have declined and fewer people are willing to exchange their lost leisure (in its broader context) for the reduced rewards. We explore these issues in their international context below.

The principal international factor causing a shift in the long-run *AS* curve is a change in the *terms of trade.* Consider what happened with many oil-importing countries when oil prices rose. A ton of cotton or a shipload of bananas purchased fewer imports, lowering what was available for absorption. (Whether the export falls in value or the import rises makes no difference; the economy has fewer real goods and services than it did before.) We consider this an *open economy aggregate supply.*[*]

Figure 12.16 suffices to show what would happen if a severe decline in terms of trade hit a country. Prices would rise, of course. But if the government tried to increase *AD* any further, it would just increase the inflation. The difficulty is that the country's productive capacity (including its ability to bring in imports) has fallen.

THE LONG RUN IN WHICH WE ARE ALL DEAD OR AT LEAST CONSIDERABLY WEAKENED

The use of the Hybrid model does not imply that we think income effects always are short term. Nor does it mean that we are dismissing out of hand the Keynesian model, in which income effects do not necessarily lead to price effects. If the price effects are a long time in coming, economic growth from higher investment might push out the long-run *AS* curve. And certainly in severe recessions, Keynes' dictum may still apply: "In the long run we are all dead." Suppose, for instance, that the long run were indeed very long and that several years of depressed income and investment caused productivity to drop; the *AS* curve would move inward. Conversely, if *AD* were stimulated and the price effects relatively slow to come, the capital base of the economy might grow and AS_{lr} move outward. Figure 12.17 shows such a situation.

---

[*] Some economists object to this usage, and your macroeconomics instructor may raise some questions. If we measure *output* according to some index of a previous year's weights, it may not fall: A ton of cotton and a boatload of bananas are still the same. But the goods they exchange for are less, altering what is available for $C + I + G$ and also the real wages that can be offered. Measuring exports by the *physical goods and services they bring,* output falls—and falls just as surely as it would if the crops were blighted. To distinguish our usage from the occasional different usage in some macroeconomics texts, we call it an *open economy aggregate supply.*

Figure 12.16 **Shifts in both *AD* and *AS* in Hybrid model.** If war or natural disaster causes a country's productivity to decline, the long-run *AS* curve shifts from AS_{lr_1} to AS_{lr_2}. Under the given aggregate demand of AD_1 prices would rise from P_1 to P_2. If the government tries to expand aggregate demand to AD_2, it produces more inflation, driving the price level up to P_3.

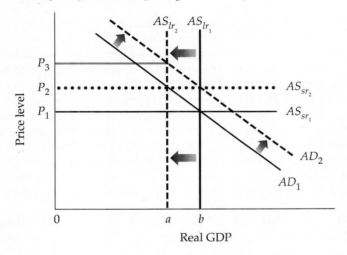

Figure 12.17 **Growth during the long run: Full employment might allow for growth in capacity.** Output falls initially from $0b$ to $0a$ due to a decline in the terms of trade. The government, however, maintains *AD* at AD_2, rather than making it fall to AD_1, which would keep prices from rising. Since prices rise only slowly, the added output over several years allows the capital base to expand such that the economy can produce $0b$, on AS_{lr_2}, with a more modest price rise to P_2, rather than to P_3.

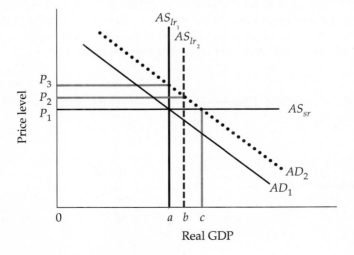

CONCLUSION

As young professors teaching at the same college, Brown and Hogendorn were amused to hear the story of the old professor who one alumni weekend received a visit from a former student. The former student looked at one of the professor's exams.

"But these are the same questions you asked us 25 years ago!"

"Yes," replied the professor, "but the answers are different."

Twenty-five years later, we aver: It is no joke, but a profound truth. Twenty-five years ago, classroom macroeconomics was *income effects,* with a few adjustments to take care of inflation when full employment neared. It was the end of the big postwar economic boom, when real growth was measured at 4 and 5% a year, when jobs were plentiful, and economists could speak of fine-tuning an economy. Some of the worries, such as short-run income effects turning into long-run price effects, were there, but were not important enough to incorporate into lower-level textbooks, or too conservative for many people's taste. Just a little $S + I$ and M and X added would suffice to make the basic points. None of this aggregate supply stuff, because in those days income effects were income effects and price effects were price effects.

The 1970s and 1980s changed that. Economics "as she was taught" simply could not handle the actual events, forcing the field to search farther and ask more searching questions. Certainly we can use the income models, and income effects are very real, as is the multiplier. They are as a whole, however, more useful for short- or medium-term analysis, or for specific situations. The long run is probably best conceptualized with the aggregate demand and supply curves. (Students should be pleased, because it is technically far easier to use AS and AD than it is to use the income models.)

We have to this point left money and exchange rates out of our considerations. Clearly, we cannot continue doing so. To begin, however, we need a good understanding of money and its relation to the foreign exchange market. Every pattern of shock and reaction seems to differ not only on whether output responds to aggregate demand, but also on whether the exchange rate is stable or not. And we have yet to look seriously at the role of monetary policy. Chapter 13 lays the groundwork to understand some of these questions.

VOCABULARY AND CONCEPTS

Aggregate demand

Aggregate supply

Aggregate supply shock

Combined marginal propensities

Contemporary model (Friedman-Phelps)

Exchange rate effect

Export schedule

Foreign repercussion effect

Hybrid Model

Import schedule

Income effect

Income elasticity of imports

Income-trade balance diagram

Injections

Keynesian model

Leakages

Long-run *AS*   *S*−*I* schedule
Marginal propensity to import   Shock to long-run *AS*
Price effect   Short-run *AS*
Price level effect   *X*−*M* schedule

QUESTIONS

1. "Trade is affected by price and income effects. We have two kinds of price effects and one kind of income effect. In the long run, however, we have only price effects." Comment.

2. The Hybrid model combines the flatness of a Keynesian *AS* curve with the steepness of a Contemporary model curve. Given the discussion, it is probably less Keynesian than it looks. Why? (Discuss the differences between the three models and explain the reason for choosing the Hybrid model.)

3. Basically, the leakages and injections model is short term and works best on the horizontal portion of the *AS* curve. Explain.

4. Draw an injections and leakages diagram using the following data: at an income of 200, $S = 20$, $M = 40$, $I = 30$, $X = 40$. I and X are exogenously determined. MPS = .2 and MPM = 0.25. What is the equilibrium level of income? Assume exports were to rise by 20; what is the new income?

5. Explain why an increase in tariffs would have no success at reducing a trade deficit in the unlikely or impossible event of having saving completely unresponsive to changes in income. Explain why a rise in tariffs might have some success in reducing a trade deficit, given that saving does indeed rise with income.

6. The foreign repercussion effect shows that leakage into imports is not as complete as leakage into saving. Explain.

7. The impact of expansion of European countries on the U.S. balance-of-trade deficit in the late 1980s would probably have been too small to significantly change that deficit. Explain, using the foreign repercussion effect and some rough-and-ready estimates.

8. "If all countries run at or near full employment, international adjustment is going to mean unemployment for trade-deficit countries and inflation for surplus countries." Show how adjustment through income effects will give that result.

9. Distinguish the kinds of shocks that affect the short-run *AS* from those affecting long-run *AS*.

10. Explain the difficulty of adjusting to a leftward or upward shift of long-run *AS*.

NOTES

[1] See *The Economist,* January 30, 1993, pp. 20 and 59.

[2] Paul R. Krugman and Richard E. Baldwin, "The persistence of the U.S. trade deficit," *Brookings Papers on Economic Activity,* Vol. I, 1987, pp. 1–55.

Chapter 13

The Foreign Exchange Market, Exchange Rates, and the Money Supply

Overall Objective: To introduce the institutional background and tools required for understanding international aspects of monetary and exchange rate policy.

MORE SPECIFICALLY:

- To show the institutions of the foreign exchange market and the difficulty any government has in attempting to control it.

- To construct a demand and supply model for currencies, and to convey an understanding of the role of monetary intervention in the foreign exchange market.

- To convey, through T-accounts, how monetary intervention leads to changes in monetary reserves and ultimately to changes in the money supply.

- To deepen understanding of the institutions through

    using the concept of transaction costs to show why foreign exchange markets are so large;

    using present value analysis to explain forward spot rate differentials.

Chapter 13 covers three important topics: (1) the workings and institutions of the foreign exchange market, (2) the basics of how exchange rates are determined, and (3) how action in the foreign exchange market may affect the money supply. These subjects are important for understanding material in later chapters: the broader monetary issues with various monetary shocks discussed in Chapter 14, and the effect of exchange rate changes covered in Chapter 15.

1. The institutions of the foreign exchange market are important, not only for their own fascination and the way the material fills in the international aspect of money and banking, but also for the way they establish limits on what policies can work and the way they shape international economic theory itself.

2. The basics of exchange rate determination are critical to theory and policy. The interrelationships of income, price level, and exchange rate changes are subtle and rather defy attempts to take them one by one. The determination of an exchange rate is not in itself a simple topic. Exchange rate stability and volatility are only partially understood, as are their determinants. The sections on the demand and supply approach and the government's role in stabilizing the value of a currency lay the basis for further understanding.

3. When monetary authorities try to fix the value of exchange rates, they produce monetary shocks that may or may not be welcome. The final part of the chapter traces the mechanics of how that comes about.

THE VALUE OF A CURRENCY

An essay question: "A currency's value is established in the foreign exchange market. Because the foreign exchange market is so efficient, so large, and so quick, governments cannot (or can no longer) decree a value. The best they can do is to target a value and, through direct intervention and supporting domestic policies, keep close to that target." Comment.

The essay question above is a difficult one, if answered with any thought. Examine the first part: The foreign exchange market, not some government decree, establishes the value of a currency. Economists and politicians sometimes express opinions that a currency's value is too high—that is, *overvalued*—or too low—that is, *undervalued.* But something in the market, or perhaps in what the government is doing, prevents the currency from reaching what they postulate is the right value. We do not understand what that is or why nothing can be done about it, so it is best to start answering with an examination of the second part of the statement: The market is so large that a decree will not work.

THE FOREIGN EXCHANGE MARKET

Like many commodities, national currencies are bought and sold in an international market. Currencies make ideal commodities for big, efficient markets. Unlike many manufactured goods, they are for the most part homogeneous—one U.S. dollar is the same as another, one French franc is the same as another. (One car or one ton of coffee is not the same as others.) Unlike agricultural commodities, they do not deteriorate (nothing like a late delivery of pig bellies or Christmas trees). And the transportation cost is virtually nothing—just a notification via electronic media. Unlike goods, however, currencies are not traded for their own sake, but for what they can buy. Ultimately, the value of a pig belly depends on what people will pay for the bacon; with currencies, there is still another step, as that currency is just a generalized claim on a nation's resources.

Few figures in economics rival in their astronomical proportions those for the foreign exchange markets. In the late 1980s those markets were handling something like US$650 billion a (working) day—which is $3 trillion a week, and something over $150 trillion in a year.

With stupendous volume and such an ideal product, we could expect the markets to be highly efficient—which they are—and perhaps even to give a realistic value to a currency based on its long-run prospects, a more debatable proposition.

THE STRUCTURE OF THE MARKET

CUSTOMERS AND BANKS   Bank patrons have a variety of instruments available to engage in buying and selling foreign exchange. The foreign exchange market falls into two tiers, one in which individuals or companies deal with banks, and one in which the banks deal with each other—retail and wholesale, so to speak. The vast majority of market participants buy and sell foreign exchange through their banks, a smaller number through securities dealers or brokerage houses (for example, Merrill Lynch). Consider a typical transaction.

The New York importer Theophilus Thistlethwaite & Sons orders 500 Scottish tartan blankets from Reekie Looms of Paisley, Scotland, at a cost of £10,000—that is ten thousand pounds sterling. The bill is *invoiced* in sterling—Thistlethwaite's obligation is legally to deliver sterling. How can Thistlethwaite pay?

1. The company could just send a U.S. dollar check, having looked up the exchange rate in the newspaper. Reekie, however, may not be pleased if in the interim the exchange rate has fallen against the dollar (so they wouldn't get enough pounds) and would dun for the remainder. They may say nothing if the dollar has risen against the pound.

2. If Thistlethwaite does a lot of business with British suppliers, it may itself have an account in Britain. It would draw a check on that account and then replenish it by sending its British bank a U.S. dollar draft—if that draft were short of the amount paid out to Reekie, the British bank would not care so long as the account was not overdrawn. In many countries—but not the United States, where such practices are prohibited by law—a company can acquire a foreign currency account in its own country and simply draw on it. Canadian companies routinely establish U.S. dollar accounts at their Canadian banks.

3. If Thistlethwaite does not do regular business in Britain, it can ask its bank to make out a check, like a cashier's check or certified bank draft, in the foreign currency. It costs more per transaction than having a foreign account, but the costs are a very small part of a large transaction like this.

4. If the two companies are unfamiliar with each other, they may choose one of a dozen or more *instruments of credit*—various letters of credit and commercial acceptances that come into play when the goods are delivered. In

essence, Reekie could send Thistlethwaite a form that, when signed, acts as a draft on Thistlethwaite's account. Usually, these are guaranteed by one or both banks involved in the transaction. They are sometimes not for immediate payment, but for payment in 30, 60, or 90 days, and may be *negotiable*— that is, they can be sold at a discount to banks. (In such a case, they would be means of finance as well as means of exchange.) Throughout the nineteenth century and well into the twentieth, such guaranteed future-payment letters, known as *bills of exchange,* were the principal means of financing trade, and a vigorous market for their discount and sale grew up in London. Indeed, the London Royal Exchange traded such bills from the 1500s until its closing in 1920, when the growth of telex and telephone transfers eliminated the need for a large bourse.[1]

THE INTERBANK MARKET   Banks wish to avoid holding excessive amounts of any one currency. A British bank, having given Reekie a credit in *sterling* (British pounds), faces a risk that the U.S. dollars it holds might fall in value. Consider this more closely.

All of the possible means by which Thistlethwaite can pay Reekie involve a bank buying dollars and selling sterling.* If the pound is worth US$1.50, then some bank ends up holding $15,000 and agreeing to pay out £10,000. In the course of a day—or, indeed, a few hours—a major bank will handle millions of dollars' worth of transactions, most considerably larger than this one. Take Lloyds, a large English bank, as an example. Some of the transactions will have Lloyds buying sterling, others selling sterling, but suppose that not very long into the day, Lloyds notices that it is selling quite a bit more sterling than it is receiving, while it is also accumulating a great many U.S. dollars. Lloyds has already established some guidelines as to how much it wishes to have of various currencies. It knows that it could get into trouble if it holds too many dollars.

1. For one thing, Lloyds wants to keep its risks down. To do so, it wishes to match its assets and liabilities so that they are in the same currency. Even if the exchange rate is £1 = $1.50, the bank does not want to see 150 million *dollars* in assets backing 100 million *pounds* of liabilities. If the dollar should slip in value, the bank would face a severe loss. While it might gain if the dollar should rise, it is not primarily in the business of speculating and is not routinely going to bet the bank on the foreign exchange market.

2. For another thing, U.S. dollars do not count as bank reserves in Britain. When Lloyds reports to the Bank of England how much it has held in reserve against its deposits, it cannot use foreign exchange as a primary reserve. If,

---

* A dollar check to Reekie would have to be cashed in a British bank; a sterling draft on Thistlethwaite's British bank would be replaced by a dollar check; an international bank draft in sterling causes the bank to buy Thistlethwaite's dollars; and any of the commercial instruments eventually ends up with a bank buying dollars.

for instance, Lloyds needed to hold 5% of its assets as reserves against deposit liabilities, it could not count the U.S. dollars.* If Lloyds is *loaned up*—that is, it has no reserves over the required 5%—it will need to convert dollars into sterling to increase its sterling reserves.

3. While not willing to bet the whole bank on speculation, Lloyds will have authorized its managers to do some limited speculation on the rise or fall of the dollar. If they are speculating against the dollar, they would, within their established *speculative limits,* reduce their dollar holdings.

4. In the very short run—a matter of hours, often—Lloyds may expect a change in its balances. Perhaps in the morning there is more demand for sterling, in the afternoon for dollars. The bank may not wish to face the transactions costs of selling in the morning and then rebuying in the afternoon, and may decide to let some imbalances ride.

In this particular case, let us suppose Lloyds decides that its need for reserves, its mismatched assets and liabilities, and its speculative feelings on the dollar all suggest it should sell off a million of them—small potatoes in the huge international market. At this point, Lloyds would enter the interbank (wholesale) market to sell.

The interbank market is a telephone- and telex-connected market, having no central bourse or city. The participants are principally the large banks and a few big brokerage houses. Regional banks in the United States buy and sell retail to the larger banks. Virtually all of the large sales are made through banks in London, New York, and Tokyo. In the late 1980s, London was doing about twice the volume of New York or Tokyo. Frankfurt, Hong Kong, Singapore, and numerous capital cities have smaller markets, usually for their own currencies against a few major ones. The Canadian foreign exchange market, for instance, handles about one fifth of the American volume, two thirds of that being in the U.S. dollar-Canadian dollar trade.** The lines are open between all major banks during the business day, and if, say, a Canadian bank doesn't find a market for its currency in Toronto, it can call New York or, early enough in the day, London. Because of the geographical spread of the three centers, the market never sleeps. When New York opens, London has already been open for five hours. When New York closes, Tokyo is just opening (and is open before the American West Coast markets close). When Tokyo closes, London is already open.

---

* The numbers are for example only. Formal reserve requirements are declining in percentage worldwide, and some countries, such as Canada, have ended them entirely. Banks still keep deposits at their central banks (around 2%) and vault cash (an amount that is growing, due to the vast number of automatic teller machines), but their size is determined by the banks.

** The remaining third is in various U.S. dollar trades against other currencies. Against third currencies, the Canadian dollar, like virtually every other currency, is converted first into U.S. dollars and then into the third currency. See George Pickering and Susan Heard, "Survey of the foreign exchange market in Canada," *Bank of Canada Review,* November 1986, pp. 3–20.

The traders work with batteries of computers and a constant flow of data. They trade either directly with other banks or through foreign exchange brokers, dealing and confirming electronically. Most banks are constantly in the market, even if they have no need to change their portfolios, looking for an opportunity to make a little money by buying and selling currencies at slightly different rates. That way, when they do enter the market to balance their own portfolios, they are up to the second on market information and their own sale is completely disguised. (That is, no one will know whether Lloyds is just speculating a bit or balancing its portfolio.)[2] Brokers try to make money on a *spread* between buying and selling rates, often very small—and they don't have to be very large when trading billions. The banks, of course, make money between the retail rates they charge their customers and the interbank rates they pay other banks. The business is highly competitive, and rates are often quoted to the ten-thousandth of a cent.

THE FORWARD MARKET   The forward market is a market in which currencies *to be delivered at a later date* are traded. Currencies traded and sold immediately are described as *spot,* presumably from "on the spot." If exporters have extended credit, however, they may wish to have a guarantee of an exchange rate when their payments come through. If Reekie had to wait six months for Thistlethwaite's payments, it might exercise its option to buy sterling *forward,* agreeing to deliver its dollar payments in six months in exchange for sterling at a rate that is set today. The development of forward markets has helped traders and investors cut risk in a period of increased exchange rate uncertainty.

Once a bank agrees to accept British pounds, it knows it has an obligation to deliver American dollars and does not want to face the foreign exchange risk. So it then looks to the foreign exchange market to sell its *forward* British pounds, in exchange for the American dollars it will deliver on maturity of the contract. That way, as its various contracts come due, it will have the proper currency and run no risk that its value will rise before the contract is due. The bank enters the forward market, which operates the same way as the spot market.

The forward market has developed enormously in the last decade. Even in the late 1970s, it was rare to find forward markets for currencies that extended more than 90 days. That limited the use of forward exchange to short-term trade financing. Banks were not long, however, in coming up with means by which investors could protect themselves over longer periods of time, and it is possible today to enter into a forward contract for periods of up to ten years.

Forward/spot swaps, a development of the 1980s, are principally agreements to buy a foreign currency *spot* and sell it *forward* at the same time. If a British investor wished to invest in U.S. Treasury bills, for instance, it could buy the dollars now and be assured that when the bill matured in 90 days it would know what it could get for the dollar through a simultaneous forward contract, or *swap.* These transactions have grown tremendously because they reduce foreign exchange risk. In the Tokyo and Toronto markets, over half of the transaction activity is in swaps, although in London and New York the percentages are closer to a quarter.[*]

FROM INSTITUTIONS TO ANALYSIS

The mechanics of the market have their own fascination, if only to indicate how large, strong, and complex the market is. But we can analytically bring it all down, perhaps with some reservations, to the venerable and durable demand and supply.

■ *WHY THERE IS SO MUCH CURRENCY TRADED*

Although the figures for currency traded are astronomical, we should no let them blind us to currency's relation to the underlying forces of trade and investment. The figures grow so large because of the structure of the market. The foreign exchange market is essentially a vast network of independent banks trading directly with one another, rather than trading through some central agent. The result of this is that the number of trades is very large.

To see this, imagine four banks with two currencies entering into trade. The number of possible trades is 6. To wit:

Algebraically, the number of lines, each representing a two-sided trade is: $n(n-1)/2$ where n is the number of traders.

As traders join the network, the number of trades rises much faster than n, since the new trader can trade with all the existing traders $(n-1)$. Adding a fifth trader raises the number of trades from 6 to 10. A new currency works in the same way—4 currencies give 6 trades, and 5 give 10 trades.

If the same banks used a central trader, however, there would only be four trades as each traded only once with the central trader. A central trader would develop if dealing was at all costly. But trading is not expensive: Given the electronic networks and computers the cost of an individual trade is very low. Therefore banks have no need to economize on the number of trades. Every time there is a new trader or a new currency, total potential trades jump greatly. The 1001st trader adds not 1, but a thousand new trades.

---

[*] There are also markets for foreign exchange on the Chicago Board of Trade. These *futures markets* allow speculators to trade currency in blocks for future delivery, much as they can corn, wheat, or pork bellies. While this market may have some influence over the price of forward contracts and offers some arbitrage opportunities, it is much smaller than the forward markets and does not, at this point, appear to be a major influence on the price in those markets.

If a central bank adds $500 million to the foreign exchange market and there are 1000 traders, that $500 million has the potential to become involved with almost 500,000 potential trades; it will not reach its potential, but the added currency is likely to enter into many transactions, swelling the total value of transactions to billions of dollars.

A DEMAND AND SUPPLY APPROACH TO THE DETERMINATION OF THE EXCHANGE RATE

Demand and supply is a highly useful tool for examining the determination of exchange rates. Admittedly, drawing demand and supply curves does not explain why they lie where we draw them, but at least it allows us to observe what the exchange rate is and what kind of efforts might be made to change it. Picture a foreign exchange market with just two currencies, the German mark and the U.S. dollar. Consider the trade in the market to represent all the trade in currencies done within a single year. The demand and supply will then tell us the price. Later we can shorten the time period considered, and use other currencies.

Figure 13.1 shows a demand and supply diagram for U.S. dollars with their price in German marks (Deutsche marks or DM). The horizontal axis is the number of dollars traded; the price of the dollar as expressed in marks per dollar is on the vertical. The demand for dollars slopes downward because at a lower price, people will be able to get more American goods and to buy up American assets

Figure 13.1 **Demand and supply of dollars.** Demand and supply schedules can be used to describe the foreign exchange market for a currency. Here, the quantity bought and sold of dollars is priced in Deutsche marks, and the equilibrium on the market is DM2.4 = $1.00.

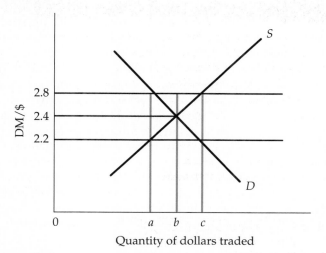

cheaply. The supply of dollars slopes upward because any attempt to persuade the Americans to put more dollars on the market requires greater incentives—they will not buy unless foreign goods, services, and assets are cheaper.

At a price of the dollar at DM2.8, well above where we show equilibrium, the Germans would not buy many American goods and assets at high prices, and so would demand few dollars, while the Americans would gladly purchase dollars to buy German goods that appear so inexpensive, and so would supply many dollars. An enormous surplus of dollars (*ac* in Fig. 13.1) would result, and the DM2.8 price could not hold. Similarly, a very low price of DM2.2 for dollars would encourage Germans to try to buy dollars, but few Americans would want to buy marks, and a shortage of dollars *(ac* in Fig. 13.1) would result. Only at the equilibrium price of DM2.4 would the market clear and exactly as many dollars would be offered as would be demanded. Traders with a good sense of the patterns of demand and supply could presumably set the price quite close to a clearing equilibrium.

Suppose we reduce the time period considered from a year to a day. Do demand and supply curves still slope? Yes; speculators, when they see the price of the mark fall below equilibrium realize the long-term implications, and buy speculatively. With a confident expectation of equilibrium, the market would still work.

THE GOVERNMENT'S ROLE IN STABILIZING THE VALUE OF A CURRENCY

Most countries try to stabilize the value of their currencies, or at least keep them from swinging too widely. The wisdom of doing so is covered in Chapter 15, but the fact of the matter is that countries are very active in manipulating their currency values. So at this point we look at the mechanics.

Countries have both direct and indirect means of stabilizing the value of a currency. Indirect means consist of (1) creating the expectation that a certain value is an equilibrium value, thus encouraging stabilizing speculation; (2) changing interest rates, which can attract or repel investment; and (3) changing price and income levels, which in turn determine the underlying demand and supply conditions for goods and services. Later chapters consider such indirect means. The direct means is to enter the foreign exchange market to influence the price of the national currency, and it is this we examine below.

A government, through its central bank or, in the case of United States, the Federal Reserve, sometimes *intervenes* in the foreign exchange market. If it purchases its own currency with foreign currencies, it drives the value of its currency up. If it sells its own currency for foreign currencies, it drives the value down.

Conceptually and expositionally we may distinguish two pure systems for handling monetary intervention: *fixed rates,* meaning the maintenance through intervention of an exchange rate within a few percent of some declared value, and *floating rates,* in which the monetary authorities never intervene in the market. In the workaday world of central banking, there are various kinds of intermediate systems—particularly intervention to slow a rise or fall in a currency—and neither pure system exists, as Chapters 17 and 18 discuss. Nonetheless, the distinction between fixed and floating exchange rates is a useful one.

INTERVENTION IN THE FOREIGN EXCHANGE MARKET

At this point consider the direct means—*intervention in the foreign exchange market.* Any government through its central bank can trade in its own currency, increasing the market's demand or supply. If the United States' monetary authorities (the Treasury and the Federal Reserve Board) saw the dollar falling and did not want it to fall, they could try to stop that fall by purchasing U.S. dollars on the foreign exchange market. If the German central bank did not want the mark to rise, it could sell more marks.

Technically, the purchases and sales of foreign exchange go through the central banks, and in the case of the United States with its Federal Reserve System, specifically through the Federal Reserve Bank of New York. Suppose, in a concerted action, the Federal Reserve Bank of New York (acting for the Federal Reserve System), and the Bundesbank (the German central bank) decided to halt the dollar's slide against the mark. Each bank would enter the foreign exchange market and purchase substantial amounts of dollars with marks. The Fed would use what marks it had already accumulated (its *foreign exchange reserves*) when the dollar was high, plus whatever it could borrow from other sources. The Bundesbank, of course, has an endless supply of marks that it can use, and it would put the dollars it bought into its foreign exchange reserves.

■ *THE FEDERAL RESERVE SUPPORTS THE DOLLAR*

One of the more dramatic examples of intervention in the last decade came during the winter of 1987–1988. The U.S. dollar came under much downward pressure in December of 1987. The *Federal Reserve Bulletin* describes the events:[3]

The announcement on December 10 that the U.S. trade deficit had jumped to a record $17.6 billion in October underlined the difficulties in reducing the U.S. external imbalance and had a strong market impact. As traders rushed to liquidate their dollar positions, the dollar gapped downward 1½ to 2 percent within a few minutes of the announcement. The U.S. authorities entered the market in concert with several European central banks, to restrain the dollar's decline. The next day, when market conditions again deteriorated, the Desk[*] reentered the market. Over the two-day period the U.S. authorities purchased $351 million against marks and yen.

And a few weeks later, after continued uncertainty in the market:

Against this background, the dollar again came under strong downward pressure as the year drew to a close. U.S. corporations and Japanese banks sold dollars in

---

[*] This means that the unit in charge of deciding whether to intervene in the foreign exchange market (the Desk) ordered the foreign exchange traders at the Federal Reserve Bank of New York to enter the market.

> *thin holiday markets, at a time when most banks in Europe and the United States were unwilling to adjust their position ahead of the year-end. The U.S. monetary authorities intervened heavily in concerted intervention operations. During the period December 16 through December 31, the Desk purchased a total of $1,707 million, approximately half of which was against marks and half against yen. By early morning January 4, the dollar had declined to record lows. . . .*
>
> In the month of December 1987, the Federal Reserve bought over $2 billion worth of U.S. currency (with marks and yen). The *Bulletin* does not indicate how much the Canadian, German, other European and Japanese governments spent, but it was considerable: All in all, it is likely that in the last quarter of 1987, central banks spent somewhere between $20 and $40 billion easing the dollar's fall.[4]

Figure 13.2 visualizes what the monetary authorities do. Here the *D* and *S* represent the market forces independent of any monetary intervention. In contrast to Fig. 13.1, the demand for dollars has fallen and the supply risen. These forces have pulled down the price of the dollar to DM2.2, from the desired rate of DM2.4. At DM2.2 0*b* of dollars would be traded. The Bundesbank and the Federal Reserve would like the price at DM2.4. To bring it there, they have to buy up the dollars with marks.

How many dollars should be bought up from the market to bring the price to DM2.4? At a price of DM2.4 the quantity supplied of dollars will be even greater than it is at DM2.2—0*c*—while the demand for dollars will be less—0*a*. To cover this gap, the monetary authorities put *ac* on the market. The value of that in marks is *ac* × 2.4, a rectangle formed by *ac* and reaching up to the DM2.4 price. A similar exercise will show that a market equilibrium of, say, DM2.6 to the dollar will call forth a sale of dollars and purchase of marks.[*]

MONETARY INTERVENTION AND THE MONETARY ACCOUNT

The monetary account of the balance of payments gives some idea of the size of the net intervention over the year. Consider the current account and the capital account as the market factors, manifesting themselves as points on the demand and supply curves. (The demand and supply curves remain their usual shadowy selves, being merely suppositions about what might have been if some other prices or quantities had prevailed.) The increase in monetary reserves (an outflow in the monetary account) would show up as the quantity of domestic currency sold (or the domestic currency value of foreign exchange).

The space *ac* in Fig. 13.2 represents not only the dollars purchased, but also the balance on the monetary account—and, by deduction, the combined bal-

---

[*] Some students show the monetary authorities' purchases and sales by shifting the demand and supply curves. There is a technical problem in handling the diagram that way, because a shift of, say, the supply curve for DMs to the right in Fig. 13.2 implies that the intervention would be the same *at any price*, and that is not what is meant at all. There is an intervention of different amounts, depending on the market's equilibrium price.

Figure 13.2 **Intervention to keep the value of the dollar up**

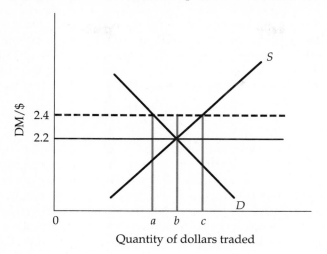

ance on the capital and current accounts (including the discrepancy). We cannot tell the week-to-week changes, but after a year we can see what the net changes have been.

Such figures are often surprising. Check once again the longer U.S. BOPS in Table 11.2 for the year 1987. Despite the drama recorded above about American foreign exchange market intervention, the *net* amount for that year was a very small $2.58 billion dollars. And in 1988 the U.S. was entering the market to hold down the price of the dollar. But that is only part of the story. Check just above in item F, *Liabilities constituting foreign authorities' reserves:* There you can see that central banks like the Bundesbank accumulated $47.72 billion in 1987 and another $40.19 billion in 1988. If we view this in terms of Fig. 13.2, taking the diagram to stand for the whole year and the Bundesbank to stand for all other central banks, *ac* of dollars amounted to $50.30 billion, of which the Federal Reserve purchased $2.58 billion and the Bundesbank (and other central banks) purchased $47.72 billion.

The monetary account shows how much the central bank or Federal Reserve borrowed or invested abroad during a given year. If it is negative, it means, as with any capital outflow, that the monetary authorities are accumulating foreign assets (or paying down foreign debt). If it is positive, it means that they are selling off those assets. If it is zero, then the capital account shows the full story of how a trade deficit was financed or a surplus invested abroad. So, if the monetary authorities do not intervene, the monetary account is zero.

More and more frequently, governments are using methods of controlling exchange rates that are difficult to classify as monetary or capital account activities. A number of central banks (South Korea's and Brazil's, notably) have been borrowing abroad from private sources and using those proceeds to purchase their own currencies on the foreign exchange market, which tends to keep their value up. Balance-of-payments statistics usually classify these as *capital* movements, but their effect is very much the same as monetary borrowing. Should these be considered as part of the intervention or the market's demand and supply? We suggest that so long as these are deliberate borrowings of the central banks to stabilize the currency, they should be considered as intervention. In some cases, such borrowings turn up in the BOPS item called *Exceptional financing*.

EXCHANGE CONTROL

Many Third World governments and some former Communist governments intervene in the market not just through buying and selling foreign exchange, but through licensing the access to foreign exchange in a system called *exchange control*. With exchange control, a country licenses the use of its currency in purchasing foreign currencies. Anyone wanting to import foreign goods, pay foreign creditors, purchase foreign services (including travel) or invest abroad has to get a license from the government, usually through the central bank. Exporters may not sell the foreign exchange they earn directly to the public, but must sell it all to the central bank. Chapter 16 discusses this at greater length.

THE MONEY SUPPLY AND FOREIGN EXCHANGE MARKET INTERVENTION

Whenever monetary authorities decide to intervene in the foreign exchange market, they set in train a series of shocks to their own money supply. Suppose we use the Bundesbank's purchases of U.S. dollars as the initial shock to the system. As the Bundesbank purchases U.S. dollars, it issues the sellers German marks. To earn some interest, it takes the dollars it purchased and buys U.S. Treasury bills. So the Bundesbank's foreign exchange reserves rise, and the new marks it issued cause the German commercial banks' reserves to rise. Then we can say:

(FD 13.1) $\qquad R_{FX}\uparrow \rightarrow R_m\uparrow \rightarrow MS\uparrow \rightarrow i\downarrow \rightarrow I\uparrow \rightarrow AD\uparrow \rightarrow (X - M)\downarrow$

That is, the monetary account turns negative when the central bank purchases foreign exchange reserves (R_{FX}). As foreign exchange reserve rise, the monetary reserves of the commercial banks (R_m) rise, and, in turn, the money supply (MS) rises. And under normal assumptions, interest rates fall, investment rises, aggregate demand grows, and because either real income or prices rise, $X - M$ falls. Chapter 12 already developed the part from AD to $X - M$, and the relationship of MS to interest rates and interest rates to investment gets full explanation (with qualifications) in first- and second-year texts. All we add here is R_{FX} to MS.

A decrease in reserves would lead in the opposite direction.

(FD 13.2) $\qquad R_{FX}\downarrow \rightarrow R_m\downarrow \rightarrow MS\downarrow \rightarrow i\uparrow \rightarrow I\downarrow \rightarrow AD\downarrow \rightarrow (X - M)\uparrow$

Why and how, then, does the purchase or sale of foreign exchange change the money supply?

When central banks buy or sell foreign exchange, they also alter their own commercial banks' reserves. The bank reserves are high-powered money and form the basis for considerable further monetary expansion or contraction. To see how the process works, we examine the T-accounts—simplified statements of changes in credits and debits in the banking system. The T-account, so named because the grid it is drawn on is in the shape of a *T*, is an economist's shorthand way of showing *changes* in bank balances, allowing the assessment of monetary impact from the patterns of changing deposits and loans in the banking system. On the left side of the T-accounts are the bank's assets (what it has or what is owed to it), and on the right side, its liabilities (what it owes others). As in any system of double-entry bookkeeping, changes on one side must always equal changes on the other.

To establish a baseline, we begin by examining a T-account when the monetary authorities do not intervene.

TRANSACTIONS WITH NO INTERVENTION

Consider for a moment how a check in dollars sent to a British bank clears. The mechanism is not the same as a normal domestic check that is sent on to the central bank. Suppose, as in the example earlier in this chapter, that Thistlethwaite of New York imports a considerable amount of blankets from Reekie Looms, and sends them a check for $1.5 million. Reekie deposits that check in its British bank, Lloyds, receiving credits for £1 million at the exchange rate of US$1.50 = £1. What does Lloyds do with the check? If Lloyds had received sterling, it would be no problem, for it would just send the sterling check on to the Bank of England, where it would receive credit, and the Bank of England would debit the bank on which it was drawn. Lloyds cannot send its dollar checks to the Bank of England, however. The Bank of England holds no account for the American bank on which the check was drawn, and will not credit a British bank for foreign currency it holds.

Unable to use the Bank of England for clearing the check, Lloyds will deposit the check in an American bank. The American bank has a regular checking account for Lloyds, and credits the check to that account in the same way it would for any other depositor. In some cases that American bank may be a Lloyds subsidiary, for most of the major foreign banks have operating subsidiaries in the United States— and most major American banks have subsidiaries in London and other financial centers. When a subsidiary is not available, or not convenient, foreign banks have working relationships with numerous American banks, called *correspondent banks*, which establish ordinary deposit accounts for them. Once the check enters the banking system it was issued in, it clears normally.

Figure 13.3 shows the British end of this set of transactions. Lloyds credits Reekie Looms with £1 million (H1) and uses the dollars as backing, increasing its foreign exchange assets by £1 million (G1). But the T-account also shows a decline

Figure 13.3 **British chartered banks T-account**

Assets			Liabilities		
G1. FX	+£1 mn		**H1.** Reekie Looms	+£1 mn	
G2. Loans	−£1 mn		**H2.** Other Depositors	−£1 mn	
(net	±0)		(net	±0)	
I1. Reserves	£1 mn		**J1.** Other Depositors	+£1 mn	
I2. Loans	+£1 mn				
I3. [Loans	+£9 mn]		**J2.** [Other Depositors	+£9 mn]	
K1. Reserves	−£1 mn		**L1.** Other Depositors	−£1 mn	
K2. [Loans	−£9 mn]		**L2.** [Other Depositors	−£9 mn]	

of £1 million in Other Depositors' accounts (J2). Why does that come about? It occurs because we are assuming that at the beginning the banking system is fully loaned out—that is, the commercial bank reserves can support no more deposits. If, for instance, the British reserve requirement were 10%, then 10% of all deposits must be in the form of reserves. If the deposits rise, but reserves do not, the banking system must build up its reserves by reducing its lending. The T-account shows that process, with loans down by £1 million (G2), as are deposits (H2). The net result is that total deposits in sterling (British pounds) neither rise nor fall (final itemization of boxes G and H).

Figure 13.4 shows the activity of the Bank of England, which in this case is none at all. A and B show no activity, as neither the liabilities of the Bank of England (the reserve deposits of British commercial banks) nor its assets have been changed by these transactions.

THE BANK OF ENGLAND INTERVENES

Now suppose that the Bank of England finds that the pound is rising on the foreign exchange market and it does not want it to do so. It enters the market and buys the $1.5 million from Lloyds. When it gets the dollars, it credits Lloyds with the £1 million and uses the foreign exchange it gained to back that credit. Figure 13.4 shows the liabilities of the Bank of England to the commercial banks rising

Figure 13.4 **Bank of England T-account**

Assets			Liabilities	
A.	±0		**B.**	±0
C. FX	+£1 mn		**D.** Commercial Banks	+£1 mn
E. T-bills	−£1 mn		**F.** Commercial Banks	−£1 mn

by £1 million (D), and the Bank's assets (held as foreign exchange, normally as T-bills in other countries) rising also by £1 million (C).

The Bank of England's purchase of foreign exchange has the same effect on the money supply as its purchase of treasury bills or bonds from the banks. Every time it buys a pound's worth, it credits the bank with *new* reserves of a pound. The middle section of Fig. 13.3 shows the reserves of the commercial banks up (I1). Initially, this allows Lloyds to make new loans of £1 million (I2). I2's higher loans create new deposits, shown as *Other depositors* in J1. The new reserves, however, are *high-powered money* (part of the monetary base) and will sustain deposits worth a multiple of their amount. If we again assume the British banks have to keep 10% of their deposits as reserves, the £1 million in new reserves would support £10 million in new deposits, which Fig. 13.3 shows as an additional £9 million to the £1 million on the first round (J2). To create these deposits, the banking system issued £9 million in new loans (I3). Both figures showing the potential expansion (I3 and J2) are in brackets.

■ *FOREIGN EXCHANGE AND BANK RESERVES: A CLARIFICATION*

The link between foreign exchange reserves and domestic banking reserves sometimes gives people difficulty. International or foreign exchange reserves are the assets a country's monetary authorities hold, enabling them to buy up their own currency, if needed, when its value slumps on the foreign exchange market. These assets, as we saw in the chapter on the balance of payments, are largely treasury bills and other short-term assets of other major countries, but also include various deposits with the International Monetary Fund, and as a secondary reserve, gold. Such reserves, along with T-bills and other claims on the domestic government, are part of the assets of the monetary authorities.

Banking reserves are reserves of the commercial banks; they are part of their assets, held on deposit with the central bank (or Fed). As such, they are liabilities of the monetary authorities. They do not include foreign exchange. Figure 13.5 shows the T-accounts of the Federal Reserve and commercial banks to illustrate the difference.

Figure 13.5 **Commercial bank reserves and foreign exchange reserves**

Federal Reserve		**Commercial banks**	
Assets	**Liabilities**	**Assets**	**Liabilities**
FX reserves		Reserves at Fed	
	Commercial bank	Loans	Customer
U.S. T-bills	deposits	Bonds	deposits
Other claims on			
U.S. government			

Note that it is the Federal Reserve that holds the foreign exchange reserves. The reserves of commercial banks, necessary to fill their reserve requirements are deposits at the Federal Reserve or central bank.

COUNTERBALANCING MONETARY POLICY: FOREIGN EXCHANGE STERILIZATION

When central banks expand the money supply through foreign exchange purchases, they often offset that monetary impact by selling T-bills. Continue following the T-account in Fig. 13.3 by supposing that the Bank of England, although it wanted to keep the pound from rising, did not want the money supply to rise. The Bank could then *sell* T-bills to its commercial banks, removing the new reserves at the same time it is creating them. Transaction E of Fig. 13.4 shows the Bank of England's assets falling by £1 million as it sells off T-bills. (Its total portfolio of assets has now changed, as it now holds more foreign exchange and fewer T-bills, but the portfolio's value is the same as it was before the Bank intervened to purchase the foreign exchange.) As the British commercial banks purchase the T-bills, the Bank of England debits their accounts (F).

Transactions K and L of Fig. 13.3 show the same transaction from the commercial banks' side. They just reverse the first-round activity (K1 and L1), and reverse the potential monetary expansion (K2 and L2). The act of removing the new reserves created by purchasing foreign exchange carries the antiseptic name of *sterilization*.

To examine what would happen if Lloyds had issued a check so that Reekie could buy something from the United States and the Bank of England had intervened to keep the price of sterling from falling, just reverse all the signs. The result should show a monetary contraction. If the Bank of England purchased T-bills, the contraction would be reversed.

PREVALENCE OF MONETARY COUNTERBALANCING

Monetary counterbalancing is a very common practice: indeed, routine. Examine, for instance, Canadian figures on foreign exchange accumulation and monetary reserves through the 1970s and 1980s, a period when the Bank of Canada sometimes bought and sometimes sold foreign exchange. The size of the foreign exchange that the Bank of Canada accumulates or depletes over a year is very large in comparison to the Canadian monetary base. In the U.S. dollar crisis of 1987 and 1988, the Bank of Canada built up its holdings of foreign exchange by $11 billion; Canadian commercial bank reserves were about $6 billion, and reserve requirements were about 5%. Could Canada have allowed reserves to triple and the money supply to rise by $440 billion? It does not seem likely, and, indeed, the Bank of Canada allowed no such thing. The reserves of Canada's commercial banks increased by less than a billion dollars in 1987 and fell in 1988, as Fig. 13.6 shows. Indeed, as Fig. 13.6 also shows, very rarely during the entire 19-year period under scrutiny did the changes in foreign exchange much affect the money supply.

Figure 13.6 **Canada: Change in FX reserves and chartered bank reserves, 1971–91.** The solid line shows the changes in the Bank of Canada's holdings of foreign exchange reserves, based on the annual balance-of-payments figures. The dashed line represents the reserves of the Canadian commercial (or *chartered*) banks. From 1970 to 1980 the increase in the reserves of deposit banks was remarkably steady—around a half billion dollars a year, despite the fact that the Bank of Canada's foreign exchange sales and purchases were extremely erratic. Only in a few years (1981–1982 and 1984–1986) do foreign exchange reserves and monetary reserves move together.

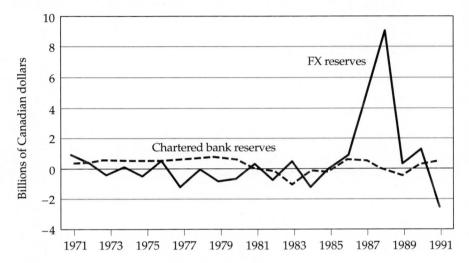

Source: International Financial Statistics Yearbook, 1990.

The means by which the Bank of Canada held the monetary reserves from rising steeply in 1987 and 1988 was foreign exchange sterilization.[*]

Figure 13.7 shows that whenever the Bank of Canada was selling foreign exchange (which would reduce commercial banks' reserves), it was buying treasury bills to reestablish banking reserves, and whenever it was accumulating foreign exchange, it was selling off treasury bills to keep banking reserves from rising.

Figure 13.7 explains, then, the steadiness of the growth of the commercial banks' reserves: The Bank of Canada used open market operations to counterbalance most of the effects of its purchases and sales of foreign exchange. (As well, it used some other methods to supplement the open market operations.)

---

[*] A technical note for Canadian students: The Bank of Canada passes on its foreign exchange to the government's Foreign Exchange Stabilization Fund, receiving government bonds in its place. An examination of Bank of Canada figures alone does not indicate the source of those bonds. The figures here are from *IFS*.

Figure 13.7 **Canada: FX sterilization changes in monetary holdings of FX and T-bills.**
As in Figure 13.6, the solid line is the change in foreign exchange reserves. The dashed
line is the change in the Bank of Canada's holdings of treasury bills. What is of
significance here is the mirror pattern of the two curves, indicating that for almost all of
the years, a loss in foreign exchange reserves was accompanied by an increase in the
growth in the T-bill holdings of the Bank of Canada and vice versa. In 1980, for
instance, the Bank of Canada had to sell over a billion dollars' worth of its foreign
exchange reserves, which, as we saw above, would extinguish a billion dollars' worth
of reserves. In that year, however, it increased its holdings of treasury bills by over $2.5
billion, far above its normal rate of increase. In 1988, when the bank bought around $9
billion worth of foreign exchange, it sold about $7.5 billion in treasury bills.

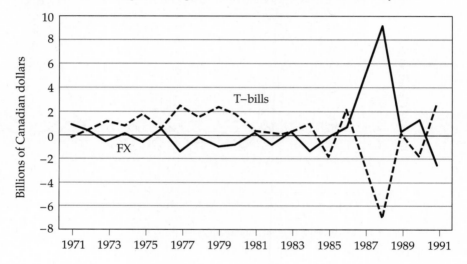

LIMITS OF STERILIZATION AND INTERVENTION

The limited availability of T-bills and similar instruments sharply restricts the
possibilities for sterilization. Intervention faces similar limitations, as well as
that of running out of foreign exchange with which to intervene. More deeply,
counterbalancing policy may very well maintain the interest rate at a level that is
not consistent with long-run real values and a sustainable trade imbalance. Let
us see why.

In the past, perhaps as late as the 1960s, it was possible for nations to intervene in the foreign exchange market regularly and substantially enough to *fix* the
value of their exchange rates within a few percentage points (usually 2.5%) of a
declared value, or *parity*. Thus in the mid-1960s people could count on the U.S.
dollar being worth 4 German marks, 5 French francs, or 0.36 pounds sterling.
While these exchange rates changed occasionally, governments declared their
currencies' par values and worked both indirectly (through interest rate and

other policies) and directly (through intervention) to maintain those values. These were described as *fixed rates.*

Twin difficulties beset the practice of monetary intervention to fix exchange rates. The most obvious is running out of foreign exchange reserves, something quite easy to do in today's world of highly mobile capital. Less obvious, but of equal importance, is the inability of most countries to sterilize inflows. In order to sterilize the inflow of foreign exchange in 1987, the Bank of Canada would have had to sell more than 7 billion Canadian dollars' worth of treasury bills; it only had around $10 billion of them. It did not—likely could not—do so; in fact it let the money supply rise, as Fig. 13.6 shows. Moreover, it refused to fix the value of the Canadian dollar, allowing it to rise some 10 cents against the U.S. dollar. By allowing the Canadian dollar to rise, it did not have to purchase as much foreign exchange as it would have at the lower price. Its reaction to the very heavy inflow of foreign exchange, in sum, was three pronged: (1) Sterilize most of the new monetary reserves created, (2) allow the money supply to rise somewhat, and (3) cut down on the amount of foreign exchange purchased and let the Canadian dollar rise.

Some governments were unsuccessful at fixing their exchange rates, even in the quieter currency markets of yesteryear. Canada in the late 1940s found that it could not seem to establish a regular expectation of how the Canadian dollar would do against the American dollar, and that numerous attempts to intervene in the market or fix the value of the Canadian dollar were unsuccessful.[5] As a consequence, the government allowed the Canadian dollar to *float,* letting the demand and supply on the foreign exchange market determine the value of the dollar; as Figure 13.7 shows, the government intervened, but only enough to slow a change.

The massive capital movements of recent years and the economic disruptions of OPEC price changes and Third World (and U.S.) debt have made intervention far less effective. The monetary authorities of the seven leading industrial nations have foreign currency holdings of something over $265 billion, although more could be raised hurriedly; remember, however, that by the mid-1980s, $650 billion was being traded *every day* and the figure is even higher now. A speculative movement against a currency is virtually unstoppable. Even the massive interventions in the fall and winter of 1987 were a small fraction of that. (The U.S. intervention, to recall, was about $2 billion in a week, and the total intervention $20–40 billion.)

THE MONEY SUPPLY WITH NO MONETARY INTERVENTION

If monetary authorities do not intervene in the foreign exchange market, they do not alter their own money supplies. This ability of floating rates to insulate money supplies from the foreign exchange market is often considered a virtue. Indeed, as Chapter 17 shows, the American movement away from fixed rates in the 1930s was intended to keep its money supply from falling. In the 1970s, the reason was usually the opposite: Countries abandoned fixing exchange rates because, like Canada, they would have created far more money than they could sterilize. However, just because the money supply is unaffected by the foreign exchange market, do not think that the monetary system is untouched even when exchange rates float. The following chapter turns, among other topics, to just that question.

CONCLUSION

The lessons of this chapter boil down to just a few:

1. A highly efficient foreign exchange market serves to move capital rapidly and in enormous sums. Knowing the details of the market and its behavior enriches this understanding.

2. We can still use fairly simple demand and supply models to describe the market. They may be a little tricky at points, but conceptually they are not difficult to use.

3. Central banks intervene in the foreign exchange market to hold the value of currencies stable or to moderate swings in their values.

4. When central banks purchase foreign exchange, they expand the reserves of their commercial banks; when they sell foreign exchange, monetary reserves shrink.

5. Monetary authorities generally counteract the effect of their purchases and sales of foreign exchange through counterbalancing treasury-bill operations. T-account analysis shows the detail. They are not always successful in so doing.

6. An inability to counteract the effect of foreign exchange intervention is one reason central banks may not try to peg the values of their currencies.

VOCABULARY AND CONCEPTS

Bills of exchange	Forward markets
Correspondent bank	Forward rate
Counterbalancing	Forward/spot swap
Covering	Interbank market
Exchange control	Intervention (in the foreign exchange market)
Fixed rates	Overvalued
Floating rates	Speculation
Foreign exchange reserves	Sterilization (foreign exchange)
Foreign exchange reserves/bank reserves	Uncovered
Forward markets	Undervalued

QUESTIONS

1. Why does the foreign exchange market exemplify a close-to-perfect market?

2. A searching question for economic theorists is whether one can use a stock concept such as demand and supply to explain a market that is quintessentially flow. Does it make sense to treat a market in which prices are changing every second as if it has one price for a year?

3. You are manager of a small scientific instrument manufacturer in Illinois and receive an order unexpectedly from a company you never heard of in Australia. How might you arrange to get paid? What would your choice be?

4. Describe the foreign exchange market. How does it differ from stock markets?

5. Draw a demand and supply curve for Canadian dollars, expressed in U.S. dollars, with the equilibrium price at US$0.87 = C$1. Then try these assumptions:

   a. Quebec voters pass a referendum calling for independence from the rest of Canada. Many Canadian firms panic and transfer funds out of Canada.

   b. The state of New York unexpectedly turns down a major contract to buy Canadian hydroelectric power, and HydroQuebec, the provincially owned electric company, fails to sell its enormous bond issue on Wall Street. Several other major Canadian issues also fail.

   In each case, show which curve would move (at least as described) and then show the necessary intervention to keep the exchange rate stable. Show also the results under floating rates.

6. Under the conditions above, what would Canada's monetary account on its balance of payments look like?

7. Show, using T-accounts, why the money supply does not change when deposits from abroad increase (and monetary authorities do not intervene). Then try the same argument without using T-accounts, as in explaining it to your uncle.

8. Show how monetary intervention increases and decreases the money supply. Are the principles involved significantly different from purchases and sales of treasury bills?

9. Explain and demonstrate what monetary counterbalancing is. Using T-accounts, show an example of (a) sterilization and (b) counterbalancing contractionary foreign exchange operations.

10. Explain how figures showing the Bank of Canada holdings of foreign exchange and treasury bills demonstrate active counterbalancing monetary policy.

11. Why is there so much activity in the foreign exchange markets? (Indicate the basis for concluding that the activity is high; then explain.)

12. Explain what covering is. Why do companies want to do so? How can they do it?

13. Why do international financial investors not routinely cover investments they have made in bonds of other countries in order to take advantage of interest rate differentials?

NOTES

[1] *The ABC of the Foreign Exchanges* is a marvelous book about how exchanges worked. George Clare published the first edition in 1892, and as of the mid-1960s Norman Crump was handling the thirteenth edition. (Macmillan). A great number of libraries have older copies; they are fascinating reading for the economic antiquarian.

[2] Mark Casson discusses the importance of information and presence in any market in *The Entrepreneur*, Oxford, Martin Robertson, 1982, chapter 9.

[3] *Federal Reserve Bulletin*, April 1988, pp. 210–211. From "Treasury and Federal Reserve foreign exchange operations," pp. 209–214.

[4] This according to a newspaper account. John Kohut, "More market swings loom if G-7 governments fail to act," *The Globe and Mail* (Toronto), May 18, 1987.

[5] See Leland Yeager, "Canada's fluctuating exchange rate," in his book *International Monetary Relations*, New York, Harper and Row, 1966. That chapter contains a good bibliography on the period.

Appendix 13.1

ARBITRAGE, SPECULATION, COVERING, AND THE FORWARD EXCHANGE MARKET

ARBITRAGE

Arbitrage is the near-simultaneous buying and selling of currencies. Because the cost of an individual trade is so small and the computers are plugged in, slight differences between currency values in different centers or with different pairs are quickly evened out.

Exchange rates between centers and between currencies remain quite close to one another. It makes no sense for a firm or individual to shop around from one center to another to see if the exchange rates are different, nor is it sensible to try to move into a third currency in order to get a cheaper rate—for example, to see if in purchasing sterling with dollars, it might be cheaper to buy francs with the dollars and sterling with the francs. The reason is that the traders have already done this, and done it with minuscule margins.* The process by which they do this is called *arbitrage.*

Traders are constantly looking out for two types of opportunities: *two-point* arbitrage and *cross-rate* arbitrage. In two-point arbitrage, the trader discovers a slight discrepancy between centers—say that the London price for sterling is a thousandth of a cent more than in New York. The trader could then purchase sterling in New York and sell it in London, picking up a thousandth of a cent on the pound. A $10 million trade could earn him all of $100; that would hardly be worth it unless he was sitting there with nothing else going at the moment, in which case the marginal cost of making that transaction would be very low indeed. In cross-rate arbitrage, the trader would look for a situation where three currencies were out of line. Suppose that the dollar had fallen one thousandth of a cent against the French franc but not against the pound sterling and that the sterling/franc rate was unchanged. The trader could then take a million dollars, buy sterling (where the dollar is still high), trade sterling for francs, and then use the francs to buy cheap dollars back again, coming out $100 ahead. Again, the margins are minuscule, but the volume of trade and its low marginal cost make it worthwhile.

Arbitrage differs from *speculation,* because in speculation there is a time difference between the purchase and the sale. If the dollar is low in Tokyo and was high in New York, or is expected to be high in New York, a speculator might pick up dollars in Tokyo and wait for New York to open. There is no certainty, however. The speculator would not do it for the tiny margins that we see on arbitrage actions.

---

* It does make sense to shop around between banks, however, because bank charges on foreign exchange transactions often vary considerably. United States charges for cashing Canadian checks—of any denomination—can be as much as $15 per check in the smaller banks. Canadian banks rarely charge more than 50 cents.

SPECULATING AND COVERING

Arbitrage is, by definition, a riskless transaction. Spanning two points in time, however, involves risk. If you buy pounds sterling today because you expect you can sell them for more next week, you have no way of knowing what the market will be next week, however good your guessing. Foreign exchange speculation is a specialized occupation, requiring much understanding of short-term market behavior. The predominant players are international banks themselves in the bank foreign exchange market and a smaller group of speculators who buy and sell on the Chicago Mercantile Exchange. Most firms try to avoid extensive risk exposure in foreign currencies.

Any exporter who invoices a buyer in a foreign currency is taking an exchange rate risk, and could see the entire profit on a sale disappear in exchange rate losses. If the exporter insists on invoicing in his own currency, then the foreign buyer faces the risk. Routinely, firms *cover* their risk. Even banks, although they may speculate, avoid heavy foreign exchange exposure and cover most of their transactions.*

There are many ways to cover. If, for instance, Reekie had agreed to sell the £10,000 worth of blankets to Thistlethwaite and taken the invoice in U.S. dollars, it would be concerned that the dollar might fall between the day it signed the agreement and the day it received the money. One way to eliminate the risk would be to borrow U.S. dollars in New York, using Thistlethwaite's *acceptance* or promise to pay as collateral. Then it would have the $15,000 and could straightaway purchase the sterling. Of course, it would have to pay interest on the loan, but it could use the sterling to pay down any debts in Scotland.

The most common way to cover is to sign *forward contracts,* as described in the main body of this chapter. Instead of borrowing dollars, Reekie would agree with its bank to *deliver* dollars at a specified date in exchange for sterling at a rate agreed upon today.

FORWARD AND SPOT DIFFERENTIALS: THE CONCEPT OF *INTEREST RATE PARITY* The prices in the forward exchange market differ from those in the spot market. A forward rate will rarely be the same as the spot rate, but will be at a discount or a premium to it; this depends principally on interest rate differentials, not speculation.

To simplify the example, suppose that, as in days of old, the Canadian dollar and the American dollar have the same value on the spot market—i.e., US$1 = C$1. Interest rates, however, differ, with the American Treasury bill (T-bill) rate at 4% and the Canadian at 8%. Figure 13.8 shows the values of the Canadian and American T-bills at the two rates. Because the Canadian discount is higher, the

---

* To *cover* a risk implies that the trader will not be hurt if the eventuality occurs. If you bet on one team winning the pennant and then have second thoughts, you can bet the same amount on its opponent. Whatever happens, you will break even. To *hedge* implies that only part of the risk is covered, as if you bet less on the opposing team than on your favorite.

farther from maturity the bills are, the less the Canadian is worth.* A bank agreeing to accept Canadian dollars and to deliver U.S. dollars in one year has, in essence, an asset in Canadian dollars. But to reduce exchange rate risk, the bank must hold that asset in U.S. dollars—the currency it must deliver. It therefore must purchase an American T-bill or some equivalent short-term asset. The bank can buy an asset that will pay it C$100,000 (Canadian dollars) in one year for US$92,593 (or for C$92,593 since the spot rate is C$1 = US$1). But if the bank agrees to deliver U.S. dollars after one year, it will have to pay $96,154 for such an asset (again, the price is the same in either currency); that is $3561 *more* to get the same number of Canadian dollars. Therefore the bank will not deliver the $100,000 Canadian, but will insist on a *discount* of $3561 dollars (again in either currency as the spot rate is the same).

Would anyone accept that discount? Of course. Those banks that are to receive American dollars and deliver Canadian dollars are in the opposite situation. They will receive US$100,000, but will be able to purchase the cheaper Canadian T-bills or other Canadian assets. They would eagerly grab up any offer that gave them that opportunity.

The result is that the exchange rate on the *forward* Canadian dollar (or forward exchange rate) falls to a discount of approximately $3561 for a $100,000 contract. This is precisely the difference between the discounted values of the American and Canadian T-bills—4% of the discounted value.

---

* The interest rates are figured as a percentage of the price that will be paid for the bill, not the face value. It is 8% of $92,592 that will produce the maturity value of $100,000.

Figure 13.8 **T-bill discounted at 4% and 8%**

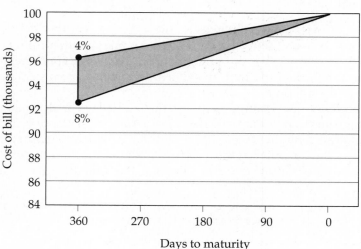

As the days to maturity decline, of course, the discount on both sets of T-bills falls, and the difference between them falls. Thus it is normal to see that countries with high interest rates have currencies that sell at a discount in the forward market, that discount increasing with the length of the contract.

Any financial newspaper will have spot and forward rates for major currencies, and they consistently show the predicted pattern, although not down to the fraction of a percentage point. Take the Canadian dollar in February of 1993 and compare its discount to discounts on other assets banks might hold.

The reason for the pattern shown in Table 13.1 is the considerable arbitrage among forward rates, T-bills, and other short-term assets. Small differences remain, partly because the assets are not completely comparable and partly because of some speculation. In this case, the smaller discount on forward than on the T-bill and commercial paper suggests some businesses are speculating that the Canadian dollar will be higher in the future.

Table 13.1   **Forward rate on Canadian dollar and short-term interest rates.** The Canadian dollar is discounted by 3%. Not surprisingly, the differences between American and Canadian T-bill rates, between short-term commercial paper in both countries, and between borrowing rates in London for those currencies are all within 0.12% of the forward rate discount.

Forward rates

	Spot	1 month	3 month	6 month
US$/C$	0.7931	0.7911	0.787	0.7809
Difference*		0.002	0.0061	0.0122
Discount (per year)**		0.030	0.0308	0.0308
Interest rates (in percent)				
U.S. T-bill		2.75	2.88	3.04
Cdn. T-bill		5.87	6.18	6.31
Difference		3.12	3.3	3.27
Commercial paper		3.08	3.1	3.2
Bankers' acceptances†		6.06	6.24	6.46
Difference		2.98	3.14	3.26
Eurodollars				
C$		6.06		
US$		3.18		
Difference		2.88		

* Spot minus forward

** (Difference divided by spot) annualized

† The standard Canadian commercial paper

Figures from the Financial Post, *February 6, 1993.*

FORWARD RATES AND COVERED INVESTMENTS Because forward cover costs the same as the interest rate differential, it is not sensible to invest in another country to get higher interest rates and then to cover, because covering will cost the same amount as the extra interest earned. The same is true for saving money on borrowing, but covering to cut the risk. We examine why through looking at an example.

Why would a Jean Jacques Canadien, facing an interest rate of 10% in Montreal, not drive down to Plattsburgh, New York, and borrow there at 7%? J.J. could certainly do so, but if he wanted to *cover* his risk, he would not save anything. After all, it is risky to borrow U.S. dollars when one's income and cash flow are generated from Canadian dollars. If the Canadian dollar falls in the interim, Jean can lose far more than the 3% he saves annually by borrowing in the United States. Certainly bank officers would not leave much of their bank's portfolio in such an uncovered position. Once the cost of cover is added, however, virtually any savings from lower interest rates disappear. And that is because the cost of selling the Canadian dollar forward very closely matches the discount on the interest rate differential.

The same reasoning works in the other direction: High interest rates may attract foreign short-term investments—but only if they are *uncovered*. If the Peorias (from Chapter 1) purchase Canadian securities, they can get 10% compared to perhaps 6% at home. However, if they want the security of knowing the Canadian dollars will buy the same amount of American dollars they did when they made the investment, they will have to sell the proceeds of their investment[*] in the forward market for their various due dates. Once investors try to cover by swapping forward, they end up paying the 4% interest differential.

Investors who move funds *uncovered* into another country have to bear the risk that the currency will fall in value before they can sell their assets. The Peorias might well decide that the size of the decline in the Canadian dollar and its chances of occurrence would be small enough for them to leave their investment uncovered. If, for instance, they could not see the Canadian dollar falling by more than 10%, and if they thought the likelihood of that occurring within the year were only 1 in 4 (0.25), then they would discount their investment by 2.5%, for a net gain of 1.5%. Clearly, the Peorias are taking a chance, but if they spread their risk over enough countries or over a long enough period, and their estimates are right, then they will come out ahead and continue to invest.[**]

---

[*] That is, the interest payments and, when due, the principal.

[**] The Peorias may lose on this particular transaction, but if their estimates are correct, they will only lose one in four times, so will come out ahead. In fact, most of us do not cover on personal investments. Author WBB has not bought forward Canadian dollars on the prospective U.S. dollar-denominated royalties from this book, the returns on the book being even less certain than the value of the Canadian dollar.

Chapter 14

Interest Rates, Trade Imbalances, and Capital Flows

OBJECTIVES

Overall Objective: To integrate interest rate analysis and monetary policy into international macro-economic theory, emphasizing the saving-investment gap.

MORE SPECIFICALLY:

- To understand the relationship of interest rates to saving and investment and to any trade imbalance.
- To understand the relationship between money supplies and the interest rate, and the conditions under which a country can have an interest rate different from world rates.
- To see why it is difficult for any but the largest economies to run monetary policies independent of other countries.
- To handle the Swan-Mundell model, which considers the relative effects of monetary and fiscal policy on a country's economy.
- To grasp how a country's economy reacts when it is in the position of having a considerable amount of foreign savings transferred to it.

Chapter 14 continues to integrate money and financial factors into the macro-economic scheme. It begins by showing how, under certain fairly standard conditions, trade imbalances tend to be self-correcting. It then proceeds to examine the role of the interest rate and capital flows in determining trade balances, focusing both on their real and their monetary roles.

SELF-CORRECTING TRADE IMBALANCES

A trade imbalance in itself can set in process a series of changes that lead to its own elimination. These rather neat models work so long as we hold that none of the changes alter the capital account—that is, the flows into or out of the capital account do not change. We have to be explicit about two variables, however: the extent to which exchange rates can change, and the degree to which price rather than income shifts as aggregate demand changes. This produces four possible situations: (1) fixed exchange rate, with price levels, not income, changing; (2) fixed exchange rate, with income responding to demand changes; (3) floating exchange rates, with price effects only, and (4) floating exchange rates with income effects.

FIXED EXCHANGE RATE, INCOME UNRESPONSIVE TO DEMAND CHANGES

The standard adjustment theory of the nineteenth century carries in its name the now nearly obsolete word for gold (and sometimes silver), *specie*. The *price-specie theory*, dating back well over two centuries, states that a nation with a balance-of-payments deficit will see an outflow of gold and therefore a contraction of the monetary base. Prices must fall, and as they fall imports will appear more expensive and exports more competitive, righting the balance of payments. Countries with surpluses, in contrast, will see an inflow of gold and an increase in prices, making exports less competitive and imports cheaper.

In its modern guise, the outflow of gold is replaced by the central bank's sale of foreign exchange, which serves to cause the money supply to decline. In turn the falling money supply depresses prices domestically, making exports more competitive and imports appear relatively more expensive than domestic substitutes.

Since we are conveniently assuming that the capital account has a net balance of zero, then every cent of the trade deficit must be matched by sales of foreign exchange (a positive sign in the monetary account). The money supply would not stop shrinking until the price level had fallen sufficiently to enable the monetary authorities to cease their sale of foreign exchange. The mechanism forces a decline in the money supply to the point where the monetary account is also zero, so the current account must equal zero. To wit:

(FD 14.1) $(X - M)\downarrow \to R_{FX}\downarrow \to R_m\downarrow \to MS\downarrow \to P\downarrow \to (X\uparrow - M\downarrow)\uparrow$

This is to say that a decline in net exports $(X - M)$ leads to a decrease in monetary reserves of foreign exchange, R_{FX}, accompanied by a decrease in monetary reserves (R_m), which in turn causes the money supply to fall, making prices lower, which cause exports to be more competitive and make imports less so, thus improving the balance of trade $(X - M)$.

FIXED EXCHANGE RATE, INCOME RESPONSIVE TO DEMAND CHANGES

The prevailing adjustment theory of the 1950s and 1960s used fixed exchange rates and an income responsive to aggregate demand changes. Once we allow income, not price, to move, the path to adjustment becomes rather different, although the trade balance still improves. Try it with a flow diagram:

(FD 14.2) $\qquad (X - M)\downarrow \rightarrow R_{FX}\downarrow \rightarrow R_m\downarrow \rightarrow MS\downarrow \rightarrow Y\downarrow \rightarrow (X - M\downarrow)\uparrow$

The trade balance worsens, leading to a decline in the reserves of foreign exchange and domestic monetary reserves, thence to a fall in the money supply, which causes income (Y) to drop, and with that drop, a decline in imports (M).

This is a difficult and costly path, but may indeed be a valid model for some periods, particularly the early 1930s, and also for some Third World debtors in the 1980s. In an attempt to cut prices to correct trade imbalances, countries in fact cut incomes. The improvement in the trade balance comes because people are too poor to afford as many imports as they used to.

It is quite possible that such a model describes at least some of the economic panics late in the last century. When the United States had a deficit and foreign lending fell off, there would be a sharp restriction in the money supply, and a resultant financial panic. This resulted in widespread business failures and recession, which caused income to drop more than it caused the price level to change. The price-specie flow model may have worked through lowering prices, but income factors were also at work.

FLOATING EXCHANGE RATE, INCOME UNRESPONSIVE TO DEMAND CHANGES

As Chapter 13 noted, monetary authorities often do not intervene in the foreign exchange market, letting the market determine the exchange rate.[*] Under a pure system monetary authorities *never* intervene, and so the monetary account is always at zero. Since our basic assumption is that the capital account does not change, we really have little choice but to state that the trade account itself must somehow balance. But how? Imagine now a country that has an inflation that has led to a trade deficit. Prices rise, causing imports to rise and exports to fall. In turn the demand for foreign exchange increases (the result of more imports) and the supply decreases (the result of fewer exports), lowering the price of the domestic currency. With higher prices for imports and better margins for exports, the trade deficit improves. To wit:

(FD 14.3) $\qquad P\uparrow \rightarrow (X\downarrow - M\uparrow)\downarrow \rightarrow D_{FX}\uparrow, S_{FX}\downarrow \rightarrow \$\downarrow\downarrow \rightarrow (X\uparrow - M\downarrow)\uparrow$

An increase in the price level leads to a decline in exports and a rise in imports. These in turn lead to an increased demand for foreign exchange and a decreased supply. The domestic currency falls sharply in value (indicated by the double arrow), and exports and imports rise again.

---

[*] The model also works for fixed exchange rates that are altered—that is, devaluation and revaluation.

Or, cutting out some of the various steps:

(FD 14.4) $(X - M)\downarrow \rightarrow \$\downarrow \rightarrow (X\uparrow - M\downarrow)\uparrow$

The difference between this floating rate scenario and the fixed rate situation (FD 14.1) is only in the path taken. Instead of depending on the whole price level to fall, it corrects directly the prices of imports and exports. The neatness of letting a currency fall in value to make a payments correction is that its path appears shorter and less encumbered by the risks of unemployment or income shifts between debtors and creditors.[*] The awkwardness, as we will eventually see, is that allowing a currency to fall may treat only a symptom.

The opposite situation, where the price level falls, producing a trade surplus, would see a reversal of the arrows.

(FD 14.5) $P\downarrow \rightarrow (X\uparrow - M\downarrow) \rightarrow D_{FX}\downarrow, S_{FX}\uparrow \rightarrow \$\uparrow\uparrow \rightarrow (X\downarrow - M\uparrow)\downarrow$

The price level falls, which makes exports more competitive and imports less so. In turn, the demand for foreign exchange declines and the supply of it rises, driving up the value of the currency on the foreign exchange market. As a result exports fall and imports rise, reversing the trade surplus.

The price level could fall due to an increase in productivity. Often too, price levels decline *relative* to other countries that are experiencing more rapid inflations, a topic taken at greater length in the next chapter. Germany and Japan, with relatively low rates of inflation, often have found their currencies rising in value. As domestic prices have moved up little, exporters have found themselves more cost competitive, only to watch the mark and the yen rise in value, removing that competitiveness.

Many economists expected that a move to floating currencies in the early 1970s would produce adjustments in the way just described. They were, as Chapter 18 shows, disappointed.

FLOATING EXCHANGE RATE, INCOME RESPONSIVE TO DEMAND CHANGES

If a country experiences rising *income,* the demand for imports will cause a rise in the demand for foreign currency, leading to a fall in the value of the home country's currency. The opposite is true if income falls.

Suppose, as it recovers from a recession, the United States finds its income rising. As Chapter 12 explained, imports would increase. But as imports rise, the demand for foreign exchange also rises (or the supply of dollars increases), driving the price of the dollar down. To wit:

(FD 14.6) $Y\uparrow \rightarrow M\uparrow \rightarrow D_{FX}\uparrow \rightarrow \$\downarrow \rightarrow (X\uparrow - M\downarrow)\uparrow$

---

[*] If the price level falls, creditors will be paid back in payments worth more in real terms than when the money was lent.

Income rises, driving up imports and the demand for foreign exchange. As the dollar drops in value, it causes price effects that serve partially to improve the trade balance.

If the United States goes into a recession, we might expect imports to decline and an improved trade balance, which in turn would cause the supply of dollars to fall and the price of the dollar to rise. We could represent that as:

(FD 14.7) $$Y\downarrow \to M\downarrow \to D_{FX}\downarrow \to \$\uparrow \to (X\downarrow - M\uparrow)\downarrow$$

Income falls and with it fall imports, decreasing the demand for foreign exchange and driving up the price of the domestic currency. Price effects in turn partially counteract the decline in the trade balance. In fact, in 1990 when the United States did go into a recession, imports fell as a portion of GNP, the trade deficit narrowed, and the dollar rose in value. In 1992, Japan followed a similar pattern, with imports falling off sharply as the economy slowed, generating a large and unwanted trade surplus.

One advantage of floating rates is that they do not subject the domestic monetary system to unnecessary shocks. It is far easier for a country to avoid a recession or an inflation if it is not bound to buy and sell foreign exchange freely. The floating rate substitutes price effects for what could be income effects. Suppose, for instance, the country sees a sharp worsening of its trade balance as exports fall off or as imports rise as it recovers from a recession. Rather than dampening that recovery through higher leakages and lower injections, the dollar falls in value, restimulating exports and import-substitutes, as in FD 14.8 below.

(FD 14.8) $$(X - M)\downarrow \to \$\downarrow \to (X\uparrow - M\downarrow)\uparrow$$

The trade balance falls, driving down the price of the domestic currency, which restimulates exports and discourages imports, helping to correct the trade deficit.

LIMITED SOLUTIONS

The paths we have been following have all led to the same solution. Admittedly, allowing unemployment to proceed as a means of ending a trade deficit (or lowering the price level) or permitting inflation to proceed as a means to end a trade surplus is a nastier path than others, but at least it leads to a solution. And again admittedly, we may decide that the benefits of the solution are not worth the cost, but at least we know where the paths lead and what happens along them and can make a reasonably judicious decision. But what if other twists and turns lie ahead, ones that will lead us back to where we started, having had only the costs? Such results are possible, although not inevitable, and a good deal of the rest of the chapter will explore them.

We have held constant the capital account in all the paths we have been following. That greatly enhances presentation of the material, but it is not in the least realistic. The capital account is vitally important and highly sensitive to interest rates. Or perhaps it is the other way around: Interest rates are highly sensitive to capital movements. It could just be that it is not the trade balance itself, but the capital balance that determines the trade balance. After all, Chapter 10 argued that it was a domestic imbalance between saving and investment that determined the trade balance. Surely that imbalance is related to interest rates and capital movements. The next section explores that relation.

REAL INTEREST RATES AND TRADE IMBALANCES

A BASIC INTEREST RATE MODEL

Economics addresses interest rates largely in terms of the money supply—that is, rates fall when the money supply rises and rise when the money supply falls. But one should not forget that at root interest rates are the price that savers get from spenders in exchange for the use of their savings, and that return on investment, like wages, is also at root a real or physical return. We measure the real interest rate as the nominal interest rate minus the rate of inflation. What that real number tries to assess is in fact the rewards to lenders in physical goods and services. Consider a model of interest determination in Castoria in which there is no money—in which everything is denominated in terms of what it actually buys, such as a beaver pelt or a standard bundle of trade goods. Interest in Castoria would be paid in pelts or trade goods, its rate obvious to all.

THE CAPITAL MARKET IN AUTARKY

The model is on the surface a simple one: The vertical axis is the real interest rate and the horizontal axis shows the funds borrowed or lent. It is set up such that the demand curve represents the demand for funds to be used for domestic investments—for fixed plant and equipment and inventories—including both private and government investment. The supply of funds represents the *net* amount of saving coming to the market; it is the sum of private and government saving.[*] In the terms we used in Chapter 10, the supply of funds is $S_p + S_g$, and the demand for funds is I_d, where S_p equals private saving, S_g government saving, and I_d domestic investment. The model accordingly shows how $S_p + S_g$ and I_d are related to the real interest rate.

Figure 14.1 views the supply of saving as responding to changes in interest rates. Normally, the demand for saving is more elastic than the supply. This is because it is difficult for people to change their saving habits, so they require a major price incentive to do so. Investors, on the other hand, may see a number of profitable opportunities and will tend to borrow more if interest rates fall.

The supply curve for saving can shift, responding to changes in demographics or tax changes, as Chapter 10 expounded. In particular, it can respond

---

[*] This differs from the typical flow-of-funds diagram in that the funds coming on the market are net of government borrowing—that is to say, it is the funds left over after the government has borrowed.

Figure 14.1 **Interest rates in autarky.** The supply of funds is S and the demand for funds is D. The intersection determines a price of i for saving, in real terms. The supply of funds is the net saving of the economy, and the demand the net demand for investment purposes. The horizontal axis is labeled *funds* in keeping with standard financial usage. Since the funds are from saving and for investment, it could also be labeled "saving and investment." Lenders are in fact yielding claims they earned but are not using for present consumption themselves. Saving and investment should equal each other at $0a$. Indeed, given that we are in autarky and no trade deficit is possible, $X = M$, so $S = I$.

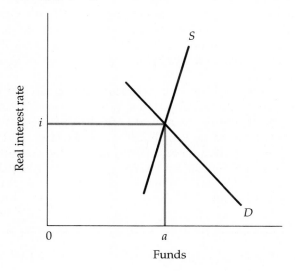

to changes in government saving, providing no fully offsetting Barro effect occurs. It also will respond to changes in income if such changes are real. As Chapter 12 noted, under conditions of unemployment and a horizontal aggregate supply curve, an increase in investment brings with it an increase in saving. Since the country is in autarky here, all new leakages would have to be in saving, so:

$$\Delta I = \Delta S$$

The demand curve for investment can shift also if expectations of the returns on investment rise. Such a shift could occur because of improved markets, technological change, or lower costs. Again, unless otherwise stated, we will operate the model without such changes.

THE MODEL UNDER PERFECT INTERNATIONAL CAPITAL MOBILITY

The enormous integrated capital markets of today make it very difficult for any country to run any kind of independent monetary policy. To see why this is so, imagine a situation of perfect capital mobility, with a capital market even more integrated than today's. Suppose all banks took deposits and made loans, not just in the domestic currency, but in an international currency as well. This currency could be the U.S. dollar, the German mark, or some kind of unit made up of a basket of currencies, such as the SDR or the ECU (see Chapters 17 and 18 for details on such units). Any individual could ask that his or her deposit be held in domestic or the foreign currency, and anyone could borrow in either. The international accounts would offer a standard international interest rate in a stable international currency and, when making loans, charge the same rate to borrowers of the same risk. Making such an imaginative flight does away with many of the practical questions of whether the typical household or firm knows what international rates are or how to access international banks. We can then assume the lenders and borrowers would decide where to do business on the basis of interest rates.

The model has not done away with domestic currencies. All lenders and borrowers will thus have to add to their interest rate decision an estimate of what they think will happen to the exchange rate (or the cost of forward cover). Financial investors therefore are careful about how much they hold in each currency. Currencies might fall in value and therefore are discounted against the more solid currencies. Canadian dollar T-bills in 1992, for instance, were discounted about 3% against U.S. dollar T-bills. Canada therefore had to pay the U.S. interest rate plus a premium.

■ *CANADIANS USE U.S. DOLLARS FOR MANY INVESTMENTS*

It is, in fact, easy for people in most countries to purchase foreign-denominated assets. Canada regularly sells domestically *Yankee bonds*—bonds denominated in U.S. dollars, and even offers preferred shares denominated in U.S. currency, as in the accompanying illustration. Even when individuals do not buy foreign accounts, their financial intermediaries may very well do so. Close to one third of all Canadian banks' assets, for instance, are denominated in foreign currencies (mostly U.S. dollars).[1]

A Canadian company offers Canadians U.S. dollar assets. An announcement from the early 1990s showing Royal Bank, a Canadian company, offering Canadians (and residents of other countries) preferred shares paying 7.625% of their purchase price in U.S. dollars. This shows how easy it is for Canadians to switch to U.S. dollars for borrowing or paying.

ROYAL BANK OF CANADA

U.S. PAY

PREFERRED SHARES

SERIES 1

DIVIDEND 7.625% U.S.

The model also assumes that the supply of funds from the rest of the world is perfectly elastic. That is, any additional borrowing the country does will not affect the international rate of interest—or at least its effect will be too small to see on the diagrams. This may stretch credulity, but it makes the diagrams much easier to read and understand and may not, as the chapter shows, be so extreme after all. Try several applications.

CASE 1: CAPITAL IMPORT AND TRADE DEFICIT   Figure 14.2 shows a situation in which the domestic demand and supply of funds would, in the absence of international lending, reach an equilibrium at i_a with saving equaling investment at $0b$. Once we allow international lending, interest rates fall to world rate levels of i_w. Domestic borrowers take advantage of the lower interest rate and expand investment to $0c$. International financial investors transfer funds into the country at world interest rates.[*] Domestic savers, seeing interest rates lower, respond with a slight decline in saving to $0a$. Since the demand for funds represents domestic investment and the supply represents domestic saving, investment comes to exceed saving by ac. That borrowing from abroad is, of course, equal to the trade deficit created as the rise in the saving investment gap $(S - I)$ matched worsening of the trade gap $(X - M)$.

CASE 2: CAPITAL EXPORT AND TRADE SURPLUS   Figure 14.3 considers the case opposite to Fig. 14.2: World interest rates are higher than the autarkal

---

[*] A *financial investor* is a person or organization whose investments are in the form of financial claims rather than physical—or real—investments.

Figure 14.2 **A world interest rate below domestic equilibrium causes an inflow of funds.** The autarkal equilibrium would be at i_a, but with capital fully mobile, interest rates are at i_w. Saving falls off slightly to $0a$. Domestic borrowers expand investment to $0c$, and international investors supply the difference ac.

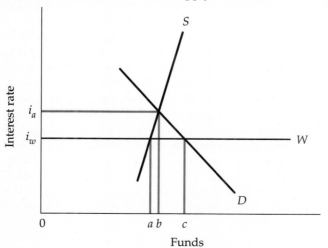

Figure 14.3 **A world interest rate above domestic equilibrium causes an outflow of funds.** Autarkal interest rates (i_a) are lower than world rates (i_w). When international lending occurs, savers increase saving by *bc*, and domestic investors cut back investment to 0*a*. The surplus of saving over investment, *ac*, is sent abroad.

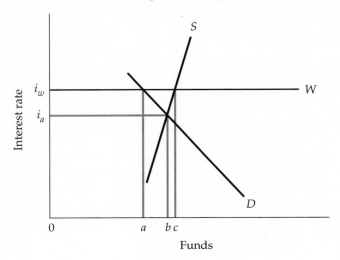

domestic equilibrium. Once international lending can take place, domestic savers respond to the higher international interest rates by saving slightly more (a rise of *bc*), while domestic investors cut back on investment from 0*b* to 0*a*. The surplus of saving over investment is transferred by the international banks to other countries. Because $S > I$, $X > M$ and the country has a trade surplus equal to its saving gap of *ac*.

TRADE IMBALANCES AS A PRODUCT OF INTEREST RATES   The analysis above places real interest rates as the key factor in determining trade balances. Whether a country has a surplus or a deficit depends on whether the world interest rate cuts across above or below the domestic equilibrium. Where they happen to lie depends on many factors exogenous to the diagram, factors that Chapter 10 discussed at considerable length. A country has a trade imbalance because at the prevailing interest rate its saving does not match its investment.

A horizontal world interest curve is relevant only in the long run. In the short run, some capital is tied up in long-term instruments, investors differ in their judgments of what will happen, and investors' knowledge of foreign opportunities is also limited. Most households and firms have a *portfolio* of holdings of real and financial assets, often in several currencies, and while they certainly shift assets in their portfolios between countries, the shifts are never as complete and dramatic as simple price models suggest. Financial investors must always cover the risk that they may be mistaken about the future course of interest rates or currency exchange rates; their movements will therefore tend to be smaller than our simple model suggests. A small interest rate differential is not going to open the floodgates overnight.

In autarky, of course, saving must equal investment, but if that equality emerges from interest rates equating demand with supply, the levels of interest would be quite different between countries. Chapter 10 showed that the forces determining saving and investment are quite strong, implying that both the demand for funds and the supply of them is quite inelastic. In autarky, the Japanese and German savers would have lower rewards and North Americans much higher rewards. Firms investing in new equipment in Japan and Germany would invest in rather low-yielding projects while their North American counterparts would have to be quite careful in selecting only the highest-yielding opportunities. Capital would therefore be less productive on a worldwide basis. In addition, low interest rates would discourage saving in Europe, and high interest rates encourage it in North America. An integrated capital market, in contrast, directs saving to where the highest outputs are, and maintains saving high in countries where demographic and cultural patterns encourage saving but investment opportunities are limited.

IS THERE JUST ONE INTEREST RATE IN THE WORLD?

Clearly interest rates really are not the same all over the world. Does this make the model above preposterous? No, it still can remain within the bounds of reason if we consider adding risk. Recall that the people in the imaginary economy have a choice as to whether to hold their assets in the domestic currency or in international units. In many cases they will choose to pay a higher rate for loans or accept lower rates on deposits because of lower risk and expectations of capital gains on exchange rate changes. Consider the situation of a country that has been running a trade deficit for some years such that its total debts are quite high and there are potential problems of paying interest on those debts. How will domestic lenders and borrowers respond?

Financial investors (lenders) will refuse to lend in domestic currency at the world rate. Domestic lenders will move their funds into international assets, and international lenders will pull their funds out. They are aware that a country's overall ability to service (pay the interest and principal on) debt depends on its size of its total international indebtedness, as well as on the expectations of what it might do. The financial investors rightly become nervous. Consider the scenarios they contemplate.

1. The government lets the value of its currency fall to try to improve the trade situation.

2. The central bank raises interest rates to put a squeeze on the domestic economy.

3. The country gets into ever-deeper financial difficulty.

Each of these possibilities increases the risks for holding assets in domestic currency. (1) If the domestic currency falls in value, holders of assets so denominated will lose more from the devaluation than they would lose in interest foregone in purchasing lower-yielding international assets. A Canadian moving $10,000 to the United States in the early autumn of 1991 would six months later have gained about $500 from the appreciation of the U.S. dollar against the Canadian dollar. Interest foregone for six months would have been less than $200. (2) If domestic interest rates rise, the value of bonds falls. International bonds, however, would be much more stable in value. If Canada had raised its interest rates by 3%, a $10,000 Canadian T-bill due in one year would have fallen $300 in value. (3) If it is going to be hard to pay debts, bonds in domestic currency will fall in value due to increased credit risk. Canadian airline shares, paper company shares, and petroleum shares all fell in the stock market. Thus a combination of interest rate, foreign exchange, and credit risk causes an outflow of funds.[*]

Often a change in perception of difficulty is not gradual, but quite precipitous. In the case of Mexico in 1982, for instance, the world's perception of Mexico's ability to continue to service its debt changed abruptly, sending interest rates on loans to Mexico sky high.

A shock to the balance of trade, or at least a sudden realization that the balance of trade was a serious problem, could set in motion a series of interest rate changes.

(FD 14.9) $$(X - M)\downarrow \rightarrow Ri\uparrow (\$\downarrow, B\downarrow) \rightarrow W+Prm\uparrow \rightarrow i\uparrow$$

A worsening of the balance of trade triggers concerns that the risk (Ri) of holding assets denominated in domestic currency ($) increases and the risk that bond prices (B) will fall, raising $W+Prm$ (world interest rate plus premium for holding the assets) and in turn domestic interest rates.

Figure 14.4 shows what happens, using the same diagrams as before. With a worsening trade balance, financial investors fear either a fall in the value of the currency or higher interest rates as monetary authorities attempt to maintain the value of their currency. As a result, they expect either the currency to fall or bond prices to fall, and accordingly must receive higher interest to hold the domestic currency. $W+Prm$ rises from i_w to I_w+. What was net borrowing from abroad of bd becomes net lending of ac. Since net lending requires a trade surplus and represents an excess of saving over investment, the trade surplus turns positive.

A flow diagram including the same information identifies the path taken.

(FD 14.10) $$i_w\uparrow \rightarrow KA\downarrow \rightarrow i_d\uparrow \rightarrow I\downarrow \rightarrow Y\downarrow \text{ or } P\downarrow \rightarrow (X - M)\uparrow$$

When world interest rates (i_w) rise, there is an outflow of private capital as shown in the capital account (KA). This causes domestic interest rates to rise and

---

[*] Technically, the *expected value* of a bond in domestic currency is lower than the expected value of an international bond. The expected value calculates the chances of a decline in the value of the bond, figuring in this case both the possible declines in value due to interest rate changes and those due to a fall in the value of the bond denominated in international currency.

Figure 14.4 **Increased risk turns a deficit into a surplus.** When the risk of a fall in the value of a currency rises, the premium demanded by world investors rises also, in this example from i_w to i_w+. With higher interest rates net borrowing from abroad of *bd* becomes net lending of *ac*.

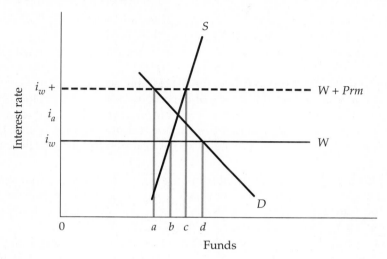

investment to fall. In turn real or nominal income falls, producing an improvement in the trade account.

In this case, higher world interest rates encourage domestic savers to place their funds in foreign assets, which forces the domestic interest rate up (by direct monetary methods or through *AD* changes), discourages investment, and lowers income or prices, improving the trade balance. One can hope that the path is easier than was Mexico's, where most of the adjustment came through lower income.

If it was expected that a country's currency might rise in value and its bonds increase in value, *W+Prm* would fall below *W*, and net lending could become net borrowing.

Our conclusion from the preceding analysis rather importantly and subtly changes the earlier conclusion that differences in interest rates determined trade balances. Now we might conclude that

1. *Differences in interest rates plus the risks of currency or interest rate changes determine trade balances.* Further, we might push that conclusion along to claim:

2. *Allowing for interest rate and exchange rate risk, all interest rates are the same.*

Arguably, the conclusions above are extreme and undemonstrated. The world is not (yet) one capital market, and national rates of saving and investment are highly correlated. Recall from Chapter 10 that during the period of the gold standard, there appeared to be more capital mobility and larger trade imbalances than there are today. Several elements combine to keep capital markets separate.

1. Even when interest rates are low, all funds do not exit because knowledge is imperfect. As Chapter 15 demonstrated, the international capital market is not homogeneous, and many lenders and borrowers have differing sets of knowledge and differing expectations of the kind of return they will get.

2. *Portfolio theory,* moreover, recognizes that in the face of uncertainty there is a value in holding a variety of assets. The uncertainty of knowing what will eventually happen to any one currency is inherent, but holding a group of currencies will reduce risk, because normally currency movements are negatively correlated—that is, if the U.S. dollar goes down the Canadian dollar goes up. So holding a variety of currencies is more valuable than staying in just one of them. Certainly, expectations and hunches cause financial investors to change the composition of and proportions within their portfolios, but they do not normally move completely out of one currency and into another.

3. Although an increase in international rates will tend to increase the entire *structure* of interest rates, they may not do so uniformly. It is the very secure and liquid assets like treasury bills and bank certificates of deposit that are most sensitive, while corporate shares or corporate long-term bonds will be less immediately affected. If the international rates rise, even with international assets available on every corner, it will only be certain funds that are shifted. We therefore modify our statement to the more realistic:

   a. *Allowing for interest rate and exchange rate risk, and differences in knowledge, all interest rates tend to be the same.*

   And we can add a corollary:

   b. *The differences in interest rates between countries reflect differences in knowledge, interest rate, and exchange rate risk.*

ADDING MONEY

Now add another ingredient to the pot: money itself. Certainly the rate of interest adjusts saving and investment, but the rate of interest is also determined by the demand and supply of money. How can they be combined? As with so many of our models, the means of combination depends on whether the response to changed interest rates is a change in real output or a change in prices.

To begin, examine a diagram closely related to the demand and supply of funds diagram: a demand and supply for money, as in Fig. 14.5. In keeping with most textbooks, we keep the supply of money under the complete control of the monetary authorities and show it as a vertical line. The demand for money, D_1, includes not only those who wish to use it for investment, but also those who simply want to hold it. Like the demand for investment, it slopes downward because people presumably will be less concerned about holding large

Figure 14.5 **The supply and demand for money.** The money supply expressed in real terms is determined by the monetary authorities and is thus vertical. As income rises, an economy normally needs more money for transactions and related purposes, so the location of D depends partly on income. As interest rates fall, people generally let their cash and noninterest-bearing checking accounts rise, so D also slopes downward.

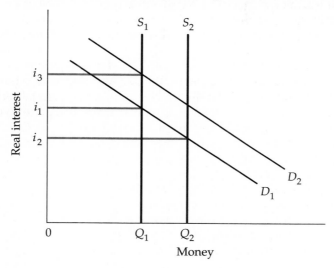

noninterest-bearing balances. If, under conditions of full employment, the monetary authorities increase the money supply to S_2 (Q_2), interest rates will appear to fall to i_2. But if price increases follow, then the *real* money supply would fall, shifting back to the left. (To deflate the nominal money supply, divide the nominal money supply by the price index, with the base year at 100.) If we postulate that output cannot rise, the real money supply would shift back to S_1.

If the money supply is reduced from S_2 to S_1 and output cannot change, the opposite should occur. We would expect that perhaps not immediately, but in due course, prices would fall to accommodate the decrease in the money supply. Money, in essence, is neutral, and it is prices that should or do adjust, as David Hume argued 240 years ago.

Twentieth-century thought, however, suggests some problems. The problem with saving flowing into investment is that it must do so through the medium of money. And money has other purposes besides converting saving into investment. The issue is known as *hoarding*. The classic miser saved a great deal of money but kept it all in the form of gold. There was no way for such saving to become investment. But misers are not necessary for the hoarding effect: The same mechanism is at work whenever the economic community as a whole begins to hold more cash or idle money balances. As more money is set aside to hold as cash or in checking accounts from which it cannot be lent, saving does not flow into investment.

Hoarding is no problem if prices are flexible. If there is less and less money available, prices should fall, leaving the real value of the available money supply unchanged. Hoarding is a problem, however, when prices do not move downward easily—which is to say most of the time. If prices do not move downward easily, then if idle money stocks build up, saving will not flow into investment. It will still equal investment, of course, but as Keynes showed with the paradox of thrift, it will be because income falls and with the decline in income saving falls also.

To see the effect of hoarding, consider Fig. 14.5 again. Because people need money for things other than investment, the demand for money shifts from D_1 to D_2, and in the absence of any change in the money supply, the interest rate rises from i_1 to i_3. Fine, if prices are flexible downward, because prices would fall and the real money supply would rise from S_1 (at Q_1) to S_2 (at Q_2). If, however, prices do not fall, a disequilibrium comes about, as people's attempted saving fails to generate new investment. As Keynes pointed out, it may be changes in income, not interest rates, that cause saving to match investment. S_1 in Figs. 14.1 to 14.4 would shift to the left because lower incomes would mean that people would save less at any given interest rate.

Monetary authorities, accordingly, try to regulate the supply of money such that the total amount of investment is close to that of saving. They replace, so to speak, the hoarded money with new. As long as they do not exceed what is hoarded, they should enable saving to equal investment without any change in the price level.

But the scope for monetary activity may be greater. Even if the problem hasn't been a sharp increase in idle money balances, increasing the money supply may still increase saving. If the increased investment draws idle resources into the economy and prices do not rise, then real income rises. As real income rises, saving rises with it until the new investment equals the new saving. The supply curve for funds in Figs. 14.1 to 14.3 would thus shift to the right as people saved more at any given interest rate. In such a situation, the movement from Q_1 to Q_2 in Fig. 14.5 would be real for both the money supply and saving. There would be no need to reduce the money supply to avoid inflation.

MONEY AND INTERNATIONAL BORROWING

If capital is perfectly free to flow between countries, can a country use monetary policy for domestic purposes? Good question, tough answer. To handle it, move from the abstract to the concrete, choosing two countries with extensive contacts, but with rather different economies: the United States and Canada. Canada has a more open economy, with 30% of its income from trade, one third of its banking assets in foreign currencies, and large amounts of debt in foreign currency issues. Typical Canadian investors are keenly aware of the U.S. financial markets and convert between Canadian and American dollars as easily as they do between Celsius and Fahrenheit. The American economy trades only 10% of its GNP and has far fewer of its assets and debts in foreign currencies. Many managers tend to regard American dollars as "real money," and others as like foreign languages—useful for others, but not for themselves. Canada would come closer to our model of perfectly mobile capital than the United States, and we start our discussion there.

Both countries, too, have been rather eclectic in their monetary and foreign exchange policies, sometimes intervening in the foreign exchange market, sometimes not, and sometimes allowing the monetary effects of intervention to carry through, but mostly counterbalancing its effects.

INTEREST RATES THAT DIFFER FROM WORLD RATES

In the 1980s both Canada and the United States also attempted to use interest rates to restrain inflation. Canada's interest rates, however, were considerably higher than those of the United States, as Fig. 14.6 shows.

CANADA   The Bank of Canada attempted to offset the expansionary impact of the government deficits by keeping interest rates high. In 1987–1988, investors became nervous about the U.S. dollar and shifted funds out of U.S. dollars. As we saw earlier, the Bank of Canada purchased many billions of U.S. dollars, to keep the value of the Canadian dollar from rising (or to keep the U.S. dollar from

Figure 14.6   **American and Canadian T-bill rates, 1960–1991.** American and Canadian interest rates were quite close to each other from 1960 to 1974. After that point, Canadian interest rates rose more than American rates and fell less steeply. The average difference for 1960–1974 shows Canada with an interest rate .07 of a percent higher, and its rate was sometimes higher and sometimes lower than the American. The average for the latter 15 years was 2.3%, with the greatest difference just short of 4% in three separate years.

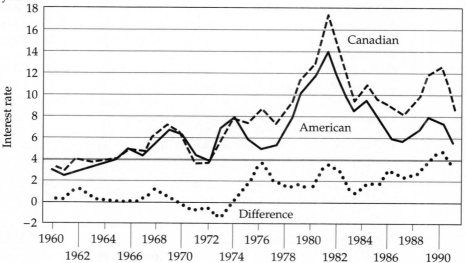

falling). Had the Bank of Canada not sterilized that inflow, the money supply would have expanded and interest rates fallen toward U.S. levels:

(FD 14.11) $$KA\uparrow \rightarrow R_{FX}\uparrow \rightarrow R_m\uparrow \rightarrow MS\uparrow \rightarrow i\downarrow$$

Presumably, as interest rates fell in Canada, fewer investors would try to buy Canadian assets, so nothing like the $11 billion that Fig. 10.6 shows flowing in would actually have done so.

The Bank of Canada, however, did not want lower interest rates because it felt that would have been inflationary. It did not want to import American inflation. Therefore it sterilized the inflow by selling T-bills, leaving the interest rate unchanged. This, of course, encouraged the capital to keep flowing in.

(FD 14.12) $$KA\uparrow \rightarrow R_{FX}\uparrow \rightarrow R_{TB}\downarrow \rightarrow \overline{R_m} \rightarrow \overline{MS} \rightarrow \overline{i}$$

As above the inflow of capital leads to a rise in the Bank of Canada's holdings of foreign exchange, but the bank then sells T-bills, leaving commercial bank reserves, the money supply, and interest rates unchanged.

The problem is that if interest rates are unchanged, then so is the incentive to move funds into Canada, so that the inflow persists. That is:

(FD 14.13) $$\boxed{\rightarrow KA\uparrow \rightarrow R_{FX}\uparrow \rightarrow R_{TB}\downarrow \rightarrow \overline{R_m} \rightarrow \overline{MS} \rightarrow}$$

Without any change in interest rate, foreign capital will continue to flow in. It cannot go on forever.

Did the sterilization work? The chart of interest rates shows that the interest rate remained high; indeed, the differential over the U.S. rate rose. But was that because the premium demanded on Canadian-dollar assets also rose? After all, the Canadian annual budget deficit is higher as a percentage of GDP and the debt service is far higher than the American, and inflation was running higher. In a sense, 2 to 3% may have been necessary to persuade people to keep investing in Canada. But a nearly 4% differential attracted a considerable amount of funds to the country, far more than the Bank of Canada was willing (or able) to purchase. (By mid-1988 only one fourth of its assets were left in T-bills; it was running out of sterilization fluid, so to speak.)[2]

As a result of its reluctance to purchase more foreign currency, the Bank of Canada had to let the Canadian dollar rise.

(FD 14.14) $$KA\uparrow \rightarrow C\$\uparrow \rightarrow (X-M)\downarrow \rightarrow AD\downarrow \rightarrow i\downarrow$$

The appreciation of the Canadian dollar, by restraining exports and encouraging imports, complemented the interest rate constraints on investment in restraining inflation. That is:

(FD 14.15) $$MS\downarrow \rightarrow i\uparrow \rightarrow \boxed{\begin{array}{c} \rightarrow I\downarrow, S\uparrow \longrightarrow \\ \rightarrow KA\uparrow \rightarrow C\$\uparrow \rightarrow (X-M)\downarrow \rightarrow \end{array}} \rightarrow AD\downarrow \rightarrow i\downarrow$$

The rising dollar, however, worsened the trade deficit. Indeed, the less the effect on investment and the rate of saving (top line), the more the effect on the trade balance. Note also that there are two effects on imports: (1) As shown, the changing Canadian dollar causes imports to rise, but (2) falling income will cause imports to fall. (In Canada's case, price won out over income, and imports rose.)

Canada's high interest rate policy affected aggregate demand both through a decrease in investment (and perhaps some decrease in consumption as saving rose as a percentage of income), and by a decrease in net exports $(X - M)$. A lower AD normally also lowers the demand for money, so interest rates would fall somewhat, although not by as much as the initial rise.

It is, therefore, difficult to say if the sterilization alone would have worked. Ultimately, it was the rise in the Canadian dollar and the market's nervousness about the future of the dollar at the higher rates that contributed to the high interest differential.

THE UNITED STATES If monetary policy is to work, it has to work quickly enough so that international capital flows do not create unwanted side effects before the intended monetary effects take hold. In the case of high interest rates, a monetary authority's object would be to end the inflation, or at least to slow it below that of its trading partners, and perhaps even to raise saving somewhat—that is, to get the top line on FD 14.15 without getting the worsened trade balance implied by the lower line. If prices fall or stabilize before a capital inflow causes a rise in the money supply or the value of the dollar, the policy will have some success. A larger and more self-contained economy than Canada's just may be able to do this.

The U.S. dollar is so fundamental to the world economy that many investors feel safe in the dollar. A vast percentage of the world's trade and debts are in U.S. dollar terms. Therefore a company can reduce its risk exposure by keeping both assets and debts in U.S. dollars. Admittedly, the company might have done better to put its assets in yen or German marks, but opportunities foregone don't show on the balance sheet. Similarly, American households count their income and carry their debts in American dollars. Perhaps they, too, would be better off to put some money in yen or marks, but that is often a rather remote idea to them. After all, we forego opportunities every day. Add to these elements the fact that 90% of American trade is internal and that foreign exchange purchases and sales are a smaller portion of banking reserves, and the United States stands a chance of being successful.

The success of the larger country could be more obvious in the case of lowering interest rates. There, to recall, lower interest rates could raise income, and with income raise saving, shifting the saving curve to the right. Once again, there are two possible effects:

(FD 14.16)
$$MS{\uparrow} \to i{\downarrow} \to \begin{array}{c} I{\uparrow}, S{\downarrow} \longrightarrow \\[2ex] KA{\downarrow} \to \${\downarrow} \to (X-M){\uparrow} \end{array} \longrightarrow AD{\uparrow} \to i{\uparrow}$$

The successful policy requires some emendation in the right side of the sequence, namely that as *AD* rises, saving rises:

(FD 14.17) $\ldots \to AD\uparrow \to S\uparrow \to \overline{i}$

The only way for this to work, even for the United States, would be to have a quick economic rebound in response to the interest rate change before too much capital left the country.

THE PROBLEM OF HIGHLY INTEREST-SENSITIVE CAPITAL MOVEMENTS

Picturing the world interest rate as a horizontal line is useful. All of the models and flow diagrams show the same pattern of monetary policy frustrated by the ready transferability of funds to other currencies. Of course it is a caricature, but so is it to pretend that central banks have a great deal of flexibility. They have some flexibility, particularly in the short run, but much less in the longer run. Is monetary policy, then, just a balancing act to keep the domestic interest rate close to the world rate plus or minus the risk premium? Perhaps.

To get another view of the problem, one that accepts a high degree of capital mobility as we suggest, we turn to examine one more approach to the subject: the external and internal balance approach.

THE EXTERNAL AND INTERNAL BALANCE APPROACH

The constraints on monetary policy posed by highly liquid capital markets encouraged Professors Trevor Swan and Robert Mundell to develop a useful model, which we will further adapt here as the *Adapted Swan-Mundell* or *ASM* model. Swan and Mundell suggested that the *external balance*—essentially the balance of the trade and capital accounts—responded more readily to changes in monetary policy than it did to fiscal policy. The principal reason for the ready response was the ability of interest rates to attract or repel short-term capital. *Internal balance*—the satisfactory resolution of inflation and employment—responded to both fiscal and monetary policy. The effect of fiscal contraction or expansion, however, was much greater on the internal balance than on the external.

On our model we broaden the meaning of the vertical axis to include more than fiscal policy, incorporating the overall economic situation, exclusive of monetary factors. This would include the level of expectations of profit and the expectations of consumers as well as the government's fiscal policy, so we call the vertical axis the *nonfinancial stance.* Anything that affects the level of aggregate demand *except* monetary policy goes on it. (Be careful here: The vertical axis is *not* the actual movement of *AD*, only what it would be if money did not matter.)

INTERNAL BALANCE

Figure 14.7 shows the differing patterns of *internal* response on the ASM diagram. Take first the structure of the diagram. The vertical axis represents the

Figure 14.7 **ASM model: Internal balance.** The distance from point *A*, where the economy is in inflation, is about the same to point *B* as to point *C*. Point *B* has the nonfinancial factors somewhat contractionary (perhaps due to a contractionary fiscal policy or pessimism among investors), counterbalanced by an expansionary monetary policy. Point *C* is at a point where investment would exceed saving were it not balanced out by a contractionary monetary policy. Any point below the internal balance line would be an expansionary one, presumably involving inflation, and any point above that line would be creating too much unemployment.

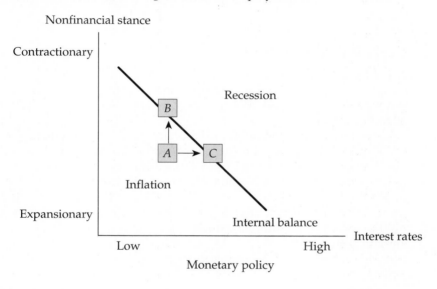

nonfinancial balance, expansionary and with a tendency to produce high aggregate demand at the bottom, and contractionary with a tendency to have low aggregate demand at the top. The horizontal axis shows monetary policy, with the highest (most contractionary) interest rates on the right and the low (expansionary) interest rates on the left. A point in the lower left-hand (southwest) corner, accordingly, would represent a combination of expansionary real factors and expansionary monetary ones; a point in the upper right (northeast) would represent a contractionary combination. A point on the upper left (northwest) corner represents an economy where, in the absence of expansionary monetary policy, a low aggregate demand would tend to create recession, but low interest rates stimulate investment and consumption to offset the otherwise sluggish economy. (Aggregate demand would be low because people might be saving larger percentages of their income and expectations of profitable investments were poor.) A point in the lower left (southeast) corner represents a situation in which the real factors (again, perhaps a highly positive outlook for investment) are restrained with high interest rates.

The line labeled *internal balance* in Fig. 14.7 shows the border between recession and inflation—presumably some ideal of low unemployment and little inflation. Any point in any of the territory to the northeast is a recessionary point, and any point in any of the territory to the southwest is inflationary. For whatever reason, interest rates may not be sufficiently counterbalancing the real pressures for expansion or contraction, and a nation can be at a position not on the border. Certainly, higher interest rates discourage investment and stimulate saving, but so do changes in expectations, in demographics, and in the microeconomic effects of taxes on saving and investment. As a result, we show the internal balance responding reasonably well to both fiscal and monetary policies.

EXTERNAL BALANCE

An external balance represents a balance on the *combined current and capital accounts.* It shows the points at which flows on the capital account exactly offset flows on the current account, so that there is no need for monetary intervention in the foreign exchange market. Anywhere along the external balance line the value of the currency is stable and monetary intervention does not occur.

Figure 14.8 shows the external balance border. The line marks out the point where the combined current and capital account equal zero. The territory to its northeast is a surplus on the capital and current accounts; everything to its southwest is a deficit. We show the external border as being steeper than the internal balance curve. The reasoning is that the capital account balance is highly sensitive to interest rate changes. The trade balance is probably not very sensitive—or at least not much more sensitive than the internal balance. But the *combination* of the two accounts causes the greater sensitivity to interest rates.

Figure 14.8's point *W* shows an external balance achieved with nonfinancial factors such that saving would greatly exceed investment (perhaps because of a very conservative fiscal policy), which holds down aggregate demand, partially counterbalanced by relatively low interest rates—like Germany at several points in the last decades. The conservative fiscal policy causes a trade surplus by reducing income, while the low interest rates encourage the capital outflow to accompany the trade deficit. (Remember, the external balance is the *combined* capital and current accounts, so that a point on the balance line can have a current account surplus matched by a capital account deficit, or vice versa.) Point *X* looks more like an American pattern, with strong budget deficits causing pressures for aggregate demand to rise while high interest rates and the accompanying high capital inflows contribute to trade deficits. The country still can stay close to external balance, if the capital inflows overcome the current account deficits. Nothing in the ASM model deals with solving a trade deficit; it just shows whether the capital and current accounts are in balance.

Note that a country can only move off the external balance line if its monetary authorities are intervening in the market. Why? So long as the monetary account is at zero, the other two accounts have to balance out. A country can only have a deficit on the combined capital and current accounts if the monetary account is positive—that is, the central bankers are selling foreign exchange.

Figure 14.8 **ASM model: External balance.** The border between an external deficit (a deficit on combined current and capital accounts, or a *CK deficit*), is quite vertical. Its vertical nature means that horizontal movements toward or away from the curve are less than vertical ones—for example, if a country is in deficit, with a policy mix at Z, then it need move only from Z to Y, while the policy affecting the real side would have to move it further from Z to W. While changes in the balance of trade would take some time, interest rates need not change enormously to cause an inflow or outflow of capital. As interest rates rise, income and/or prices will fall with some effect on correcting the trade imbalance, but the principal effect will be an inflow of short-term capital. As they fall, the opposite will occur.

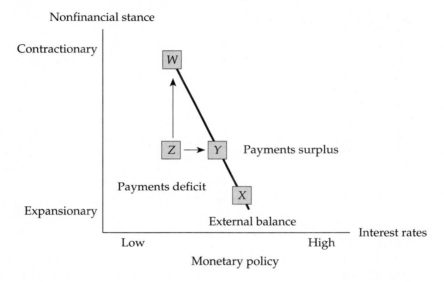

EXTERNAL AND INTERNAL BALANCES TOGETHER

Put the two curves together and difficulties stand out. Figure 14.9 has four zones. In Zone 2, outside both the external and internal balance lines, there is both a recession and a payments surplus. The solution to both problems is policies that encourage greater investment and/or consumption for the nonfinancial axis and lower interest rates for the monetary axis. Zone 4 shows both inflation and a payments deficit; contraction through encouraging more saving and discouraging investment, accompanied by higher interest rates (which also encourage saving and discourage investment) is surely the way to right both the internal and external balances.

So far no problem. Suppose, however, a nation is in Zone 4 at point C; unable to control the budget or other nonfinancial factors raising aggregate demand, it opts for a very tight monetary policy, trying to move to point D. If it gets anywhere outside the external balance line, however, it enters Zone 3, generating a surplus on the combined current and capital accounts, partly as a result of the decreased economic activity and partly as a result of the short-term capital

Figure 14.9 **ASM model: External and internal balances.** When both boundaries between internal and external balances appear on the same diagram, two anomalous zones appear (Zone 1 and Zone 3), where policies that improve one balance make the other worse. An increase in interest rates moving the country from *C* to *D*, for instance, improves the internal balance but produces a high capital inflow.

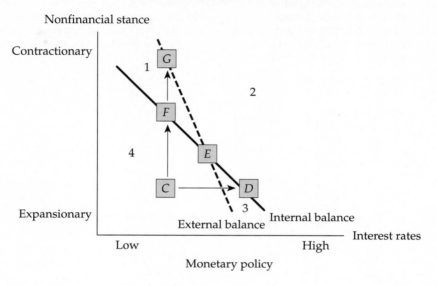

inflow. Now suppose it is able to use fiscal policy (and effectively increase aggregate demand) and moves toward point *F* on the internal balance; it is now in Zone 1, with internal balance but still a payments deficit. If it persists in using fiscal policy, it is going to have to move all the way to *G* to reach external balance, and at that point it will be in a major recession. The reason is that the low interest rates are failing to attract capital (or repelling too much domestic capital). Zones 1 and 3, accordingly, are very troublesome because the solution to the internal problem and the external problem call for opposite policies.

In some senses, all nations should aim for point *E*, which is where the external and internal balances cross; that is not an easy matter. Monetary policy must keep interest rates where they help create just the right economic incentive to invest, while yet moving short-term capital in a way to keep the balance on the current and capital accounts neutral. If monetary policy alone cannot bring about a balance, it is up to other policies affecting nonfinancial elements to do so. There is no way, for instance, to move from point *C* in the preceding example (Fig. 14.9) to point *E* (equilibrium) without using policies affecting both axes. Yet fiscal policy is very hard to use strictly to regulate GNP—government taxes and expenditures have multiple purposes, and possibly regrettably, macroeconomic management is not normally a high priority. Moreover, even effective fiscal policy may not work, as Barro effects may counteract it, requiring the institution of other, rather slower-acting policies such as tax reform. It is highly unlikely the government could work directly and quickly to change any of the other factors affecting the nonfinancial axis.

The ASM model is an interesting tool, and you can try to place actual policies at points on the diagram. American economists have often suggested that Germany through the 1980s had a positive balance of payments only because it constrained its economy too much. This would be a point between *E* and *G* in Fig. 14.9. United States policy in the 1980s had reasonably good internal balance, but poor external balance, placing it between points *E* and *F* on Fig. 14.9. Canada in the late 1980s had high interest rates, greater inflation than the United States, large fiscal deficits, and trade deficits, placing it in Zone 4, about the height of point *C*, but well to its right. The policy prescription would therefore be to decrease the fiscal deficit and lower interest rates.

SHOCKS ARISING IN THE CAPITAL ACCOUNT

Earlier in the chapter we examined how a change in international interest rates could turn a trade deficit into a surplus. We turn now to a topic related analytically: What happens when a country becomes more attractive to international financial investors? This may not be due to interest rate policy, but because of an unusually good investment climate, or in some situations, because that country is owed money. In such a case we would expect an inflow of capital. The question is whether the country should *accommodate* it—that is, allow the current account deficit to increase—or in some way try to frustrate it. One typical way would be for the monetary authorities to buy up the foreign exchange provided by financial investors and sterilize its effect on the money supply. The monetary account would serve to counterbalance the capital account. The issue demands closer attention.

HOW INVESTMENT FROM ABROAD CREATES A TRADE DEFICIT

Investment from abroad expands the money supply or else drives up the value of a currency. Either path produces a trade deficit to match the incoming loans. Canada in the 1950s and Western Europe in the 1960s were in the situation of receiving very substantial amounts of private capital inflows. In most cases, these funds were not very sensitive to short-term interest rates, but they *were* sensitive to the possibility of long-term gains. The impact of a capital inflow, whether under fixed or floating exchange rates, is to create a trade deficit. Case 1, Fig. 14.2, showed a situation in which world interest rates fell. Assume in this case that a country looks more attractive because the risk of investing there falls, so *W+Prm* (world interest rate plus premium) falls with it. On a flow diagram we would see

(FD 14.18) $Ri{\downarrow} \to KA{\uparrow} \to R_{FX}{\uparrow} \to MS{\uparrow} \to i{\downarrow} \to Y{\uparrow}$ or $P{\uparrow} \to (X - M){\downarrow}$

As the risk of investing in the country falls, capital enters. Under fixed exchange rates, the capital inflow forces the central bank to buy foreign currency, raising the money supply and lowering interest rates. If income stays fixed, this leads to a rise in prices; if it does not, to an increase in income. Either leads to a decline in $X - M$.

The path is shorter under floating rates:

(FD 14.19) $$KA\uparrow \rightarrow \$\uparrow \rightarrow (X - M)\downarrow$$

Under floating rates, the inflow of capital raises the price of the currency, which in turn causes exports to fall and imports to rise. This occurs regardless of the assumption about income.

Note that investments made abroad, like Britain's at the end of the last century, create their own trade surpluses, in flow diagrams that look like those above, but with the arrows reversed.

THE REAL TRANSFER

Back in the 1960s and 1970s, Germans used to complain, "The Americans are taking over our country. Their capital keeps pouring in and we are heavily indebted to them. We must save more of our own money!" All interesting thoughts, except that Germany at the time was running a trade surplus. Germany was not borrowing *in real terms* (that is, goods and services). What was happening was that as capital flowed into Germany, the Bundesbank bought it up, and placed it in U.S. dollar Treasury bills. At the same time it sterilized the inflow so the money supply did not grow. Without economic expansion, the Germans did not develop a trade deficit. And the German central bank's investments in U.S. Treasury bills earned considerably less than what the Germans paid in interest and profits on the investments the Americans made.

The problem Germany faced goes by the name *the real transfer*. A real transfer is the movement of goods and services that match an initial capital movement. If Canada borrows $100 million from the bond market in New York, there is a financial transfer. If the trade deficit increases by $100 million, that is a real transfer. If it does not, something has occurred to offset the $100 million. If, for instance, loans are $100 million, but the actual trade deficit is $75 million, then somehow $25 million must have been offset, either in some other part of the capital account, or in the *monetary* account. Rule out the offsetting activity from some other part of the capital market, and concentrate on the use of the monetary account. That is:

(FD 14.20) $$KA\uparrow \rightarrow R_{FX}\uparrow \rightarrow R_{TB}\downarrow \rightarrow \overline{MS}$$

With a capital inflow, the central bank's reserves of foreign exchange (R_{FX}) rise. The bank then sterilizes that by selling Treasury bills, meaning its reserves of T-bills fall (R_{TB}). The action leaves the money supply constant.

The Germans could have rid themselves of their surplus by accepting a *real transfer* from the United States. They could achieve this by allowing an inflation. The Bundesbank undoubtedly would have argued that an inflation was too heavy a price to pay to stimulate the inflow of goods and services. But the

Germans had other options: They might, for instance, have ended agricultural protectionism and imported American farm goods. Instead, Germany chose to add American portfolio investments and Treasury bills to its portfolio.

CONCLUSION

In theory and under some conditions, trade deficits set in train a series of changes that lead to their own correction. Under a fixed exchange rate system, trade deficits tend to produce deficits on the combined current and capital accounts, which leads monetary authorities to sell their foreign exchange reserves. As a result, the money supply falls, and either falling incomes or falling price levels lead to an improvement in the trade balance. Under floating rates, the decline in demand for a currency leads to a fall in its value, and thence to the improvement in the trade balance. The opposite happens with trade surpluses.

Since capital flows are sensitive to interest rate differentials, attempts to correct trade imbalances through interest rate policy often have only limited success. The same applies to attempts to use monetary policy to constrain domestic investment. The more sensitive the capital inflow to interest rates, the more interest rate changes cause the capital account to change and the less they cause the current account to change. Whether with fixed or floating rates, the result is the same.

Fiscal policy may be more effective than monetary policy in controlling domestic economic activity. The ASM model compares the effectiveness of monetary policy with fiscal and other policies that might control aggregate demand.

The self-correcting mechanisms only work if the capital account does not change. The models in which interest rates determine trade imbalances easily incorporate capital flows. They show that trade imbalances are closely related to the difference between domestic and world interest rates. They show that a trade imbalance can be sustained for long periods of time, but they do not indicate whether a given trade imbalance needs to be corrected. Again, we must make a judgment as to the costs and benefits of maintaining a trade imbalance.

Financial movements of capital can induce real changes. An inflow of foreign capital will tend to produce a trade deficit so that the financial flow also becomes a real flow of goods and services. An outflow of capital tends to produce a trade surplus to match the amount of net capital outflow. Often countries' actions tend to block the real transfer from taking place, with untoward consequences.

VOCABULARY AND CONCEPTS ————————————————

Adapted Swan-Mundell model	Hoarding (of money)
Capital account shock	Internal balance
Credit risk	Nonfinancial stance
External balance	Perfect capital mobility
Financial investor	Portfolio approach

Price-specie theory
Real interest rates
Real transfer
Self-correcting mechanism

Specie
Sustainable trade imbalances
Swan-Mundell Model

QUESTIONS

1. Why is the assumption that the capital account will *not* change important to the argument that trade deficits are self-correcting?

2. "Trade deficits would be self-correcting, if only governments would stop doing their darndest to prevent correction." Comment, showing how fixing exchange rates and counterbalancing monetary policy prevent adjustment.

3. "Of the various problems a nation faces, an unwanted trade imbalance is probably the least serious. It is far better to have a trade deficit and full employment than a surplus and unemployment." Of course, but under what circumstances would that be the set of choices available to countries?

4. What paths seem the most difficult to follow for self-correction of trade imbalances? Why?

5. Trace how trade surpluses correct themselves.

6. "The domestic supply of saving must always equal the domestic demand for saving under autarky, but not in an open economy." Explain, using the demand and supply of funds model.

7. What is the rationale for having a horizontal $W+Prm$ curve? (Students comfortable with diagramming can try one that is upward sloping.)

8. Trace through what happens if a country tries to maintain an interest rate that is higher than the world interest rate plus the premium both when real income cannot rise and when the expansion will stimulate growth.

9. Some economists believe that counterbalancing monetary policy is ultimately impossible. Indicate why it might be so in a world of perfect knowledge and perfect capital mobility, and why imperfect knowledge might give it some chance to work.

10. Canada and the United States were able to control inflation through interest rate policy, but it was not, as the textbooks usually suggest, through cutting investment, but through cutting net exports $(X - M)$. Explain and demonstrate.

11. "'Capital flight' is not the product of selfish millionaires, but improper interest rate policy." Discuss, showing how a central bank can find itself intervening to counter a major capital account outflow while its country's trade imbalance is not in itself that serious.

12. While on the surface floating rates seem to give a country an ability to pursue its own monetary policy, is that freedom merely illusory?

13. "There may be several interest rates in the world, but adjusted for the same risk, there is only one." Comment.

14. Is a sustainable trade imbalance whatever the market thinks is sustainable, or what economists think the market should think is sustainable?

15. Coming into the latter quarter of 1991, the Fed increased the money supply, despite the approximately 5% inflation rate. Picture now what happens on an ASM model.

   a. Assume that the Fed considers the unemployment a sign of being off internal balance and monetary policy the correct prescription; on which side of the internal balance line would the United States lie?

   b. The United States has seen a slowly

improving trade balance and a capital inflow that has been largely private in the first half of 1991. Indeed, the dollar has risen in the foreign exchange market against most currencies. Where would you place the United States in relation to the external balance line? (Remember, external balance is not the trade balance, but the combined current and capital accounts.)

c. How will you move the point where the United States is when interest rates fall?

d. Many observers believe that the United States is in fact bound for trouble because its inflation rate is higher than that of most of its trading partners and that monetary policy is not the appropriate policy. Where would these observers place the United States, and how would they see the movement to lower interest rates?

e. Will the United States move off the external balance line?

16. Canada in late 1991 was coming out of a recession, like the United States somewhat sluggishly, but with a lower rate of inflation (perhaps 2%) and a very conservative Bank of Canada. While the current account deficit had improved during the recession, the inflow of private capital had remained high and had driven the Canadian dollar higher than it had been in years. Where would you place Canada on an ASM?

a. Given the Bank of Canada's assessment that long-run internal balance required continued tight money.

b. Given a substantial fiscal deficit but otherwise sluggish nonfinancial position.

c. Given a trade deficit and a probably undesirably high Canadian dollar.

17. "So long as the trade imbalance is sustainable, countries should enable real transfers to follow private capital flows." Comment.

NOTES

[1] The Bank of Canada Statistics Monthly reported $607 billion worth of commercial bank assets, $191 billion of them in foreign currency-denominated assets (July 1991). The percentage has been as high as 35%.

[2] Canadians interested in the detail might note that the Bank of Canada passes its foreign exchange holdings on to the Treasury, which issues it longer-term bills. Reading the Bank of Canada's balance sheet is not as instructive as reading the listings in *International Financial Statistics*, which lists the holdings of the *monetary authorities*, and which combines and nets out the Treasury and Bank of Canada's accounts.

International Financial Markets

Overall Objective: To deepen and expand understanding of integrated capital markets through a close examination of the institutions and microeconomic functions of those markets and their macroeconomic implications.

MORE SPECIFICALLY:

- To show the allocational and efficiency functions of the capital market.
- To present the basic structure of the international market with a deeper examination of its Eurocurrency operations.
- To demonstrate through T-accounts that the Eurocurrency market does not expand national money supplies, but that it could have some important implications for liquidity, and hence for monetary policy.
- To explain how changes in liquidity, securitization, risk bundling, transparency, and the role of financial intermediaries have affected monetary policy and control.

This chapter provides a deeper look into the workings of international capital markets. It supplements and expands Chapter 14, showing on the microeconomic side a capital market that is far less perfect than the earlier chapter might imply, and on the macroeconomic side additional ways in which international capital markets frustrate domestic monetary policies.

The first section of the chapter explores the functions of the international financial markets as they direct saving to investors. The second part examines the international financial markets, with particular emphasis on the Eurodollar market. The third and last section probes the way in which changes in the international capital markets have altered domestic monetary and banking policies.

WHAT CAPITAL MARKETS DO

THE MATCHING PROCESS

In a very basic sense, a market matches the needs of sellers to those of buyers and establishes the price at which trades occur. In a capital market, lenders have preferences as to (1) the maturity of the loans they make, (2) the ease and security of liquidating any assets they purchase, (3) the amount and kind of risks they wish to bear, (4) the regularity of payments they wish to receive, and (5) the price they can get for lending capital. Theoretically, lenders might offer their funds for a highly customized bond, tailored just to their individual lending needs. Borrowers, however, may have quite different sets of desires and may wish to issue securities quite different from what lenders desire.

Lender and borrower can make an agreement by varying any part of this mixture of features. Typically, the economist would suggest that the feature to change would be the price. Thus the borrower may give exactly what the lender wants on the first four features, but pay low interest. It is quite likely, however, that a better overall arrangement will come by changing the nature of the loan instrument itself rather than solely the interest rate. For instance, both borrower and lender may compromise on the maturity, and on who shoulders certain risks, and come up with a more satisfactory interest rate.

Suppose, for instance, that a Canadian resort development wanted to borrow from the United States. It might prefer to pay in Canadian dollars, once a year, and borrow with a 20-year bond. It is likely, however, that it could get a lower interest rate if it paid in U.S. dollars, quarterly, with a 15-year bond. This would mean that the foreign exchange risk, the problems of having the interest ready four times a year, and the risk of refinancing after 15 years would all fall on the company. Management would have to decide if the lower interest rate were worth the increased costs.

Examine the matching process of lender and borrower more closely.

LIQUIDITY AND ITS MATCHING

Liquidity is the ease with which an asset can be turned into cash. It can emerge from short maturity assets, as, for instance, a savings account or a deposit "on call" (that is, a deposit that the borrower can retrieve on very short notice), or from having a good resale or *secondary market* for long-term assets. The holder of a 90-day U.S. Treasury bill, for instance, cannot receive payment from the government until the period expires, but would have no problem selling the bill to someone else who would be willing to wait. Similarly, a company depositing money in a bank may receive a negotiable *certificate of deposit,* which it could sell to any other company, should it need the money sooner than expected.

For an asset as secure as a U.S. T-bill, the main risk in purchasing the bill is that the interest rate will rise in the interim so that the value of the bill falls. Typically, then, a T-bill presents very little *credit risk* (the borrower will pay for sure), but has *interest rate risk.* For less secure assets, buyers take the credit risk that the market's assessment of the likelihood of repayment will change (as in a Brazilian bond), and so they may have to sell at a discount to what they expected.

Liquidity is less in smaller markets. Suppose you hold a five-year corporate note from an obscure Finnish corporation you know personally to be reliable. You are faced with the need for some cash and go to sell the note; you find very few potential buyers who also know the reliability of the firm. You have to wait, holding your price, until a knowledgeable buyer with a desire to invest comes along; alternatively you can sell at a considerable discount to people who, lacking knowledge of Finnish companies, consider the investment risky or who do not feel that this type of investment, however secure, fits their investment portfolios at this time. Such secondary markets are described as *thin*.

Liquidity is higher in larger markets because the secondary markets are much more active. The volume of sales in stock and bond markets is very much greater. The more unusual assets (such as convertible Swedish krona-denominated bonds) have very small secondary markets and so are less liquid. The larger the market, however, the more likely it is that even the more unusual assets will have decent secondary markets. Borrowers will have lower costs in good secondary markets because they may issue a longer-term security, yet the lender may treat it as only a somewhat riskier short-term commitment.

POOLING RISK AND MATCHING RISK

A capital market serves to pool risk such that an individual lender is not tied to the chance, however remote, that the borrower will be unable to pay. The market serves to pool risk in the same way that insurance pools risks of accidents. It was not unusual in centuries past for many loans to be made on a person-to-person basis. Nineteenth-century probates (settling of a deceased's estate) show many notes issued to neighbors or relations. Today, the same function is performed by banks or other financial institutions. The lender does not depend on the ability of a few people to pay up, nor on his ability to judge their ability to pay. (Nor does he face the prospect of having to push a relation into bankruptcy to get back his money.) Instead, the lender and thousands of other lenders place their money in a bank and the bank relends that money to thousands of people; each person's risk is spread among thousands of loans. The only risk is that the bank itself will make too many wrong judgments—a risk, but not as large a risk as an individual's lending to two or three other individuals. Pooling also works to reduce other forms of risk, such as that the interest rate will change.

Banks are only one form of risk pooling. Syndicated loans, in which many banks participate as part of a "syndicate," were popular for a time and were a favored means for financing Third World debt.* Mutual funds, life insurance arrangements, and pension funds similarly allow the saver to accumulate relatively small amounts of saving and, through the fund or company, lend that saving to a wide variety of borrowers.

The money invested in corporations is also a loan to many much smaller units within that corporation, and in that sense is risk pooling. If we lend to Chi-Chi's Mexican Restaurants, part of a chain, we lend to a corporation with hun-

---

* Such loans led to considerable problems because the same risks were pooled—20 little parts of loans to Brazil instead of one big loan of 20 times the size availed the banks little default protection. See the following section on assessing risk.

dreds of restaurants, pooling the risk of an individual restaurant's failure. If we lend to a McDonald's franchisee, we are dependent upon that particular restaurant's success. The alternative way of achieving the same risk diversification obtained by buying into Chi-Chi's would be to invest a few dollars in each of hundreds of restaurants. Similarly, we could lend to a conglomerate, or we could lend to each of the component parts. In this sense, the management of the company performs a risk-pooling service.

Some lenders are risk averse, preferring low returns and security to high returns. Others are more willing to take risks in order to get much higher gains. The same family, in fact, may be both risk averse and speculative, depending on what is needed for its entire portfolio of investments—some quite secure investments or some rather speculative ones. If the risk-seeking lender can be connected with the high-risk company, both borrower and lender benefit. The borrower need not pay the rates necessary to attract the risk averse, while the lender has found a borrower willing to pay high rates. Because not all investors have the same knowledge or expertise, an investment that might be very risky to one buyer might appear quite safe to another; if the borrower can be matched with the expert lender, the borrower's costs may be lower.

ASSESSING RISK AND GAIN

Under neoclassical assumptions, the market should have perfect information for the period under consideration. Even if the success of each loan is not predictable, the success of a large group of loans should be, so the market could pool the risks, much the way an insurance company can pool the risks of an accident occurring. Such assumptions are useful in some kinds of modeling, but from a practical (as well as theoretical) point of view, it is germane to approach the capital market as having rather imperfect information. If the market is to work well, the lender must have a good idea of the risk involved in making the loan—risks of default, of late payment, of payment in a devalued currency, and the like. If it is a pool of risk the lender is about to participate in, it should be reasonably clear to the lender the approximate risk involved in the entire pool. Lacking information, a lender will demand a very high rate of interest even from what might be, were the information known, the safest of borrowers.

The ability to perceive how a loan is related to the underlying risk is known as *transparency*. If a loan is transparent, the lender can understand and assess the underlying risk. If Uncle Reg lends money to Cousin Carrie, he is in a position to judge what she uses the loan for, her other assets, her past history, and his means of putting pressure on her to pay up should she prove reluctant to pay. If the loan is to a company that owns other companies, which relend the money to other companies, the loan may not be very transparent at all.

One of the functions of a capital market is to assess the risk, to make transparent what might be quite opaque. Bond rating services, stockbrokers, credit rating companies, investors' reports, newspaper reports, auditing investigations, government monitoring, and bank assessments of creditability are typical means of assessing risk. As the market has become more complicated and more international, and in the process, less transparent, the ability to assess risk has fallen.

The Third World debt crisis provides an example of what occurs when transparency is lost. It has become clear that neither the banks nor the borrowers understood the size of the risk they were taking. Much of the debt was incurred through syndicated loans, in which one bank would persuade 10 or 20 other banks to join it in making a loan. Since no one bank was incurring a great risk, the underlying soundness of the loan was not closely investigated. Frequently, banks made loans to government-owned corporations, whose loans were guaranteed by the country's government or government bank. Since a guarantee does not appear directly on the books (being a *contingent liability*, contingent upon the government corporation defaulting), it was unclear how much the government was about to owe when its corporations defaulted. Moreover, because experience with loans to the Third World had been good in the previous few decades, banks were not inclined to investigate closely their exposure. While today teams of specialists calculate country-by-country exposure to combat the opacity of the loans, they did not do so before default became a likelihood, rather than a remote possibility.

THE COSTS OF USING THE MARKET

As a financial market performs its functions of matching the needs of borrowers and lenders (often reshaping the loan packages), finding lenders and borrowers with complementary needs, increasing liquidity, pooling risks, assessing the risks involved, and ultimately setting a price, it creates a considerable benefit and a substantial cost. The market recovers its costs and charges for its benefits. Loan fees, brokerage fees, underwriting fees, differences in the rates a financial institution pays for money and what it charges are typical examples of the ways the market takes its reward. Other companies sell their information to subscribers—as, for instance, Standard and Poor's credit ratings.

THE ECONOMIC FUNCTIONS OF THE CAPITAL MARKET

A well-functioning capital market increases the efficiency of the economy. It gives the lender a combination of risk, reward, and security that fits individual needs while providing borrowers with a different combination (or matches them with lenders who want the same combination the borrowers do) more suited to the borrowers' needs. The market serves to adjust the product (the loan instrument) and the price to work out a compromise satisfactory to all parties. In such a situation, saving should flow from those who are willing to save to the projects that have the highest benefits (risk and yield combinations) at the lowest risk. As noted, the nineteenth-century family had a rather restricted set of opportunities to invest. The modern family can place its saving at the service of any place in the world, and has sophisticated institutions to help assess risk, limit downside risk, and move the money for them.

In an international context, a well-functioning international market might function to move saving from nations with high saving to nations with high returns. As Chapter 10 noted, however, it moves less capital in net terms than one would expect.

If the growth of the international capital market has not made that much difference to the flow of saving between countries, what has it done? It may, as above, have some negative effect on government saving because it makes borrowing less costly. Alternatively, the effect may be principally microeconomic. The international capital market functions, like the domestic, to pool risks, to match preferences of lender and borrower, and does so by providing a great variety of financial instruments in highly liquid markets. The French invest in Germany, Germans in France in accordance with the differing knowledge and needs of French and German lenders and borrowers, much as French and Germans buy each other's cars, alcohol, and appliances. The effect is to lower the costs of borrowing in both nations, but not to change the pattern of flow. In many senses, trade in securities can be compared to intraindustrial trade with differentiated products. Each instrument is another product, seeking some fairly narrow market segment, worthwhile to develop only in large international markets. Just as intraindustrial trade does not alter trade balances greatly, so trade in debt instruments does not much alter net flows of capital.

THE INTERNATIONAL CAPITAL MARKET

EXTENT OF INTEGRATION OF NATIONAL MARKETS

The international capital market consists of interlinked national capital markets, with the principal centers at London and New York and to a lesser extent Tokyo.[1] While the markets are highly integrated, they remain partially separate in some areas. Each national capital market is under the regulation of its national authorities. Securities issued in the United States, for instance, must follow American rules on disclosure of information; those issued in Britain follow British law. American markets cannot issue, for instance, what are known as *bearer bonds,* bonds that state merely that the company will "pay to the bearer" such and such an amount upon presentation of the bond or a coupon cut from the bond.[*] Most European countries allow bearer bonds. Nothing prevents an American brokerage house, however, from selling its clients securities issued in Britain according to British law. (After all, if the United States prevented that, its citizens would still be free to contact a British firm directly and the American brokerage firm would simply lose business.)

All large banks are international in scope, accepting deposits or selling certificates of deposit to people from many nations and lending in turn to international clients. National (or nationalist) banking laws often give preference to national banks in commercial banking—the acceptance of deposits and providing

---

[*] The reason is that bearer bonds are excellent ways to escape taxation or to hide illegal proceeds.

of ordinary banking services to the public—but are less restrictive with investment banking. Jean Claude Canadien may not be able to walk into a branch of New York's Citibank in Montreal and deposit a check, but JCC Enterprises could certainly deal with the Citibank office to arrange to purchase a $100,000 certificate of deposit in New York.

National laws, similarly, may restrict the ability of pension funds or trust accounts to invest in foreign assets. Such laws, presumably to protect pensioners from having their funds badly invested in questionable securities, can also serve to protect domestic borrowers from having to pay internationally competitive rates.

Nationals may also have more knowledge of their own markets. Finns can assess the prospects of a Finnish firm better than can Americans because they have been watching local firms more closely and have sources of knowledge not easily available to the foreigner. Because their knowledge is better, they are better able to assess the risk and prospects of a Finnish firm, and therefore their cost of lending is less.

National markets also have different tax regulations and rates, different accounting systems.

The differences in national laws and differences in ability to assess risk provide a certain viscosity to the flow of capital between nations that domestic markets do not possess. In most instances, however, that viscosity is not great and is certainly declining.

Separate national currencies are no longer a great barrier to international investment. As we show in the section below on the Eurocurrency markets, financial institutions can issue or back securities and loans in currencies other than that of their own nation. Moreover, the tremendous growth of the *forward exchange* market allows an investor to cover an investment over long periods—up to 10 years in some cases. Twenty years ago, the longest coverage was one year, and 90 days was the norm. While investors may face a discount in purchasing the forward contract, they can eliminate the (downside) risk associated with the foreign exchange movement.

The enormous improvements in communication networks and in the computerization of financial flows have served to integrate the world's financial markets to an extent never seen before. Information travels much faster, and the amount of capital that can be mobilized in a short time has expanded vastly. The vast bulk of the hundreds of billions of dollars worth of foreign currency traded every day is investment related: short-term speculation, coverage on exchange risk, financing of trade, or longer-run cross-border investments. All the major banks are in the major international financial centers, gathering information and spreading it about their own networks, so information (or rumors) spread quickly and concerted action is easy.

AN OVERVIEW OF THE INTERNATIONAL MARKETS

International capital markets have all the complexities of national markets compounded by international elements. When investors place their money in foreign banks or buy securities in another country, using the currency of the other country, we refer to that activity as *cross-border,* or *traditional.* (So we get cross-border loans and deposits and cross-border purchases and sales of bonds.) Activity in such markets has grown considerably. But there is a second, rather unusual market, where the accounts are kept and securities issued not in the currency of the country, but in some other currency. An American company can deposit or borrow U.S. dollars in London, or issue securities denominated in German marks in London as well. This second kind of market is called the *Eurocurrency market.*

THE EUROCURRENCY MARKET

Eurocurrency consists of issues of loans, deposits, and securities denominated in currencies other than the currency of the nation in which the deposit is made or the securities are issued. Like any national market, the Eurocurrency market has bank loans, securities for short, medium, and long term, the last usually called bonds, and a great variety of instruments among these. Unlike national markets, however, the debt is not denominated in the home currency.

When a security is issued or a loan made in a currency other than that of the nation in which it is issued, it is called a *Eurocurrency* debt. A British bank taking deposits in U.S. dollars and lending in U.S. dollars is making *Eurodollar* transactions. An American investment house syndicating securities denominated in Japanese yen (but not issued in Japan) is selling *Euroyen* securities. A European company attempting to borrow long term and issuing bonds denominated in SDRs (see Ch. 17) is also in the Eurocurrency market.

No logical reason exists why debt should have to be denominated in the currency of the debtor or the currency of the creditor. Indeed, it need not be denominated in any specific currency at all. Companies issue bonds in both SDRs and ECUs (see Ch. 18), and medieval European merchants often stated debt in terms of coins of known quality but no longer minted, or just used fictitious units.[2]

Virtually every major industrial country has a Euro-version of its domestic currency.* Bank deposits and loans, particularly of shorter duration, are predominantly in U.S. dollars, hence the phrase Eurodollar market, which often applies somewhat loosely to all the Eurocurrency markets. Because the longer-run value of the U.S. dollar is uncertain, many longer-term securities are issued in currencies other than the U.S. dollar. A borrower wishing to pay a low interest rate may choose to issue its debt in a currency expected to be stable or to rise in value. Manitoba Hydro, the provincially owned electric utility, for instance, has borrowed in Japanese yen. The corporation thereby trades off a lower interest rate against the risk that the currency will not rise in value. Manitoba Hydro, for instance, gets its revenue in Canadian and American dollars, which have fallen in value against the yen, so has found its debt burden rising as it has had to pay more to buy the yen to service its debt.

---

* *The Economist*'s weekly tables list Australian dollars, Belgian francs, Canadian dollars, French francs, German marks, Dutch guilders, Italian lira, Japanese yen, Spanish pesetas, Swedish crowns, Swiss francs, British pounds, and U.S. dollars.

LONDON AND NEW YORK   The difficulty of dealing with a number of separate national capital markets, even if closely linked, is that with the exceptions of London and New York, each is rather thin. The smaller national markets simply lack the scale and scope of the big ones.

Before the First World War, London was the chief financial market for the world. In the interwar decades, New York gradually came to overshadow London as the most important financial market. The dollar remained strong, while sterling faltered, and all London's financial acumen could not attract a large amount of foreign deposits denominated in sterling. British exchange control during the Second World War and into the postwar period made the position of the London banks even worse. While London withered as a market, New York waxed stronger. Was London to disappear as a major international financial center? No, thanks to the invention of a new class of financial instruments— Eurodollars.

ORIGINS OF THE EURODOLLAR MARKET   In the 1950s a momentum began to build in Europe for a new kind of capital market, one free of the limitations of using only domestic currencies to denominate debt. The impetus came from a number of governmental decisions that by hindsight seem unwise in their impact on the New York and London capital markets. Basically, both the British and the American governments were concerned about the amount of short-term lending their banks were making abroad and restricted them, through controls and taxes, from lending more. The British restrictions came in 1957 and the American in 1963 with the effect of sharply reducing the loans the two biggest capital markets in the world could make. The American market remained open for Canada and many Third World countries, but the Japanese and the Europeans lost their source of short-term dollar financing. Where could they turn to borrow and lend in the world's major currency?

For years, London banks had checking accounts in foreign currencies, principally dollars. Any individual or business could open a dollar account with a London bank, depositing dollars and writing checks in dollars. In the 1950s many Communist bloc countries had begun to make dollar deposits in London to have the security and liquidity associated with dollars, yet to avoid the scrutiny and possible freezing of their funds that would occur were they to hold dollars in an American bank. London banks realized that they could use such accounts to provide the basis for lending dollars rather than sterling. They could thereby avoid the restrictions on the foreign lending of sterling and at the same time take advantage of the world's demand for dollar-denominated loans and deposits. They began to promote the idea of making dollar deposits with them and in turn they would make dollar loans. Soon the name Eurodollars came to apply to such transactions.

Most investors were not interested in putting dollars into London simply for current account use. Rather, they wished to make short-term deposits for periods of a few weeks to a few months. While the British did pay some interest on the regular external checking accounts, investors sought higher returns, and London was ready with a variety of means for providing what was sought. It soon developed deposits for money on call (whenever the depositor requested), 30, 60, and 90 days, and followed the American lead immediately when in 1961 American banks developed the certificate of deposit.[*]

The popularity of Eurodollars grew rapidly. They were convenient—that is to say, the *transaction costs* of borrowing or lending were lower. European borrowers of dollars did not need to develop contracts with American banks and could instead deal with their own banks. American banks and corporations with dollars to lend found it much easier to lend these dollars to European banks than to try to place the dollars themselves in Europe. They thus avoided the problems of credit risk and lack of knowledge concerning local markets and conditions. The aggravating difference in business hours between Europe and America could be avoided by Europeans who dealt in dollars with European banks. Finally, there was also a crucial competitive factor. British banks found that dollar-denominated deposits were an excellent way to attract additional deposits, and by running leaner operations, they could reduce the spread between what they paid for deposits and what they charged for loans below what New York could.

Again, U.S. regulations were partially to blame for the early boost to the Eurodollar market. (They certainly were not the entire cause of the market's growth, because it remains vigorous today after all the regulations that contributed to its rapid growth have been relaxed.) The Federal Reserve regulated the interest rates, time periods, and reserve requirements on time deposits. American banks had to hold 5% of all time deposits as reserves, while European banks could use their discretion, which frequently meant they carried no reserves specifically for the Eurodollar deposits. This meant that a U.S. bank with a $100,000 savings deposit could lend only $95,000 of it, while the European bank with the same deposit could lend it all. At 10% interest, the European bank would earn $500 more a year, and could therefore undercut the American's price.[**] American banks also could not pay interest on the shorter-term deposits (for example, CD deposits of less than 90 days). Moreover, when interest rates rose sharply in the 1970s as a response to worldwide inflation, American banks found themselves up against a regulatory ceiling on interest rates they could pay to secure funds. Many of their big depositors therefore just moved their money to the Eurodollar market, which was not so constrained.

American banks did not want to miss out on the Eurodollar action, and large numbers of them moved to London to accept Eurodollar deposits and issue loans. All the major banks and many smaller ones (forming joint banks to operate abroad) opened London banks.[3]

---

[*] A certificate of deposit or CD is a negotiable interest-bearing certificate indicating that a fixed sum has been deposited and will be paid back on a given date.

[**] Some writers confused the reserve requirement on checking accounts (at that time around 18%) with those on savings (then 5%). Eurodollars are a near money, competitive with CDs and short-term savings deposits, whose reserve requirements were 5%.

THE EURODOLLAR BANK LOAN MARKET TODAY

The London Interbank Market   Some banks, particularly the London banks, have been successful at collecting Eurodollar deposits, but frequently do not have ready places to lend the money. A vigorous market developed in which banks with surplus Eurodollars could lend (sell) them to other banks with ready borrowers. The market is much like the foreign exchange market, with large amounts of Eurodollars traded in blocks, and frequently going through several banks on their way to the final borrower.

The Size of the Market   Estimating the size of Eurodollar bank loans presents a number of difficulties. The figures usually cited are for new loans made during a given year and attempt to avoid double-counting loans that are made from one bank to another before being lent to a final borrower.[4] R.B.R. Johnson's figures showed great early growth—a rise in the stock of Eurocurrency loans from 103 billion U.S. dollars in 1970 to just under 1.3 trillion U.S. dollars in 1980.[5] Growth has slowed since, and 1990 levels of net new Eurocurrency loans were around $115 billion.

LONGER-TERM SECURITIES   While Eurodollar deposits and loans were the principal short-term instruments in the Eurocurrency market, the securities market developed somewhat differently. It began with the issue of bonds—long-term securities—denominated, at first, mostly in dollars, but soon in a variety of other currencies as well. The advantages of issuing a Eurocurrency bond lay in the ability to tap an international capital market with one bond issue, rather than the more complex and considerably more expensive method of issuing *parallel bonds* in several national markets. They also had more freedom from national rules, which lay most heavily on the issue of bonds to nationals in the country of issue; a Dutch firm issuing Eurodollar bonds and selling them in France was far less constrained than if it offered guilder bonds in the Netherlands and incidentally sold some in France as well.

The medium-term markets developed more slowly than either the short- or long-term markets. Secondary markets were thin, forcing many buyers to hold securities until their expiration. It is only in the last decade that the medium-term markets for securities have grown vigorously and come to fill out the market. The secondary market for securities has thickened substantially: Between 1980 and 1986, the secondary market grew by 60%, while the primary market grew by only 45%.[6] The British and European banks have been particularly innovative in their approach to the medium-term market. One invention was the *floating rate note* or *FRN*, where the borrower is guaranteed receipt of a certain amount of capital, but the interest rate it pays goes up or down depending on market conditions. Normally such rates are expressed as percentages above a base rate, which in the case of the Eurodollar markets is the *London Interbank Offer Rate*, or *LIBOR. LIBOR* (pronounced Lye-boar) is the interest rate banks pay each other to borrow short-term funds in the Eurodollar market.[*] At times, about 40% of the overall Eurobond market has been made up of FRNs.[7]

SIZE AND CHARACTERISTICS   To some extent Eurocurrency loans have been replaced by medium- and long-term securities, part of the process of securitization discussed below. Eurobonds (including medium-term securities) were over $212 billion in 1989 and around $180 billion in 1990. (In 1986, the IMF estimated the Eurocurrency bond market, including the medium-term notes, to hold 618 billion U.S. dollars' worth of debt.) Figure 15.1 shows the recent activity in the international capital markets, including both Eurocurrency and traditional issues.

Figure 15.2 shows how the composition of Eurobonds has changed, according to the currency of their denomination. The U.S. dollar has declined in importance and the European Currency Unit (or ECU, a unit of value weighted according to a number of European currencies) has increased in usage.

MONETARY ANALYSIS OF THE EUROCURRENCY MARKETS

As the Eurodollar market grew, people began to wonder how to analyze its monetary effects. Some thought it might cause a multiple expansion of deposits,

[*] A floating-rate note in the United States would normally be expressed as a percentage over the Treasury-bill rate.

Figure 15.1 **International capital market 1987–1990.** This figure shows the new capital market issues in each of four recent years. Note how Eurocurrency bonds (E-bonds in the chart) and Eurocurrency bank loans (E-loans) have come to displace the traditional foreign loans—that is, loans made to foreigners in domestic currencies or bonds issued in domestic currencies for foreign parties. Note also that bonds are tending to replace bank loans. *Other* refers to some bank loan issues, some of which are in Eurocurrencies.

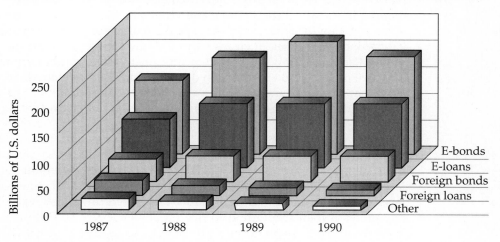

Source: International Financial Markets, *IMF, Vol. 2, Table S.1, 1989, 1991.*

Figure 15.2 **Eurobond currency composition changes, 1981, 1990**

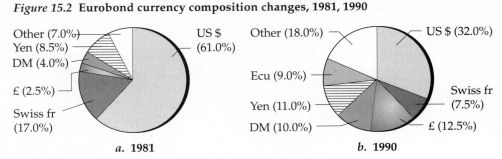

a. **1981**   *b.* **1990**

Source: The Economist, *August 25, 1990, from Bank of England figures, p. 83. See also International Monetary Fund,* International Financial Markets *(annual publication), Table 1-12.*

as in domestic monetary markets. Others dismissed that idea, but could see that there might be some other significant effects. To see why, examine Eurodollars on T-accounts.

EURODOLLARS ON T-ACCOUNTS   An examination of Eurodollars on T-accounts reveals that they can have no effect on the money supply in the United States or abroad. Examine first the sections of British and U.S. banks above the dotted lines. Begin with the decision of Pechiney, a French aluminum firm, to place $100,000 of the dollar balances it has accumulated in the United States and for which it has no immediate need in a Eurodollar deposit. Accordingly, it writes a check on its U.S. bank, Chase Manhattan, and deposits it in a London Bank, Lloyds. Lloyds then creates a Eurodollar deposit for Pechiney. Figure 15.3 shows this deposit as 1A. Lloyds then backs this new deposit with the $100,000 it just received. As with any foreign currency deposit, Lloyds must place that deposit in an American bank and it chooses Citibank. So we see the $100,000 appear as Lloyds' asset in 1B and as Citibank's liability (to Lloyds) in 2B. Once Citibank has the check, it clears it through the banking system and the bank on which Pechiney drew its check, in this case Chase Manhattan, is debited by $100,000 in 2A. Neither American deposits nor reserves change.

What happens when a borrower spends the Eurodollars? Again, American reserves do not change. We examine two cases, both of which have the same ending.

A Loan Whose Proceeds Are Spent in the United States   Suppose the Irish toolmaking firm, Toolan-Digh, wishes to import an automatic lathe from the Massachusetts firm of Turner and Turner. We start with the T-accounts we developed above and continue below the dotted line. Toolan-Digh's treasurer negotiates a loan through an office of Lloyds' bank in Dublin. Lloyds takes Toolan-Digh's promise to pay $100,000 as an asset (3A). It does not create a deposit in Britain for Toolan-Digh, but allows Toolan-Digh to draw on Lloyds' U.S. deposit. When Toolan-Digh buys the lathe from Turner and Turner, it draws

---

Figure 15.3

Eurodollar deposits of British banks

Assets		Liabilities	
1B. Deposit in U.S. Bank	+$100	**1A.** Pechiney	+$100
3A. Loan to Toolan-Digh	+$100		
3B. Deposit in U.S.	−$100		±0

U.S. banks

Assets		Liabilities	
Reserves	±0	**2A.** Pechiney (at Chase)	−$100
		2B. Lloyds (at Citibank)	+$100
Reserves	±0	**4A.** Lloyds (at Citibank)	−$100
		4B. T&T (at 1st Boston)	+$100

down the Lloyds account at Citibank by the $100,000, causing Lloyds to reduce its assets (3B). In the American banking system, the deposit that was at Citibank now belongs to Turner and Turner, which has its account at First Boston, so the Federal Reserve debits Lloyds (4A) and credits First Boston (4B).

All accounts still balance: Lloyds has a deposit from Pechiney of $100,000 backed by a promise to pay of Toolan-Digh of the same amount. The U.S. banking system has seen a deposit move from Chase to Citibank to First Boston, but no increase or decrease in deposits or reserves.

A Loan Whose Proceeds Are Spent Outside the United States   Assume now that Toolan-Digh bought from an English supplier. Will that change the British money supply? No, but let us see why by following the transactions in Fig. 15.4. The establishment of Pechiney's Eurodollar deposit remains the same, but when Toolan-Digh gets its dollars, it asks Lloyds to credit it in sterling. Lloyds complies by granting it an account in its regular or sterling account of the sterling equivalent of the U.S. dollars lent (£67,000) (1A, Fig. 15.4) and backing that account with the U.S. dollars it has got from Pechiney (1B). Presuming that British banks have no excess reserves, the new deposit Lloyds creates causes Lloyds' deposits to exceed the amount its reserves can support, so Lloyds will have to rebuild its reserves.

Lloyds builds its reserves by cutting down on lending (2A), in so doing keeping some of the reserves it gets from other banks when loans are repaid. It thus accumulates another £67,000 in reserves (3B). That would cause Lloyds' loans to fall and its reserves to rise. Those reserves, however, would be coming from another British bank, so total bank reserves would not rise. The reduction in Lloyds' lending would have a chain reaction throughout the system until deposits fell by £67,000 (2B).

Figure 15.4

British banks' sterling accounts

Assets		Liabilities	
1B. Foreign Exchange	+£67	**1A.** Toolan-Digh Deposit	+£67
2A. Loans	−£67	**2B.** Other Deposits	−£67
3A. Other British Bank Reserves	−£67		
3B. Reserves of Lloyds	+£67		
4B. Reserves (Barclays)	−£67	**4A.** U.S. bank deposit (at Barclays)	−£67
4C. Reserves (Lloyds)	+£67		

Lloyds could sell its U.S. dollars to some other bank to secure more reserves. Should it sell off its U.S. dollars to another British bank, that bank in turn would have insufficient reserves, and it would contract loans in the same way Lloyds did. Whether Lloyds does contract its loans or some other British bank does, Toolan-Digh's new deposit will cause some other equivalent deposits to disappear from the system. (It has to, if it is fully lent out.)

Should Lloyds sell its U.S. dollars to an American bank, it would purchase the American bank's sterling deposit in another British bank, Barclays in our example. The items numbered 4A–C show this. Once Lloyds had purchased the sterling, the Bank of England would credit Lloyds (4C) and debit Barclays (4B), which would in turn debit its American bank customer (4A). The deposit would disappear from Barclays, again balancing out the new Toolan-Digh deposit. Neither British deposits nor reserves have changed.

Is There a Multiple Expansion of Eurodollars?   The process outlined above poses another question: Is there a multiple expansion, not in domestic money supplies, but in Eurodollars themselves—one akin to the expansion of the domestic money supply? The answer is that a multiple expansion is possible, but likely to be very small because of the very great leakage from the system. Recall that the only reason reserves in the domestic banking system can be a small fraction of total deposits is because money that is lent and withdrawn always returns into the system. Only when it leaks out into cash is it not returned. The money multiplier is determined by a formula based on 1/RR + leakage, where RR is the reserve requirement and leakage is the money not redeposited. Eurodollar reserve requirements are low, but leakage is near 100%.[8] Only a very small part of Eurodollars is ever returned to the market. Would, for instance, Turner and Turner turn around and deposit its proceeds from Toolan-Digh in the Eurodollar market? Probably not, because T&T would use most of the proceeds for paying labor and materials, and even if it did generate some temporarily idle cash available for short-term investment, it might put those funds in the American CD market, purchase U.S. T-bills, or find some other short-term facility.[*] As a result, the multiplier has remained around 1.[9]

LIQUIDITY, NEAR MONIES, AND WEALTH   Eurodollars, in their shorter-term lengths, are not in themselves money, but *near money*. Except for a very small amount in checking accounts, they must be converted to checking accounts or cash to purchase anything. Moreover, people making Eurodollar deposits know that they are temporarily giving up the use of that money's claim on goods and services, while those who make checking deposits presume that all of those deposits are available instantly. So in the narrower definitions of money—the M1s—Eurodollars are excluded as are savings accounts, treasury bills, and CDs.

Eurodollars, however, almost undoubtedly increase liquidity and may increase wealth. An increase in liquidity means that firms that normally held large balances in checking accounts can hold smaller balances—that is, the firm does not need to hold money for precautionary motives. A larger number of transactions could therefore take place on the same monetary base—velocity rises. It is also possible that the added assets of the Eurodollar market give people more wealth, and therefore affect their spending habits.

Both wealth and liquidity effects depend on the Eurodollars being net additions to the world's assets. Eurocurrency assets may just substitute for national assets: General Motors chooses a London CD instead of a U.S. CD; the wealthy Gil Tedge puts his saving in a 20-year Eurocurrency bond instead of a 20-year American bond. So some domestic bonds and some CDs remain unsold and total assets do not expand. In such cases, neither liquidity nor wealth expands. We must have some indication that there are net changes.

Many of the Eurodollar instruments had shorter maturities than were allowed in the United States—30-day certificates of deposit, for instance, and call deposits. The improvements in the secondary market have also increased liquidity. It is possible to argue that if buyers in such markets have come from other markets, liquidity may have decreased elsewhere. It would seem, nonetheless, that on balance the Eurocurrency market has increased liquidity. Note, however, that the Eurodollar market is only part of a general increase in liquidity and consequent instability in the money velocity.

A wealth effect could emerge if a party that normally kept money in a checking account placed that money in a Eurodollar account, enabling the banking system to allow another party to use the checking deposits. The new Eurodollar depositor would feel just as wealthy as before and almost as liquid. A new borrower, with his new account, would not feel wealthier, of course, but the people he paid might feel so as the borrower drew down his checking account and

---

[*] For a time in the late 1960s, central banks were purchasing U.S. dollars to keep the dollar up and placing their accumulated dollars in the Eurodollar market. Since many of their purchases arose from Eurodollar loans, the redeposits contributed to the expansion of the Eurodollar deposit and produced a multiplier of greater than 1.

money moved to those of his suppliers and employees. There would thus be two sets of parties feeling that the same deposit was theirs. Again, that can only happen if the Eurodollar deposit is a substitute for a checking account, not for another near money.

INTERNATIONAL CAPITAL AND NATIONAL POLICY

CHANGES IN THE INTERNATIONAL CAPITAL MARKET

All capital markets, national or international, are experiencing four major changes:[10] (1) increased *liquidity*, (2) increased *securitization*, which is a move away from using banking intermediaries, (3) *risk unbundling*, in which the various risks involved in a single loan are separated, and (probably) (4) a decrease in transparency. At the same time the markets are undergoing these changes, the organization of the market itself is changing as the lines between banks and other financial institutions are blurring.

1. *Liquidity*. Changes in communication, computerization, and the increasing sophistication of modern finance allow large amounts of capital to be mobilized very rapidly. The ease with which financiers have been able to raise the capital to take over large corporations is just one of many illustrations of the ability of modern markets to generate capital funds.

2. *Securitization*. As noted earlier in the chapter, lenders can place their money with banks and let the banks do the lending for them, or they can lend directly to the borrower through purchasing securities. One of the current trends is for more and more corporations and government borrowers, which used to borrow through banks, to borrow through securities; the process is known as securitization. A company with a good reputation, working with an investment banker or brokerage house, can arrange an issue of securities and pay smaller fees than it would through a bank.

The development of high-yielding, somewhat less secure bonds, known inappropriately by the term junk bonds has been a key element in the takeover battles of recent years.* In addition, many industries that suffered greatly during credit crunches in the past have reduced their dependence on bank credit through leasing and other securitized programs. Today apartment housing is often financed through selling the units as condominiums, and shopping malls by selling shares in long-term leases. Banks, rather than using deposits to support housing loans, often sell off securities to finance the mortgages. Roughly one third of all U.S. mortgages are financed through issues of securities rather than through bank deposits.[11] Corporations with heavy capital costs have cut their

---

* The bonds do not receive a high rating from bond-rating companies and thus are ineligible to be purchased by many trust and pension funds. They are somewhat riskier, but they pay well enough to keep buyers coming.

dependence on banks by selling part of the organization to a leasing company (financed by a new issue of stock) and then used the proceeds of the sale to expand in another area.*

3. *Unbundling of risk.* It used to be that a lender took all the risk involved in a loan: (a) *credit (or default) risk,* which is the risk that the borrower would not repay, (b) *interest (or market) risk,* the risk that interest rates would rise before the loan was due, depressing the present value of the loan, (c) *scheduling risk,* the risk that the payments would come, but not on schedule, and (d) *foreign exchange (or currency) risk,* the risk that the currency of payment would fall in value. The lender may not have wanted to take all these risks, and may have been in a better position to judge, and shoulder, some of the risks rather than others. (The executive who can judge the soundness of Saab-Scania may not be able to judge what will happen to interest rates.) Today, the capital market can often sell the different risks separately.

One set of techniques involves a financial institution making the judgment on the credit risk, but selling the interest rate risk. An example is a bank selling securities on mortgages or other loans, where it agrees to pay the purchasers' interest, whether or not the underlying loan defaults.[12]

Another common technique is the swap. Chapter 13 noted the use of swaps for foreign currency, but financiers use the technique to trade interest payments. Swaps arise when a bank has a need for a certain type of income—fixed or variable, one currency or another—yet finds that the loan that best suits its customer does not best suit the bank's needs. Rather than tell the borrower to find another bank, which may have more difficulty in judging the credit risk, the bank makes the loan, then trades off some of the loan's elements to another bank. An example of this is shown in Fig. 15.5. Markets for the swapping of interest rate payments are very active and are handled through brokers. From their inception in 1982, interest rate swaps grew to over 300 billion U.S. dollars in 1986, and over 2.3 trillion U.S. dollars by 1991.[13]

4. *Reduced transparency.* A number of the changes that are occurring in financial markets today have the effect of making it harder to assess underlying risk. Financial institutions are probably carrying more contingent liabilities, agreeing, for instance, to buy up unsold securities, to support a secondary market, or to guarantee securitized transactions. The health of the intermediary is much harder to judge when liabilities are only contingent upon a failure somewhere else. The practice of syndicated loans virtually stopped after Third World debt defaults, but has begun again in a small way, and various risk pooling and other innovative financial devices often make it quite difficult to perceive the underlying risk. Moreover, a number of economists fear that in the process of short-

---

* As an example, Union Carbide sold one of its plants to a new company it created, then leased back the plant. The new company raised money through stockbrokers and paid its shareholders with the rents from Union Carbide. Union Carbide took the money from the sale of the plant and used it to invest elsewhere. Look, Ma, no banks.

Figure 15.5 **An interest rate swap.** Chase Manhattan lends money to Company 1, a Canadian company wishing to pay fixed interest in Canadian dollars. The loan does not fit Chase's portfolio wishes precisely, so it seeks a swap. Chase finds the Bank of Nova Scotia, which has lent U.S. dollars at a variable rate to one of their American borrowers, a loan, too, that does not fit "Scotiabank's" portfolio. The loan above the line represents the situation of both banks before the swap. The two banks agree to swap the payments, while each keeps the credit risk (and the customer). The resultant situation is that shown below the line. If need be, either bank could find another bank with which to swap only the currency or fixed versus variable interest, separating the risk even further.

Chase Manhattan	**Bank of Nova Scotia**
Loan in Canadian dollars, fixed interest to Company 1	Loan in United States dollars, variable interest to Company 2
Loan to Company 1 variable interest, United States dollars from Company 2	Loan to Company 2 Fixed interest, Canadian dollars from Company 1

circuiting the banks, the information gathering and risk assessment in the market have declined. The riposte to that suggestion is that the separation of credit, interest, and exchange rate risk places risk with specialized holders, each better able to assess the risk than a more generalized institution.

5. *Changing roles of intermediaries.* As the markets have changed, so have the institutions in the market. There has been a blurring of the traditional lines between a commercial bank—which accepts deposits, holds reserves, and makes loans—and an investment house or merchant bank—which underwrites and places securities issues. In the United States, where the 1932 Glass-Steagall Act sought to separate the deposit-taking banks from merchant banks, banks have used holding companies to buy investment houses and investment houses have set up banks. Abroad, where the lines were less clear but still visible, the process has also occurred. It is a necessary adjustment to the changes in market liquidity.[14]

IMPLICATIONS OF THE CHANGES

MONETARY POLICY For many countries in the world, monetary policy has become exchange rate policy. Canada's 1987–1989 attempt to keep its interest rates 3–4% higher than U.S. rates, much higher than its historic spread, attracted a great deal of short-term capital and may not have had a significant effect on choking domestic investment, much of which is financed from abroad. While initially logical sounding, the reasoning is rather more complex.

While much economic theory assumes that raising the interest rate affects the economy evenly, cutting off only the lower-yielding investments, that may not have been what was occurring. According to the *capital availability theory*, banks do not rely exclusively on interest rates, but *ration* the quantities of loans they make. In a period of economic expansion, banks do not immediately raise interest rates to ration credit; instead, they ask their customers to delay receiving loans until the money is available. A queue thus forms, and bankers lend the money as available. (Rationing and queuing are quite common in many industries during boom periods, as the firms have to consider not just the short-run advantage, but their long relationship with their customers.) Such behavior has interesting international implications.

Investment borrowing may be highly price inelastic, since it is a derived demand from increased consumer spending or foreign spending. (Ask an executive from most firms if a 1% rise in the interest rate is going to change the firm's plans. Few will admit their decision is so finely tuned.) Instead, lower money supplies rationed credit, and tended to target those industries most dependent on bank credit—for example, construction and some forms of new capital investments. While quite willing to invest, builders or potential housing buyers were met with requirements such as banks refusing to lend more than 50% of the value of a house, which essentially cut many of them out of the market. As such industries have come to use securitization to sidestep extensive use of bank credit, they have become less sensitive to changes in the money supply. Since reducing the money supply no longer has the same rationing effect, interest rates must be raised much higher to induce firms to postpone investment plans.[15]

Many borrowers, unhappy with domestic interest rates, can borrow abroad at lower rates. So long as they are willing to shoulder the foreign exchange risk, they can have their funds to invest. The funds they borrow give them command over resources domestically, and given relatively full employment (or a vertical *AS*), will squeeze some other group out. The mechanism by which this occurs varies according to the way exchange rate policy reacts to the capital inflow. Chapter 14 analyzed this kind of event as a shock to the capital account. Given full employment, it will result in a rise in the value of the currency on the foreign exchange market, or an inflation domestically.

Both an inflation and a rise in the value of the nation's exchange rate have the same effect—they hit exports and import-competing goods. The effect of monetary policy, then, is not so much to squeeze domestic investment, but to squeeze out the exchange-rate-sensitive sector. Aggregate demand falls (or slows in its expansion) not because, as traditionally expected, investment falls, but because exports fall and imports rise. To wit:

FD 15.1

$$i\uparrow \rightarrow \begin{cases} \$\uparrow \\ I(\uparrow) \rightarrow AD\uparrow \\ KA\uparrow \rightarrow MS\uparrow \rightarrow I\uparrow AD\uparrow \rightarrow P\uparrow \end{cases} \rightarrow (X\downarrow - M\uparrow)\downarrow$$

A rise in the interest rate fails to cut domestic investment, restricting instead exports and import substitutes—that is, net foreign investment. In the top line, the currency rises; in the bottom line, a capital inflow yields a rising money supply, which counteracts the higher interest rate. In the middle line, the inflow of capital is sterilized, but investment proceeds anyway, again raising prices. The rise in interest rates does dampen AD, but by squeezing exports and import substitutes, not new domestic investment. Because it worsens the trade balance, the domestic investment proceeds at the cost of foreign borrowing or disinvestment.

FISCAL POLICY   Seen on a Swan-Mundell diagram, the changes described turn the external balance line more vertical, and the domestic balance line more horizontal, increasing, in turn, the policy conflict areas of (1) inflation and external inflow and (2) recession and external outflow. Figure 15.6 shows this change.

One might well ask whether smaller nations have a monetary policy at all, since money supply change appears mainly to be an exchange rate policy, and largely defensive at that. The weakening of monetary policy puts added burdens on fiscal policy, which is recognized as being less flexible, more politicized, and far harder to control than monetary policy.

SUPERVISION AND MONITORING   Authorities find it far harder to monitor and regulate the financial markets than before. Certainly one problem is the number of different countries and conflicting jurisdictions. Perhaps more important has been the increase in securities, by nature harder to monitor than bank loans, the rise in contingent liabilities, and the newer and more complex financial instruments developed. Declining transparency and increasing liquidity are like a flood of dark water to those charged with monitoring financial markets.

Figure 15.6 **Changes in policy responsiveness.** Easier international borrowing and lending means that monetary policy is less effective in controlling investment, meaning the internal balance is harder to change, giving a flatter internal schedule. Funds, in the meantime, are more responsive to small international interest rate differences, making the external balance steeper.

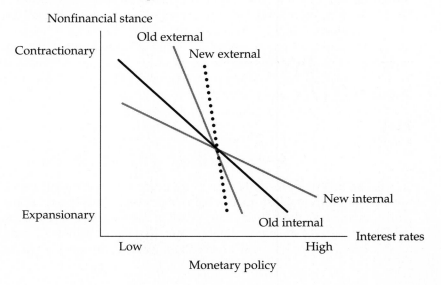

After a number of Third World countries defaulted on their debt in the early 1980s, the problem of the solvency of major commercial banks became very serious, leading to a more far-reaching plan, the Basle Agreement. It merits more detailed consideration.

THE BASLE AGREEMENT

Most banking regulation has focused on bank reserves, reflecting the older concerns that banks would lack the liquidity to deal with a sudden crisis. Thus the government would require the amount of reserves needed. Liquidity in the 1990s, however, is hardly a problem, as banks have large amounts of assets in T-bills and other short-term assets. More important is solvency—that failure of borrowers to repay a bank's loans will cause the bank's liabilities to exceed its assets. Consider this on a simplified bank balance sheet, Fig. 15.7. Assets (the bank's loans, short- and long-term financial assets, and physical assets) equal the bank's liabilities (principally what it owes its depositors) and net worth—what it owes its shareholders. The net worth is the value of what shareholders own: their *equity*.

Staid has $825 million in assets and an equal amount in liabilities. Twenty-five million dollars of the shareholders' equity is in buildings and other physical equipment and another $300 million dollars is in Treasury bills. Now suppose the bank is forced to show that $100 million of loans cannot be collected, as in the middle section of the figure. Loans would fall to $400 million, and equity, which is assets less liabilities, to $25 million, as shown in the middle segment of the balance sheet. What if it has to take another loss of $50 million? Down go the assets to $350 million, but liabilities cannot fall that far. The bank still owes $700 million to depositors; if shareholder equity is negative, as the third segment shows, the bank is bankrupt.

We drew Staid in bold strokes and presented a very conservative bank, with liquid reserves in equity at a very high 25% of all assets, when in 1982 these figures were closer to 3% to 5%. In the mid-1980s many banks kept declaring that their

Figure 15.7 **Staid National Bank**

Assets		Liabilities	
Loans	$500	Deposits	$700
T-bills	300	Equity	125
Buildings, etc.	25		
Loans	400	Deposits	700
T-bills	300	Equity	25
Buildings, etc.	25		
Loans	350	Deposits	700
T-bills	300	Equity	−25
Buildings, etc.	25		

loans were worth their full face value when they and their regulators knew otherwise, while they scrambled to set aside loan reserves (potential equity) to cover the losses. Otherwise, many major banks would have been declared insolvent, a situation that would have produced a major financial panic, to say the least.

To prevent banks from becoming severely overextended in the future, central bankers from the G-7 countries made the Basle Agreement (or Accord) of 1988. In essence, the central bankers decided to pressure commercial banks in their countries to maintain higher equity. More specifically, the Basle Agreement calls for banks to maintain at least 8% of a weighted calculation of their assets as capital. This capital is in two tiers. The first tier of 4% must be shareholders' equity (the net worth of Staid National Bank). The second tier may contain additional equity, but it can also have funds set aside for reserves against losses (which belong to the shareholders until the default takes place) and subordinated debt. (Subordinated debt is borrowings that stand last in line among debts for payment if the bank becomes insolvent.)

The weighted calculation of a bank's assets counts loans as 1, some higher-risk municipal bonds as .5, many municipal, state, and provincial assets as .2, and debt of the G-7 governments as 0. Anything else is counted, along with loans, as 1. To make things more difficult, banks are also supposed to count their *contingent liabilities*—for instance, the liability they assume when they guarantee a note—and most of these are as 1.

To build up their equity, particularly reserves against loan losses, banks must take some of their earnings and place them in liquid assets, rather than distributing them as dividends, using them to buy equipment or buildings, or placing them in illiquid holdings. In the United States, the reserves must be built out of profits (that is, after-profits taxes are paid before the money is put into reserves); many other countries' tax laws do not consider as profit the money going to create loss reserves.[16] In any case, building reserves takes time and is costly in terms of income foregone. In practice, the G-7 countries (and several other countries) have not instituted the requirement all at once, and are gradually increasing the amount of capital a bank is to hold, pushing toward the agreement's level. In other cases, they are still discussing how to count some items, particularly the various contingent liabilities.

The Basle Agreement may have far-reaching effects because it effectively supplants reserve requirements for control over lending. If a bank does not reach the required 8% when its central bank believes it should, the bank can do nothing but buy T-bills or hold excess reserves. This will produce a more secure banking system, but further reduce the role of banks in lending. Borrowers instead will go directly to the public with commercial paper, furthering the move to securitization.

Slowly, the national authorities are coming to share information and to establish some common standards.[17] The market, however, is changing so rapidly that supervision is difficult and new gaps open up as others are closed. As one writer commented recently, "the gaps in supervision remain alarming."[18]

CONCLUSION

Changes in the international financial markets have been great, and phrases like "financial revolution" and "Big Bang" may not be too far off the mark. On a microeconomic level, the changes have served to increase competition, lower the costs of loans, and apportion and divide up risk to those most willing to assume it. Such changes are not an unmixed blessing because the development of so many new instruments and the rapid change in the market have reduced transparency of some activities, making it harder for authorities and individual investors and borrowers to assess risk. While the increased internationalization of the markets has created a great deal more activity, much of that activity is churning—many trades for small profits or small reductions of risk—or superior allocations of existing capital flows among lenders and borrowers. For all its size, the capital market has not markedly increased net flows of capital over what could be predicted without taking the capital market changes into account. (This is particularly true of the period after the Third World debt crisis.)

On a macroeconomic level, the internationalization, securitization, and increases in liquidity have made monetary policy far less effective in reining in investment, particularly in smaller nations, where interest rate policy has become mostly exchange rate policy. Fiscal policy then becomes the principal macroeconomic tool, and it is an awkward tool.

VOCABULARY AND CONCEPTS

Basle Agreement
Capital availability argument
Capital (equity) requirements
Certificates of Deposit (CDs)
Contingent liability
Credit risk
Cross-border transaction
Currency swap
Eurocurrency (Eurodollar) loan
Eurocurrency (Eurodollar) bond
Eurodollar deposit
Eurocurrency deposit
Instrument
Interest rate risk
Interest rate swap
LIBOR—London Interbank Offer Rate
Liquidity

London interbank market
Matching process
Medium-term Eurocurrency notes
Near money
Risk assessment
Risk pooling
Risk unbundling
Risk aversion
Secondary market
Securitization
Swaps
Syndicated loans
Thin market
Transaction costs
Transparency
Unit of account

QUESTIONS

1. Describe what the matching process is, what is matched, and what its economic functions are. How would the world be poorer if it functioned poorly?

2. What makes a market thin? Why are secondary markets important? Illustrate with a discussion of medium-term Eurocurrency securities.

3. What does it mean to pool risks? How does that help the economic process? What is a particular danger of pooling risk?

4. What is *transparency*, and what are the indications that it has declined in international lending? What suggests that it may in fact be greater?

5. How might the great segmentation (borrowers and investors with different needs finding specialized instruments) of the international capital market lead to a large gross flow of capital, but much smaller net flow? How does it compare to intraindustrial trade?

6. What is a swap, and how does it contribute to the matching process? Does it make international investment more or less secure?

7. Distinguish traditional cross-border foreign loans and bond issues from Eurocurrency issues.

8. Explain why a large market in Eurocurrency loans and bonds has arisen. (Do not rely on simple historical description, except insofar as that illustrates the conceptual points.)

9. Explain why Eurodollars do not have a substantial impact on the money supply.

10. Explain how Eurodollars could (a) increase the velocity of the money supply, (b) increase consumption, or (c) increase investment. (For c, comment on the thesis that monetary policy does not restrain domestic investment when the capital market is so highly integrated.)

11. How have changes in liquidity, securitization, and risk unbundling affected the international capital market? Be sure you explain each term.

12. How have the changes in the international capital markets come to affect domestic monetary policy?

13. Chapter 14 showed how difficult it was to use monetary policy to change the rate of domestic saving and investment. How has this difficulty modified or magnified that conclusion?

14. The last sentence of the chapter is rather glum. ("Fiscal policy then becomes the principal macroeconomic tool, and it is an awkward tool.") Do you agree?

NOTES

[1] See Adrian Hamilton, *The Financial Revolution,* New York, The Free Press, 1986.

[2] Paul Einzig, *The History of Foreign Exchange,* London, Macmillan, 1964, p. 83.

[3] The history of the market has been covered in a number of places. An early analysis is Paul Einzig, *The Eurodollar System,* Macmillan, London, 1965. See also R.B.R. Johnson, *The Economics of the Eurodollar Market,* London, Macmillan, 1983, Chapter 2; Gunter Dufey and Ian Giddy, *The International Money Market,* Englewood Cliffs, N.J., Prentice Hall, 1978, Chapter 1; Jan S. Hogendorn and Wilson Brown, *The New International Economics,* Reading, Mass., Addison-Wesley, 1979, Chapter 5.

[4] See R.B.R. Johnson, *The Economics of the Eurodollar Market,* Chapter 3.

[5] R.B.R. Johnson, *The Economics of the Eurodollar Market,* Chapter 3.

[6] Maxwell Watson et. al., *International Capital Markets: Development and Prospects,* Washington, D.C. International Monetary Fund, 1988, p. 36.

[7] See Adrian Hamilton, *The Financial Revolution,* p. 57. Hamilton also mentions numerous other floating-rate instruments.

[8] See John Hewson and Eisuke Sakakibara, "Eurodollar deposit multiplier: A portfolio approach," *IMF Staff Papers,* July 1975.

[9] Economists agree that the multiplier, in the sense we have used the term above, is close to 1. See Dufey and Giddy, *The International Money Market*, Chapter 3, or R.B.R. Johnson, *The Economics of the Eurodollar Market*, Chapter 9, and the articles to which they refer. The word *multiplier* is sometimes used to describe the relation of the amount of Eurodollars of a given term (for example, all deposits or loans under one year) to the base in U.S. dollar holdings, but this is a relationship (and not a very stable one) whose links of causality with the Eurodollar market are not clear. An increase in U.S. dollar holdings of foreign banks does not lead to greater Eurodollar deposits, and possibly does not even stem from them. See the sources noted for a fuller discussion.

[10] International capital markets change rapidly. Those interested in recent developments may wish to check one of two regular reviews of the market. (1) The IMF publishes an annual survey in January of each year, entitled *International Capital Markets*. It contains a general discussion, often some background study, and a number of important tables and statistics. (2) Every year in the last week in March *The Economist* publishes a survey of world banking. Those interested in following the market closely can see if their library subscribes to *Euromoney*, a monthly magazine for the financial public.

[11] In the United States, "mortgage pass-throughs have grown from minuscule proportions of all residential mortgage debt in the early 1970s to about one third, or $600 billion, in mid-1987." Thomas Simpson, "Developments in the U.S. financial system since the mid-1970s," *Federal Reserve Bulletin*, January 1988, pp. 1–13. Quotation from p. 10.

[12] Christopher James, "Off-balance sheet banking" *Economic Review*, Federal Reserve Bank of San Francisco, Fall 1987, pp. 21–36. Thomas Simpson, "Developments in the U.S. financial system since the mid-1970s," cited above.

[13] Steven D. Felgram, "Interest rate swaps: Use, risk, and prices," *New England Economic Review*, Federal Reserve Bank of Boston, November–December 1987, pp. 22–32; Watson, *The International Capital Market*, p. 36, comments on these as a securitization of risk. The 1991 figure is from Morris Goldstein, David Folkerts-Landau, Mohamed El-Erian, Steven Fries, and Liliana Rojas-Suarez, *International Capital Markets: Developments, Prospects, and Policy Issues*, Washington, International Monetary Fund, 1992, p. 74.

[14] The institutional changes are quite extensive and largely beyond the scope of this chapter or book. See Hamilton, *The Financial Revolution*, Chapter 4.

[15] The credit-rationing argument and the argument that higher interest rates now squeeze exports and import substitutes are from Chapter 3 of Watson, *International Capital Markets*. In brief and more explicit form they are in Russell Kincaid, "Policy implications of structural changes in financial markets," *Finance and Development*, March 1988, pp. 2–6.

[16] This may explain why foreign banks have somewhat higher loss reserves.

[17] See Watson, *International Capital Markets*, pp. 37–39.

[18] See Hamilton, *The Financial Revolution*, Chapter 9. The quotation is from p. 219.

Chapter 16

Exchange Rate Adjustment

OBJECTIVES

Overall Objective: To tie foreign exchange policy into open-economy macroeconomics, examining it in detail.

MORE SPECIFICALLY:

- To show how purchasing power relates to exchange rates.
- To explain the circumstance under which an exchange rate can be altered to correct payments imbalances and the conditions under which alteration may not work.
- To demonstrate why changing the exchange rate alone is often (or normally) not effective.
- To consider the possibility that devaluation will have completely opposite effects to those normally supposed, as shown in the Marshall-Lerner effect.
- To note how delayed effects of devaluations, as shown in the J-curve, can confuse policy.
- To consider once again why protectionism will not work to end trade deficits.

Previous chapters have examined the effects of saving and investment, of income and prices, and of monetary and fiscal policies on a country's international position. Chapter 16 examines how changes in the exchange rate itself affect a country—that is, it examines exchange rate shocks. The chapter has four main sections:

1. An exploration of the relationship of price levels to exchange rates. This relationship is very complex and not fully understood.

2. An examination of how governments may deliberately change exchange rates to achieve economic objectives. The opportunities to do so successfully appear to be limited.

3. A probing of some of the difficulties involved when exports and imports prove not to be very responsive to price changes, including an examination of the infamous Marshall-Lerner effect.

4. And finally, some analysis of protectionism and adjustment.

WHAT VALUE SHOULD AN EXCHANGE RATE HAVE?

What value should an exchange rate have? Start with a basic widely accepted view. *An exchange rate should have a value that will help achieve a sustainable trade imbalance: That is, its value should promote the price adjustments to allow a trade deficit or surplus consistent with the efficient allocation of capital in an open economy.* The exchange rate need not produce balanced trade, but it should keep trade deficits within the ability of the country to pay the costs of what it must borrow to sustain them. And it should keep surpluses down to the point where they do not weaken the surplus country's capital base. Well and good, but has it other roles to play? The statement, after all, is basically a microeconomic statement, suggesting no macroeconomic role. Try two opposing macroeconomic views.

1. *It makes no difference what an exchange rate is so long as it does not change.* The important thing is to have the *price level* and *interest rate* correct. The economy should shape itself around the exchange rate, much as it did before the First World War. Attempts to use the exchange rate as a macroeconomic tool are dangerous because in themselves they distort the price system and are ultimately unsuccessful.

2. *Exchange rates are part and parcel of macroeconomic adjustment procedures. When small amounts of inflation help to achieve full employment, it is sensible to adjust the exchange rate, rather than to try to push down the price level to achieve proper microeconomic balance.* While occasionally they may be used as tools, for the most part they act as equilibrating mechanisms and do so successfully.

The first statement is tough and implies the exchange rate adjustment may have disequilibrating effects: It may make things worse. The second is accommodating, seeing the exchange rate principally as a means for adjusting to economic changes that have already occurred. They form the principal focus for the chapter. To understand them well, however, it is best to take a long look at the relationship of price levels and exchange rates.

■ *DEVALUATION, DEPRECIATION, REVALUATION, AND APPRECIATION*

The four concepts are all related to changing the value of a currency. Under a system of fixed rates, a country may *devalue* its exchange rate by setting a lower price at which it will intervene in the foreign exchange market. It may *revalue* (raise upward) its exchange rate by setting a higher intervention price. Under floating rates, a country can use interest rates to attract capital, forcing its exchange rate to *appreciate*. Similarly, it could lower interest rates, causing its exchange rate to *depreciate*.

UNDERVALUATION AND OVERVALUATION: PRICE LEVELS AND EXCHANGE RATE VALUES

A currency that is too high in value is said to be overvalued, and one that is too low is undervalued. But who judges, and on what basis can such judgments be made? One can cite the wisdom of the market, noting that currencies under attack with central banks intervening heavily to support them must be overvalued. But that rather begs the question as to how the market achieved its wisdom. Ultimately, and rather imprecisely, the question usually comes down to relative levels of inflation, modified by important considerations of investment climate.

THE THEORY OF PURCHASING POWER PARITY (PPP)

We cannot just find out what a franc buys in France and what a dollar buys in the United States and compute from that what the exchange rate will be. Every traveler knows how hard it is to make comparisons of living standards. A thousand Thai baht buys far more in Thailand than the $25 it costs, particularly when those purchases are foods, haircuts, housing, or domestic service. (The income of $1300 per person actually purchases a great deal more than it could in the United States.) The problem is that we cannot move a basket of personal services, housing, or tropical fruits to the United States costlessly and sell it. Hence we cannot compare what the baht buys and what the dollar buys and conclude from that something about the exchange rates. It is tradable goods and services that are important in determining exchange rates, not all goods and services.

While we cannot use purchasing power in the way described, there is massive evidence that one can compute changes in exchange rates from changes in purchasing power. In the short run, tradable goods and tastes change more slowly than do price levels. And one can choose a price index involving more tradable goods—the wholesale index rather than the cost of living index. We now have a new proposition: The percentage change in the price level of one nation compared with the percentage change in the price level of another determines the alteration in the relative values of their currencies. As an example, suppose France had an inflation that doubled its wholesale price index and the United States had no inflation. Then if the French franc was initially at US$0.20, we would expect that it would now fall to US$0.10.

Usually, however, all nations are inflating at the same time, though some at more rapid rates than others. That is too hard to do in the head, so we need a formula.

(Eq. 16.1)
$$\frac{PP_a}{PP_b} \times \frac{Ca_0}{Cb_0} = \frac{Ca_1}{Cb_1}$$

where PP_a = index of the purchasing power of currency a in the current period, with the base year set at 100.

PP_b = index of purchasing power of currency b in the current period, with the base year set at 100.

Ca_0 and Cb_0 = value of currencies a and b in terms of each other (Ca/Cb) in the base period, and

Ca_1 and Cb_1 = value of currencies a and b in current period.

As an example, suppose the United States had an inflation of 100% over a given period and France had one of only 50%. In the initial period the exchange rate was Fr5 = US$1.00. To handle this example, make both countries' price indexes 100 in the base year and determine the new price index: The new French price index is 100 + 50 = 150, and the American is 100 + 100 = 200. (Be careful to express the figures on a base of 100; otherwise the formula would predict that a country with a 2% inflation would see its currency halve in value against a country with a 1% inflation!)

Then:

(Eq. 16.2)
$$\frac{150}{200} \times \frac{5}{1} = \frac{3.75}{1}$$

The French franc would tend toward a value of 3.75 to the dollar.

Gustav Cassel first put forth the theory of purchasing power parity in a series of articles published during the First World War. The war had unleashed inflation, but inflation that varied from nation to nation. Cassel figured that simple adjustment of exchange rates would restore the prewar trading relations. The nations, however, attempted to restore prewar gold parities and prewar price levels and only adjusted exchange rates when they were forced to. Indeed, the creation of many new states in Central Europe and the destruction of older industries and establishment of newer ones may have fundamentally altered the relationship of domestic to international purchasing power, making purchasing power theory useless.

Cassel's ideas, whether followed or not, made good sense, and the theory of purchasing power parity is in common use among bankers as an important indicator of foreign exchange movements. No modern bank report on foreign exchange is complete without some purchasing power observations, and they have a remarkably good track record in predicting the extent of exchange rate movements. The statistics can be frustrating and debatable at points, but the method has been remarkably durable. It must, of course, be used with considerable caution because, as Chapter 14 explained, interest rates are also important determinants of exchange rates.

■ *PURCHASING POWER PARITY AND THE CANADIAN DOLLAR*

Figure 16.1 shows purchasing power parity used to explain the difference in the values of the U.S. and Canadian dollars and demonstrates both the strength and weakness of the PPP approach.

Figure 16.1 Purchasing power parity: C$ and US$, 1980–1991. The solid line shows the actual exchange rate of the U.S. dollar in Canadian dollars.[1] The dotted line is a predicted exchange rate, based on the ratio of the rates of inflation in both countries, as explained in Eq. 16.1. From 1980 to 1987, PPP worked very well. The predicted rates, based on relative rates of inflation, while hardly down to the last cent, are quite good. Were a bank to have predicted the 1986 rate on the basis of inflation indicators alone, it would have been right on. Only in 1985 would the predicted rate have been more than 4 cents off. After 1987, however, the Canadian dollar rose in value (or the U.S. dollar fell), departing widely from its predicted purchasing power value. A banker speculating on the U.S. dollar remaining near 1.25 Canadian dollars would have lost 10 cents on the dollar. Relative purchasing powers are only one determinant of a currency's value.

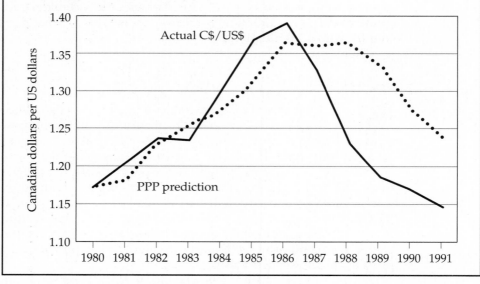

CAN PURCHASING POWER DRIVE EXCHANGE RATE VALUES?

To this point, we have been arguing, essentially, that it is a change in relative price levels that determines the exchange rate. Given other countries' inflations at zero, then:

(FD 16.1) $$\Delta P\downarrow \rightarrow \Delta\$\uparrow \ \text{ or } \ \Delta P\uparrow \rightarrow \Delta\$\downarrow$$

That is: A change downward in the price level causes the value of the currency on the foreign exchange market to change in an upward direction, or an upward change in the price level causes the currency to fall on the foreign exchange market. While no one would doubt that in the long run this relationship is true, how close a relationship, and how quickly it comes about, is not at all clear, as Figure 16.1 showing the Canadian situation after 1987 indicates.

TRADE MAKES UP A SMALL PORTION OF TOTAL CURRENCY TRADE   As Chapter 13 noted, the total of goods and services traded plus the *net* movement of capital[*] is less than 7% of the trillions of dollars that move through the foreign exchange markets. Some writers have dismissed the purchasing power theory on just those grounds: The vast amount of activity in any period is related to speculation, covering, and short-term investments.[2] How, then, can the tail wag the dog?

The counterargument is that a better analogy would be a little gear driving a bigger one, with the real factors (trade and net capital movement) being the small gear. The low transaction cost of currency trading means that every $10 billion of additional trade can produce a vastly larger amount of foreign exchange activity. After all, if trade were unimportant, the announcement of a large U.S. trade deficit would hardly cause the panic on the foreign exchange markets described in Chapter 13.

STATISTICAL PROBLEMS Statistical problems of figuring purchasing power parities are such that we cannot know, except in a very general way, what the real purchasing power parity should be. Key questions surround which price index to use, what base years to choose, and how to include products that are not in the index. Generally, the cost of living index is a poor choice because it reflects a great number of prices of goods that do not come into trade at all. Nor do the weights of goods in the index match at all what is traded. Preferred indexes are those such as wholesale prices or manufactured goods, but every index has a problem. The IMF calculates no fewer than six different series for assessing the extent of overvaluation among developed countries. Three are based on differing price indexes, and three on differing labor cost and value-added indexes.[3]

The choice of base year is important—in which year was trade normal? Worse, in advanced nations many of the traded goods are newly invented goods, not in the indexes, or certainly not in the index in the original year of comparison. Moreover, since each country has many trading partners, it is best to use an index *weighted* according to the amount of trade with each partner, and in itself that creates another set of choices. As with many figures, the closer one looks, the slipperier the figures appear. That does not mean indexes are useless, particularly since computers these days can run many different sets of choices, giving a range of possible answers, if not one with the precision to aid a foreign exchange trader.

■ *A SHORT STATISTICAL STUDY*

Statistical problems are endemic in economic policy. Just because the answers may give us a range of possibilities any of which may be correct does not mean we cannot use them. At least the statistics create reasonable parameters for discussion. Consider the case of a student working on the Korean economy, which in the late 1980s went from having very substantial trade deficits to even more impressive trade surpluses. He decided to examine whether the Korean *won* had fallen in value in real terms over those years. The problem was tricky because Korea's

---

[*] The net capital movement is equal to the sum of all deficit countries' current account deficits, or all surplus countries' surpluses. It is, of course, much lower than the total trade in the year.

pattern of trade had changed greatly; Japan, for instance, was a far more important partner in 1987 than in 1981. Moreover, the rates of inflation both within Korea and among its trading partners differed over the period. Nonetheless, the choice of base year and weights to give to each trading partner made little difference to the overall pattern of movement of the real value of the Korean won.

The student tried three different base years for the inflation and two different base years to determine the weights to give to each country. The choice of base year to measure from (that designated as 100 for the purchasing power index) made a large difference in the amount of undervaluation, but not in how it changed. The choice of weights for each country made little difference. As the diagram is set up, any point at 0 means that the inflation and changes in currency values have exactly offset each other. (Technically, $\Delta PP_K / \Delta PP_o = 1$, where ΔPP is the change in purchasing power, stated as an index, K is Korea, and o is a composite index of Korea's trading partners.) While no one would want to trade foreign exchange based on such predictions, the pattern of rise and decline is much the same for any series, becoming somewhat more pronounced over the time period. By 1987 the won was undervalued in comparison to the 1976–1981 period on all five measurements. So, despite a rather unpromising set of conditions for measurement, the results certainly suggest why Korea saw such a great turnaround in its trade balance.[*]

Figure 16.2 Korea: Index of PPP valuations using different weights and base years. BYr = Base year, W = Weight. 85BYr & W means choosing 1985 as a base year and using weights from that year. 87BYr and 85W means choosing 1987 as a base year and 1985 for weighting the various countries. Note that the base year makes the principal difference, and the weighting of the currencies is of less importance. The pattern of moving toward undervaluation, climbing into overvaluation, and then declining sharply again is the same under all five combinations.

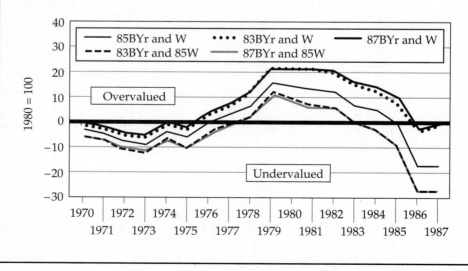

---

[*] Price was not the sole factor. Korea also had major changes that raised the return to saving.

PURCHASING POWER AND POPULAR UNDERSTANDING

While the reader may be nodding sagely at the observations above, the concept is not readily grasped by the public at large. During the debate over the Free Trade Agreement between the United States and Canada, the issue came up a number of times. Three cases illustrate the difficulties of grasping the idea.

1. Many Canadian harvester teams (sets of combines and operators who harvest grain on contract with farmers) travel the American Midwest. A television special showed an American competitor complaining bitterly that the "cheap Canadian dollar" (US$0.80 at the time) gave an unfair advantage to the Canadians because the Canadian dollar was only 80% of the American. It is a common enough interpretation. It should suffice to point out that the Canadian dollar was 80% of the American because American prices were 80% of Canadian.

2. During a Canadian public meeting on the Free Trade Agreement, an economist responded to a question by stating that he expected the Canadian dollar would rise in value. Many in the audience were disturbed by what they expected would be a loss in competitive position. "No," replied the economist, "it would reflect an improved competitive position." Few seemed to follow. What the economist expected was that an improvement in Canadian productivity would lower Canadian costs and hold down inflation, which would cause Canadian costs to fall relative to the American. In turn, the Canadian dollar would rise.

3. Some exporters object to floating exchange rates because of the uncertainty they give. But if the exchange rate reflects changes in purchasing power, they give more certainty. The tendency of exchange rates to follow relative inflations eases the problem of corporate planning. A Canadian exporter planning to increase plant size in order to further penetrate the U.S. market need not be *overly* concerned with the effect of inflation. If Canadian costs rise faster than American, the Canadian dollar will tend to adjust to that difference. Lingering worries continue over the degree to which it will not adjust.

LESSONS FROM PURCHASING POWER PARITY IDEAS

The purchasing power parity model highlights three important aspects of the price level problem:

1. Price level increases are relative to prices in other nations. Often a country with a trade deficit needs only to keep its inflation less than its trading partners' to restore purchasing power parity. Like a steady tennis player who just returns all shots and waits for the opponent to err, this nation holds back inflation while its trading partners let theirs plunge on. To a considerable extent this was true of the United States in the mid-1970s as its trading partners outinflated it and so strengthened the dollar. Still, the causes of inflation are so political and so deep seated that the inflation prone and the stability prone remain just that way. Germany, with its deeply rooted fear of inflation,

has constantly had smaller price increases than its less austere trading part-ners, leading to steady upward pressure on the German mark.

2. Purchasing power parity shows the policy options of the government noted at this chapter's beginning—to change the purchasing power of the currency with respect to domestic goods and services or to change the value of its cur-rency with respect to foreign currency.

3. Purchasing power explanations are only partial. Interest rates, investment climate, and expectations also play important roles. We know from Chapter 14 that Canada increased its interest rates well above American rates and borrowed more from abroad after 1987, and that it sterilized the 1987–1988 inflows so that its interest rates remained high.

With some idea of the value exchange rates might achieve without any cen-tral bank interference, we can ask what will happen if, in fact, the exchange rates do change and whether central banks should intervene in the market to maintain them at some estimated ideal value.

EXCHANGE RATE SHOCKS: CORRECTING PAYMENTS IMBALANCES

Can a devaluation improve a trade deficit? The simplicity of devaluation is that it immediately changes the price relationships between the domestic econ-omy and the rest of the world. Moreover, it does so *without* the difficulties of trying to push down a price level. Wages do not have to fall (in nominal terms) nor do prices. Almost immediately, the prices of exports rise as do the prices of import substitutes, making exports and import substitutes more profitable. Resources should then flow into exports and industries that compete with imports.

But price effects, whether a devaluation or a lowering of the price level, cannot end the trade imbalance unless they also change $S - I$ and $Y - A$. How can a price effect that changes the relation of exports and import substitutes to the prices of other goods also change saving or investment?

It can do so if there are many unemployed resources because income rises and with the rise in income comes increased saving. Take the problem in the form of an injections and leakages diagram. Figure 16.3 shows a situation in which a devaluation raises exports and lowers imports, thereby shifting $X - M$ upward. As it does so, it increases real income, and as real income increases, so does saving.

(FD 16.2) $\$\downarrow \rightarrow (X - M)\uparrow \rightarrow Y\uparrow \rightarrow S\uparrow$

But what if the country is already at full employment or is at a natural rate of unemployment—that is, as high an employment as can be achieved *in the long run* by expanding aggregate demand? Figure 16.4 shows this by marking the full-employment real income. No shift in $X - M$ alone will allow a solution to the trade problem. All possible equilibria that will solve the trade problem lie to the

Figure 16.3 **Devaluation on an injections and leakages diagram (with substantial unemployment).** A devaluation causes $X - M$ to shift upward. Because substantial unemployment exists, as aggregate demand rises real income increases, raising saving. The $X - M$ curve shifts along the $S - I$ curve. As a result $S - I = 0$ at the same point as $X - M$ does.

Injections and leakages

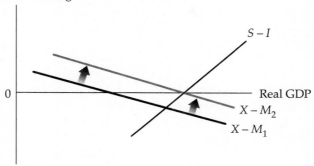

right of the full-employment point. In such cases, inflation will ensue, making exports more costly and imports cheaper, and $X - M$ will move back to its original position (but with the price level higher in the economy).

To modify the flow diagram, we could say:

(FD 16.3) $\$\downarrow \rightarrow (X - M)\uparrow \rightarrow P\uparrow \rightarrow (X - M)\downarrow$

Figure 16.4 **Devaluation at full employment I.** Figure 16.4 shows a devaluation sufficient to bring a trade balance at full employment. As in Fig. 16.3, $X - M_1$ rises to $X - M_2$ (the postdevaluation line), and it appears that saving should rise. Unfortunately, the point of equilibrium, marked by the arrow, is substantially to the right of the full-employment point, noted by a vertical dashed line. Unless we can figure some way that $S - I$ will shift upward to cross $X - M$ at the full-employment line, we cannot simultaneously solve the employment problem and the trade problem.

Injections and leakages

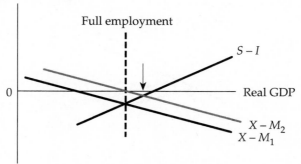

A decline in the value of the currency on the foreign exchange market causes the trade balance to improve and leads to an increase in the price level (given a fixed output), which in turn reverses the initial effects, causing $X - M$ to fall again.

Figure 16.5 shows the result we need: Some way has to be devised or discovered that will cause $S - I$ to rise as $X - M$ rises.

If a price effect moves $X - M$, can it also shift the $S - I$ curve? The answer is a qualified yes. As price effects move more resources into exports and import substitutes, which we will call the traded goods sector, that sector will crowd out investment, some consumption, and possibly some government spending. (Or as some economists write, the traded goods sector will crowd in.) The normal route for this would be a general rise in prices as aggregate demand rises, but higher increases for the traded goods sector. A higher money income means a greater demand for cash balances, and real interest rates will rise. In turn, this will choke off further investment and perhaps encourage some increased saving. Using the flow diagrams,

(FD 16.4) $\$\downarrow \to (X - M)\uparrow \to Y\uparrow$ or $P\uparrow \to i\uparrow \to I\downarrow, S\uparrow$

This is to say that a decline in a country's currency value (1) lowers the price of foreign exchange and so expands the trade sector $(X - M)$ and (2) in turn, the expanding trade sector raises the costs of investment. Only through this income-interest rate effect can devaluation shrink absorption, and bring S and I closer together.

This is not a particularly attractive solution, since it involves inflation. Clearly, if the monetary authorities decide that high interest rates are needed, it would be better if they just raised the rates, rather than waiting for inflation to perform the task. Moreover, we have not calculated what would happen to international capital flows. The increase in absorption could be largely accom-

---

Figure 16.5 **Devaluation at full employment II.** Only a simultaneous movement of $X - M$ and $S - I$ can solve both the trade deficit and employment problems simultaneously. In the diagram, $X - M$ shifts from $X - M_1$ to $X - M_2$, while an increase in saving or a decrease in investment causes $S - I_1$ to shift to $S - I_2$.

Injections and leakages

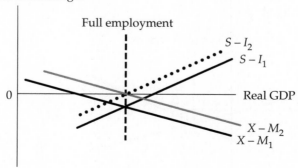

modated by increased foreign lending—hence little improvement in the trade deficit.

We have one other case in which $S - I$ will rise. If income increases temporarily, we could see short-term equilibrium at a point greater than full employment without inflation. The Hybrid model shows that real income can rise temporarily as a result of an increase in aggregate demand. Figure 16.6 shows this, with AD shifting from AD_1 to AD_2, and in the short run causing income to rise to $0b$.

Represented on a flow diagram:

$$(\text{FD 16.5}) \qquad \$\downarrow \rightarrow (X - M)\uparrow \begin{cases} \rightarrow Y\uparrow \rightarrow S\uparrow \\ \\ \rightarrow P\uparrow \rightarrow (X - M)\downarrow \end{cases}$$

The short-run effect is in the top line, as income and saving rise. The long-run effect is in the bottom line. While the short run leads to an apparently stable improvement, the long run leads nowhere.

Figure 16.4 showed that devaluation shifts $X - M$ upward, but that inflation will continue if $X - M = S - I$ to the right of full employment. Typically $S - I$ would fail to shift because the government increased the money supply, preventing the price of money from rising. As people leave the workforce and

---

Figure 16.6 **Devaluation produces a short-run rise in output.** The devaluation causes exports to rise and imports to fall such that aggregate demand rises from AD_1 to AD_2. This shift causes a short-run rise in employment, raising income from $0a$ to $0b$. That is only a temporary change, however, as people leave the workforce and those remaining can command higher nominal wages. As short run gives way to long, the price level rises from P_1 to P_2, and a new short-run AS curve will establish itself at P_2. If the country had a trade deficit at $0a$ before, it will have it there again, but at a higher price level.

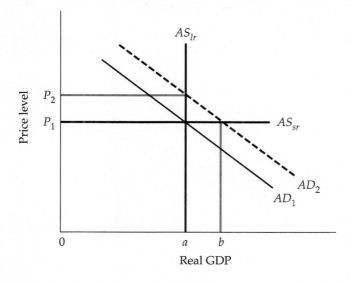

the country moves onto its long-run *AS* curve, $X - M$ will gradually move back to its deficit position, and the devaluation will have produced little but temporary help and a greater inflation. Figure 16.7 shows this move.

Effects such as those in which a devaluation turns into an inflation are often slow to show themselves. If the short run is long enough, or for some reason the long-run effect is unlikely to occur, the devaluation could be successful. Start with several situations in which it almost undoubtedly would work.

DEVALUATION (OR MANAGED DEPRECIATION) AS ADJUSTMENT

Devaluation may not always be an optimal or even a very good solution *if* it in itself contributes seriously to inflation. We begin, however, with some situations where devaluation is almost always the best solution.

THE ONCE-AND-FOR-ALL DEVALUATION AFTER GREAT INFLATION
Devaluation is an important means to reestablish a country's trade competitiveness after it has suffered a severe inflation. Cassel's original idea to use purchasing power as a guide to reestablishing exchange rates after general severe inflation was sound, and post–World War I Europe was almost an ideal place to use such a policy. Different rates of inflation in each of the countries, different borders, and vastly changed economic conditions had thrown the prewar exchange rates vastly out of alignment, and the simplest approach might have been a once-and-for-all resetting of exchange rates, with the high inflation countries devaluing. Instead, some of the countries undertook the monumental task of trying to force their price levels lower, a task they failed to accomplish.

Figure 16.7 **Devaluation followed by inflation.** Because the relationship of saving to investment is changed only temporarily by the devaluation, the effect is also temporary. $X - M$ rises from $X - M_1$ to $X - M_2$, but as inflation continues, exports decline and imports rise, and $X - M_2$ shifts back to $X - M_1$. Note that the horizontal axis is in real terms.

Injections and leakages

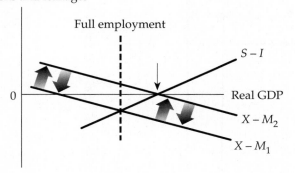

DEVALUATION AFTER EXCHANGE CONTROL   Devaluation is also effective after a country has gone through a period of exchange control. Typically, the country with exchange control has undergone considerably more inflation than its trading partners. Foreign exchange has been scarce and therefore costly. Consider the experience of Peru after the Second World War. The Peruvian currency in those days was the sol, and in 1945 it was worth about 15.5 U.S. cents, or 6.5 soles to the dollar. Under pressure from powerful urban interest groups, the government tried to keep the price of imported food and other essentials down by fixing the exchange rate at the 1945 level, even though inflation was moving along at 30% a year or so. As Peruvian prices rose, imports appeared cheaper, and many people wanted to import. Lacking sufficient foreign exchange, the government established an exchange control system, rationing foreign exchange and issuing permits to purchase it only to those it favored. Exporters suffered because the government insisted they turn over all their foreign exchange earnings and receive only 6.5 soles per dollar. Exports of mining products and cotton fell considerably.

Figure 16.8 demonstrates what happened.

Exchange control, in effect, causes a hidden devaluation by making the black or grey market price for imports very high. By discouraging exports, it decreases the foreign goods available. So the formal devaluation that follows may not in fact lead to an increase in price levels. It is simply a necessary and effective policy.

The next situation is one where devaluation might work, but the wisdom of using it is more questionable.

DEVALUATION TO STIMULATE A LAGGING ECONOMY   For a nation with substantial unemployment far to the left of where AS_{sr} and AS_{lr} meet, devaluation looks like an attractive way to increase national income. Some nations have used devaluation for just that purpose. France in the late 1920s under the pretext of going on the gold standard purchased gold extensively, thereby increasing the supply of francs and holding down the value of the French franc.[4]

The difficulty with using devaluation to stimulate income comes in the hidden assumption of the income diagram—the horizontality of the aggregate supply curve. The devaluation will increase real income only insofar as there is a pool of unemployed labor (and other idle factors) that, because prices are rigid in a downward direction, cannot be employed at current prices and wages. Besides, income that comes from a trade surplus, while it does cut foreign debt, does not by definition contribute to absorption. So it is only the added consumption from the multiplier effect that is a net contribution to absorption. That is, you cannot eat (or absorb) your exports.

Perhaps it is best that devaluations are not often successful in stimulating large increases in income because such policies are successful only insofar as they make beggars of their neighbors. France's trade surplus in the late 1920s was Britain's deficit, and whatever additional *AD* was created in France came at the

Figure 16.8 **Peru under exchange control, 1945–1950.** The Peruvian government rationed its expected foreign exchange receipts (represented as dollars) at the line marked *Quota*. At a price of 6.5 soles to the dollar, exporters were forced to limit their exports, and they brought in only the Quota amount of dollars. Demand, however, was great at 6.5, amounting to Q^*. Since that amount could not be supplied, all those who wanted dollars between the Quota and Q^* could not get them. Measured by the scarcity, the sol was actually worth no more than about 5 cents or 21 to the dollar. (This would be a guess for the actual situation, but the black market price was even higher.) So when devaluation did come about in 1948–1950, the sol went to about 14 per dollar or 7 cents. Was that a decline in value from 15 cents (6.5/$) or a rise from 5 cents (21/$)? Exports did recover, and whatever chaos has descended upon that unhappy country since, economic policy in the 1950s was on the whole successful.

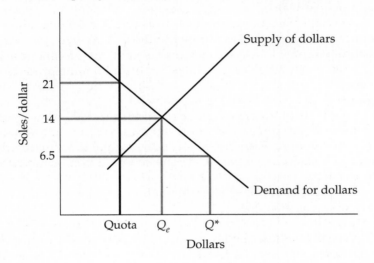

expense of lower *AD* in the United Kingdom. If the policy makers are going to be Keynesian, there are surely better ways to expand aggregate demand than beggaring one's neighbor.

DEVALUATION AS A CAUSE OF INFLATION

It is possible that the price effects of devaluation could in themselves cause inflation, undoing to a greater or lesser extent the price adjustment they are seeking to make. This would be most awkward, yet it can occur. Consider several possibilities.

LIMITED PRICE EFFECTS OF DEVALUATION   Unless they follow exchange control, devaluations usually have price-level effects. The rise in price of imports will almost undoubtedly shift AS_{sr} upward, and AD may also shift to the right because more export will be sold and more import substitutes bought at existing domestic prices. How far will the price rise? One argument says that, even though the price level rises, it should not rise as much as the prices of traded goods. That, after all, is where the pressure for increased prices originates. Any inflation that would completely undo the effects of the devaluation would remove the stimulus for the price increases. The domestic inflation would dampen the price effect of devaluation, weakening its effectiveness.[*]

Consider the possible inflationary effects of a devaluation in the United States during the Reagan years. If the U.S. dollar had fallen earlier and further than it did, and the trade balance moved toward surplus, the goods and services from abroad that amounted to 2 to 3% of GNP would no longer be available. Unless absorption fell, there would be inflation. That inflation would partially undo the effect of the devaluation, perhaps requiring another devaluation. Yet eventually, the policy would be successful.

Consider the question in percentage terms. The U.S. imports about 10% of its goods and services. A fall in the value of the dollar by 20% could increase the price of imports by that amount, but that would be only a 2% increase in all costs. Even that is unlikely because oil prices are stated in dollar terms and many other exporters to the United States would hold their prices down. In an economy such as Canada's, which imports far more and would likely pay the full amount of the price increase, the change is not enormous. Twenty percent of 39% is 6%. That increase is far less than the 20% decrease in the Canadian dollar. Even if that 6% did cause some further rounds, it is unlikely it would reach 20%. In such a case, although the decline in the dollar would cause some increase in the price level, it would be insufficient to counter the exchange rate effect.

A MICROECONOMIC ARGUMENT FOR HIGHER PRICES   There is still a stronger argument against devaluation, one that sounds at first hearing a bit off the wall—namely that any devaluation will raise all domestic prices by the percentage of the devaluation. The reasoning is based on two things: (1) that the high correlation between purchasing power and exchange rate changes may be one in which the exchange rate drives the purchasing power and (2) that, with the prices of exports and imports higher, the opportunity costs for any potentially exportable good or any potential import substitute rises. The first argument is a debater's point in the sense that correlations do not show which of two factors is the independent variable. The second point is of more interest.

We can show the opportunity cost argument with the demand and supply models from earlier chapters. Essentially, the price of imports determines not only prices of imported goods, but also those of import-competing goods as well. Figure 16.9 is simply a variation of the ones Chapter 4 showed to illustrate the effects of a tariff.

The effect is similar for exports. As exports rise in value, it is not only the exported widgets themselves, but all the widgets that were sold domestically that rise in price.

---

[*] Such an effect cannot exceed whatever it is dampening; if you drop a ball, the second bounce cannot be higher than the first one.

Figure 16.9 **The limit price argument.** Before devaluation, the price of imported widgets is P_1. After devaluation it is P_2. It is not just imported widgets Q_1Q_4 that will rise in price, but all the imported widgets and domestic widgets as well: $0Q_3$. Devaluation, accordingly, increases prices across large sectors of the economy.

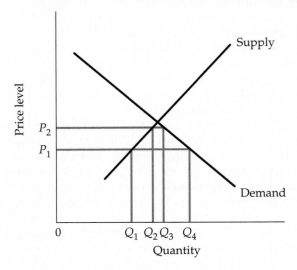

The argument, then, holds that the price-level change will equal the devaluation, canceling out any advantage:

(FD 16.6) $\$\downarrow \rightarrow$ $\begin{array}{l} \rightarrow (X-M)\uparrow \\ \\ \rightarrow P\uparrow \rightarrow (X-M)\downarrow \end{array}$

The dollar falls in value. The first line shows that the exchange rate effect leads to an improvement in the balance of trade. The second line, however, shows that prices are driven up, such that the price-level effect cancels out some or all of the first line's effects.

Note that these are partial equilibrium arguments. Could a 20% devaluation cause *all* prices to rise by 20%? That is unlikely. If the money supply is unchanged, it is even more unlikely. Certainly, the velocity of money could rise, but that is not a limitless phenomenon. If incomes do not rise or do not rise sharply, people will have less money left over for other goods after purchasing their widgets, and the prices of *other* goods should fall. Aggregate demand should rise, as explained above, but the impact on prices would ordinarily be much less than the percentage of devaluation.

Examine the question in terms of an AD/AS diagram.

Figure 16.10, using the Hybrid model, illustrates both macro and micro elements to the argument. Before devaluation, long-run AS is AS_{lr_1}, AD is as shown, and the price level is P_1. After devaluation, AS_{sr} rises to AS_{sr_2}, and the price level

Figure 16.10 **Cost-push factors in devaluation.** A devaluation of 20% to a currency in a country with imports 30% of GNP could have two different results. The upward shift of AS_{sr} represents substantial cost-push inflation, producing substantial unemployment. The shift of AS_{lr} to the left, however, represents the loss in goods and services available, and, without a cost-push element, produces a smaller price and income effect.

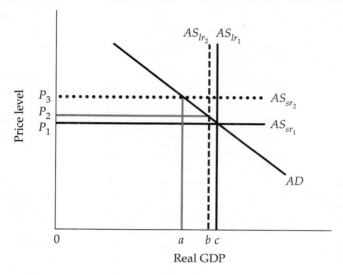

increases by the full amount of the devaluation—from P_1 to P_3, which in the example above was 20%. These price increases are too high to allow the market to clear at former output levels, given the level of aggregate demand, and output falls from $0c$ to $0a$.

AS_{lr_1} represents the actual decline in goods and services available after the devaluation, which is only 6% in the example above. The actual price increase experienced depends on the slope of AD.[5] The lower rewards for working do not cause many people to leave the workforce. With employment nearly the same, output will not fall nearly as much as the limit price argument implies.

The problem is that in the short run the producers of exports and import substitutes are having to bid resources away from their existing uses by offering higher prices. They can do so, given the devaluation. But price rigidity slows the transfer of those resources as prices do not fall elsewhere in the economy. Unemployment is thus much more severe in the short than in the long run and the government will be sorely tempted to increase aggregate demand to alleviate it. If AD rises, then a price-level effect will undo the exchange rate effect.

DEVALUATION AND INFLATIONARY EXPECTATIONS   Add now another element: *expectations.* Suppose that devaluation has been frequent. Labor unions and managers expect a certain degree of inflation and set their bargain and their prices (to the extent they can) with a degree of inflation built in. People who might only demand a real 2% increase in wages will find themselves demanding

10% if they expect an 8% inflation. Exporters and producers of import substitutes know that they will come in for a period of low margins with perhaps some unemployment as inflation increases costs and the exchange rate does not change. But periodic devaluations reduce that constraint. That is, indeed, what devaluations are supposed to do to keep the economy operating efficiently. The problem is that it removes any constraints on the next round of wage and price increases. Figure 16.11 shows a process of escalating inflation.

Now, *if* workers could not expect a devaluation and *if* firms could not count on raising prices, they would order their affairs differently. Moreover, *if* governments cannot count on devaluation to end payments problems, they, too, will try to keep inflation down. So, goes the argument, a fixed exchange rate, tied to a currency of a low-inflation country, will feed back into more moderate wage demands. While there may be some temporary unemployment and bankruptcies as those firms who doubt the government's will are shown to be wrong, eventually the cost-push elements will be controlled.

Figure 16.11 **Devaluation and inflation with rational expectations.** This figure adds expectations to the mix. Assume, as in Fig. 16.10, that devaluation has produced a temporary increase in income to $0c$, followed by a gradual adjustment of employment levels and prices that has moved the short-run aggregate supply curve from AS_{sr_1} to AS_{sr_2}. Output now falls back to $0b$, where the long-run AS curve is placed. Since saving is lower at a lower real income, the current account deficit would return. In the next round of wage settlements and price setting, employees and companies set their prices deliberately high, anticipating greater inflation and another devaluation. The short-run AS curve then rises to AS_{sr_3}. Output falls to $0a$. The lower real income may help the trade balance by causing investment to decline, but it is unacceptably low. The government could restore full employment at output level $0b$, but would soon find the price level at P_3; worse, it would still have a trade imbalance, just as it had at $0b$ before. If it devalues the currency again, AD rises to AD_4. But again AS shifts to AS_{sr_4} at P_4, and round after round continues.

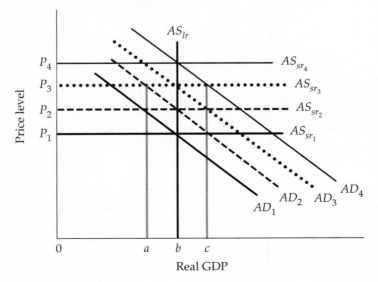

We have not given the argument above all its theoretical vestments. It has a following among both European central bankers and international organizations. Most of the models, usually mathematical, show that it is important for the government to have a *credible commitment,* or to achieve credibility, and for the anticipations to be consistent with what the government will do. Credible policies show two important effects: a moderation of the inflation and a reduction in dislocation. We have spoken of the former, but let us address the latter.

If wages and prices are set too high, expecting an increase in aggregate demand that does not occur, unemployment will be considerable, lasting a long period of time, and capacity utilization will fall, reducing profits. If wages and prices are set too high for exports in anticipation of a devaluation that does not occur, then those industries will experience unemployment, poor capacity utilization, and perhaps bankruptcy. If people respond fairly quickly to the unemployment by lowering wages and to the undercapacity by lowering prices and bargaining harder on wage deals, realizing that their expectations were proving wrong, then the dip in employment and profits may be short. Economists call this *adaptive expectations.* If, however, everyone believes the government and immediately jumps to the solution, there will be very little displacement. Wages and prices will not rise much and the government will not be tempted to expand aggregate demand to catch up with the rising costs. Economists describe this as forward-looking rational expectations with credible commitment. Devaluation will be unnecessary. As a consequence, the economy fares better.[6]

While this may seem a very rosy prediction, it is a key factor in the reasoning many countries have for joining the European Monetary System (described in Chapter 18), which ties their currencies to the German mark. It clearly lay behind the strategies of John Major in the United Kingdom and of Ireland, where it is cited as being a major factor in the decline of inflation and control of the trade deficit. In 1991 Sweden joined the European Monetary System to try to end its successive rounds of devaluation and inflation.

The Irish case is of particular interest. After the very large current account deficits Ireland ran in the 1970s and early 1980s (discussed in Chapter 10), it began to fix its exchange rate against an average of European rates.[*] It was then able to cut its rate of inflation (to less than 3% in 1990) and achieve current account surpluses from 1987 onward. Growth rose to 5% a year. Unfortunately, unemployment, which was running around 15%, continued at those high rates. Note, however, that unemployment did not worsen, nor is there any evidence that it is responsive to macroeconomic measures. Certainly, the use of high aggregate demand in the 1970s and early 1980s had little or no effect on its level.[7]

HANGING TOUGH   The final decades of the twentieth century are witnessing a move away from Keynesian aggregate demand adjustment, with the notable

---

[*] Previously, Ireland had fixed its exchange rate to the British pound, which meant frequent devaluations or periods of depreciation against other currencies.

exception of the United States. The reasons may be practical rather than theoretical; policy makers are concluding that expanding aggregate demand, particularly through lowering interest rates, no longer works, and may even have reluctantly concluded that rates of unemployment are naturally much higher than most people would like to think. A view that an economy must adjust to an exchange rate, rather than vice versa, is consistent with other policy objectives. Employers argue to their employees that further wage increases are impossible because price increases are impossible since they expect no inflation or devaluation and "international competition is tough." If they do grant higher wages, the government is immovable, having tied its hands by selecting a fixed rate (and an independent central bank governor).

Whether this is a tough new world or simply the old one looked at more realistically is moot.

REVALUATION (UPWARD VALUATION)

To this point the discussion has centered on devaluation. Partly, this derives from the ease of explaining models in just one context. But countries adjust their exchange rates upward as well as downward, and not all of the models can be reversed.

In the great exchange rate crisis of 1971–1972, it was not the United States that devalued, but Germany, Japan, and Switzerland that revalued. Why should it be the countries with heavy current and capital account inflows that make the change? After all, while a heavy capital inflow is not to an economist a good thing, it is not as bad as having a heavy outflow. Often the onus is on the troubled debtor, not the grumbling creditor.

The answer lies in what we saw in Chapter 14: It is impossible for most countries to sterilize a heavy inflow on the balance of payments. The central bank must sell the treasury bills that it has into what is, with the exception of the United States and Britain, a small market. The supply of treasury bills is limited, and so is the sterilization. The deficit country, meanwhile, can go on creating money and particularly so when the government itself is running a deficit, continually creating new treasury bills for the central bank to buy. So it was the creditor countries that cracked first under the strain.

Germany and Switzerland did not want their money supplies to rise and create an inflation. That might have corrected the payments problems, but they viewed the cost of inflation as too great. They therefore opted for revaluation to make their exports less competitive and increase their imports.

THE JOKER IN THE DECK: MARSHALL-LERNER EFFECT AND J-CURVES

To this point, the short-run problem of most significance has been that of the unemployment that might be generated if the short-run *AS* curve rises after devaluation. There is another quite serious effect, also short-run and also dangerous. It is possible that an exchange rate change will have a short-run price effect opposite that expected. As production and consumption fail to respond positively to price changes, but lag behind, a trade imbalance may become significantly worse before it starts to get better. We see why in the section below.

THE NECESSARY DEMAND CONDITIONS

Up to now, we have assumed that devaluation or a planned depreciation will have price effects to help end a trade deficit. What if it did not? Such a thing is possible, although there is some debate as to its likelihood. The Marshall-Lerner theory (after Abba Lerner, who took one of Alfred Marshall's models to illustrate these points) conjures up a specter to haunt policy makers who try devaluations. What the M-L theory says, in essence, is that a devaluation will not work if the demand for a nation's exports and that nation's demand for imports are highly inelastic; to be more precise, the two elasticities, added together, must exceed 1, or the devaluation will make the trade balance worse. As the flow diagram would express it:

(FD 16.7) $$\$\downarrow \rightarrow (X - M)\downarrow$$

It is perverse for a decline in the value of a currency to cause a worsening of the trade balance, but it might happen.

Take a simple example. Suppose the U.S. dollar and the Canadian dollar are, as they were for a number of years, at par—a U.S. dollar equals a Canadian dollar. Suppose further that the Canadians spend about $100 million a month on imports from the United States and the Americans spend $100 million on imports from Canada. Now suppose Canada devalues its dollar by 20%. Will the devaluation increase Canadian exports and decrease imports?

Suppose the Canadian demand for imports is highly inelastic—indeed, it has an elasticity of zero. It certainly would be low in the very short run because almost all the imports have already been ordered and virtually all are invoiced in U.S. dollars. The Canadians would therefore import the same quantity of U.S. goods, and would have to pay 20% more for them. The result: 120 million Canadian dollars on the market where there had been only 100 million before.

And to make things more difficult, suppose the Americans had a demand for Canadian exports of zero elasticity.[*] Since the Americans do not need any more imports from Canada, they will pay only 80 cents for the Canadian dollar—and only 80 million U.S. dollars are put on the market. Those dollars equal 100 million Canadian dollars at the new exchange rate of US$0.80 = C$1. The result: a trade deficit of 20 million Canadian dollars. Summarized in Table 16.1, it is Set 1, the first pair of comparisons.

---

[*] This is actually unlikely even in the very short run because most of the invoices are also in U.S. dollars.

Table 16.1   **Effect of 20% devaluation of Canadian dollar under different elasticity assumptions**

Set	Importer	Elasticity	US$		C$	Balance of trade
1	Canadian	0			120	
	U.S.	0	80	=	100	−20
2	Canadian	0			120	
	U.S.	1	100	=	120	0
3	Canadian	1			100	
	U.S.	0	80	=	100	0
4	Canadian	.75	85	=	102	
	U.S.	.75	92	=	115	+13

Now suppose the demand elasticity of Canada's imports was still zero, but that its exports had an elasticity of 1—that is, a 20% decrease in price triggers a 20% increase in volume, which means total revenue is unchanged (Set 2 in Table 16.1). In such a situation, Canada's importers would respond by placing 120 million Canadian dollars on the market, but the American importers would offer the same 100 million U.S. dollars. The value in Canadian dollars of those $100 million is C$120. The balance of trade is unchanged. The chart shows this in the second pair.

Or we could suppose as in the third pair that the elasticity of Canada's imports was 1, and that of the United States for Canadian exports was zero. In that case we find 100 million Canadian dollars trading for 80 million U.S. dollars. The US$80 million is worth C$100 million, which again gives us no change in the trade balance.

The two extreme examples with an elasticity of zero and the other of 1 just meet the *Marshall-Lerner* condition that *the sum of the two elasticities must at least equal 1 for the balance of trade to improve.* The same would be true of any other combination of elasticities—for example, 0.5 for each of the demands.

Anything that adds up to more than 1 will improve the balance of trade. Set 4 shows a situation in which both the demand for imports and the demand for Canada's exports are inelastic (0.75), but the effect is quite positive. Canadian importers reduce their consumption of American goods to US$85 million, worth 102 million Canadian dollars. The U.S. importers from Canada will spend 15% more Canadian dollars, but need only purchase them at 80 cents, so will offer 92 million U.S. dollars. The trade balance improves by C$13 million.

ELASTICITIES IN PRACTICE—AN ASSESSMENT

Most economists agree that nearly always there exist the minimum elasticities required to avoid the *Marshall-Lerner bind.* A.C. Harberger's studies have shown that the short-run elasticities of demand for imports into a typical country are at least as high as 0.5 or 1, while the elasticity of demand for the same typical country's exports is at least 2 and usually higher. The result is that the Marshall-

Lerner minimum conditions (that the sum of the elasticities of the demands for a nation's imports and exports exceed 1) are almost always satisfied.

Theoretically, a number of factors contribute to the adequacy of the elasticities. The first is the question of time. The longer the time period, the higher the elasticities. In the very short run (usually a few months) elasticities are probably very low. As noted in the discussion of Canada above, the currency of invoice is important. Most trade is invoiced in U.S. dollars, and therefore a country devaluing against the U.S. dollar will find that its imports, already ordered or on the way, do not fall, and its importers simply have to fork up the extra money to pay for these imports. The saving grace here, however, is that exports are also invoiced in U.S. dollars, so the U.S. importers cannot reduce the amount of U.S. dollars they have agreed to pay. Accordingly, the situation will tend toward the very minimum Marshall-Lerner condition with the sum of the elasticities close to 1.

The opposite occurs if the nation devaluing is also the nation of the currency of invoice—the United States would find that import prices would not rise immediately, but export prices would not fall either. Again, the Marshall-Lerner condition would be just barely met.

The demand for imports is usually far more elastic than that for the goods themselves. The reason is that as imports fall in price, they not only increase the total sales of the good, but also displace domestic supplies.

Elasticities of imports are also fairly high because of the increasing amount of substitutability. A great deal of trade, as Chapter 3 showed, is intraindustrial—that is, trade within the same industry, as automobiles for automobiles, appliances for appliances, or airplanes for airplanes. Because such goods are close substitutes, elasticities are high.[8]

THREE LAST BRACING THOUGHTS ON MARSHALL-LERNER

1. *If devaluations will not work, lowering the price level will not work either.* Almost all the discussion of Marshall-Lerner is in the context of devaluation, yet the alternative of deflation (price effects only) depends equally on the two elasticities of demand for imports being high enough. The world is in a fine state if neither deflation nor depreciation works, because all that leaves for policy is the reduction of national incomes.

2. *If income effects eventually become price effects, recession will not work either,* because the price system will ultimately adjust. As prices of exports fall because of highly inelastic demand, foreign exchange receipts will fall, and as import prices rise, import demand will not be choked off enough. The only reason why lowering the price level might look as if it would work is that it is a more gradual process than devaluation and might avoid the downward section on the J-curve, to be explained below.

3. *If devaluation does not work, an increase in the value of a nation's currency will work.* That suggestion takes the breath away. Logically, this is true, yet no nation has ever proceeded to carry this out, which suggests that few people believe that Marshall-Lerner conditions prevail.

J-CURVES

Typically, a country that devalues its currency sees a fall or no improvement in its trade balance for several months or longer, and then an improvement. If we plot the trade balance against the time period, the result looks like a J as in Fig. 16.2. Since Marshall-Lerner type effects are most likely in the very short run, it is quite possible that a country's trade deficit will worsen immediately after a devaluation or depreciation of its currency. It is likely that the full effects of the price change will take some time to work their way through the economic system. Some of the nonprice changes noted above may take even more time to be effective. As the months move on, the trade balance ceases to worsen; then, as the elasticities rise, it begins to improve, often quite rapidly. In such cases, the devaluing country must have the foreign exchange funds to prevent further declines in its currency over the initial few months after devaluation.

If the bottom of the J is deep or wide, such that recovery does not appear to be taking place, the country may be tempted to devalue again. Or under floating rates, the market itself may perceive that no improvement will come forth and force a further depreciation. J-curve becomes added onto J-curve in such a situation, which can worsen rapidly, as Fig. 16.13 shows.

If a country faces a J-curve effect, it must have the foreign exchange funds to prevent further declines in its currency over the initial few months after devaluation. Otherwise it might face new pressures for devaluation and put itself once again in the downward-sloping part of the J. One of the problems suggested for floating rates has been that without monetary intervention, the exchange rate will keep declining, putting the country into situations where the demand and supply of imports are highly inelastic. Such a pattern has been suggested for the United States in the 1980s, although a recent article argues strongly against that interpretation.[9]

Figure 16.12 **J-curve effect.** The country devalues at point *a*. The ensuing months see the balance of trade worsen to point *b*, whereupon it improves. At point *c* it is the same as it was when devaluation occurred. At point *d*, the trade deficit ceases. The critical period is *a–c*, the width of the J.

Trade balance

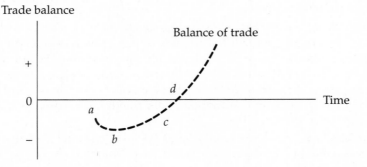

Figure 16.13 **Repeated devaluations and successive J-curves.** A series of repeated devaluations or declines in the value of a currency cause a series of J curves to form. Because the market (or central bank) does not wait until the curve begins to turn upward, it keeps introducing new price declines. As a result, the balance of trade appears to worsen, following the line more or less tangent with the edges of the J-curves.

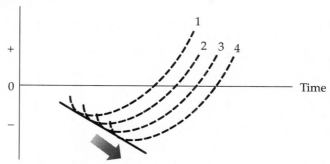

SUCCESSIVE J-CURVES: THE EXPERIENCE OF NEW ZEALAND

New Zealand provides some evidence of both kinds of J-curves, as shown in Fig. 16.14. In the early 1980s New Zealand let the N.Z. dollar fall and saw some response in improved trade. Like Sweden, however, New Zealand was unable to control its inflation. In the later 1980s it let the dollar tumble. We can see some lagged effects of this strategy, but again, the underlying problems were not solved.

PROTECTIONISM AND ADJUSTMENT

A final way, often suggested, to correct a payments deficit is to increase trade barriers. But attempts to protect an economy from import competition cannot over the long haul aid the trade balance. The fundamental need is to change $S - I$, but all protectionism does is to reduce the volume of trade. The effect of the restricted imports will be to cause prices to rise or the exchange rate to fall, in either case making it more difficult to export.

Take the example of the United States seeking to protect domestic industries threatened by imports and also to increase its exports. If we look at the exchange rate alone as an adjustment mechanism, protection would cause a decline in the quantity of dollars spent for imports. With fewer dollars, the dollar rises and other currencies fall. The result is that other countries will buy fewer U.S. products than before and the United States will buy less from abroad, assuming normal elasticities satisfying the Marshall-Lerner condition. Thus any interference with trade sets in motion a correcting mechanism.

Figure 16.14 **New Zealand: J-curve 1979–1985.** The New Zealand dollar depreciated in value considerably during the 1979 to 1985 period, as indicated by the solid light line, which corresponds to the value of the N.Z. dollar on the right-hand axis. The trade balance, which is measured along the left-hand axis, followed the dotted lines. There appear to be three J-curves in this period, one following the depreciation of the N.Z. dollar during 1979, a second following the slide of the dollar in 1981, and a third following its continued slide in 1982. The 1984 devaluation did not show a significant J effect.

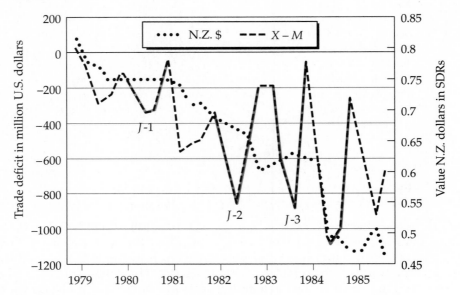

The particular importance of this point for the United States in the 1980s is that a high dollar stimulated imports and eroded exports, leading to a rise in protectionist sentiments. But the urge to protect, if followed through, *would appreciate the currency still more, with further stimulus to imports and harm to exports.* The mechanism works both to limit the effectiveness of the protective measures and to damage the export sector.

Suppose the United States were able to hold the dollar from rising; what would happen then? The price system will do the work. With the dollar not rising in value as imports are restricted, the price level would rise, and rise faster than the U.S. trading partners', whose exports to the United States would be falling. As aggregate demand remained high, pressures on the price level would be upward. Moreover, the increase in protectionism would decrease efficiency and move the aggregate supply curve to the left, compounding the problem.

The conclusion: Protectionism does not work to improve a trade balance. Either it forces the currency to rise in value in relation to others, or it causes the price level to rise. On top of it all, it makes the economy less efficient, worsening productivity.

CONCLUSION

Exchange rate adjustment can, in some situations, effectively counterbalance past increases in the price level and adjust a country's trade competitiveness—that is, bring it closer to a trade balance. Extensive studies of purchasing power parities show that exchange rates do indeed tend to follow differences in purchasing power. Cause and effect are unclear, however—is it the price level driving the exchange rate or the other way around? Thus exchange rate changes can be destabilizing and set in train unwanted price and income effects. The problem is compounded because a devaluation or managed depreciation that works in the short run may not work in the long run, and continued devaluations may signal an acquiescence to wage and price pressures that encourages more reckless behavior on the part of firms and their workers.

Individual nations need not act in isolation, however. Together, many nations can design international systems that will survive crises and introduce a predictability into international macroeconomic policy and banking that is beneficial, domestically and internationally. Sometimes they can act together strongly enough to convince the markets of their correctness, or at least of the folly of opposing what a group of countries wants to do. The next two chapters take up the questions of international policy and systems.

VOCABULARY AND CONCEPTS

Adaptive expectations
Appreciation
Credible commitment
Depreciation
Devaluation
Hidden devaluation
J-curve

Marshall-Lerner condition
Overvaluation
Purchasing power parity
Revaluation
Undervaluation
Limit price

QUESTIONS

1. Why is it difficult to establish the comparative values of two currencies by measuring what people can actually buy with each?

2. What are the arguments for and against the idea that purchasing power ultimately determines exchange rates?

3. What are some of the statistical problems involved in using purchasing power parity? To what extent do they affect the possible use of conclusions drawn from such estimates?

4. Demonstrate, using the $S - I = X - M$ framework, the conditions under which a devaluation would help improve a balance of trade and in which it would not.

5. Using the AD/AS framework, explain how a devaluation might improve the balance of trade in the short run, but not in the long run.

6. In their younger days, Brown and Hogendorn were far more optimistic about the way in which changes in the values of currencies could correct trade deficits. Why might they have grown far more cautious (that is to say, even changed their minds)?

7. Figure 16.10 shows two arguments: (a) Prices will rise because goods in the trade sector are

more expensive, and (b) All prices will rise by approximately the value of the devaluation. What are the initial changes in output and price level under each assumption? What happens if the government and monetary authorities increase *AD* to increase employment, at least as far as 0*b*? Given that open economy output has fallen to 0*b*, and price stability is a goal, what would be an appropriate long-run response for *AD* management? In which situations will the balance of trade improve, and why?

8. What did he mean when the economics guru proclaimed:

"A devaluation and a deflation
Are One.
A devaluation, a deflation, and a recession,
Are One."?

9. Explain the conditions under which a devaluation would tend to work to right a balance of trade deficit, and under what circumstances it would not do so.

10. "A country that has had extensive exchange control may not have any serious price consequences from devaluation." Why?

11. What are the reasons for suspecting that a devaluation could cause an inflation? Would that inflation be so large as to overcome the exchange rate effect? How are such arguments linked to ideas of cost-push inflation?

12. What is the role of expectation in inflations stimulated or validated by devaluations?

13. Explain the Marshall-Lerner effect and why it might be present only for the short run. What is the relation of the Marshall-Lerner effect to the J-curve?

14. Explain what a J-curve is and how it can complicate the beneficial effects of devaluation.

15. "Consider the match between the basic general equilibrium theoretical conclusions on trade and the macroeconomic mechanisms. Neither shows that protectionism helps improve a trade balance. Rather, overall trade declines." Explain and evaluate.

NOTES

[1] The purchasing powers were figured using the U.S. Wholesale Price Index, and after that series stopped, the U.S. Finished Goods Producer Price Index, and the Canadian Industrial Selling Price.

[2] This is one of the arguments mounted against purchasing power parity in Lawrence Summers and Chris Carroll, "Why is U.S. national saving so low?" *Brookings Papers on Economic Activity*, Vol. 2, 1987, pp. 607–635.

[3] *International Financial Statistics* has a table, Real Effective Exchange Rates, located shortly before the country tables that shows the results of using the various indexes. See Chapter 18 for further discussion of this topic.

[4] See Leland Yeager, *International Monetary Relations*, New York, Harper and Row, 1986, pp. 285–286.

[5] More precisely, it depends on the elasticity of *AD*. If the elasticity of *AD* is less than 1, prices will rise more than the percentage shift in AS.

[6] A typical and accessible (for students with some mathematical background) use of the different types of expectations is in Ralph C. Bryant, John F. Helliwell, and Peter Hooper, "Domestic and cross-border consequences of U.S. macroeconomic policies," in Ralph

Bryant et al., eds., *Macroeconomic Policies in an Interdependent World,* IMF and Centre for Economic Policy Research, 1989, pp. 59–115. The latter part discusses expectations.

[7] See Jeroen J.M. Kremers, "Gaining policy credibility for a disinflation," *IMF Staff Papers,* March 1990, pp. 116–145. See also *The Economist,* May 25, 1991, p. 111.

[8] In the short run, trade that is intrafirm may be less elastic. A firm that builds a plant in one country to supply a plant in another cannot quickly switch when the exchange rate changes. That is a situation that is particularly important in the trade of intermediate goods. See, for instance, Jane Sneddon Little, "Intrafirm trade: An update," *New England Economic Review,* Federal Reserve Bank of Boston, May/June, 1987, pp. 46–51.

[9] The Federal Reserve Board's Ellen E. Meade concluded in a recent article that the J part was relatively shallow (for the United States) and that we cannot explain the U.S. balance-of-payments problem as a series of continuing J-curve effects. The article has some general discussion of interest also. "Exchange rates, adjustment and the J-curve," *Federal Reserve Bulletin,* October 1988, pp. 633–644.

Chapter 17

International Macroeconomic Policy I

Overall Objective: To develop a systemic approach to international economic arrangements, stressing the interrelationships of the exchange rate system with national economic responses and policies.

MORE SPECIFICALLY:

- To develop a historical background to understand the successes and failures of the gold standard, the interwar period, and the Bretton Woods system.

- To relate the exchange rate systems, domestic policies, extent of flexibility, sustainability of trade imbalances, and degree of international cooperation to the functioning of the arrangements in each period.

- To demonstrate the basic elements of the Bretton Woods system, including the adjustable peg, the International Monetary Fund, and reserve currencies.

To this point the text has looked at economic policies largely from a national viewpoint, rather than from an international perspective. Its concern has been, for instance, how a fixed or a floating rate affects an individual nation, not how a *system* of floating or fixed rates affects all nations. Chapters 17 and 18 change perspective, looking at issues and institutions that affect the entire system. The question at hand is what kind of international currency arrangement effectively helps trade and international investment, yet at the same time promotes growth, high employment, and price stability. That in itself is a tall order for domestic policy, but in an integrated world domestic policy alone will not achieve it. To see how it might be done, the text turns to look at the international system itself.

AN INTERNATIONAL SYSTEM

In a *system,* the parts are related so that a change in any one part affects another. Moreover, a system is usually comprehensive, so that it includes all elements that mutually affect one another. One part of any international arrangement, for instance, is the type of exchange rate system. Fixed rates, in comparison with floating rates, require more reserves, another part of any international system. After all, if monetary authorities never intervene in the foreign exchange market, they do not need to hold any foreign exchange reserves. What Chapter 17 does is to define the elements of the system and then view their development in historical perspective. Chapter 18 looks at the present system and toward the future.

The following are the elements of the system:

1. *The exchange rate system:* the extent to which and patterns by which exchange rates change.
2. *Rules or guidelines:* the prescriptions for domestic economies to adjust to international disturbances.
3. *Economic flexibility:* how easily and quickly domestic price and employment patterns adjust to changes.
4. *Sustainability of imbalances:* the extent to which private capital markets, monetary reserves, and governmental borrowing and lending allow imbalances to persist.
5. *International cooperation:* the extent to which several governments harmonize their macro or micro policies to work internationally toward reducing or accepting payments imbalances.

The way in which these elements of the system have evolved over the last century shows how the system as a whole worked, and provides essential background for thinking of the future. We turn to that now.

THE INTERNATIONAL SYSTEM UNDER THE GOLD STANDARD

The classic gold standard, 1870–1914, had permanently fixed exchange rates, a few well-understood rules about how to handle payments troubles, a limited reserve base of gold, more price flexibility in countries' economies, little need for international coordination of policies, and, withal, quite high levels of international trade imbalances. Trade and capital movements grew rapidly during the period and price levels were stable or falling. The gold standard was also associated with a series of financial panics and recessions, which may have unnecessarily reduced economic growth and employment. The following section explores how and why it worked.

THE GOLD STANDARD IN ITS PRIME

Before the advent of paper currency and central banks, coinage was in gold or silver (*specie*), and a nation's monetary base was directly dependent on the availability of the circulating gold and silver. A deficit on the capital and current accounts would lead to an outflow of specie and a shortage of currency. In many parts of the American colonies coins were often absent and trade took place as barter or notations in traders' books. Wampum is a common feature in the wills from New Amsterdam. In Africa, the cowrie shell, worth a tiny fraction of an ounce of gold, came to act as money.[1]

As bank notes (currency issued by private banks and the government) came into use in the nineteenth century, banks and governments found they could keep as reserve gold worth only a fraction of the notes they issued, establishing, in essence, the kind of fractional reserve system we present today as deriving from checking accounts.[*] Those people transferring funds abroad exchanged their notes for gold, which they could in turn convert to a foreign currency. If there were a deficit on current and capital accounts in such a situation, the outflow of gold would cause multiple contractions, as the bank notes issued would have less backing, and prudent banks would cease to issue new notes as existing notes were retired.[**] Or as happened from time to time, customers would demand gold from their banks all at once, causing a run on the banks and financial panic.[†]

The late nineteenth and early twentieth centuries brought the growth of central banking, the appearance of bank notes issued by the government and central banks, the growth of checking accounts, and a decline in privately issued bank notes, establishing the domestic monetary system more or less as described in introductory texts. Bank notes were redeemable in gold. Central banks, however, held gold to back their bank note issue and reserve liabilities (the money they owed to the commercial banks that held reserves with them, similar to modern member bank deposits). The gold a central bank held, however, was only a fraction (usually a large one) of its total assets. Whenever the nation had a deficit on the current and capital accounts, customers would be seeking gold from their banks, and their banks in turn would seek gold from their central bank. Again, the money supply would contract by some multiple of the gold outflow.

---

[*] Before checking accounts were common, banks issued their own notes. A lender would receive bank notes, fractionally backed by gold, and these notes circulated as currency. It is only in the twentieth century that bank notes have become monopolies of the central bank and government.

[**] A person requesting a loan from a bank would be given notes redeemable at the bank, not a checking account. The borrower would spend those notes. When the loan was due, the borrower could pay back the notes (in which case a prudent bank would not relend them).

[†] Silver gradually disappeared as a reserve. The ratio of silver to gold, as officially set, was about 15:1, but new finds of silver in the late nineteenth century brought the price of silver down (say 20:1), and producers could sell it to the government, getting one ounce of gold for every 15 of silver, rather than for 20 on the market. Debate over the use of two reserve metals (*bimetallism*) raged in the United States, partly because the issue of paper money would be larger if silver was held as a reserve. One of the most famous speeches of American history was that of William Jennings Bryan, thrice Democratic candidate for president, in which he declared: "You shall not crucify mankind upon a cross of gold!" This was, in essence, a plea to avoid the deflationary aspects of a gold standard.

The gold standard, at least in its classic form, existed for only about half a century. Until 1870, the United States had currency that was not redeemable in gold—the so-called greenbacks first issued to finance the Civil War.* By 1870, there were clear signs that greenback convertibility would be restored, hence the 1870 date for the beginning of the gold standard. The essence of the gold standard was the legal obligation of countries to buy and sell gold to all comers at some fixed price. Around 1900, the United States was doing this at approximately the same price that had been in use since long before the Civil War, namely $20.67 per ounce.** Anyone visiting an office of the U.S. Treasury was able to sell gold to the Treasury in the form of coins, bars, or gold dust, collecting the fixed price of $20.67 an ounce minus only a service charge of a quarter of a percent. Anyone with dollars in hand could visit that same office and buy gold at the identical price, but with the one-quarter percent charge added on.

Meanwhile, other countries through their own legislation guaranteed that they too would purchase and sell gold at some fixed price in terms of their own currency. In Britain, by an act of George III dated June 1816, the gold price was established at £4.2477 per ounce.† A little thought will show that the mutual agreements to buy and sell gold at fixed rates meant that the exchange rate of one currency in terms of another was also fixed.

Consider what ensued if the dollar started to fall in value against the pound sterling in the foreign exchange market in London, then the largest in the world. Holders of dollars never needed to accept a highly unfavorable rate. Instead, they could take the dollars to a bank or office of the Treasury, redeem them in gold, then ship the gold to Britain, selling it for pounds sterling. Say that in 1900 the amount of a debt to be paid in London was £1000. Americans would find that a gold bar weighing 123.274 grains would be worth exactly £1000 if sold in London. By American law they could buy this bar for exactly $4866, including service charges. The *mint parity* of the pound to the dollar was thus $4.866 to £1. If they were to purchase one such bar and ship it by sea to London, the additional cost of shipping and insuring might amount to $26, making the total cost $4892. As long as the price of pounds on the London foreign exchange market remained above £1 = $4.892, traders would benefit by shipping gold instead of using the foreign exchange market.

Conversely, British buyers of dollars would ship gold to the United States any time their £1000 sterling were to buy them less than $4840 on the foreign exchange market. There was thus a floor for the price of a pound at $4.840 and a

---

* Bills redeemable in gold had gold-colored backs.

** This was not the usual avoirdupois weight, but a slightly heavier troy ounce—12 of which make up a troy pound, which is lighter than the 16-ounce avoirdupois pound. Yes, trivia fans, an ounce of gold is heavier than an ounce of lead, but a pound of gold is lighter than a pound of lead!

† Once again there is a complication. The British definition of gold was "standard gold," that is, eleven-twelfths pure and one-twelfth alloy. The United States used a different definition, namely nine-tenths pure and one-tenth alloy. Before calculating the exchange rate, this discrepancy had to be resolved—and of course that was done by clerks using longhand arithmetic, who doubtless would have sold their inheritances for electronic calculators.

ceiling of $4.892, with 5.2 cents (about 1%) spread between the two prices known as *gold points*. Because the spread was determined by shipping costs, which fell throughout the period, it gradually diminished to around 0.5% at the outbreak of the First World War. See Fig. 17.1.

By the last quarter of the nineteenth century, it was seldom necessary for the typical trader or even bank actually to ship any gold. Instead, specialized *bullion* dealers acting in the role of arbitrageur would ship gold whenever the spread opened too widely.

TRADE IMBALANCES UNDER THE GOLD STANDARD   A remarkable thing about the gold standard period was the degree of trade imbalance it allowed. So long as people believed that the system would work, they were willing to tolerate trade imbalances much larger than they have in recent decades. Examine one estimate shown in Table 17.1.

Figure 17.1 **The gold standard holds the price of the pound down.** The figure below illustrates how the gold standard worked. Suppose, as in the example above, mint parity is $4.866 and transportation charges were about 0.5%. With the demand for pounds at D_1, there is insufficient incentive either to ship gold to Britain or to export it from Britain. If, however, the demand for pounds increased to D_2, it would be cheaper for those buying pounds to eschew the foreign exchange market and buy gold and ship it to Britain instead. Once the pound reached $4.892 in the foreign exchange markets in New York or London, dealers would begin to purchase gold in the United States and ship it to England. How much would they ship? Enough to fill the gap between demand and supply at the upper gold point—*ab*. Conversely, if the pound fell in value below $4.84, dealers would ship gold from Britain at the lower gold point. Sales of gold thus served to fix the price of the dollar and pound to a narrow range.

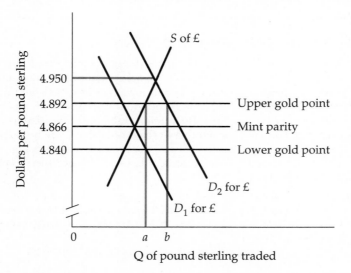

Table 17.1   **Trade imbalances as percentages of GNP under gold standard and in the postwar period[2]**

Country	Average current account balance
	Gold standard
United Kingdom	4.5
Federal Republic of Germany	1.8
Italy	0.6
Sweden	−2.7
Norway	−2.5
Denmark	−2.6
Australia	−3.7
Canada	−7.7
	Postwar (1948–)
United States	0.0
Japan	0.7
Federal Republic of Germany	0.9
France	0.2
United Kingdom	0.0
Canada	−1.5
Belgium	0.0
Norway	−2.1
Finland	−1.6
Greece	−3.1

■ *CONVENIENCES OF THE GOLD STANDARD*

The true golden age of the world's money markets made trade and international investment easy. Private citizens of all occupations and nationalities could exchange major currencies without fear of a change in value—and in fact, no major currency *did* change in value throughout the period. It was a time of almost unbelievable convenience for foreign trade and investment, with currencies exchanged against one another at fixed rates that were not expected to, and did not, change from year to year and decade to decade. What is more, the rates were in part selected for ease of calculation. Consider these typical gold standard rates from 1913:

- German mark = one British shilling
- U.S. dollar = 50 British pence, thus 2 U.S. cents = one British penny
- Italian lira = 10 British pence = US$0.20 = 1 Austro-Hungarian crown
- Russian ruble = US$0.50
- Swedish crown = Norwegian crown = Danish crown = US$0.25

RULES, RESERVES, AND ADJUSTMENT
UNDER THE GOLD STANDARD

Under the gold standard, adjustments to international imbalances were supposed to be made quickly. Unfortunately, many times such adjustments were to income rather than involving declining price levels. The nineteenth-century financial histories of both Canada and the United States are filled with panics that came about when British banks called in North American loans and credit dried up precipitously.

By the early years of this century, and perhaps throughout the entire period, however, central banks were acting to dampen (not counter) the contractionary effects of outflows or the expansionary effects of inflows. In those days, the principal monetary tool was the discount rate offered by the central bank for loans to other banks. If central banks wanted to cushion the fall in the money supply, they would lower the discount rate, encouraging the commercial banks to take advances from them and hold the advances as reserves. Thus there is substantial evidence that as early as 1890 reserves remained much steadier than the strict gold standard rules would have led us to expect, showing that partially counterbalancing monetary policy has been with us for over a century.[3] Indeed, one of the principal reasons for forming the Federal Reserve System was partially to insulate the United States from the bank panics and ensuing recessions that had occurred whenever gold flowed out of the United States. In a sense, bankers came to value predictability in the domestic credit markets over predictability of international reactions.

A tradeoff sacrificing some of the automaticity of the gold system for stability in domestic currency markets was not a bad one, so long as the central bankers paid attention to the medium and longer term, raising interest rates when needed to conserve the gold stock. They could, in essence, take the sharp edge off a panic, allowing the market more time to adjust, if necessary, to higher interest rates. Indeed, so long as gold served both as a base for the monetary system and for international transactions, the bankers had little choice but to allow the longer-term adjustments.

Dampening the effects of gold outflows and inflows required some form of monetary reserves that were not immediately monetized. As yet the distinction we made in Chapter 14 between domestic banking reserves and international or foreign exchange reserves had not emerged. Gold served to back both, but the link was not as direct as in earlier times, since the emerging central banks could regulate how much gold was required to back a given money supply.

END OF THE GOLD STANDARD

During the First World War, it became increasingly difficult to buy and sell gold. At first it was merely unpatriotic to put a strain on one's country's finances by buying gold. Britain used many means to pretend that it would still redeem currencies in gold, yet making sure it did not have too many takers. What is clear is that by the end of the war the old standard was dead.[4]

THE GOLD STANDARD AS A SYSTEM

The gold standard had credible fixed exchange rates, backed by the widespread assumption that while central banks might occasionally follow counterbalancing policies, a gold outflow would cause a domestic contraction that would end any threat to the currency's viability. Domestic economies did indeed adjust, and there is ample evidence of stable or falling price levels from 1870 through the First World War. The private capital market flourished and was able to support trade imbalances that were very large by modern standards. Since all countries played by the same rules and had flexible domestic prices, little international cooperation was required to keep the system working.

THE TWENTIES AND THIRTIES: THE GOLD-EXCHANGE STANDARD AND PEGGED RATES

THE WAY THE SYSTEM WORKED

After the collapse of the gold standard during the First World War, most countries never achieved full *gold convertibility*. High rates of inflation, persistent unemployment in Europe, and international debt problems characterized the 1920s. The modern system of fixed exchange rates with central banks actively intervening in the foreign exchange market came into existence during this period. The system, however, was fraught with problems in an age of difficulties. Its difficulties were precisely those that planners after the Second World War sought to avoid. So that we are not condemned to repeat this particular history, it is good to look more closely at the interwar period.

The First World War and its associated inflations and economic dislocations brought about the demise of the gold standard. Many of the European countries substituted paper money and cheap coinage for gold and denied what was then called convertibility—the right to turn currency into a gold equivalent.[*] (The United States allowed this right until 1933.) No longer could a Frenchman go to his bank and get gold for francs; he would have to have his bank buy whatever currency he wanted on the foreign exchange market. Central banks began the pattern described in this book of intervening in the foreign exchange market with foreign exchange. They would sell some gold directly to another nation's central bank, receive credit for the gold in that nation's currency, and then use that credit to buy up their own currency. Gold became much more an intergovernmental medium. In addition, many nations began holding some amounts of foreign exchange as reserves. British sterling bills, for instance, paid interest and were somewhat more liquid than gold. While foreign exchange reserves (principally U.S. dollars and British sterling) were under 25% of all reserves, the 1920s marked the beginning of what came to be called the *gold-exchange standard*.

---

[*] *Convertibility* today means the ability to change a currency into foreign currency without having an exchange license—the absence of exchange control.

The 1920s were further complicated by frequent changes in the value of currencies, a hyperinflation in Germany, a constant strain placed on the international system by high French and British war debts owed to the United States, and reparations payments the Germans owed to the French and British. Without gold convertibility, the values of currencies in foreign exchange markets could fluctuate, and central bank intervention was not always consistent or regular. The British pound, for instance, fell to as low as $3.60 from its par value of $4.80. When it was restored to $4.80 under Chancellor of the Exchequer Winston Churchill in 1925, Britain was plunged into a severe recession. Any purchasing power parity study would have shown that a $4.80 pound was sharply overvalued. Churchill expected the British price level to fall, which it did not, recession coming on instead, and the move eventually cost him his place in the government.[5] The French franc was very unstable during most of the period, with some pegging, but with much heavy speculation against it. The German mark, suffering from the hyperinflation of 1922–1923, fell to about 4 trillion to the dollar.

In short, the gold standard in the 1920s was what one specialist called a façade.[6] In fact, it was a mixture of floating exchange rates with frequent and extensive intervention to peg the exchange rate, with many of the pegs (or par values) set at inappropriate levels.[7]

WAR DEBTS, REPARATIONS, TARIFFS

During the First World War, Britain and France had borrowed large sums of money from the United States, principally from the government. When the war was over, they demanded enormous reparations from Germany to cover the cost of the war. Eventually, they scaled down their demands to just what they would have to pay the United States for war debts. For this to work, the Germans had to develop a trade surplus with the United States and use the dollars so gained to pay Britain and France, who would then repay the United States, with whom they needed balanced trade. The United States could be paid back for the goods and services it had transferred to France and England during the war by goods and services from Germany.

Consider the following model of the situation, as illustrated in Fig. 17.2. In the first line Germany has a trade surplus of 1 billion U.S. dollars. The German trade surplus means that German income exceeds German absorption (and saving exceeds investment) by $1 billion. But Germany has agreed to pay Britain a vast amount of money as reparations—a form of unrequited transfer. So the German savings are transferred to Britain in the second line. Germany's current account would show a trade surplus and an outflow under unrequited transfers of $1 billion, giving it a balance of zero.

Britain has balanced trade, so presumably it is absorbing just what its income is. The $1 billion in payments from Germany comes in under the unrequited transfers. The $1 billion to the United States goes out under the capital account. Britain therefore has a current account surplus, offset by a capital account deficit, thereby

Figure 17.2

Germany		Britain		United States	
Trade	+ $1 billion	Trade	$0 billion	Trade	− $1 billion
Transfers	− $1 billion	Transfers	+ $1 billion	Capital	+ $1 billion
		Capital	− $1 billion		

reducing its indebtedness abroad. Britain's current absorption is unchanged, but it is able to use the transfer from Germany to reduce its net indebtedness.

The United States, in order to use the German savings, runs a trade deficit of $1 billion, which it pays for with the $1 billion in loan repayments from Great Britain, which is under the capital account. The United States has $1 billion more dollars worth of goods and services to use, but sees its foreign assets fall by $1 billion—which is what it wants if it is to get paid back.

The only way this could have worked is if the United States had run a trade deficit and Germany a surplus. United States domestic investment had to exceed U.S. domestic saving ($I_d > S_d$) for imports to exceed exports ($M > X$). The world did not work that way, unfortunately. The United States raised tariffs considerably in 1922, making it harder for Europe to export, and reducing the volume of trade.[*] Sterling was probably overvalued in 1925, making exports difficult; the German economy was in chaos; and only the franc, some of the time, was undervalued. Domestic price levels showed little sign of decline, and neither massive devaluation nor deflation was practical.

Instead, what interest and reparations payments there were came from private lending. Europe had higher interest rates than the United States and its national and municipal governments frequently sold bonds on the New York markets. When the dollars so gained were converted to domestic currencies, the governments bought them and used them to repay the U.S. government. Thus a private capital flow helped pay the public debts. It was, in a sense, a house of cards, and it collapsed after the October 1929 stock market crash on Wall Street. That particular financial panic might have been just a historical curiosity instead of a world trauma, had it not removed a key card from the pile. The private loans to Europe stopped, and with their cessation, gold began to flow out of Europe—first from Austria, then from Germany, then from France.

Looming over it all was the Smoot-Hawley Tariff. President Hoover had originally intended lower tariffs, but the momentum in congress produced sharply higher tariffs. In itself, however unwise, the tariff would merely have made the world less efficient and lowered trade, not worsened trade balances. Coming as it did, when it did, it decreased the chances of any country developing a trade surplus with the United States and spread despair in Europe.

---

[*] As Chapter 2 noted, tariffs reduce the volume of trade but do not in themselves necessarily or even usually alter trade balances. The smaller volume of trade, however, made the service (interest and the amount of the loans paid back) that much larger as a percentage of all exports.

THE GOLD-EXCHANGE SYSTEM AND FINANCIAL COLLAPSE

The collapse of the international monetary system did not follow immediately after the October Wall Street crash, nor after the Smoot-Hawley Tariff. It fell more like a pile of cans than a house of cards: a period of uneasiness (1930) followed by one can, then two, then the whole pile coming down over the summer of 1931. Like so many macroeconomic phenomena, it was real and monetary at the same time. As loans from New York dried up and no signs of new ones were forthcoming, the inflow of dollars to Europe ceased. As their currencies began to fall in value, European central banks tried to intervene, but they lacked the gold or foreign exchange to do so successfully. Nor could they isolate their own money supplies from the outflow of gold and their monetary base; instead, they let interest rates rise with the hope that it would keep funds from exiting. Banks failed and people panicked (rightly so), withdrawing their money from the banks.

The problems were especially great for Britain because many foreign banks (including central banks) held sterling as reserves. When the foreign central banks came to intervene in the foreign exchange market, they sold the sterling for gold, and used the gold to buy dollars to intervene. Every time the Austrian bank spent a million pounds of its sterling reserves, it used up not only a million pounds of its foreign exchange reserves, but a million pounds of Britain's gold reserves as well. So the roughly 20–25% of reserves that were in foreign exchange disappeared, causing international reserves to fall sharply. As the process continued, Britain's ability to redeem currencies in gold came under doubt. Several central banks cleared out their holdings of sterling bonds, including the Bank of France. Despite a considerable number of loans, arranged hurriedly with the U.S. Treasury, the pressure against the pound proved too great and Britain announced it would no longer redeem currencies in gold (on September 15, 1931).

The declining monetary bases in Europe and the attempts to keep capital from fleeing by raising interest rates caused investment to fall sharply, just at a time when it needed to be encouraged. The result was a recession that turned into a full-scale depression.

Pressure was transferred to the United States. The United States had no problem with trade deficits, but it was the last place any private citizen could buy gold, and gold was a safe haven for assets in this period. As a result, banks and the U.S. Treasury lost gold and the money supply fell. Yet the Federal Reserve only replaced part of the lost reserves.[*] As a consequence, interest rates rose in the United States throughout 1931 and 1932, turning the recession into a depression. Finally, in 1933, the United States, too, ceased to redeem currency in gold, severing the link. Gold became exclusively an intergovernmental medium, but even in that case few governments stood ready to sell gold at the simple request of another.[8]

---

[*] It claimed, perhaps rightly, that it needed to keep the gold in order to back its issue of currency notes and that it could not hold more Treasury bills. That constraint was removed shortly, but the Fed still did not reflate the economy.

THE GOLD-EXCHANGE STANDARD AS A SYSTEM

The international system of the 1920s was an unstable system during an unstable period. Temporarily pegging exchange rates left considerable uncertainty about where the price would be in the future. The severance of the domestic monetary base from inflows and outflows of capital meant that governments were under less pressure to expand or contract as the balance of payments dictated. The good side of this was that certain unnecessary recessions could be avoided, but the down side was that governments, businesses, and labor were under no great pressure to keep the price level down. Also on the good side, the United States was able to sterilize all gold inflows and so avoid inflation. On the down side, the European countries trying to develop a trade surplus with the United States were forced into deflationary policies or into frequent devaluations. Economies, in a sense, became less flexible, although whether the inflexibility caused the frequent devaluations or the reverse is unclear.

International cooperation began, at least in a series of attempts to solve the war debts issues. Relations between the Bank of England and the Federal Reserve Bank of New York were also strong and consultation regular. There was, however, no international institution to provide any additional reserves, or any formal procedures for central banks to borrow from one another.

Key to the difficulties of the 1920s system was the unsatisfactory reserve base and ultimately, the unwillingness of central banks to lend when private capital could or would no longer do so. We can argue, in a what-it-could-have-been way, that had the Federal Reserve stood ready to help Britain out in the early 1930s, private capital would not have panicked. There never would have been a run on the sterling, nor the ensuing collapse of world reserves.

THE GREAT DEPRESSION

Released from the need to redeem currencies in gold, governments were free to reflate and increase demand. But the prevailing wisdom was not Keynesian; it would be nearly a decade before Keynes' ideas were well understood. The freedom was, therefore, not well used. The currency experience of the 1930s was a mixture of floating rates, pegged rates, and experiments in exchange control, the last in Nazi Germany. Few observers at the time, or indeed, since, have considered the 1930s' experiments with floating rates successful, since they appeared to disrupt trade and foreign investment.

The outbreak of the Second World War brought exchange control in virtually every country except the United States. Chapter 16 discussed exchange control. Recall that the par value is maintained by rationing foreign currencies through a system of licenses and that exporters are required to turn in any foreign exchange and accept the government's official value for it, despite much higher black market rates. Such a system has effects similar to quotas on imports, but it also includes any other use of foreign exchange—for travel, repayment of loans, or remittance of profits. It seriously distorts the price system and may, perhaps, have been justified during the war, but its use in peacetime made little sense.

The system in the 1930s lacked international cooperation, a generally agreed upon set of rules, stable exchange rates, and any reserves but gold. Domestic problems were so serious that they always took precedence over international cooperation or coordination.

THE BRETTON WOODS SYSTEM: 1947–1973

The Bretton Woods Conference of 1944 introduced major changes to the international monetary system, changes that were to endure for 25 years. As the Second World War finally turned in favor of the Allies, the governments of Britain and the United States turned some of their thoughts to the postwar economic and political order. Many of our current international institutions were designed to prevent a rerun of the 1930s. The United Nations, particularly its Security Council, was intended to keep any new Hitler from power. The *International Monetary Fund* and the associated understandings, known as the *Bretton Woods system,* were intended to control or eliminate the currency speculation, frequent changes in currency values, and lack of means to make economic adjustments characteristic of the previous three decades. The British, French, and Americans had begun discussions on the postwar economic order as the war progressed, but in 1944, a final conference was held at the orange-roofed Mount Washington Hotel in the New Hampshire mountain resort of Bretton Woods. Representatives of some 44 nations attended, but the principal action was between the British delegation, headed by none other than John Maynard Keynes, and the American, headed by a Treasury official, Harry Dexter White.

The conference hammered out two important features of the postwar world, the International Monetary Fund and a set of rules for an exchange rate system known as the *adjustable peg.* We examine both of these, starting with the adjustable peg.

EXCHANGE RATES UNDER THE BRETTON WOODS SYSTEM

Under the Bretton Woods adjustable peg, governments fixed their currencies in terms of gold and used their foreign exchange reserves (and borrowings from the newly created IMF) to keep their exchange rates from falling below their target. While technically the currencies were fixed to gold, in practical terms they were fixed to the U.S. dollar, which served far more than gold did as reserves and as a means for intervening in the foreign exchange market. When the value of their currency rose toward the target ceiling, the governments would buy back the foreign exchange (largely U.S. dollars), replenishing their reserves and repaying their loans. In the 1950s Britain, for instance, defined the pound in terms of gold such that £1 = $2.80. It would allow fluctuation around that par value of about

1% (2.8 cents) either way, giving a floor price at $2.772 and a ceiling at $2.828. If the pound fell toward the floor or hit the ceiling, the Bank of England would intervene in the market, *pegging* the rate.

The diagram for showing intervention looks very much like the gold standard diagram. The difference is that instead of private dealers moving gold when a gold point was reached, the Bank of England itself intervened to purchase or sell sterling in the manner we described in Chapter 14. Figure 17.3 below shows a situation similar to that shown in Fig. 17.1 where the demand for sterling has risen. This time, however, it is the Bank of England that intervenes to sell *ab* of sterling and peg the exchange rate to 1% on either side of the *par value* of $2.80.

When, however, the fixed rate became untenable, the country would change the rate, this being the adjustable element. Thus in 1967, after several years of attempting to maintain the old rate, Britain devalued the pound from $2.80 to $2.40. It removed the peg, so to speak, and repegged the rate at a point it thought it could defend. Figure 17.4 shows the situation in which Britain found itself in 1967. After a number of years in which the demand and supply of the pound had kept the price at around $2.80, demand for the pound fell sharply, from D_1 to D_2. The amount of intervention the Bank of England would have to undertake to peg the pound at $2.772 or above would be enormous. So instead, Britain announced that henceforth, it would peg the exchange rate to within 1% of $2.40, rather than $2.80. That is a devaluation and downward adjustment of the peg.

Nations announced their par values and only changed them if they had a *fundamental disequilibrium*—and then this would be done in consultation with the IMF. One reason for the consultation was to prevent the kind of competitive

---

Figure 17.3 **Central bank intervention pegs the pound within 1% of par value.** Market pressures force the demand for pounds to rise to D_2, increasing its price to $2.90. To counter that pressure, the Bank of England purchases *ab* of pounds at the price of $2.828 to keep the price within the agreed-upon bounds.

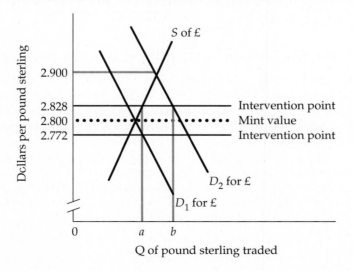

devaluations that had occurred in the 1920s, when nations sought to stimulate their economies by devaluing, as described in Chapter 16. Another reason was to have international advice in seeking alternatives to revaluing the currency.

Nations were also to strive to remove the exchange controls they had placed on their currencies during the depression and the war. The agreement set no specific dates, but by the mid-1950s most industrial countries had removed all significant controls. (Britain freed almost all transactions, but until the 1970s still clung to a restriction on how much British residents could take abroad.) Third World countries persisted in using exchange control.

The whole thrust of the adjustable peg system was toward pegging, not adjustment. Governments were to try to use domestic monetary and fiscal policies to correct payments difficulties, and repegging was to be only a last resort. Keynes himself helped design the International Monetary Fund system and supported the thrust toward exchange rate stability. A recent book by a leading monetarist argues that Keynes put considerable value on stable expectations for government policy as means for keeping capital costs down and investment up; support of stable exchange rates was consistent with that goal.[9]

The system worked well until the late 1960s. A strong U.S. dollar, which was produced by consistent American trade surpluses, high U.S. gold reserves, and a low rate of U.S. inflation anchored the system. Countries in fact were pegging their currencies to the U.S. dollar and holding dollars rather than gold as reserves. While the high rate of U.S. private investment abroad caused deficits on the combined capital and current accounts throughout the period, other countries welcomed the increase in foreign exchange reserves (at least through the

---

Figure 17.4 Adjusting the peg: Britain devalues the pound. Under an adjustable peg, Britain was able to move the rate at which it pegged the pound. With demand for sterling persistently at D_2, rather than D_1, efforts to peg the pound at $2.870 would have been very difficult, but at $2.40 successful.

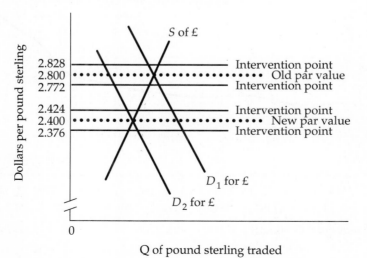

1950s). The rise in dollar holdings abroad, moreover, was not so rapid as to cause undue expansion of the money supply in other countries.

Figure 17.5 shows the wholesale price index for finished goods in the United States during that period, indicating the low rates of inflation before 1965.

SPECULATION AND THE ONE-WAY OPTION   Difficulties with the Bretton Woods system arose when the U.S. price level increased sharply in the late 1960s, as Fig. 17.5 shows. Its balance of trade worsened, and it had become obvious that the U.S. gold supply was not going to be used to back the currency. As the inflation and trade balance problems continued, they put serious strains on the system, strains that were aggravated by great currency speculation that was endemic in the system.

To see why speculation was high, consider the case of Great Britain in 1967, when it devalued the pound. Up to the very day on which the pound was devalued (a Sunday, of course, when markets are closed), the Bank of England was buying enormous quantities of pounds in a last-ditch attempt to maintain the rate at the level of £1 = $2.772. By doing so, the Bank of England (and other

---

Figure 17.5 **United States: Wholesale price (finished goods) index, 1951–1980.** Between 1951 (the Korean War) and 1967 the wholesale price level for finished goods rose about 10.5%. That is an average rate of less than 0.75% a year. Given the upward bias of a price index, deriving from its failure to reflect quality changes, there was probably no inflation at all. The dollar provided an excellent anchor for the whole system. But the upward turn afterwards, as the chapter later shows, set the whole system adrift.

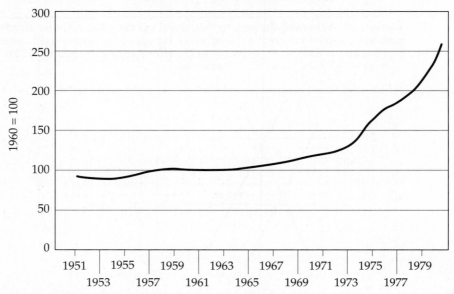

Source: International Financial Statistics Yearbook, *1981.*

monetary authorities who pitched in to help) set up a situation whereby speculators might win but could not lose.

An example will show this *one-way option*. Imagine yourself the treasurer of Transatlantic Enterprises, a London-based subsidiary of an American company that in 1967 had £50,000 in cash assets. You suspect the pound will be devalued on the weekend as it has been battered heavily for several weeks. So you convert all £50,000 into dollars at the rate of £1 = $2.772, receiving $138,600. If the devaluation does not occur, you can buy back whatever sterling you need on Monday at a rate very close to what you sold them for, less rather minor bank charges. After all that pressure, the pound is not going to rise to its ceiling and certainly it is not going to be revalued upward, so the risk of loss from an upward movement of the pound is minuscule. But if the pound is devalued, then you stand to gain. Had it been the weekend of October 27, 1967 you would have awakened Monday morning to find the pound down to £1 = $2.40, and you could then have repurchased your £50,000 for $120,000, a neat $18,600 profit; that is 13% for one weekend. The one-way option was that you can't lose but you can win, and it encouraged enormous speculative currency movements.

The one-way option forced governments to be dishonest about their exchange rates. To avoid massive speculations, finance ministers and undersecretaries never spoke of devaluations except in the most condemning of terms. If on Monday the ministers met to decide whether to devalue on Friday, no minister emerged from the meeting to give an inkling of what had transpired. No comment would be made beyond the firm assurance that "the government is prepared to defend the existing parity at all costs." For this reason, a government defending a fixed rate continues to issue reassuring statements, often wholly untrue, right up to the very hour of the devaluation. As long ago as 1551, the Duke of Northumberland, in charge of English finances, denied firmly that the pound would be devalued at the very time he was arranging its devaluation. Over 400 years later, on May 9, 1969, the German government announced that the existing par value of the mark was "valid for eternity." Eternity lasted just under five months, as the mark was raised in value on September 24, 1969.

Under a floating rate system, the one-way option disappears. Since the central bank does not regularly intervene, the exchange can move up or down, much as do shares on the stock market. If the pound had been floating in 1967, it would already have been in the $2.40 neighborhood, and nobody could have made 13% on a weekend. Speculation, of course, continues, as it does in the stock or commodities markets, but the "heads I don't lose, tails I win" aspect of adjustable parities disappears.

While speculation was a problem, particularly near the end of the adjustable peg system, governments acted together to provide other central banks with considerable financing to peg their exchange rates. The system was designed so that scrambling to find additional finance to fight speculation (as Britain had to do in 1931) would not be necessary. There would be a ready, reasonable, and sufficient source of additional reserves. That source would be the International Monetary Fund.

THE INTERNATIONAL MONETARY FUND

THE DESIGN OF THE SYSTEM   At Bretton Woods, the British, led by Lord Keynes, advocated a powerful institution that could create new international reserves in the same way as a central bank can expand the domestic money supply of a country. Countries wishing to settle debts could make a limited amount of overdrafts (borrow) from a so-called clearing union. When they borrowed, the clearing union would credit the countries' accounts with *bancor*, which the nations could then turn over to surplus countries in exchange for their currencies. In essence, each nation would agree to receive the bancor much as it took gold. The bancor could also be used to back domestic currency issues and be held as reserves of the central bank. The clearing union could expand world reserves as needed by the stroke of a pen, as Fig. 17.6 shows.

The United States pushed through a much more conservative proposal. Each member nation of the IMF was assigned a quota that bore some general relation to the value of its wealth and trade.* The quota was expressed as a certain amount of gold and its own currency. This became the property of the Fund. The Fund could in turn lend these reserves to countries having difficulty defending their exchange rates. Not only would this increase the stability of exchange markets, but it would give the Fund some degree of control over its members. If members violated a rule of the Fund—one such was not to devalue by more than 10% without prior consultation—then the Fund could deny loans to that country. The IMF soon organized a secretariat and technical staff to help make studies and offer advice. The power to send or withdraw a technical mission gave additional control over member nations. Finally, the IMF was given a very special weapon (never actually used) called the *scarce currency clause*. This allowed the Fund to declare scarce the currency of a country with a large trade surplus. It might do this if the surplus country were accumulating large amounts of reserves and showing no sign of trying to reduce that surplus. If the currency was declared scarce, all other countries could apply discriminatory exchange controls against the offender.

Such power, although certainly not enabling the IMF to dictate policy, was considerable, and the Fund's designers were not careless about its control. They were not about to adopt a one-country, one-vote rule, such as that employed in the United Nations General Assembly. Nor did the idea of key members (as in the UN Security Council) appeal to them. Instead, voting in the IMF was appor-

---

* The actual figure was based on payments to the International Postal Union, a handy proxy.

Figure 17.6 **Clearing union**

Assets	Liabilities
Loan to debtor nation +100	Bancor +100

tioned according to the quotas, the vote being directly proportional to the quota size. Early in the fund's existence, this meant that the United States, with 24.3% of the votes, and Great Britain, with 11.5%, could control the Fund. Quotas have been altered considerably since. Figure 17.7 shows them as of 1992.

LENDING OPERATIONS OF THE IMF One of the main functions of the IMF is to lend money to nations that are having difficulty keeping their exchange rates from falling. Such loans have served to stave off many a devaluation, giving time for the nation to make adjustments, and convincing speculators that the nation had enough backing to keep its currency from falling. By the end of 1991, the Fund had lent around SDR 115 billion, over two thirds of that lent after 1981. (The SDR, explained in detail below, is a unit of account based on a basket of major currencies. In 1991 it averaged $1.37.)

HOW THE FUND WORKS: THE BASIC STRUCTURE The Fund is, as noted above, a pool of currencies. When it started, the Fund assigned each member a *quota*, which was to be filled one quarter with gold and three quarters with *the nation's own currency*. As the Fund's needs rose, quotas were raised several times, each requiring the one quarter gold and three quarters currency. Recent increases in the quota have used foreign exchange in place of the gold. (That is, Germany could give three quarters in marks, and one quarter in francs.)* The Fund encouraged central banks to include the gold and foreign exchange deposited with the Fund as part of their official reserves. Each nation could borrow from the Fund an amount equal to 125% of its quota. That borrowing was divided into five tranches (*tranche* is French for *slice*, but usage rhymes *tranche* with *ranch*). A borrowing country could get the first tranche (the *reserve tranche*, called in the old days the *gold tranche*) simply by asking for it; after all, it was the country's gold to begin with. When, however, the country desired to borrow more than the gold tranche, it had to ask the Fund. The IMF's permission to bor-

---

* That foreign exchange may be in any hard currency normally used as a reserve—dollars, yen, or German marks are fine, but no Haitian gourdes or Peruvian intis.

Figure 17.7 **IMF quotas, 1992**

Country	Percentage votes
United States	19.1
Germany	5.9
Japan	5.9
France	5.4
United Kingdom	5.4
Saudi Arabia	3.7
Italy	3.3
Canada	3.1

row became more and more difficult as the nation borrowed the each successive tranche up to the *supertranche,* the last 25%. That basic system continues today.

Technically, the IMF describes a nation's borrowing as a purchase, because the borrowing nation pays for the foreign currency it buys by depositing its own currency with the Fund. When Argentina borrowed SDR 292.5 (about US$400) million worth of foreign currency in 1991, for instance, it paid for it with 417.69 million Argentine pesos. Whenever it pays back the foreign exchange, it will, to use the Fund's word, repurchase its own pesos.[10]

The total assets of the Fund in 1991 were around SDR 91 billion, which seems an impressive sum. However, much of that 91 billion was not truly usable.

1. Many currencies it holds are soft, so hedged about by exchange restrictions that they are of little or no use in making international payments. Others are hard enough, but so unimportant no one wants them anyway—for example, the Guatemalan quetzal or the Thai baht. In the early years of the Fund, loans were almost exclusively in U.S. dollars. As of 1987, the Fund had used 55 currencies (yes, including the quetzals and Malaysian ringgit, but only in very small quantities); most of the lending is in the currencies of the developed nations, particularly U.S. dollars.

2. Roughly one quarter of the Fund's assets are likely to be already lent out at any given time. As repayment is scheduled over three to five years, this portion of the IMF's assets is effectively immobilized. The IMF does earn some small interest on its loans, but it is unimportant.

3. Finally, much of the Fund's holdings are unusable because these are the currencies under attack. If the Argentine peso is facing difficulties and the Fund's holdings of pesos are high, it makes no sense to lend out the pesos just used by Argentina to purchase foreign currency. It would be absurd for the Fund to lend Britain foreign exchange to support the pound, and then turn around and lend pounds to some other country, because that would put downward pressure on the pound. With the U.S. dollar falling in value in the late 1980s, the Fund has reduced its lending of U.S. dollars.

MODIFICATIONS TO THE ORIGINAL SCHEME   The Fund has come under considerable pressure to expand its lending operations and at the same time has sought sources of funding beyond quota increases to help meet this pressure. As a result, the basic structure of the Fund's finances has changed considerably, although the bulk of these changes occurred after 1973. To note the early ones and the trends, however:

Borrowing by the Fund   The Fund in 1962 made an agreement, continued to this day, with 10 industrial nations (the Group of Ten) called the *General Arrangements to Borrow* (GAB), a credit line that presently can amount to SDR 18.5 billion.[11] (Again, if a major currency is under attack, it cannot be used. If the U.S. dollar should need aid, the 4.25 billion of the U.S. line of credit would be useless.) Originally, the GAB could only be used to finance loans to the Group of Ten, but since 1983, some of the money can be used for weaker countries. None of the money borrowed is part of a country's quota. Additional sources of funding developed later are discussed in the following chapter.

Standby Arrangements   From its very early days the Fund has frequently negotiated *standby arrangements* with countries, in which it agrees that *if needed*, it will lend to a nation out of its various facilities. It established such arrangements originally in 1952, because the use of the tranches beyond the reserve tranche is not automatic and requires time to negotiate. A standby arrangement is evidence that a country has immediate access to foreign exchange, which may well calm the markets for its currency, even if this exchange is never used.

ADVISING OPERATIONS OF THE FUND   The founders of the IMF could hardly have envisaged an organization with 167 members,[*] nor could they have foreseen the needs and difficulties of new nations. The IMF soon learned, however, that it could not play the role of a private banker with a spendthrift customer and simply deny loans when the nation asked for more help. The *conditionality* of the upper credit tranches gave the IMF an opportunity—or perhaps forced upon it a duty—to do more than just deny loans; it had to give counsel and advice and monitor that the advice was taken. The IMF would send advisors, who would suggest certain programs—following them would secure new loans, while ignoring them would lead to the denial of new loans.

The IMF faces frequent criticism for the type of advice it gives. Often the advice is sound enough, but is politically unpopular. Suppose the Fund must advise Brazil, a nation suffering from high inflation, sagging exports, and a growing debt problem. It might call for the reduction of a government deficit, devaluation and elimination of exchange control, and the elimination of subsidies on fuels and food. Such a program would tend to shift income toward the rural areas, where food was produced, toward people who had not been able to secure import licenses, toward exporters and producers of import substitutes (but not to those who were dependent on imported materials), and toward those on more fixed incomes. These are the groups that are politically weak, or else they would have had these advantages already. The advice hurts the strong and helps the weak (not necessarily the poor and the rich, just the well-organized and the unorganized), and is sure to bring howls of rage from the labor unions and industrialists dependent on import licenses. Even if the IMF orders just what the finance minister wants to do, he or she must pretend to do it only with extreme reluctance. Obviously, in many situations, the IMF may not be able to have many of its policy recommendations accepted at all.

---

[*] In 1944 there were only three independent countries in Africa (Ethiopia, Liberia, and South Africa), three in the Caribbean (Cuba, Haiti, and the Dominican Republic), and three in the Far East (Japan, China, and Thailand). The Communist countries did not join.

RESERVE CURRENCIES

When central banks hold a currency widely, that currency is known as a *reserve currency*. The principal reserve currency in the 1920s was sterling. In the 1930s and for a period after the Second World War, those countries continuing to use sterling as a reserve were part of what was called the sterling area. Sterling's weakness (constantly under pressure to fall in value) made it less attractive than the dollar, and as noted above, the dollar became the principal reserve currency after the war. In more recent years, central banks have kept wider portfolios of foreign currencies, particularly the stronger German mark, Japanese yen, and Swiss franc.

The difficulty with using currencies like the mark or Swiss franc as reserve currencies is that their domestic financial markets are small, and compared to the dollar and sterling markets, rather illiquid. A nation seeking to buy a considerable amount of German marks (in the form of German government bonds) could drive up bond prices and drive them down when it sold off the marks. Moreover, if the German government tried to keep the mark stable by intervening in the foreign exchange market, German reserves would undergo a number of shocks that would make it difficult for the Bundesbank to keep the mark stable. In the larger, more liquid U.S. (and Eurodollar) markets, such changes would be a ripple, not a wave.

A curious property of those nations whose currencies are used as reserves is that their trade deficits are, in effect, covered by the central banks that pick up the excess foreign exchange reserves. Whenever other countries buy up dollars to keep their own currencies from rising (i.e., the dollar from falling), their reserves, and hence world reserves, rise automatically. So whenever the United States ran a deficit on the capital and currency accounts, world reserves tended to rise, leading to rather special problems.

The U.S. trade deficit of the mid-1980s provides an illustration. From 1984 through mid-1987 that deficit was covered by large private capital inflows from abroad, but in the latter part of 1987, foreign central banks began to pick up billions of dollars, accounting for a great deal of the SDR 84 billion rise in world reserves discussed in the following chapter. The dollar, however, was not an ideal reserve because it was tending to fall in value, so the central banks were buying up an asset declining in value. The U.S. trade deficit, in essence, was paid for by central banks investing in U.S. Treasury bills. The Americans gave hope from time to time that they would end the deficit, but the Europeans and Japanese complained that the additional reserves so created were preventing adjustment and letting the U.S. deficit plunge on.

SPECIAL DRAWING RIGHTS (SDRs)

Worries about whether the U.S. dollar could continue to be a strong reserve base caused economists to try to think of some means to replace the dollar as a reserve. The reliance on the dollar as a reserve currency was much in discussion in the 1960s. As foreign holdings of dollars swelled and the U.S. gold base shrank, some bankers feared a repeat of the 1931 British scenario. Others were just annoyed that the United States was in a position to run deficits indefinitely. This was before the period when the United States had a trade deficit, but the combined current and capital accounts had been in deficit for many years. Indeed, the United States had to run a deficit on the combined current and capital accounts if world reserves were to expand. If the United States sensibly stopped doing so, then world reserves might shrink. What could the world possibly use if the dollar ceased to be appropriate? In an attempt to replace U.S. dollars as foreign exchange reserves and avert a possible crisis similar to that of 1931, central bankers agreed to create a special drawing right (SDR). The SDR is a unit whose value is determined by a basket of key currencies. But it is also a right to draw foreign exchange from another central bank, acting almost like gold.

In 1967, the IMF and the Group of Ten created the SDR system. Its details are as follows:

1. A new category of reserves called special drawing rights was established separate from the general accounts of the IMF but still part of the Fund's operations.

2. Any IMF member was eligible to participate and any member could opt out.

3. The initial allocation of SDRs, made on January 1, 1970, was 9.4 billion. Subsequent allocations occurred in 1979, 1980, and 1981, bringing the total issued to 21.4 billion. Officials thought that decisions on the further creation of the new SDRs would be made every five years. However, only token opposition will suffice to stop new creation, since an 85% positive vote of the IMF must approve. The formula used to allocate the new reserves was based on voting strength in the Fund; hence, rich countries benefited far more than poor.

4. Holders of SDRs (which must be central banks) can exchange them for foreign currency directly with another country. As this resembles the way gold used to be employed as a reserve, the SDRs were not surprisingly nicknamed "paper gold." Initially, the SDRs were even defined in terms of gold, with the dollar designation being understood to mean the dollar at $35 per ounce of gold. However, in 1974 after the dollar had begun to slide and the gold price rose, the IMF began to express the value of the SDR as a moving average of major currencies. (The weights at present are U.S. dollar 40%, German mark 21%, Japanese yen 17%, French franc 11%, and British pound 11%.) SDRs are little affected by currency devaluations (other than that of the dollar, which is 40% of the basket). They hold a substantial advantage over gold in that interest rates (60% of the weighted average of short-term interest rates in America, Japan, Germany, and Britain) are paid to any country that holds SDRs in excess of its initial allocation, that interest rate in effect being paid by the countries using the SDRs and thus holding less than their quota. This seems to make a great deal more sense than

the use of gold, which not only bears no interest, but takes up storage space, must be guarded, and has many industrial uses.

5. The transfer of SDRs occurs on the accounts of the IMF. The paying country is debited and the recipient country is credited. Thus there are no pieces of paper called SDRs, just numbers in books and on computers. There is no requirement for corrective action or IMF supervision, as with the Fund's credit tranches. However, even though the IMF need not approve a transaction involving SDRs, the recipient country must agree, and does have the right to refuse acceptance.[*]

■ THE SDR AS A UNIT OF ACCOUNT

Because it is more stable than any single currency, the SDR is often used as a unit of account, just as if it were dollars or pounds. In such cases, people usually write "SDR 200 million." For a number of years the *Balance of Payments Statistics* used SDRs, but has reverted to using dollars. Many IMF accounts are still kept in SDRs. We occasionally use the SDR instead of dollars in these chapters. Its price has varied in recent years ranging between $1.10 and $1.40.

---

6. A country may use all its SDRs, but the average daily holdings by a country over a five-year period must be no less than 30% of its average daily allocation of SDRs. The result is that a country using no more than 70% of its allocation has no problems, and the SDR is good as gold. If it uses 80% for six months, it must *reconstitute* (buy back) enough SDRs to reach 40% of its allocation in some subsequent six-month period. It would do so by exchanging holdings of foreign currency for the SDRs of some other country.

SDRs as reserves have never become as important as economists expected; indeed, no new ones have been issued since 1981. The reasons are several:

1. Central banks are doing quite well relying almost exclusively on foreign exchange for reserves. As gold has become a secondary reserve asset, nations have come to rely almost exclusively on foreign exchange reserves, despite the higher risks of holding a fluctuating currency. Virtually all nations have sundered the tie between gold or foreign exchange reserves and their domestic currency and money issues.

2. As the United States ran enormous trade deficits in the mid 1980s and persuaded other nations' central banks to buy up many of the surplus dollars, world reserves grew very large. They (not counting gold) jumped by 20% in

---

[*] There is one exception: When a country is "designated" by the IMF—ordinarily this would be a country with a very large and growing stock of reserves—then it *must* accept SDRs in exchange for its own or some other convertible currency. The obligation ends when the designated country has acquired SDRs up to three times its own allocation. For example, a country that was allocated $100 in SDRs after designation would be obligated to accept $200 worth of additional SDRs from other countries. After the required maximum figure is reached, the designated country can continue to accept the SDRs of others if it wishes, but it does not have to. This clause has never been used.

1987. Because the tie with gold no longer exists, foreign central banks that buy U.S. dollars can only turn them in for more U.S. dollars, so they are left with the choice of letting their own currencies rise in value or increasing their holdings of dollars. In some senses, the United States has not needed reserves because it has been able to persuade, cajole, or force other nations to accumulate dollars.

3. Most of the problems faced by the international monetary system are problems of adjustment, not problems of inadequate reserves. Additional reserves per se would not end the U.S. deficit or solve the problems of Third World indebtedness.[*]

4. More reserves could be inflationary. By postponing adjustment, deficit countries would continue in deficit, and the surplus countries would be forced to maintain high trade surpluses and/or to let their price levels rise, as argued in the previous chapter. Even the non-oil less developed countries, many of whom were heavily indebted, did not use their SDRs to the fullest possible extent, retaining 40 to 60% of their allocations. Actual patterns of retention appeared to be determined by portfolio considerations of the balance between foreign exchange and SDR holdings and the risk and interest on each. An increase in SDRs would not, and did not, automatically lead to their being spent to perpetuate a deficit.[12]

BORROWING: SWAP LINES

By the mid-1960s, the resources of the IMF looked small compared to the speculative movements of currencies that countries were experiencing. The IMF worked well enough for small Third World countries, but it would not have the resources to fight a run on a major currency. As a response to this problem, most of the industrialized countries developed short-term arrangements for lines of credit with each other called *swap lines*. Most of these are bilateral agreements to lend each other up to several billion dollars if called upon. Many of these arrangements have been in place since the early 1960s, although they have to be renewed as frequently as four times a year. The mechanism by which the swap lines work is of at least academic interest.

Should a swap be drawn upon, it would work as follows, using the case of Germany and the United States: Suppose in a period of crisis the United States wishes to obtain $100 million worth of marks. The terminology used is to "activate a swap line," which is jargon for "to borrow." The Federal Reserve System, which administers the U.S. swaps, credits the dollar account of the Deutsche Bundesbank (BB) with $100 million (Step 1 in the T-account, Figure 17.8). Simultaneously, the Fed would obtain a credit (a new deposit) of DM170 million (at $1=DM1.70) in the Bundesbank (Step 2). Naturally, neither the Bundesbank

---

[*] This is not to say that they might not be *part* of the solution. If new SDRs were issued to heavily indebted nations, for instance, they (or 70% of them) could be used to pay off the debt. Such a simple solution, however, carries with it a large number of problems. Most economists would like some mixture of increased adjustment ability along with some debt relief.

nor the Fed can simply issue new liabilities without backing them with assets. In this case, the backing is the foreign credit they are in the process of receiving. Hence the Bundesbank can credit the Fed with DM170 million because it has just received $100 million from the Fed, and the Fed can credit the Bundesbank with $100 million because it has the DM170 million (Steps 3 and 4).

To this point the swap looks like a double loan, and the reader may be wondering how the United States is to get any benefit. That comes when the Fed spends the marks in support of the dollar, but Germany does not spend the dollars. As the Fed buys up excess dollars from commercial banks, the marks paid are transferred from the Fed's account at the Bundesbank to those of the German commercial banks (Step 5). In the United States, however, the $100 million stays put in the Bundesbank's account at the Fed, and hence creates no further credit repercussions.

As part of the agreement, the two central banks pledge to reverse the transaction three months later at the identical rate of exchange, thus removing any fear of loss of value. Should the swapped currency not be used immediately, it would be placed in interest-bearing time deposits or treasury bills. Following consultation between the central banks, each is free to draw upon the swapped foreign currency to conduct stabilizing operations in the foreign exchange market.

THE END OF THE BRETTON WOODS SYSTEM

The end of the Bretton Woods system came in 1973. Continued U.S. inflation was pushing the purchasing power parity value estimates of the U.S. dollar far out of line from the German mark, Swiss franc, and currencies closely tied with them. The OPEC oil crisis was driving up the cost of U.S. imports. United States gold reserves, still important in that period, were falling, and doubt was considerable that they would ever be used anyway. The rising tide of inflation was lifting the system's anchor off the floor, and with the chain at its bitter end, a round of speculation against the dollar ensued. The governments called a hurried conference in Washington in December of 1971. Meeting in a room at the centrally located Smithsonian Institution, the central bankers and treasury and finance officials

---

Figure 17.8 **Swap line T-account**

United States

Assets		Liabilities	
1. Credit at BB	+$100 mn	3. Deposit of BB	+$100 mn

Germany

Assets		Liabilities	
4. Credit at Fed	+DM170 mn	2. Fed Res	+DM170 mn
		5. Fed	−DM170 mn
		5. Commercial Banks	+DM170 mn

realigned currencies, noting as usual that the arrangement was "for eternity." The *Smithsonian Agreement* was shaky at the start, failing to engender confidence or change governments' policies.

In January of 1973, speculation on the Swiss franc rising caused a large movement of funds into Switzerland that the Swiss could not sterilize. Rather than face an inflation, the Swiss allowed the franc to float upward. While such a move is reasonable from the experience over the last decade and a half, it exposed the weakness of the Smithsonian Agreement. Within a few weeks there surged a veritable tidal wave of speculation out of weak currencies and into German marks, Swiss francs, and Japanese yen. The Bundesbank alone purchased $6 to $7 billion worth of currency in a week. Currencies were once again realigned, but the new alignments did not hold. Finally, on March 11, 1973, governments announced that they would no longer peg their currencies. Eternity had lasted little more than a year. The Bretton Woods period, begun with a bang, closed with a whimper.

THE BRETTON WOODS SYSTEM: AN ASSESSMENT

Under Bretton Woods, at least in its heyday, exchange rates were fixed, but could be adjusted. Domestic flexibility had declined considerably, as few countries saw prices falling, and high levels of unemployment were not tolerated. As a consequence, there was far more pressure for international cooperation and building up of reserves. The cooperation, through the IMF, helped in adjustment (in its approval of exchange rate changes and in its advisory capacity) and in the ability to maintain trade imbalances. The sharp increase in the holdings of U.S. dollars allowed a large expansion of international reserves and while perhaps excessive at times, was important in keeping reserves at high levels. Indeed, when the United States no longer would redeem dollars in gold, it was gold, not dollars, that ceased to be the international reserve!

The Bretton Woods system was a good one for its time. It worked in a period when international capital flows were modest compared to the present markets, when one financial market and one currency dominated, and where that currency's purchasing power was quite stable. It worked in a period when full employment levels could be achieved with only modest inflation and when a slowing of growth could bring income adjustments without large-scale unemployment. Times have changed, however, and the Bretton Woods system could not survive the changes. What would replace it in the decades to follow? And what kind of system can we now build? Turn to the following chapter.

VOCABULARY AND CONCEPTS ─────────────────

Adjustable peg	Bullion
Bancor	Bullion dealers
Bretton Woods system	Clearing union

Conditionality
Financial panic
Fund quotas
Fundamental disequilibrium
General Arrangements to Borrow (GAB)
Gold convertibility
Gold standard
Gold-exchange standard
International Monetary Fund (IMF)
Keynes Plan
Mint parity
One-way option

Pegging
Reconstitution
Reparations
Reserve currency
Reserve tranche
Smithsonian Agreement
Special drawing rights (SDRs)
Standby arrangements
Supertranche
Swap lines
Systemic approach
Tranche

QUESTIONS

1. Explain the elements of the international system and how they are interrelated.

   a. Take each element of the system and show what it was like under the gold standard, in the 1920s, during the Great Depression, and under Bretton Woods.

   b. Examine how each part was interrelated under any one of the systems, with particular interest in the gold standard and Bretton Woods periods.

2. Explain what the gold standard was and how it worked in its prime.

3. What were some of the key benefits of the gold standard? Its most severe problems?

4. How automatic were adjustments under the gold standard?

5. Explain what the gold-exchange standard was.

6. How was Germany to pay reparations to Britain and France and they to repay the United States for the wartime loans?

7. "The Smoot-Hawley Tariff in itself would not have changed trade balances, which are driven by differences between saving and investment, but it did make the war debts harder to pay." Explain.

8. Analyze the gold-exchange standard as a system, showing its benefits and difficulties.

9. Explain the adjustable peg. Under what circumstances could it be adjusted? Why was adjustment so much controlled?

10. "The whole thrust of the Bretton Woods system was toward pegging, not using the exchange rate to make adjustment." Explain and evaluate.

11. Why might speculation be worse under fixed than under floating rates?

12. Explain the basics of the IMF: how funds are collected, how they are lent, and the conditions for lending.

13. How does the IMF differ from a central bank? (Contrast it with the Keynes Plan.)

14. How would the IMF prevent the kind of runs on currency that occurred in 1931?

15. What are SDRs? Why did economists think they should be created? What are the rules governing their creation and use?

16. Why have SDRs never been as important as anticipated?

17. Why did the Bretton Woods system collapse?

NOTES

[1] Readers interested in the topic may wish to read Jan Hogendorn and Marion Johnson, *The Shell Money of the Slave Trade,* Cambridge, Cambridge University Press, 1986.

[2] See Tamim Bayoumi, "Saving-investment correlation," *IMF Staff Papers,* June, 1990, pp. 360–387.

[3] Arthur I. Bloomfield traces the relationship of the discount rate to the reserve ratio in 11 European nations. "The fact that, for five of the eleven [central] banks examined, discount rates and reserve ratios did *not* characteristically move in opposite directions—even on an annual average basis—indicates that the link between discount rate changes and movements of gold was not so close or general under the pre-1914 gold standard as is supposed." *Monetary Policy Under the International Gold Standard, 1880–1914,* New York, Federal Reserve Bank of New York, 1959.

[4] "The date when England 'returned to gold' after the war is a landmark in world history, but it is very difficult to determine the date when England left the gold standard to which she returned in 1925." W.A. Brown, Jr. in Ragnar Nurkse, *International Currency Experience,* Geneva, League of Nations, 1944, Vol. II, p. 28. Quoted in Leland Yeager, *International Monetary Relations,* New York, Harper and Row, 1966, Chapter 15.

[5] All predicted by Keynes in his pamphlet, *The Economic Consequences of Mr Churchill* (originally published in 1925), in *The Collected Writing of John Maynard Keynes,* Vol. IX, London, Macmillan, 1972, pp. 207–230.

[6] W.A. Brown, Jr., in Nurkse, *International Currency Experience,* used that word on p. 154.

[7] For a good summary of the whole period see Leland Yeager, *International Monetary Relations.* For more depth see the eminently readable Nurkse volumes, cited with the W.A. Brown reference.

[8] See again Yeager, *International Monetary Relations,* and the Nurkse *International Currency Experience.*

[9] Allan Meltzer, *Keynes's Monetary Theory: A Different Interpretation,* Cambridge, Cambridge University Press, 1988.

[10] Borrowings and repayments, described as purchases and repurchases, are in the beginning pages of the IMF's *International Financial Statistics,* a monthly publication available in almost any university library. They are not in the annual yearbook.

[11] The basic arrangements are described in the Introduction to each month's *International Financial Statistics.*

[12] Robert G. Murphy and George M. Von Furstenberg, "An analysis of factors influencing the level of SDR holdings in non-oil developing countries," *IMF Staff Papers,* June 1981, pp. 310–337.

Chapter 18

International Macroeconomic Policy II

Overall Objective: To convey an understanding of how international monetary systems serve the world in which they operate, evaluating the current arrangements and exploring suggested alternatives; and to suggest that the problems of international adjustment, like those of trade, are ultimately related to domestic flexibility.

MORE SPECIFICALLY:

- To describe the elements of the post–Bretton Woods system (or systems), particularly the exchange rate adjustment mechanisms and types of international coordination.

- To show what kinds of changes the IMF has had, and why they have been made.

- To evaluate the present system in terms of the systemic criteria delineated in the previous chapter.

- To consider the exchange rate options suggested for the future and their pros and cons; and to know the principal arguments for and against fixed exchange rates.

- To convey an understanding of the $N-1$ problem and both the advantages and dangers of coordination.

- To reveal the extent of reserves in the present system and why they are not presently a problem.

- To show how increased domestic flexibility would ease international adjustments.

BEYOND BRETTON WOODS

ELEMENTS OF THE POST–BRETTON WOODS SYSTEM

Some economists feared that the collapse of the Bretton Woods system would unleash once again the havoc that followed the crumbling of the international monetary system in 1931. It didn't. The industrial nations were not in a period of recession at the outset, and they were quite willing—probably too willing—to use the freedom from international constraint to pursue their own monetary policies. The system as set up is basically what this book has shown in

Chapters 10–16, so it need not bear extensive discussion here. Continued historical analysis, bringing matters up to the early 1990s, is, however, fundamental to a consideration of any changes in the system.

Taking each part of the international system as described in the last chapter, the post–Bretton Woods system consists of the following:

Exchange Rate System. In the initial period after the collapse of Bretton Woods, almost all currencies seemed to float against one another. Central banks were intervening in the market to control or establish trends, but no official parities were established. Gradually, however, governments sought more stability. Today, no single exchange rate system prevails. Most European currencies have been fixed to one another through the *European Monetary System* (discussed below); other currencies have been closely tied to the dollar, some to the yen, and still others float. Normally, the dollar, the ECU (a European currency unit, discussed below), and the yen float against one another, although frequently monetary authorities intervene in the markets to try to influence the value of the currencies. Currencies might be fixed for a while and then changed, since outside the European Monetary System there are no rules. In some cases, the degree of tying is unknown: The Canadian press was full of (incorrect) claims in 1990 that the Canadian dollar was being tied to the U.S. dollar at around 86 cents; the government claimed otherwise, but the public was unsure.

The box on the next page shows the IMF's assessment of how each currency was handled—the extent of fixing and against what currency.

Rules and Guidelines. Attempts have increased to reach common understandings of how governments are to react to unusual changes in the value of their currencies on the foreign exchange market; attempts at international coordination of policy have also increased.

Economic Flexibility. The ability of governments to push prices down or even to hold prices was severely questioned in the 1970s. Some greater flexibility may be emerging, but its absence is still striking.

Sustainability of Trade Imbalances. Although trade imbalances have been less than in the gold standard period, many countries, including the United States and much of the Third World, have been able to run substantial trade deficits. When the private capital market has failed, monetary and government funds have frequently, though grudgingly, been used to maintain the trade imbalances. A shortage of reserves is not a serious problem, given the large amount of U.S. dollars held as reserves.

International Cooperation. The extent of international cooperation has been much greater in recent decades.

■ *PREVAILING EXCHANGE RATE REGIMES*
   AND THEIR FREQUENCY

Peg: single currency (46 countries). The country links its exchange rate to the value of a major currency—usually the U.S. dollar or the French franc—but does not change the rate frequently. About one half of all developing countries have such an arrangement.

Peg: currency composite (40). A composite, or basket, is usually formed by the currencies of major trading partners to make the pegged currency more stable than if a single-currency peg were used. Currency weights may be based on trade, services, or major capital flows. About one fourth of all developing countries have composite pegs.

Flexibility limited vis-à-vis single currency (4). The value of the currency is maintained within certain margins of the peg. This system is currently used by four Middle Eastern countries.

Flexibility limited: cooperative arrangements (10). This has applied to countries in the exchange rate mechanism (ERM) of the European Monetary System (EMS), and is a cross between a peg and a float: EMS currencies have been pegged to each other, but float otherwise.

More flexible: adjusted to indicator (5). The currency is adjusted more or less automatically to changes in selected indicators. A common indicator is the real effective exchange rate that reflects inflation-adjusted changes in the currency vis-à-vis major trading partners. This category also includes cases where the exchange rate is adjusted according to a preannounced schedule.

More flexible: managed float (22). The central bank sets the rate, but varies it, sometimes frequently. Adjustments are judgmental, usually based on a range of indicators, such as international reserves, the real effective exchange rate, and developments in parallel exchange markets.

More flexible: independent float (27). Rates are market-determined. Most developed countries have floats—partial for EMS countries, but the number of developing countries included in this category has been increasing in recent years.

Source: David Burton and Martin Gilman, "Exchange rate policy and the IMF," *Finance and Development*, September 1991, p. 20.

PROBLEMS POSED BY FLOATING RATES

The era of floating rates was not greeted with the dread that had accompanied the floating rates of the 1930s. Germany and Switzerland, after all, had allowed their currencies to float to keep down inflation, and many people thought that the U.S. dollar should have been lower in value. Countries that had used floating rates, such as Canada, which had floated its currency (in violation of IMF rules) in 1949 and never declared a par value, had had a relatively good experience. Given the size of speculative funds and the increased liquidity of capital markets, pegging rates seemed impossible. Moreover, many economists were convinced that market-determined exchange rates would be more stable, lacking the one-way option, and more reflective of underlying costs than government-determined rates—and this included the influential conservative economist, Milton Friedman.

A great deal of professional opinion—and particularly the opinion of the central bankers—has moved away from the earlier optimism about floating rates. The reasons are several:

1. International trade and investment are more costly and complicated when currencies change frequently in value. Certainly the development of long-term forward instruments has allowed world trade and investment to continue to expand. But forward coverage is not free, and for the smaller firm, it is complicated. Travelers, who sometimes could use such coverage, cannot be bothered (in the sense that the bother is a cost) and sometimes get stung, holding a declining currency. Moreover, truly long-run investments cannot be covered.

   This is not to say that given the fact that nations have different rates of inflation, the investors would prefer fixed rates; that would distort costs even more. If British Industries builds a plant in Canada to serve the North American market and the Canadian inflation is more than the American, British Industries is certainly better off if the Canadian dollar can fall in value. What we are saying is that floating rates are the lesser of two evils, and it may be possible to avoid getting into situations where that choice must be made.

2. Financial, tax, and cost accounting problems are considerable under floating rates, and the solutions to the problems are often rather awkward. A money-losing (in Deutsche marks) German subsidiary of an American company, for instance, could turn up on the accounts as improving the company's profits because of a requirement to revalue the whole German plant in dollars because the Deutsche mark has risen. In a sense, the German subsidiary has helped the parent—if the parent is about to or can sell it, but that may not be an option. While management might understand the ambiguity, recognizing that in one sense the plant has contributed to profits and in another it has not, tax collectors cannot be equally philosophical, assessing a profits tax that is both paid and not paid.

   Again, a floating rate may be preferable to fixed rates, given disparate rates of inflation, which have their own accounting problems. And again, the better solution is little or no inflation in all major countries and no changes in exchange rates.

3. Currency movements under floating rates have not proved as sensible as anticipated. Despite the fact that the free market is at work, some currencies appear overvalued and some undervalued—in the judgment of most economists. Whether this is the fault of speculators or of countries' increasing reliance on interest rate policy is unclear, but very large current account imbalances are offset by large short-term capital inflows. Either the market has been often in error, or the economists and central bankers are wide of the mark.

Moreover, several economists have argued convincingly that rational economic decision makers can cause exchange rates to *overshoot*. The arguments center on the timing of the response of spot and forward exchange rates, interest rates, and prices, the details of which need not concern us here.[1] Stock markets, commodity markets, and to a lesser extent, bond markets all show patterns of overshooting, and however inconvenient, it seems to be true also of foreign exchange markets. Suffice it to note that information in markets is asymmetrically distributed, and much key information is unknowable, meaning that expectations are important in short-term movements. There seems no logical reason, for instance, why the Canadian dollar should have plunged from 87 to 72 and then back up to 80 U.S. cents in the course of three months. If it was going to settle near 80 cents, why did it plunge all the way to 72 cents?

Again, it is unlikely that the Bretton Woods system as it stood could have produced better exchange rates. As two IMF economists commented, "The hybrid system that has been in place since 1973 has proved resilient to large shocks to the international monetary system; it is doubtful whether the Bretton Woods system would have withstood the two major oil price increases. . . ."[2]

4. A floating rate may give a country the ability to keep on inflating without suffering any more severe consequence than the continued fall in the foreign exchange value of its currency. Any pressure for price stability exerted by the outflow of reserves under a fixed exchange rate system is thereby ended.

   In truth, the argument cuts both ways. By cutting loose from fixed values, Germany and Switzerland have avoided inflations. Fixed rates restrain inflation only when the low inflation country can anchor the system. Otherwise, it can spread inflation.

5. Finally, we note again the arguments of Chapter 16 dealing with the inflationary effects of devaluation and its contribution to inflationary expectations.

MOVES TOWARD GREATER EXCHANGE RATE CERTAINTY

G-5 AND G-7   In 1967, the finance ministers of the five leading industrial nations—the United States, the United Kingdom, Germany, Japan, and France—began a series of annual, and sometimes more frequent, meetings to discuss world economic matters of mutual interest. These countries became known as the *Group of Five* or *G-5*. In 1975, the heads of state began to attend also, leading to the phrase *economic summit*. In 1975 and 1976, Italy and Canada joined the economic summit, giving rise to the *Group of Seven* or *G-7*. The G-5, particularly through their *G-5 forum*, begun in 1982 and attended also by the heads of the central banks, continued to work informally and more effectively than the more ceremonial meetings of the G-7. The sense that the action lay in the G-5 forum led Canada and Italy to press to join the forums, which they began to do in 1987. In addition to country representatives, two European Community officials and the managing director of the IMF attend most meetings.* G-5 can still meet separately, but Canada and Italy send observers anyway, and in no case is any decision binding. Most of the meetings have dealt with economic coordination, a topic explored at length later in this chapter, but part of the summits' concerns has been exchange rates.

The G-5 accepted the floating exchange rates that followed the collapse of the Smithsonian Agreement, concentrating instead on coordination of fiscal and, to a more limited extent, monetary policy. Certainly they discussed exchange rates and possible systems, but the countries never committed themselves to any joint action. In 1985, however, at meetings at the Plaza Hotel in New York, the G-5 decided on joint action to push down the value of the U.S. dollar. Since then, joint management of exchange rates has been a regular topic, and presumably the G-7 is coordinating some joint efforts to manage exchange rate values. The Plaza Accord appears to mark (and it is early to say) a change in attitude and a movement toward international management of exchange rates. Whether we are to carve the RIP on the tombstone of floating rates depends on how much the corpse stirs.

THE EUROPEAN MONETARY SYSTEM

Disenchantment with floating rates came first in Europe, where there are many currencies. After all, the United States has only one currency over an area larger than Western Europe and a population nearly as large. With trade in the 10% of GNP range, only a small percentage of transactions have to be made in floating rates and covered in the forward markets. Europe, in contrast, was having to face such activities for 30 to 50 percent of its trade. Imagine the difficulties of trade within the United States if the area east of the Mississippi were divided into six different states with different currency units. Europe has struggled with the problem since the end of the First World War, making a number of attempts at increasing exchange rate stability. The latest of these is the European Monetary System, founded in 1979, which in the summer of 1993 experienced major and perhaps mortal troubles.

INSTITUTIONAL ARRANGEMENT WITHIN THE EMS In its the initial years saw only limited coordination, as the members adjusted to economic shocks in different ways, some of them inflationary and some contractionary. From 1983 to about 1987, the member countries concentrated on internal monetary stability.** Such an attention to monetary matters was characteristic of much policy at the time, including the policies in the United States and Britain, not at that time

---

* *G-10* refers to the industrial nations that lend the IMF money under the General Arrangements to Borrow. G-77 refers to a group of Third World countries who want an input into international economic policy. Since a group of 77 proved rather awkward, a smaller G-24 has been organized.

** The members of the EMS are all EC members with the exception of Greece and Portugal. In addition, Norway, Sweden, and Finland have sworn to follow EMS rules.

in the EMS. During this period the EMS developed the *exchange rate mechanism (ERM)* where the currencies of the countries were tied to a central rate in a *wide band* (2.25% either side of the weighted average); it is this part of the system that collapsed in 1993 when the band was widened to 30%. To keep their currencies within this band, the countries had to try to minimize divergences in economic performance. In 1987, the central banks of EMS countries developed swap lines that were virtually unlimited for the very short run, allowing considerable intervention in the foreign exchange market. The countries were also to work together on interest rate policies and to allow somewhat more fluctuation within the wide band.

In many senses, the EMS has been a miniature of the old Bretton Woods adjustable peg. Instead of having a low-inflation, strong currency, the American dollar as the anchor, the German mark has served. And the mark has indeed put a brake on the system. Officially, the unit of account is the ECU, or *European Currency Unit,* a weighted average of all the member currencies. *The Economist* noted that the average rate of inflation of the eight full members of the EMS has been 3.5%, ranging from Holland's 1% to Italy's 6.75%. The European Community members outside the EMS have had an average inflation of 10.25%. Perhaps they did not join the EMS because they had higher inflation rates—or to put it another way, because they did not feel they could come to grips with their higher inflation rates.

The whole EMS system floats against currencies outside the system. Within the system, currencies move against one another, but the countries have tried to keep them from straying too far through the use of monetary and fiscal (to some extent) policy, and through intervention in the foreign exchange markets. Until 1993, currencies had changed in value, usually without the same speculation that was characteristic of the adjustable peg. In the summer of 1993, however, many currencies were pushed to their floor values, and, sensing the one-way option, speculation became intense.

Like the Bretton Woods adjustable peg that worked while the dollar was sound, the EMS probably worked because it was tied to the German mark, a low-inflation currency. It also worked because the number of countries involved has been small and willing to run economic policies that reinforced their exchange rate policies. The EMS differed from the Bretton Woods system, however, in that the dollar assets generally paid the lowest interest rates. The strain on the ERM came when the low-inflation country experienced higher inflation and also began to run high interest rates, attracting enormous capital inflows.

Unlike the Bretton Woods system, however, the EMS has been looking toward further stability and an eventual single currency for all of the European Community. While the accomplishment of this objective seems distant, it is of great interest. The plan alone was bold. In December of 1991 the European Community heads of state held a meeting at Maastricht in the Netherlands to agree upon a treaty to provide the legal and political framework for a European monetary union. Such a union would have a single currency (the ECU) and a single central banking system. The new common monetary authority, the European System of Central Banks, with its European Central Bank would be something like the American Federal Reserve System—the *Euro-Fed*—with each country's central bank having a representative on the board and with a president appointed by the governments. The ECB would control the money supply and, like the Federal Reserve, handle intervention in the foreign exchange market to control the external value of the new currency. The date for completing such arrangements was to be January 1, 1999, a date now much in doubt, as a later section discusses.

FURTHER DEVELOPMENTS OF THE IMF

The IMF ceased to be the dominant institution it had been in the heyday of Bretton Woods. The industrial countries, free of the need to peg their exchange rates, did not need to borrow. When they did decide to borrow to informally peg their rates, the IMF could not match the resources they could obtain through bilateral arrangements. The IMF became much more concerned with Third World governments who required fewer reserves and had fewer borrowing options. Nonetheless, there was a very considerable pressure applied on the Fund's resources. This led to modifications in its funding sources and in its lending terms.

ADDITIONAL SOURCES OF FUNDING   In the post–Bretton Woods period, the Fund has found three additional sources to provide it with funds.

1. In 1974 and 1975, the Fund arranged a special *oil facility* where oil exporters lent it foreign exchange to be relent to countries struggling with the higher oil prices; those arrangements are presently finished, all loans having been repaid to the lenders.

2. In 1977, the Fund borrowed additional funds under the *Special Financing Facility,* and this continues at present, with nearly SDR 3.5 billion lent to the fund.

3. In 1988, the Fund began to borrow money from various monetary authorities to be used for the *Enhanced Structural Adjustment Facility,* described in the next section.

4. In addition, the Fund has a number of bilateral agreements. It has a SDR 9.6 billion loan from Saudi Arabia, and a much smaller amount from Japan.

NEW LENDING FACILITIES   The IMF has found it necessary to lend Third World countries considerably more than is authorized in their original quotas.[3] To do so, a series of facilities has been established. The Fund's lending categories have expanded well beyond the basic credit tranches.[4] Its accounts list an impressive array of special lending facilities:

- Compensatory Financing Facility, and its successor the Compensatory and Contingency Financing Facility
- Buffer Stock Financing Facility

- Oil Facility
- Credit Tranche Special Financing Facility
- Credit Tranche Expanded Access
- Extended Facility Ordinary Resources
- Extended Facility Special Financing
- Extended Facility Enlarged Access Resources

These facilities arose from a series of economic shocks that put extraordinary pressure on countries, mostly less developed ones. Nations found that their ordinary loans were not enough to cover the pressures brought about by rapidly changing primary product prices and the considerable economic shocks of the 1970s and 1980s. The oil facility was to help nations who were importing oil heavily when the price rose in 1972. The compensatory financing facility was to help some nations whose exports fell sharply in value as the industrial nations contracted demand after the oil price rise. The buffer stock facility was to help nations involved in international commodity agreements pay for storage and surpluses in years when prices were falling. Each problem called forth another response, and in some cases, additional credits were approved also. As the Third World debt problem became serious in the 1980s, the IMF was pressured to increase its lending to deeply indebted countries and expand its credit tranches, resulting in the Enhanced Structural Adjustment Facility. Not all facilities are open to all countries, but some are able to tap a number of them. Mauritania, for instance, is using six of the nine facilities.

THE PRESENT SYSTEM AND ITS WEAKNESSES

EXCHANGE RATE STABILITY

After nearly two decades of living with some, often considerable, degree of exchange rate instability, few economists doubt that more stability would be better. Trade has been made more complicated and international investment more difficult. While most economists expected that exchange rates would settle at points that would reflect price level differences, and maybe they do, that path is long and twisting. Governments and producers in the trade-sensitive sectors of the economy have to struggle with substantial swings in the value of currencies. That stable rates would be better is not in question. What is less certain is whether the benefits would outweigh the costs. After all, trade has continued to expand, and international investment is very extensive, despite the difficulties of dealing with floating rates.

ECONOMIC FLEXIBILITY

Given that trade and investment do not appear to suffer greatly, perhaps the costs of floating rates are a reasonable price to pay for avoiding the costs of adjustment. *Any* adjustment of income, price level, or exchange rate is difficult. Given a fixed income, it involves a shift of income between borrowers and lenders, between savers and spenders (which includes the government), the trade-sensitive sector and the rest of the economy. Given a real income responsive to aggregate demand, saving must still rise faster than absorption or investment. The problem is that exchange rate changes rarely stop with just a shifting of resources between the domestic and trade-sensitive sectors. The forces they unleash themselves create inflation and unemployment, which is what changing the exchange rate was supposed to avoid.

In a sense, the ultimate solution to payments problems is not macroeconomic but microeconomic: the development of institutions and understandings that allow adjustment. Institutional change, for instance, could come in a different form of wage and employment contracts, making a different kind of tradeoff between regular employment and wages. Another change might be greater government control over its own saving and expenditures to reduce its reliance on monetary policy. The key question here is whether the adoption of a more rigorous international system of fixed rates and responses according to rules, as under the gold standard, can force institutional change or affect expectations in such a way as to stimulate institutional growth. The chapter explores these questions further.

TOLERANCE FOR TRADE IMBALANCES

As we have noted, trade imbalances were much higher at the turn of the century than in the last decades. Clearly, the lenders expected repayment and the borrowers expected to pay, and to a very great extent those expectations were fulfilled. By historical standards, today's governments are extraordinarily nervous and conservative. So many of the imbalances between saving and investment may reflect much longer-term factors, particularly if demographics and long-run growth prospects are key elements. Two cases in point are the United States and Canada. Both have run large current account deficits in the 1980s, yet both have been recipients of substantial inflows of private capital. And despite the doom-mongering of economists throughout the decade, no sudden collapse has occurred, and at least as of 1992, both countries' current accounts were showing marked improvements. Should the stress on policy making then be for more settled expectations and extra reserves, such that trade imbalances could be prolonged?

INTERNATIONAL COOPERATION

International cooperation can play an important role in keeping stable expectations. It can (1) establish rules and guidelines to participating countries, (2) provide additional reserves if a nation wishes to keep its exchange rate stable in a period when the market is forcing it down, and (3) plan coordinated macroeconomic policy. Since the establishment of the IMF, the world has had the first two forms of cooperation. More recently it has seen some of the third. Note that if the world has more international cooperation on policies, it can make adjustment easier and prevent beggar-thy-neighbor behavior. It is difficult at this point to sum up whether there is sufficient international cooperation in the current system.

Our thoughts then must turn to the future and to what kind of system is likely to emerge in the 1990s.

PLANNING FOR A NEW EXCHANGE RATE SYSTEM

THE FIXED VERSUS FLEXIBLE RATE DEBATE

What, then, is the best exchange rate system? The answer is not obvious, but in the interest of at least seeing what it is we cannot see, review what we have developed about the two systems. It is a favorite topic for international economics essays, and a useful theoretical exercise. From a practical point of view, most systems under use or serious discussion involve elements of both fixed and floating rates. The theoretical debate also has a tendency to contrast ideal constructs, or to take an ideal of one and a weak form of the other, but here consider both the ideal and the actual, rather weaker form.

THE IDEAL FIXED RATE   An ideal fixed exchange rate would never change—or at least the participants in the market would believe that to be so, so we will call it a credible fixed rate. We will also postulate that the reserve unit (gold, dollars, SDRs, or something new) is stable in value. Its chief advantages are:

For microeconomics:

1. Trade and travel are much simpler, not requiring extensive forward cover or risk exposure.

2. Investment, both short and long term, is much safer because neither investor nor borrower faces significant exchange rate risk.

3. International corporate planning is far easier because there is no need to consider what will happen to the exchange rate.

4. The valuation of corporate assets, as well as the taxes they incur, is far easier, and undoubtedly less misallocative, if the exchange rate is stable.

For macroeconomics:

1. To maintain a fixed exchange rate, a country will almost undoubtedly have to figure out how to borrow at reasonable rates or restrict its economy. It is therefore most likely that countries will follow policies that lead to price stability.

2. A fixed exchange rate encourages conservative expectations in the price level and in itself becomes a self-fulfilling prophecy.

THE IMPERFECT FIXED EXCHANGE RATE   The imperfect fixed rate is not completely credible, as devaluations and revaluations occur. We also cannot trust that the reserve base will be noninflationary.

Many of the microeconomic advantages are reduced. We still must cover for trade and travel. Short-term investment still faces a risk of change. Direct or stock market investment might actually be better off, as the next section argues. Macroeconomic advantages are also weakened. If the country feels that it never need restore old price levels, and can instead devalue its currency, it has less incentive to keep price levels down. Moreover, if the quantity of underlying reserve assets increases greatly, there will be inflationary pressures. Economic historians have noted how in the sixteenth century the inflow of gold from the New World (combined with large Spanish trade deficits as the Hapsburgs sought to hold their land in the Netherlands) contributed to European inflation. More currently, we noted how the increased inflation in the United States undermined the Bretton Woods system.

IDEAL FLOATING RATES   An ideal floating rate would tend to follow purchasing power parity fairly closely, and market speculation would in fact tend to keep it fairly stable.

Microeconomic advantages:

1. There has been little evidence that trade and investment have been seriously hampered by the extent of floating rates. The options of covering are available and the markets very active.

2. Some companies could plan better with a floating rate because the foreign exchange rate changes will adjust to differential inflation rates.

Macroeconomic advantages:

1. A declining exchange rate is a clear signal to the public that the country is in serious trouble. In a sense, it is more alarming than a rise in the price index, and therefore may call forth action.

2. The avoidance of unnecessary swings in the money supply may be of great importance to some countries, where the inflows and outflows are large portions of the money supply, and counterbalancing policy difficult.

3. Creating unemployment in an attempt to hold prices down is a poor way to correct a trade deficit. Similarly, an inflation is a poor way to handle a trade surplus.

4. Provided that the changes to the exchange rate are suitably backed by domestic policies, a floating rate can restore competitiveness to the trade-sensitive sector more quickly and in a longer-lasting way than can alternative policies.

THE IMPERFECT FLOATING RATE   The imperfect rate frequently moves far away from its purchasing power parity for no apparent reason. When it rises or falls, it overshoots. The government does not put into force suitable domestic policies to reinforce what it is trying to do with the exchange rate.

The imperfect floating rate has no microeconomic advantages. It makes trade and investment much harder, and given its unpredictability, does not aid long-run investment.

On the macroeconomic side, the price effects of the declining exchange rates feed into the price level and into wage and price expectations, worsening inflation and nullifying any price benefits of the initial exchange rate change. Rising exchange rates might tend to push prices down, but if prices are rigid, would lead also to some unemployment.

An exchange rate that moves in ways that are hard for the public to understand is hardly going to be a sign to them of rising inflation or other problems that need fixing.

OPTIONS FOR THE NINETIES

The objective of having predictable and stable exchange rates is in itself a good one; the question has always been whether the tradeoffs required are too costly. The options under consideration today are several:

1. Target ranges, or *bands* around a central announced nominal exchange rate. The band would be 5 to 10% around a declared value and bolstered by domestic monetary and fiscal policies designed to bring prices in line with those of the most slowly inflating countries.

2. Target ranges around real exchange rates, with nominal devaluation allowed to account for differences in price levels. Such systems usually also involve supportive domestic monetary and fiscal policies. Advocates of such policies are more concerned with the adjustment difficulties of sticky wages and prices and more skeptical of monetarist or rational expectation effects.

Central to both sets of proposals is the idea of having a *target zone* or *target range,* considerably broader than the Bretton Woods 2%. With a broader range, speculators would have less of a one-way option because the currency would rarely be at the bottom or top, and even if it were, the speculator would face the chance of a fairly large movement in the opposite direction. Suppose the pound sterling in 1967 had a target zone of between $2.50 and $2.75 and had been not at the floor of $2.772 but at $2.65. Under the Bretton Woods system the speculator could lose only about 2 cents on the pound, and likely a lot less. Under the target range, the speculator stands a chance of losing more than 2 cents on the pound if the pound rises. And even if the pound is devalued, will it fall much below $2.65?

With a wide band, too, a country can devalue or revalue without upsetting the market too much, so long as the currency is not at the floor or ceiling. If the pound were at $2.60 with a floor of $2.50 and a ceiling of $2.75, it is unlikely the market would react sharply to a lowering of the range to $2.40–$2.65.

The target range proposals give more certainty to a currency value, and probably they are most useful over a longer period of time. Traders would still have to cover, but long-run investors and travelers would feel more comfortable. A traveler is not likely to get too upset about a 5% change in the value of the local currency. A long-run investor, similarly, is not basing its strategy on something as small as a 5% currency change over a 10-year period. An import firm, however, may lose all its profits with the 5% change.[*]

If the target range can change, of course, then long-run advantages are lost. To be credible, the system must have relatively few changes in target ranges. A system of creeping target ranges, like many creeping creatures, would not be especially pernicious, but would provide little benefit either.

NOMINAL TARGET RANGES

The European Monetary System uses nominal target ranges, fixes the values of currencies within those limits, and allows changes in valuation, after consultation. If it did not allow the revaluations, the high-inflation countries (France and Italy in particular) would have to slow their inflations to the levels of Germany and the Netherlands, something that would not be easy. G-5 and G-7 decisions to intervene in the foreign exchange markets have also set a range (not made public) for currency values.

The principal advantage of nominal targets is in the extent to which they discourage inflationary expectations. That, in turn, depends on (1) the key-currency nation itself having a low rate of inflation and (2) very infrequent devaluations. In turn, the countries themselves must be prepared to run policies that are not inflationary. In the mid-1980s, it was in vogue to have monetary targets, the assumption being that a stable money supply would keep prices from rising. Practical difficulties in defining a measurement of money and the annoying tendency of the velocity of money to change proved discouraging.

A more promising approach is to target *nominal GDP* rather than money supplies. If real GDP rises faster than the nominal, prices will fall; if it rises more slowly prices will, of course, rise. But if the target for nominal GDP is a realistic assessment of what the country can produce, prices will not change greatly. What is more, countries have a reasonable guide as to government policy.

Despite their appeal, nominal target ranges for currencies have their drawbacks:

1. However desirable, the world has not seen policies to reinforce the target currency ranges. In such situations, intervention is a waste of money. The 1987 Louvre Accord (of the G-5) agreed on an unrealistically high range for the U.S. dollar, one that U.S. policy (at least subsequent) did not justify. G-7 countries picked up something like $100 billion, but the stock market crash of October caused such a run on the dollar that it fell anyway. Central banks found them-

---

[*] If the trader holds a currency risk for 90 days, the 5% is 20% a year. The 10-year investor, however, views 5% over 10 years as only 0.5% per year.

selves holding devalued dollars. Britain lost perhaps £1 billion, West Germany DM 4 billion, and Japan ¥600 billion, "a gift from the taxpayers of Britain, West Germany, and Japan to the American government," commented *The Economist*.[5]

2. Insofar as a tradeoff exists between inflation and unemployment, and the economy decides to move toward higher employment and suffer the ills of some inflation, it should not also suffer the losses associated with an overvalued exchange rate in the name of rather nebulous gains from exchange rate stability. Much of the argument, therefore, is over the extent of that tradeoff. Does a tradeoff between inflation and unemployment exist? If it does, how much is it? Does exchange rate stability lower expectations of price increases and therefore achieve lower wage settlements and ultimately lower price increases? Can it do so without persistent high unemployment?

3. It is not the nominal, but the real exchange rates that should be—or in fact are—set and defended. The use of nominal exchange rates may be a kind of charade, with long-run adjustments being set close to the real exchange rate levels. This does not come close to giving an investor any assurance, however, since the decisions made by the meetings, however effective they may be, are not bound to any previously announced rule. In 1995 the G-7 may decide that the yen is at 140 to the dollar and in 2000 that it is 100. Why not admit at the outset that it is the real rate that will be defended (and of course, is easier to defend)?

REAL RANGES AND THE FUNDAMENTAL EQUILIBRIUM EXCHANGE RATE

A *real exchange rate* is a rate defined according to purchasing power parity. A mixture of intervention and economic policy could perhaps more successfully target and defend a real target than a nominal one. A current problem serves as a good basis for discussion of the problem.

In 1991 the Canadian dollar stood at over US$0.89, its highest price since 1972, and a number far off purchasing power parity. As a result, Canadian exports were suffering and exporters were being squeezed between higher domestic costs and lower Canadian dollars. Canadian competitors with imports, similarly, found their costs rising while competing imports were falling in price. Had the Canadian government targeted a real exchange rate, it would have intervened to keep the Canadian dollar from rising.

Fixing real rates would help investors whose investments were not tied to nominal values—those in direct investment, shares, or convertible securities. A Canadian firm could make its plans on *real* factors and be less concerned about the effect of inflation. Whether or not Canadian inflation is higher than the

American, the firm can be confident costs will not be distorted by an overvalued (or undervalued) exchange rate. In turn, the allocation of investment will be better, and with less risk, the amount of investment will be higher.

Note, however, that those investing in assets with fixed payouts—bonds and loans—do not gain from targeted real rates. They are no better off than they are under untargeted floating rates. They would still have to cover or be exposed to considerable risk. Funds moving through such channels would be discouraged.

The Canadian case illustrates yet another problem: By how much do we modify purchasing power parity to take into account investment flows? Nineteen eighty-nine was a year of high domestic Canadian investment, despite the high interest rates. A goodly portion of that investment was associated with the Free Trade Agreement with the United States, and a considerable portion was from abroad. As domestic investment rises above domestic saving, we would expect a trade deficit, which the higher Canadian dollar facilitates. Since the foreign borrowing appears sound in that it is going to domestic investment and to foreign-exchange-producing (or -saving) operations, the borrowing should be no problem. How should we account for this in our system?

The Institute for International Economics' John Williamson, who espouses real target zones, has put forth the idea of a *Fundamental Equilibrium Exchange Rate,* or *FEER.* A FEER is basically a purchasing power parity exchange rate, modified by long-run investment aims.[6] We might view it as the trade balance that would occur, given that interest rates more or less accurately reflected opportunity costs. Where there is inflation, we could assume that the interest rate *adjusted for inflation* was also close to the natural rate.

A FEER approach to the 1989 Canadian dollar would figure the purchasing power parity, then take a look at long-run trends (and aims) in Canadian foreign investment patterns, and modify the purchasing power rate accordingly. Clearly Canada can sustain foreign borrowing at small percentages of GNP indefinitely, so any purchasing power calculation has to look at the base year to see how much of a current account deficit Canada was able to handle comfortably in the base year, and, if it can still handle the deficit on a continuing basis, not seek a Canadian dollar so low as to eliminate the trade deficit.

FEERs can also handle any shifts in the competitiveness of a country that are not due to purchasing power shifts.

The FEER has a certain attraction, but many economists and central bankers remain nervous about it. The uneasiness comes from a number of problems:

1. In itself, it accepts differing rates of inflation, and therefore targeting FEERs does nothing for holding down world inflation rates. Moreover, exchange rate adjustment may *validate* inflationary expectations and weaken the credibility of the central bank's resolve to end the inflation.

2. The way of calculating FEERs may be ultimately too arbitrary to suffice as a target. Anyone can identify a nominal rate: A *real* exchange rate, however, is a statistical beast, and it comes in many forms. The calculation of purchasing

power parity itself depends on (1) a measure of inflation and (2) a weighting of exchange rates.

International Financial Statistics has six different measures of real rates (for major countries only), each based on a different index: Two are on labor costs (relative labor unit costs, relative normalized labor unit costs) and four on price indexes (relative value added deflators, wholesale prices, export unit values, and consumer prices). By those figures, the FEER value of the U.S. dollar for 1990, compared to a 1985 value of 100, could be as high as 74.8 (using an index based on unit values of exports), or as low as 56 (using an index based on relative unit labor costs). Consumer and wholesale price indexes both suggested a 69.6 value. Worse, by the middle of 1992, the only 1991 figure available was that based on consumer price indexes; this renders them of little use to those trying to make policy.

3. Without the use of supporting policy, choosing a real target range is only somewhat more sensible than choosing a nominal one. One of the reasons the Canadian dollar in 1989 was high was that Canadian interest rates were fighting an inflation, while American interest rates were lowered to fight possible recession, opening up a 4% gap in interest rates. Were Canada to have fixed its real exchange rate, then it would have had to buy large amounts of U.S. dollars, beyond what it could effectively sterilize. The proper policy answer was to reduce the large Canadian budget deficit, and without that a real target alone means little.

None of the three sets of criticisms is unanswerable. If the G-7 has intervened without supporting policy, it is not because any economist has advocated it. Williamson himself is quite keen on international cooperation in monetary and fiscal areas and the targeting of more than exchange rates, and such is an integral part of his latest blueprint plan. In that plan he and his associate Marcus Miller argue that fiscal policy should be used principally to regulate the domestic economy, while monetary policies and targets should be used to target real exchange rates.[7]

The high Canadian dollar is an effect of an incorrect fiscal policy. Whatever the FEER of the Canadian dollar, it is lower than 86 cents, and if it is targeted to be lower, almost the only option available is a contractionary fiscal policy. As for holding down world inflation, that too may be better handled as part of a package of policies; it is, in essence, foolish to place the burden of fighting world inflation on exchange rate policy. While exclusive reliance may be foolish, exchange rate stability may have a role to play.

The statistical problem reduces the clarity or transparency of a target range policy, but statistical problems are endemic in economic policy. Just because the answers may give only a range of correctness does not mean we cannot use them. Those answers may prove to be surprisingly consistent, as Chapter 16 showed in the presentation of material on the Korean won.

COORDINATION

To what extent should governments coordinate their macroeconomic policies?[8] Given the relatively slow domestic adjustments, some coordination between countries could be helpful to contain deflation or inflation. Under a system such as the gold standard, where every country followed well-accepted rules, there would be little need for meetings to decide on some plan of coordinated economic policy. But in most plans for any new system, policy coordination plays a large role. We examine that now.

THE *N* MINUS ONE (*N* − 1) PROBLEM

Countries can act independently so long as one, presumably a large one, takes a passive role. Consider a family of seven people coming to divide a pie into seven pieces. Each person can change the size of his or her slice of pie (up to a reasonable limit), depending on mood or taste. So long as self-sacrificing or diet-conscious Mother does not object, everyone else in the family can claim a slightly larger piece of pie. Indeed, some members may want smaller and others larger pieces, so that Mother rarely faces the problem. If, however, it works out that the last piece is too little or too large, then the family has a coordination problem, and may have to discuss the question. The problem has a name, currently fashionable: the *N minus one (N − 1) problem*. *N* is the number of pieces (7) whose size can be determined and *N* − 1 (6) is the number of pieces whose size can be determined independently.

If the pieces of pie are all roughly equal, the group will be under fairly considerable pressure to coordinate, or establish clear parameters. If, however, one member always has a very large piece, then coordination may not be as important. If Father, being a giant, always has roughly half the pie, and the other six only 8.3%, Father might not notice or care too much if sometimes he had 44% and sometimes 56%, which gives the others a chance to have up to 9.3% each. Since some frequently do not want their full 8.3% share, there may be only rare occasions for coordination, when Father gets too much or too little.

However homely, the *N* − 1 analogy and its corollary, which we will dub *the big slice,* serve to describe well the coordination problem facing the world. To illustrate how the big slice kept the need for coordination down, consider how the United States through the 1950s and mid-1960s just kept the dollar fixed to gold, while all other countries changed their exchange rates. The United States, being the *n*th country and the giant, never changed its exchange rate against the rest of the world. If other countries raised their interest rates, the United States was large enough that it could tolerate an outflow of short-term capital without major changes to its interest rates.

When young and boisterous with a sense of stewardship over what it liked to call the Free World, the giant let other countries change their exchange rates, interest rates, and fiscal policies without reacting much to them. So long as the other countries trusted the giant to be reasonable, they did not mind the occasional adjustments they made to his demands. The American inflation of the 1960s, its soaring budget deficits, and its large current account deficit changed the easy relationship. The giant could no longer face changing pieces of pie with equanimity, nor could the other members happily swallow pieces of pie that were much larger or smaller than they anticipated. Pressure mounted for some kind of coordination.

RULE-BASED OR PROCESS-ORIENTED POLICIES

A rule-based approach for international coordination establishes what countries must do when given situations develop. For instance under Bretton Woods, if their exchange rate came to the top of its par value, they were to intervene, buying foreign currency until it fell. Under rule-based coordination, a country facing persistent trade deficits might be required to lower its nominal GNP target. A process-oriented policy, to use the phrase of Yale's Richard Cooper, would not hold a rule as to when to intervene, but would have a set consultative process for making that decision. It is more like the decision of the Federal Reserve Board to change interest rates: No hard and fast rule exists, but the process by which the decision is reached is well established.

Under a rule-based system, countries would agree to follow a set of rules. Their actions would be predictable, and in turn that would lead to better investment decisions and more stable economic relations. Typical of such would be criteria concerning nominal or real exchange rates, the size of fiscal deficit relative to GNP, growth of money supply, size of current account deficit, or, popular recently, growth of nominal GDP.[9]

The problem with the rule-based systems is the problem of sovereignty: The values of coordination have to be large (and clear) compared with the values of controlling one's own economy for countries to get themselves tied up in a series of macroeconomic rules. It is hard to imagine the United States agreeing to a treaty that would hold its deficit down to some given percentage of GDP, or even to just holding down the growth of domestic demand. However desirable the goal, congress would surely feel that such ends are the national responsibility. After all, getting congress to approve the IMF was not that easy, and congress never did approve either the aborted International Trade Organization or GATT.[*] The gains from coordination, moreover, are not so clear as to inspire visionaries to leap to a new international system that constrains them too much domestically. Even if all countries did agree to rules, the ability to reinterpret rules, especially with no particular penalty for breaking them, is considerable. The amazing financial legerdemain the United States has used to keep its fiscal deficit conforming with the Gramm-Rudman requirements is a case in point. A rule-based system is probably not a serious political contender, at least in a formal sense.

---

[*] Note, too, that it is not only American sovereignty, but congress's power vis-à-vis the executive, that is at stake.

If the world is to have more economic coordination, it is surely going to come about through the meetings of the G-7, particularly the G-7 Forum, and other policy-level international meetings. Meetings are already frequent, particularly on monetary matters, and topics discussed have expanded.[10] In the earlier years of summit meetings, the topics were principally monetary and exchange rates, but in recent summit meetings the topics have dealt more with fiscal than monetary policy. Fiscal policy is more political than monetary policy, which is almost always in the hands of monetary authorities, somewhat insulated from political processes. Political authority, if only in the form of the pomp of summit meetings and in the sense of some tradeoff among political leaders, is important if any international meetings are to have any impact on fiscal policy. It is quite possible that some of the rules suggested above—particularly the growth of aggregate demand or some of the monetary aggregates—may become (or are) important elements or guidelines in the discussions. If one or more of the guidelines is not met, the policy makers will be under some degree of international pressure to make concessions elsewhere. Whether or not the accords reached at such meetings will have success, particularly when they reach deep into domestic politics, remains to be seen.

LIMITS AND DANGERS

A number of economists are unenthusiastic about a great deal of coordination. Take a former chairman of the President's Council of Economic Advisors, Martin Feldstein:

> *I believe that many of the claimed advantages of cooperation and coordination are wrong, that there are substantial risks and disadvantages to the types of coordination that are envisioned, and that an emphasis on international coordination can distract attention from the necessary changes in domestic policy.*[11]

What if the international decision is wrong? It might, for instance, call for more fiscal expansion for Germany and Japan, when they feel strongly (and correctly suppose) that such will cause more a rise in prices than any increase in income and consequent rise in imports. As such it might inaugurate a period of worldwide inflation. A policy that is right for some countries might not be right for them all. Moreover, some international coordination, as *The Economist*'s Clive Crook pointed out, has given the world one of the worst possible economic policies: the MFA, or Multi-Fiber Arrangement. And as European Community members increase their coordination of both monetary and fiscal plans, will they create another monster like their Common Agricultural Policy?

The benefits of coordination remain, in some senses, rather nebulous. Like certain subatomic particles, theory suggests they exist, but whether they can be found and whether, as Feldstein suggests, they are worth the trouble and distraction is hard to say. In any case, at present the world is experimenting with more coordination. We can only trust that it stimulates fiscal and monetary propriety, rather than providing excuses to abandon it.

THE MAASTRICHT TREATY IN PERSPECTIVE

A DESCRIPTION OF THE TREATY   The Maastricht Treaty to create a single European currency and monetary authority provides a specific set of answers to the questions raised. Whether correct or not, they are of great interest. Consider the elements of the treaty:

1. It establishes three stages of increasing coordination of policy as necessary preparation for a single currency. Governments are to meet four criteria on inflation, exchange rates, interest rates, and fiscal deficits. In the first stage (1992–1993), governments work on their own to meet the criteria, in the second (1994–?) the EC oversees their work and progress, and in the third (no later than January 1, 1999), the single currency and single monetary authority come into effect.

2. The criteria to be met are:
    a. Inflations cannot exceed by more than 1.5% the inflation rates of the three best-performing EC members.
    b. Long-term interest rates cannot be more than 2% above those of the three countries with the lowest inflations.
    c. The exchange rate must be held within the EMS' band.
    d. The combined deficits of central, state, and local governments must not be more than 3% of GDP, and total public debt should not be more than 60% of GDP.

Depending on how well countries meet the criteria, a decision will be made in 1996 when to start the third stage. In addition, any country joining must make its central bank independent of government direction.

Britain had proposed the establishment of the ECU as a hard currency, but one that would circulate side by side with national currencies. If successful, it would gradually replace national currencies.[12] In a sense, the ECU would act much as gold did during the true gold standard, when people in any country could use either banknotes or gold itself. The British idea was a good idea but was not accepted. With the failure of the ERM in 1993, it may again be on the table.

HOW DOES THE MAASTRICHT TREATY ANSWER THE POLICY QUESTIONS ABOVE?   The Maastricht Treaty provides one set of answers to the questions we have raised. They are not necessarily correct for Europe or for the world, and it already seems they are impractical, but the answers are clear.

Q: Should coordination be rule based or process based?
A: Rule based.
Q: Should monetary policy accommodate price increases?
A: No.
Q: Should we use real or nominal exchange rates?
A: Nominal ones.
Q: Should exchange rate bands be narrow or wide?

A: Narrow.

Q: Does a tradeoff exist between inflation and unemployment?

A: No.

Q: How do we solve the $N - 1$ problem?

A: We make the independent central bank the last party.

Q: Does international coordination distract attention from necessary changes in domestic policy?

A: No, the changes in domestic policy must occur first.

Q: What happens if Europe is wrong, and countries suffer unusual amounts of unemployment?

A: The same thing that happens if New England suffers unemployment while the West Coast booms. Prices fall and people move.

Q: Isn't that going to make it harder in Europe, where the population is not so mobile and language and culture differences are great?

A: Perhaps.

Q: What happens if there is a recession and governments cannot use fiscal policy to help and the European Central Bank refuses to expand the money supply?

A: Unemployment rises, but eventually prices will adjust to the level of money. Governments may fall, too.

Q: What happens if there is a very large wage push and aggregate supply shifts upward?

A: That would be short-run AS; long-run AS is determined by productivity and the size of the work force. We would expect that without the ability to pass on higher wages in the form of higher prices and exchange rate devaluations, different wage bargains would be struck. Otherwise there will be much unemployment.

Q: These answers seem very conservative. Whatever happened to Keynes?

A: Keynes died in 1946. He favored exchange rate stability, and it would be hard to know what he would say after the stagflations of the last two decades. He may have been right for the 1930s, and his followers right for the 1950s, but the world has changed.

Q: Does the EC advocate these policies for the rest of the world?

A: No. It is clear that, however good they may be for Europe, the ECU will have to float against the dollar and the yen, with perhaps a more flexible approach. If Europe is successful, perhaps the others will follow.

THE COLLAPSE OF THE ERM The collapse of the ERM looked something like the 1931 monetary crisis. Starting in September of 1992 with the Swedish kronor, speculation against weaker currencies in the ERM (and toward the Deutsche mark and guilder) knocked them one by one out of the ERM. Sweden, Portugal, Spain, Britain, Ireland, and Italy were forced into devaluation or temporary withdrawal. When speculation turned against the remaining Danish, Belgian, and French currencies, the countries decided to relax the rules and establish a 30% wide band. The other rules on interest and inflation rates, technically still in force, would presumably be guidelines only. With the August announcement, it appeared Maastricht was dead. What caused the collapse?

1. Germany was key. The expenses of unification had caused fiscal deficits, and the Bundesbank was using tight monetary policy to fight inflation. A stable currency with high interest rates caused funds to flow into Germany, yet Germany attempted to sterilize the entire inflow. Germany was not going to let its price level rise.

2. The commitment of governments to the Maastricht guidelines was not credible. Votes on the ratification of the treaty were only narrowly and grudgingly in favor.

3. It was clear by 1992 that most countries wished to use monetary policy to stimulate their economies and were not about to wait for price levels to fall in order to raise the real money supply. Nor could they have tolerated the size of trade deficit that would emerge should *AD* rise. Countries would not live with the answers given to the questions on unemployment in the dialogue above.

4. The ability of an international system to discipline domestic economies is doubtful, particularly in the absence of domestic institutional changes that would make prices more flexible. Price flexibility is not about to be changed by a smattering of Thatcherist limitations of labor, an anti-trust case here and there, and talk of social contracts and union-management cooperation; this is particularly true if the size of governments, the number of regulations, and world class agricultural protectionism are unchanged.

Is there a moral? Perhaps: The establishment of a rigid international system when the domestic systems are also rigid is bound to fail.

RESERVES AND ADJUSTMENT

Perhaps we are too much worried about what are in historical perspective fairly small payments imbalances. Microeconomics indicates that world welfare will be improved if capital moves to where it has its highest returns, so large trade imbalances may very well be improving welfare. If investments are more productive in one country than another, then output will rise. But even if the reason for the high return on capital is that some other people want to use it for consumption, it could improve welfare. Take the case of the United States. Surely, we should be concerned if the individual actions of millions of people cause a trade deficit that ultimately may be more costly than they think it will be. Perhaps the economist's role is to make appropriate jeremiads decrying such behavior. But it is not certain that the economic system is so much askew that such behavior worsens welfare, or that the generations doing the spending are not later going to make up for it in saving. To the extent we hold with such views, then we had better be prepared to live with high trade imbalances.

How can the world manage with higher trade imbalances? As ever, with a mixture of private and government lending. However we put it, if the Japanese have a surplus and the Americans a deficit, we have a loan. If Japanese banks lend money to Americans, or Japanese corporations advance trade credits, that lending sustains an American trade deficit and a Japanese trade surplus. If Japanese banks refuse to extend credits, but the Bank of Japan buys U.S. Treasury bills, the Japanese are still lending money to the Americans. If the Bank of Japan accepts SDRs from the Americans, that is its asset (a promise to pay by some other government) against sustaining the trade deficit. The concern here is that while normally the private capital market will do the job, that market occasionally collapses, creating in itself unnecessary disruption.

A collapse in the private capital market was the principal source of the panics of the nineteenth century and of the chaos that brought on the Great Depression. When private international capital inflows drop, the monetary authorities step in with their own funds. Lacking the easy ability to create new reserves they have in domestic markets, they must rely on their foreign exchange reserves or on what they can borrow.

Consider again the founding of the Bretton Woods system. What Keynes wanted was fixed exchange rates, with deficits normally supported through private capital borrowings. Since from time to time private capital was not forthcoming, he sought some system whereby monetary authorities could replace the presumably temporary drop in private capital with assets of their own. The Keynes Plan was essentially just a way of creating new financial assets to give to lending countries—only instead of being bonds held by private holders, they would be assets held by the central banks. The new assets would not, however, be a claim on the particular country that was borrowing, but on any other member of the system, much as are SDRs today. The advantage of Keynes' plan was that the new reserves would be flexible. The current system, however, depends much on having a given level of reserves in place in case something happens. We examine that issue now.

RATIONALE FOR RESERVES

Reserves are foreign-exchange-denominated liquid assets held by central banks. They can be converted readily into foreign exchange and used to support the nation's currency on the foreign exchange market. The presence of large amounts of reserves allows more time for economies to adjust, but at the same time reduces the pressure for rapid adjustment. Those economists who have argued for limited international reserves (for example, a return to the gold standard) desire a system in which governments are forced to react quickly to unusual current account deficits or surpluses. Governments would accordingly have to encourage wage, price, or income flexibility. Those economists who accept as inevitable considerable price and wage stickiness prefer ample reserves.

A nation with extensive foreign exchange reserves can maintain a given level of imports (or foreign investments) despite serious trade difficulties. If the problems are cyclical, the nation need only wait until the trading situation turns around. If adjustment is required, the nation has time to lower the price level or to hold the inflation level down below its trading partners' until their price increases restore purchasing power parity. If devaluation looks like the only plausible solution, then the nation can devalue and have the reserves to wait for the balance of trade to reach the right-hand side of the J-curve.

THE AMOUNT OF RESERVES IN THE SYSTEM

Total reserves available at the end of 1991 were about 672 billion SDRs. (The SDR was worth US$1.37 in 1991.) About 93% of reserves take the form of foreign exchange (Treasury bills and other short-term assets of other countries); about 4% is foreign exchange the nation has deposited with the International Monetary Fund and can withdraw without question; and the remaining 3% is in SDRs. Figure 18.1 shows the pattern of reserves since 1971.

Gold is presently counted as a *secondary reserve* because it is not as liquid as it used to be and because it is hard to establish its value. Monetary authorities hold about 940 million ounces of gold. At 1992 market prices, that would be somewhat over $310 billion, but if a country tried to sell much gold at any one time, the price of gold would plummet.[*] The IMF reports both the total ounces of gold and the book price of gold at its official price of SDR 35 an ounce. Figure 18.2 shows the amount of gold reserves, measured in ounces.

PROBLEMS WITH RESERVES

The problem with having a great deal of reserves is that it can be inflationary. As noted in Chapter 16, the surplus country, if near full employment, will tend to have often irreversible price effects if the deficit country refuses to contract. The deficit country, unfortunately, will not contract because it fears income, not price, effects. The argument for additional reserves becomes, in essence, an argument about the speed of adjustment and who should bear its cost.

With large reserves, it is the surplus country that pays the cost of a lack of adjustment by the deficit country. The creation of additional reserves allows the deficit country to maintain a trade deficit, thereby absorbing the saving of the surplus countries. The surplus country forgoes the consumption or domestic investment of goods and services in return for investments abroad it may not want to make. If, on the other hand, the surplus country allows inflation to make the adjustment, it suffers from the costs of that inflation.

The situation is further complicated by the use of foreign exchange as reserves.

RESERVE CURRENCIES   When central banks hold a currency widely, that currency is known as a *reserve currency*. The principal reserve currency in the 1920s was sterling (British pounds). In the 1930s and for a period after the Second

---

[*] The leading gold producer, South Africa, has a yearly production of gold that in 1987 was worth about 6.3 billion SDRs. The total stock of gold in the monetary coffers is nearly 50 times that. Another way to put it would be to imagine that the $100 billion or so in foreign exchange that was used to support the U.S. dollar late in 1987 had been raised by selling gold—the gold market would have been flooded with 10 times its usual selling volume.

Figure 18.1 **World reserves 1971–1991.** World reserves are principally and increasingly foreign exchange reserves, the cross-hatched area. While SDRs were of some importance as reserves when they were first introduced, they have declined as a proportion of total reserves. The deposits of countries at the IMF have also remained a small part of reserves.

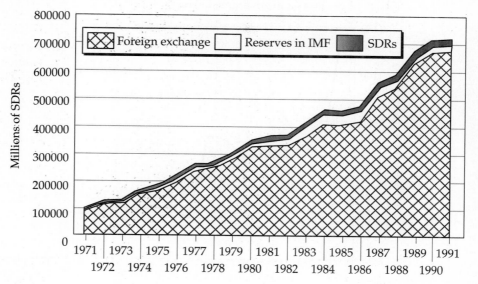

World War, those countries continuing to use sterling as a reserve were part of what was called the *sterling area.* Sterling's weakness (constantly under pressure to fall in value) made it less attractive than the dollar, and as noted above, the dollar became the principal reserve after the war. In more recent years, central banks have kept wider portfolios of foreign currencies, particularly the stronger German mark, Japanese yen, and Swiss franc.

A curious property of reserve currency nations (that is, those nations whose currencies are used as reserves) is that their trade deficits are, in effect, covered by the central banks that pick up the excess foreign exchange reserves. Whenever other countries buy up dollars to keep their own currencies from rising (that is, keep the dollar from falling), their reserves, hence world reserves, rise automatically. So whenever the United States runs a deficit on the capital and currency accounts, world reserves tend to rise, leading to rather special problems.

The ability of, put abstractly, the reserve currency nation and, put concretely, the United States to run trade deficits without end and never generate the trade surplus to pay them back is a form of *seigniorage.* Any authority that can issue notes can pay people with money it issues, and so long as the money remains in circulation and is not turned back for redemption, the authority never has to pay. The ability to issue notes is now that of national governments and they get the rights and considerable value of seigniorage. By analogy, the United States has seigniorage because it can run up debts internationally and no

Figure 18.2 **Gold held as reserves (by weight), 1971–1991.** Since the end of the Bretton Woods system, gold has ceased to play an active role as a reserve. Holdings of gold dropped sharply in 1971, due largely to selling of gold to cover the large payments problem and the heavy speculation of that year. Gold holdings fell again in 1978 at the second oil crisis, as nations again tried to handle some speculation. But for a decade now, gold has just sat in governments' reserves.

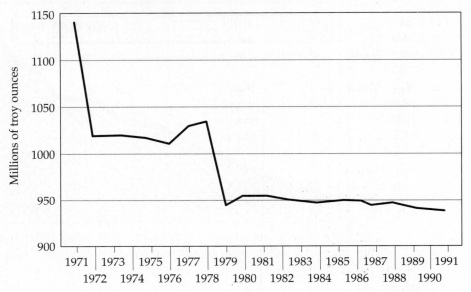

country can turn in those dollar claims for U.S. goods so long as no U.S. trade surplus develops.

The United States can rightly claim that it is quite willing to run trade surpluses, but if other countries believe that the only way that is to be done is by themselves running inflations larger than the U.S. inflation, the point is moot. It is, in a way, an ironic reversal of the 1920s situation, in which the United States would not run a trade deficit to allow the war debts to be repaid. But with the United States in the power position in both cases, it is not the United States, but the rest of the world that has to, but will not, adjust.

THE DEGREE OF DOMESTIC ECONOMIC FLEXIBILITY

SYSTEMS AND SOLUTIONS

Whatever the international system for rules and exchange rates, it must work with the domestic economic systems. The harder it is to change price levels or to shift resources from producing one thing to producing another, the more difficult it is to adjust to change. No international economic system in itself will work well if resources cannot be easily moved. Perhaps conversely, any reasonable system will work well if resources can move easily. The problem is not the international system, but the microeconomic and institutional base.

For a country to correct a trade imbalance it must do two things: (1) transfer resources into or out of exports and import substitutes and (2) change the ratio of saving to investment (and income to absorption), which will alter the incomes of savers and spenders. If the path to doing so involves much unemployment and/or inflation, welfare losses, and political and social strife, then adjustment is far more costly than it need be. Indeed, it may be more costly than perpetuating the payments imbalance. The problem is that given domestic inflexibilities, any path toward payments correction seems more costly than it needs to be.

TRANSFERRING RESOURCES

A country with a serious trade deficit will need to transfer resources into exports and import substitutes and at the same time increase the rewards for saving or decrease them for investing. A country seeking to reduce a trade surplus would want to do the opposite. Consider the issue in an economy of two sectors:

1. The first is the *trade sector,* composed of those industries or firms that produce exports or goods that are highly competitive with imports.

2. The second is the *nontrade sector,* which includes those industries favored by natural protection, such as lawyers and government employees, but also those industries that are so highly protected that a large change in the price of foreign exchange will not affect them.

To end a trade deficit, a country must shift resources into the first sector and out of the second. Wages and returns to capital in the trade sector must rise, and they must fall in the nontrade sector. If prices and wages go down in the nontrade sector, the trade sector can pick up those resources without raising wages and prices. But what if wages and returns to capital in the nontrade sector are rigid?[13]

What could very well happen would be that wages would not fall in the nontrade sector, and prices would not likely fall much either. Worker and capital immobility and the possibility of a revival of the industry, should the exchange rate change again, would keep people in the queue waiting to be rehired. As an example of immobility, consider that textile workers in Britain failed to migrate to the expanding auto and electronics industries in the 1920s.[14] The trade sector would find its employees from new entrants into the workforce, paying a premium wage. One sector sees inflation, the other unemployment, because there are limited means to get wages down in the nontrade sector or resources from it to the trade sector.

The transfer of resources will be more difficult if those in the shrinking sector have the political power and will to shore up the older industries. As the first part of this book made abundantly clear, industries that find themselves less competitive due to international changes fight tooth and nail to maintain their old positions.

FLEXIBILITY AS A SOLUTION

The question of domestic flexibility is unavoidable. We offer no specific solutions because that would be getting outside the range of our expertise and scope. They could be market solutions; some kind of social contractual solution in which labor, government, and business work together; or the market improvement approach, in which the government seeks to provide more information and subsidies for changing occupations. They are little different, in sum, from the kinds of solutions offered for those displaced by the decline of protection.

Within our expertise, however, we can note that international flexibility contributes to domestic inflexibility. The argument Chapter 16 raised about the expectations effects of devaluation is a case in point. If the international system consistently bends to favor domestic inflexibility (at least that of the more powerful of its members), it reduces the need for internal discipline. If prices can rise forever, we do not have to find the means for ever lowering them. If adjustment can take a generation, we have no reason for figuring out how to make it in less time. Perhaps that is as it should be, but economists, as usual, are divided on the issue.

THE TALL ORDER

Chapter 17 began by asking what kind of international system effectively helps trade and international investment, yet at the same time promotes growth, high employment, and price stability. We return, as a kind of summary, to what the chapter also described as a tall order.

No international system alone can work without some degree of domestic flexibility. Some systems, however, tend much farther toward *accommodation* and others toward *discipline*. An accommodating system accepts domestic price levels and differing degrees of wage and price flexibility. The danger in accommodation is that it might become validation—not merely an acceptance of the past, but a blessing on it in such a way that it continues. A disciplinary system constrains domestic policy far more. Its danger is that the domestic economies simply will not adjust easily to its constraints, and the cost of constraint will be very high. Evaluate now some of the major historical systems and suggested future systems by these criteria.

THE GOLD STANDARD

The gold standard, at least in its heyday, was heavy in discipline. Stable exchange rates undoubtedly made for easier trade and capital movements. The disruption to the money supplies of many countries, however, was undoubtedly unhealthy, and by 1914 many countries were partially counterbalancing gold flows. The high level of private capital flows, moreover, allowed high trade imbalances, which also would allow accommodation in the medium run. It was clear, however, that the long-run implications were that countries would maintain their exchange rates and would tend toward having similar price-level changes.[*]

THE BRETTON WOODS SYSTEM

The Bretton Woods system, as it emerged in its first decade, was only slightly more accommodating than the gold standard. The Bretton Woods system tried to have accommodation without validation. Countries with *fundamental disequilibria* could change their exchange rates, but a pattern of repeated adjustments was not anticipated. It was once-and-for-all adjustment of the kind described in Chapter 16. Reserves were to be supplemented by short-term borrowings from the IMF in case the private capital market failed, but this was intended to help avoid such temporary panic situations as occurred in 1931.

The Bretton Woods system did not work well when countries became hooked into differing rates of inflation. Very likely this occurred as aggregate demand management, fairly successful in the 1950s, ceased to be so effective as prices began to rise in anticipation of the government raising aggregate demand to accommodate the price rises. Such pressures differed between countries, leaving some countries with perpetually higher rates of inflation than others. Moreover, the widespread acceptance and great size of U.S. dollar reserves was not anticipated, nor was the seigniorage that the United States enjoyed as its trade account began to worsen. It is hard to imagine that any international agreement in the 1960s would have forced the United States or Great Britain to run lower inflations, or Germany and Japan to run higher ones. The accommodation in the system to inflation was, in reality, a tacit abandonment of the original plan. It was already so much abandoned, in fact, that the collapse of the Smithsonian Agreement had little immediate effect.

Bretton Woods did not anticipate the extent of the adjustment problems of Third World countries. Indeed, the phrase had not yet been invented in 1948, when most of the present-day Third World was still under colonial control. The system was oriented toward the kinds of problems Europe had experienced, which was certainly a priority concern of the day. The response was therefore rather *ad hoc*.

THE CURRENT SYSTEM

The current system, with its floating exchange rates, lack of targets, and frequent meetings for coordination, very likely leans too heavily toward accommodation. Interestingly, a number of European countries have begun to fight that accommodation by tying their own hands and joining the Exchange Rate Mechanism (ERM) of the European Monetary System. Perhaps seeing the Irish

---

[*] We cannot say they would have stable price levels, because the system would work if they all inflated at about the same rate. In fact, the gold standard functioned well during a period of stable (or falling) prices. The extent to which it *caused* that stability is debatable.

success in reducing inflation and price levels, Britain announced it would join, and even Sweden decided to join in 1991. It seems unlikely the United States would ever agree to tying its own hands like that.

The question then is whether the G-7 meetings and other forms of coordination and persuasion are going to be enough to bring discipline rather than accommodation.

SUGGESTED SYSTEMS

Most systems advocated today are less likely than the current system to encourage wage and price increases. In a sense, they lie between the rigidity of the gold standard and the extreme flexibility of floating exchange rates. Those approaches advocating fixed real rates do not suggest rolling back wage or price increases, but instead supplementing the fixed real rate with other guidelines that should prevent a continued validation of price increases. Those approaches advocating fixing nominal rates lean more closely toward the old gold standard's tough line that prices, not exchange rates, should do the adjusting. Similarly, the rule-based systems are more likely to avoid inflation than those that are coordinated or process-based. Of course, the more conservative systems, while effective against inflation, carry with them the higher probability of serious unemployment.

WHICH SYSTEM SHOULD THE WORLD HAVE?

To achieve domestic growth and high employment rates without high inflation, a system that accommodates but does not validate is better than one that disciplines but is enormously costly. That is particularly so if the cost is not a one-time cost as firms and unions learn that it is costly to themselves to push up prices in anticipation of inflation and devaluation. Just as clearly, however, a system that controls inflation and stabilizes exchange rates without producing frequent periods of unemployment and poor growth is superior to one that encourages inflation.

The underlying assessment criterion is the flexibility of the economy. The shorter the period of unemployment and the more flexible prices and wages, the easier it is to grow without inflation and adjust to changes without great cost. The longer and deeper the unemployment, and the more rigid the price system, the more costly is the adjustment. This suggests that long-run policy might concentrate on increasing domestic flexibility rather than devising new international systems. That is healthier both domestically and internationally. We heartily recommend such an approach.

VOCABULARY AND CONCEPTS ——————————————————

Accommodation versus discipline
Economic summit
ECU, European Currency Unit

Enhanced facilities
European Monetary System
Fundamental equilibrium

Exchange rate (FEER)
Facilities (borrowing)
   Oil
   Special financing
   Enhanced
   Structural Adjustment
G-5 forum
Group of Five (G-5)
Group of Seven (G-7)
Lending facilities
   Compensatory Financing
   Buffer Stock Financing
   Oil
   Credit Tranche
   Special Financing

Expanded Access
   Extended facilities
Louvre Accord
$N - 1$ problem
Nominal target ranges
Nontrade sector (Nontrade-sensitive sector)
Plaza Accord
Post–Bretton Woods system
Process-oriented policies
Real target ranges
Rule-based policies
Seigniorage
Target ranges
The big slice
Wide band

QUESTIONS

1. Outline the elements of the post–Bretton Woods system and discuss their interrelationships.

2. "Floating rates worked better than they did in the 1930s, and perhaps they did as well as any system could have, but there must be a better way." Comment on what the quotation affirms and indicate why it shows some frustration.

3. What are the moves that have been made toward greater exchange rate certainty and why have they been made?

4. Discuss the EMS and how it achieves exchange rate stability within the system.

5. How has the IMF adjusted to the changes of the post–Bretton Woods era?

6. "In a sense, the ultimate solution to payments problems is not *macroeconomic* but *microeconomic*." Comment, explaining what the authors mean.

7. Contrast the ideal fixed and floating rates with their real-life counterparts.

8. Compare John Williamson's suggested real target ranges with the more commonly advocated nominal target ranges. What seems to you to be the better system?

9. "Insofar as a tradeoff exists between inflation and unemployment and the economy decides to move toward higher employment and suffer the ills of some inflation, it should not also suffer the losses associated with an overvalued exchange rate in the name of rather nebulous gains from exchange rate stability." Comment. (What exchange rate system does this argument support, and why? What would you say to argue against it?)

10. Distinguish rule-based and process-oriented coordination and discuss what coordination of economic policies exists presently.

11. What is the $N-1$ problem? How does international coordination solve it?

12. Discuss the amount of reserves in the system. Indicate why it is not at present a vitally important issue.

13. What is seigniorage and why might it be important for reserve-currency countries?

14. "No international economic system in itself will work well if resources cannot be easily moved. Perhaps conversely, any reasonable system will work if resources can move easily. The problem is not the international system, but the microeconomic and institutional base." Do you agree? If so, why, or, if not, why?

15. The danger in accommodation is that it might become validation. So those who fear valida-

tion are chary about accommodation and prefer more disciplinary systems. Explain, and show the extent to which the various systems in the past 100 years have mixed accommodation and discipline.

16. In international monetary matters there appears to exist considerably more trust than in trade matters. Is this so, and what might cause that difference?

NOTES

[1] The standard article is Rudiger Dornbusch, "Expectations and exchange rate dynamics," *Journal of Political Economy*, December 1976. See also Robert A. Driskill, "Exchange rate dynamics," *Journal of Political Economy*, April 1981.

[2] Joycelyn P. Horne and Paul Masson of the IMF, "International economic cooperation and policy coordination," *Finance and Development*, June 1987, pp. 28–31.

[3] The lending facilities are also discussed in the introduction to *International Financial Statistics*. Detailed discussions of each, as it was put in place, are available in the International Monetary Fund's newsletter, *IMF Survey*.

[4] Although some of these facilities date back to the Bretton Woods period, the majority came after 1973.

[5] *The Economist*, January 16, 1988, p. 66.

[6] See John Williamson, *The Exchange Rate System*, Washington, Institute for International Economics, 1985; also "The case for roughly stabilizing the real value of the dollar," *American Economic Review, Papers and Proceedings*, 1989, 79:2, pp. 41–45; also John Williamson and Marcus Miller, *Targets and Indicators: A Blueprint for the International Coordination of Economic Policy*, Washington, D.C., Institute for International Economics, 1987.

[7] John Williamson and Marcus H. Miller, *Targets and Indicators: A Blueprint for the International Coordination of Economic Policy*, Washington, D.C., Institute for International Economics, September 1987.

[8] We draw from a number of sources. A fine summary article is Jacob A. Frenkel, Morris Goldstein, and Paul Masson, "International coordination of economic policies: Scope, methods, and effects," Chapter 4 of Wilfried Guth, moderator, *Economic Policy Coordination*, IMF, 1988, pp. 149–200. The other essays and comments in the Guth book are also quite valuable. See also Andrew Crockett, "Indicators and international economic cooperation," *Finance and Development*, September 1988, pp. 20–24; Jocelyn P. Horne and Paul R. Masson, "International economic cooperation and policy coordination," *Finance and Development*, June 1987. John Williamson's views on targets and indicators are in Williamson and Miller, cited above. The

Economist's (or, more particularly, Clive Crook's) somewhat dyspeptic view of the whole process is in *The World Economy*, a series of articles included in *The Economist*, Sept. 26, 1987. Also suggested: Richard N. Cooper, "Economic interdependence and coordination of economic policies" in Ronald Jones and Peter Kenen, eds., *Handbook of International Economics*, Amsterdam, North Holland Press, Vol. 2, Chapter 23. Advanced undergraduates, at least those able to follow the conclusions of economic modeling, could benefit from the essays in Ralph C. Bryant, et al., eds., *Macroeconomic Policies in an Interdependent World*. The articles in the Guth and Bryant books each have very considerable bibliographies.

[9] Rule-based systems make good bases for econometric simulations. Two of interest, in materials noted above, are those of Williamson and Miller and those of Frenkel, Goldstein, and Masson. William H. Branson, "International adjustment and the dollar," in Guth, *Economic Policy Coordination*, also has an accessible model.

[10] See Jacques J. Polak, "Economic policy objectives and policymaking in the major industrial countries," and Günter Grosser, "Empirical evidence of policy coordination among major industrial countries since Rambouillet summit of 1975," both in Guth, cited above.

[11] Martin Feldstein, "Distinguished lecture on economics in government: Thinking about international economic coordination," *The Journal of Economic Perspectives*, Vol. 2, Spring 1988. Quoted in Frenkel, Goldstein, and Masson.

[12] Some of the material is from *The European Monetary System: Developments and Perspectives*, IMF Occasional Paper No. 73, January 1991.

[13] The two-sector analysis is based on Mark Casson, *Economics of Unemployment: An Historical Perspective*, Cambridge, Mass., MIT Press, 1984. Casson notes that A. Pigou, E. Cannan, and H. Clay, all British economists of the 1920s, held a kind of two-sector disequilibrium model.

[14] See Casson, *Economics of Unemployment: An Historical Perspective*.

Chapter 19

Foreign Direct Investment and Multinational Firms

The theories behind foreign direct investment (FDI) and multinational firms belong more to industrial organization than to the models we have developed in this book. FDI is a key factor in modern international economics, and the theories for its existence have developed such that a short exploration is in order.[1]

Foreign direct investments (FDI) are investments outside the investor's country in which the investor exerts a degree of control over the company. Normally the investor in such case is not an individual, but a foreign corporation (whose ownership, however, may be widespread). The management in the home (or investor) country has considerable direct control over the subsidiary, normally including the right to determine the board of directors and management. In most cases, the foreign subsidiary is registered as a separate company for legal and tax reasons, and the parent (investor) company owns 100% of its shares. In a significant minority of cases, the foreign investment is a *joint venture*. The foreign company may be paired with a domestic company; it may be two or more foreign companies, or it may be domestic investors holding only portfolio interests. Portfolio investments are those in which the investor has no control—bonds, preferred shares, or small amounts of common shares.

Economists usually describe a multinational firm as a large firm with sub-stantial operating units in several countries. They include many large manu-facturing firms like General Motors, Exxon, and Nestlé, as well as a number of service firms, in retailing (Woolworth, active for decades), food service (McDonald's and Mr. Donut), or financial services (Sun Life and all the big auditing firms). The United Nations estimated that by 1985 foreign direct invest-ment amounted to well over $600 billion. By the mid-1980s about half of the flow and about 40% of the stock of FDI was in services, although measurement presents something of a problem.[2] Where and why did investment of such magnitude arise?

ORIGINS OF MULTINATIONAL FIRMS

Alfred Chandler has argued that the modern firm rose with the rapid improve-ments in transportation and communications occurring after 1840 that we described in Chapter 1.[3] With the exception of a few large trading companies, the typical early nineteenth-century firm was a partnership or sole proprietorship in which the owners were the managers and directly oversaw the work of their workers and employees. When business was bad or the owners saw better opportunities, they closed one firm and began another; when they died, the firm ceased to exist. A hay rake making its way from the manufacturer to the final buyer would pass through many hands—a barge owner or carter, a whole-saler, perhaps another set of transporters, and the final merchant. The original owner had no way of knowing who the final purchasers were and little knowl-edge of how much was caught up in inventory along the way.

The spread of the railways and telegraph created new sets of opportunities by providing ready communication to allow the considerable growth of service industries, many of those investments in the selfsame transportation and com-munications industries. The first decade of the twentieth century saw extensive FDI in what we think of as utilities: street railways, electrical networks, rail-ways, and telegraph and telephone systems, most of them originally private and foreign owned.

THE CHANGING PATTERN OF FOREIGN DIRECT INVESTMENT

FOREIGN DIRECT INVESTMENT BEFORE THE SECOND WORLD WAR   In the early years of the twentieth century, Britain was the dominant investor, with the United States second, but by the end of World War II, the positions had changed.[*] American investment abroad appeared to explode after the war. Measured by historical or book value, it expanded 170% between 1950 ($12

---

[*] Britain lost much of its older investments as it cut down its foreign assets to pay for the supplies it needed to fight two world wars. Exchange control from the 1930s through the 1960s also limited the amount of capital that the government would allow to be placed abroad.

billion) and 1960 ($32 billion) and another 140% (to $78 billion) in the next decade. It followed from this limited perspective that the MNF was something new and explosive on the world scene. More careful work, however, has rather dampened the sudden-explosion theory, though it remains popular with more journalistic writers. American investment abroad in the 1970s and 1980s—as a percentage of America's GNP or as a percentage of American exports—was remarkably similar to pre-Depression and pre–World War II figures. Indeed, U.S. FDI in 1914, 1929, 1970, and 1987 amounted to close to 7% of GNP.

AN INTERPENETRATION OF DIRECT INVESTMENTS

Direct investment has shown considerable growth in the last decade, but growth based on *interpenetration*, rather than a one-way outflow from a few countries into all others. It is the same kind of growth that we have seen in intraindustrial trade and in portfolio investment—relatively small net movements, but much trading of goods and mutual exchange of capital.* The U.S. and the United Kingdom alone accounted for just under two thirds of all foreign investment in 1960; by 1985 that dominance had declined to less than half and smaller countries had increased their investments. At the same time, the United States had become a target for new investment, as shown in Fig. 19.1.

THE U.S. FOREIGN DIRECT INVESTMENT POSITION

The interpenetration of multinational firms shows quite clearly in American statistics. American firms have continued to grow abroad, but the number of foreign firms operating in the United States has expanded considerably. Estimates vary greatly, as shown in Fig. 19.2, but American FDI abroad and foreign FDI in the United States are probably close in size and around half a trillion dollars each. Foreign companies operating in the United States employ about 4.5 million people, roughly 16% of the workforce, and have important market shares in manufacturing, mining, and commercial real estate. The leading investors in the United States, in order, are Great Britain, Japan, and Canada.[4]

The large American current account deficit is, of course, closely related to these changes. Foreign investment in the United States enabled the trade deficit to be as large as it was, or to put it the opposite way, Americans let go of some of their domestic assets in order to borrow from abroad.

Before examining the trend, we have an important note of caution: Measuring the value of direct investments is difficult. Until recently, the U.S. government used historical book value—that is, assets were valued according to

---

*Interpenetration is not a new phenomenon either, as it was present in the nineteenth century. Much has been made of Singer's establishment of sewing machine manufacturing in Scotland in 1868 as the first continuously operating American multinational. Clark Thread of Paisley, Scotland, however, constructed a large factory in Newark, New Jersey, in 1865, and the company has been operating continuously in Newark since that date.

Figure 19.1 **Foreign direct investment, 1975 and 1985.** The upper two pies show that FDI rose 2.5 times between 1975 and 1985, changing in composition. While American investment increased, the U.S. no longer dominated FDI, as FDI rose more sharply from Western Europe, Japan, Canada, and Australia. The lower two pie charts show the areas in which the FDI has been made. Interestingly, foreign investment in the developing countries has remained the same percentage of all investment over the entire decade.

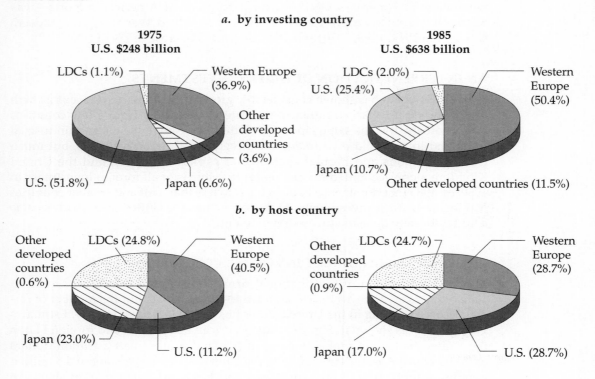

Source: United Nations Centre on Transnational Corporations, Transnational Corporations in World Development *(New York, 1980).*

the price the firms paid to get them. A $10 million plant erected in 1970 was worth just that, less depreciation, not its replacement cost. Now government researchers present two other measures: (1) the book value at replacement cost (*current cost valuation*) and (2) an estimate of the market value of the shares of the subsidiary (if there were a market), known as *market share valuation*.[5] Figure 19.2 shows several attempts at the measurement of FDI in this way.

The FDI figures present rather a puzzle. Given that the United States ran such large current account deficits during the 1980s, it stands to reason that its net indebtedness should increase. Just as a scion of a wealthy family cannot continue to spend more than he receives without running down the value of his inheritance, the United States could not continue to run current account deficits

Figure 19.2 **Three estimates of U.S. foreign direct investment.** Two of three different estimates of the American net direct investment position show the United States with a positive position, although it has fallen greatly over the years. The reason the U.S. historical and current cost estimates (top) differ more than the foreign equivalents is that most U.S. investment is older and made before the big inflations of the 1970s. Historical cost methods understate the value of American FDI.

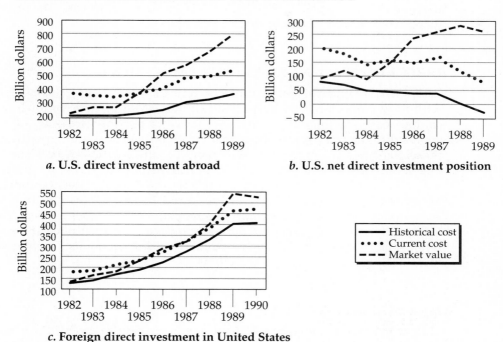

a. **U.S. direct investment abroad**

b. **U.S. net direct investment position**

c. **Foreign direct investment in United States**

Source: Landefeld and Lawson, and Scholl, Survey of Current Business, *May and June 1991.*

without falling into net indebtedness. Strange to say, the figures are very inconclusive about this.[6] We would expect net factor receipts (NFRs) to turn negative, but American NFRs, although they have fallen, are still strongly positive.

THE THEORETICAL CHALLENGE OF MULTINATIONALS

Despite their early origins, it was the 1960s before multinational firms received either a name or widespread attention. Business writers praised the efficiency-producing, capital-moving, and technology-transferring form of organization. Some political scientists sounded notes of caution; others sounded alarms. What manner of beast was this *multinational firm?* How did it differ from a domestic firm? Could the economist help? Perhaps, but where was the theoretical foundation to understand this phenomenon? When economists went to their toolboxes to try to address some of the issues raised, they found their tools were at best awkward and their arguments unconvincing. International trade theory was firmly based on highly competitive markets and *independent* exporters and importers, yet it was clear a great deal of trade occurred between affiliates of the same firm. Classical economics postulated single-product, single-location entities, and in truth, explained the existence of *any* firm awkwardly. The profession, it appeared, would have to go back to the drawing boards.

DIRECT INVESTMENT AS A CAPITAL MOVEMENT

Early interpretations of foreign direct investment saw it as a capital movement—with those areas having a surplus of capital exporting it in various forms to capital-scarce regions. It was an alternative to portfolio investment, but responded to the same forces. If so, then much of the current interpenetration of investments is hard to explain. Why would a single nation be both the host to FDI and an investor abroad itself? Why has the bulk of FDI gone to countries with adequate capital? Why does the relationship between those countries that are moving resources abroad (as measured by the balance on the current account) have so weak a connection to foreign direct investment flows?[*] Viewing FDI simply as a form of capital flow, responsive to interest rates and risk premiums, has not been particularly helpful.[7] Instead, economists have turned to ideas dealing with market imperfections.

MARKET IMPERFECTIONS

Market imperfections lie at the heart of the modern theory of the MNF. The problem facing economic theorists as they began to discuss the MNF in the 1960s was that economic theories, which are for the most part based on highly efficient markets, did not seem to explain why there should be an MNF. *If markets were efficient, there would be no need for an international firm.* A firm could sell its technology or product expertise to a foreign firm; it could place any surplus capital in a highly efficient capital market; and it could sell its managerial services, much as do many of the international engineering firms. Active markets exist for all these things. Yet those markets operate side by side with integrated firms that move their capital, their specialized technologies, their product developments, their managerial skills entirely within the firm. In addition, if markets were efficient, the firm would have no need to vertically integrate (that is, to own its source of raw materials or outlets for its products) because independent firms

---

[*] The current account balance, which is the difference between exports and imports plus or minus gifts, measures the amount of resources a nation transfers to the rest of the world. If it is not positive, then the nation is absorbing resources from the rest of the world. We find only a limited connection between the amount of resources the nation is actually transferring and the extent to which it transfers these resources in the form of foreign direct investment.

could handle those operations perfectly well; yet some firms chose to integrate vertically, while others did not. How might a theory encompass these issues?

THE THREE PILLARS OF AN ECLECTIC THEORY OF THE MNF

The basic theory of the multinational firm jelled in the mid-1970s.[8] It is perhaps best summarized, and certainly most plainly put, in the University of Reading's John Dunning's *eclectic theory.* Dunning based his interpretation of the multinational firm on three pillars.

1. The MNF possessed a unique asset, enabling it to collect a rent either by producing at a lower cost or by selling at a higher price than competitors.

2. The MNF could not sell its rent, at least not and get a great return on it, because *transaction costs* were high. It therefore found it more profitable to develop foreign markets itself, *internalizing* what could be an external market.

3. The MNF had to have a cost advantage to produce in more than one country; otherwise it would merely import and export.[*]

THE IMPORTANCE OF UNIQUE ASSETS   Charles Kindleberger hypothesized that the MNF always has some unique asset that gives it a limited monopoly, enabling it to receive some economic profit.[9] Such a market structure, with limited monopolies giving a small edge in a basically competitive market is sometimes described as *monopolistic competition.*[**] The unique advantage may be a special product, a patented technology, an ability to raise capital cheaply, or just superior managerial skills that are not easily copied. Ford, for instance, had a brand name and reputation as well as special skills at mass manufacture and marketing. Since none of these could be copied easily, Ford was able to set itself up in Europe, competing successfully with domestic manufacturers while enduring the expense of the more complicated management structure required for international operations.

Another way of putting this is to say that the unique asset produces a rent, with the value of the rent deriving from the economic profits. Using the unique-asset approach, we suppose that the advantage the firm gets is insufficient to give it a "monopoly" in the industry as a whole. Its unique product may only appeal to part of the market, or its cost advantage only work over a restricted range of output.

---

[*] Dunning's theory was eclectic in the sense that he took each element from separate theoretical bodies. The idea of the unique advantage came from Kindleberger and Hymer (see note 9), with a basis in monopolistic competition theory. The idea of transaction cost goes back to Ronald Coase and the "institutionalists" of Chicago in the 1920s and 1930s. The idea of the locational advantage is straight out of classical economics. For a full statement of the theory, with many applications, see John H. Dunning, *Explaining International Production,* London, Unwin Hyman, 1988.

[**] The concept of monopolistic competition is normally associated with product differentiation and substantial entrants into an industry. That is, it lies somewhere between perfect competition and oligopoly. We use it, however, in a way closer to Edward Chamberlin's definition, in which entry is not closed, but still relatively few firms compete, selling differentiated products.

Take the case of a firm with certain production skills giving it a cost advantage that for the foreseeable future will be insufficient to have a major effect on the market price.[*] The firm is thus a price taker, viewing a horizontal demand curve—one, however, that is determined by other firms' costs and lies above its own average cost curve. Figure 19.3's left diagram shows the line at E as being the efficient firm's cost and the line PP as being the cost of other firms in the industry. The difference between the market price and the firm's cost times volume sold is economic profit; such profit in turn we assume to arise solely from the unique cost advantage. The firm maximizes its profits at output $0A$, earning an amount equivalent to the shaded box per year. The value of its cost-cutting technique, of which there is only one, is in the right-hand diagram. The vertical supply curve at a stands for the single patent, and its value, per year, is the economic profit it generates—the shaded rectangle on the right has the same area as the shaded rectangle representing profit in the left figure. Because the unique production skill will not disappear if it gets zero price and will not increase if it gets a much higher price, it has a completely inelastic supply curve, and in such situations any returns due to that invention can be considered a rent.

The profit may be generated because unique product advantages enable the firm to sell at a higher price, facing a higher demand curve than other firms. Figure 19.3 does double duty here: Consider PP the price our firm can get because of its unique product and E the prices other firms get. The firm with the unique product therefore gets a profit equal to the shaded rectangle, which

---

[*] The cost advantage comes, let us suppose, from the dynamic leadership of the present management and splendid industrial relations. Neither of these advantages can be duplicated easily, either for other firms to use or for rapid expansion of the existing firm, which might destroy the very dynamism and industrial relations that have given the firm its advantage.

Figure 19.3 **The rent produced by a unique advantage.** The economic profit a firm earns from having a unique advantage, the shaded box on the left part of the diagram, is equivalent to the annual rent to that advantage, shown by the shaded box on the right side. Since there is only one unique advantage, it has a vertical supply curve. The demand for that advantage is a derived demand from the extra profits the advantage generates.

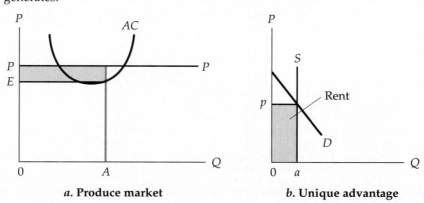

a. **Produce market**   *b.* **Unique advantage**

again produces a rent equal to the shaded rectangle in the right-hand figure. The rent in this case goes to the unique product advantage.

The theory in its original form never stated *why* the firm did not sell its rental income. After all, if the value of the rent in Fig. 19.3 is known for one year, we could project future rents, discount them to the current year, and establish a price for the unique asset. If the market were nearly perfect, the asset that produced the rent could be sold as easily as selling a bond. To wit: The unique-asset explanation cannot alone explain why a firm would operate across borders.

As theorists began to examine the MNF more closely, they realized that they needed a better explanation for the existence of the firm—domestically or internationally. Indeed, as theory developed, most specialists concluded that the theory that explains the MNF is not very different from the theory required to explain the domestic firm. After all, any strictly local or national firm can sell its patents, license its name brands, rent out its managerial expertise, or avoid vertical integration *domestically*, yet many do not. The question is not why we have multinational firms, but why we have firms?[10]

TRANSACTION COST AND INTERNALIZATION   Logically, the reason firms cannot sell their unique assets is because the market is not perfect, or even very good in some cases. The ideas behind such an approach stem from a 1937 article by Ronald Coase that developed the idea of *transaction costs*. Coase noted that using a market carries costs, which he called the transaction costs. He described the costs as being of several kinds:

1. *Brokerage costs:* the costs of matching a buyer and a seller and coming to an agreement. In some instances our economy has separate brokers, as in the real estate or stock market; in other cases, the buyers or sellers take on the costs themselves, as in a manufacturer's agent coming to a plant, or a delegation from a company going to a trade show to shop for equipment or merchandise.

2. *Contractual costs:* the costs of drawing up a contract that adequately covers the foreseeable problems or conflicts.

3. *Risk costs:* the cost of the chance that income will be foregone when the firm charges another a lower price than it could have, or that the firm has paid a higher price than was necessary.

4. *Taxation costs:* Firms that can write off losses from a new division against profits from an old division are at an advantage compared to a new firm or a firm with a single line of goods, which does not receive any tax advantages until it begins to earn profits.

Against these transaction costs, Coase suggested there were costs of doing things internally—*the administrative costs.* Today, we would think of these as the problems of additional administrative levels, of a slowdown or breakdown in the decision-making process, of an inability of management to understand new operations, or of unnecessary commitment of capital to low-yielding operations.

According to Coase, the limits of a firm would be determined by the balance between transaction costs and administrative costs. A firm would follow an *internal* route if transaction costs exceeded administrative costs and would follow an *external* route if the reverse were true. Coase referred to following the internal route as *internalization.*

LOCATIONAL ADVANTAGES AND THE ECLECTIC MODEL   Dunning's third pillar was important in that it explained why the firms would operate abroad in the first place. If there were no locational advantages, the firm would simply export from its home nation. Dunning's theory does not imply that the MNF causes a geographic dispersion of production; rather it explains why dispersed production facilities are owned by a single firm. To put it in specific terms, the third pillar explains why Canada produces automobiles, but the first two pillars explain why Ford, General Motors, and Chrysler own the car plants.

STRENGTHS AND WEAKNESSES OF THE ECLECTIC MODEL   The eclectic theory has a certain durability and resiliency that keep it current. It appears, for instance, to be at root of the analysis in the United Nations Centre for Transnational Corporations' 1988 study of multinationals, and functioned well for Alan Rugman's analysis of Canadian multinationals.[11] Nonetheless, the last decade has seen a considerable number of advances in thought on each of Dunning's eclectic pillars.

1. A single unique asset does not suffice as an explanation. The value of any unique asset itself is short lived. It is rather the process by which a stream of assets is created that is of importance.

2. Used crudely, transaction cost analysis gives a circular reasoning. The existence of multinational firms in the automobile industry demonstrates that transaction costs are high; therefore high transaction costs cause multinational firms. To avoid circularity, the analysis must identify what causes transaction costs to be high. The last decade has seen considerable progress in identifying such causes.

3. Locational advantages are probably declining in importance. The thrust of much new trade theory is to explain trade that is intraindustrial, intrafactoral, and often intrafirm. As Chapter 3 showed, such analysis downplays a factor-proportions approach, with its increasing-cost implications, in favor of specialization arguments that feature decreasing costs with expanding output. Specialization becomes the cause of, rather than the result of, trade. Because specialization drives costs, it is possible to conceive of a part of the world in which all the nations have virtually identical factor proportions, but multinational firms still exist.

BEYOND THE ECLECTIC MODEL: INFORMATION, RISK, AND COORDINATION

UNIQUE ASSETS AND RENTS   The early literature was rather vague on what constituted a unique asset. Clearly patentable technology or copyright material would qualify, but it was often unclear just what a company's unique asset was. Phrases like "managerial know-how" or "marketing expertise" represented a groping toward the explanation of something rather less tangible than a patent. An ability to come up with successful new products, a skill in coordinating the flow of goods from manufacturer to consumer, a good reputation for paying off debt, a certain genius in identifying market needs, or good supplier relations may be closer to what a firm has that is unique than any one instance of success.

As the definition of a unique asset moves away from a single item to something less concrete, it moves to what is essentially the production of information or a skill in coordination. Because the coordination and the information are *continually being produced and renewed*, the use of the concept of rent to describe them is inappropriate. A rent is a return on something that will not disappear if it gets no return at all. Surely, the latest computer program will not disappear if the law allows it to be copied freely; but just as surely, the stream of new computer programs will dry up. Classical economics has difficulty in handling streams of unique items; if it treats them as single inventions, it must use the techniques of rent with a vertical supply curve. If it treats them as similar items possessing a positively sloped supply curve, it falsifies their nature, implying that tomorrow's invention is the same as today's. The money a pharmaceutical firm makes on a patented drug, for instance, has only some characteristics of a rent: A removal of patent protection will not cause the drug's disappearance, and an increase in protection does not guarantee that some firm will develop an equally effective new drug. But few would argue that pharmaceuticals as a group would be developed without some reward for the inventor.

Harold Demsetz has argued that many of a firm's unique advantages in reputation, in inventiveness, or in reliability are earned, and that their returns in terms of higher prices or lower costs are their rewards, as well as incentives for other firms to do likewise. When brand names, new inventions, or particularly good reputations stand as barriers to entry, they also serve as important stimuli to produce new information and maintain good reputations. The rewards are thus not rents, but legitimate payments.[12]

The Demsetz approach stands against the idea that the multinational firm in itself is a means of perpetuating an unnecessary monopoly. The rent received for a new invention, insofar as it is an essential reward to encourage new invention, is called an *efficiency rent*. Attempts to reduce those rewards, as, for instance, by forcing firms to license others to use their patents, will ultimately cause a reduction in the flow of new inventions or of corporate reliability. The international scope of a firm merely increases the incentive for it to keep up its stream of unique assets. We explore these questions farther as we turn to examine information, coordination, and risk.

INFORMATION

Public Good and Asymmetrical Characteristics of Information   From an economic point of view, information is quite unlike most other goods and services. It has, as Mark Casson[13] noted, the characteristics of a typical *public good.* A public good in technical terms is not solely a publicly produced good; rather it shares characteristics with such goods. The chief characteristic of a public good is that it can be given away or sold and yet the original possessor will still have it. Fire protection and public parks have the essential public-goods characteristic of being used by many people, yet not appreciably diminishing in quality as more people use them.

The problem with public goods, and one of the reasons why so many are publicly provided, is that they are difficult to charge for; once created they are used by very many people and it is very difficult to establish fees—or to collect them. Typically, we say that public goods are nonrival, meaning that many people can share them at once without significant diminution of pleasure, and we say they are nonexclusive, meaning that it is hard to keep people from using them for nothing. Another way of saying it is to note that some people, free riders, can use the good who have not paid anything toward its creation.

Information has the characteristics of a public good, but only a limited amount of information is provided publicly. A firm that possesses information of value to others has a unique asset which, following the usual characteristics of public goods, can be sold without diminishing its stock. That piece of information could presumably be sold many times and still have the same value. It could be, for instance, a special recipe, a joke, a new invention, a piece of valuable market news, a special insight into the political situation. The problem is how to sell the information—and what to sell it for.

The sale of information presents even more difficulty than just keeping away free riders. One difficulty arises because of an *asymmetry* in the holding of information. The Neoclassical model always assumes that both buyer and seller have adequate information about the product, but if the good that is being sold is in itself information, it is hard to maintain a pretense that the buyers know what the information is, or else they need not buy it.[14] The buyer of information will not necessarily want to buy something that is of uncertain value—the legendary pig in a poke. Yet in very many cases the revelation of the information in itself robs that information of value: Once the buyer knows it, why should he pay for it? Furthermore, once the buyer knows what the information is, what is to prevent him from reselling it at lower rates than what the original possessor of that information is charging? Without some sort of control over the use of that information, firms will not let others know what information they have.

If information is hard to sell as information per se, the firm discovering it will likely try to gain its value in other ways. It may try the legal route of acquiring patent or copyright protection, but that can be cumbersome. Failing that it may in itself act on the information it has (such as buying up a crop it has found out to be in short supply) or embody that knowledge in a product. While the product may or may not get patent protection, there would be at least a short period before imitators copied the product, and with luck, perhaps some barriers to entry could be erected. The need for self-exploitation of the value of information becomes, in a sense, the reason for the foundation of the firm.

Licensing Across Borders   Very often firms license across national borders where they would not license within the same country. If they can restrict the licensee from selling back into the home market, then they do not risk losing sales to their own licensee. Even then, licensing problems are considerable.

A recent study of the market for licensing technology shows just how many difficulties there are.[15] Potential buyers are uncertain about the value of new information. In addition, they are concerned that technology may change, leaving them at a disadvantage compared to their competitors, and may wish to purchase a license, not only for current technology, but for future improvements, a greater uncertainty. The licensor is reluctant to make a license for current and future technology because it will have to share the fruits of any technological break-through with a licensee without being able to renegotiate the contract. The licensor, accordingly, has less incentive to improve its licensed product or technology.

The licensor is also anxious to get in on any improvements the licensee might make to the licensed product or technology and tries to write a contract whereby any such improvements come back to it automatically and without any payment. The licensee does not like this type of contract because if it makes any key improvements, it will not be rewarded for them. It therefore has less incentive to make improvements.

Things That Cannot Be Licensed The market for technological licenses is highly efficient when compared to the markets for other forms of information. Consider the problems in selling an understanding of what a given market will want in the coming year, the information that the coffee crop in Brazil is bad, that unusually large shiploads of bananas are on their way to Boston, that the teenage trend-setting rock group will be wearing diagonally striped clothes, or that the statements of a new restaurant owner on his ability to pay are correct. Any of this information could be extremely valuable, but it is only valuable for a short period of time, far too short to achieve copyright or patent protection, if indeed, it would legally qualify for protection. If the market fails, or is quite expensive to use, *and* the information is valuable, the firm will tend to follow internal routes for the generation and processing of such short-lived and easily copied information. The firm is therefore a *technically efficient* transmitter of information.

The ease with which information moves within a corporation may also be the cause of some of the extensively horizontally integrated agricultural trading firms. Coffee, grain, and tobacco buying are dominated by a few horizontally integrated firms, with rather limited vertical integration. In his study of the grain traders, Harvard's Richard Caves theorized that it was the extensive horizontal communication network, allowing ready communication about buying and selling conditions in many countries, that was one of the keys to extensive horizontal integration.[16]

COORDINATION Whenever two parties working in isolation achieve a lower output than they can working as a team—that is, they have a synergy—coordination has a value.[17] The problems of teamwork, however, are considerable—the prevention of shirking, the individual distribution of a reward that by its very nature is joint, and the allocation of risks among the participants are considerable.

Coordination occurs in many ways: the timing of shipments of goods (as, for instance, bananas or petroleum), the coming on stream of separate plants, or the introduction of new products. Much of this is necessarily planned administratively, whether between firms or within one firm.

Coordination can and does occur between firms or within firms. As with the sale of information, the issue is whether independent firms can achieve coordination as inexpensively and effectively as can a single firm, which internalizes the process. In some cases, it appears that it is more efficient to coordinate within a firm, and in others interfirm coordination works effectively.[18]

RISK   As Coase noted, risk is an important determinant of transaction costs. A closer examination of risk may indicate just how key it is to understanding multinational firms.

Risk is a cost that, like garbage, people will pay to get rid of. The market is in a sense a market for the removal of risk. In itself, the market is less than perfect for some kinds of risks, and when risk is combined with information and coordination problems, transaction costs can rise sharply.

Highly efficient and very organized markets exist for risk. At the same time, information and its public-good nature, and the large amount of risk that responds to no known actuarial figures, make some forms of risk very hard to pass off. How would a company sell the risk, for instance, to a new product that it had just developed? (To whom could it explain its idea without having it taken? Whom could it convince to take the risk on a product, if that person doesn't know much about it?) In such situations, a firm may internalize risk, in essence self-insuring.

Risk and Internalization   A number of risks disappear entirely when both parties to the risk are internalized. Such risks are typically those where one party's gain matches another's loss and the two parties pool their risks. Such risks usually pair an upside risk against a downside risk in such a way that the upside risk disappears. An upside risk is the chance of losing out on some considerable gain. Downside risk is the more normal idea of risk, namely, the chance of losing something one already has.

Typical of these double-risk situations:

1. A licensor worries that what it charges for the license is too low, while the licensee worries that what it paid is too high. Should the license prove very successful, the licensor suffers from having charged too low a price. If the licensed product is much less successful than expected, the licensee has paid too much. If the licensor owns the licensee, the only risk is that the product will not do well.[19]

2. The signatories to any contract run the risk that unforeseen and uncovered eventualities will benefit one of the parties at the other's expense. Most contracts cover a number of obvious contingencies—what the responsibilities of each party is should some change come up. A contract signed, for instance,

between an energy company and a buyer might carry a *contingency provision* that the price paid will be changed if oil prices change and specify the extent of that change. Unfortunately, no contract can specify all contingencies. Some are unforeseen and unforeseeable. Others are hopelessly remote—if event *a* occurs, followed by event *b*, and finally event *c* occurs, what do we do? The lawyers could spend a year writing the contract and still not specify all the possible contingencies. Any contract, it follows, is incomplete in that it cannot specify all contingencies.[20] If both parties are within the same firm, then it is unimportant to write out any mutual obligation, and the firm need not try to plan the unplannable.

3. Buyers and suppliers, tied closely together, create risks for one another in their quality control, in their delivery times, and in their technological and marketing skills. Difficulties with either side of the arrangement can cause serious losses for the other. If buyer and supplier are in the same firm, the risk remains that quality will be inappropriate, goods will be delivered in inappropriate quantities, the firm will make technological or marketing errors. But the risk that one party will bear them to the other's benefit disappears.

4. Risks between licensor and licensee of making improvements in a product without being able to get a decent return for the work are eliminated if a single firm owns both.

5. Moreover, the licensing company does not have to worry about a licensee underselling it in the home market if it owns the licensee. (If the licensee has lower costs, it makes sense for the company to source the good at its lower-cost facility, but the gains will go to the parent company.)

Another set of risks may be placed, not against a risk that cancels them out, but against enough risks that the chances fall—that is, the firm itself becomes large enough to self-insure. As Shakespeare's Antonio, the Merchant of Venice, noted:

> My ventures are not in one bottom trusted,
> Nor to one place, nor is my whole estate
> Upon the fortune of this present year.

Caves suggested that the small number of international grain traders is related to risk. The size of an individual shipload of grain is extraordinarily large, easily swallowing up a year's production of some of North America's richest counties. Only the largest grain traders have enough ships going that they can afford the loss or delay of a few. Domestically, however, where shipments are smaller, trading companies are far more numerous.[21]

Information reduces risk, and normally knowledge flows more freely within the firm than between firms. Hence in situations where knowledge is important for planning, risk falls when internal routes are followed, as we noted in a previous section.[22]

CONCLUSION

In many situations, the only practical way a firm can cut risk, exclude free riders, and appropriate a significant amount of the value created by generation of new information and coordination is to embody that information into a good and sell it itself. The complications and uncertainties of licensing and the difficulties of legal enforcement of contracts limit their use. Transaction costs, in other words, are high, and it is more efficient for the firm to establish itself abroad than it is to license another company to produce there.

VOCABULARY AND CONCEPTS

Brokerage costs
Contingency provision
Contractual costs
Coordination
Direct investment
Downside risk
Eclectic theory
Efficiency rent
Embodiment (of information or coordination)
External routes
Foreign Direct Investment (FDI)
Internal routes

Internalization
Interpenetration
Licensing
Market imperfections approach
Multinational firm (MNF)
Portfolio investment
Public good
Rent
Risk costs
Transaction costs
Unique assets
Upside risk

QUESTIONS

1. "There is nothing either historically or analytically to suggest that multinational firms are a post–World War II phenomenon." Explain and evaluate.

2. Why has the idea that direct investment is inherently a *capital* movement been rejected?

3. Explain Dunning's eclectic theory of multinational firms, outlining its three pillars, particularly the need for having both unique assets and high transaction costs.

4. The unique-asset approach in itself has limitations; indicate what they are, discussing the question of whether the assets are one-time and whether they produce true rents. Are the rents they produce good things or bad things?

5. What is the role of information and coordination in the modern theory of the firm—particularly the international firm?

6. How does the emerging theory of the MNF adjust the eclectic approach to be more flexible?

7. Why is licensing internationally often more difficult than direct appropriation through embodiment?

8. If U.S. direct investment abroad has been underestimated, what implication does that have for the current account deficits of the 1980s? Explain.

NOTES

[1] The basic theoretical framework for this chapter, elaborated at much greater length, is in Wilson B. Brown, *Markets, Organizations, and Information*, Toronto, John Wiley, 1992.

[2] *Transnational Corporations in World Development*, New York, United Nations Centre on Transnational Corporations, 1988, pp. 4–6, 439–424.

[3] Alfred D. Chandler, Jr., *The Visible Hand: The Managerial Revolution in American Business*, Cambridge, Mass., Belknap Press, 1977.

[4] Steve D. Bezirganian, "U.S. affiliates of foreign companies: Operations in 1989," *Survey of Current Business*, July 1991, pp. 72–85. Russell B. Scholl, "The international investment position of the United States in 1990," *Survey of Current Business*, June 1991, pp. 23–35. Jeffrey H. Lowe and Raymond J. Mataloni, Jr., "U.S. direct investment abroad: 1989 benchmark survey results," *Survey of Current Business*, October 1991, pp. 29–55.

[5] J. Steven Landefeld and Ann M. Lawson, "Valuation of the U.S. net international investment position," *Survey of Current Business*, May 1991, pp. 40–49. The market share valuation is based on an index of share prices in the host country, not on the prospects or profits of the American subsidiary.

[6] The problem was noted by Michael Ulan and William G. Dewald, "The U.S. net international investment position: Misstated and misunderstood," in James A. Dorn and William Niskanen, eds., *Dollars, Deficits and Trade*, Norwell, Mass., Luwar Academic Publishers for the Cato Institute, 1989, and Robert Eisner and Paul J. Pieper, "The world's greatest debtor nation?" in *The North American Review of Economics and Finance*, Vol. 1, No. 1.

[7] A good review of earlier theory is in John H. Dunning, *Explaining International Production*, London, Unwin Hyman, 1988, pp. 120–139.

[8] John McManus, "The theory of the international firm," in Gilles Paquet, *The Multinational Firm and the Nation State*, Toronto, Collier-Macmillan, 1972, pp. 66–93. Wilson B. Brown, "Islands of conscious power," *MSU Business Topics*, Summer 1976, pp. 37–45. J.H. Dunning, "Trade, location of economic activity and the multinational enterprise: A search for an eclectic approach," in B. Ohlin et al. eds., *The International Allocation of Economic Activity*, London, Macmillan, 1977.

[9] Kindleberger's ideas were in part based on those of his student, Stephen Hymer, whose thesis on the subject was published some years later. See Charles P. Kindleberger, *American Business Abroad*, New Haven, Yale, 1969, Chapter 1.

[10] See in particular Mark Casson, *The Firm and the Market*, Cambridge, Mass., MIT Press, 1987.

[11] Alan Rugman, *Megafirms*, Toronto, Methuen, 1985.

[12] Harold Demsetz, "Barriers to entry," *The American Economic Review*, March 1982, pp. 47–57.

[13] Mark Casson, *Alternatives to the Multinational Enterprise*, New York, Holmes and Meier Publishers, 1979, Chapter 3, pp. 45–55.

[14] Kenneth J. Arrow, "Economic welfare and the allocation of resources for invention," in National Bureau of Economic Research, *The Rate and Direction of Inventive Activity*, Princeton, 1962.

[15] See Richard Caves, Harold Crookell, and J.P. Killing, "The imperfect market for technology licenses," *The Oxford Bulletin of Economics and Statistics*, August 1983, pp. 249–267.

[16] Richard E. Caves, "Organization, scale, and performance of the grain trade," *Stanford University Food Research Institute Studies*, Vol. XVI, No. 3, 1977–78, pp. 107–123.

[17] Mark Casson, *The Entrepreneur*, Martin Robertson, 1982, pp. 41–56.

[18] See Wilson B. Brown, *Markets, Organizations, and Information*, Chapter 8.

[19] See Wilson B. Brown, "Islands of conscious power," *MSU Business Topics*, Summer 1976.

[20] Oliver Williamson lays heavy stress on the problem of incomplete contracts. He notes that the "what ifs" multiply greatly once managers start looking very far into the future. See his *Markets and Hierarchies*, The Free Press, 1979.

[21] Richard Caves, "Organization, scale, and performance of the grain trade."

[22] On the freer flow of information within firms see Oliver Williamson, *Markets and Hierarchies*, New York, Free Press, 1975.

Name Index

Thompson, T. Scott, 141, 266
Tirole, Jean, 242
Tryon, Ralph W., 399
Tullock, Gordon, 121, 141
Tyson, Laura D'Andrea, 262, 266, 302–304

Ulan, Michael, 639

Vaitsos, Constantine V., 351, 361, 363
Van Bael, Ivo, 265
Van Duren, Erna, 188
Vanek, Jaroslav, 66, 102
Vaughan, Michael B., 40
Venables, Anthony J., 361
Vermulst, Edwin A., 265
Vernon, Raymond, 97–98, 104
Villanueva, Delano, 399
Viner, Jacob, 317–318
Von Furstenburg, George M., 589

Vousden, Neil, 141

Walker, Franklin V., 141
Wan, H., 321, 361
Warr, Peter G., 363
Wasson, Chester A., 104
Watson, Maxwell, 530–531
Weintraub, Sidney, 362
Weiss, Leonard, 103
Wellisz, Stanislaw, 188
Wells, Louis, Jr., 97–98, 104
Wenders, John T., 141
Whalley, John, 361
White, Harry Dexter, 573
Whitney, Peter D., 362
Wigle, Randall M., 102
Willett, Thomas D., 361
Williamson, John, 605–606, 622–623
Williamson, Oliver, 639

Willmore, L.N., 363
Winglee, Peter, 102, 139, 141, 234–235, 265, 303, 362
Winters, L. Alan, 361
Woglom, Geoffrey, 399
Wonnacott, Paul, 361–362
Wood, Adrian, 102
Wyckoff, Andrew, 235

Xafa, Miranda, 102, 139, 141, 234–235, 265, 303

Yamamura, Kozo, 305
Yankelovich, Daniel, 212, 235
Yeager, Leland, 472, 560, 589
Yeats, Alexander, 187
Young, Leslie, 141

Zysman, John, 302–303

Subject Index

Absolute advantage, 28
Absorption in balance of trade, 370–371
Accommodation, 618–620
Ad valorem tariffs, 106–108
Adapted Swan-Mundell (ASM) model, 496–501, 526
Adaptive expectations, 551
Adjustable peg system, 573–577, 619
Administered markup pricing, 182
Administrative costs, 631–632
Administrative protection against imports, 157–158
Advertising and protectionism, 184–185
Africa, economic integration in, 348–349
African-Caribbean-Pacific (ACP) states, 344
Agglomeration, economies of, 79, 82, 83
Aggregate supply, 444–448
Aggregate supply and demand models, 424–427, 446–447, 548–549, 551–552
Aggregate supply curves, 444–446
Agricultural surpluses, 205–208
Agriculture
    protectionist standards in, 164–165
    protectionist tariffs for, 191–192, 201
Airlines and protectionism, 184
Allied Coordinating Committee for Strategic
    Export Control (COCOM), 298–299
American Selling Price (ASP) case, 200
Andean Trade Preference Act (ATPA), 345
Antidumping Act of 1921, 237–239
Apparent tariffs, 109–111
Appreciation of currencies, 533
Arbitrage, 473
Asia, economic integration in, 349–350
ASM (Adapted Swan-Mundell) model, 496–501, 526
Australia-New Zealand Closer Economic
    Relations Trade Agreement
    (ANZCERTA), 332
Autarky, 27, 38–39, 482–483
Automation costs, 86

Balance of payments, 400–421
    and foreign exchange, 460–462, 540–552
    in real-world countries, 409–418
    and trade imbalances, 401–403
Balance-of-payments accounting, 401–416.
    See also Capital accounts; Current
    accounts; Monetary accounts;
    Unrequited transfers
    discrepancies in, 407–408, 411, 413, 414,
        419–420
    double-entry items in, 409

Balance-of-payments statements, 400, 401
Balance of trade. *See also* Trade deficits;
    Trade imbalances; Trade surpluses
    absorption in, 370–371
    and capital markets, 395–397
    current account and, 403–404
    in goods and services, 404
    government consumption in, 374–377
    and income, 439–443
    merchandise (visible), 404
    protectionism in, 224–225
    and saving, 379–381, 395–397
        and investment, 373–377
Bank customers in foreign exchange market,
    452–453
Bank loans, Eurocurrency, 516–521
Bank notes, 563
Bank of Canada, 466–468
Bank panics, 563, 567, 571
Bank reserves, 463–469, 515. *See also*
    Reserves
Banks
    central, 5n, 406–407, 458–459, 515, 563,
        567
    commercial
        in capital markets, 524; equity main-
            tained by, 527–528; in
            Eurocurrency market, 516–517;
            foreign assets of, 5–6; in foreign
            exchange, 452–455; international
            scope of, 511–512; liquidity of, 527;
            T-accounts of, 463–465
    correspondent, 463
    foreign, 184
Bargaining and protectionism, 225
Bargaining tariffs, 125
Barro effects of saving decline, 382–384
Barter, 357
Basle Agreement, 527–528
Basle Convention, 170
Benelux union, 327
Big slice corollary to N–1 problem, 607
Bills of exchange, 453
Bimetalism, 563n
Bonds
    bearer, 511; Euro-, 516–518; expected
        value of, 488n; junk, 522; parallel,
        516; Yankee, 484
Border-tax adjustments, 181–183
Bretton Woods Conference, 196
Bretton Woods System, 573–577, 608, 613,
    619
    economic system following, 590–598

Brokerage costs, 631
Brother-in-law theorem, 122
Budget deficits, 378–384
Buffer stock facility of IMF, 597, 598
Bullion dealers, 565
Buy American laws, 159, 162–163
Buy backs in countertrade, 357–358
Buy Provincial acts in Canada, 163

Canada
    balance of payments of, 414–415
    Bank of, 466–468
    Barro effect in, 383, 384
    and Caribbean, trade between, 345
    foreign exchange in, 484
    foreign repercussion effect in, 437
    and Mexico, trade between, 342
    monetary policy in, 492–495
    purchasing power parity in, 535–536
    timber case of, 256
    and U.S., trade agreement of, 315,
        332–339
Capital
    accumulation of, 387–394
    domestic and foreign bases of, 387–390
    growth of, 281
    human, 67, 91
    importation of, 63
    mobility of, 483–487. *See also* Capital
        movement
Capital accounts, 406, 410–415, 460–462, 496,
    498–503
Capital availability theory, 524–525
Capital consumption allowance, 388
Capital costs, 74
Capital flows. *See* Capital movement
Capital-intensive production, 57–70
Capital markets
    in autarky, 482–483
    functions of, 506–511
    intermediaries in, 524
    liquidity in, 507–508, 521, 522
    matching process in, 506–509
    supervision and monitoring of, 526–527
    types of
        Eurocurrency, 513–522; internation-
            al, 511–527; national, 511–512,
            514
    using, costs of, 510
Capital movement, 5–7, 16, 17. *See also*
    Capital mobility
    in currency trading, 536–537
    and exchange rates, 501–502

642